THE 12TH SS

VOLUME TWO

The History of the Hitler Youth Panzer Division

Hubert Meyer

STACKPOLE
BOOKS

0 11557 03199 7

Published in 2005 by
STACKPOLE BOOKS
5067 Ritter Road
Mechanicsburg, PA 17055
www.stackpolebooks.com

www.jjfpub.mb.ca

Printed in the United States of America

10 9 8 7 6 5 4 3 2 1

FIRST EDITION

Library of Congress Cataloging-in-Publication Data

Meyer, Hubert, 1913–
  [Kriegsgeschichte der 12. SS-Panzerdivision "Hitlerjugend". English]
  The 12th SS : the history of the Hitler Youth Panzer Division / Hubert Meyer ; translated by H. Harri Henschler.— 1st ed.
      p. cm. — (Stackpole Military history series)
  Originally published in English as: The history of the 12. SS-Panzerdivision "Hitlerjugend". Winnipeg, Man. : J.J. Fedorowicz, 1994.
  Includes bibliographical references and index.
  ISBN 0-8117-3199-5
  1. Waffen-SS. SS-Panzerdivision "Hitlerjugend," 12. 2. World War, 1939–1945—Regimental histories—United States. 3. World War, 1939–1945—Tank warfare. 4. World War, 1939–1945—Campaigns—Western Front. I. Meyer, Hubert, 1913– History of the 12. SS-Panzerdivision "Hitlerjugend". II. Title. III. Series.

  D757.5612th .M4913 2005
  940.54'21422—dc22
                                        2005001216
  ISBN 978-0-8117-3199-7

Table of Contents

PART II

The Division during the Defensive Battles against the Allied Invasion in Normandy (continued from Volume I)

CHAPTER 5.4

Preparation of Operation 'TOTALIZE' and Defense Against It. Fighting in the Bridgehead of Grimbosq on 7 and 8 August 1944

The actions by Aufklärungsgruppe Olboeter in the area east of the Vire at the dividing line between Panzergruppe West (from 3.8. onward "Panzer-armee West", then 5. Panzerarmee) and 7. Armee offer some insight into the developments there. These had come about as a consequence of the American "COBRA" and the British "BLUECOAT" operations. Events were moving quickly toward a critical peak and demanded decisive countermeasures from the German leadership. The gravity of the situation was clearly expressed in an order of the OKW of 2 August 1944. The countermeasures, as a consequence, were accordingly severe. The text follows verbatim:

> The enemy breakthrough on the western wing of the beachhead front can only be parried by a decisive counterattack of strong German Panzer forces.
>
> Our superior tactical experience must be used to return the situation to a positive state. The combat-inexperienced and difficult-to-move Infanterie Divisions must not be brought into this torn wing, while the bulk of the Panzer units is tied down at the still coherent main line of defense in infantry defense further to the east, and remains there. Thus, the Führer has ordered:
>
> 'The front line between the Orne and Vire rivers is to be curled inward to the north, using mainly Infanterie Divisions. If necessary, a new main line of defense, with the front line pulled back, must be established along a general line Thury-Harcourt-Vire-Fontenermont, and held.
>
> 'The Panzer units in action at that front until now must be pulled out and moved to the left wing as a complete body. The attacks by these, at least four, Panzer units must destroy the enemy tank forces which have broken through to the east, southeast and south. Without any regard to the enemy breakthrough in Brittany, contact must be established with the western coast of the Cotentin peninsula near Avranches or north of it.'[1]

The acting chief of the Wehrmacht operational staff, General Warlimont, carried the OKW order for the counteroffensive to Supreme Commander West on 2 August. He explained the order and its impact on Panzerarmee West at its command post during the following day. This conversation was recorded in a file note for the war diary of Panzergruppe West as follows:

Meeting with the acting chief of Wehrmacht operational staff, General der Artillerie Warlimont (Gen. W.) on 3.8.1944.

Present:Supreme Commander Panzerarmee West (S.C.)
    commanding General I. SS-Panzerkorps,
    Chief Panzerarmee West,
    Ia Panzerarmee West,
    Oberstleutnant i.G. (general staff) von Kluge,
    Major i.G. Buchterkirch, staff of inspector general of the Panzer
troops.

S.C. provides a briefing on the present situation at Panzerarmee West.

   . . .

S.C.: It appears that the situation at Panzerarmee West and 7. Armee cannot be held in the long run.

Gen. W.: However, positions have been held there until now. If this can be done for another month or two, the battle of this summer has not been lost. The English people have been promised the end of the war for this year. If that does not occur, there is one more big chance for us (significant impact on morale by V 1s)!

S.C.: The situation at 7. Armee demands that an overall decision must be taken.

Gen. W.: If the Normandy front of 120 kilometers cannot be held, then it won't be possible further back at all (Seine-Marne-Westwall). There can also be no question of it since no supply system is in place there. It is necessary to pull four Pz.-Divs. out of the Panzerarmee West sector in order to push through to Avranches and cut off the Americans.

Commanding Gen. I.SS-Pz. Korps: If the SS-Divisions are pulled out south of Caen, the enemy will attack there and break through.

Gen.W.: The SS-Divisions there are not in the right spot since they are, immobile, part of the front line and the enemy's point of main effort is not there.

S.C.: Advancing Infanterie Divisions must be put into action as soon as possible. However, the SS-Divisions must be put in readiness to the rear in order to prop up the front. The principal question remains how we can hold the front in the long run in view of the enemy being vastly superior in materiel.

Gen.W.: Two more SS-Brigades can be brought in from Denmark.

S.C.: Bringing up these SS-Brigades takes 8–10 days. That is too long. Pulling out the SS-Divisions from the present front line and action into the direction of Avranches takes at least three to four days. No-one knows what the situation there will be by then.

Karte 7: Operation TOTALIZE
Abwehrkämpfe vom 8.-11. August 1944

Map 7: Operation TOTALIZE
defensive battles August 8-11 1944

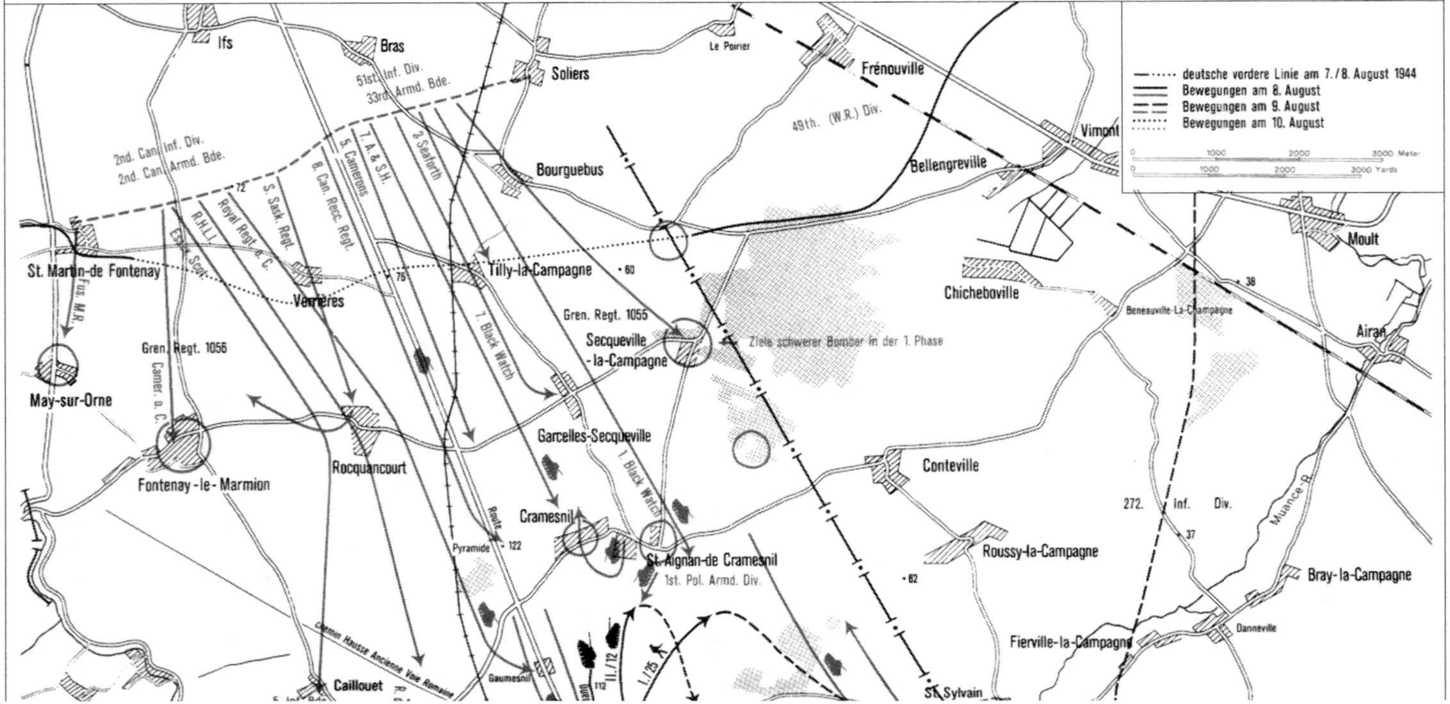

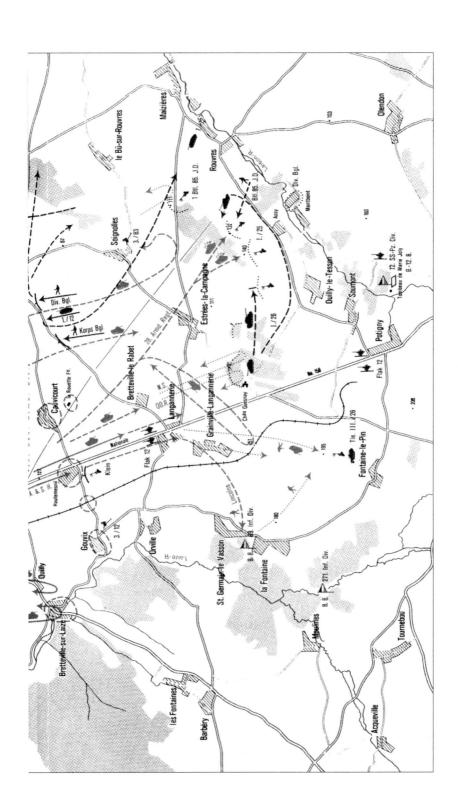

Gen.W.: . . . Within the foreseeable future, the impact of action by completely new weapons will be felt. There, too, the perpetrators of 20 July have slowed things down . . . The first 1,000 new fighters will enter combat during the second half of August.[2]

This order meant that, in addition to 2. and 116. Panzer Divisions which had been attached to 7. Armee as early as the end of July, and to 21. Pz.-Div. and II. SS-Panzerkorps which were in combat against the English in the area northeast of Vire, 1. and 12. SS-Panzerdivisions were to be pulled out for the counterattack. Thereafter, the Caen sector would be stripped of all Panzer forces.

Among the Infanterie Divisions, scheduled to relieve the Panzerdivisions in the Caen sector, was 89. Inf.-Div. The following report on its condition may indicate what could be expected of it. It was a division in the '44' structure and, according to the assessment of its first general staff officer ". . . well equipped with personnel and materiel, judged against the conditions of the time." The division had two Infanterie regiments of three battalions and a Füsilier battalion, mobile on bicycles, each. Further, it had one Pionier battalion, whose 1. Kompanie was also mobile on bicycles, and one field reserve battalion. The Artillerieregiment had four Abteilungen of which two were equipped with light German field howitzers 10.5 cm and one with heavy French 15.5 cm field howitzers. The fourth Abteilung was an anti-tank/anti-aircraft Abteilung with 8.8 cm guns. The Panzerjäger companies of the Infanterie regiments had 5 cm and 7.5 cm Pak. The Panzerjägerabteilung had available one company with 7.5 cm Pak, while the assault gun battery and the Flak-Kompanie were still being moved up. Based on the experiences of "EPSOM" and "GOODWOOD", the provision of anti-tank weapons for the western theater of war was totally inadequate. The division's commanders and officers were mostly front line experienced, and a similar core of NCOs and men, as well as young, quickly trained replacements with a good attitude, as stated in the report by the first general staff officer. After the start of its formation in March 1944 in Norway, the division was moved by rail into the area northeast of Rouen in early July. There, it relieved parts of 17. Luftwaffe-Feld-Division. It continued its combat training, moved to the area southeast of Dieppe at the end of July, and was then sent toward the invasion front. Thus, time for training had been very tight. Nevertheless, the Ia judged: At the time the order for action arrived, ". . . the Division was ready for offensive missions. Leadership and troops were aware of their own value in battle and looking forward to action."[3]

On 31 July, when the success of the American offensive had become obvious by the capture of Avranches, General Eisenhower urged that the German Panzer units be tied down on the eastern wing. He sent a radio message to General Montgomery on the same day in which he said, among others:

Bradley (supreme commander of the First US Army, Author) has sufficient infantry to secure all terrain gained and enable the tank forces to continue their pressure and encircle the enemy. Through energetic action by the Canadian Army, in order to prevent withdrawal of enemy forces from the Caen area, as well as Dempsey's [Second British Army] and Bradley's coordinated attack, it will be possible to clear the terrain west of the Orne once and for all.[4]

The Canadian Army had received respective orders from Montgomery as early as 21 July. It then saw the opportunity to become active again.

Tilly-la Campagne, which had already been attacked several times without success, was planned to be captured by the newly arrived 4th Canadian Armoured Division, together with parts of the 2nd Canadian Infantry Division. Through this, the Canadians wanted to decisively reduce the possibility of German observation of the Canadian assembly area south of Caen for a major attack along both sides of the road Caen-Falaise. As well, the new division was to be given an opportunity to gather its first combat experiences. Repeated attacks by parts of both divisions on 1 August were repelled by the "Leibstandarte". However, the observation post in the church of St. Martin-de Fontenay, which had been reinforced into a strongpoint and was defended by a unit of the "Hohenstaufen" Division, was captured. Montgomery demanded further action by the Canadians in order to tie down German forces in that sector. Two more Canadian attempts to capture Tilly through surprise attacks during the following night were fought off, causing significant losses.

During the night of 3–4 August the Canadians tried to destroy the mining towers and the pit installations immediately south of St. Martin-de Fontenay. This operation, too, failed. The silence on the German side during the following day let the enemy assume that the positions had been abandoned, as was the case west of the Orne near St. André on 4 August. Because of the threatening developments on its left wing, Panzerarmee West had pulled back the main line of defense along a line from the northern tip of Forêt de Grimbosq to the southern edge of Aunay. The Canadians attacked May-sur-Orne from St. André-sur-Orne in the late afternoon of 5 August. The defenders were ready and repelled the attack, causing severe losses to the attackers. Another attack in the evening also failed. Further attacks on Tilly-la Campagne, undertaken during the same day were also repulsed, with significant losses to the attackers.

The actions of that day merely brought the enemy the dearly paid-for recognition that the existing German positions were manned as before and energetically defended.[5]

These results could not satisfy General Montgomery. In his Directive No. M 516 of 4 August 1944 he ordered the Canadian Army to mount a major attack from the Caen area in the direction of Falaise. Specifically, he said:

Objective of the operation:

    a) Breakthrough through the enemy positions south and south-
    east of Caen in order to capture as much terrain as is necessary
    to cut off the enemy forces which are now facing the Second
    Army, and to impede their withdrawal to the east, if not mak-
    ing it impossible altogether.

    b) In a general way, to destroy enemy personnel and materiel in
    preparation for the greatest possible enlargement of the suc-
    cess.[6]

An essential factor for the preparation and execution of the operation, as well as defending against it, was the terrain. What did it look like?

Between Caen and Falaise stretches an elevated plain which is bordered in the east first by Route Nationale No. 13 and then by Route Départemen-tale D 40 from Vimont to St. Pierre-sur-Dives, the western border is formed by the Orne valley. Route Nationale No. 158 leads in a straight line across the highest points of this gently undulating terrain for a distance of twenty-four kilometers from Caen-South to Potigny. Thereafter, with a few bends to avoid the sources of the Laison river, it runs the distance of nine kilometers to Falaise. It starts in Caen-Vaucelles at an elevation of approximately thirty meters and rises to seventy-six meters near Tilly-la Campagne, 122 meters at Cramesnil, 127 meters south of Cintheaux, 132 meters southeast of Grainville-Langennerie and 183 meters north of Potigny. It then drops to 160 meters in Potigny and 139 meters at the Laison northwest of Soulangy, climbing to 152 meters at the crossroads 1.5 kilometers northwest of Falaise. The road then crosses the Ante valley, which is only at sixty-two meters, by way of a high bridge and reaches the walls of Falaise with the old castle where William the Conqueror was born in the year 1028. Only the Laison valley cuts through the high plateau east of Route Nationale No. 158 from the southwest to the northeast, bordered by a number of villages and wooded areas along the banks and slopes. The deep valley of the Laize river approaches the road near from the west to within fifteen kilometers, and the open terrain on that side of the road is reduced to two kilometers. The river valley is covered with extensive forests. The terrain west of the Laize is bro-ken and thus not suited for a sweeping tank attack. On the other hand, the terrain east of Route Nationale offers good possibilities for evasion in an east-erly direction as soon as one has passed the Muance valley west of St. Sylvain. Although there is no major road cutting all the way through the terrain, the network of roads is quite suitable there for armored units. In general, it can be stated that the terrain was excellently suited for a major attack by tank and motorized forces in the year 1944, especially its northern section. It did not offer the defender a natural obstruction ahead of his front line.

The II Canadian Corps, which was scheduled to carry out the operation, had been constantly reinforced since the end of Operation "GOODWOOD".

At the beginning of August 1944 it consisted of the 2nd and 3rd Canadian Infantry Divisions, the 51st British Highland Division, the 2nd Canadian and the 33rd British Armoured Brigades, and the 1st Polish Armoured Division. Strongest possible air support had been promised for the planned operation. The plan of attack assumed that the German main line of defense in the attack sector ran from la Hogue via Tilly-la Campagne to May-sur-Orne, and that a rear position had been partially prepared along the general line St. Sylvain-Hautmesnil. It was further assumed, correctly, that the German command expected an attack there so that no surprise was possible in that respect.

Only the timing and available materiel could not be known to the German side. The formation of a bridgehead across the Orne to the rear of the left wing of the German defensive front line, before the start of the major attack, was seen as an important prerequisite for the successful breakthrough across the forward German positions. The operation, named "TOTALIZE", was to be carried out in three phases:

Phase 1: Night attack by two infantry divisions—2nd Canadian and 51st British—and two tank brigades—2nd Canadian and 33rd British—without air preparation to break through the German positions between la Hogue and Fontenay-le Marmion;

Destruction of reserves possibly assembled there and making the terrain in the May-sur-Orne-Fontenay-le Marmion area and the wooded area southeast of la Hogue impassable. At the start of the attack, a short fire attack by medium artillery on the forward enemy positions. Under its cover, tanks and infantry, mounted on armored vehicles, were to advance on the first attack objectives.

Phase 2: 4th Canadian Armoured Division and 3rd Canadian Infantry Division were to break through the rear position between St. Sylvain and Hautmesnil;

All available medium bombers and heavy daylight bombers, as well as fighter-bombers, were to support the attack, strong artillery was available, on call.

Phase 3: The two tank divisions, 4th Canadian and 1st Polish Armoured, were to enlarge the breakthrough after Phase 2 and capture the dominating hills north and northwest of Potigny (183 and 1945), then seek and maintain contact with the German troops facing them.[7]

In Directive No. M 517 of 6 August 1944, General Montgomery made clear the significance for the German side of the sector southeast and south of Caen. He described it as the "hinge" of the German front. It would be extremely troublesome to the German command if the positions along both sides of the road to Falaise, or even the city of Falaise were lost ". . . during the next day or the two next days . . ." He ordered the First Canadian Army to start the attack during the night of 7–8 August and, if possible, to take and hold Falaise.[8]

On the side of the defender, only 89. Infanteriedivision was facing the two armored divisions, three infantry divisions and two tank brigades of the attacker in the sector from la Hogue to the Orne northwest of St. Martin-de Fontenay. At the Orne, 271 Infanteriedivision was adjacent. Its positions stretched along the river to two kilometers north of Thury-Harcourt and consisted only of a chain of strongpoints. The 89. Inf.-Div. had only begun relieving "LAH" on 5 August. On that day, 271. Inf.-Div. had pulled back to the west bank of the Orne, and on the following day to the steep east bank, in the course of shortening the front line. While 89. Inf.-Div. had taken over the reinforced positions of "LAH", 271. Inf.-Div. had to rely on its own resources. The only reserve of the general command of I. SS-Panzerkorps, in charge of this sector, was the "HJ" Division. Its Aufklärungsgruppe Olboeter was in action in the Vire area under the command of II SS-Panzerkorps. However, the order for the counterattack near Mortain provided that this division, too, would be moved there. The Schwere SS-Panzerabteilung 101, as mentioned previously, was part of Kampfgruppe Wünsche. During the next days, the 89. Inf.-Div. would have been without any support by Panzers or mobile anti-tank forces in case of an enemy attack.

As already noted, the plan for Operation "TOTALIZE" envisaged the formation of a bridgehead across the Orne behind the left wing of the German defensive position. The withdrawal of the front line of Panzerarmee West to the west of the Orne, in order to save forces, offered a good opportunity for this. The 53rd (Welsh) Infantry Division and 59th Infantry Division of XII Corps were able to swiftly follow the withdrawing infantry divisions since they could use the undamaged bridges near Evrécy and Avenay.[9]

They were ordered to establish the Orne bridgehead in four phases:

Phase 1: 59th Infantry Division is to form a bridgehead across the Orne near Brieux, 5.5 kilometers north of Thury-Harcourt, with support from the tank unit 107th Battalion Royal Armoured Corps.

Phase 2: 53rd Infantry Division is to take over Brieux bridgehead.

Phase 3: 59th Infantry Division is to establish a bridgehead near Thury-Harcourt and capture Hill 205, one kilometer west of Meslay, and Hill 192, southeast of 205.

Phase 4: If the attack by 59th Infantry Division from the bridgehead progresses well, 53rd Infantry Division will attack past it and advance on Falaise. If the hills are not captured by 59th Division, 53rd Division will capture them and then attack further in the direction of Falaise.[10]

On 6 August, from 18.40 hours on, the 271. Inf.-Div. observed enemy rocket fire in the Grimbosq (nine kilometers west of Bretteville-sur Laize) and Thury-Harcourt sectors. Enemy assault squads attacked in other sectors of the front line of I. SS-Panzerkorps. During the night 6-7 August, the 176th Infantry Brigade of 59th Infantry Division, supported by the tank unit 107th RAC, succeeded in crossing the steep banks of the Orne near Grimbosq and south of it after a two-hour barrage, and established two bridgeheads. In the morning of 7 August, two tank companies crossed the river near le Bas, immediately west of Brieux, to support the infantry. The Füsilierbataillon of 271. Inf.-Div. mounted a counterattack in the early morning hours to eliminate the bridgehead near Grimbosq. It was repulsed, causing high losses, as was a second attack which was noted in the reports of the opposite side.[11]

Since the 271. Inf.-Div. had no prospects of a decisive success with its own forces against the obviously strong enemy, supported by tanks, the general command sent Kampfgruppe Wünsche into a counterattack. The Kampfgruppe, after the pull-out of Aufklärungsgruppe Olboeter, consisted of the staff of the Panzerregiment, the staff of I. Abteilung with 3. Kompanie (Panthers) and 8. Kompanie (Panzer IVs), one company of heavy Panzer-abteilung 101 (Tigers), I./26 and III./26 without the staff and one company. The I. Panzerabteilung of "LAH", which belonged to the Kampfgruppe, had moved to the west together with the Division.

During the course of the day, the enemy had enlarged his bridgehead and fortified his positions. The bridgehead stretched from Lasseray (one kilometer north of Grimbosq) in an arc via the eastern edge of Grimbosq—eastern edge of Brieux to south of Brieux where the destroyed bridge across the Orne and the river crossing were located. The enemy had advanced securing forces up to the Forêt de Grimbosq. The front line of the 271. Inf.-Div. had been ripped open along a width of several kilometers. Speed had become a matter of urgency.

During the march to the assembly area, the Panzers of Kampfgruppe Wünsche came under attack from fifty-four Mitchell bombers. Flak fire damaged thirty-six bombers, some so severely that they were unable to return to England.[12] After the Forêt de Grimbosq had been cleared by III./26, the Kampfgruppe assembled in its southern and eastern sectors for the attack. The III. Artillerieabteilung had been attached to it as support. The attack started at 19.00 hours. Initially, it progressed well. Panzers and infantry penetrated into Grimbosq and Brieux. Parts of I./26 were able to advance to the bridge in le Bas, as reported by Unterscharführer Förster. He took up position there with two guns of the Panzerjägerzug of 4./26. However, he was forced to blow up these two captured Russian guns (nicknamed "Ratsch-bumm") when all ammunition had been used up. During the violent fighting, twenty-eight tanks were knocked out, two of them by III./26. The attack then stalled in the barrages from the enemy artillery. The grenadiers dug in and the Panzers took up favorable ambush positions.[13] The enemy had excellent observation possibilities from the hills west of the Orne, e.g. Hill 162 west of Goupillières. In contrast, Grimbosq is located at an elevation of only 100 to 120 meters. The German artillery was unable to observe the Orne valley and the river crossings.

Former members of 3. Kompanie of Panzerregiment 12 report on the armor battle, first Sturmmann Hermann Linke:

It was in the late afternoon of 7 August 1944. We were driving down a lane in the forest. Gradually, the wood thinned. But what we saw next could not be called a forest any more. Only tree stumps were left. All of the trees had been ripped apart by the artillery to a depth of approximately 200 meters. Outside of the forest was a large orchard. In it, there was not one tree either which had not been shredded by artillery fire. We took up position at that edge of the wood. In a valley ahead of us, some 800 meters away, flowed the Orne.

The attack started in the evening, together with the infantry. As the Panzer engines were started, the enemy artillery fire set in again. The barrages were increasing in ferocity and soon we could not see any more grenadiers. Suddenly, the Panzer to our left took a hit and caught on fire immediately. To our right sat the Panzer of Untersturmführer Alban. My commander, Oberscharführer Mende suddenly said: 'Alban has left his Panzer and is leaping from Panzer to Panzer. He must be crazy to leave his vehicle during this artillery barrage'. When he had reached us, Alban shouted: 'Disengage!' They probably did not want to transmit this order by radio.

Then, there was a terrible bang. A shell exploded immediately next to our Panzer. Immediately, we all thought of Untersturmführer Alban. Mende said to the driver: 'Drive back slowly, maybe we can give Alban some cover that way!' But we could not see anything of Alban. So, Mende ordered to drive forward again, hoping to spot Alban.

Then we saw him. He was leaning against a tree stump, dead. I had never been a hero, but now I had to get out. I jumped to my killed Zug leader and secured his pay-book and other papers he carried with him.

The enemy had observed our movements and concentrated his fire on us. The fire was so heavy that we were not able to take our killed Zug leader with us. In order not to get knocked out ourselves, we had to pull out as quickly as possible.

By carrying the order to disengage in person, Alban had probably saved all our lives and had sacrificed his own. He was a brave soldier and a shining example for his men.

Next, Unterscharführer Heinz Freiberg:

Our order was to secure Grimbosq and a section of terrain at the edge of town. First, Untersturmführer Bogensberger, Unterscharführer Frey and I received orders to relieve the Tigers of the Korpsabteilung, securing inside the town. However, the only street was so narrow that the Tigers had to be pulled out first before we could reach our position. We waved a greeting to the Tigers as they drove by us and then started out. Frey was at the point, then came I and behind me, Bogensberger. On our way, we encountered grenadiers of the Krause Kampfgruppe. They reported that the Tommies had pushed forward immediately after the Tigers pulled out, and already occupied half of Grimbosq. The thick smoke and fog allowed us no visibility at all, but it also hid our presence from the enemy. Despite that, tremendous fire, particularly from infantry weapons, was directed at us and our grenadiers suffered high losses. Then, the order to withdraw to the edge of town came. So, we drove back to our new position with the grenadiers. There, a Tiger joined us, but it departed again right away after an ineffectual explosion close-by. It was likely that its mission was just to ensure we had reached the right position.

Thus, we were sitting with three Panzers of our Kompanie on a piece of road some 200 meters long. Frey was at the point, I was in the middle and in the rear, next to a house, Bogensberger. He had a very good field of fire to the right. During a suddenly mounted artillery attack, Frey was wounded. He then drove back with his Panzer.

So, only Bogensberger and I were left in our position together with our crews. The detonations of the explosive shells suddenly stopped and we were covered with smoke grenades. This meant that we had to watch out especially carefully. It was clear to all of us that something would happen after the smoke. And that was just the way it went. As soon as the veil of smoke had lifted we came under a hail of tank and anti-tank shells. My vehicle received violent fire from the other bank of the river. I kept my Panzer on the move by constantly driving back and forth, so as not to get hit. Despite that, we managed to knock out one anti-tank gun and a truck. Throughout that time, Bogensberger radioed in regular intervals to find out how we were.

When these questions stopped, I looked to the rear and saw Bogensberger's vehicle sitting immobile, its gun hanging down on the right. His Panzer was under constant fire from super heavy machine guns. As we drove up to Bogensberger's Panzer, we took a hit to the turret which knocked off all our spare track links. The shell fragments had also damaged the periscope. That meant, open the hatch and take a chance at looking around. I could not believe my eyes when I spotted, on the right, three enemy tanks which had taken up positions approximately 800 meters away. Only their guns showed over top of the embankment. Nothing else to do but into gear and fifty meters forward again. The periscope was quickly replaced so that we could 'see' again. That was really necessary since two anti-tank guns were setting up position on the opposite bank. They were knocked out with six explosive shells.

Since Bogensberger had still not answered on the radio, I had my radio operator get out and run back to Bogensberger's Panzer. After a short time he returned, wounded, and reported that Bogensberger and all of his turret crew had been killed. Now, we were all on our own, since we had no radio contact with anyone. In order to disengage without being observed we had to get off the road and drive around a slope through swamp-like terrain. This, we managed to do. However, we came under fire from the side which had been free of the enemy until then. Still, we succeeded in regaining the road some way behind Bogensberger's Panzer and picked up twelve wounded comrades, some of them critically. With our Panzer, which had taken seven hits, we set out slowly. But soon after the village we lost the left track which had also been hit. The damage was repaired within fifteen minutes and we continued on our way.

Soon after, we met the Abteilung commander to whom I reported on the situation. After handing over the wounded, I was ordered to drive back, despite the Panzer being badly damaged, and take up positions again near the entrance to Grimbosq. Another order, to tow Bogensberger's vehicle out during the night, was not carried out since the order to withdraw arrived before midnight. We were not at all angry about that.[14]

The general command ordered the continuation of the attack for the next day in order to smash the bridgehead. During the night, the enemy reorganized his forces. The commander of 43rd Tank Brigade went to the front himself and sent the two badly battered companies back into action. In addition, he brought up a third company to the river. It crossed the Orne at first daylight. Another unit of the Brigade, the 147th RAC, was assembled to relieve the 107th RAC. The bridgehead was to be held by all means. Because of the enemy reinforcements and German losses, the attack of 8 August was not successful either. A report by Hauptscharführer Friedrich Heubeck, a forward observer of III. Artillerieabteilung, gives an indication of the bitterness of the fighting. He wrote:

At first, we moved forward at good speed until our counterattack stalled under enemy fire. The infantry had dug in and was ordered to hold the positions they had reached. Since an enemy counterattack was to be expected, I calibrated my fire, preparing for a barrage. It was not long at all before the counterattack with strong tank support started. The Grenadierkompanie, where I was, suffered very high losses. In order to stop the tank attack, or at least to make it more difficult, I ordered firing of smoke grenades and anti-tank shells. That showed some success. My observation post was located in a hollow and I had to climb out every time to correct the fire. Then I spotted enemy tanks coming through the wall of smoke. One of them made me out and hammered a shell right in front of my feet. I was somewhat lucky, after all. The severity of the wounds was only established later in hospital. A bullet had lodged in my left lung, a piece of shrapnel was stuck in my right chest, pieces of shrapnel were found in my left and right arms, but it could have been even worse.

Since the position could no longer be held and almost none of the infantry men were still alive, I ordered my two uninjured radio operators to destroy the radio equipment and to get out. I was not able to go with them. The two took me to a house close-by. Soon after, I saw the first Englishmen outside the windows. I did not want to fall into their hands alive. Then I heard track noises from a German Panzer, heard German words. The door opened, my two radio operators came in and told me that there was a Tiger outside to pick me up. While retreating, my radio operators had encountered the Panzer. They had told the crew about me and they really got me out. We returned without losses. I still managed to report to Obersturmbannführer Wünsche at the command post. Later, I found myself in the field hospital where I was immediately operated on.[15]

The fighting near Grimbosq on 7 and 8 August had caused significant losses:

| | Killed | | | Wounded | | | Missing | | |
	Officers	NCOs	Men	Officers	NCOs	Men	Officers	NCOs	Men
Pz.Rgt.12	3	1	6	-	6	8	-	-	-
I./26	-	2	5	-	8	48	-	-	-
III./26	-	-	7	-	3	17	-	-	7
III./AR12	-	-	-	-	1	-	-	-	-
Total	3	3	18	-	18	73	-	-	7

The total losses were twenty-four killed, ninety-one wounded and seven missing. This amounted to a total of 122 losses.[16] The enemy personnel losses are not known. The Kampfgruppe lost nine Panthers, the enemy twenty-eight tanks.

Thanks to the quick reaction by 271. Inf.-Div. after the formation of the bridgehead, in particular the determined counterattack by Kampfgruppe Wünsche, the dislodging of the left wing of 89. Inf.-Div., facing north, had been prevented. However, the enemy succeeded in tying down Kampfgruppe

Wünsche and prevented it from being available for action at the northern front on 8 August. The enemy had not been able to establish, as ordered, a bridgehead near Thury-Harcourt, not to even mention their other wide-ranging goals.

While the battles near Grimbosq were still going on, decisive developments had occurred at the northern front of I. SS-Panzerkorps. At 21.40 hours on 7 August, the Heeresgruppe ordered that the "HJ" Division also set out to reinforce the Panzergruppe in action with 7. Armee. The directed assembly area was around la Capelle, northwest of Condé. The chief of staff of I. SS-Panzerkorps reported that one Panzergrenadierbataillon, one Artillerie and one Werfer Abteilung, one Panzerkompanie, one Batterie of 8.8 cm Flak and one Kompanie of four-barrel Flak [an error—it must have been a 2 cm single barrel] could be available as early as the night of 7 to 8 August. The elements in action near Grimbosq could probably follow on 8 August from 10.00 hours on, after the bridgehead had been eliminated.[17] An hour later, at 23.45 hours, Brigadeführer Kraemer reported to the Panzer-armee that bombs were constantly being dropped between Boulon and Grimbosq. Heavy artillery fire was concentrated on the German main line of defense. He judged this to be the preparation for a major attack and requested that the "HJ" Division not be withdrawn but left with the Korps. Another hour later, Oberstleutnant von Kluge, a son of the Feldmarschall, advised the Armee that the "HJ" Division continued to be available to the Panzerarmee. However, all measures were to be taken to prepare for a move into the sector of 7. Armee. This decision, which ran counter to the demands of the OKW, would have significant consequences. The general command continued to have available an armored unit if the enemy attack really came on the next day. However, it was split into three groups of which two were tied down in action, one of them many kilometers distant.[18]

Several important personnel changes, the timing of which cannot be determined exactly, must be mentioned before the rapid developments of the next ten days monopolize all attention. Three new commanders were transferred to the Artillerieregiment and took on their duties: Sturmbann-führer Oskar Drexler as Regimental commander; Haupt-sturmführer Hage-meier as commander of I. Abteilung and successor to Sturmbannführer Eric Urbanitz who had taken over the Korpsartillerieabteilung at the end of July; Sturmbannführer Günter Neumann as commander of II. Abteilung and suc-cessor to Sturmbannführer Schöps who had been killed on 27 June. Sturm-bannführer Karl Bartling, who had led the Regiment on an acting basis since the beginning of July, took back the command of III. Abteilung.

CHAPTER 5.5
The Canadian-British Operation 'TOTALIZE'. Defensive Battles near St. Sylvain and at the Laison Sector from 8 to 11 August 1944

The descriptions of the events which led to the establishment of the British bridgehead near Grimbosq, and of the German counterattack, have anticipated the developments in the sector of 89. Inf.-Div. It had taken over the positions of "LAH" Division on both sides of Route Nationale No. 158 which runs from Caen to Falaise. The main thrust of the Canadian-British "TOTALIZE" operation was directed against this division. The picture of the situation, which the enemy used for the planning of the operation, was improved during the first days of August. During the night of 5–6 August, a soldier of 89. Inf.-Div. deserted to the enemy. In addition, an ambulance of that Division got lost and ended up in the Canadian positions. This allowed the enemy to determine that the "LAH" Division had been relieved. However, he did not know that it was on the march to Mortain but assumed that it probably had taken up a second line.[1] That impression was possibly reinforced by the fact that Kampfgruppe Wünsche had set up sixty-five dummy Panzers in the area around Billy and Conteville (3.5 kilometers north of St. Sylvain) as well as north and northwest of St. Sylvain during the night of 2–3 August.[2]

The enemy apparently drew the conclusion from this changed picture of the situation that it would be possible to break through the German positions more rapidly than if "LAH" Division had still held them. Thus, the two Allied tank divisions were to be brought up to the 'starting line' as early as the morning of 8 August. Additionally, it was assumed that they could push through directly to their ultimate attack objectives in Phase 2. Accordingly, the 4th Canadian Armoured Division had to capture Hills 180 (immediately east of St. Germain-le Vasson), 195 (two kilometers southeast of it), and 206 (two kilometers west of Potigny). Attack objectives of the 1st Polish Armoured Division were Hills 165 (two kilometers west of Olendon), 170 (two kilometers southwest of Olendon), and 159 (three kilometers north-northeast of Falaise). The 3rd Canadian Infantry Division was to be ready during Phase 2 to advance via Bretteville-le Rabet and capture Hill 140 which dominated the Laison sector west of Rouvres. In its place, the infantry divisions had to take over the securing of the flanks. The supreme commander of the First Canadian Army anticipated a great victory which would bring a quick end to the war.[3]

On 7 August 1944 at 23.00 hours, as scheduled, the aerial bombardment of the villages on the flanks of the combat sector, where the armored units would break through, started. They were: la Hogue, Secqueville-la Campagne, Garcelles-Secqueville, St. Aignan, Cramesnil, Fontenay-le Marmion and May-sur-Orne. A total of 1,020 Halifax and Lancaster bombers dropped 3,462 tons of bombs on these villages. The rising smoke soon obscured visibility so that the last third of the bomb load was not dropped for security reasons. Ten aircraft were shot down by German Flak.[4] Grenadierregiment 1055, in action with 89. Inf.-Div. on the right, reported a German bombing raid on the enemy positions opposite, which showed good results. The men came out of their foxholes to watch this spectacle, not seen for a long time. In reality, this was not a German air attack but enemy bombs missing their mark. A few minutes later, Grenadierregiment 1056, which was in action to the left, reported a massive enemy bombing attack on the German main line of defense and well into the main battlefield. During the bombing attack, an infantry Zug had left its positions and moved forward to evade the bombs. There, it encountered an enemy who was ready for attack and totally surprised. After the end of the bombing, the Zug had returned unharmed, bringing along enemy prisoners.[5]

One half hour after the start of the bomb attack the armored enemy units mounted their attack. The 51st Highland Division, together with the 33rd British Armoured Brigade, attacked in three columns east of the road Caen-Falaise. In each column, four vehicles were driving side by side with only one meter distance between them, the vehicles behind followed at a distance of three meters. Each column had a heavily armored spearhead of two platoons of Sherman tanks, two platoons of flail tanks for mine removal, and one platoon of tank assault engineers. These latter had as their mission the marking of the attack sector with tape and lights. The main body followed behind the spearhead. It consisted of a large number of tanks and an infantry battalion in armored vehicles. These were various types of vehicles which had been 'borrowed' from other units. Among others, the main body of each column had heavy machine guns, anti-tank guns and bulldozers. The columns were made up of approximately 1,900 men each, with 200 armored vehicles. Behind the three narrow columns of the Division followed a group of tanks as their support. Further, this group was to secure space for the deployment of the armored units and to win a starting base for the infantry attacking on foot. In the same formation, the 2nd Canadian Infantry Division, together with the 2nd Canadian Armoured Brigade, attacked in four columns to the west of the Route Nationale.

Searchlights were beamed at the cloud cover to facilitate orientation. In addition, radio beams and driving by use of compass, which had been practiced, were to help maintain direction.[6] In order not to endanger their own troops, enemy artillery did not fire at the start of the attack. It opened fire, however, at 23.45 hours. Initially, 360 guns laid a barrage of 3,700 meters width on both sides of the Route Nationale. This wall of fire moved forward at ninety meters per minute. A total of 720 guns was available for the various tasks. The artillery fire reached all the way to the command post of 89. Inf.-

Div. which was located in the vicinity of Bretteville-sur-Laize. With its start it was clear that the expected major enemy attack had begun.[7]

Despite all the technical precautions, most of the columns lost direction and reached their attack objectives with considerable delays. That was partially a result of deteriorating visibility due to haze, smoke and dust thrown up by the tracked vehicles, partly also due to defensive fire from individual pockets of resistance and of the artillery. Contact within the columns was occasionally lost although the tail lights of the vehicles had been turned on. Individual vehicles ended up in other columns and were fired at by their own troops. The point vehicles of one attack group dropped into a bomb crater and blocked the way.

In the attack sector of the 51st Division the armored groups were successful in capturing Garcelles, St. Aignan and Cramesnil during the night. The woods immediately south of St. Aignan were occupied in the morning hours of 8 August. The attack on la Hogue was initially bloodily repelled with the help of the neighbor on the right, 272. Inf.-Div. When Hill 75 west of Secqueville, which had also been held with support from 272. Inf.-Div., was lost, the parts of 89. Inf.-Div. in action there moved into the prepared secondary position on both sides of St. Aignan. The enemy thrust then hit also the left wing of 272. Inf.-Div. The forest east of Secqueville was lost. A counterattack by an Infanteriebataillon was fought off. The 272. Inf.-Div. pulled back its left wing to the line Chicheboville-Conteville. After St. Aignan was lost, British tanks attacked from there to the east but were repulsed near Conteville and Poussy.[8]

One strong point, particularly bitterly fought for, was Tilly-la Campagne. Stacy wrote about it:

> Tilly-la Campagne, then held by 89. Infanteriedivision, was defended for some time in a manner reminiscent of the 'Leibstandarte'. The first attack by the 2nd Battalion of the Seaforth Highlanders was beaten back. Then, a part of the 5th Seaforth went into action. The resistance faltered when a company of the 148th Regiment Royal Armoured Corps [tank company] showed up around seven o'clock. In the end, the bloodstained ruins of Tilly fell into British hands.[9]

To the west of the Route Nationale, the columns of the Canadian Armoured Brigade and the 4th Canadian Infantry Brigade also had problems orienting themselves. The Royal Regiment of Canada pushed past Rocquancourt to the east instead of west of the village. The Royal Hamilton Light Infantry, which should have advanced even further to the west, thrust right through the center of the village. The 3rd Battalion The Essex Scottish completely lost its way. The fourth Canadian column, the 8th Canadian Reconnaissance Regiment was stopped shortly before reaching its objective, Hill 122. The Royal Regiment of Canada finally reached its goal of Gaumesnil after a considerable delay. The Royal Hamilton dug in approximately 1.5 kilometers northwest of Gaumesnil. Supposedly, they had found their attack objective, the quarry at the intersection of the road St. Aignan-Bretteville-sur-Laize and the old Roman road, occupied by Panzers and self-propelled guns. The most westerly Canadian column, the Essex Scottish, had only been able to re-assemble at 08.55 hours in the vicinity of Rocquancourt. It came under fire, lost a considerable number of vehicles and only reached its attack objective, Caillouet, around noon.[10]

The infantry of the 6th Canadian Infantry Brigade, attacking on foot, also had problems. Most successful was the South Saskatchewan Regiment. It advanced closely behind the moving barrage and penetrated into Rocquancourt, capturing the village at 00.45 hours. The attack of Les Fusiliers Mont-Royal battalion on May-sur-Orne was fought off. The same fate awaited The Cameron Highlanders of Canada battalion which attacked Fontenay-le Marmion. Trusting the effect of the bomb attacks, neither of the two had received any artillery support. It became evident that the bombers had not been able to completely break the 89. Infanteriedivision's determination to resist. Finally, May-sur-Orne was captured at approximately 16.00 hours with support from flame thrower tanks. Fontenay-le Marmion, too, was only captured in the early afternoon of 8 August, following bitter and eventful battles, with the support of the Saskatchewans who attacked the German defenders from Rocquancourt into their deep flank and the rear.[11]

Around noon of 8 August, the attackers had generally reached the objectives laid down for Phase 1. They were only lagging behind on the western wing. Thanks to aerial bombardment by more than 1,000 bombers, the concentrated action by more than 600 tanks and more than 700 artillery guns, the superior Canadian-British forces had achieved a great success. They had managed to break through the positions of 89. Infanteriedivision at a width of approximately six kilometers. The Infanteriedivision, just moved into the positions and without Panzers and heavy mobile anti-tank weapons, had not been able to withstand that assault.

As scheduled for Phase 2, the enemy could now advance into the depth of the terrain along the road Caen-Falaise. He was close to a battle-deciding, huge success. Only those parts of the worn-out 12. SS-Panzerdivision not already in action at other hot spots could be thrown at the enemy: at that time one Panzerabteilung with thirty-nine Panzer IVs, one Kompanie of heavy SS-Panzerabteilung 101 with approximately ten Tigers, one Kompanie of Panzerjäger IVs, one Panzergrenadierbataillon (Kampfgruppe Waldmüller), the Division- and Korpsbegleitkompanie (escort companies), three Artillerieabteilungen (without one battery "Wespen"—wasps) and Werferabteilung 12. In addition, parts of III. Flakkorps and Werferregiment 83 were still in action in the sector of I. SS-Panzerkorps. It was obvious that these forces would not be able to withstand the attack by strong tank units with their usual air support.

In the course of 7 August, the Division—without those parts in action—had been moved from the area Vieux Fumé-Maizières-St. Sylvain-Bray-la Campagne into the area south of Bretteville-sur-Laize, i.e. west of the Route Nationale. This was done in order to be closer to the center of the Korps sector and in the vicinity of the hot spot which was taking on form through the establishment of the enemy bridgehead near Grimbosq and Brieux.[12] The bombing raids of the late evening had also caused alarm at the Division. Contact was sought through scouting parties with the units of 89. Infanteriedivision in action at the front line so as to learn immediately of any developments. During the night, Sturmbannführer Waldmüller moved one Panzerjäger Zug forward to Cintheaux at the Route Nationale.

Even before dawn on 8 August, the Divisional commander, Oberführer Kurt Meyer, drove to the front with several messengers to establish a personal understanding of the development of events on the spot. The first incoming reports were alarming. According to them, a breakthrough across the positions of 89. Inf.-Div. along a wide stretch seemed to have occurred. Several strong points were supposedly holding out. There was no contact with them. Garcelles was still in German hands, however, tanks were reported in St. Aignan. The situation in Rocquancourt and May-sur-Orne was unclear. If the enemy had broken through the total depth of the main battlefield on a wide front, a new defensive front line could only be established, given the existing ratio of forces, behind the Laison sector and on both sides of Potigny. That could be done only with the help of 85. Infanteriedivision which was advancing and whose point units had reached the Trun area. It was necessary to gain time and to stop the enemy as far north of that line as possible, or at least delay his advance.

Bretteville-sur-Laize was impassable due to massive bombardments. Oberführer Meyer drove cross-country to Cintheaux where he encountered Waldmüller's Panzerjägerzug. The village was under artillery fire. He spotted German soldiers, in complete disarray, moving south along both sides of the Route Nationale. Here is Panzermeyer's report:

> For the first time during those long and cruel years of nations killing each other I see fleeing German soldiers. It is impossible to talk to them any more—they have gone through the hell fire of the raging battle and stumble emaciated, their eyes full of terror, past us. Mesmerized, I stare at the leaderless soldiers. My uniform sticks to my skin. Cold sweat of responsibility breaks from all pores. Suddenly, I know that the fate of the city of Falaise and thus the safety of the two armies depends on my decision. I am standing upright in my Volkswagen, driving in the direction of Caen. More and more shaken soldiers are moving in the other direction, fleeing to the south. Without any success I am trying to bring the moving front line to a stop again. The terrifying bombing raids have unnerved the units of

89. Infanteriedivision. Shell fire covers the road and sweeps it clean. The flight only continues to the left and right of that straight road. I jump from the car and stand alone on the road. Slowly, I walk toward the front line and speak to the fleeing comrades. They hesitate, stop, look at me incredulously as I stand, armed with a carbine, on the road. These boys probably think that I have lost my mind. Then, they recognize me, wave their comrades to come closer and organize the defense on the hill of Cintheaux. The village must be held at all cost in order to gain time for the two Kampfgruppen. Time is of the essence.[13]

The Divisional commander met the supreme commander of 5. Panzer-armee, General Eberbach, in Urville. He, too, had wanted to get a direct impression of the situation of the front line units in their immediate vicinity. The supreme commander agreed with Panzermeyer's assessment of the situation and supported his decisions for a counterattack. In the meantime, the Division had been ordered by I. SS-Panzerkorps to stop the enemy breakthrough in a counterattack and, if possible, to throw it back. Thus, it ordered:

Kampfgruppe Waldmüller, reinforced by II. Panzer-abteilung and one Tigerkompanie, is to capture the hills south of St. Aignan in a counterattack;

the Korpsbegleitkompanie (escort company) is attached to Kampfgruppe Waldmüller, is to move to the right of it and join its attack;

the Divisionsbegleitkompanie with attached 1. Kompanie of SS-Panzer-jägerabteilung 12 is to capture, advancing by way of Estrées, the hill west of St. Sylvain, and will be attached to Kampfgruppe Waldmüller;

Kampfgruppe Wünsche is to immediately break off the counterattack near Grimbosq and Brieux, disengage from the enemy, occupy the hills west and northwest of Potigny and will defend the narrow passage between Laison and Laize;

the Artillerieregiment with attached Werferabteilung 12 is to support the attack from positions in the vicinity of the Route Nationale;

the Flakabteilung is to establish an anti-tank barrier on both sides of the Route Nationale in line with Bretteville-le Rabet;

the Aufklärungsgruppe under the leadership of Untersturmführer Wienecke is to maintain contact with the left wing of 272. Inf.-Div. and reconnoiter into the gap assumed to exist from there to the west;

the Divisional command post will be set up in la Brêche du Diable below Tombeau de Marie Joly (1.5 kilometers east of Potigny);

the Divisional commander will remain with Kampfgruppe Waldmüller.

No verified information can be offered regarding the strength and positions of the Luftwaffe Flak and the Werfers. It is merely known that, on 8 August, 3. Batterie of Werferregiment 83 of Werferbrigade 7 was in position near Soignolles, securing a sector from St. Sylvain to Urville (both inclusive) in a depth of 7.5 kilometers (thus including St. Aignan). Both batteries of I. Abteilung were probably in action in the vicinity.[14]

Kampfgruppe Waldmüller was sent off to Bretteville-le Rabet without delay to assemble there. The attack was scheduled to start at 12.30 hours.

In the meantime, the enemy had completed his preparations for Phase 2. The 1st Polish Armoured Division and the 4th Canadian Armoured Division had advanced to the assembly areas of the infantry divisions in the morning hours of 8 August. The infantry divisions had left these areas at the start of the attack. At dawn, the Poles assembled in the area southeast of Cormelles (three kilometers southeast of the Orne bridge in Caen). The Canadians assembled in the area between Fleury-sur-Orne and the Route Nationale, except for one tank unit which was located east of the road.[15]

The start of the attack, for the tank divisions, had been scheduled for 13.55 hours. The time period of 12.26 hours to 13.55 hours had been set aside for the preparatory bomb attack. The rearward line for the bomb drop ran from the northern edge of Robertmesnil (1.2 kilometers southeast of St. Aignan) via the northern edge of Gaumesnil to the southern edge of the quarry 1.5 kilometers west of Gaumesnil. The attacking units would only be able to approach this line with the end of the bomb attack. The advance to the starting line did not come about without delays caused by artillery fire and infantry fire from strong points which were still holding out, in particular from the hills west of Verrières.[16]

The 1st Polish Armoured Division was led into the sector east of the Route Nationale around 10 A.M. It rolled on into its assembly area which it reached in time for the start of the bomb attack.[17] It was to join the attack by the 4th Canadian Armoured Division on the east and advance to Hill 165 (two kilometers west of Olendon), Hill 170 (three kilometers southwest of Olendon) and Hill 159 (three kilometers north-northeast of Falaise).

The plan of attack for the 4th Canadian Armoured Division envisaged that the 4th Armoured Brigade, advancing east of the Route Nationale, would by-pass Cintheaux and Hautmesnil to the east. It would first capture Bretteville-le Rabet and then advance on Hills 195 and 206 northwest and west-southwest of Potigny. In order to achieve this, the Brigade had formed a spearhead consisting of the Canadian Grenadier Guards (tanks) and The Lake Superior Regiment (armored infantry) under the command of Lieutenant Colonel W.W. Halpenny. Its mission was to occupy or capture the hills near Potigny. It received orders at 08.45 hours to advance from its assembly area north of Troteval Ferme (one kilometer north of Verrières). However, it only started out slowly, probably because of congestion along the route of advance, around noon.[18]

The 10th Infantry Brigade had been given the objectives of capturing Cintheaux and Hautmesnil and then to clear the attack sector of any centers of resistance.[19]

The 8th US Air Force showed up over the target area at 12.55 hours. The Canadian artillery had been issued signal shells one hour previously. Their red smoke was to mark the targets and the artillery was able to open fire just in time. The attack objectives of the 678 airborne four-engined bombers were St. Sylvain, Cauvicourt and the Ferme La Ruette located one kilometer southeast, Hautmesnil, Gouvix and Bretteville-sur-Laize. The batteries of III. Flakkorps, in position in the target area, opened fire despite themselves coming under enemy artillery fire or being caught in the hail of bombs. They were successful in shooting down nine four-engined bombers.

Their massive and well-aimed fire also hit one of the lead bombers. It carried out an emergency bomb drop before having reached its target, thus causing the aircraft of its own squadron following behind to drop their loads of bombs short, i.e. on their own troops assembled for the attack. A large number of bombers was forced off course so that only 492 aircraft were able to drop their loads of bombs, a total of 1,487 tons. Several other aircraft may also not have reached their action area for other reasons. There was an additional erroneous bomb drop on their own troops. One of the lead bombers had made a mistake in identifying its target and dropped its bombs on the southern outskirts of Caen, Faubourg de Vaucelles, through which a Canadian battalion was driving at the time. This caused approximately 100 casualties. The Polish anti-aircraft unit lost eight dead and twenty-eight wounded. The total Allied losses on the ground were approximately sixty-five dead and 250 wounded. In addition, four guns and fifty-five vehicles were lost. Much worse, however, was the confusion which had been caused.[20]

The Poles started their attack hesitantly at 13.30 hours. The II Canadian Corps reported that the two tank divisions had crossed the starting line at 13.55 hours.[21]

Into that advancing attack by the Poles and Canadians thrust the counterattack of Kampfgruppe Waldmüller. The Divisional commander, who directed the counterattack from the spearhead, reported on it:

I met Waldmüller north of Bretteville-le Rabet. Together we drove to Cintheaux to determine the present situation. Wittmann's Tigers were already in position in cover of a hedge east of Cintheaux without having taken part in the fire fight so far. Cintheaux was under artillery fire while the open terrain was fairly free of fire. From the northern edge of the village we spotted massive tank columns north of the road to Bretteville-sur-Laize. The tanks were assembled in packs. The same picture offered itself south of Garcelles and at the edge of the forest southeast of the village. Seeing these concentrations of tanks almost took our breath away. We could not comprehend the behavior of the Canadians. Why did those overwhelming tank forces not push on their attack? . . .

Waldmüller and I agreed that we could not let the tank units start out against us. The enemy tanks must not be allowed to drive another attack. An enemy tank division sat attack-ready on either side of the road. That attack could not be allowed to get started-we must attempt to grasp the initiative.

I decided to defend the village of Cintheaux with all the forces already in action there, to attack at lightning speed east of the road with all available soldiers and thus to upset the enemy plans. I determined the forest southeast of Garcelles as the target of the attack . . .

During the last briefings with Waldmüller and Wittmann we watched a single bomber approaching. It flew across the terrain several times and then set a visual marker. The bomber appeared to us to be some sort of airborne command post. I immediately ordered the attack so that the troops would be out of the bombing sector. Once more I shook Michel Wittmann's hand and mentioned the extremely critical situation. Our good Michel laughed his boyish laughter and climbed into his Tiger. Until that moment, 138 enemy tanks had become his victims. Would he increase that number of victories or become a victim himself?

The Panzers rolled speedily northward. At high speed, they crossed the open areas and took advantage of small breaks in the terrain to fire. The Panzer attack pulled the grenadiers forward. Widely dispersed, they advanced on the target of the attack. I was located at the northern edge of Cintheaux while the enemy artillery laid concentrated fire on the attacking Panzers. Michel Wittmann's Panzer raced right into the enemy fire. I knew his tactic during such situations: Get through! Don't stop! Into the dirt and reach a free field of fire. All the Panzers hurled themselves into the steel inferno. They had to prevent the enemy from attacking, they had to disrupt his timetable. Waldmüller pursued with his infantry, the brave grenadiers following their officers.

During the all-destroying artillery fire a machine gunner yelled at me, pointing into a northwesterly direction. Lost for words in the face of the terrific Allied power I watched an endless chain of large four-engined bombers approaching. Ironical laughter from some young grenadiers let us forget that terrible danger for a fraction of a second. A typical boy from Berlin shouted: 'What an honor, Churchill is sending one bomber for each of us!' Indeed, the boy was right. More bombers came flying at us than there were German grenadiers lying in the dirt there! There was only one escape: Get away from the village and into the open terrain! As quick as lightning the defenders of Cintheaux leapt into the green fields north of the village and waited for the dropping of the bombs. We had guessed correctly: Village after village was leveled. It did not take long before large fires blazed into the skies. With a certain amount of glee we observed that the Canadians were also being looked after by the American bomber fleet . . .

The last waves flew overhead of the strongly attacking Waldmüller Kampfgruppe without dropping a single bomb on the Panzers. The bombers attacked their targets as ordered without concern for the, by this time, changed situation . . .

As Kampfgruppe Waldmüller approached the woods, it immediately engaged Polish infantry. The grim duels of Panzers against tanks were fought by the fighting vehicles of the 4th Canadian Armoured Division and Michel Wittmann's Tiger's.

At times, the Tigers could hardly be recognized. Very well-directed artillery fire hammered down on the Tigers and Panthers [read: Panzer IVs]. In the meantime, we had moved back into our old positions in the ruins of Cintheaux. The village immediately came under an attack from due north and was under direct fire from Canadian tanks. Action on their flanks by a few Tigers of the Wittmann group kept the Sherman tanks away from Cintheaux. We observed massive enemy movements in the direction of Bretteville-sur-Laize one kilometer in front of us. One attack after the other faltered at our strong front line. We were unbelievably lucky—the opposite side did not carry out one single concentrated attack. The Divisionsbegleitkompanie reported its position west of St. Sylvain. It was battling the spearhead of the 1. Polish Armoured Division and it had knocked out several tanks. The Poles no longer dared to leave the Cramesnil forest . . .

The battle had already been lasting for hours. The wounded assembled south of Cintheaux. They were transported away under enemy fire.[22]

Sturmmann Helmut Wiese took part in the attack by Kampfgruppe Waldmüller as the driver of a Panzer IV of 5. Kompanie. He gave an account of his experiences:

After inspecting our target, discussing possible danger spots and driving tactics, we mounted and informed Arno, our gunner, Karl, our loader, and Egon, the radio operator. Their first combat action was now before them. Ready to go, ready to fire. 'Panzer, march!' Our nerves tight to the breaking point, each alone with his thoughts, complete silence inside the vehicle, only the engine was humming. So we crawled and crept slowly toward the hilltop. What was waiting for us on the rear slope? Otto [Panzer commander

Unterscharführer Otto Knoof] was standing in his hatch. 'Slowly, a little higher!—Stop! Turret three o'clock, aim at the edge of the woods!—Again, nothing—Helmut, let's go, march!' I geared up and opened the throttle all the way. We crested the hilltop, I spotted the edge of the woods and steered toward its left corner. We wanted to go around it so we could see what was behind it. Then, a violent rattle on the outer walls, machine gun and rifle fire. Our turret MG was firing. I recognized a rapidly firing enemy machine gun, spotted the flat helmets. De-clutching on the right, aiming the hull MG, firing—all that happened in a flash. There, at the corner of the woods, enemy soldiers moving a gun into position! Report to the turret, again aiming the hull MG. Our gun was firing with the Panzer moving at full speed. 'Stop! Stop! Back! Back! Faster!' Otto shouted that order. I knew the engine was at full speed, it could not go backward any faster. I turned toward the instruments, we were way past the maximum allowable number of revolutions, the time was sixteen minutes before sixteen hours. Just as I was about to look out of my sight slit I was blinded by a flash of light. There was a bang as if a soda pop bottle had smashed into a stone floor. Hit to the forehead, alive, those were my thoughts. Then, the Panzer was shaking as if in the grip of a giant fist, brightness, howling, shrieking noises, totally inhuman. Smell of sulfur, complete silence. Then, Otto's voice: 'Bail out, Panzer's on fire!' I unlatched my hatch, pushed it open, it moved only a few centimeters. Flames immediately blazed through the opening. The turret skirt sat above. I saw how Egon, our radio operator, pulled his legs from his hatch. That was the way. Across the transmission, the radio, my breath stopped, it was getting so hot, I had to get out, I could not take it any more.—Far away, a face. Arms stretching toward me. Shouts: 'Helmut, get out!' Pulling, ripping, fresh air. I was outside, jumped off, letting myself drop.—Egon had come back and pulled me out. Thanks, comrade! Egon helped me to get up, I was standing again. Bullets whistled by and hit the hull. We leapt to the side away from the enemy, there was Otto. What about Arno and Karl? Otto pointed to the turret, its side hatches were still closed and yelled: 'Both were killed outright, I was still inside!' I could not believe it. Arno Eltus from Königsberg in East Prussia, my gunner. Since Hasselt we had been together with Otto, always in the same Panzer. We lived through our first actions, victories, always the three of us together. And now he was gone, just left inside the turret. What a terrible realization.

Dark smoke billowed from the open hatches. We ran into the direction of our front line. Suddenly I heard: 'Helmut, you're on fire!' I rolled on the ground, Otto and Egon helped extinguish the flames. Again, machine gun bullets were whistling by us. We ran and ran. Finally, we reached the rear slope, found German soldiers, houses. A squad of soldiers addressed us but I did not hear or comprehend anything. I could see but not recognize, felt pain, severely burning pain. Then it turned all black around me and silent. I made out that I was in a room, was lying on the ground, unable to move, in pain, moaning. Someone was looking after me but I could not see him. Then, I suddenly understood. The voice said: 'Quiet, stay calm. You're at our dressing station, and safe.' Again, everything turned black. Suddenly, Otto appeared and said: 'I'll get you out of here at nightfall and take you along.' That made me happy. Again, all was dark. The floor was shaking, noise from the engines, voices shouting: 'The Panzers are getting out!' I was deeply disappointed, Otto had promised he was going to fetch me. Then, daylight shone through the door, strange uniforms appeared, a clear questioning voice: 'Who be here from the 'As-As'?' Infantry bullets, artillery explosions, being rapidly loaded into an ambulance, severe pain, another blackout. The tent hospital in Caen, transport by ship, I lived through that as in a trance and was mostly unconscious. On 21 August, in Leeds, I realized and understood that I had been captured. I could tell from my hospital documents that the dressing station where I had been taken had been handed over to members of the 1st Polish Armoured Division in the morning of 9 August.[23]

The Poles attacked with two tank units, the 2nd Tank Regiment and the Lancers Regiment, at the point. Each unit consisted, in accordance with the structure of British and Canadian armored divisions, of three companies with eighteen Sherman tanks each. Of the thirty-six tanks from two companies of the 2nd Tank Regiment attacking as the first wave, twenty-six were knocked out soon after the start of the attack. Two officers had been killed, most of the tank drivers burned. The 24th Lancers advanced more carefully. They stopped inside a wide hollow and waited for the results from their forward reconnaissance. Because of the intensive fire from artillery and Panzers, the unit did not dare attack. Still, it lost fourteen tanks. After that, it pulled back behind the Canadian positions. At 15.10 hours, the Poles had reported to II Canadian Corps that twenty Tigers were in action in the area southeast of St. Aignan-de Cramesnil, dominating the terrain on the other side of the road leading through the village with their fire. The Poles also reported that they had suffered losses and were regrouping.[24]

The Canadian attack also started slowly. In the course of the afternoon, however, and after bad losses, it achieved small gains of terrain. Gaumesnil withstood the assault by superior forces for some time but was captured at 15.30 hours by The Royal Regiment of Canada which belonged to the 4th Infantry Brigade of the 2nd Canadian Infantry Division. Presumably, the town could only be captured after the few Tigers, which had been engaging the attacking Canadian tanks, had been knocked out. Among them was also the commander of the Tigerabteilung, Hauptsturmführer Michel Wittmann.

The medical officer of Schwere Panzerabteilung 101, Hauptsturmführer Dr. Wolfgang Rabe, M.D., observed the battle of the Tigers from some distance away. Four of them had taken up positions along a country lane leading in a northerly direction from Cintheaux, approximately 300 meters away from the Route Nationale. They were sitting between a high, thick hedge and a row of low bushes running parallel on its left. Dr. Rabe wrote:

> Wittmann and four or five Tigers were east of the road leading to Caen. I was off to the side. The Tigers came under fire, reported to be directly from English 15 cm guns. Several Tigers went up in flames and I tried to determine whether anyone was getting out. Since I could not see anybody, I assumed that some had left the Panzers by way of the ground hatch and I tried to get closer. That was not possible either since, as soon as I left the ditch in an easterly direction, I came under fire. We waited for another one or two hours, to see if any crew member might still show up. Toward evening I drove over to Brigadeführer Kraemer (chief of staff of I. SS-Panzerkorps, Author) and reported to him on what had happened. He directed me, as I was the longest serving officer of the Abteilung, to lead the remnants of the Abteilung back and assigned me to Wünsche.[25]

When Obersturmbannführer Max Wünsche learned that Michel Wittmann was missing, he had a search started for him. Untersturmführer Horst Borgsmüller reported:

> I was given an order to search for Wittmann and his crew to the right and left of N 158. My driver, Sturmmann Klein, and I drove first in the direction of Hautmesnil. Dusk was setting in and I could not make out any details. After some time we came under machine gun fire from the right of the road. The search of the terrain and the dressing stations was unsuccessful. I heard from some Grenadiers that Tigers had been knocked out by enemy anti-tank guns to the right of the road. Obersturmführer Wendorf of the Tigerabteilung could not tell me anything either. On orders from Hauptsturmführer Isecke I drove once more in the direction of Grainville during the night. The command post of Obersturmbannführer Mohnke was located there. He warned me against driving on since the enemy had already closed in. We tried to go on for a short distance. Then flares shot into the sky and we came under fire, again from the right.[26]

Some French citizens from St. Aignan-de Gaumesnil saw a Tiger sitting in that area at a country lane leading from St. Aignan to Gaumesnil after the fighting had stopped. Four more Tigers were seen along the country lane from St. Aignan to Cintheaux. One of those had its turret ripped off. The battle diary recorder of the Tigerabteilung, Rottenführer Herbert Debusmann, was assigned to collect ammunition in that area while still a prisoner of war in 1947. He still found all five previously mentioned destroyed or immobilized Tigers as well as two Panzer IVs in the vicinity. The turret of one Tiger, with the number 007, had been ripped off. It had been the commander's Panzer. Obersturmbannführer von Westernhagen, the Abteilung commander, had not taken part in this battle, sidelined by an illness. Among other matters, Herbert Debusmann related in his report:

> The turret of '007'—it was in the very rear of the four Panzers—was lying on the ground several meters away from the hull. I do not believe that the question whether Michel Wittmann was in this Panzer can be answered. The fact was that he disliked using a staff Panzer or commander's Panzer since they carried approximately thirty fewer shells, because of their ground-to-air radio equipment, than the other Panzers. Some 1,500 meters away from that spot, in the direction of Caen but further away from the Route Nationale, sat another Tiger of 2. Kompanie. It had not been knocked out but looked completely serviceable. It showed no damage to the tracks and I could not determine any other mechanical defect. The Panzer had not been blown up and was still carrying its full supply of ammunition.[27]

Since no members of the Tiger crews who fought near Cintheaux survived the war, maybe not even the Normandy battles, nothing totally reliable may ever be established regarding the last battle of Michel Wittmann.

The Argyll and Sutherland Highlanders of Canada, of the 4th Canadian Armoured Division, and The South Alberta Regiment—the reconnaissance unit of that division—captured the bitterly fought-for town of Cintheaux at 18.00 hours. Two companies of the Argylls advanced further along the Route Nationale and took Hautmesnil. The command post of I./25, part of Kampfgruppe Waldmüller, was located south of the intersection of the road from Cauvicourt to Gouvix with the Route Nationale. While Sturmbannführer Waldmüller accompanied the attacking troops, the adjutant, Untersturmführer Willy Klein, had established a base there with members of the staff company and stragglers of 89. Inf.-Div. That base was held against all attacks on 8 August.[28]

The 3. Batterie of Werferabteilung 12 was in position approximately two kilometers further west. Under the command of Obersturmführer Bay it fought off all attacks until evening. The Batterie chief was seriously wounded, but it was possible to pull out the battery at the fall of darkness.[29]

The enemy movements in the direction of Bretteville-sur-Laize, which the Divisional commander had observed, were part of the attack by the 2nd Canadian Infantry Division on that town. Supported by artillery and a tank unit, two battalions captured the town. However, in the evening they withdrew to the higher northern bank of the Laize river. During this withdrawal they suffered severe losses from German artillery fire.

After the enemy had advanced to Bretteville-sur-Laize and had taken Hautmesnil, the left flank of Kampfgruppe Waldmüller was open. It did not have a contact on the right either. Thus, it could no longer hold the line it had reached with its counterattack and where it had later changed over to defense. At approximately 16.00 hours General Eberbach considered a withdrawal, during the night of 8–9 August, to a line Moult (2.5 kilometers southeast of Vimont)-St. Sylvain-les Moutiers (three kilometers southeast of Grimbosq). He also contemplated throwing into battle the newly arriving parts of 85. Inf.-Div. The general command of I. SS-Panzerkorps agreed with these intentions. "HJ" Division would move to a line St. Sylvain-Bretteville-sur-Laize (exclusive), 271. Inf.-Div. would mainyain contact on the left. Further, it was planned to move the approaching 85. Inf.-Div. into a second position along a line Condé-sur Ifs-Grainville.

That decision was based on outdated reports and an incorrect picture of the enemy. However, the units fighting at the front line did not have a clear picture of the enemy situation since there was no longer a continuous front. Communications frequently broke down during the heavy fighting, or reports were only rarely provided. The Ia was forced to trust that the Divisional commander at the front had an overall view of the situation and would contact the Divisional command post if significant decisions were required.

Three conversations, held between Feldmarschall von Kluge and General Eberbach in the evening, indicate the gravity of the situation, and the difficult struggle to find solutions. These exchanges were recorded in the war diary of 5. Panzerarmee. General Eberbach (GE) informed the Feldmarschall (FM) on the situation at 21.00 hours:

> GE: At I. SS-Pz.-Korps: the enemy air preparation there is worse than on 18 July. It lasted throughout the night (having started last night at 10 P.M.) The enemy has penetrated the main line of defense, with a large number of tanks, approximately 500.
>
> FM: What, 500 tanks?
>
> GE: Yes, at Chicheboville alone there were 200 constantly throughout the day. The enemy broke through our main line of defense there and advanced to St. Aignan. It was only recaptured in a counterattack. Then renewed carpet bombing, 'HJ' smashed to

the point where only individual Panzers returned. The enemy advanced further south to Gaumesnil and continues to push on. The I. SS-Pz.-Korps has established a defensive line of Pak and Flak which it has held until now. It is questionable if this line can be held tomorrow when the enemy attacks in earnest. The new Inf.-Div. has practically been reduced by 50 percent, the same holds true for the 'HJ'. I would be happy if I could assemble twenty Panzers tonight, including Tigers. At 271. Inf.-Div., the attack continued throughout the day. Parts of 'HJ' are in action there. They suffered heavy losses from enemy barrages . . .

Facing LXXXVI.A.K. are the 7th English Armoured Division, 8th English Armoured Brigade, 27th English Armoured Brigade, 50th and 53rd English Infantry Divisions. During fine weather tomorrow, the enemy will resume his attacks and attempt to further break through in the direction of Falaise . . .

FM: We have to accept the fact that the decisive time here will be tomorrow or the day after.

Thereafter, the Feldmarschall searched for possibilities to reinforce I. SS-Panzerkorps. If the front line north of Falaise did not hold, 7. Armee and the left wing of 5. Panzerarmee were threatened with encirclement and destruction. As a last resort, troops which were also indispensable there, would have to be used. The Feldmarschall again called General Eberbach at 22.20 hours and 23.30 hours.

22.20 hours: long distance telephone conversation between Feld-marschall von Kluge and General Eberbach:

FM: If one of the Panzer divisions, which I took away from you, was returned to you, what would you then be lacking most?

GE: Above all, I lack Panzers.

FM: Do you have a commander who understands how to handle Panzers? Where is the 'HJ' command?

GE: The commander of 'HJ' telephoned me this afternoon from St. Aignan. He was there to organize the defense.

FM: That is 'Fast Meyer'! Have you had any news from him since?

GE: No news. That was before the carpet -bombing.

FM: Early or during the night?

GE: I am referring to the carpet bombing which took place again at around noon. I have had no more news from him since.

FM: If I were to send you a Panzer unit, would that help you?

GE: Yes, Sir, it would.

FM: Do you have a man who could lead it?

GE: Yes, Wünsche.

FM: He is still there? Well! I'll see if I can still send you a Panzer-abteilung.

GE: If it would be possible.

FM: Maybe one more Panzerabteilung from AlenÁon. During the night, of course.

GE: Maybe we are lucky and have fog. Could it come to Falaise? I would have fuel available there.

FM: Yes, I will call you again right away.

23.30 hours: Continuation of the telephone conversation Feld-marschall von Kluge and General Eberbach:

FM: Has the situation got worse or better?

GE: One cannot say better. The enemy seems to be reorganizing his units. He carried out all his attacks with tanks and without infantry. Based on the evening reports I have the impression that he is moving forces away, even from opposite LXXXVI. A.K., in order to put them into action in the main breakthrough area at the Caen road in the direction of Falaise. I believe that he will attack tomor-row more intensely and on a wider front, extending from the left wing of I.-SS-Pz.-Korps to LXXXVI. A.K. The enemy has advanced with very strong elements from Hautmesnil to Langannerie. I hope that it will be possible to destroy the enemy, reported not to be very strong (twelve tanks), in Langannerie tonight and to hold the line St. Sylvain-Bretteville.

FM: Which forces will you use to do that?

GE: With parts of LXXXVI. A.K. (Kampfgruppe), parts of 'HJ'. No contact with Meyer, only Wünsche is there until now.

FM: The Panzers of 9. Division will set out from Argentan to Falaise so that they will be half way tomorrow morning. That is a dif-ficult decision for me, largely giving up on an order issued to me. I cannot think of another solution, I have no other forces left. If this keeps going the same way tomorrow, we will be unable to stop it.

Arrange for an efficient superior officer of Panzerarmee 5 com-mand or of I.-SS-Pz.-Korps to be at the railroad crossing 800 meters south of Falaise along the road from Argentan to Falaise, road fork south of the rail line, at 05.00 hours. I understand that these forces will not be sufficient in the long run.[30]

The Panther Abteilung of 9. Panzerdivision (Heer), scheduled to pro-vide the reinforcement, had only approximately one dozen battle-ready Panzers. For that reason, II. SS-Panzerkorps was ordered to release one Panz-erabteilung of 9. SS-Panzerdivision "Hohenstaufen". At 23.50 hours, the Korps reported that the Abteilung was tied down in the front lines and that,

instead, Schwere SS-Panzerabteilung 102 with, at that moment, thirteen battle-ready Tigers was being sent off.[31]

By the evening, the enemy had advanced east of the Route Nationale
with forty to fifty tanks and reached the area north of Langannerie. There,
Flakabteilung 12 had stopped him. The enemy now stood in the deep flank
of Kampfgruppe Waldmüller. In the meantime, Kampfgruppe Wünsche had
reached the Potigny area by way of Tournebu and Ussy. It had started to prepare for defense along a predetermined line north of Potigny. The Divisional command became convinced that defense was possible only on the
high terrain north of the Laison sector. Kampfgruppe Waldmüller, threatened by encirclement, had first to fight its way there. Thus, the Division
ordered:

> Kampfgruppe Waldmüller (reinforced I./26) will defend itself on the
> hills north of Maizières, north of Rouvres to Hill 140 inclusive, north-
> west of Assy. For this, 1. Kompanie SS-Panzerjägerabteilung 12 will be
> attached to it;
>
> Kampfgruppe Krause (reinforced I./26) will defend itself in the sector
> of the hills north of Ouilly-Hill 183 at the Route Nationale;
>
> III./26 will defend itself on the high terrain around Hill 195 (three kilo-
> meters northwest of Potigny) and will absorb all arriving stragglers of
> 89. Inf.-Div.;
>
> Panzerregiment 12 with attached heavy SS-Panzerabteilung 102 will
> assemble in the Quesnay forest (two kilometers northwest of Ouilly).
> From there, it will carry out limited attacks to enable the setting up of
> the defenses and prevent a breakthrough by enemy tank forces along
> the Route Nationale;
>
> Artillerieregiment 12 with attached Werferabteilung 12 will take up posi-
> tion south of the Laison in such a manner that it can go into action
> anywhere in the sector of the Division;
>
> Flakabteilung 12 will take up positions along the Route Nationale north
> of Potigny with the two 8.8 cm batteries so that it can destroy enemy
> tanks which have broken through. The 4. Batterie (3.7 cm) and the
> attached 14./26 (2 cm) are available for air defense;
>
> Aufklärungsgruppe Wienecke will establish and maintain contact with
> 272. Inf.-Div.;
>
> the Divisionsbegleitkompanie will leave Kampfgruppe Waldmüller and
> assemble in Montboit (1.5 kilometers east of Ouilly) as Divisional
> reserve;
>
> the Divisional command post will remain at la Brêche-du-Diable.

The first parts of 85. Inf.-Div. would not arrive in the combat area before
the morning of 9 August. The defense of the hills north of the Laison was
able to ensure an orderly assembly according to plan. At 22.00 hours, the
artillery of "HJ" Division was in position, the Panzerregiment had assembled
in the Quesnay forest. The I./26 and III./26, without Aufklärungsgruppe

Olboeter which was still approaching from Vire, prepared for defense in the predetermined sectors. During the night, Flakabteilung 12 and the parts of III. Flak-Korps in action south of Langannerie changed positions.

The Kampfgruppe of I./25, under the command of Untersturmführer Willi Klein, which had defended itself resolutely in the southern section of Hautmesnil against all attacks, withdrew from its position shortly before dawn on 9 August and joined with I./25 near Soignolles. When daylight arrived, observation from the village church tower indicated that I./25, together with the attached Korps and Divisional escort companies and the 1. Kompanie of Panzerjägerabteilung, were encircled. Sturmbannführer Waldmüller sent his adjutant with two men to the Divisional command post to obtain further orders. They met Oberführer Meyer at the Route Nationale, reported the situation near Soignolles and requested further orders. The Divisional commander ordered defense north of the Laison sector and sent a message to Waldmüller that his Kampfgruppe would be brought out by Panzers.[32]

The 89. Inf.-Div. organized its units during the night 8-9 August. The remnants were primarily sent into defensive action west of the Route Nationale. The right wing was located near Grainville, its front facing northeast. From there, the front line in the morning of 9 August ran south of Urville and further along the eastern edge of the hills behind the Laize to the area of Bretteville-sur-Laize.[33] The 271. Inf.-Div. also moved its front line to the rear and established contact on the right with 89. Inf.-Div. south of Bretteville. From there, the forward positions ran in a westerly direction through the Forêt de Cinglais—from the western edge of the forest in a southwesterly direction one kilometer south of les Moutiers—via la Maisonnière to the Orne river, one kilometer northwest of Croisilles.[34] During the night, 272. Inf.-Div. strengthened the positions it had moved into at noon of 8 August, improved anti-tank measures, reorganized the artillery, and brought all available reserves behind the left wing.[35]

The results of Attack Phase 2 were disappointing for the Canadian command. Despite the immense expenditure of air force and tanks it had not been possible to reach the second attack objective, the hills northeast and north of Falaise and near Potigny. After the breakthrough across the positions of 89. Inf.-Div., it was above all the few Panzers of II. Abteilung, a few Tigers, 1. Panzerjägerkompanie, as well as the grenadiers of I./25 and the two escort companies with their heavy weapons, who prevented the breakthrough in the depth. The commanding general of the II Canadian Corps, General Simonds, ordered his two tank divisions to continue their attack during the night, using lowest possible light sources, in order to gain favorable starting positions for the next day. He ordered the 4th Canadian Armoured Division to further enlarge the bulge in the front near Langannerie. The 1st Polish Armoured Division was ordered to reconnoiter in the direction of the attack and to prepare for an attack on Cauvicourt (one kilometer east of Hautmesnil) at first light and to capture it.

Contrary to this order, the Canadian Grenadier Guards tanks withdrew to Cintheaux and Gaumesnil after dark, as they had been taught during training. Around dawn they advanced again to attack Bretteville-le Rabet. The third tank unit of the 4th Canadian Armoured Brigade—the British Columbia Regiment—with the attached Algonquin Regiment was ordered by the brigade commander to capture Hill 195 by dawn. To the surprise of both sides, the execution of that order took place in a manner completely different from what was expected.

The 01 of the "HJ" Division, Obersturmführer Meitzel, had been assigned to the Panzerregiment. In the early morning hours of 9 August, he attempted to establish contact, from Quesnay, to Kampfgruppe Waldmüller which was reported near Hill 140. He drove along the southern slope of the ridge of hills in a captured English light armored reconnaissance vehicle and then turned north toward Hill 140. To his surprise, he came under fire from there and spotted Canadian tanks instead of German infantry. Luckily, his reconnaissance vehicle was not hit so that Meitzel was able to turn around and report to Obersturmbannführer Wünsche. The Divisional commander observed that event from Tombeau Marie Jolie through his binoculars. Feeling apprehensive, he immediately telephoned Obersturmbannführer Wünsche in the Quesnay forest, told him of his observations, and requested more detailed information. Wünsche had already alerted his Panzer Kampfgruppe and was waiting for Meitzel to return. After Meitzel's observations had been reported to him, the Divisional commander drove at high speed to the command post of the Panzerregiment. There was a danger of an enemy tank unit breakthrough across the position which was still being built and where, especially in that sector, not one single German infantryman was deployed.

Max Wünsche immediately sent out two Panzer platoons with orders to destroy the enemy who had broken through, and to capture Hill 140.

Meitzel drove back in his reconnaissance vehicle in order to gain a more detailed picture of the enemy. He reported on it later:

> As I approached the attacking tanks once again, my armored car was hit. I was hurled out into the air, then slammed into the turret of my vehicle and broke my right arm. A few moments later I was captured by a Canadian tank crew.
>
> I had barely reached the Canadian hedgehog defensive position on Hill 140 when our 8.8 cm guns started to fire on Canadian tanks and infantry. Tigers and Panthers advanced in order to encircle the positions on the hill. One Canadian tank after the other was knocked out and ended up in smoke and flames. Some crews which had lost their tanks tried to reach a small wood close-by and escape the blazing 'hedgehog' of exploding tanks. They took me along. Soon after, the wood came under sustained attacks from fighter-bombers to relieve the hard-pressed Canadians. My suggestion to

the Canadians, to break through to our command post, was refused, with thanks. Only after further fighter-bomber attacks did they change their minds.

I arrived at our command post again in the late afternoon with twenty-three Canadians and a broken arm.

Among the prisoners was Captain J. A. Renwick. From the interrogation, during which the Captain from the British Columbia Regiment provided no tactical information, and from the questions the Canadians had directed at the previously captured Obersturmführer Meitzel, the following picture of the situation evolved: The German counterattack at noon of 8 August had stopped the enemy attack near St. Sylvain and Hautmesnil. In order to recapture the initiative, the 4th Canadian Armoured Division had apparently sent the 28th Armoured Regiment (British Columbia Regiment) and two infantry companies of the Algonquin Regiment for a night attack on Hill 195 northwest of Potigny. That action was probably meant to open up the narrow passage between the Laison and the Laize, enabling a rapid breakthrough to Falaise. Because of an error in orientation during the night, the combat group had captured the unoccupied Hill 140 instead of Hill 195. Obersturmführer Meitzel had been asked for the ". . . wide asphalt road . . ." which they had looked for in vain. During the night, the enemy force had thus overtaken the Waldmüller Kampfgruppe which had moved to Soignolles and had orders to capture Hill 140.

The "HJ" Division learned later that Bataillon Waldmüller had been pushed to the east and awaited darkness in broken terrain in order to reach the German lines during the night. The Divisionsbegleitkompanie had encountered a similar fate. It had been overtaken by the Poles. Both arrived in their predetermined areas, totally exhausted, in the evening of 9 August. The men of Bataillon Waldmüller dug in on Hill 140 and to the west of it, reinforced by two bicycle companies of 85. Infanteriedivision.[36]

The entries in the war diaries of the other side portray the following picture, as relayed by Stacy.

The combat group of the British Columbia Regiment with the attached Algonquin Regiment started its attack to capture Hill 195, near Potigny, from Gaumesnil in the early morning hours of 9 August. Initially, it encountered only minor resistance. East of the Route Nationale it met the "Halpenney Force" combat group, assembling for the attack on Bretteville-le Rabet. The commander of the British Columbia Regiment, Lieutenant Colonel D.G. Worthington, wanted to avoid the enemy who was located near Bretteville. He swung to the east, planning to turn westward later. Because of the restricted visibility of the early morning, the combat group became disoriented as it marched cross country. A single tank section found the right direction, advanced between Bretteville and Estrées and reached Hill 151 (two kilometers north of Hill 195). When the section leader noticed that he had lost contact with his unit, he turned around. The main body of the combat group continued to roll in a southeasterly direction. At 06.45 hours it reported that its objective was 1,800 meters away and that it was preparing to capture it. At 07.55 hours, the combat group reported its location as Hill 195 which it had found free of the enemy. It now awaited reinforcements. In reality, two Canadian tank companies, less one section, and two infantry companies were located on the wide round top of Hill 140, one kilometer northwest of Assy. The remainder of Worthington's combat group was located to the rear as a reserve.[37]

Between 08.08 and 08.41 hours, the combat group reported contact with the enemy and that ten tanks had been knocked out. It requested artillery support. The Brigade asked for the location of the enemy. It was reported as approximately 450 meters south of the Canadian position. The Brigade directed fire into the indicated area. When it then requested a report on the accuracy of the fire it did not receive any answer. Since no reports were coming in from the Worthington combat group, the Brigade ordered the 21st Armoured Regiment (tanks) at 10.00 hours to assemble near Gaumesnil and advance to Hill 195 in order to reinforce Worthington. It took two hours for the unit to bring back its elements which had been assigned to other units. The Regiment started out after 14.30 hours. At 16.05 hours, it reported that it had reached the road connecting Soignolles and Bretteville. When the Regiment attempted to cross the open terrain between Estrées and Bretteville, it encountered strong resistance and lost twenty-six tanks.[38]

A squad of armored half-tracks was sent by the 10th Infantry Brigade before noon to the Worthington combat group to transport back the wounded. When it returned, however, even its leader could not give reliable information on the location. During the course of the day, tanks were spotted at quite a distance. They were assumed to be Polish. At first, they opened fire on the Canadian troops. However, when yellow smoke signal markers were fired, they stopped firing. Thereafter, these tanks were observed coming under fire from German Panzers. They withdrew after having lost several fighting vehicles. At 15.00 hours, eight battle-ready tanks arrived at the Brigade, sent back by Worthington. They had made it back unchallenged and had not caused any counter measures. The combat group came under renewed attack at 18.30 hours. The attack was repelled by infantry and the crews of the knocked-out tanks. At approximately that time, Lieutenant Colonel Worthington was killed by a mortar shell. At dusk, when another German attack advanced, a portion of the combat group surrendered. The remainder withdrew and was taken in by the Poles.[39]

During these battles for Hill 140, which were carried out with great valor on both sides, the 28th Armoured Regiment lost forty-seven tanks and 112 men, of whom forty were killed and thirty-four captured.

On 9 and 10 August, the Algonquin Regiment lost 128 men, of whom forty-five were killed and the same number captured. Most of these losses probably occurred on 9 August.[40]

The I./25 had set up defenses during the night 8–9 August in the area around Soignolles. The 1. Kompanie of the Panzerjägerabteilung was located there as well. The Divisionsbegleitkompanie had moved into a defensive position between St. Sylvain and the Ch‚teau du Fosse, located approximately one kilometer southwest of the town. The Muance creek, running on its right wing in a northeasterly direction, offered sufficient protection from tanks. The Korpsbegleitkompanie was in position to the left of the Divisionsbegleitkompanie. Around noon, the 1st Polish Armoured Division attacked Kampfgruppe Waldmüller. The Panzerjägerkompanie knocked out a number of enemy tanks. The Korpsbegleitkompanie was wiped out by that attack, the Divisionsbegleitkompanie was overrun from the south at approximately 14.00 hours. However, it was able to hold on and withdraw to the woods two kilometers southeast of St. Sylvain in the evening. Unterscharführer Leo Freund of the Divisionsbegleitkompanie reported on the battle:

> We moved into a position between St. Sylvain and the Ch‚teau du Fosse. The position was located in the middle of open terrain. In front of us was a wide and easily observed field of fire, in our back a huge harvested grain field, the sheaves standing upright. A wooded area was behind the grain field. The enemy attacked in the afternoon. We could see the tanks rolling toward us a long distance away. However, the first push was directed at our neighbor on the left, the Korpsbegleitkompanie. But then, all hell broke loose in our corner also. Suddenly, enemy tanks were sitting among our fox holes. One of the tanks was even right next to the Kompanie command post, located in a fair-sized camouflaged depression in the ground, covered with tree trunks. The two 7.5 cm Pak guns, attached to the Kompanie, fired without pause at the enemy tanks now coming at us from dead ahead. After several of them had been knocked out, the others stopped, suddenly and as if frightened, but to our relief. They opened fire on the two Pak guns. In the meantime, two of the tanks driving around among our positions, had been destroyed, including the one next to the Kompanie command post. The other two or three immediately withdrew in the direction of the chateau. Our two Pak guns had been silenced by the concentrated enemy fire. But suddenly, the forward observer of our I.G. Zug, Unterscharführer Kurt Breitmoser, appeared next to me and yelled: 'Let's go, come over to the Pak!'
>
> The two guns were sitting not far from us. One of them was destroyed, but the other still seemed in working order. However, all

the crews were casualties. We loaded for the first time and Kurt Breitmoser pointed the gun deliberately at the tank closest to us. Direct
hit! We were able to fire two more shells, then there was a sudden
bang and we were hurled backward a few meters, landing in the
sand. I was unharmed, but Breitmoser had been wounded in the
head. His face was covered with blood and he hurried back to find a
medic. However, it did not take long before Breitmoser showed up
again, his head bandaged up to the eyes. In answer to our surprised
looks and questions he only said: 'There's no way I can leave you
alone here, even if there isn't a helmet to fit me.'

During the evening we withdrew eastward across the grain field to
the wooded area. The enemy infantry first tried to pursue us. However, after our MGs had set the sheaves of grain on fire with tracer
bullets, the enemy attack, carried out with great superiority, was
fought off.

Inside the wooded area we felt as if we were in a mouse trap. All
around us was open terrain and we were glad that we could move to
Condé-sur-Ifs during the same night.[41]

After the fall of darkness, I./25 and the attached Panzerjägerkompanie
were also able to disengage from the enemy and arrived in the new sector
during the night. The Divisionsbegleitkompanie formed the rearguard and
withdrew to Condé-sur-Ifs at approximately 23.00 hours.[42]

In the history of the 1st Polish Armoured Division, reports on the battles
of 9 August 1944 state that the 1st Polish Armoured Regiment (tanks) came
across the burned-out Canadian tanks near Hill 140. The unit continued its
attack. It was able to surprise the German infantry and push into the ravine
near Rouvres at the Laison river. Although the tanks were not accompanied
by infantry, they took some prisoners. These picked up their weapons again
and fired on the dismounted crews. During the confusion, Major Stefanow-
icz saw no alternative but to retreat. He ordered the wounded loaded onto
the tanks and drove back to his starting position. He lost twenty-two tanks,
twenty-four men were killed or wounded. He reported that his unit had
destroyed thirteen German Panzers, ten guns, fourteen mortars and four
Pak.[43] No reports from the German side are available on the battle near Rouvres since the bicycle battalion of 85. Inf.-Div. was in action there. It can only
be confirmed that two Paks of the Divisionsbegleitkompanie were knocked
out during the preceding fighting. The reported destruction of thirteen German Panzers must be based on an error.

A description of the course of the fighting on 9 August 1944 at the
neighboring divisions must be given here. At 272. Inf.-Div., 9 August proved
to be relatively quiet. Toward evening, several enemy attacks from Bellengreville were repelled. Later, the enemy penetrated into Béneauville south of
Vimont and was stopped with the last available reserves at the 981 Regimen-

tal command post. The 272. Inf.-Div. handed over the Troarn sector to 346. Inf.-Div. The freed-up Füsilierbataillon was moved behind the left wing of 272. Inf.-Div. as a reserve. The left boundary of the Division with I. SS-Panzerkorps was moved and, from then on, ran from St. Sylvain (I.SS)-le Bû (LXXXVI)-Maizières (I.SS) to Vendeuvre (I.SS). The new main line of resistance ran from east of Vimont via Hill 86 (west of Moult)-northwestern edge of the forest north of Navarre-northwest of Billy-western edge of Fierville-Hill 50 (southeast of St. Sylvain)-northeast of Soignolles.[43]

Throughout 9 August, platoons, squads and individual men arrived at 89. Inf.-Div. They had held on to strong points during the previous day and had withdrawn during the night. They were returned to their regiments. The Füsilierbataillon was dissolved and distributed to the two Infanterie regiments. The enemy achieved several deep penetrations along the whole length of the Divisional front line during the day. These were either cleared up through counterattacks or cut off. The Divisional command post was moved from Potigny to St. Loup (4.5 kilometers north of Falaise).[44]

The 271. Inf.-Div., in its new positions, was also attacked by infantry and tanks but was generally able to hold on.[45]

The war diary of 5. Panzerarmee offers an indication of the considerations by supreme commands of the Armee and Heeresgruppe B during 9 August 1944. After a visit to the divisions by General Eberbach, 5. Panzerarmee reported to Heeresgruppe B at 09.55 hours that it would be necessary, during the coming night, to withdraw the LXXXVI. A.K.—in action to the right of I. SS-Panzerkorps—across the Dives. A withdrawal of I. SS-Panzerkorps to a line north of Maizières and north of Rouvres was contemplated since a Polish tank division was reported in the area of Soignolles and south of it.

In a change to his order of the previous day, Feldmarschall von Kluge ordered that the Pantherabteilung of 9. Panzerdivision, which had just arrived at I. SS-Panzerkorps, be immediately returned to 7. Armee. The 5. Panzerarmee requested at noon that this Abteilung remain in the forest of Ouilly, where it had been stopped, until the evening since the infantry could not withstand the attack by itself. The Schwere SS-Panzer-abteilung 102 under Sturmbannführer Hans Weifl arrived at I. SS-Panzerkorps before noon. It was attached to the "HJ" Division. At 15.20 hours, Feldmarschall von Kluge informed General Eberbach that he ". . . had to take over command of the assault group on Avranches on the personal order of the Führer." During this temporary action, SS-Oberstgruppenführer Sepp Dietrich was to command 5. Panzerarmee on an acting basis. During that occasion the Feldmarschall emphasized that ". . . it was the express wish of the Führer to carry out the planned assault on Avranches. He, himself, was as certain as ever that a success could lead to a turning point in the situation, a failure to the collapse of the whole front." For that reason, the Feldmarschall ordered the immediate departure of the Pantherabteilung of 9.Pz.-Div. He refused the requested withdrawal of the right wing of the Armee behind the Dives. At

21.20 hours, 5. Panzerarmee reported to the Heeresgruppe that the total Panzer inventory of I. SS-Panzerkorps was only fifteen Panzer IVs, five Panthers and fifteen Tigers (after Tigerabteilung 102 was assigned). Stopping a breakthrough toward Falaise by the superior enemy was no longer possible.

In its daily report of 9 August 1944, 5. Panzerarmee stated its intention to move into the following line east of the Orne:

> Western edge of Moult-western edge of Airan-western edge of Bray-la Campagne-western edge Fierville-western edge of the forest southeast of St. Sylvain-edge of the woods 800 meters northwest Hill 111-Hill 88-southern edge of Estrées-southern edge of Grainville-northern edge Bois de St. Germain-Cingal-Thury-Harcourt-St. Pierre-Lesay. It further expressed the fear that, if the enemy attacks continued at the previous level of force at I. SS-Panzerkorps and LXXIV. Korps adjacent on the left, those lines could not be held with the available forces.
>
> Massive movements of tanks on the road Caen-Falaise in a southerly direction gave rise to the expectation that the enemy would continue his attacks to break through in that area with new, strong forces. At the front line of I. SS-Panzerkorps ". . . three to four large enemy tank units were observed.[46]

The supplement to the daily report of 5. Panzerarmee contains changes in the Panzer strength of I. SS-Panzerkorps and information on the distribution of the Panzers. "HJ" Division had, in the meantime, reported the following Panzers battle-ready in its sector: ten Panzer IVs, five Panthers and eight Tigers. The 89. Inf.-Div. reported three Panzer IVs, and 271. Inf.-Div. seven Panzer IVs. The ten Panzer IVs reported by the two Inf.-Divs. were provided, without question, by Panzerregiment 12, so that the Division had a total of twenty action-ready Panzer IVs. One of the two Tiger companies of Schwere SS-Panzerabteilung 102 was assigned and moved to 271. Inf.-Div. in the evening. Its seven Tigers were, however, not included in the supplement to the daily report. Thus, I. SS-Panzerkorps had available an action-ready total of twenty Panzer IVs, five Panthers and fifteen Tigers. The 2. Kompanie of Panzerregiment 12 (Panthers) was still on the march from the area around Vire.[47] Despite the high losses he had suffered on 8 and 9 August, the enemy had still available a multiple of that figure of tanks. The forward line of the II Canadian Corps, in the evening of 9 August, ran from St. Sylvain via Soignolles-Langannerie-St. Germain-le Vasson to Urville. The attacks of the day had not resulted in any noteworthy gain of terrain, despite the fact that no reinforcements, other than the bicycle battalion of 85. Inf.-Div., had taken part in the fighting. In contrast, the Corps had suffered significant losses, particularly in tanks. General Simonds, the commanding general, insisted that the attack was pushed ahead. He ordered the 4th Armoured Division again to capture the high terrain northwest and southwest of Potigny (Hills 195 and 206) and, if the situation was favorable, to advance in the direction of Falaise. The 1st Polish Armoured Division was ordered to capture Hill 140 and advance across the Laison to the hills immediately north of Falaise.

The infantry of the 4th Armoured Division was scheduled to first take Hill 195 and then the tanks would push forward from there to Hill 206.

The Argyll and Southerland Highlanders of Canada started a silent attack during the night of 9 to 10 August 1944. They ". . . simply advanced in a row toward the hill, up the slopes to the peak and dug in there." That is the way it is stated in the history of that battalion. At dawn all of the battalion was prepared for defense and all counterattacks, which started at that time with rocket launcher support, had been repelled. In the meantime, The Lincoln and Welland Regiment had advanced on the right flank of the Argylls and occupied Hill 195 which lies opposite St. Germain-le Vasson. As a result of that progress, the 22nd Armoured Regiment was ordered, in the early morning of 10 August, to Hill 194 in order to advance to Hill 206. According to the Canadian report, during the issuance of orders north of Hill 195, a violent German counterattack took place in which remote controlled "Goliath" Panzers took part. The attack was fought off, but the 22nd Armoured Regiment lost several tanks. A Canadian artillery observation aircraft spotted twenty-four 8.8 cm guns. In view of that massive anti-tank capability, the planned attack on Hill 206 was abandoned. The 22nd Armoured Regiment remained on Hill 195. The 21st Armoured Regiment was also moved there as further reinforcement.[48]

As the Divisional commander, Oberführer Kurt Meyer, wrote in his recollection of events, he hurried to Hill 195 after the din of firing had woken up him from a short nap. There, he witnessed the counterattack by III./26, several Panzers and the remote controlled Panzers. The enemy had broken through the defenses, which were only based on individual strong points, and was about to capture all of the hill. The Canadian spearheads had been thrown back and the hill was held.[49]

The war diary of 5. Panzerarmee noted for 10 August that the enemy had succeeded in occupying Hill 195 south of Grainville. Continuing, it was further stated that the prevailing impression was that, after reorganizing and concentrating his forces, the enemy would start a major attack on 11 August. In addition, it was noted that the constant firing on enemy tank assemblies had caused shortages of ammunition, in particular for the light and heavy field howitzers. The available amounts would, on no account, be sufficient for the expected major battles.[50]

The occasionally contradictory reports and statements are probably based on the fact that Hill 195 has a rounded top, approximately 1.5 kilometers wide, running southwest-northeast for approximately two kilometers, before it drops off more markedly in the west toward the Laize valley and in the east toward the Route Nationale. One may assume that the Canadians

were holding the highest point of the top while Kampfgruppe Olboeter was
in position at its southern slope, holding on to that position. Olboeter, himself, had probably arrived only during the night with the Aufklärungsgruppe
from the area east of Vire. Holding that position was decisive for further
developments. Without doubt, the observed 8.8 cm Flak guns were an important support in anti-tank activities. However, the high construction of the
guns reduced them to only restricted usefulness against tanks. Only at long
distance were they able to fight tanks effectively without being knocked out
quickly by them. Once spotted however, they were favorite targets for
artillery and fighter-bombers. The Flak combat squads, consisting of two 8.8
cm Flak guns, had not been a success. Instead, they had suffered dispropor-
tionately high losses. The 8.8 cm Flak batteries with four 8.8 cm guns and
several 2 cm Flak guns were much more effective against low level air attacks
if they could operate from the depth of the field, approximately four kilometers back. The Canadian decision to initially discontinue the attack on
Hill 206 because of the 8.8 cm guns they had spotted is thus difficult to
understand. Since the position of these guns had been located, they could
also have been neutralized by artillery. Very likely, however, more guns were
assumed to be there which had not yet been detected. Possibly, however, the
major reason for that decision was the large overestimation of the strength
of the German forces after the annihilation of the Worthington combat
group near Hill 140 on the previous day.

At 10.00 hours, General Simonds conducted a briefing with his divisional commanders and issued the following orders for the continuation of
the stalled attack: The 3rd Canadian Infantry Division, which was located farther to the rear and had not yet seen serious combat during that operation,
would attack at 16.00 hours with the attached 2nd Armoured Brigade and
the support of two army artillery units and the artillery of the 1st Polish
Armoured Division. As its first objective, it would have to achieve the crossing of the Laison east of Potigny in order to then capture the dominating
range west of Epaney (Hill 175). The 3rd Division was to follow behind the
1st Polish Division, capture Hill 140, cross the Laison and advance on Sassy.

During the previous day, the Quesnay forest had already proved to be a
major obstacle. Panzers dominated the open terrain to the east, north and
west from there. Thus, Quesnay forest had to be captured first. That mission
was handed to The North Shore Regiment (on the east) and the battalion
The Queen's Own Rifles of Canada (on the west) as well as the battalion Le
Régiment de la Chaudière following behind them. The "HJ" Division had
fought against them in June and at the beginning of July near Caen.

The attack only started at 20.00 hours. It encountered the "mass" of the
Panzerregiment which consisted of only 23 Panzers by then. The only
infantry in the Quesnay forest was a part of Kampfgruppe Krause. Infantry
and Panzers waited until the enemy had come very close before opening fire.
Because of the small distance between attackers and defenders, the artillery

was unable to fire effectively. The spearhead companies of The Queen's Own Rifles were cut off. All officers and NCOs were lost. A corporal, just promoted, assembled the remnants. The battalion withdrew with the approval of the 3rd Canadian Infantry Division. It had lost twenty-two killed and sixty-three wounded. The North Shore Regiment, which had suffered severe losses from misdirected Allied bombs, consisted of only three companies. It went around the northern edge of the Quesnay forest and penetrated into the woods despite the heavy fire from rocket launchers. According to Canadian reports, several small squads reached the southern edge of the forest. They withdrew after coming under Canadian artillery fire. The communications system within the battalion broke down and the attack was broken off. The battalion lost twenty-two killed and fifty-eight wounded.[51]

The 1st Polish Armoured Division had been ordered to follow behind the 3rd Canadian Infantry Division, to capture Hill 140, cross the Laison, and then take Sassy. To do that, the 3rd Rifle Brigade was assembled in the area around Estrées. The history of the Polish Division indicates that the attack was put off due to heavy German artillery fire. However, it is likely that the deciding factor was the failure of the attack on the Quesnay forest. The 9th Battalion of the Brigade did not receive the counter-order and started an attack on Hill 111, located 1.5 kilometers northwest of Hill 140, in the evening. Together with it, the 10th Rifle Regiment and a tank reconnaissance unit, consisting of three Cromwell tank companies, attacked. The tanks were at the point. During the advance they came under artillery fire but did reach Hill 111 with one company. According to Polish reports, hand-to-hand combat with German troops took place there. The Poles suffered significant losses. A second attack was also repelled. Only after reinforcements arrived was Hill 111 captured as night fell.[52] It is questionable if the Poles were indeed on Hill 111 Northwest of Hill 140. The positions of the left wing of I./25 were located on Hill 140, certainly not Hill 111. It is possible that Hill 111 (two kilometers northwest of Rouvres) was meant, although the mention of Hill 140 contradicts that. In position on Hill 111 near Rouvres was the bicycle-equipped Grenadierbataillon of 85. Inf.-Div. In addition, 1. Kompanie of Panzerjägerabteilung 12 was in action for anti-tank defense. It was the backbone of the valiantly fighting Grenadierbataillon. Sturmmann Walter Gömann reported on the action of the Panzerjägers:

> On 10 August, when 1. Kompanie encountered the Polish tank division, I was there as a combat supply driver. I was hauling fuel for our Panzers which, because of the fighter-bomber activity, was not an enjoyable job. We were very happy when our armorer, Unterscharführer Ortlep, came to the front in order to readjust the guns. He had just installed the cross hairs on the muzzles and was looking for a prominent landmark. As he was doing that, he spotted two enemy tanks and knocked them out within three minutes.[53]

The diary of Untersturmführer Helmut Zeiner, at the time Zug leader in
1. Kompanie, indicates that, on 10 August, the Kompanie chief, Obersturmführer Georg Hurdelbrink, and his gunner, Rottenführer Fritz Eckstein,
knocked out eleven tanks, and Obersturmführer Rudolf Roy knocked out
seven tanks. Untersturmführer Zeiner's Panzer was not ready for action, it
had to be taken back to the workshop in the morning. During the previous
day, he had knocked out one tank from his position at the edge of the forest—presumably in the area of Hill 111.[54]

The Polish war history reports that German units undertook a counterattack during the night. They by-passed the Polish positions (near Hill 111)
and reached Soignolles with weak forces. The Polish battalion held on to its
position until the night of 11–12 August. The study by Oberstleutnant i.G.
Kurt Schuster, the Ia of 85. Inf,-div. shows that Grenadierregiment 1053 and
III. Artillerieabteilung moved into their predetermined positions in the
evening of 10 August. Some of those positions had to be taken by an attack.
The right wing, advancing across the predetermined forward line, repelled
an enemy reconnaissance unit, supported by tanks, in the area northwest of
le Bû-sur-Rouvres.[55] This supports the theory that Hill 111 in question was
the one located northwest of Rouvres.

The attack by the 1st Polish Armoured Brigade and the 3rd Canadian
Infantry Division with the attached 2nd Canadian Armoured Brigade had
been fought back by the battle-weary remnants of the "HJ" Division and the
approaching Grenadierregiment 1053 of 85. Inf.-Div. They had inflicted considerable losses on the enemy. That success was thanks to the perseverance
of the Panzergrenadiers and Grenadiers, but primarily to the Panzers and
Panzerjägers as well as the artillery. The outstanding successes achieved by 1.
Kompanie of Panzerjägerabteilung 12 since 8 August were recognized by
awarding the Knight's Cross to the Kompanie chief, Obersturmführer Georg
Hurdelbrink, one of his Panzer commanders, Oberscharführer Rudolf Roy,
and a gunner, Rottenführer Fritz Eckstein.

In addition to the men in combat at the front line, the motorcycle messengers, drivers of supply vehicles and the repair services contributed significantly to the achieved success. The two reports following will illustrate the
accomplishments of those men. Sturmmann Paul Kamberger reported:

> At the beginning of August 1944 I was detailed with my side-car
> motorcycle from the command Abteilung of the Division staff to the
> supply Abteilung. My co-driver was my comrade Gerd K. We were
> supposed to take turns during the many drives. We were not overly
> happy with the assignment in the knowledge that, as one went far-
> ther away from the vicinity of the front to the rear, the skies got
> busier. Those pests were hated by all vehicle and motorcycle drivers.
> Frequently, during the next weeks, I had to deliver messages to the

front or to the rear bases. Those drives often took more than one day. During dawn, one was able to cover maybe one or two kilometers, driving slalom around burning or burnt-out vehicles wrecks, which had been caught during the night, and past bomb craters or pieces of vehicles scattered about. Then, when daylight came, the comrades from the other field post number showed up, those damned fighter-bombers. Driving alone was like being blind during a new moon night: You could not see or hear a thing. You only noticed that someone was sitting on your neck when the asphalt on the right and left was riddled by bullets from on-board weapons. And then you were still lucky, the pilot had aimed poorly! Then one had the time it took the aircraft to veer off and approach again, to find cover. The duel of pilot against motorcycle messenger did not always end in our favor! How often did we have to wait until the fighter-bomber and his friends sought another field of activity after determining that, apparently, nothing else could be found in this area.

During one of my runs I lost Gerd, my co-driver. We were passing a column of Panzers, being waved past by each of the Panzer commanders. Suddenly, the last but one Panzer gave a small jerk, or was that maybe just my exhausted imagination after the long drive? Slowing down and driving off to the side between the trees brought me back to being wide awake immediately. I had missed a small dip in the ground, Gerd's leg, hanging out of the sidecar, got caught on a tree trunk-and there we had a nice mess! I drove him to the closest field hospital, his leg broken, and from then on I was alone with my guilty conscience.[56]

Sturmmann Heinrich Peyers remembered it this way in a letter:

On 10 August 1944 we found ourselves in a bombing raid. The largest part of the Kompanie had been scattered. Kurt Fritzsch and I were to fetch ammunition and provisions from supplies in my VW-Kübel. Although the supply troops had already moved, I found them as darkness fell. Together with my sergeant, I loaded our crate and drove back to the command post, this time on the main road Falaise-Caen in the vicinity of Bretteville. The command post was located in a manor house which was connected to the main road by a tree-lined lane. Some two to three kilometers from our command post I met some men from a Heer division who had previously been together with us. The told us that they had been ordered to withdraw but that our unit was still in the same position as in the afternoon. Barely one kilometer farther on I suddenly found myself on the road between two tanks. I first thought they were ours, but then a Tommy looked out of the turret hatch. You can imagine how quickly I was gone in my vehicle. Regrettably, I could not go back but had to start my escape forward. I had planned to reach our lines by driving along a country road, one I had used with Kurt Fritzsch in the afternoon to avoid aircraft. It seems that the tanks had alerted the infantry by radio of my approach. In any case, a group of infantrymen was waiting for me, hammering my car with their submachine guns. Thank God, I was so fast that their presents slammed into the rations and the motor behind me. Then I got caught by an armored car which they had driven across the road. That was the start of my captivity. After numerous interrogations and other chicaneries I was finally moved to England on 20.8.1944.[57]

The enemy did not attack the unit on the right, 272. Inf.-Div., on 10 August. Only loose contact existed with it through Aufklärungsgruppe Wienecke. Assemblies of infantry and tank units near St. Sylvain and Soignolles were battled by the Divisional artillery with good results.[58] The day brought intense enemy attacks and continued crises to 271. Inf.-Div. On its left wing, the enemy succeeded in penetrating with tanks near le Moncel and Croisilles (four and two kilometers, respectively, northeast of Thury-Harcourt). A possible breakthrough to the road Thury-Harcourt-Falaise threatened to roll back the Divisional front line. The Division succeeded in setting up a sparsely manned new defensive front south of the line Espins-Thury-Harcourt and to reinforce it by the following day.[59]

The enemy found himself forced to break off Operation "TOTALIZE" and to reorganize his forces for a future continuation of the attack. The spearhead troops of the II Corps were on Hill 195, three kilometers northwest of Potigny. In the evening of 10 August, they were fifteen kilometers away from their starting position. They had only managed to form an eight kilometers wide corridor (between St. Sylvain and Bretteville-sur-Laize) in the direction of Falaise, their major attack objective. It was another eleven kilometers to Falaise. This German defensive success, with all due respect to the valor of the soldiers of 89. and 271. Inf.-Divs. and the attached rocket launchers and Luftwaffen Flak, was primarily thanks to the decimated "Hitlerjugend" Division which, according to the opinion of the enemy, was "only a shadow of its former self" when he started that operation. Every member of the Division knew that he stood in a position decisive for the outcome of the battle, and that every individual had to count.

Based on available enemy reports, the supreme command of 5. Panzerarmee assessed the situation in the evening of 10 August 1944 as follows:

There are strong enemy reconnaissance probes along the whole front and massive assemblies of tanks and infantry are observed in

Bellengreville, Conteville, St. Sylvain, Soignolles, Estrées, Grainville, Urville, Barbery and south of les Moutiers. These villages are under constant and concentrated artillery fire, observed to be very effective. This indicates that the enemy has used today to determine the exact manpower situation of our own main line of defense. The enemy is also assembling for more attacks aimed at breaking through our lines. Renewed major attacks are thus to be expected on 11 August.[60]

Soon after midnight on 10 August, the enemy again attacked the positions in the Quesnay forest, just as the relief by parts of 85. Inf.-Div. began. He was able to achieve a penetration. A counterattack, probably by I./26, started at 02.40 hours. It was able to restore the previous situation by noon. Approximately at noon, thirty tanks were observed advancing from Grainville to the southwest. They were effectively battled by concentrated artillery fire. German Panzers knocked out 11 tanks. The enemy attack was broken off.[61] Presumably, this was the relief of the 4th Armoured Division by the 3rd Armoured Division on the opposite side.

The sector of the Division was completely taken over by 85. Inf.-Div. during the night 11–12 August. The hand-over took place at 21.00 hours on 12 August. The senior general staff officer of 85. Inf.-Div., Oberstleutnant i.G. Kurt Schuster, wrote about this later in a study:

In order to avoid unnecessary losses to enemy activity during relief activity during the day, and to provide the troops, tired out from the march, a chance for a short rest period, the parts of 12. SS-Panzerdivision which were to be relieved, remained in their positions for one more day. This, despite the heavy losses they had suffered during the major battles of the previous day, and is an exemplary display of comradeship of the front line soldier.[62]

The "HJ" Division moved into an area northeast of Falaise as Korps reserve. One company of Panzers, the remnants of Schwere SS-Panzerabteilung 101, Schwere SS-Panzerabteilung 102 (less one company) and two self-propelled rocket launcher batteries were attached to it. The Korps reserve had available, combat-ready, seventeen Panzer IVs, seven Panthers and eleven Tigers. In addition, it had two companies of Panzerjäger IVs (tank destroyers) of SS-Panzerjägerabteilung 12. The number of battle-ready Panzerjägers is not known.[63]

During the period of 8 to 12 August 1944, the "HJ" Division suffered the following losses. The losses during the fighting near Grimbosq are not counted here. They have already been detailed previously.

	Killed			Wounded			Missing		
	Officers	NCOs	Men	Officers	NCOs	Men	Officers	NCOs	Men
8 August									
Pz. & Pz.-Jg.	1	3	11	1	13	25	-	1	5
Pz.Gren.	1	1	18	3	6	40	-	-	15
Art. & Werfer	-	2	20	1	6	43	1	-	1
Total Day	2	6	49	5	25	108	1	1	21
9 August									
Pz. & Pz.-Jg.	-	4	10	1	4	18	-	-	-
Pz.Gren.	-	1	13	-	6	24	-	4	36
Art. & Werfer	-	-	1	-	1	8	-	-	-
Total Day	-	5	24	1	11	50	-	4	36
10 August									
Pz. & Pz.-Jg.	-	-	1	-	-	2	-	-	-
Pz.Gren.	-	-	3	-	2	11	-	-	1
Art. & Werfer	-	-	-	-	-	3	-	-	-
Total Day	-	-	4	-	2	16	-	-	1
11 August									
Pz. & Pz.-Jg.	-	1	2	-	1	2	-	-	-
Pz.Gren.	-	-	2	-	-	1	-	-	-
Art. & Werfer	-	-	1	-	-	3	-	-	1
Total Day	-	1	5	-	1	6	-	-	1
12 August									
Pz. & Pz.-Jg.	-	1	3	2	5	10	-	-	-
Pz.Gren.	-	-	1	-	-	1	1	-	-
Art. & Werfer	-	-	-	-	-	4	-	-	-
Total Day	-	1	4	2	5	15	1	-	-
8–12 August	2	13	86	8	44	195	2	5	59

The total losses were 101 killed, 247 wounded and 66 missing. This amounted to a total of 414 losses.

The totals are for: "Pz. & Pz.-Jg.": SS-Panzerregiment 12, SS-Panzerjäger-abteilung 12 and Schwere Panzerabteilung 101; "Pz.Gren.": Divisionsbegleitkompanie, I./25 and I./26; "Art. & Werfer": SS-Panzerartillerieregiment 12 and Werferabteilung 12. The lists of losses of Schwere SS-Panzerabteilung 101 and I./26 are not complete. Of the missing on 9 August, two returned to their unit on 16 August and one on 27 August.[64]

After the end of the battles in the Laison sector, the staff of SS-Panzergrenadierregiment 26 was also withdrawn and moved to the area where it had been located at the start of the invasion. Obersturmbannführer Wilhelm Mohnke, the Regimental commander, was assigned disciplinary responsibility for all elements of the Division withdrawn for refitting. The combat-ready parts of the Division, forming the Korps reserve, consisted of:

    Operations squadron of the Divisional staff,

    Divisionsbegleitkompanie in the strength of one Zug,

    Staff of SS-Panzerregiment 12,

    I./SS-Panzerregiment 12 and 7 battle-ready Panthers,

    II./SS-Panzerregiment 12 and 17 battle-ready Panzer IVs,

    I./SS-Panzergrenadierregiment 25 with the strength of approximately 2 companies,

    I./SS-Panzergrenadierregiment 26 with the strength of approximately 2 companies,

    III./SS-Panzergrenadierregiment 26 (armored personnel carriers), with the strength of approximately 2 companies;

    SS-Panzerartillerieregiment 12, without the two light field howitzer batteries of II. Abteilung which had been eliminated by bombs, Werferabteilung 12 with 3 batteries;

    SS-Flakabteilung 12 with 1 battery of 8.8 cm Flak, 1 battery of 3.7 cm self-propelled Flak and one -Kompanie of 2 cm self-propelled Flak (14./26);

    SS-Panzerjägerabteilung 12 with 2 companies Panzerjäger IVs, Aufklärungsgruppe Wienecke of SS-Panzeraufklärungsabteilung 12, the radio operations platoon and parts of the communications company of SS-Panzernachrichtenabteilung 12 (communications).

CHAPTER 5.6
Operation 'TRACTABLE'. Defensive Battles North of Falaise and in the Falaise Encirclement from 13 to 19 August 1944

The basic concept of the Allied invasion plan envisaged the encirclement and destruction of the German troops fighting in western Normandy, west of the Seine river from its mouth to Paris, and north of the Loire river from Orléans to the estuary. The breakthrough of the US First Army near Avranches fulfilled an important requirement for the execution of that plan.

The German leadership recognized the threatening danger and ordered a counterattack by at least four Panzer divisions in order to cut off and destroy the enemy forces which had broken through to the south. In preparation, the Panzer divisions were to assemble in the area northeast and east

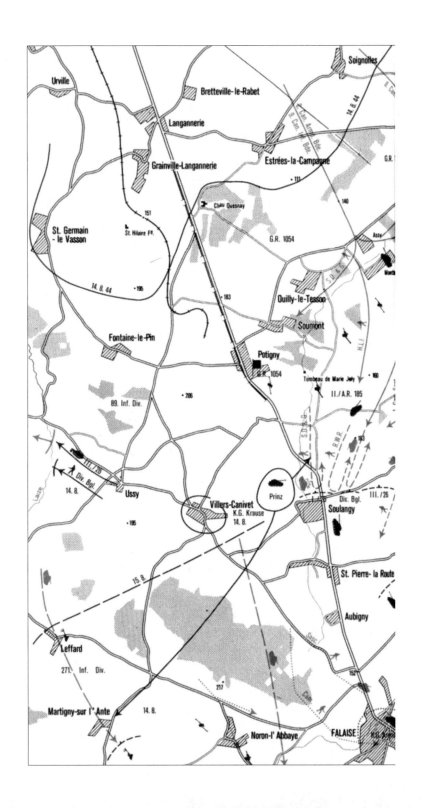

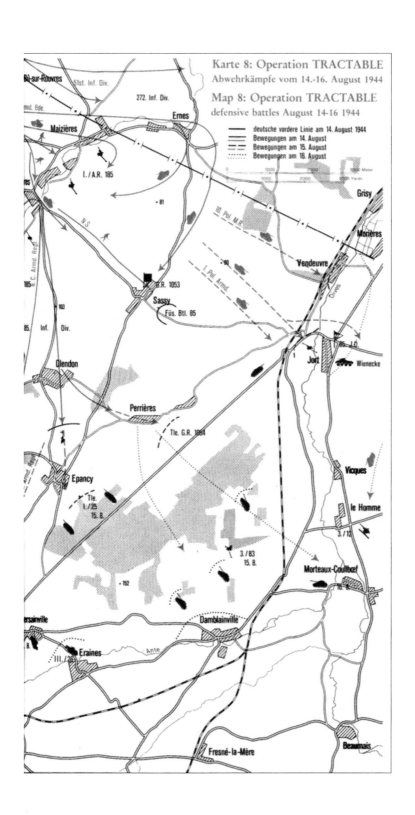

Karte 8: Operation TRACTABLE
Abwehrkämpfe vom 14.-16. August 1944

Map 8: Operation TRACTABLE
defensive battles August 14-16 1944

deutsche vordere Linie am 14. August 1944
Bewegungen am 14. August
Bewegungen am 15. August
Bewegungen am 16. August

of Mortain and then, advancing via Mortain and to the north of the city, break through to Avranches. The counterattack by 116. and 2. Panzerdivisions and 1. and 2. SS-Panzerdivisions started during the night of 6 to 7 August 1944. Mortain was captured. A gain of a few kilometers to the west was achieved on the right wing. Through the "ULTRA" radio intelligence, the enemy was informed, in detail, of the German plans and the strength of the troops in action. During the course of 7 August, when the visibility improved and was, finally, excellent, the Americans were able to effectively deploy their superior air force. The attack by the German Panzer divisions had been promised the support by 1,000 fighters. That was not realized to anywhere near that extent. The counterattack soon stalled. In the meantime, General Patton and a part of his Third US Army had broken out into the open terrain near Avranches and swung to the east. Its spearheads crossed the Sarthe river near Le Mans. All German Panzer divisions deployed in Normandy, except for the "HJ" Division, were then located behind the left wing of 7. Armee and on the left wing of 5. Panzerarmee, well west of the Orne. Thus, the Allied supreme command saw the possibility of encircling them already west of the Dives. On 11 August, General Montgomery issued a new directive-M 518. It stated, inter alia:

> . . . Intentions
> 8. It remains unchanged, as indicated in Figure 5 of M 517. It must clearly be our intention to destroy the enemy forces between Seine and Loire.

> The outline of the plan
> 9. For the moment, the plan outlined in M 517 will be modified as indicated below. We will now concentrate our forces in order to encircle the main enemy forces so that we can possibly destroy them in their present location.

> First Canadian Army
> 10. The Canadian Army is to capture Falaise. That has first priority. It is vital that it happens quickly.
> 11. The Army will then capture Argentan with armored and mobile forces.
> 12. A firm front line to the east between Falaise and the sea must be held.

> Second British Army
> 13. The Second Army will advance its left wing to Falaise. That is of primary and vital priority. Sufficient forces will be made available to the Corps on the left to allow it to push forward, rapidly, to Falaise.

14. After Falaise has been taken, by either the Second Army or the Canadian Army, it will be held by the Second Army.

15. From Falaise, the Second Army will operate to the west and south . . .[1]

The new directive differed from Directive M 517, issued on 6 August, mainly in two points, regarding the Falaise area: The Canadian Army had been unable to capture Falaise until then and it appeared questionable whether it would succeed in that at all within a short period of time. That is why the Second British Army was also ordered to rapidly advance on Falaise and take the town if the Canadians had not been successful in doing so. The Second British Army had originally received orders to advance with its strong right wing to the Seine by way of Argentan, l'Aigle, Dreux and Evreux. Now, it was to capture the area around Falaise with a strong left wing and then advance to the west and south. Obviously, the encirclement of the German forces west of the Orne was planned.

THE DEFENSIVE BATTLES NORTH OF FALAISE FROM 13 TO 16 AUGUST 1944

General Montgomery's Directive M 518 clearly indicated that the city of Falaise would be of special significance in the coming battles. There was no effective east-west road between the two major points of Argentan and Falaise. That was clear to the German supreme leadership as well as to the command of I. SS-Panzerkorps and the Division which was in action in that sector. The forces available for the defense of the area north of Falaise would barely be able to carry out that difficult mission. The right border of I. SS-Panzerkorps ran between Ernes and Maizières-south of le Bû-toward the southern tip of the wood north of le Bû and further along the eastern edge of St. Sylvain. The forward line of 85. Inf.-Div., in action on the right in the Korps sector, was the same as that of "HJ" Division on the day of the handing over: southern tip of the wood north of le Bû-Hill 111 (two kilometers northwest of Rouvres)-northwestern edge of the adjoining forest-Hill 111 (2.5 kilometers northwest Assy)-northern edge of the Quesnay forest. The 89. Inf.-Div. maintained contact at the Route Nationale. The front line ran from there via the southern slope of Hill 195-eastern edge St. Germain le-Vasson-northern edge of Placy-northern edge of Thury-Harcourt. The Laize immediately west of St. Germain formed the dividing line between 89. and 271. Inf.-Divs.[2]

Infantry divisions were positioned in the front lines. Experience had shown that they had insufficient anti-tank weapons. A natural tank obstacle would significantly increase their defensive strength. To a limited extent, the valley of the Laison was such an obstacle. The location of the main line of defense to the north of the valley was advantageous for the "HJ" Division. With its Panzers and Panzerjägers it possessed freedom of movement for its offensive defense there and was not dependent on a few narrow river cross-

ings. The Laison creek would have been a favorable main line of resistance
for the 85. Inf.-Div. It cannot be determined why 85. Inf.-Div. had to take over
the positions of "HJ" Division. It is conceivable that the 272. Inf.-Div., adjacent
on the right, was unable to extend its left wing still farther to the south.

The 85. Inf.-Div. had been established from February to May 1944 north
of the Somme as a Division of the 25th Wave (Note: German divisions were
raised in waves, i.e.: at least several at one time. Translator's note). Its senior
general staff officer, Oberstleutnant i.G. Kurt Schuster, wrote in his study in
the year 1946:

> . . . When leaving for action at the invasion front, the Division was
> fully prepared for defense, and prepared for offense with limita-
> tions. The Division, above all, did not have sufficient armor-piercing
> weapons (no Pak at the Grenadierregiments, no assault guns) and
> not enough artillery . . .

On the day the invasion started, the Division was combat-ready. On
orders of Armeeoberkommando 15 (AOK), it had moved into the highest
stage of readiness in the early morning so that it would be ready to march
within two hours.

> The marching orders, impatiently and eagerly awaited by the troops,
> did not arrive for some time. The troops remained far away from
> combat action for almost two more months . . .[3]

The combat troops started their march to the invasion front in the
evening of 31 July. The foot-soldiers were transported by massed vehicles into
the assembly area south of the Seine. The river was crossed at seven ferry
locations north of Rouen and between Quillebeuf and Gd. Couronne during
the period of 4 to 6 August 1944. Despite the considerable enemy air activity,
thanks to efficient discipline and camouflage, the troops suffered no significant losses. That, although the crossings stretched into dawn because of the
short nights. After assembly in the area east and southeast of Bernay, the
Division marched, in very small groups, along secondary roads on both sides
of the main route of advance; Bernay-Orbec-Livarot-Falaise. The main road
was heavily used by the supply traffic for the combat troops. As early as the
afternoon of 6 August, the spearhead of reinforced Grenadierregiment 1053
reached le Mesnil-Jaquet (nine kilometers west of Falaise). The Division was
assigned to I. SS-Panzerkorps. Previously, it had been ordered into action
with II. SS-Panzerkorps. Because of the imposed radio silence, the order to
change direction did not reach the Regiment until the early morning hours
of 9 August. This is another example of the disastrous impact of the wrong
picture of the enemy by Fremde Heere West. But, it also clearly shows how

the existing difficulties during the advance could be overcome despite the destroyed bridges and enemy air supremacy.[4]

The only reserve of I. SS-Panzerkorps consisted of the "HJ" Division. Its combat-ready parts had the strength of a Regiment Kampfgruppe and were, in addition, worn-out. Thus, it is more correct to speak of a "Kampfgruppe 'HJ' Division". It was located in the area north of Falaise, ready to be sent into action at the respective hot-spots.

Although the previous Canadian plan of breaking through to Falaise by forming strong points on both sides of the Route Nationale had not led to success, the II Canadian Corps adhered to it. The orders for Operation "TRACTABLE" stated, regarding the enemy picture and action:

The focal point of the German defense is located in the area of the Quesnay forest and Potigny. To the east, the German positions extend along the Laison. Anti-tank defenses are carried out by 85. Inf.-Div. and 12. SS-Panzerdivision "HJ" in the left portion of this sector. "HJ" Division is defending the Laison sector to Condé-sur-Ifs.[5]

At the present, there is no definite indication on which other units can be freed in the west to support 'HJ'. At this time, 'HJ' is the one outstanding, first class unit between us and Falaise. . . . The area across which 'HJ' is distributed cannot be exactly determined. It appears, however, that it has moved into positions behind the shield formed by infantry of 271., 89., and 85. Infanteriedivisions. . . . In the Quesnay area, III. Bataillon of Grenadierregiment 1054 has been spotted in the forest south of the village. Prisoner statements seem to confirm the assumption that two battalions, significantly reinforced by tanks of 'Hitlerjugend', are in position there.[6]

To be put into action:

The 4th Canadian Armoured Division with attached 8th Infantry Brigade in the eastern attack sector to attack the enemy positions on the hills north of the Laison valley between Maizières and Montboint. Attack target of the 4th Armoured Brigade is Versainville (2.5 kilometers northeast of Falaise). It will be followed by the 8th Canadian Infantry Brigade as the first wave. It will clear the Laison valley from Maizières to Rouvres, its attack objective is Sassy. The 10th Canadian Infantry Brigade will follow as the second wave. It will overtake the 8th Brigade and capture the villages of Perrières and Epaney northeast of Versainville. Also in the second wave will be the 3rd Canadian Infantry Division to the west of the 4th Armoured Division. The attached 2nd Canadian Armoured Brigade will take Hills 170 and 175, west of Epaney. The 9th Canadian Infantry Brigade will clear the Laison valley from west of Rouvres to Montboint inclusive.

Support by artillery and air force:

The attack will take place during the day. In order to eliminate observed fire from all German weapons, the artillery will provide smoke screens ahead of our own front line and on the flanks. This will be followed, in the course of the attack, by a moving wall of fire from smoke and explosive shells. Fire will be concentrated on observed gun positions.

Strategic bombers will attack the fortified Quesnay forest two hours after the start of the attack, as well as Soumont (northeast of Potigny), Fontaine-le Pin and several areas west of the attack sector. Immediately prior to the start of the attack, medium bombers will attack gun and mortar positions, as well as tank ambush positions in Maizières, Rouvres and Assy.

Start of the attack: 14 August, 12.00 hours.

It was planned that the 4th Armoured Division would capture the bridges across the Ante creek near Damblainville and Eraines during a third attack phase. Then, taking advantage of the success, to advance south and southeast and link up with the XV US Corps in the area around Trun.[7]

In the afternoon of 11 August, a scouting party of the 18th Armoured Car Regiment—a reconnaissance unit—reported that German troops appeared to be withdrawing in the Urville sector (three kilometers southeast of Bretteville-sur-Laize). The II Corps thus ordered the 2nd Infantry Division, an infantry brigade reinforced by a tank unit, to cross the Laize at Bretteville and attack toward the south. The brigade, further reinforced by artillery and another tank unit, reached the hills north of Moulines in the morning of 12 August. By evening, the town had been captured, with considerable losses. Several Tigers of 2. Kompanie of Schwere SS-Panzerabteilung 102 supported the defense by the parts of 271. Inf.-Div. in action there. During the following day, the Canadians formed a bridgehead across the Laize near Clair-Tizon (five kilometers west of Potigny). In the evening they attempted to enlarge it but were repelled with heavy losses.[8]

At 13.00 hours on 12 August, the enemy started an attack with tanks and infantry on the left wing of LXXXVI. A.K. German artillery fire forced the tanks to turn away to the west. Enemy infantry managed to penetrate into the northern sector of le B°. Seven tanks were knocked out.[9]

In the evening of 13 August, an officer of the 8th Reconnaissance Regiment lost his way with his armored car and drove into the German positions. The officer was killed during the encounter, his driver was captured. A document from the 2nd Canadian Division was found on the dead officer. It contained the fundamental points of the Canadian attack plan. Based on the document, in Stacy's opinion, a Panzerjägerkompanie was sent into action above the Laison in the Canadian attack sector even before the start of the attack. In Schuster's study, the capture of the document is confirmed, but not the presumed reinforcement.[10]

During the night from 13 to 14 August, Kampfgruppe Krause (I./26 and Divisionsbegleitkompanie) was moved from Olendon (eight kilometers north-northeast of Falaise) to Villers-Canivet (six kilometers northwest of

Falaise). As well, parts of the Artillerieregiment in action with 85. Inf.-Div. and III./26 were brought in to eliminate the enemy bridgehead near Clair-Tizon. In the morning of 14 August, III./26, with the attached Divisionsbegleitkompanie, attacked the bridgehead from the area northwest of Ussy. The enemy was thrown back across the river. The positions of the Divisions-begleitkompanie subsequently came under carpet bombing, but no losses were suffered. Parts of the Kompanie set up a blocking position west of la Cressonerie (1.2 kilometers west of Ussy).[11]

In the course of 13 August the general situation had further deteriorated. The XV US Corps had penetrated into the area south of Argentan. AlenÁon, the supply bases of 7. Armee, was in enemy hands. An armored reconnais-sance party of SS-Panzeraufklärungsabteilung 12, whose cadres were refitting in the area around Rugles (fifty-five kilometers northeast of Argentan), recon-noitered on 13 August from l'Aigle via Ste. Gauburge, Ste. Colombe to Sees. Near Marmouille it encountered an American column driving in a southerly direction. The scouting party, led by August Zinflmeister, at first fired at two trucks, equipped with anti-aircraft guns, with machine pistols at close range. The gun of the armored car had jammed. The enemy answered the fire with bazookas and infantry weapons. Because of the repeated jamming of the gun, the scouting party had to withdraw. In le Mesnil-Froger it came under enemy artillery fire. The Aufklärungsabteilung reported the results of the reconnais-sance mission to the Division and the Korps. It constructed securing positions and continued to carry out combat reconnaissance. The fear of imminent encirclement was confirmed to the Division command. It had become all the more important to hold the northern front on both sides of Falaise.[13]

In the morning of 14 August, Oberführer Kurt Meyer, together with Obersturmbannführer Max Wünsche, scouted the terrain north of Falaise. Their intention was to determine where to set up rear positions in the even-tuality of an enemy breakthrough during his expected renewed attack on Falaise from the north. Hill 159 (three kilometers north of Falaise) domi-nated the city and the Ante sector, adjoining on the east, from the north. The Panzerregiment and Panzerjägerabteilung 12 were scheduled to set up strong points, when ordered, on that flat hilltop and at several prominent spots south of the road St. Pierre-sur-Dives. Since the Division command reckoned with the possibility of an enemy breakthrough at the right border of the Korps, it took special precautions. The Panzerspähtrupp (scouting detail) of Untersturmführer Albert Wienecke received orders to maintain contact with the command post of 85. Inf.-Div.at the Dives crossing near Jort. As well, it was to observe and report developments at 272. Inf.-Div. adjoining to the right. The 3. (8.8 cm) Batterie of Flakabteilung 12, under the com-mand of Untersturmführer Hartwig, was deployed on Hill 66 immediately east of Couliboeuf to block the Dives crossings on both sides of that town.

In the morning of 14 August, the Canadian divisions assembled for the attack along the road from St. Sylvain to Bretteville-le Rabet. The "starting line", which was to be crossed at "X" hour, ran through Soignolles and immediately north of Estrées. In his order of the day, which arrived during the assembly, General Crerar, the supreme commander of the First Canadian Army, emphasized once more the great importance of the operation. ". . . Hit him immediately, hit him hard, and continue hitting him. Through today's operation we can significantly contribute to expedite the Allied victory . . ."[14]

At 11.37 hours the artillery started firing marker shells for the medium bombers. Shortly thereafter it fired smoke screens which were meant to give cover to the flanks and the front of the advancing columns. In succession, the bombers attacked the German positions in Montboint, Rouvres and Maizières for a quarter of an hour. Taking part in that action were twenty-five Mitchells and twenty-eight Bostons. At 11.42 hours, on orders received by radio, the tank columns began moving. Clouds of smoke and dust covered the battlefield and hampered the tank drivers' orientation. They were mostly using the sun as a marker. At the same time, the German anti-tank forces on the hills south of the Laison were blinded by the smoke and dust. The tanks and infantry following behind on armored vehicles were able to very quickly break through the German infantry positions north of the Laison. They reached the valley after a short time. Although the creek is only narrow and not very deep, the valley proved to be a significant obstacle to the tanks. When the AVRES—special tanks to remove obstructions—finally arrived, they were able to construct crossings quickly, using fascines they had brought along. Other tanks found opportunities to cross in Rouvres.

Simultaneously with the attack by the 4th Armoured Division and the 3rd Canadian Infantry Division in the sector of 85. Inf.-Div., the 51st British Highland Division started its attack to the east of them. It captured le B° on the left wing of 272. Inf.-Div. in the sector of LXXXVI. Korps and continued to advance to the southeast. The tanks of the 4th Canadian Armoured Brigade took advantage of that thrust. Swinging wide, they found Laison crossings north of Ernes and in the village itself. They then turned to the southwest, thus pushing into the flanks and the rear of the artillery in position southeast of Maizières. It was destroyed in a short fight.

The tank attack in the Maizières-Rouvres sector south of the Laison only re-started in the late afternoon. The delay was mainly caused by a mixing of the units. Olendon and Sassy were taken toward evening. The 4th Armoured Division reported in the evening that it had captured fifteen officers and 545 NCOs and men.[15]

The 85. Inf.-Div. had deployed its reserves, Füsilierbataillon 85 and two Pionier companies of Pionierbataillon 185, to prevent an enemy breakthrough. They were able to hold rear positions south of Sassy and south of Olendon.

Contact with the 272. Inf.-Div. adjoining on the right was lost in the afternoon. A gap of almost five kilometers in width had been created up to

Condé-sur-Ifs. The command post of Grenadierregiment 980 was located there. It defended the village valiantly. The 272. Inf.-Div. brought in all available tank hunter squads, Pak and captured tanks. The enemy who had penetrated into the village was thrown back and the village cleared.[16]

The attack in the sector of the 3rd Canadian Infantry Division followed a similar course. The infantry on armored vehicles arrived at Ch,teau Montboint ahead of the tanks and was held up by machine gun fire. The MG positions were overcome by flame throwers mounted on tracks. One of the two Tigers in action there was reportedly knocked out.[17] During their further advance, the Canadians reached Hills 175 (two kilometers west of Epaney) and 184 (two kilometers northeast of Soulagny) and 160 (two kilometers south of Montboint) before nightfall against the tenacious resistance by Grenadierregiment 1054, the Tigerkompanie and a group of Panzers from Panzerregiment 12.

At 14.00 hours, the attack by heavy bombers on villages along both sides of Route Nationale commenced. A total of 3,723 tons of bombs were dropped by 417 Lancasters, 352 Halifax and forty-two Mosquito bombers. Two aircraft were shot down, one of them probably by Allied anti-aircraft guns.

As already on 8 August, a portion of the carpet bombing hit Canadian and Polish troops, in particular in the areas around St. Aignan and Hautmesnil. The losses were significantly higher still than on 8 August and they caused confusion and bitterness.[18]

At 272. Inf.-Div. the attacker advanced to Bonnoeil (12.5 kilometers northwest of Falaise) and his tanks reached Leffard (eight kilometers northwest of Falaise) in the afternoon. When a crisis occurred in the evening, the Kampfgruppe of Panzerregiment 12 was moved behind the threatened right wing of 271. Inf.-Div. and assembled in the area around Martigny-Pierrepont (two kilometers south of Leffard). It remained under the command of the "HJ" Division. The commander of II. Panzerabteilung, holder of the Knight's Cross Sturmbannführer Karl-Heinz Prinz was killed on 14 August 1944 near Torps, two kilometers west of Soulagny.[19]

In the early afternoon the I. SS-Panzerkorps requested approval from 5. Panzerarmee to pull back the main line of resistance to the line Sassy-Aubigny (2.5 kilometers north of Falaise)-Noron (3.5 kilometers west of Falaise). The Armee ordered the Korps at 15.30 hours to hold the line Ernes-Soulagny-Bonnoeil under all circumstances for the remainder of 14 August. Otherwise, the only major road to the west would be cut off. Brigadeführer Kraemer believed that he could not hold that line since the enemy was already located in St. Germain, three kilometers east of Bonnoeil, and was attacking with superior forces (three infantry divisions, one armored division, two tank brigades). The 5. Panzerarmee requested from the Heeresgruppe that the 21. Panzerdivision, in the west, be pulled out and moved behind I. Panzerkorps in order to prevent a breakthrough of the enemy to Falaise.

Toward evening, I. Korps reported to 5. Panzerarmee that the front had been penetrated in numerous locations and that the existing main line of resistance could no longer be held. In the course of the night, the Korps would withdraw to a line from the southern edge of the woods northwest of Vendeuvre (connecting there with LXXXVI. A.K.)-Hill 78 (one kilometer southeast of Sassy)-Hill 175 (two kilometers northeast of Soulagny)-Glatigny (one kilometer southwest of Soulagny)-Leffard-Tréprel-le Val-la Hère (connecting there with LXXIV. A.K.). In case the Panzers of 11. Panzerdivision promised to the Korps for the following day, did not arrive, it would be unable to hold Falaise against a renewed enemy attack. In the course of the evening, Feldmarschall von Kluge arrived at the Armee command post. He approved the requested move of the 21. Panzerdivision behind the I. SS-Panzerkorps.[20]

Only weak forces were still available for the continued defense of the sector west of the Dives and north of the Ante—on both sides of Falaise. The 85. Inf.-Div. had lost the bulk of its infantry and artillery. It could no longer establish a cohesive front line. The 89. Inf.-Div. had suffered only minor losses. Although the 271. Inf.-Div. had taken significant losses, it was still at a relatively high combat-readiness and capability. The Kampfgruppe of the 12. SS-Panzerdivision had been further weakened by partition. Still, it formed the only mobile reserve of the Korps.

The Infanteriedivisions moved into new positions during the night. These could be manned, in many cases, only as strong points. In its left sector, the positions of the 272. Inf.-Div. ran from the western edge of Vieux-Fumé via Magny-la Campagne-Favières-Hill 79 (1.5 kilometers east of Ernes)-western edge of the forest northwest of Vendeuvre. Contact with the right wing of the 85. Inf.-Div. was to be sought near Hill 80 (one kilometer southwest of Vendeuvre).[21]

The 85. Inf.-Div. established a line of strong points with small groups of infantry, Pioniers and one company of Feldersatzbataillon 185 (field reinforcement battalion) on the hills immediately west of the Dives between Vendeuvre and Bernières-d'Ailly, and along the northwestern edge of the wooded area on les Monts d'Eraines. The mixed Luftwaffen-Flakabteilung, in action in the sector of that Division, was pulled out during the night despite the objection by the Division. Its mission had been to block the Dives crossings on both sides of Jort.[22]

In the left sector of the Korps, at the 271 Inf.-Div., almost unnoticed by the enemy, it had been possible to set up a fairly cohesive main line of resistance from Leffard via Pierrepont to Tréprel and to man it with three Kampfgruppen. The artillery went into position with three Abteilungen in the area Noron-St. Martin-de-Mieux-Fourneau-le Val, and with one Abteilung around Rapilly. An anti-tank front was set up in the Noron area along the road from Falaise to Pont-d'Ouilly using the remaining anti-tank guns in order to prevent a tank breakthrough to Falaise.[23] A Tigerkompanie of Schwere SS-Panzerabteilung 102, with several Panzers, was also in action there.

The "HJ" Division pulled back its Panzergruppe to the previously explored positions north and northeast of Falaise. The two companies of Panzerjägerabteilung 12 were in ambush positions, split into several small units, on the northwest slopes of the Monts d'Eraines and in the woods southeast of Epaney. They formed the anti-tank element of the Grenadiers of the 85. Inf.-Div. in action there at several strong points. The Panzers of Panzerregiment 12 set up ambush positions on Hill 159 (three kilometers northeast of Falaise). Grenadiers of 85. Inf.-Div. who had lost their units were incorporated into the defensive front line. During the night of 14-15 August, Kampfgruppe Krause moved to Soulagny (five kilometers northwest of Falaise on the Route Nationale). The I./26 prepared for defense at the northern edge of Soulagny on both sides of the road. Two Tigers of Schwere SS-Panzerabteilung 102 were in position there to support I./26. The Divisionsbegleitkompanie was adjacent on the right. Its positions were located in the open field. Its neighbor on the right was III./26. Stragglers of the 85. Inf.-Div. were incorporated into the positions there as well. The III. Abteilung of Artillerieregiment 12 took up positions southeast of Falaise behind the Ante. A depot, holding ammunition for heavy field howitzers, was located by chance. That meant that sufficient ammunition was available for a while. The Panzer scouting party of Untersturmführer Wienecke remained in position near Jort, the 8.8 cm Flak battery of Untersturmführer Hartwig near Morteaux-Couliboeuf. The I. Abteilung of Werferregiment 83 was also in action in the Falaise sector. The firing position of 3. Batterie was located north of Damblainville and covered the sector Damblainville-Jort-Olendon. Nothing is known about the actions of the other two Abteilungen of the Regiment. They were, probably, also in action in the sector of I. SS-Panzerkorps.

In the course of 14 August, Montgomery once again changed his Directive M 518 of 11 August 1944 regarding the capture of Falaise. The First Canadian Army now received the order to take Falaise. Previously, it had been left open whether that mission would be carried out by the First Canadian or the Second British Army. At the same time, and with particular emphasis, the Army was ordered to thrust to the southeast and capture Trun, thus linking up with General Patton's forces coming from the south. At that time, the Americans stood immediately south of Argentan, approximately twenty-five kilometers southeast of Falaise. The boundary between the British/Canadian 21st Army Group and the American 12th Army Group ran approximately thirteen kilometers south of Argentan. General Patton, the supreme commander of the Third US Army, was determined to attack across that boundary to the north. The supreme commander of the American Army Group, General Bradley, prohibited the action, and General Eisenhower approved that decision. It is likely that an excellent opportunity was wasted.[24]

In the morning of 15 August, the First Canadian Army continued its attack. At approximately 11.00 hours, the enemy attacked the positions of III./26 and the Begleitkompanie with infantry and fifteen tanks. In the afternoon, I./26 in Soulagny also came under attack from infantry, tanks and flame thrower tanks. While Soulagny could be held, the 1st Battalion Canadian Scottish Regiment, attacking from Hill 175, managed to gain a foothold on Hill 168 after a long, bitter battle. The supporting tanks of the 1st Hussars were prevented from following their infantry by the two Tigers. A report by the other side stated on the action of the Grenadiers of III./26 and the Begleitkompanie: ". . . they prefer death to surrender." The Canadian battalion lost thirty-seven killed and ninety-three wounded in that battle. Those were the most serious losses it had suffered in one day until that time. The III./26 lost four killed, thirteen wounded and twenty missing. The Begleitkompanie suffered five wounded.[25]

In the evening, The Royal Winnipeg Rifles and the 2nd Armoured Brigade attacked Soulagny from the direction of Hill 184. The attack was supported from the north by the Stormont, Dundas and Glengarry Highlanders. The enemy was able to penetrate deeply into the village. However, with the support of a Tiger, he was thrown back again. The enemy lost ten tanks.[26] The commander of the Tiger reported on that action:

The company chief of the Grenadiers came over. He asked us to drive forward in our Tiger and get his men out. They were still holding fast in their foxholes along the Route Nationale and had long since been outflanked. Despite his orders to block any attack near St. Pierre, our commander immediately agreed. An infantryman himself, he understood the plight of those men.

After a fast cross-country drive in the direction of Soulagny, we saw what was happening with the Grenadiers. The company chief quickly briefed us on the extent of his positions and then disappeared to join his men. After a short period of observation, our presence paid off. The reported tanks showed up between the houses of Soulagny. We made out six Shermans, driving line astern slowly past the positions, covering the foxholes with constant fire. It was true that no-one could have made it out of there. It would only have been a question of hours before the last of the Grenadiers had paid with his life for holding out. Finally, when all six tanks showed themselves in all their bulk, our commander gave the order to fire. In accordance with time-tested tactic, the commander fired first on the point tank and then at the one to the rear. There was total confusion. The tanks had been playing that game a few times already without being bothered by anyone. Now, suddenly, two of them stood in flames. We did not leave them any time to think. The other four tanks, too, were set on fire in a short time. They had hardly found time to locate our position and fire a few shells. Suddenly, from the opposite direction as the tanks, a column of armored personnel carriers appeared on the battlefield. In the light of the late afternoon sun we could clearly recognize the white stars on the vehicles. Otherwise, there might have been doubts if our own Panzergrenadiers were possibly attacking from that direction.

But there was no question now. In quick succession, our explosive shells and machine gun salvos hit the fully loaded armored personnel carriers. Within a short time, the whole column sat burning and smoking in the open terrain.

There was nothing to be feared from that corner for the next few hours. Terrible, how quickly those men, as young as we, had been surprised by death in the middle of their impetuous and youthful zest for action! But next, it was back to our starting position at St. Pierre, as directed in our original orders.[27]

The 4th Armored Brigade attacked in the direction of Hill 159 from the Olendon area, by-passing Epaney to the west. There, the Panzers of Obersturmführer Max Wünsche were waiting for the enemy. The enemy attack gathered momentum only in the course of the afternoon. Oberführer Kurt Meyer reported on the battle for that important hill outside Falaise:

> . . . Within a short time, the hill is a boiling mass. Shell after shell drills into the ground, laying open the innards of the hill. Our Panzers are sitting in dispersed ambush positions. They are waiting for the dark shadows which will soon have to push out of the black wall of smoke and dust. The first enemy tanks sit burning in the terrain. Enemy infantry is nailed to the ground by well-aimed MG salvos. Do we have any nerves left? Can we still be called human? Our gaze returns time and again to the wall which is nourished by steel and fire. We no longer hear the whistle, the bursting, the roar and the disgusting howl of exploding shells. Every movement in the wall makes our breathing stop. Is there another mass of tanks pushing out of the wall? Will yesterday's spectacle repeat itself? Will we find ourselves lying under the screaming tracks of rattling tanks? None of all that happens. The enemy tanks keep their distance—they do not overrun us. They are stalled in front of Hill 159 . . .[28]

The III. Artillerieabteilung played a significant part in the defensive success.

Further to the east, the enemy attacked Perrières and Epaney. Both villages were lost. However, the tenaciously fighting parts of Grenadierregiment 1054, with the support of 12 Panzerjägers of the "HJ" Division, succeeded in preventing a breakthrough to the south.[29]

The 1st Polish Armoured Division had repeatedly attacked the Quesnay forest on 14 August and was repelled, suffering losses. During the following night, the Germans withdrew from the forest and it was occupied by the Poles. On 15 August, the division, on orders of the II Canadian Corps, moved to the eastern wing. It then would advance via Jort and Trun to Chambois and there join up with the spearhead of the Americans attacking from the south. The 10th Mounted Rifle Regiment (PSK), the armored reconnaissance unit of the division, equipped with Cromwell tanks, scouted in the direction of Jort and Vendeuvre. That sector was defended by a Pio-nierkompanie of 85. Inf.-Div. Three Pak of that division were located in the Jort bridgehead. After the withdrawal of the Luftwaffe Flak-Abteilung from the Vendeuvre bridgehead, only Panzerfausts were available as anti-tank weapons there. The Pioniers in Vendeuvre blew up the bridges across the Dives when the first tank approached. Attempts to ford the river failed, with the loss of one tank which was knocked out by a Panzerfaust. The company of the Polish reconnaissance unit was relieved by the 9th Polish Battalion, an infantry battalion. During the night of 15–16 August it succeeded in forming a bridgehead. The Poles attacked near Jort, supported by Canadian artillery and tank destroyers. The western bridge across the Dives had been blown up, the other prepared for demolition. Despite the marshy banks outside the town, the Poles managed to bring two tanks across the river, and to pull a further six across, using steel cables. Thus, they stood in the rear of the German bridge guards on the eastern bank who held their positions into the night. During that attack, the tanks and tank destroyers on the western bank were reported to have been engaged by two German Tigers. Three Polish tanks were knocked out during the battles, some by Panzers, others by Pak. Five tanks were damaged. One Tiger was reported knocked out. It is improb-able that Tigers were in action there. The Tigerkompanie was fighting, in the afternoon, near Soulagny, northwest of Falaise. Panzerjägerabteilung 12 was in action in the eastern sector. The 1st Polish Armoured Regiment and the 1st Polish (Highland) Battalion (infantry) were brought up to reinforce the troops attacking Jort.[30] The Wienecke Panzer reconnaissance unit, located near Jort, constantly reported to the Division the development of the situation which grew more and more threatening. The "HJ" Division was unable to reinforce the defenses of the 85. Inf.-Div. there. Later, contact with the Wienecke Panzer reconnaissance unit broke off. Polish reconnaissance forces, which had crossed the Dives north of its position, attacked the Wie-necke unit and destroyed it. Untersturmführer Wienecke, three NCOs and nine men went missing. One wounded NCO was able to escape. Albert Wie-necke was initially taken prisoner but managed to escape. After a long time of crisscrossing enemy-held territory, he was able to secure civilian clothing and make his way to the German lines. His report to the Divisional staff was very valuable but, at the same time, cause for concern.

The 272. Inf.-Div., adjoining on the right of the 85. Inf.-Div., had moved into new positions during the night to 15 August. It sought to establish contact near Hill 80 (2.5 kilometers west of Vendeuvre). That movement was still under way in the morning of 15 August. Only around noon was a securing front line established, but it was given up in the course of the afternoon when the Poles attacked Vendeuvre.[31]

As on the right wing of I. SS-Panzerkorps, an extremely critical situation also developed on its left wing on 15 August. Tanks advanced during the course of the afternoon west of the Route Nationale from the north, and reached the Falaise-Pont d'Ouilly road. A report by the 89. Inf.-Div. that the enemy had penetrated into Falaise turned out to be wrong. However, in the evening, parts of the 4th Canadian Infantry Brigade stood one or two kilometers west of the city. Further to the west, at the 271. Inf.-Div., the enemy attacked during the day, focusing the attack near Leffard and Tréprel. The defensive positions, established during the previous night, were broken through at both points. Martigny was abandoned after bitter fighting. Parts of Infanterieregiment 977 set up a blocking position southeast of the village and, in cooperation with the anti-tank barrier, forced enemy tanks, attacking on the hills west of Noron, to turn away. On the Division's western wing, tanks pushed into Pierrepont and advanced to the high terrain south of Tréprel. Withdrawing troops set up a blocking position on the road Pont d'Ouilly-Falaise and were able to stop the enemy attack there.[32]

At twelve noon, I. SS-Panzerkorps reported to 5. Panzerarmee that the 85. Inf.-Div. was almost annihilated and only had one-and-one half battalions and two 8.8 cm guns available. Further, that the 12. SS-Panzerdivision only had 15 Panzers left. The promised Panzers of 11. Panzerdivision and the promised personnel reinforcements had not arrived. The Korps complained about the inadequate support by III. Flak-korps. The batteries were quite far to the rear, some of them still south of Falaise, deployed to combat aerial targets and not available for ground action. The Korps proposed that all Flak forces within its sector be reorganized into Flak combat units. That request was approved by III. Flakkorps. It is questionable to what extent it could still be carried out. That process proves that, during combat on 14 and 15 August, the 8.8 cm Flak, feared by the enemy—contrary to his assumption—did not play a role in anti-tank action.[33]

In view of the extremely critical situation, 5. Panzerarmee ordered, on its own since Feldmarschall von Kluge could not be reached, at 21.00 hours the withdrawal of LXXXVI. A.K. behind the Dives to a line Houlgate (at the Dives Channel estuary)-le Ham-Cléville-Mezidon (seven kilometers north-northwest of St. Pierre-sur-Dives)-western edge of Courcy-hill one kilometer east of Morteaux-Couliboeuf-southern edge of the forest south of Perrières-northern edge of Versainville-southern edge of Aubigny-Hill 203 (?) 1.2 kilometers east of Pierrepont-Pont d'Ouilly.[34]

The pullback of the front line of LXXXVI. A.K. led, at the same time, to a shortening of the front. That made it possible to withdraw one Grenadier-regiment of the 272. Inf.-Div. and move it to the left wing as a reinforcement. The battalions, however, were able to go into action in their new sectors only one after the other. During the night of 15–16 August, the 85. Inf.-Div. established a new defensive front of strong points along the line Lieury-Courcy-Louvagny. It was manned by approximately 300 survivors of Artillerieregiment 185. They had been assembled during the previous night and organized for such a mission. The Division collected the remains of its infantry during the night 15–16 August, supplied them and reorganized them under the leadership of the commander of Grenadierregiment 1053.[35]

At that point, "HJ" Division should have linked up. After the withdrawal of the infantry of the 85. Inf.-Div., which had fought in the wooded terrain of the Monts d'Eraines together with Panzerjägerabteilung 12, no forces were available for that. The 8.8 cm Flakbatterie of Untersturmführer Hartwig was deployed on the right wing of the "HJ" Division, on the eastern bank of the Dives near Morteaux-Couliboeuf, without contact on the right. The Dives crossing near Couliboeuf was secured by a few Panzers on the western bank. The two Panzerjäger companies, together with some stragglers from 85. Inf.-Div., formed a bridgehead on the hills immediately north of Damblainville. The crossing near Eraines was guarded by III./26 of Sturmbannführer Olboeter. The majority of the Panzers—approximately ten—stood near Versainville. The Krause Kampfgruppe prepared for defense at the -northern and western edge of Falaise. It consisted of I./26, the Divisionsbegleitkompanie and two Tigers of Schwere SS-Panzer-abteilung 102.

The remnants of 89. Inf.-Div. defended a narrow sector west of Falaise. The 271. Inf.-Div. fortified its positions, into which it had moved during the afternoon and evening of 15 August, during the course of the night. It deployed all available heavy weapons on the right wing to cover Falaise.

General Crerar, supreme commander of the First Canadian Army, ordered the II Canadian Corps on 15 August, to start an attack by its two armored divisions on Trun, after the capture of Falaise. Consequently, General Simonds issued orders to the 4th Canadian Armoured Division in the morning of 16 August, not to carry out the planned attack on the high terrain north of Falaise. Instead, to cross the Ante near Damblainville, to advance farther along the road Falaise-Trun and so to close the gap between the First Canadian Army and the Third US Army. The 1st Polish Armoured Division was ordered to attack alongside the 4th Armoured Division from the area around Jort in a southeasterly direction and to also establish contact with the Americans.[36]

During the night of 15–16 August, the Poles established a bridgehead across the Dives near Vendeuvre. During that operation, they were harassed by German aircraft which dropped parachute flares and, afterwards, light fragmentation bombs. Polish engineers built a temporary bridge and a Bailey bridge across the Dives. That allowed the whole of the 10th Polish Armoured Brigade to advance into the bridgehead which had been established in the morning by joining up the Vendeuvre and Jort bridgeheads. The parts of 85. Inf.-Div., in position opposite, covered the Polish positions and assembly area with intensive and effective mortar fire. In the course of the day, the 3rd Canadian Infantry Division relieved the Poles in the bridgeheads, thus freeing them for the attack on Trun. In the afternoon, the 8th Polish Battalion (the infantry battalion "Bloody Shirts") started an attack on Barou-en-Auge, Norrey-en-Auge and Hill 151 (probably Hill 159, two kilometers southeast of Norrey). It pushed into the gap between the left wing of 85. Inf.-Div., near Louvagny, and the securing positions on the right wing of "HJ" Division. Untersturmführer Hartwig moved his 3. Flakbatterie into a new position in order to be able to fire on the enemy appearing in his flank. As they set up the position, they surprised Polish tanks and knocked them out. Untersturmführer Hartwig was mortally wounded. The Poles reported having captured Hill 151 (159?) by evening.[37]

The enemy attacked to the north along both sides of the Dives from the Vendeuvre area. His thrust disrupted the movement of Grenadierregiment 980 which had been ordered to establish contact with the right wing of 85. Inf.-Div. behind the Dives. The enemy captured St. Pierre-sur-Dives, advanced to Ouville (3.5 kilometers north of the city), but was thrown back to St. Pierre by a counterattack.[38] Simultaneously, tanks attacked in an easterly direction. They, too, were repulsed and pulled back to St. Pierre. Captured enemy documents indicated the direction of the thrust as toward Lisieux by way of Livarot.[39]

The attack by the 4th Canadian Armoured Division on 16 August got under way only slowly. Despite the vastly superior attacking forces, it made little progress. Untersturmführer Borgsmüller of the Panzerregiment provided a report on the mood of the troops:

Around noon I had to go and look for Panzerjägers in the forest of Monts d'Eraines. They were reported above Ste. Anne-d'Entremont (three kilometers north of Damblainville). In fact, that is where they were. An Untersturmführer received me with these words: 'Do you want to see tanks?' He pointed to the road. They were sitting down there, lined up in rank and file. Regrettably, they were not our Panzers. The road, as far as one could see, was full of tanks. My God, when they start their attack! Why did they not do just that? If only we had had such an opportunity! Now, back to the command post.

That almost went wrong. Exactly where we had driven only a few minutes previously, at the road junction near Hill 138 (two kilometers southwest of the town), we ran directly into tracked enemy vehicles. Enemy infantry was standing alongside. We were not separated from them by even ten meters. I yelled at the driver: 'Get away to the left!' He reacted immediately and we raced at full throttle along the country lane in the direction of Damblainville toward the cover of a slope. Then we heard the salvos from the enemy's automatic weapons. They hit the ground to the right and left of our BMW. I could almost feel the bullets hitting my back, but luck was with us.[40]

The Panzerjägers and the few infantrymen accompanying them prevented an enemy breakthrough to Damblainville. In the course of the day, the enemy succeeded in breaking through the line near Versainville. With a few Panzers, the Panzerregiment fought off a breakthrough to the Ante.[41]

There will be reports further on regarding the progress of the battle for the city of Falaise. Before that, developments at 89. Inf.-Div., 271. Inf.-Div. and in the general situation must be described. No reports are available for 16 August on 89. Inf.-Div. The enemy report on the situation on the German side stated: ". . . Tonight it was reported that the Bois du Roi is free of the enemy with the exception of a few individual riflemen and stragglers. Members of Grenadierregiment 1056 were taken prisoner . . ."[42] The regiment mentioned was part of 89. Inf.-Div. At first, the enemy did not attack on the sector of 271. Inf.-Div. Only toward evening did a strong enemy combat group of infantry and tanks break into the right wing. The anti-tank guns in position there were initially lost but were recaptured by their crews. Finally, the villages of Noron and Miette (one kilometer southeast of Noron at the Ante crossing) were lost.[43]

At the Eberbach Panzergruppe, the enemy pushed to the north and northeast in the course of 16 August with strong infantry and tank forces by way of La Ferté-Macé (twelve kilometers west of Carrouges). In the sector of the breakthrough between Alençon and Argentan, the enemy succeeded in capturing Ecouche and in advancing in the direction of Falaise with strong armored units to a point that the British and American spearheads were only eighteen kilometers apart. In the opinion of Supreme Command West ". . . an encirclement of the bulk of 5. Panzerarmee, 7. Armee and Panzergruppe Eberbach . . ." was in the making.[44] Feldmarschall von Kluge telephoned Generaloberst Jodl in the afternoon and stated: ". . . It would be a disastrous mistake to embrace a hope today which cannot be fulfilled, and no force in this world is able to do that, not even through an order which is issued in that respect. That is the situation! . . ." Generaloberst Jodl replied that the sense of the Feldmarschall's words was clear to him, and that a short radio massage along those lines would be sent. Feldmarschall von Kluge continued, saying that he required a certain freedom of action so that he could lead back the armies across the difficult Orne sector.[45] A Führer order arrived in the afternoon approving the withdrawal across the Orne and the Dives. The cornerstone of Falaise was to be held.[46] Based on that, Feldmarschall von Kluge ordered the 5. Panzerarmee: ". . . It is essential that the bottleneck in the north and in the south be held, with sufficient cover. To do this, it may become necessary to move one Panzerdivision into the break-through sector of St. Pierre. It is further planned to assemble the bulk of the Panzer units in the area east of Evreux on both sides of the Eure . . ." [47]

The commander of 21. Panzerdivision, Generalmajor Feuchtinger, reported to I. SS-Panzerkorps at 11.30 hours. The bulk of his division, sched-uled to assemble south of Falaise in the Bois de St. André, was still west of the Orne. The Korps intended to put the division into action at the focal point of Morteaux-Couliboeuf in order to keep the bottleneck open. The Armee approved that plan. For the coming night, the Korps ordered the withdrawal of the front to the line Mittois (four kilometers east of St. Pierre-sur-Dives)-Lieury-northern edge of Courcy-northern edge of Morteaux-Couli-boeuf-northern edge of Damblainville-northern edge of Falaise-Les Loges (eight kilometers west-southwest of Falaise), with contact to the neighbor on the left.[48] Because of the deteriorating situation, 272. Inf.-Div. had to pull back its left wing to Fourneaux-le Val (three kilometers southeast of Les Loges).[49]

THE DEFENSE OF FALAISE FROM 16 TO 18 AUGUST 1944

The city of Falaise had lost some of its importance, for both sides, since a breakthrough from the west to the east was no longer possible because of the closeness of the front. In addition, Montgomery had moved the focal point of the Allied attack to the Dives after the breakthrough to Falaise by 15 August had been unsuccessful. Despite that, Falaise was of extreme impor-tance to secure the flanks during the eastward withdrawal of the troops still to the west of the Orne.

The old city of William the Conqueror is located on a plateau above the Ante valley. The whole northwestern boundary of the city is formed, then as today, by the medieval city-wall. It had a wide gap where the road from Caen enters. Between that road and the old fortress, located in the southwestern corner, the city-wall was broken by two gates: the Porte des Cordeliers and the Porte Philippe Jean. Through those gates, narrow roads led down into the Ante valley. The old fortress sits on top of steep rocks which gave the city its name. The Route Nationale No. 158, coming from Caen, leads through the city in a continued southeasterly direction to Argentan, Sees and AlenÁon. Important connecting roads led to Falaise from Trun in the southeast and from St. Pierre in the northeast. The road from Thury-Harcourt was, in places, less well constructed. A wide connecting road came from Flers, in the west, via Pont-d'Ouilly, another one from Putanges in the south. Thus, Falaise was even then a road junction center of importance and, because of that, one of the major attack objectives of Montgomery's 21st Army Group.

On the day of the start of the invasion, Falaise was attacked once by fighter-bombers. The civilian population suffered five killed and a dozen wounded. Soon after, a bomb carpet was dropped on the city, causing signif-icant losses and destruction. As the front was approaching the city, Canadian

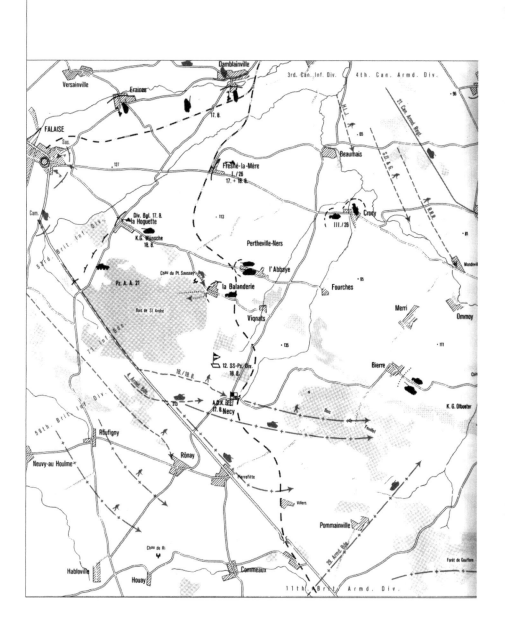

Karte 9: Kämpfe im Kessel von Falaise
vom 17.-19.8.1944
und Ausbruch aus dem Kessel vom 19.-20.8.1944

Map 9: Fighting in the Falaise Cauldron
August 17-19 1944
and the break-out from the Cauldron August 19-20 1944

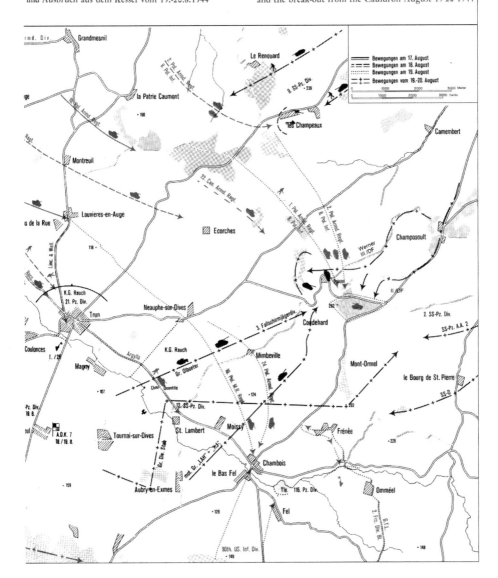

artillery repeatedly covered it with barrages. During the night of 12-13 August, 144 bombers attacked Falaise in order to block the southern entrances to German troops. As if by a miracle, no-one was hurt. Most of the inhabitants had, in any case, left the city. Only the mayor had stayed. [50]

The responsibility for the defense of Falaise had been given to Sturmbannführer Bernhard Krause. His Kampfgruppe consisted of I./26, the Divisionsbegleitkompanie, and two Tigers of Schwere Panzerabteilung 102. He had approximately 150 men available. The Kampfgruppe set up strong point defenses along the old city-wall, facing north and northwest. The Divisionsbegleitkompanie took over the right sector, I./26 the left sector. Two 7.5 cm anti-tank guns were available as anti-tank weapons. They were both moved to the Route Nationale. One went into position on the right side of the road at the bridge across the Ante. The road was blocked by a barbed wire barricade. The second gun sat at the Porte Marescot where the Route Nationale leaves the old city in a southeasterly direction. The Kampfgruppe command post was located in the vicinity of the railroad station.

The order to capture the city of Falaise was issued to the 6th Infantry Brigade of the 2nd Canadian Infantry Division, reinforced by two companies of the 27th Armoured Regiment. The brigade had suffered heavy losses during the battles near Clair-Tizon and la Cressonnière from 11 to 14 August. In the morning of 16 August, its battalions mustered the following strengths: Les Fusiliers Mont Royal 558 men, The Queen's Own Cameron Highlanders of Canada 667 men and The South Saskatchewan Regiment 625 men. The two companies of the 27th Armoured Regiment had at their disposal ten and eleven tanks, plus three reserve tanks, for a total of twenty-four. In addition, parts of the 2nd Anti-tank Regiment were attached. Artillery fire support was provided by the 4th, 5th and 6th Field Regiments.[51]

The weather in the morning of 16 August was foggy, but then it cleared up and turned into a hot day.

The commander of the 2nd Canadian Infantry Division, Major General C. Foulkes, arrived at the command post of the 6th Infantry Brigade, which was led by Brigadier H.A. Young. Foulkes issued the order to advance with all possible speed on Falaise. Together with the 27th Armored Regiment, the brigade developed the plan for the capture of the city. Two battalions would advance along the two major roads leading through Falaise: in the southern section the Rue Paul Doumer with its extension Rue des Ursulines, and in the northern section the Rue de Caen with its extensions Rue Georges Clemenceau and Avenue Aristide Briand, i.e. the Route Nationale No. 158. The hills west of the city were occupied by the 4th Infantry Brigade. The plan of attack envisaged:

The South Saskatchewan Regiment (infantry), supported by "B"-Squadron of the 27th Armoured Regiment, attacks along the road Villers-Canivet, continuing along the northern road.

The Cameron Highlanders (infantry), supported by "A"-Squadron of the Armoured Regiment attack from the northwest past the 4th Infantry Brigade and advance along the southern road.

Start of the attack 13.00 hours.

Thus, half of the day was already lost. During the previous evening, the Camerons had not made any preparations for scouting and reconnaissance. That caused a delay of at least one hour. A crossing move by the 8th and 9th Armoured Regiments in the Villers-Canivet area caused a traffic chaos which added another one hour delay. When the Camerons advanced through the southern section of the Bois du Roi, they came under mortar fire. The battalion commander, himself, had to lead the troops forward. A further one hour delay was encountered. Thus, the start of the attack was postponed by two hours to 15.00 hours. Despite that, there was insufficient time to brief the units and determine the cooperation between infantry, tanks and artillery.

The Saskatchewans started their attack at the time as ordered, but came under fire from 8.8 cm guns and machine guns from the area of the crossroads 1.5 kilometers south of Aubigny. The fire originated from Tigers 001 and 241 of Tigerabteilung 102 of Sturmbannführer Weifl, and their close-in infantry support. That strong point had already been spotted in the morning and the expectation had been that the 4th Brigade would have eliminated it. At 15.30 hours, the position came under concentrated artillery fire. Under its cover, the tanks of "A"-Squadron, which accompanied the Saskatchewans, advanced. Two tanks were knocked out, the others pushed past the position. Soon after, the two Tigers and their close-in support were ordered to withdraw to the northeastern edge of Falaise.[52]

As the Canadians approached the suburbs of Falaise along the Route Nationale, they came under fire from the anti-tank gun and machine guns in position at the bridge. One tank was knocked out. The battalion commander, Lieutenant Colonel Clift, went forward to determine the reason for the delay in the advance. He took the rifle away from one of the infantrymen and fired at the gun crew. According to his observations, he took out three men. The remaining men had then blown up the gun and withdrawn.[53] Sturmmann Heinrich Bassenauer, a member of that gun crew, reported:

> To the left and the right of the road—from the orchards above—the Canadians were closing in. The machine gunner of our anti-tank gun aimed effective fire on the enemy. He then changed position and was badly wounded by enemy rifle fire. I took over the machine gun and set up position on the top floor of a carpenter's shop, next to the bridge at the city-wall. From there I had a good field of fire and could effectively fight the attackers. The first Canadian tank showed up from behind a bend in the street. It was knocked out by our anti-tank gun. My machine gun nest was spotted by the enemy

and I changed position. On the way, a shell hit the gable of a house and I was wounded by shrapnel. I was carried out of the position. Rottenführer Mahraun, the commander of our anti-tank gun, was brought to the main field dressing station one half hour later, suffering from a bad head wound. With his voice rattling and breaking, he asked for Obersturmführer Hartung, our company chief, to report to him that he had knocked out three enemy tanks.

Together with him, I was transferred to the field hospital by an ambulance bus. The road led up a hill where, suddenly, we saw two burning Canadian tanks sitting to the right of the road. To the left, on a down-slope, was a whole pack of tanks. The Canadians let us pass without hindrance, but then fired a machine gun after us. However, we soon reached a wooded area which offered us cover. The fire had not caused any damage.[54]

Sturmmann Leo Freund reported on the progress of the fighting in the sector of the Divisionsbegleitkompanie, adjoining on the right:

On 16 August, the enemy attacked Falaise without pause. We were able to fight off all attacks, although the enemy charged our positions at the edge of the city time and again.

Suddenly, in the afternoon, a new attack wave was made up completely of Negroes! That was the first time we were facing Negroes. We stared at that specter, as if paralyzed by shock. The first of our men, their faces distorted by terror, began to retreat. As he realized the situation, our company chief, Obersturmführer Guntrum, ordered me to immediately report the new development to Sturmbannführer Krause. I raced past the cathedral,down a long straight street with a slight up-slope. On the left of that street, in a cellar, was the command post of Sturmbannführer Krause.

After I had jumped down the few steps into the cellar, terror still on my back, I stood in front of Sturmbannführer Krause and started to stammer my report. He calmly pushed me down on a stool and spoke in a fatherly voice: 'Calm down first, my boy, and then tell me what is happening with your bunch.' After a shot of schnapps, I managed to report about the Negroes and also of the fear which had engulfed us all, and that the Negroes had probably already penetrated into Falaise.

As cool as you please, Sturmbannführer Krause then issued his orders for the counterattack. Since he had no reserves at all, he carried out the counterattack with the men of his staff, maybe twenty men altogether. Indeed, the Negroes had already penetrated into Falaise, i.e. into the desert of rubble which was Falaise, since, other than the cathedral, almost no buildings were still standing. Everywhere we saw the black heads appear from behind the chunks of masonry. But, we also found our men in the ruins and when they recognized 'Papa Krause', as we soldiers called him, all their terror disappeared and a strong counterattack formed. Now it was the turn of the Negroes to experience terror and they quickly fled the ruins of Falaise. We were able to move back into our positions at the northeastern edge. Thanks to Sturmbannführer Krause, we had learned from another experience.[55]

At 17.30 hours, the Saskatchewans and their tanks had gained a foothold on the eastern bank of the Ante and penetrated into the city.[56] Their advance along the Rue de Caen was stopped by a machine gun, in position in the Rue du Camp Ferme, and firing down Route Frédéric Galleron and the Rue des Cordeliers. That machine gun squad subsequently changed its position to lot No. 7 of the present Rue de Caen. Its resistance was only broken when Shermans set the block of houses on fire. Once the Saskatchewans had reached the square in front of the church of St. Gervais, they turned northeast and advanced, with the tanks, along Rue Gambetta. A small group of Grenadiers was hiding behind some concrete blocks which had previously been used as cover against shrapnel by the Feldgendarmerie (military police). They let the tanks pass and then opened fire on the infantry following behind. Three comrades were killed in that spot. The Saskatchewans combed all the streets in the northeastern section of the city. They were stopped, time and again, by individual Grenadiers. In his "Histoire de Falaise", Dr. German wrote about these battles:

> . . . Night was slowly falling on the ruins of Falaise. The skeletons of what used to be our houses at one time stretched black into the sky, illuminated by the red glow of the fires which had been started by the fighting. That background made the hunt for humans, of whom each was at one time the hunter, at another time the prey, even more sinister.
>
> What valor did these Canadians show who had come across the ocean to defend freedom, advancing down our streets, knowing that any piece of broken wall could hide one of those excellent riflemen who rarely missed his target. Did we not equally have to admire the valor of the eighteen year old, young Germans who remained quietly in their positions until the Canadian tanks and infantry advanced—at a ratio of thirty to one—waiting for the most promising moment to fire. They knew well that such delay increased the uncertainty of their survival, and they accepted death in the defense of their fatherland. . .[57]

By midnight, the Saskatchewans had occupied the largest—northern—section of the old city. Until that time, their losses amounted to fourteen killed and numerous wounded.[58] They were then ordered by the Brigade to clear the eastern suburb of German soldiers. Thereafter, they were to prepare for defense along the rail line—it was later closed down—which ran around Falaise in a wide bend, with their front line facing east. A counterattack by Panzers was expected for the next morning. When the Saskatchewans advanced on the Guibray district, they were forced to the ground by fire from a Grenadier squad. It had initially been in position in the park of the Ch,teau de la Fresnay at the edge of the Vallée du Marescot, then in the vicinity of the railroad station and finally in the Jardin Public. From there, a rifleman in a tree fired into the open carriers. The Canadians could only advance further after he had been overcome. At the same time, that column came under machine gun fire from the south side of the Rue Georges Clemenceau until it had crossed the intersection with the Route de Livarot (today, Avenue Général Leclerc). The column then advanced along that street to the railroad crossing which it reached at approximately 03.00 hours on 17 August. In the face of resistance by individual Grenadiers, it captured the railroad crossing on the road to Trun one hour later. The completely exhausted Canadians set up defenses primarily at those two railroad crossings.[59] At that time, Eraines was still occupied by German troops. The parts of Kampfgruppe Krause which had been in action in the northern section of the city had withdrawn fighting, as ordered by the Kampfgruppe commander at approximately 2 A.M., to the eastern edge of the city and then to Fresné-la Mère (six kilometers east of Falaise). There, the Pitscheck Kompanie set up a securing line along the railroad embankment. The Divisionsbegleitkompanie became the reserve of the Kampfgruppe.[60]

The two Tigers, led by Untersturmführer Schroif, which had been withdrawn from the crossroads south of Aubigny at noon, had also taken part in the fighting in the northeastern sector of the city. They were in action mainly at the Eglise St. Gervais, then in the southern section of the city. With the fall of darkness, they withdrew to the southern edge of the city. Thereafter, they were ordered to Villy (three kilometers east of Falaise) where they arrived on 17 August at 02.30 hours, with mounted Grenadiers. After taking on supplies, they went into position at the northern exit from the town at dawn, together with two assault guns, or possibly Panzerjägers.[61]

In the western sector of Kampfgruppe Krause, the Camerons attacking there made only very slow progress. The bridge across the Ante at the Place de la Mutualité was blocked by a barrier of girders and rocks. It was covered by fire from machine guns which were in position below the Porte Philippe Jean along the streets Venelle de la Brasserie and Venelle de la Pipinière. The ten Shermans which supported their attack got stuck in the wet and soft ground of the bomb craters.

Bulldozers were called in. They were unable to get by the stationary column. The Camerons would have to attack the city, at a higher elevation, across the Ante without tank support. The battalion commander of the Camerons thus ordered the attack broken off. Attempts to find a way to get around further to the south were in vain.

The battalion Les Fusiliers Mont Royal was scheduled to follow behind the Camerons after the start of the attack. However, a scouting party of the 14th Hussars reported German Panzers near the Ch,teau d'Aubigny at 13.00 hours. Those were several Panzers which had been ordered to forcefully reconnoiter in the vicinity of the Route Nationale north of Falaise. In order to cover the flank against that threat and against the two Tigers at the crossroads south of Aubigny, the Mont Royals went into position with the attached three reserve tanks at the eastern edge of the Bois du Roi. When the battalion The Royal Winnipeg Rifles of the 3rd Canadian Infantry Division and the Tigers withdrew, the Mont Royals were moved forward into the assembly area of the Camerons northwest of Falaise. They remained there, awaiting further orders.[62]

Under cover of darkness, four companies of the Camerons crossed the Ante but were unable to advance further. The bulldozers made their way there along detours and removed the barriers, allowing the tanks to cross the creek. In the meantime, it was 02.00 hours on 17 August. The attack on the German positions at the Porte Philippe Jean ran into such ferocious resistance from the Grenadiers that it was broken off. The Camerons then bypassed the old Ch,teau to the south at the base of the steep cliffs. There, the advance was greatly impeded by the craters and rubble caused by previous air attacks, and by the fire from a few Grenadiers. Finally, after daybreak, the Canadians were able to cross the expanse of rubble and ruins. They reached the square at the church Sainte-Trinité at 07.30 hours where an exchange of fire took place near the prison.[63]

Orders were issued at the Brigade at 07.30 hours. They stated that the Saskatchewans would hold the line they had reached at the railroad embankment and that the Camerons would advance to St. Clair (two kilometers south of Falaise). The Fusiliers Mont Royal were given the mission to clear the city. If required, reinforcements would be provided to them from the 4th Infantry Brigade.[64]

The Camerons started their attack at 11.45 hours from the Rue Paul Doumer. The spearhead was formed by a company of the 14th Hussars (reconnaissance unit). It was followed by the attached Sherman company. At the end of the Rue des Ursulines, where it runs into the Rue Lebailly, a Grenadier fired Panzerfausts from a window of house No. 2 at the marching column. He knocked out a tank and an armored reconnaissance vehicle. A little further on, where that street joins the road to Argentan (Avenue Aristide Briand), the column came under fire from individual riflemen who had withdrawn from the Guibray district. However, that fire did not delay the advance. The Camerons reached St. Clair at approximately 12.30 hours and cleared out Couvrigny. In that village, their advance had been delayed by a Waffen-SS rifleman in a tree, probably a straggler of Kampfgruppe Krause. They were only able to resume their advance after he had been killed by the machine gun fire from a carrier.[65]

In the meantime, the Fusiliers Mont Royal began clearing the southern section of Falaise. Apparently, the parts of Kampfgruppe Krause in action there had lost contact to the Kampfgruppe during the night so that the order to withdraw to Fresné-la Mère did not reach them. Individual groups, even individual men, fought on, using only their own resources and without any contact with each other. Ten Canadians and four Grenadiers were killed during hand-to-hand combat in the Ch,teau de la Fresnaye. A group of Grenadiers, which had gradually withdrawn to the block of houses bordered by the Rue des Prémonstrés, the Rue Saint-Jean, the Rue des Ursulines, the Rue Lebailly and the Avenue Aristide Briand, offered especially tenacious and lasting resistance.

Those men, with their rifle and machine gun fire, made the two major routes of advance, the Rue Georges Clemenceau and the Rue des Ursulines, almost impassable for all non-armored vehicles. In order to provide supplies and reinforcements to the parts of the Brigade in action south of the city, the Canadians had to eliminate that pocket of resistance as quickly as possible. In the course of a concentrated attack, the men gradually withdrew to the Ecole Supérieure de Jeunes Filles. It was an old building with thick walls, part of the Saint-Jean-Baptiste abbey. According to statements by civilians and a prisoner, the strong point in the school was occupied by fifty to sixty Grenadiers. They were well equipped with weapons and with enough provisions to last for several days. From the top floor of the building, the Grenadiers dominated, in addition, several streets in the southern section of the city, in particular the main route of advance. The Canadians brought up tanks which shot holes in the thick wall surrounding the school grounds. At 18.00 hours, a group of ten Canadians tried to push into the school square and the building. They were repulsed, suffering losses. Then, the assault party of the Canadian reconnaissance unit undertook such an attempt with the same result. Following that, a systematic attack on the pocket of resistance was ordered to start at 02.00 hours.[66]

After nightfall, two young Grenadiers managed to make their way to the German troops outside of Falaise. Since no-one had wanted to leave their comrades the two had been selected by drawing lots. They reported to the Divisional commander that the surrounded men in the Ecole Supérieure would resist to the last, and conveyed their greetings to their comrades. [67]

The only survivor of the Ecole Supérieure who could be reached, was Rottenführer Paul Hinsberger, a medic. He reported on the progress of the fighting:

. . . Our fighting strength inside the Ecole, without the wounded, may have been about forty men. That was not sufficient to man all the windows. By the hour, the number of combat-ready men decreased. The group of our wounded in the cellar continued to grow. Those with minor wounds remained in the ranks of the fighters, only the badly wounded wanted to be in the cellar . . .

He continued in his report, stating that it had been possible, with the help of a captured Canadian medic, to hand over the seriously wounded German and one Canadian soldier to the Canadians during a break in the fighting before the end of the combat. During that, he was taken prisoner of war by the Canadians. No confirmation could be found for his opinion that a breakout by the survivors—except for the major casualties—had been planned, but failed.[68] The war diary of the 6th Canadian Infantry Brigade contains a report on the conclusion of the battle in Falaise:

. . . The Fusiliers Mont Royal started their attack at 02.00 hours. Approximately 100 men took part in it, supported by anti-tank guns and Bren carriers. With the help of mortars and anti-tank guns, the school was eventually set on fire and the defenders came out. A small number of enemy bombers dropped flares and bombs on the area during the attack, causing some confusion. The building was occupied by members of 12.SS who fought staunchly to the end. With the exception of four, who were able to flee into the sector of the South Saskatchewan Regiment, no prisoners were taken. At 05.00 hours we found several piles of dead Germans in the vicinity of the building, and burnt corpses inside the house . . .[69]

The battle by that small group of young soldiers of the Division is an outstanding example of the gallantry and willingness to sacrifice themselves of the men of "HJ" Division. That, in particular, during the critical and nearly hopeless situation when, in other places, the combat spirit waned. The defense of the ruins of Falaise during two days and two nights brought about a decisive gain of time for the divisions fighting between Falaise and the Orne and, initially, west of the Orne.

No memorial tablet bears witness of the fighting by the Tiger crews and the men of "Hitlerjugend" Division, in particular of the battle in the Ecole Supérieure. However, in his "Histoire de Falaise", Dr. German has erected a memorial which will outlast time itself.

That example alone refutes the claim by a renowned British author:

. . . Everywhere, the SS-troops forced the less enthusiastic troops in the front lines to remain in their positions by firing, from the rear, on anyone who tried to surrender or retreat. To an increasing extent, the SS units used regular Wehrmacht uniforms as a protective shield behind which they tried to escape. This practice explains why troops of such obviously low qualification fought with such desperate bravery against a hopelessly superior enemy . . .[70]

After the last resistance in Falaise had been extinguished, the Mont Royals were inserted between the Camerons in St. Clair and the Saskatchewans at the rail line at the eastern edge of the Guibray district. During the night, another anti-tank company moved in so that, as of 12.00 hours on 18 August, the sector ". . . bristled with anti-tank guns . . .", as stated in the war diary of the 6th Brigade.[71] The Canadians had no idea that a maximum of only ten Panzers were still facing them in the area around Falaise. They were in no position to counterattack. The constantly repeated attacks from inside the defenses, with limited objectives, had led to an overestimation of the German Panzer forces.

STRENGTHENING THE NORTHERN FLANK OF THE FALAISE ENCIRCLEMENT FROM 17 TO 19 AUGUST 1944

The description of the fighting on both sides of Falaise ends with the evening of 16 August. At that time, the II Canadian Corps saw the enemy situation as follows:

> . . . The picture is confused. It is not clear what the bag contains. It is possible that the enemy was able to withdraw significant parts of his infantry at the cost of his tank units. A large portion of the SS may also have sneaked out, leaving the Wehrmacht troops to their fate. The latter appears to be the case in our sector of the front. The 'Hitlerjugend', which had been the Korps reserve, was split into a number of Kampfgruppen. They are held ready, along the whole front, as operational reserve with a small pack of tanks each. Except for a few stragglers, we saw nothing of the 'Hitlerjugend' during our advance today. The present location of that division or its Kampfgruppen is unknown.[72]

As ordered, the parts of "HJ" Division located east of Falaise withdrew to behind the Ante sector during the night 16–17 August 1944. They blocked the crossings which were usable by vehicles near Bloqueville, Damblainville and Eraines. For that mission, the two companies of Panzerjägerabteilung 12, the remaining Panzers of the Panzerregiment, several Tigers and III./26 were available. From 2 a.m. onward, the bulk of Kampfgruppe Krause withdrew from Falaise and assembled in Fresné-la Mère. The Pitscheck Kompanie moved into securing positions along the railroad embankment, facing toward Falaise.[73]

In the course of the day, the 4th Canadian Armoured Division attacked the Ante sector. In the early morning, the Argyll and Southerland Highlanders captured Damblainville against weak resistance by forward guards. The Algonquin Regiment attempted to cross the Ante and capture the hills at the opposite bank. Although the old stone bridges had not been blown up, the Canadians were unable to cross the creek. They were held down along the narrow approaches to the bridges by machine guns and mortars. The tanks were unable to deploy. They came under fire from tank hunters of Panzerjägerabteilung 12 who were sitting in elevated ambush positions south of the Ante. Unterscharführer Alfred Schulz, Panzer commander in 2. Kompanie, reported:

> The tanks were sitting in a wide hedge. Ahead of us, the terrain dropped off, rising again slowly at the far side of the wide valley. Early morning fog drifted across the low ground. There, we awaited the enemy attack. I scanned the terrain intensely. Suddenly, I spotted three enemy tanks, just outside a wooded area, approximately 2,000 meters distant. I raced forward, planning to get all three of them by myself. I could not observe the result of my fire since the smoke from the discharges lingered for a long time ahead of my gun barrel. It was possible that, because of the fog, I had estimated the distance incorrectly. The enemy tanks opened fire on me and I became the prey. In the open terrain, I made a good target and was almost knocked out. When my firing distance had shrunk to 1,800 meters, the tanks disappeared into the wood. I do not know whether I hit one of them. Just as I wanted to drive back to my ambush position, the Panzer stopped. The motor had packed it in. We sat, without any cover, in the open field. I asked to be towed back to the position, but none of the vehicles in the vicinity had a towing cable. I sent my loader and my gunner to Panzers of the Panzerregiment farther away. The gunner returned without a cable. The loader never arrived at the Panzer IV, approximately one kilometer away, where he was going. He is missing to this day.
> We were coming under MG fire from the right. I had to blow up the Panzer. I sneaked toward it, leapt inside with one jump, and packed the explosive charges into the engine compartment. Despite the MG fire, I had to get out of the Panzer. Two enemy tanks opened fire on it. I could not have waited one second longer.[74]

Untersturmführer Schroif and his Tigers also took part in that fighting. At approximately 16.30 hours, he observed some thirty-five tanks attacking Damblainville from the north. He opened fire and the tanks turned off to the east. At approximately 18.00 hours, he destroyed a fuel supply column, consisting of an armored reconnaissance vehicle and three trucks, with his Tiger 241. He forced three tanks to turn away. [75]

The left sector of "HJ" Division was generally quiet. The Panzers and III./26 in action near Eraines came under artillery and fighter-bomber fire. The Divisionsbegleitkompanie watched, from Fresné-la Mère, a long column of tanks and armored personnel carriers roll along the horizon from the area north of Falaise in the direction of Morteaux-Couliboeuf. After dark, the Divisionsbegleitkompanie moved to la Hoguette to extend the left wing of the Division.[76]

To the south of Falaise, the Aufklärungsabteilung of 21. Pz.-Div. secured toward the city. Further to the west, a gap had been created during the night. The 89. Inf.-Div. in action there had been wiped out, except for small remnants. When the artillery no longer had any ammunition, it was pulled out of the encirclement area. All four Abteilungen reached the southern bank of the Seine during the following days, complete and without losses. The heavy infantry weapons and "non-essential personnel" followed the same process.[77] At 271. Inf.-Div., the left neighbor of 89. Inf.-Div., a Kampfgruppe led by the commander of Infanterieregiment 977 still held the strong point Corday (five kilometers southwest of Falaise) through 17 August. In the evening, the Divisional staff established contact with the command post of 7. Armee in Nécy. The supreme command approved the pullout of the remnants of the Division and their assembly and re-grouping outside direct enemy effective range. The LXXIV. A.K. took over its sector. [78]

The situation east of the Dives went through a threatening development. In the evening of 16 August, two Kampf-gruppen had been sent into action to stop the attack by the Polish Armoured Division from the Jort bridgehead in the direction of Trun. The Kampfgruppe von Luck consisted of Panzer-grenadierregiment 125, Feldersatzbataillon 200, Panzer-pionier-bataillon 200, and I. and II. Abteilung of Artillerie-regiment 155. Its orders were to move into the area Vaudeloges (five kilometers northeast of Morteaux-Couliboeuf)-Norrey-en-Auge (three kilometers farther south)-les Moutiers-en-Auge (three kilometers south of Norrey).[79] During the move, it encountered the Poles advancing toward Trun. They had already reached Norrey-en-Auge the previous evening. The Cromwell tanks of the 10th Polish Rifle Regiment (reconnaissance) attacked from les Moutiers in the direction of Trun. They came under effective fire from Kampfgruppe von Luck. Four tanks were knocked out. Two damaged tanks were able to retreat under cover of artificial smoke. The two tank units of the 10th Polish Armoured Brigade reached Hill 259 (probably immediately east of le Haut-de-la-Cambe, approximately two kilometers east of Montreuil) by evening "after heavy fighting".[80]

The second Kampfgruppe of 21. Pz.-Div. was led by Oberst Rauch. It consisted of the worn-out Panzergreandierregiment 192, I. Abteilung of Panzerregiment 22, which still had eight combat-ready Panzer IVs, and III. Abteilung of Panzerartillerieregiment 155. That Kampfgruppe was attached to "HJ" Division. It received orders to throw back the enemy advancing from the north on Trun through a counterattack and to keep the east-west passage through Trun, where the major roads crossed, open.[81]

The attack by the 4th Canadian Armoured Division against the Ante sector proved to be difficult. However, since a small bridgehead had already been established near Couliboeuf during the previous day, the II Canadian Corps changed its orders. The 4th Canadian Armoured Division received directives to move the focal point of its attack farther to the east and to cross the Dives near Couliboeuf. In order to do that, it was relived by the 3rd Canadian Infantry Division. The Divisionsbegleitkompanie had observed the moves connected with that operation. The Canadian tank division advanced along secondary roads from the Dives bridgehead toward Trun in the afternoon. Presumably, Kampfgruppe Rauch was still being assembled. The Canadians, in any case, encountered only weak resistance and reached Louvières-en-Auge toward evening. They stopped there to rest and to prepare for the attack on Trun the next day.[82]

The forces of 5. Panzerarmee were insufficient to keep open the northern opening of the bottleneck to the encirclement area. Thus, the supreme command requested from Feld-marschall von Kluge the immediate provision of two Panzerdivisions from the Eberbach Panzergruppe to I. SS-Panzerkorps for a counterattack to the north. It also appeared necessary to withdraw the 7. Armee in one movement across the Orne. The Feldmarschall approved the request.[83] At the boundary between I. SS-Panzerkorps and the LXXXVI. A.K. to the right, the situation had also developed critically during the day. The enemy found a gap. He pushed with strong forces in the evening near Ste. Marie-aux-Anglais and les Authieux (seven kilometers northeast of St. Pierre-sur-Dives) at the LXXXVI. A.K. whose left wing was without support farther to the south. The I. SS-Panzerkorps pulled back its right wing to Montviette (five kilometers west of Livarot) and demanded that the neighboring Korps establish contact there under all circumstances. It was hoping to be able to hold the line MontpiÁon-Grandmesnil (2.5 kilometers south of Ammeville)-les Moutiers-Beaumais-southwestern corner of the Bois de St. André. The Armee promised the Panzerkorps that two Panzerdivisions would be brought in during the night in order to cut off the breakthrough near Morteaux-Couliboeuf. Their arrival could hardly be expected before the start of the enemy attack on Trun.[84]

Since the enemy was already located deep in the right flank of "HJ" Division, it evacuated the positions behind the Ante sector during the night 17–18 August. The III./26 blocked the river crossings near Crocy. The Kampfgruppe Krause secured near Fresné-la Mère, as previously, and Kampfgruppe Wünsche near la Hoguette.

For 18 August, the II Canadian Corps received orders to establish contact with the US troops attacking from the south. Further, to block the Dives sector in order to prevent a breakout by the almost encircled German troops.

A major change took place in the German supreme command on 18 August 1944. The Supreme Commander West, who was the supreme commander of Heeresgruppe B at the same time, Feldmarschall von Kluge, was relieved and ordered to the Führer headquarters to report in person. On his way there he took poison. In a farewell letter to Adolf Hitler, he implored him, in case Feldmarschall Model was unable to master the situation, and if the new weapons did not show the expected success, to end the hopeless battle. Von Kluge assured the Führer that he had felt closer to him than he may have believed, and that he was departing this life in the knowledge of having done his duty to the last.

Feldmarschall Model arrived at the command post of 5. Panzerarmee at 09.00 hours for a briefing with Oberst-gruppen-führer Dietrich, General Eberbach, General Kuntzen, General Gause and—representing Oberstgruppenführer Hausser—Oberst von Gersdorff. The supreme commander of 7. Armee did not want to leave his position with the troops during that extremely critical situation. After receiving the reports on the situation at the Armeen (armies) and Panzergruppe Eberbach, the Feldmarschall ordered:

It is initially important to establish a front line again, whether before or behind the Seine, depends on the development of the situation. The worse solution would be behind the Seine.

To do that, it is important that, while the flanks are being reinforced, the 7. Armee and the Gruppe Eberbach be moved out of the front curve.

During the withdrawal operation, Gruppe Eberbach will be attached to AOK 7. It will then fight in the Trun area, thereafter in the area around Vimoutiers so that a front line can be established behind the Touques river. The 7. Armee must be behind the Dives on 20 August, behind the Touques on 22 August. When that has been achieved, the reinforcement of the flanks can be pulled out. As support on both sides of Trun on 19 and 20 August, Gruppe Eberbach requires:

to the north: II. SS-Panzerkorps with 2., 9., 12. SS-Pz.-Divs., and 21. Pz.-Div.,

to the south: XXXXVII. Pz.-Korps with 2. and 116. Pz.-Divs.

Immediately free are 1. SS- and 10. SS-Pz.Divs. They will start marching initially into the area north of Laigle, and from there into the area south of Mantes. The remains of 17. SS-Pz.-Gren.-Div. and of the Pz.-Lehr-Div. are to start moving into the refitting area east of Paris as soon as possible. Of the general commands, I. SS-Pz.-Korps and LVIII. Pz.-Korps will be withdrawn first . . . General command LXXXIV. A.K. will be sent by AOK 7 to direct the fighting between LXXXI. A.K. and Paris.

As far as possible, the Panzer units are to be pulled out for refitting even while the present objective, the establishment of a new front line, is being carried out.[85]

Apart from artillery fire and fighter-bombers attacks, the enemy did not attack the northern front between Dives and la Hoguette which was held by the "HJ" Division. The sunny weather and good visibility assisted enemy air activity.

The spearhead parts of the British 53rd Infantry Division had reached the area south of Falaise in the evening of 17 August. On 18 August they advanced in the direction of Nécy and Pertheville. At approximately 15.00 hours, Obersturm-bannführer Wünsche, who was located with his Kampfgruppe near la Hoguette, ordered the Divisionsbegleitkompanie, which was down to a combat strength of only 15 men, to move into a securing position near la Balanderie. He directed it there himself. Untersturmführer Stier, who led that small Kampfgruppe after Obersturmführer Guntrum had been pulled out (on orders of the Division) with a broken collarbone, had available two armored personnel carriers and two Panzerjäger IVs. Unterscharführer Leo Freund reported on a small encounter which took place there in the afternoon:

The Divisionsbegleitkompanie was located near the village of la Balanderie on 18.8.1944. After we had fought off several scouting parties, an enemy armored personnel carrier drove right into our position. It was driving on a narrow road with a steep embankment on one side. After we opened fire on the armored vehicle from close distance, the driver lost control of it and steered it up the embankment. It toppled over to the side and came to rest on its top on the road. During the attempt to set it back on its wheels, the commander slid out of the turret. The top of his skull had been cut off as if by a saw. The other crew members surrendered. After they had buried their dead comrade, we sent them into captivity. The armored personnel carrier was undamaged. It was handed over to Sturmbannführer Krause who used it as his command vehicle.[86]

In the early hours of the afternoon, Untersturmführer Schroif had been pulled out of a securing position near the Ch,teau two kilometers east of la Hoguette. He had been ordered to the junction of the railroad and the road west of l'Abbaye where Tiger 124 was located, unable to move. The Panzer was towed to the southern edge of the village. Two Tigers (001 and 124) guarded the northwestern exit of the village to the west, together with the two Panzerjägers. Around 17.00 hours, tanks approached the securing position but were repelled. The Abteilung ordered Tiger 124 blown up after dark, then to march via Vignats, where the Abteilung command post was located, to Nécy and refuel the Tigers of 1. Kompanie. Thereafter, a joint withdrawal to Brieux.

At approximately 23.00 hours, the securing position was pulled back to the railroad embankment east of the village.[87]

The focal point of the attack by the II Canadian Corps on 18 August was east of the Dives. There, three divisions attacked: furthest to the east, the 1st Polish Armoured Division; in the center, the 4th Canadian Armoured Division; in the west, along the Dives, parts of the 3rd Canadian Infantry Division. The Poles had been given the objective to link up with the 90th US Division in Chambois. They started out at 02.00 hours together with the 2nd Polish Armoured Regiment and the 8th Polish Battalion. Marching at night, along secondary roads and country lanes through broken terrain, they lost their way. At dawn, they reached les Champeaux, which is located ten kilometers north of their attack objective, Chambois. The Poles encountered German troops there who knocked out several of their tanks. Just when the Polish attack gathered momentum again, they were attacked by American aircraft. The Polish tanks and the accompanying mounted infantry were stuck in a hollow and suffered significant losses. Only the third wave of attacking aircraft recognized the tanks as their own and broke off the attack. One company of the 10th Polish Mounted Rifle Regiment reached Hill 124 (2.2 kilometers north of Chambois) in the evening. They determined that Chambois was still in German hands and observed a large number of vehicles withdrawing along the road from Chambois to Vimoutiers. After a few fire attacks on the German columns, the company withdrew to its starting position.[88]

In the course of the day, the 4th Armoured Brigade crossed the road Trun-Vimoutiers and reached the area west of Ecorches by midnight. It was slowed down by individual Kampfgruppen fighting their way out of the closing encirclement, as had happened to the Poles. The 3rd Canadian Infantry Division attacked from the bridgehead Morteaux-Couliboeuf along the eastern bank of the Dives. The spearhead of the 7th Infantry Brigade, the Royal Winnipeg Rifles, reached the area immediately northwest of Trun. At the same time, the Lincoln & Welland Regiment of the 4th Canadian Armoured Division pushed into the city from the north. The Regina Rifle Regiment, which also belonged to the 7th Infantry Brigade, occupied Mandeville. The Stormonts of the 9th Infantry Brigade advanced into the area of les Cordiers (one kilometer east of Crocy), the Highland Light Infantry to east of Beaumais.[89]

Since the enemy was thus located in the deep right flank of the "HJ" Division, it became necessary to withdraw its parts securing to the east, north and west. Kampfgruppe Rauch had stopped the Canadian attack south and southeast of Trun and was holding that line. The III./26 was ordered to prepare for defense on both sides of Roc (one kilometer south of Guêprei).

The Wünsche and Krause Kampfgruppen were initially ordered to move to Bierre. In addition, the "HJ" Division ordered all non-essential elements to move out of the closing encirclement. The Artillerieregiment designated the Stabsbatterie (staff battery) of III. Abteilung as well as 7. and 8. Batterie, which had to hand over their ammunition to 9. Batterie. They were able to make their way out of the encirclement area. The Nachrichtenabteilung (communications) was ordered to withdraw to the area around Orbec. That did not come about, as will be reported later. The Flakabteilung was ordered to disengage from the enemy, together with its staff and 4. Batterie (3.7 cm), still in action, and the attached 14./26 (2 cm). It was to move out during the following night and assemble behind the Touques.[90]

The difficulties which had to be expected during the march out of the encirclement area, were described by 5. Panzerarmee in its daily report with terse words. It is stated there:

> ... At the exits from the pocket, as well as inside it, constant air and fighter-bomber attacks, hunting down even individual men on foot, make any movement or assembly of the units, or an attack by them, impossible. The communications systems are largely destroyed ...

The report stated, regarding the enemy situation:

> ... Enemy forces are reported in Champosoult, Champeaux, Ecorches, Trun, Fontaine, Ommoy, and on the advance in a south-easterly direction via St. Lambert and Aubry. The enemy is reported on the attack also from the south, out of the Argentan area, and from Urou east of Argentan toward Crennes. As well, he is reported pushing from Silli (-en-Gouffern, Author) to the north and north-east. Along the Falaise-Argentan, the enemy is reported in Pierrefitte, there is a major enemy breakthrough near Neuvy ...[91]

The American attack encountered determined resistance in the sector east of Argentan. Parts of 116. Pz.-Div. and the Panther-Abteilung of 9. Pz.-Div. repulsed the attack of the 80th US Division immediately east of the city. The 90th US Division was able to make some progress, however, parts of 116. Pz.-Div. were able to stop it immediately south of Chambois.[92]

Another overview of the situation in the sector northeast and north of Morteaux-Couliboeuf should be provided here. Kampfgruppe von Luck of the 21. Panzerdivision had received direction to establish defenses in the sector of the hills northeast and east of Grandmesnil, and north of Monteuil. The northern part of that line could be held on 18 August. In its southern part, the Poles had managed to break through to les Champeaux during the night. As Generalmajor Feuchtinger, the commander of 21. Panzerdivision, reported—the dates, however, had to be corrected—a replacement battalion of "HJ" Division under Sturmbannführer Waldmüller arrived in the St. Gervais area during that day. It planned to drive on to the Division by way of Trun. Since that was no longer possible, Generalmajor Feuchtinger took control of the battalion himself. He directed it to occupy the forest 1.5 kilometers south of St. Gervais and to block the lanes and roads leading from west to east. It is improbable that the mission could be carried out since the Poles had advanced from Hill 259 to les Champeaux. The attachment of the battalion to 21. Panzerdivision is the cause of the 'Front Line' map of 19. August of the Supreme Command West, "HJ" Division being incorrectly shown to the east of Morteaux-Couliboeuf, i.e. outside the developing encirclement.

Unterscharführer Köpke of 1. Kompanie of SS-Panzer-grenadierregiment 25 reported on that replacement battalion in a letter of 20 October 1946: The withdrawn core personnel of the battalion had been moved to Orbec, their original area before the invasion. There, the companies had been reinforced by reserves which had come from replacement units of the 4. SS-Polizei-Panzergrenadier-Division (police). In addition to the men, there were also Zugführers and Gruppenführers. Eberhard Köpke wrote: ". . . They were, especially the NCOs, really on the ball. Two old Hauptscharführer, as Zugführer, did a great job. The best, however, was whom we got: a new Kompanieführer, a great guy from Transylvania, who was absolutely outstanding . . ." The battalion marched off in the direction of Trun. On the march, the column was broken up since the roads were congested with troops coming out of the encirclement area. Sturmbannführer Waldmüller remained outside with the bulk of the battalion. Parts of it pushed into the not yet fully closed encirclement, to the Division.[93]

While the enemy did not attack on the northern front of the encirclement area on 18 August, the 53rd British Infantry Division advanced from the area southwest of Falaise along the road from Falaise to Argentan. In the evening it reached, supported by the 4th Armoured Brigade, the area of Rùnai, ten kilometers southeast of Falaise. The 2nd Battalion The Monmouthshire Regiment, one of the three infantry battalions of the 160th Infantry Brigade, was ordered to take possession of the high terrain south of Nécy in a night attack. It is likely that other battalions also received similar orders. That development was not known at the "HJ" Division. It still assumed that its left flank was secured by Panzeraufklärungsabteilung 21 and the remnants of 271. Inf.-Div. The Divisional command post was located immediately north of Nécy. The command post of Kampfgruppe Wünsche was in Fourches. The Kampfgruppe had orders to move to the area around Bierre during the night. During the move it encountered, totally unexpected, enemy forces which Obersturmführer Meitzel had not found when he scouted in the area of the new command post during the afternoon.

Untersturmführer Fritz Freitag, the orderly officer of the Panzerregiment, reported on the unexpected encounter:

> . . . After the vehicles had been refueled again and the marching orders made known, we moved out around midnight. The marching sequence was: commander Panzerregiment. adjutant Panzerregiment, commander Panzerjägerabteilung, radio armored personnel carrier, and then the rest. I was riding in the captured armored reconnaissance vehicle of the Regimental commander at the point. The English vehicle offered seats only for the driver and one other. Thus, I sat on the roof and wrapped myself in a blanket since it had turned bitterly cold and it was still the middle of a dark night. There was not a glimmer of light anywhere. Single JU 88s darted across very low above, and dropped their load on the other side. We recognized them only by the bluish exhaust flames. The brave comrades from the Luftwaffe were not to be envied. Even if they sneaked up with their engines throttled, heavy defensive fire welcomed them. The green, red, and yellow trails of the tracer bullets from the English anti-aircraft guns set off a proper fireworks on the night horizon.
>
> On 19 August 1944 at approximately 04.00 hours, just before dawn, we drove through a hollow, not far from Brieux where our new command post was located. Infantrymen were coming toward us, marching past us one after the other. I looked down from my high seat but could only make out the lighter areas of their faces under the steel helmets. Behind our scout vehicle came the Volkswagen with the Regimental adjutant Isecke and the Regimental physician Stiawa. Behind it was the Volkswagen with the commander of the Panzerjägerabteilung, Hanreich.
>
> The typical Volkswagen motor noise seemed to have made the approaching infantrymen suspicious since, all of a sudden, they opened fire at close distance. Hand grenades exploded, the fuel tank of a car blew up. The shouts of the wounded mixed into that hellish concert, and all that in a narrow hollow, eerily lit by the burning car. We did not have to contemplate for long whom we were facing. I have probably never before slid off the vehicle roof into the fighting compartment as quickly as I did then, when the air was full of 'flying lead'.
>
> We could not turn around, and that would have been useless in any case since we could not have made it by the burning car. So, open the throttle slowly and carefully ahead. As dawn came, we were at the entrance to Brieux, driving around a road bend. We were in for a shock when we spotted two Sherman tanks and several

machine gun carriers with dismounted infantry approximately fifty meters ahead of us at a crossroads. Canadians [probably English]!

We could not turn around, that would invariably have earned us a 7.5 cm tank gun hit. But, our captured English reconnaissance vehicle fooled the comrades from the other field post number for the first moment. They kept standing at the crossroads and watched us approach. That reasoning raced through our brains like lightning. Instinctively, the driver opened the throttle. The Canadians standing on the crossroads scattered in all directions. Then, around the next corner, and onward! Behind us followed a Volkswagen which had also taken advantage of that moment of first surprise. The machine gun fire which they sent after us when they had recovered from the initial surprise, went barely over our heads. The next bend in the road provided us with safety for a while. That provided some time for rational consideration of the situation. Our two vehicles were all by themselves. The Regimental commander, his driver and I in the English scout vehicle, and the Regimental adjutant, the Regimental physician and the driver in the VW-Kübel. Six men altogether. A quick exploration of the map indicated that we were located on the road between Nécy and Brieux.

Stiawa, our doctor, had apparently been hit during the wild firing in the hollow. But, we had no time to check him out carefully and put a dressing on him. We laid him on the back seat of the Volkswagen and went on. The scout car was in the lead. Somewhere we would have to get through, it was impossible that Canadians were everywhere. They had reached Brieux only at dawn, after all.

Isecke, the Regimental adjutant, and I sat on the left and right of the engine in the rear of the scout vehicle, our machine pistols at the ready. We tried our luck along the next lane leading south. But we had barely left the cover of a hedge when MG fire came whistling at us from about 150 meters away. Thankfully, it went just above our heads. Like lightning, Isecke and I were in the ditch and fired back. Our reconnaissance vehicle withdrew behind the hedge again.

We tried a few other spots to find out if the Canadians had not left a gap anywhere through which we could escape. However, 'flying lead' welcomed us everywhere! Wünsche and I set out on foot to find a favorable spot. We reached the major road which led to the Dives crossing near St. Lambert. Just as we discussed what to do next, two Tigers came rolling toward us. They, too, must have been at a lost position in the depth of enemy territory and were trying to establish contact with their own lines. We waved and yelled, but the two massive crates droned past. Immediately after, we heard the burst of shells being fired and their explosions. The two of us did not have a thick skin such as those two, and we could not fight our way out with explosive shells either. With anger burning in our stomachs, and a mighty rage at those two Panzer commanders, we started back toward our comrades. After arriving there, we decided to wait for darkness and then to simply race under its cover through the Canadian security line. No sooner said than done. Everything we needed was taken from the two vehicles, charts, binoculars, weapons, compass, and two chocolate bars which had somehow found their way there.

In the meantime, it was the middle of the morning, and the sky was slowly clouding over. The two vehicles were well camouflaged at a hedge. A French farm boy watched us doing that, but we chased him off.

We hid in old foxholes near a hedge. The two drivers in one hole, Wünsche and I in another, Stiawa and Isecke in their own. Each hole was within shouting distance from the others. We were able to keep an eye on the hiding place of our vehicles from there. Only then did we find time to examine Stiawa and put a dressing on him. He had only been grazed, not badly, and was able to walk with some help.

In the early hours of the afternoon, some Canadian reconnaissance vehicles with mounted infantry suddenly appeared, soon there was a whole platoon. The French boy we had chased off in the morning led them to the hiding place of our vehicles. The Canadians removed the camouflage and took our two vehicles away. Furious and helpless, we had to watch them do it. They did not search for us for any length of time, probably thinking that we had taken off a long time ago. So, there we sat, with nowhere to go but down, as they say. That was the end to our race through enemy lines after dark. With well-founded discretion, we moved into new hiding places. During the move we lost sight of our two drivers. A small thicket offered wonderful cover, and we slipped into it.

There were only four of us left. The commander, Wünsche, his adjutant Isecke, Dr. Stiawa and I. We made extensive use of the daylight before dark to memorize our way on the map and the respective compass directions, and to commit that portion of the map to memory. Through my many scouting parties and reconnaissance missions, I had become very adept in doing that. It really paid off later during the night. Our plan was to make our way through the Canadian guards by night and arrive at our own lines again at dawn. That did not seem too difficult, but we had not expected that the enemy had already advanced to such an extent that we were practically in the enemy's back country. Otherwise, we would surely have thought of grabbing some vehicle in order to be able to move faster. But, as said, we did regrettably not know that at the time, and it is easy to talk later . . .[94]

The Divisionsbegleitkompanie also moved with the column of Kampfgruppe Wünsche, mounted on six Flakpanzers. Unter-scharführer Leo Fre-
und experienced the march as follows:

> . . . The night was fairly dark, and the Panzers were driving closely
> one behind the other, so as not to lose contact. I sat on the third
> Flakpanzer. We had been traveling for some time when the column
> drove through a small wooded area along a narrow path. Massive
> trees could be made out on the left and right. Suddenly, there was a
> loud explosion. The Panzer at the point stopped, flames were lick-
> ing up on its outside. The second Panzer immediately opened fire,
> aimless along the path and into the woods. No enemy could be spot-
> ted. With difficulty, the five Flak-panzers backed out of the wooded
> area, in the sad knowledge of having lost the commander of the
> Panzerregiment . . .[95]

The attachment of Schwere SS-Panzerabteilung 102 was canceled on 18
August. It was given orders to move into the area south of Vimoutiers during
the following night in order to support the planned attack by II. SS-Panzerkorps from the outside to keep the "bottleneck" open. Untersturmführer
Freitag reported previously that two Tigers rolled past him in the morning of
19 August. They were apparently able to open their path by firing. That was
not true for all. An English report on the action by the 2nd Monmouthshires
near Nécy described an encounter with three Tigers of the Abteilung:

> . . . At approximately 06.00 hours we heard tank noises in the north.
> Some of us thought that those were Sherman tanks, but their unmis-
> takable rattle could not be heard. A few minutes later, three German
> Tigers came into view. They immediately came under fire from all
> available weapons, machine guns and pistols, but they rolled undam-
> aged through 'D'-Company and reached the crossroads which was
> occupied by 'C'-Company and the battalion staff. The road was
> blocked by the armored personnel carrier of the artillery observer.
> The point Tiger rammed it and pushed it through the wall of a
> barn, until it had enough room to pass. The Tiger then attacked the
> carrier of the commander which had been hastily and unceremoni-
> ously abandoned. When the path was open, the Tiger continued
> toward 'B'-Company. A keen radio operator had warned that com-
> pany. Soon after, we heard three loud bangs. The battalion staff
> believed that the Tigers had opened fire with their 8.8 cm guns, but
> a few minutes later the chief of 'B'-Company called to express his
> regrets that one had got away. That was an understatement. The
> point Tiger had missed the brackets holding the 'Hawkins grenades'
> deployed in the vicinity of the command post. The second Tiger,

however, detonated two of them and slipped into the road ditch. The third tank, driving at top speed as did the others, ran into the other Tiger stopped in front of him and which had, in the meantime, been hit by a PIAT (anti-tank grenade launcher). Its gun muzzle was wedged tight under the baggage carrier of the second tank. The hit from the PIAT had not penetrated the armor, but both crews bailed out in all haste. Those crew members who survived were taken prisoner . . .[96]

The commander of the Tiger which got away was Obersturm-führer Kals. The two other Panzers were commanded by Untersturmführer Schroif and Unterscharführer Glagow.[97]

Even before the skirmish with the Tigers, some vehicles ran into the advancing English near Nécy in the dark. After an exchange of fire, the wounded commander of SS-Panzerjägerabteilung 12, Sturmbannführer Jakob Hanreich, and his escort were taken prisoner. The English report quoted above stated on that:

> . . . His extreme arrogance and offensive attitude almost led to his sudden death a few times. However, he was duly transported to a prison camp without suffering further damage . . .

The battle noise alerted the Divisional operations staff at its close-by command post near le Mesnil-Guérard at the southeastern edge of the Bois de St. André. It moved hastily to the area of Bierre.

The replacement unit of the Flakabteilung , which drove out of the encirclement area during the night of 18–19 August, was not left unscathed either. Sturmmann Hans Krieg of 4. Batterie wrote on that in a report:

> . . . We set out during the night. It was slow going. Repeatedly, the roads came under artillery fire, but we had no losses. At dawn, we drove on somewhat faster in a northeasterly direction. To the left and right sat bombed and knocked-out vehicles, guns and bloated dead horses. It was a hopeless picture. After some time we caught up with a horse-drawn artillery column which moved along the road ahead of us. It was under violent artillery fire. We drove our cross-country vehicles off the road, which led up a range of hills, into the terrain. A medic climbed on our tractor and looked after our wounded comrades. As we approached a farm, our Abteilung commander, Sturmbannführer Fend, shouted at us: 'Get ready for close combat!' The commander of the gun and I took over the operation of the gun. The others jumped off and took cover behind the radiator armor. To our side we spotted Canadians. We fired explosive and anti-tank shells at them. The Abteilung adjutant, Untersturmführer

Kolb, directed the fire from the driver's cab. He observed that we set
several armored vehicles on fire.

Then we drove on. In no time, all available spots on the vehicle
and the trailer were taken over by infantrymen who wanted to get
out with us. We could no longer see our battery. A self-propelled
gun-carriage of the Fallschirmjägers (paratroopers) also joined us.
The road leading up the hill was full of retreating infantrymen.
They all wanted to catch a ride but found no more space. On the
hill we waited for our other guns, but only tractors with 2 cm guns of
14./26 arrived. We had to keep going, to get our wounded to the
dressing station. The road was under fire from tanks. We drove off
the road through a tree nursery of small firs. None of our five vehicles was hit. One vehicle with the wounded stayed behind in the
next village, the others drove on. Outside the range of enemy fire
we waited in vain for the members of our battery until the evening.
During the night we drove on to Louviers where we joined our battery supply unit on 20 August. After a few days, other comrades
returned, but without vehicles and guns . . .[98]

In the afternoon of 18 August, General Simonds had ordered the 3rd
Canadian Infantry Division to close up and to hold the east bank of the Dives
from Morteaux-Couliboeuf to Trun. The 4th Canadian Armoured Division
was scheduled to advance from Trun, and the 1st Polish Armoured Division
from les Champeaux, to Chambois in order to establish contact with the
Americans there. The 4th Canadian Armoured Division had been ordered to
clear out the area north and northwest of Trun before the advance.[99] In the
morning of 19 August, General Simonds ordered the 2nd Canadian Infantry
Division to move out of its positions near Falaise and to take over the northern sector of the 3rd Canadian Infantry Division in order to be able to effectively block all arterial routes. He ordered the 4th Canadian Armoured
Division to link up in the south with the 3rd Canadian Infantry Division and
to block the Trun-Moissy sector. The 1st Polish Armoured Division was scheduled to take over the sector from Moissy to Hill 262 (three kilometers northeast of Chambois) and there establish contact with the Americans who were
reported in possession of that hill.[100]

In the course of the night to 19 August, the "HJ" Division set up a line of
strongpoints, facing north, with its remaining weak forces. Kampfgruppe
Rauch of 21. Pz.-Div. held the sector between Neauphe-sur-Dives and the
Dives river south of Trun. The I./26 secured along both sides of the road
Trun-Argentan immediately south of the Dives crossing. Parts of Kampfgruppe Olboeter (III./26, Divisionsbegleitkompanie, two Tigers, two Panthers, five Flakpanzers and two assault guns) secured around Roc and
southeast of Bierre. At approximately 16.00 hours, the Begleitkompanie
moved a stationary scouting party, on orders of Sturmbannführer Olboeter,

into the area north of Roc. At approximately 20.00 hours, it was reinforced, on orders of the Ia, by the rest of the Begleitkompanie, one Flakpanzer and two assault howitzers. Enemy scouting and assault parties were repelled.[101] The Divisional command no longer had contact with Kampfgruppe Rauch. Contact with Kampfgruppen Krause and Olboeter was maintained through orderly officers. Contact with the general command of I. SS-Panzerkorps had been broken. The Divisional command post was located in the area of la Londe, approximately two kilometers northwest of Villedieu-lès-Bailleul.

On 19 August, St. Lambert-sur-Dives was one of the focal points of the fighting. In the morning, led by Major Currie, one company of the Argyll and Southerland Highlanders of Canada and one company of the 29th Reconnaissance Regiment attacked the village, located on the Dives river. They captured the northern section of the village. Despite the fact that reinforcements had arrived, they withstood repeated counterattacks only with difficulty. Parts of horse-drawn and motorized divisions escaped through the gap, which still existed there, on 19 August. From the afternoon on, they were being chased by the fire from Canadian artillery which had moved positions in the meantime. After heavy fighting with withdrawing German troops, the 10th Polish Mounted Rifle -Regiment (reconnaissance unit) reached Chambois at approximately 19.00 hours and met the 2nd Battalion of the 359th US Infantry Regiment there. The Poles were later reinforced by the 24th Polish Armoured Regiment, which attacked from the northeast. A Polish combat group, consisting of two tank units and three infantry battalions, captured Hill 262 near Coudehard in the course of the day against variably strong resistance from withdrawing German troops. The combat group was cut off from its connection to the rear. It did not reach its original attack objective, Hill 262 south of Mont Ormel. It prepared for defense on the wooded hill which allowed an encompassing view of the encirclement which had by then been closed.[102]

The situation at the southern arm of the closing pincers had developed as follows: The Groupe Tactique "L" of the 2ème Division Blindée (combat group of the 2nd French Armored Division), attached to the 90th US Infantry Division, had supported the American attack on 18 August against le Bourg-St. Léonard. At 23.00 hours, it received orders from the 90th US Infantry Division, to advance in the morning of 19 August ". . . along all available roads from Exmes to the north and northwest. This, in order to first capture the high terrain around Omméel and to prevent the enemy from using the road from Chambois to the east. Thereafter, in cooperation with the 3rd Battalion 358th Infantry Regiment, to take possession of the high terrain immediately northeast of Chambois and to prevent the enemy from using the road from Chambois to Mont-Ormel . . ." Additionally, this would secure the right flank of the 90th Division along the line le Bourg-Exmes-Croisilles. [103] Général Leclerc, the commander of the French armored division, then secretly directed the commander of the combat group, along the lines of a directive issued by Général de Gaulle, not to engage too strongly so that he could disengage if necessary. If so ordered, he was to be able to quickly return to the mass of the division. Its mission was to liberate Paris, and it had to arrive there within twenty-four hours.[104]

In accordance with that directive and the order from the 90th Division, Colonel de Langlade started the attack at 16.00 hours on 19 August after an artillery fire attack of 1,800 shells. He crossed the Dives against weak resistance, occupied Frénée and advanced to the road Chambois-Vimoutiers.

As darkness fell, he withdrew again behind the Dives, against the order of the 90th Division. Thus, the road between Chambois and Mont-Ormel was not cut off. Also, because of the foothills of Hill 262 South, located between the road and the French positions, the road could not be controlled by fire. That gap gained significant importance in the days to follow.[105]

The encirclement was closed. However, the eastern front of the surrounding ring was not without gaps and was manned at varying strength. The Kampfgruppe of the "HJ" Division, which secured an approximately seven kilometers wide sector of the northern front, was encircled together with remnants and Kampfgruppen of other divisions. The situation was known to the Divisional command only in broad terms. The commanding general of LXXXIV. A.K., Generalleutnant Elfeld, and his chief of staff, Oberstleutnant i.G. von Criegern, arrived at the Divisional command post toward noon. The Divisional command learned from them that the general command of the I. SS-Panzerkorps was located outside the encirclement and was thus attached to LXXXIV. A.K. He had no further forces to command since 85. and 89. Inf.-Divs. had been decimated and their remnants, as those of 271. Inf.-Div., had marched off.

The two command posts were consolidated in a farm house. That resulted in a strange picture, but telling of the situation. The two "command units" were situated in the living room of the house, a long, narrow room stretching all across the house. In its two narrow walls were windows, at the center of one wide wall was an open fireplace. Next to it, a door led to the kitchen through which one reached the living room. In the middle of the room, along its long axis, sat a long table. Alongside it stood benches of equal length, without back rests. At the fireplace side sat Generalleutnant Elfeld and Oberstleutnant von Criegern. They made up the "Korps command post". Opposite, sat Oberführer Kurt Meyer and Sturmbannführer Hubert Meyer, making up the "Division command post". Several orderly officers, messengers and drivers were scattered throughout other rooms of the house and adjoining buildings.

Through a fortunate coincidence, the command post of 7. Armee was found in a small quarry at the eastern edge of Villedieu-lès-Bailleul. Generalleutnant Elfeld and Oberführer Meyer set out for there to report, to receive a briefing on the situation, and to receive orders. They advanced, in leaps and starts because of artillery fire, and reached the command post after some time. The supreme commander, Oberstgruppenführer Paul Hausser sat at the edge of a ditch and studied the map. Close-by were his chief of staff, Oberst i.G. (general staff) von Gersdorff, Oberstleutnant i.G. von Kluge, the chief of Panzergruppe Eberbach, and Major i.G. Heinz Guderian, the Ia of 116. Panzerdivision. Oberst von Gersdorff had taken part in the situation briefing with Feldmarschall Model. He had arrived, on foot from Chambois, at the command post and given his report. The counterattack by II. SS-Panzerkorps, ordered for 19 August had to be delayed by one day. Shortages of fuel and congested roads had prevented the units from reaching their assembly areas. The encirclement was obviously complete, the intention to keep the "bottleneck" open was outdated. Based on the changed situation, Oberstgruppenführer Hausser ordered the breakout from the encirclement for the night of 19-20 August, making use of the planned counterattack of II. SS-Panzerkorps. To do that, he took command of all troops inside the encirclement. The orders for the breakout were as follows:

3. Fallschirmjägerdivision is to move out of its assembly area north of Montabard (five kilometers west of Villedieu) at 22.30 hours. It will break through the encircling ring in the area of St. Lambert, if possible without firing;

"HJ" Division will initially hold its securing line and follow the Fallschirmjägers after the breakthrough had been achieved;

1. SS-Panzerdivision and 116. Panzerdivision are to move out after midnight and break through the encircling ring near Chambois. The Panzers of "HJ" Division will join those of "LAH" Division;

XXXXVII. Pz.-Korps, with 10. SS-Panzerdivision and 2. Panzerdivision (Heer) and LXXIV. A.K. with 277., 276. and 326. Inf.-Divs. will follow, securing the flanks and the rear.

Oberstgruppenführer Hausser reported his decision to the Heeresgruppe by radio. He requested that II. SS-Panzerkorps attack early on 20 August in the general direction of Trun in order to take in the troops breaking out. The Armee staff planned to follow the 3. Fallschirmjägerdivision during the breakout.[106]

On their return journey to the command post, through increasingly heavy artillery fire, Generalleutnant Elfeld and Oberführer Meyer encountered the commanding general of II. Fallschirmjägerkorps, General der Flieger Meindl, and General-leutnant Schimpf, the commander of 3. Fallschirmjäger-division. They discussed the details of the plan for the breakout. The Fallschirmjägers wanted to break through, using the compass and without firing, south of Coulonces and near Magny in two spearheads, in the direction of the hills east of Coudehard. They intended to keep a four to five kilometer wide gap open there. Their artillery would fire the last of its ammunition during the course of 19 August, blow up its guns and join the foot soldiers of the rearguard regiment during the breakout. Individual 8.8 cm Flak and Pak guns were to be taken along. Where possible, enemy positions were to be avoided.[107] The "HJ" Division made its last two Tigers available to the Fallschirmjägers for the expected fighting after dawn.

After returning to the Divisional command post, orders were issued to the commanders of the Kampfgruppen. The I./26 with the operations group would follow behind the Fallschirmjägers across the Dives near St. Lambert. Sturmbannführer Olboeter was directed to follow with his Kampfgruppe and cover the rear. Sturmbannführer Oskar Drexler, commander of the Artillerieregiment, received the difficult mission of having the remaining parts of his regiment move all vehicles of the other units out of the encirclement after the breakout by "LAH" near Chambois had been achieved. The road Chambois-Vimoutiers would then be available for that. There were no usable roads in the northern part of the breakout sector.

The Division assigned a liaison scouting party to the Fallschirmjägers with orders to report when the breakout had been successful. Messengers from all Kampfgruppen remained at the Divisional command post to carry the orders to move out. The troops got rid of all non-essentials. All vehicles not in running order and immobile guns were blown up. The troops awaited the next day with apprehension.

CHAPTER 5.7
Breakout from the Falaise Encirclement on 20 and 21 August 1944

As ordered, 3. Fallschirmjägerdivision started out from its assembly area—the forest north of Montabard—for the breakout on 19 August 1944 at 22.30 hours. East of the Argentan-Trun road, its spearhead already had to avoid enemy tanks. The commander of 3. Fallschirmjägerdivision, Generalleutnant Schimpf was wounded. General Meindl took over the command of the division. The spearhead reached the Dives at approximately 00.30 hours on 20 August. The small river was crossed south of the mill one kilometer southeast of Magny. Immediately thereafter, the Fallschirmjäger encountered a number of tanks which opened fire. In St. Lambert, too, heavy fire opened up. At the spearhead, General Meindl initially advanced in an easterly direction and then followed the course of the Ruisseau du Foulbec. At first light, he reached the area of Coudehard, a large community consisting of numerous individual farms and hamlets. That made it difficult to determine his exact position. Ahead, General Meindl observed a dominating range of hills. A group of 20 tanks was driving from the west, from where loud battle noise could be heard, toward the hills. At that time, at 05.30, daylight came. An attack on the enemy positions on the range of hills appeared possible only with Panzer support. In the direction of his attack, the wooded Hill 262 (North) was located half-right, Hill 243 to half-left. The road from Trun via Boisjos to Vimoutiers wound through a cut between the two hills. Just ahead of the cut, a country lane from St. Lambert joined the road near la Cour du Bosq. That road had to be opened by force. The General wanted to attack Hill 262 from the north. He reported his intention to Oberstgruppenführer Hausser.[1]

What had happened in the meantime at the "HJ" Division which had been ordered to follow behind the Fallschirmjägers after the successful breakthrough? No report from the liaison scouting party of the Division, which accompanied the Fallschirmjägers' attack, had been received at the Divisional command post by midnight. Neither could loud battle noise be heard from the direction of the attack. Had the Fallschirmjägers only sneaked through, or had they found a sufficiently wide gap through which they could move unhindered? It was important that the "HJ" Division Kampfgruppen crossed the Dives before daylight. Behind the river, at least strong enemy securing forces could be expected. Generalleutnant Elfeld approved the departure of the Infanteriegruppe for 2 A.M. It consisted of approximately fifty men: Generalleutnant Elfeld, Oberstleutnant i.G. von Criegern, Oberführer Kurt Meyer, Untersturmführer Kölln with several NCOs and men of the Divisional staff, as well as the staff of I./26 under the leadership of Sturmbannführer Krause. Another group of I./26 followed closely behind. The members of the "HJ" Division wore camouflage suits, belts with haversacks and gas masks, and small arms. There was a solemn farewell to the men who would break out in the few remaining vehicles with the motorized group after daybreak. Would they ever see each other again?

The General, his chief of staff, Oberführer Meyer, and his Ia marched with the spearhead. They were using a footpath leading east. It started behind the farm which had housed the command posts. At first light, the point reached a nursery of small fir trees one kilometer west of Aubry-en-Exmes. At the crossroads near Point 124, the spearhead turned into a northnortheasterly direction, toward St. Lambert. When they reached the northeastern edge of the tree nursery, Sturmbannführer Hubert Meyer noticed that contact had been lost and that Oberführer Kurt Meyer was missing. He requested permission from the General to re-establish contact himself and search for his commander. The commanding general agreed and offered to wait. When he reached the crossroads, the Ia noticed a German Panzer unit southeast of the tree nursery in the open terrain. It had deployed in a widely scattered formation in order to attack in an approximately easterly direction. The terrain was dominated by a wooded ridge of hills—the Forêt de Gouffern, which was reported to be in enemy hands. The deployment could not remain undisturbed for long. The Ia spotted his commander on a Panzer IV near a barn approximately 200 meters from his position. He ran toward the Panzer and barely managed to climb on as it began to move. He noticed a man in camouflage uniform on the Panzer's skirt. It turned out that he was dead. The Panzer must previously have come under fire. Enemy artillery opened fire again. The Oberführer sat in the front, next to the turret. He had lost contact and joined the Panzers since he was afraid of not finding his group again. He was glad that his men were in the vicinity. Both men quickly jumped from the moving Panzer and ran back to their infantry group. Generalleutnant Elfeld and Oberstleutnant von Criegern had wanted to make use of the time to scout the way ahead. They had gone forward. The group, which had stopped, immediately continued its march—as previously, in file, but with somewhat greater distance between the men. However, they did not find the officers who had walked ahead.

During further advance, battle noise was heard in St. Lambert. Because of that, the group kept further west and reached the Dives near Ch,teau Quantité, one kilometer northwest of St. Lambert. It first crossed a culvert and then the narrow, deeply carved bed of the Dives without encountering the enemy. At the crossing point lay abandoned and knocked-out vehicles and dead horses. They rarely saw dead soldiers. The Ch,teau, by which they passed then, was marked as a collecting point for wounded soldiers by a large Red Cross flag. It was obviously overcrowded since many wounded were lying in the open. The group advanced further in a northeasterly direction toward the northern entrance of St. Lambert. The road to Trun was under fire from enemy tanks to the northwest. It was crossed with leaps and jumps. The village sign "St. Lambert" burned itself into memory, the houses in the vicinity were shot to pieces, there was rubble everywhere. Behind the village, orchards bordered by hedges, and pastures, offered cover for the medium distance. Occasionally, tanks appeared, difficult to spot over the hedges and between the trees. The men took cover, to the right or the left alongside the hedges, driven by the machine gun fire from the tanks.

It appeared that the Fallschirmjägers had been unable to break through. Loud battle noise could be heard from the northeast and north. Numerous tanks were taking part, moreover, there was artillery fire. Since the Infanteriegruppe had no Panzerfausts and no heavy weapons, there was no choice but to evade the tanks. At a distance of five kilometers, a dominating hill (Hill 262 South) stood out against the horizon. It was considered to be free of the enemy. Everything depended on reaching it. Stragglers of the Heer, most of them without weapons, wanted to join. Oberführer Meyer accepted only those who were still armed or managed to find weapons again. Broken up into numerous small groups of five to six men each, they advanced from hedge to hedge, and through them, constantly covering and observing, mostly moving stealthily, sometimes leaping and running. On the pastures and in the ditches lay dead men, caught by enemy fire. They also saw groups of soldiers who had thrown away their weapons and were waving white rags attached to sticks, indicating their willingness to surrender. A disgraceful, never before seen picture.

After a chase which lasted for hours, the spearhead group reached the Chambois-Vimoutiers road south of Hill 262 (South), immediately south of the junction of the path from Sourdevals. Completely exhausted, they took cover in the road ditch and waited for the comrades following behind. Oberführer Meyer was missing once again. After several minutes, he arrived, accompanied by his orderly officer, Untersturmführer Kölln, and his Cossack, Michel. His head wound had opened up again. Thus, he could not keep up when the last blocking position had been broken through, running uphill. While the group was still collecting its strength in the ditch, a Sherman tank approached along the road from the direction of Chambois. It stopped at a farm approximately 100 meters distant. The men held their breath. After a short while, which seemed like an eternity, the tank rolled back again. The road appeared to be open. As a body, the men jumped across and ran up the steeply climbing slope of the hill, as fast and as long as they possibly could. Woods and scattered underbrush offered cover against observation, impeding progress at the same time. The difference in elevation of 130 meters over a distance of 500 meters had to be overcome. When the group assembled on the hill—which was, in fact, free of the enemy—only about a dozen men were gathered. They were Oberführer Meyer, Sturmbannführers Bernhard Krause and Hubert Meyer, Untersturmführer Kölln, several NCOs and men, as well as Michel, the Cossack. The other subgroups had lost contact in the broken terrain. The tanks driving to and fro forced evasion in various directions. A look into the boiling basin from above showed the hell which the men had escaped.

After the group had had some rest and scouted the surrounding area, it started out again. It was uncertain where and when German troops would be encountered. It appeared safest to initially march along the ridge in an easterly direction. The final objective was the Seine. Time and again, they stopped and observed. In the early hours of the afternoon, they spotted German vehicles, 1.5 kilometers to the north, driving in the direction of the encirclement. They may have been units of II. SS-Panzerkorps which were ordered to break the encircling ring in an attack from the east. After a lengthy march, the group encountered a blocking position of Panzeraufklärungs-abteilung of 116. Pz.-Div. It was taken to le Mesnil-Hubert where the command post of SS-Panzergrenadierregiment "Deutschland" was located. There, Obersturmbannführer Günter Wisliceny briefed the commander and the Ia on the situation.

On 20 August 1944, at approximately 04.00 hours, II. SS-Panzerkorps started an attack from the area south of Vimoutiers in the direction of Trun. The 9. SS-Pz.-Div. "Hohenstaufen" advanced on the right. It encountered parts of the 1st Polish Armoured Division near St. Gervais and les Champeaux (seven and nine kilometers northeast of Trun respectively). With its few Panzers and assault guns, and the remnants of the decimated Panzergrenadier companies, it was unable to throw back the ready-for-defense enemy in the broken terrain.[2] To the left of "Hohenstaufen", 2. SS-Panzerdivision "Das Reich" attacked: on the right the SS-Panzergrenadierregiment "Der Führer" along the road Fresnay-le Samson-Champosoult-Coudehard, in the center the Panzeraufklärungsabteilung toward Survie, and to the left SS-Panzergrenadierregiment "Deutschland" via le Mesnil-Hubert toward St. Pierre-la Rivière. The attack by III./"DF", led by Hauptsturmführer Heinz Werner, initially advanced only with difficulty since its neighbor on the right—"Hohenstaufen"—was still hanging back. Moreover, shot up vehicles impeded his armored personnel carriers. The II./"DF", advancing next to it on the left, had to repel violent attacks by Polish tanks from the area of Hill 262 (North). The Aufklärungsabteilung in the center gained ground rapidly. The "Deutschland" Regiment on the left wing advanced only slowly against determined resistance in broken terrain. At 15.00 hours, III./26 captured the road fork one kilometer northwest of Hill 262 (North) with the support of one Panther and two Panzer IVs. The Poles were driven back into the woods near Point 262 and lost several tanks. In the restricted space, two armored units defended themselves (the 1st and 2nd Polish Armoured Regiment), as well as two infantry battalions (the 8th and 9th Polish Infantry Battalion) and two companies of the 1st Polish Infantry Battalion. That opened up the road Champosoult-Boisjos. Simultaneously with II. SS-Panzer-korps, General Meindl also attacked with several Kampf-gruppen of 3. Fallschirmjägerdivision and Kampfgruppe Olboeter from inside the encirclement. That action opened the road Coudehard-Boisjos. Soon after, the first vehicles rolled into the opened breach. At 15.30 hours, Regiment "Deutschland" succeeded in fighting open another breach in cooperation with Panzers attacking from inside the encirclement near Chambois. That opened up the Road Chambois-Vimoutiers.[3]

The breakout of Kampfgruppe Olboeter is described in the reports below. Unterscharführer Leo Freund of the Divisionsbegleitkompanie wrote:

In the early morning hours, we advanced toward the encircling ring in Trun. The four Panzers formed the spearhead, followed by us, the Divisionsbegleitkompanie, on the Flak-Panzers. The first resistance we encountered was soon overpowered, and other units of the Wehrmacht immediately streamed into the enemy front line which had been ripped open. Among them was a Fallschirmjägerkompanie which joined us right away. We almost thought that we had succeeded when we came under fire from all sides. It was only then that we realized how deeply staggered the encircling ring was already, and that we were standing in the middle of the enemy. After the first Flak-Panzer had been knocked out from the flank, we of the Begleitkompanie left these lightly armored vehicles. The attack advanced, unstoppable, under cover from our Tigers and Panthers.

Suddenly, however, our situation appeared hopeless. Coming out of a wooded area, we had to cross a large, rising, pasture, with one enemy tank sitting next to the other on its crest. At that moment, the superiority of our Tigers and Panthers showed itself. They performed a precision piece of work and knocked out seven to eight of the enemy tanks, one after the other.

Sturmbannführer Olboeter judged that the moment had come to break through that opened gap. Standing in the turret of a Panther, he signaled us to follow him, and his Panther raced toward the burning enemy tanks. But he did not get very far. A hit shook the Panther and, to our surprise, Sturmbannführer Olboeter jumped out of the turret, apparently unharmed, and ran back to the other Panzers in a wooded area. We, however, sought cover in a ditch running straight across the pasture. The duel of armor started over again, shells howled through the air across our heads. One of us had left a Panzerfaust lying at the edge of the ditch. A horrible coincidence caused that Panzerfaust to be set off by a bullet or a shrapnel, and it exploded in the ditch. One of our comrades was ripped apart and almost all of us were splattered with blood and pieces of flesh. But, that was like a signal for us. There was no holding us back anymore. Shooting from the hip, we ran toward the burning enemy tanks, leaped across the enemy infantry positions, got past the tanks and had it made. Many of our comrades stayed behind in that pasture. Apart from the Fallschirmjäger comrades, seven men from the Divisionsbegleitkompanie gathered on the other side of the enemy positions.[4]

Sturmmann Theodor Waitschat of 12./26 experienced the breakout as follows:

At dawn, several Panzers, tank destroyers, armored personnel carriers, and many men on foot from all branches, including even two marines, gathered in the assembly area. After a short briefing on the situation we set out, first in a southeasterly direction. Later, we swung to the east where, apparently, a weak spot had been detected. At top speed we drove through several Canadian infantry positions. Some of them surrendered and ran with us. The dirt cover of the dug-in infantry and anti-tank positions was easily blown away by our tank destroyers. After two hours, we had broken through the enemy positions. Some of the infantrymen, hanging on to the armored personnel carriers for the ride, were torn off. I had already been wounded in the encirclement and, after a lengthy march, was finally cared for at a dressing station.[5]

A Zugführer of 5. Panzerkompanie, Oberscharführer Willy Kretzschmar, wrote on his experiences:

The hard rubber plate of our Panzer's right driving wheel had been defective since 18 August. Our driver, Kurt Schreiner, fixed the drive shaft in a makeshift fashion with a heavy wire. We were able to drive again, but it was impossible to steer to the right. The driver could move the vehicle to the right only by selecting the reverse gear and braking the left track. Using that provisional arrangement, we reached the edge of the encirclement at approximately 10.00 hours on 20 August. As we advanced, concentrated fire from tanks, Paks and Flak hammered at us from ahead. We fired off a portion of our ammunition and then pulled back. At that time, six Panzers of our Abteilung were still battle-ready. During the withdrawal, our Panzer stopped. The motor was still running, but there was no power transfer to the driving wheels. After a quick inspection, our driver determined that the gear-box had been ripped and the oil was draining out. With a heavy heart, I decided to blow up the Panzer. A one-kilogram explosive charge, set off in the fighting compartment, hurled the turret approximately fifteen meters into the air. The fact that we had lived unharmed through our last action had, finally, to be credited to our driver's skill. Without our Panzer we felt like infantrymen without rifles. On foot, we followed the withdrawing Panzers, always under cover of ditches or hedgerows, taking full cover every time there was an artillery fire attack. We caught up with our remaining Panzers in a hollow. Only four Panzer IVs and three tank destroyers were left.

After darkness had fallen, we set out for the final break-out. Grenadiers of our Division and several Fallschirmjägers were at the point. The Panzers and tank destroyers followed, and at some distance behind came soldiers of our Division and of the Heer who did not want to be taken prisoner. There may have been 2,000 to 3,000 men following us. It was a fairly dark night. We directed the Panzers in the right direction with signals from our flashlights. Then we came under infantry fire, we were right in front of the enemy positions. Our Panzers fired their turret machine guns and explosive shells, and drove at high speed through the enemy lines. All Panzers made it undamaged. The infantry losses are not known. Regretfully, during the further march that night, crossing unknown terrain, we had to leave one Panzer after the other: one got stuck in the mire, another toppled into a ditch, a third got hung up on a tree trunk. In the early morning, our widely dispersed small group reached our own lines: Panzer IVs of the "Das Reich" Division assembled for relief action. At around 9 A.M. we came to a strong point of our Division, in the process of moving out. I was taken along by the NCO in charge of our supply company, since my left ankle had given up its service—a souvenir of Russia 1941. It was approximately 13.00 hours. Soon after, enemy tanks appeared.[6]

Sturmmann Willy Schnittfinke of 5. Panzerkompanie was not as lucky. He had been wounded and was transported in the co-driver's seat of an armored personnel carrier. He wrote:

"Our armored personnel carrier, full to the bursting point with soldiers, raced at top speed in the direction of the Dives. A shell must have exploded in that tangle of men. I heard the bang, felt a blow to my right shoulder. I saw the driver jump off and somehow managed to also get out of the wreck tumbling into the ditch. A medic motorcycle, racing south along a narrow path on this side of the Dives, stopped and picked me up. A few meters later it was also hit. I waded through the Dives and ran, probably not very fast anymore, up the bank on the other side. I met a Heer officer who was checking his compass and said that the 'bag' was probably closed now after all. I spotted an enemy tank sitting, off to the left at the edge of the woods, turning its gun toward us. The explosive shell went wide, only a few shrapnels hit me in non-vital parts of my body. I crawled into a straw stack and hid, before losing consciousness. When I came to, in the evening, a bespectacled GI was standing in front of me, demanding in broken German, that I put up both my hands. As he soon noticed, that was impossible. Thus, I became a POW.[7]

Sturmmann Karl Musch, from one of the two four-barrel Flak units of the Artillerieregiment, experienced the breakout in this manner:

. . . With Oberscharführer Heuser and Oberscharführer Wolf, our two gun commanders, we broke out of the encirclement. Since we no longer had a gunner, a Luftwaffe NCO jumped up on the seat with us. We fought for our lives against tanks and enemy infantry. After the last shell had been fired, we continued on foot through hedges and ditches full of dead soldiers in the direction of the Divisional assembly area. We came under fire from tanks and I took a piece of shrapnel in the right shoulder. The heavy loss of blood weakened me to the point where I could no longer walk. Two comrades of my Zug took me between them and in that manner we continued to an isolated farmhouse. Since we had hardly eaten during the previous days, we were given a hearty meal, over which I fell asleep. After some time, my comrades woke me. It was time to move on. However, I could not carry on. So they caught a horse in a pasture and tied me on its back. Thus, we continued. Toward evening, we reached the assembly area . . .[8]

It has already been mentioned that Oberstgruppenführer Hausser accompanied the attack of the Fallschirmjäger spearhead on foot. General Meindl reported to him his intention of attacking Hill 262 from the north. The supreme commander agreed and informed Meindl that he was in contact with parts of a Panzerdivision with which he wanted to take part in the last stages of the breakout. During that attack, contact between the two Kampfgruppen was lost. Untersturmführer Max Anger, at the time adjutant of I. Artillerieabteilung, was a member of the Panzer Kampfgruppe. He described the events of the day as follows:

> . . . The order for the breakout from the encirclement reached us in the Bois de Feuillet, north of Montabard. Without hurry and with deliberation, we decided what was non-essential, what was needed, what would be loaded and how we would assemble. Hauptsturm-führer Hagemeier said: 'Let's take a bath first and dress in our best gear so that we'll be clean if anything happens to us.' It was probably meant as a joke, to overcome the seriousness of our situation. But, he was to be so right!
>
> The columns started their march in the morning of 20 August. After leaving Montabard forest we fanned out in a wide front across the open terrain. There was no enemy air force, despite the fact that we offered a fantastic target during great visibility conditions. The mood was good. In some of the 'Wespen' ["wasps"—light, self-pro-pelled field howitzers], the men were singing. It was a rare picture, we had only seen that many armored vehicles on the opposite side. Next to our armored personnel carrier, Olboeter was riding in the turret of a Panzer. We had crossed the Rue Départemental 916 in the direction of Chambois when there was a sudden stop in the vicinity of Tournay. Any number of units, including units of the Heer, were driving about aimlessly. For the first time, after all these many campaigns, I heard the call: 'SS to the front!'
>
> We were able to move out and continued to advance to the east. We came under well-aimed fire from the range of hills to the north and suffered losses. Between Chambois and St. Lambert we swung to the north and across D 13. The enemy fire was extremely well aimed, our losses were increasing. We were driving in the direction of the slope along a country lane through terrain offering some lim-ited cover when the column suddenly stopped. Hagemeier jumped off our armored personnel carrier and ran forward twenty meters to a bend in the lane. An infantry bullet killed him. We loaded him onto an ammunition trailer. In that spot I met one of the last battery commanders, Untersturmführer Rudolf Heller from Eger.
>
> I ordered the few 'Wespen' to take up positions along both sides of the lane. Then I tried to reconnoiter by myself since there was

neither leadership nor contact. Alone, I crawled through the terrain covered with low bushes uphill. On the way, in a road ditch, I met Oberstgruppenführer Hausser and another officer. Hausser was the person I least expected there. It was approximately 11 A.M. I was ordered to suppress enemy forces in recognized locations, from my present position. I leaped, crawled and ran back, like a rabbit and I was chased like one. From off to the side of our firing position I could accurately observe our shells exploding. They were well aimed at the range of hills west of Mont Ormel. Somehow, we managed to disengage and I tried to re-establish contact with the spearhead. But then there was another well-aimed fire attack and it was all over for me. Untersturmführer Kronegger of the staff of AR 12 dragged me to an armored personnel carrier.

I was unable to observe further developments. I was lying on the floor and heard a great number of chirping sounds at the outer wall. We probably curved through the terrain for about half-an-hour, under constant fire. Then it was definitely over. Our armored personnel carrier stopped and within seconds all those who were not wounded, including Kronegger, had been dragged out of the vehicle. I never heard from Kronegger again. Under guard, our driver took the armored personnel carrier to the main Canadian dressing station at Trun. Arrival there was at approximately 16.00 hours.[9]

Together with many other comrades, Hauptsturmführer Hagemeier found a dignified resting place in the German war cemetery at la Cambe.

In the further course of these battles, Oberstgruppenführer Hausser was seriously wounded. However, Obersturmführer Kurzbein, chief of 5. Batterie of the Artillerieregiment, succeeded in bringing the Armee supreme commander out of the encirclement, in an armored personnel carrier, in the Mont Ormel area. When Hausser regained consciousness he asked Kurzbein where he was. Kurzbein reported his rank, name and position and indicated their location and that, fortunately, they were out of the encirclement. Oberst-gruppen-führer Hausser replied to that: "I will bring you before a court-martial. How could you transport a supreme commander from the field of battle without his agreement?" Regrettably, there is no record on how the conversation continued. It is probable that Kurzbein was able to explain that he had picked up the general seriously wounded and unconscious on the battlefield and had thus been unable to secure his permission. In any case, court-martial proceedings did not take place.(10) In a note, composed by Oberstgruppenführer Hausser after the war, the events were described as follows:

Enemy tanks blocked the way at the northern foothills of Mont Ormel, 1.5 kilometers north of Coudehard. They set a line of vehicles on fire so that the road was completely obstructed. At the same time, strong artillery fire from an unknown direction set in.

We had to wait for darkness. We were able to assemble a small Panzer Kampfgruppe, supply it with fuel from damaged vehicles and prepare to break out during the night. During that activity I was wounded by mortar shrapnel.

We assembled again at approximately 21.00 hours. The night was cloudy and rainy. I cannot recall our route. In any case, we reached the Aufklärungsabteilung of 2. SS-Pz.-Div. before dawn on 21 August. By way of the general command II. SS-Pz.-Korps, I hastened to the forward command post of 7. Armee at le Sap. There, General von Gersdorff had already been able to inform the Heeresgruppe.[11]

The 1. SS-Pz.-Div. and 116. Pz.-Div. had been directed to open the encirclement at a second location through an attack on Chambois. They succeeded, as already mentioned, in the afternoon of 20 August. The parts of the Artillerieregiment remaining in the encirclement—with the exception of the armored self-propelled guns—tried to break out there after blowing up the guns which had been rendered immobile. Even during the approach to the Dives, many vehicles were lost and casualties suffered. An organized march along the Chambois-Vimoutiers road did not come about. The marching group dissolved into many small, even tiny, groups which tried to fight their way through on their own. Some were successful, others took heavy losses or were taken prisoner. The heavy vehicles proved to be a severe impediment during the move.[12]

Among those who tried in vain to escape the encirclement area in their vehicles was also the very competent and highly esteemed commander of the Nachrichtenabteilung, Sturmbannführer Erich Pandel. Regarding his fate, Sturmmann Werner Halbroth reported in a letter to Mrs. Pandel:

. . . We left the Falaise area on 18 August with orders to fight our way to Orbec. By chance, we arrived at the Armee command post (Hausser) on 19 August. I was present when he received orders to break out of the Argentan-Falaise encirclement. From there we then walked back to our vehicle. During that walk, for the first time, I heard your husband speak of death as a certainty. I remember very well that I replied at the time: 'It won't happen that quickly!' We drove in the Volkswagen through the night to the location of our planned breakout. Early in the morning of 20 August I drove, with Roehsing in the rear seat and your husband in the right front seat next to me, forward to scout the road and reconnoiter. What occurred on that mission at a slope of one of the hills has been described to you by Clemens in a few words. Without warning we came under mortar fire and received a direct hit to the vehicle right at the start of the barrage. Clemens received a minor wound. Your husband either jumped on his own from the vehicle or was hurled out by the blast of the shell. I was hardly scratched and able to stop the car after a few meters. I then jumped from the car, into cover for a moment, and reached your husband after a few leaps. I found him lying on his left side, with a massive wound in the back, right upper arm and shoulder, as well as a large wound in the chest, probably caused by a shrapnel smashing through from the back. After having called him by rank repeatedly, I checked for his pulse which was already quite weak. After another desperate call he opened his eyes, stretched his left hand toward me and said: 'Werner, good bye, and give my love to my dear wife.' With those words, a life in full flower was extinguished. However, I could not believe it should be so and called to him again several times, in the presence of Roehsing who had come over in the meantime. I checked for the pulse again, but all the checking was in vain.

His wedding band, the death's-head ring, the identification tag and his other papers had already been lost on 8 August, a day which I have already mentioned to you. Your husband had several unimportant papers on him. I left them with him in the hope that someone would find him and bury him, which I hope has been done. Roehsing and I were not able to prepare a grave for him ourselves. I can no longer recall the name of the village. However, if I returned to Normandy, I could find the village again without any problem at all.

May I describe to you my own fate in a few words. I was seriously wounded myself on 20 August, transported to a German dressing station and taken prisoner there a few hours later. Semiconscious, I was moved by airplane to England where I then spent a year-and-a-half in hospital . . .[13]

The fallen Sturmbannführer Erich Pandel was found by English soldiers on 20 August and buried near Aubry-en-Exmes, as indicated in an English list of dead.[14]

Many vehicles and soldiers on foot moved through the open breaches during the night 20–21 August. Even during the day, groups and individuals still made their way out. At 07.00 hours, General Meindl and the rear guard of 3. Fallschirmjägerdivision arrived at the securing positions of Hauptsturmführer Werner in the area west of Champosoult. From noon on, only a few stragglers showed up there. Thus, the "Das Reich" Division was ordered in the afternoon to pull back to the east at dusk and to leave securing forces along the line le Bosc-Renoult (seven kilometers east-southeast of Vimoutiers)-le Sap. The Division was to assemble in the area around la Follelière (four kilometers south of Orbec). It moved out as ordered. With that, the battle for the Falaise encirclement came to an end.[15]

There were stragglers left inside the encirclement. They did not give up trying to find their way back to their units. A small group, with Obersturm-bannführer Max Wünsche, was also still inside. It had encountered the enemy in the Brieux area during the night of 18 August while pulling out and had been scattered. It stayed under cover during the daylight hours of 19 August. After darkness had fallen, the group started out again in an easterly direction. Dr. Stiawa, who was wounded, had to be supported by two men all the time. At dawn on 20 August, the four men took cover in a beet field and were able to find some meager sustenance eating beets. They spent the whole day in a ditch there, covered by brush, soaked to the skin, and cold. They were able to observe the activity at a near-by English command post. During the following night they continued their cross-country march, using the compass. Before dawn on 21 August they encountered an enemy outpost. The group was scat-tered by fire from the outpost. They were able to meet up again later, with the exception of Dr. Stiawa whom they searched for in vain. It turned out later that he had been wounded and taken prisoner. Max Wünsche had been shot in the calf and suffered from severe pain in his shoulder. It appeared to be a broken bone caused by a bullet. The arm was put in splints, using the primi-tive means available. A scouting sortie determined that the group was located in the Forèt de Gouffern, a large forest south of Bailleul. They marched on by day, but returned to their starting point around noon since they had to fre-quently evade obstacles and enemy troops. After a short rest, the three men set out again. However, in the afternoon they were forced to seek a hiding place since they kept spotting the enemy. Hauptsturmführer Isecke encoun-tered Americans combing the woods and barely escaped. He was unable to find his two comrades again later and tried to make his way on his own dur-ing the night. That, he managed to do until the morning of 24 August. After a long march during the night he had crawled into a thicket and fallen asleep, exhausted. American troops were combing the terrain in wide infantry cordons. He was roughly woken up and led off into captivity.

Max Wünsche and Fritz Freitag waited in vain for several hours for Georg Isecke's return. Finally, they started out, continuing in an easterly direction. They oriented themselves by the noise of battle which could be heard in the distance. That had to be the front line. They marched across an open field, through the assembly of a Canadian tank unit, without being spotted. Even before dawn on 22 August they apparently reached the no-man's land and believed they would find German troops any moment. Then the tanks rolled past them and the two stragglers realized that they were still in the enemy rear areas. They went to sleep in a truck loaded with knapsacks. In the morning they exchanged their tattered uniforms and underwear for those of the Luftwaffe which they found in the knapsacks. During that, it turned out that Max Wünsche's arm was not broken but only dislocated. After several extremely painful attempts, Fritz Freitag was able to bring the arm back to its normal position. They put on camouflage jackets over the

Luftwaffe uniforms. Fritz Freitag sewed on the sleeve markings. In the meantime, Max -Wünsche found a can of pork meat and some crispbread. Their starved stomachs could only manage a few mouthfuls.

Nearby, they found a German car, a Kfz. 2, which was fully intact. They decided to continue their march motorized. Fuel and provisions were loaded, together with pistols and machine pistols. One soldier from a group of Heer stragglers joined them. Enemy soldiers showed up, combing the terrain. That forced another overnight stay in the German truck. Untersturmführer Freitag described in his own words what happened then:

> . . . In the light of dawn of 23 August 1944 we climbed down from our elevated sleeping accommodations. We grabbed two horses, still in harness, and used them to pull the knocked-out vehicles to the side, so as to free our car. A rifle stock replaced the ignition key. Then, in the bright light of the morning, we were on our way in the direction of St. Lambert on the Dives where the only still usable Dives crossing was located. From the top of a small hill we surveyed the plains behind us. Abandoned German vehicles were sitting everywhere. In between them, Canadians were driving around in their jeeps and in captured vehicles, looking for booty. The same activity was taking place on the plains ahead of us. Thus, we did not attract any attention in our car. The guys were even waving at us and we, quite cheekily, waved back at them. In that manner, always driving cross-country, we reached the main road leading to St. Lambert. On that road sat an endless column of vehicles waiting to drive across the bridge in St. Lambert. Our boldness, however, did not extend to the point where we would mix with them. Being careful always prevents porcelain from being broken, as they say, and many dogs will finally catch the hare. Thus, we preferred to set up quarters right next to the road. The car was camouflaged and all the important items were taken along. Behind a hedge we found a pile of straw where we made ourselves comfortable. The sun was burning down on us with searing heat. We put our feet up, fixed sandwiches with thick slices of pork meat. Canned chanterelles and chocolate completed the meal. Afterward, we puffed big cigars of which we had sufficient reserves. However, missing was a healthy cup of firewater which would have helped our digestion. As a replacement, there was a can of condensed milk which we slurped with enjoyment. In that manner we spent the rest of the forenoon. An in-depth study of the maps gave us an understanding of the route we had to take. However, the maps were blank on the other side of the Dives crossing, only directional arrows indicated the main directions.

> We wanted to get to Coudehard and then use the wide main road leading from there to Orbec and Lisieux. Without question, we had

to expect heavy enemy supply traffic on this side. But we wanted to drive our car only at night when, as is well known, all cats are gray. If we could manage to link with an English column, nothing could really go wrong. With some justification, we hoped that we would continue to be lucky.

Around noon, three Frenchmen walked past our hiding place and noticed us. However, they made as if they had not seen us and walked on without stopping. Not expecting anything good to come, we immediately broke off our siesta, packed our gear and changed location. Not far, only into the closest hedge. As it turned out, that was a brier hedge. If we wanted to get under cover quickly, we had no choice but to work our way into it. However, that paid off.

We had not been stuck inside our thorny 'chambre séparée' for long when Canadians came racing up in their jeeps, straight toward our previous hiding place. However, the birds had flown away, now they were grinning silently.

The columns which had waited along the road in the morning had disappeared. Only now and then a single vehicle or a lonely motorcycle messenger passed down the road. Apart from them, it was deadly silent. The afternoon passed slowly. Toward the evening we became active again, loaded our car which was still sitting in its previous spot, and drove off. It was still light. Since none of us had any headgear, we did not attract any attention in the vehicles coming opposite. The Canadians, too, were driving captured German vehicles.

We made our way to St. Lambert unimpeded. In the middle of the street in the center of town stood a Canadian military police-man, in a white cap and white gauntlets, directing traffic. As bold as anything, Wünsche started blowing the car horn and the Canadian promptly indicated the direction to us. Darkness was slowly falling. Our car had no headlights. So I had to signal to enemy vehicles coming opposite with my flashlight. Unfortunately, it had a loose contact. With every jolt of the car, the light went out and only came on again after some forceful shaking of the flashlight . . .

During an attempt to get by one of the many knocked-out and burnt vehicles sitting on the narrow road, the car of the three stragglers slid into the road ditch. All efforts to bring it back on the road were in vain. In the hope that Canadians would pull out their vehicle in order to open up the road for themselves, the stragglers found a hiding place. Fritz Freitag's report continued:

. . . As daylight broke on 24 August, our crate was still sitting in the same spot. We noticed only then that we were in the immediate vicinity of several farms. Thus, we did not dare work during the day and retreated again into our hiding place, a depression in the ground, grown over with bushes. The beginning day brought some rays of sun. Their warmth visibly braced us up. In the course of the morning, we emptied several cans of meat and other delicacies, and puffed big cigars in between. With our stomachs full, and feeling secure, all three of us fell asleep. Suddenly, a din of voices and a loud 'Hands up! Come on!' The barrels of six submachine guns and rifles were pointed at us. We could not even grab our weapons from the ground next to us. Captured![16]

Obersturmbannführer Max Wünsche, awarded the Oak Leaves of the Knight's Cross for his outstanding leadership and personal valor, reported on his fate after his capture:

Based on the first impressions after being captured I had to assume that I would simply be executed. However, I was put into a wire cage sitting in a flooded meadow. After the first shock had passed, there was nothing else to do but to patiently await the future. I had immediately been separated from my comrades. After a first, short interrogation I had to spend all of the day and also the following night more often lying in the water than standing or squatting, since my strength was giving out. Only during the next day was I driven, accompanied by a captain and two sergeants, for some forty kilometers in a vehicle. The captain, who spoke German quite well, answered my question where I was being taken, to a dressing station or a hospital: 'No, you're going to a senior officer or a commander.' I saw, with surprise, a large number of vehicles and tents and was told that we had reached our destination. After a short waiting period I was told to get out. From a command vehicle I saw the very man dismount whom they called simply 'Monty'. He was General Montgomery, a black beret on his head. A short report by the captain was followed by Montgomery's reply, which totally startled me when it was translated:
'We will treat the German prisoners in accordance with the Geneva Convention, but not the SS. They will be treated as what they are: political vermin, political dirt.'
When I wanted to answer that, I was told to shut up with the words: 'You have nothing to say! Move out!' Even the captain with me was obviously surprised but did not dare say anything. I was led away again and driven off with the same accompaniment, in the direction of the coast. It was a long and torturous drive since I was in considerable pain. As it turned out later, it was not only the wound in my calf, but also the once dislocated arm, torn ligaments and del-

toid muscle which caused me pain, as well as my thighs which were chafed raw and festered. Thus, I was glad when we finally arrived at the coast and I was handed over to a navy officer. He greeted me with the words: 'You are my guest.' He was the commander of the ship which would take me to England. First, I was looked after by a medical sergeant who washed and shaved me, and dressed my wounds. Then, there was something to eat. For the first time, after seven days, I had something warm in my stomach. I was led to a cabin where I could lie down and finally sleep for a while. Time and again, I had to think of the comrades who were left God knows where, and of those who were still stuck in the encirclement. We traveled throughout the night and arrived in Plymouth while it was still dark. The commander said: 'Sorry', and the military policemen who received me were whispering among themselves. A tent became my lodging for the next hours. My shoes were taken off and I had to lie down on the bare floor. Flood lights were beamed at me, two men stood in the tent entrance, their submachine guns aimed at me. In the course of the day I was taken to a hospital where I was thoroughly examined. From there, I was taken to a civilian hospital where I had to stay for seven months.[17]

The battle of the Falaise encirclement was, indisputably, a severe defeat for the German forces in the west. The losses were very high. Reliable figures have not yet been established. The lists of losses for the "HJ" Division offer a nearly complete picture. The reports on losses of I./26 are incomplete, those for the Nachrichtenabteilung are missing.

Losses during the battles in the Falaise area and the Falaise encirclement in the period 15–22 August 1944.

| Date | Killed | | | Wounded | | | Missing | | |
	Officers	NCOs	Men	Officers	NCOs	Men	Officers	NCOs	Men
15.8.	-	1	8	1	7	37	1	2	32
16.8.	-	-	4	-	3	34	-	3	16
17.8.	1	-	1	-	4	15	-	1	24
18.8.	1	3	2	1	1	17	-	2	43
15.-18.8.	2	4	15	2	15	103	1	8	115
19.8.	-	1	6	2	1	12	4	7	34
20.8.	1	4	10	1	16	45	7	28	326
21.8.	-	-	2	-	1	44	-	7	85
22.8.	-	-	-	-	2	4	-	1	32
19.-22.8.	1	5	18	3	20	105	11	43	477
15.-22.8.	3	9	33	5	35	208	12	51	592

The total losses were 45 killed, 248 wounded and 655 missing. This amounted to a total of 948 losses.[18]

Most of the 655 missing were likely taken prisoner. Some were able to flee from imprisonment, others had been dispersed and reached their own units again after days or weeks. Among the missing there is surely also a significant number of killed whose death was not observed and reported by comrades of their own units. More than half of the missing were members of the Artillerieregiment and the Werferabteilung, i.e. 387 officers, NCOs and men. It is probable that most of them were captured as they tried to get out of the encirclement with their heavy vehicles along the congested roads or even cross-country.

Those units which had been pulled out after the withdrawal from Caen, and moved back to their previous areas, were still combat-ready after the encirclement battle. However, they had only received a small part of the required personnel replacements. Thus, they were not refitted at all when they were sent into action against General Patton's troops which had broken through toward the Seine river. More on that later.

The following were located outside the encirclement before it was closed:

the staff of Panzergrenadierregiment 26 with parts of the Regimental units, core personnel of II./26;

the staff of Panzergrenadierregiment 25 with parts of the Regimental units, core personnel of II. and III./25 and the majority of the reinforced I./25;

the core personnel of Panzeraufklärungsabteilung;

the core personnel of Panzerpionierbataillon;

crews of the Panzerregiment, without Panzers, and the repair facilities;

two batteries of heavy field howitzers;

one battery of 3.7 cm Flak;

the Feldersatzbataillon (field replacement training -battalion);

all of the supply units.

On 1 June 1944, "HJ" Division had 20,540 officers, NCOs and men. From the start of the invasion to 20 July it lost 6,164 killed, wounded and missing.[19] From then on, to the end of the encirclement battle, it suffered significant new personnel losses. The total losses to 22 August amounted to approximately 8,000 men. The existing strength of the Division on that day was approximately 12,500 men and not 500 men, as repeatedly reported in the relevant literature. The approximately 2,500 men of the supply units were part of the existing strength. Since the Division had lost almost all combat-ready Panzers, Jagdpanzers, armored personnel carriers and the bulk of guns of the Artillerieregiment, it was no longer ready for action as a divisional fighting unit. It had to be pulled out and refitted as quickly as possible. When Oberführer Meyer and the Ia arrived at the command post of I. SS-Panzerkorps in the afternoon of 20 August, they—who had been believed killed—were warmly welcomed. The chief of staff then briefed them on the overall situation. It was much less than hopeful. They received orders to assemble the embers of the Division coming out of the encirclement east of the Seine. The units of the "HJ" Division which had already been pulled out previously were in combat near Evreux and Pacy-sur-Eure under the command of Obersturmbannführer Mohnke. They were to remain in action until further orders arrived.

The men of the "HJ" Division asked themselves how the completion of the encirclement could have come about, despite the fact that they had held the northern front of the developing encirclement with their remaining strength. The origin of the battle of the encirclement lay with the failed counterattack near Avranches. The battles of 7. Armee are not the subject of this book. In order to judge the ensuing rearguard action of that Armee and of Panzergruppe Eberbach and the left wing of 5. Panzerarmee, several publications must be awaited: Part IV of the divisional history of "LAH" by Rudolf Lehmann and the history of 116. Panzerdivision by Heinz Guderian. However, the statement, that the order by OKW of 16.8.1944 to withdraw behind the Orne was issued too late, is certainly justified.

Fortunately, some measures and events on the opposite side also led to a delayed and incomplete closing of the encirclement. The inadequate cooperation of the two army groups played a decisive role in that. In the area where the pincer was to be closed around the German armies, the dividing line between the British-Canadian and the American army groups ran from Tinchebray (eleven kilometers west of Flers) via la Ferrière (ten kilometers southeast of Flers)—approximately three kilometers south of R,nes (17.5 kilometers southwest of Argentan)—immediately north of Sées (twenty kilometers southeast of Argentan). On 11 August, Montgomery ordered Argentan to be the Canadian, and the line Sées-Carrouges to be the American attack objectives.(20) When the XV. US Corps reached the area south of Argentan on 12 August, the First Canadian Army was still located ten kilometers northwest of Falaise and thirty-five kilometers northwest of Argentan. Montgomery did not change his decision, probably because he expected a rapid success of the "TRACTABLE" Operation. The "HJ" Division foiled that plan through its determined resistance. Finally, when the American army group ordered the First US Army on 17.8. to ". . . capture the Chambois-Trun area and advance far enough to the north to establish contact with the British . . .", there were delays, caused by changes in the issuance of the orders.[21]

Finally, the 4th Canadian Armoured Division advanced only hesitantly in the direction of Chambois and did not advance beyond St. Lambert. Obviously, parts of the division were pushed to the east by attacks from German troops breaking out, and they crossed the Polish attack sector. In addition, the Poles, because of an orientation error, lost their direction toward Chambois and turned up in les Champeaux, ten kilometers north-northeast of

Chambois. On 19 August, 91 Polish Sherman tanks stood on Hill 262 (North) while only thirty-six were in action immediately east of the Dives between St. Lambert and Chambois.[22] But even those were too far removed from the narrow river, which formed a considerable obstacle to the tanks.

The Groupe Tactique of the 2ème Division Blindée had not carried out its mission since its division had concentrated its attention on Paris. Thus, the Chambois-Vimoutiers road was only temporarily disrupted on 19 August, but not during the following night and on 20 and 21 August. That fact allowed many units to break out, among them the group of the Divisional staff.

It may be difficult for the outsider to understand why the encircled troops did not force the breakout through a methodical attack by strong units which would have smashed open a wide gap. It must be remembered that all units along the encirclement ring were in action. There were no free reserves available. The troops had to disengage, attracting as little attention as possible, from their sectors for the breakout. There was no time for a methodical assembly since the enemy increased pressure as soon as he detected withdrawal movements. The roads and lanes were congested and could not be used for an assembly. Thus, only parts were available for the initial thrust, the other units had to hold their positions for some time yet. There was a shortage of fuel and ammunition. The artillery had fired most of its shells. The troops had received neither fuel nor ammunition since 15 August. The main radio operations of the command staffs were almost totally destroyed. Orders and reports could be transmitted only by messengers or orderly officers. Because of the road conditions, that often took hours even across short distances. Thus, the most important requirement for a unified command of all encircled units by one single authority during battle was missing. An attack by a Panzer unit had to overcome a significant obstacle— the Dives. That could only be tried during the day and in the face of masses of enemy tanks and artillery, ready for defense. Such an undertaking had to fail, even if the enemy air force did not show up because of bad weather. The order for the breakout took account as much as possible of these requirements and circumstances. The developments are certain proof of the superiority of a tactic of missions compared to the tactic of issuing orders.

With the breakout from the Falaise encirclement, the invasion battles came to an end for the "HJ" Division. It had stood at the focal point of the fighting for two-and-one-half months and performed extraordinary feats. From 7 June to 8 July it kept Caen—first in the attack, then in defense—out of the hands of a numerically vastly superior enemy who had made the city one of his most important operational objectives. He was finally able to capture the northern section of the city under heavy losses on 9 July, but not the Orne crossing. The decimated Division prevented the breakthrough of the Guards Armoured Division near Vimont on 18 and 19 July and, with that, contributed to the failure of the "GOODWOOD" Operation. On 8 August near St. Sylvain, it thrust itself at the enemy who had broken through the positions of 89. Infanterie-division, and stopped the offensive by two armored divisions, two infantry divisions and two tank brigades in the Laison sector. The Division succeeded in that despite the fact that two battalions and one Panzer unit were initially still in action at other spots, and became available only later. When Operation "TRACTABLE" launched the battle for Falaise on 14 August, the "HJ" Division only had seven Panthers, seventeen Panzer IVs and eleven Tigers of the two Korpstigerabteilungen, approximately ten Panzerjägers as well as two weak Panzergrenadier battalions and an almost complete artillery regiment with little ammunition. Only III. Abteilung was well supplied. That Kampfgruppe defended Falaise and the hills north of the Ante against a vastly superior enemy until the evening of 16 August. Through that action it prevented the formation of an encirclement west of the Orne, and a resulting catastrophe. The even further decimated forces held the northern front of the contracting encirclement ring west of the Dives until 19 August. That enabled many units—in particular the infantry divisions of 5. Panzerarmee—to move eastward before the encirclement was closed off. The men of the "Baby Division", once ridiculed by the enemy, had gained his respect and could justly be proud of their unit and their achievements.

The Battles between the Touques and Seine Rivers from 21 to 25 August 1944

It was reported in the previous chapter that, in the early hours of the afternoon on 20 August, the operations group of the "HJ" Division encountered securing positions of the 116. Panzerdivision outside the encirclement. From there they were taken to the command post of SS-Panzergrenadierregiment "Deutschland" in le Mesnil-Hubert. After a short period of rest and a briefing on the local situation, Oberführer Kurt Meyer and Sturmbannführer Hubert Meyer were taken to the command post of I. SS-Panzerkorps. The chief of staff, Brigadeführer Fritz Kraemer, briefed them on the overall situation and informed them on the battle zones of the parts of the Division fighting outside the encirclement. They learned that the Aufklärungsabteilung under the command of Sturmbannführer Bremer had had hostile contact for days with the American forces which had advanced to the Seine near Mantes. He had apparently been able to significantly contribute, through action by his armored reconnaissance vehicles on a wide front, to deceive the enemy regarding the situation on the German side and to prevent enemy assaults to the north. The parts of the Division coming from inside the encirclement were to be assembled in the areas around Pacy-sur-Eure and around Evreux. General Eberbach had providently prepared outside assembly areas for the "encirclement divisions" where provisions were available. The 7. Armee, too, had established assembly areas. Without one knowing what the other was doing, these areas did not cooperate. Still, the troops breaking out and the stragglers found help initially, and their own units subsequently, as has already been reported in one case.[1]

In the morning of 20 August, a firm and stable front line existed in northern France only at the Channel coast up to Houlgate, at the mouth of the Dives, where the enemy had not attacked, and from there at 711. and 346. Inf.-Divs. eastward to St. Julien (twelve kilometers southwest of Lisieux). Only a few strongpoints were holding out in the area northeast of Trun. In the area southwest of Vimoutiers, the II. SS-Panzerkorps was on the attack.

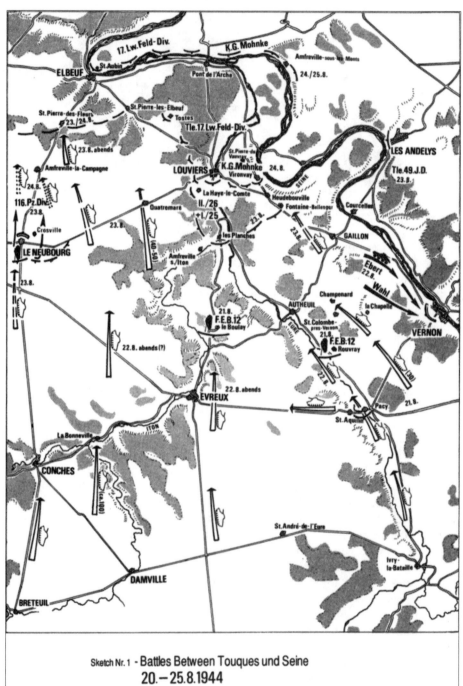

Sketch Nr. 1 - Battles Between Touques und Seine
20. – 25.8.1944

Along a general line Gacé-l'Aigle-Verneuil-Dreux-Pacy, Kampfgruppen of several infantry divisions were in securing positions, with Kampfgruppe Wahl on the left wing. That Kampfgruppe consisted of parts of 17. SS-Panzer-grenadierdivision "Götz von Berlichingen" and parts of 1. and 10. SS-Panzer-divisions, and 2. and 116. Panzerdivisions, assembled in haste. It attacked the left flank of the Americans advancing in the direction of the Seine northwest of Mantes. Remnants of 352. Inf.-Div. and strike forces were fighting that enemy west of Paris.[2]

It was the intention of the enemy to encircle the forces still in Normandy south of the Seine, and to destroy them. Thereafter, to advance to the north and, if possible, bring the same fate to the troops in action in northeastern France along the Channel coast. The Second British Army and the First Canadian Army were ordered by General Montgomery on 20 August to initially destroy the German forces inside the Falaise encirclement, and then to advance to the Seine at top speed. At the same time, the Twelfth US Army Group would attack to the north across the line Mantes-Dreux-Verneuil, while the right wing would advance along the southern bank of the Seine. The XV. and IX. Corps, under the command of the First US Army, were scheduled to carry out that attack.[3]

Only elements of the "HJ" Division took part in the fighting between Touques and the Seine. They had been moved to their previous areas in mid-July and partially in August, to be refitted there. Since personnel replacement arrived only in insufficient numbers, and material replacement hardly at all, it had been impossible to set up combat-ready units again. The strongest in numbers was the Feldersatzbataillon, led by Hauptsturmführer Urabl. It was located in Châteauneuf (twenty kilometers southwest of Dreux). Obersturm-führer Harro Lübbe reported on the activity in that battalion:

> . . . I was scheduled to become the battalion adjutant of the Felder-satzbataillon. However, Hauptsturmführer Urabl needed company commanders and initially used me for that post. The replacements which I then trained were partly transferred from the Luftwaffe, as was my senior NCO and the training NCOs. After I had taken parts from all companies of the battalion to the front near Caen at the beginning of August, traveling by truck at night, new replacements arrived. They were mostly older men. Approximately ten officers from the regular SS, among them Sturmbannführers and Ober-sturmbannführers, who had volunteered for front duty, came to my company. They were given combat training for the upcoming action. Naturally, they were not used in accordance with their rank in the general SS but in accordance with their standing in military training. I always put great emphasis on practicing being overrun by enemy tanks and firing the Panzerfaust . . .

On 14 August, the Bataillon left Châteauneuf to march into action between the Eure and Seine rivers. Since there were not enough vehicles, high Norman two-wheeled carts were requisitioned for the supplies, pulled by one horse. The companies were driven to the positions in several groups, one after the other. On the way, Hauptsturmführer Urabl incorporated dispersed Wehrmacht groups, in particular motorized ones, into his Bataillon. The stragglers were, for the most part, glad to have re-established contact. Some of them left again during the night, either to reach their own units again or to reach safety behind the Seine.[4]

The parts of Panzergrenadierregiment 26, which had been pulled out for refitting, were located in the area northeast of Dreux. North of them, around Pacy-sur-Eure, was the Pionierbataillon. The repair companies, the supply units and the Panzer-less crews of the Panzerregiment were situated in the area of le Neubourg and southwest of Elbeuf. The parts of Regiment 25, which were to be refitted, were probably stationed around Orbec. The other core personnel and supply units which had been pulled out, had withdrawn from their original areas to the north behind the line Dreux-Verneuil when the American troops approached. The supply units set up small combat groups which formed a thin screen toward the south.

On 20 August, parts of I./25 and of II./25 fought near Livarot. After a successful attack, through which encircled units of other divisions were freed, they were pulled out and moved into the planned assembly area. Unterscharführer Eberhard Köpke wrote in a letter on that "removal":

> . . . After we had accomplished our mission, the question was how we would get back again. At that moment our invaluable drivers entered the picture, Toni and Diehl, with all their vehicles. Regrettably, we lost all but the field kitchen vehicle during the numerous encounters with the enemy. Then, the whole company continued the trip on the field kitchen vehicle. In the cab alone, there were ten men. In that manner we continued along the rain-muddied country lanes in the direction of the Seine. One Zug had previously lost contact. It had made its way through on foot. Thus, we were a total of more than 60 men with our weapons and equipment . . .[5]

Hauptsturmführer Hans Siegel, who had suffered second degree burns on 27 June near Cheux, reported on the activity in the "base" of II. Panzerabteilung:

> . . . At the end of July/beginning of August, Hans Siegel returned there. He had been released prematurely from the hospital in Claíron near Paris, both of his hands still bandaged. On orders of Obersturmbannführer Wünsche, he took over command of the base. His tasks were:

to organize the base,

to train replacements arriving from the homeland,

to replace weapons and material through repairs, possibly new acquisitions,

to set up a temporary hospital, to be commanded by the walking wounded Dr. Jordan (in a walking cast due to a wound in the leg),

to establish a soldiers' recreation center,

to secure the fuel and ammunition dumps,

to build defensive positions in cooperation with the local commander in Elbeuf,

to secure the supply of the fighting units with ammunition, fuel, provisions, and goods.

As the front came closer it became necessary to move all supplies to the Seine and across the river to the east bank, and to secure them there. That had to be done without vehicles of their own and under constant air attacks. During that operation, Obersturmführer Gaspard Gillis, a Flemish volunteer who had arrived from home quite recently, offered advice and distinguished himself through his circumspection and energy. The next morning, after our briefing, he came to me and asked that I inspect his 'horse-drawn wagons'. Eight one-horse carriages were standing on the right, another eight on the left, the two-wheeled French carts lined up cleanly in rank and file. Elderly Frenchmen were holding the horses by their halters, facing me motionless. 'At ease!—I thank you, Gillis.'

Then we set out. First we transported clothing and equipment along the bank for three to four kilometers toward the valley, to the vicinity of a bombed bridge across the Seine. It was hanging into the water, blocking boat traffic. It was a sunny day. Enemy aircraft were constantly in the skies above, driven off by our 8.8 cm Flak, manned by crews of the Luftwaffe and the Arbeitsdienst (labor service), whom I had visited some days previously to establish contact. At the storage area itself we had our own guards with machine guns on anti-aircraft tripods.

Then, in the night, when fuel barrels and ammunition were carted down and the storage area increased frighteningly in size, Gillis had an answer again. 'How will we get the stuff across the more than 100 meters wide river, Gillis?—'With rowboats, Hauptsturmführer, I have already organized them, with schnapps and tobacco!' Indeed, Gillis transported everything, piece by piece, barrel after barrel, shell after shell, across the river . . .[6]

On 21 August 1944, the supreme command of 5. Panzerarmee reported the fighting strength of its divisions to Heeresgruppe B. Indicated for the "HJ" Division were: ". . . 300 men, 10 Panzers, no artillery . . ." These figures

can only be an estimate for the units which had broken out of the encirclement and were ready for combat. The combat strength of "Kampfgruppe
Mohnke" cannot be included in them. Based on that information, mistaken
conclusions regarding the losses in the Falaise encirclement have been
drawn. It is completely useless as a basis for such considerations.[6a]

While the encircled Divisionskampfgruppe was breaking out of the
Falaise pocket, "Kampfgruppe Mohnke" had its first enemy contact. Standartenführer Wilhelm Mohnke, commander of SS-Panzergrenadierregiment
26, reported to Oberstgruppenführer Sepp Dietrich, supreme commander
of 5. Panzerarmee, several days later regarding events on 20.8.1944:

> . . . Using quickly assembled parts of Feldersatzbataillon 12 and parts
> of Panzerregiment 12, a securing line was initially established from
> Heudebouville (six kilometers southeast of Louviers, Author) to the
> road Louviers-Evreux.
>
> Based on information from the Armee that 'Gruppe Wahl' had
> started an attack on Vernon, the securing line was moved forward
> during the night 20/21 August to le Goulet [perhaps le Boulay, six
> kilometers northeast of Evreux?]-Rouvray [six kilometers northwest
> of Pacy].
>
> During the attack and the forward move of the securing line, a
> total of fifteen Sherman tanks were destroyed. After weak German
> securing forces still located near Pacy had been pushed aside and
> the enemy had achieved a breakthrough across the line Pacy-
> Evreux, he attacked with tank forces (30) and infantry from the
> Chapelle area [probably la Chapelle, eight kilometers west of Ver-
> non]. He was able to penetrate and assembled strong forces in the
> Champenard-Ste. Colombe area (six and seven kilometers south of
> Gaillon respectively] for an attack . . .[7]

Concerning the course of the fighting on 21 August, Standartenführer
Mohnke reported merely that three enemy Pak had been destroyed.

In an order issued by the supreme command of 5. Panzerarmee on 21
August it was stated, i.a.:

> . . . During the continuation of the operation it is important that
> forces be reduced in the western Normandy sector and transferred
> to the eastern wing. To enable that, a withdrawal to the line
> Deauville (at the Channel coast)-Lisieux-Orbec-l'Aigle will be car-
> ried out during the night 21/22 August. . . . The I. SS-Panzerkorps
> with 2. Pz.-Div., 1. and 12. SS-Pz.-Divs. is to be pulled out immedi-
> ately and assembled in the Pacy-Evreux area . . . difficult-to-move
> supply units, repair companies, etc. area to be withdrawn as soon as
> possible and marched into the area north of the Seine . . .[8]

The daily report of the Armee, of 22 August 1944 stated i.a.:

. . . The enemy attacked the positions of LXXXI. A.K. on a wide front from the area south of Pacy-Breteuil [one kilometer north of Verneuil] to the north with two armored divisions. He broke through the positions and his units on the right are now located immediately northeast of Evreux. Strong tank forces are on the advance from Pacy in the direction of Evreux. Near Bonneville [five kilometers southwest of Evreux], the enemy attacked with approximately 100 tanks. According to unconfirmed reports, units of the tanks have penetrated to a position southeast of le Neubourg. An attack by assembled remnants of 1. and 12. SS-Pz.-Divs. and weak parts of 344. Inf.-Div. against the breakthrough area at Bonneville is under way . . .[9]

On that day, the Aufklärungsabteilung—probably as did others—formed a Kampfgruppe to secure the southwestern entrance of Louviers. It consisted of two armored reconnaissance vehicles and approximately twenty Luftwaffe stragglers. Unterscharführer Ebert scouted with his armored reconnaissance vehicle via Gaillon toward Vernon, where he had contact with the enemy.[10]
Standartenführer Mohnke's report on that day stated as follows:

. . . On 22 August, the enemy attacked with approximately 90 tanks, strong artillery, and constant air force support. He was able to break through the Kampfgruppe's defensive line in three places.
During that attack, the enemy lost, partly in close combat with Panzerfausts, a total of: twenty-five Sherman tanks, one 'Dreadnought' tank and ten carriers.
After leaving behind strong forward outposts, the Kampf-gruppe moved to a new line of defense during the night of 22/23 August: southern bend of the Seine-Fontaine Bellenger [six kilometers southeast of Louviers]-les Planches . . .[11]

On 23 August at 12.45 hours, Feldmarschall Model ordered the forward line of LXXXI. A.K. to be advanced to Conches-Evreux. Remnants of 116. Panzerdivision, of 1. and 12. SS-Panzerdivisions and of 2. Panzerdivision would be put into action for that attack. They were still in action at other locations and could not be brought up in time. During a telephone conversation with Oberstgruppenführer Sepp Dietrich, supreme commander of 5. Panzerarmee, at 15.20 hours, the Feldmarschall ordered that the attack had to be carried out regardless of circumstances. Sepp Dietrich replied that he understood the situation and knew what was important. However, since the units available for that attack consisted of only a few battalions, small in numbers, and a maximum of thirty Panzers, he considered the attack against an enemy, superior in armor and particularly in the air, as not promising. At 16.00 hours, the Armee reported to the Heeresgruppe that the attack, as ordered, from the area on both sides of le Neubourg under the command of General Graf (Count) Schwerin had started. In the evening, at 20.15 hours, LXXXI. A.K. reported that the enemy had broken through the positions of 116. Panzerdivision south of le Neubourg and knocked out four Panzers. At 18.00 hours, le Neubourg had been captured. The Division had withdrawn to the hills near Crosseville (immediately north of le Neubourg, Author). The scheduled attack had not developed. In order to prevent an enemy breakthrough across the southern front, Oberstgruppenführer Sepp Dietrich then ordered II. SS-Panzerkorps, which had to hold the western front, to pull the 2. SS-Panzerdivision out of the front during the night. It was to move to LXXXI. A.K. to support the counterattack against the enemy penetration near le Neubourg, scheduled for the next morning. The Division had still available two Panzergrenadier battalions and 12 Panzers.[12]

The small Kampfgruppe of the Aufklärungsabteilung of "HJ" Division, located near Louviers, was reinforced, on 23 August, by one 7.5 cm Pak and one 2 cm Flak. Some American artillery was already firing into the city. The Kampfgruppe secured at the edge of the city during the day. In the evening it moved to a small wood near Vironvay, three kilometers southeast of the city.[13]

A report by Obersturmführer Emil Maître, the commander of 4. Kraftfahrkompanie (transport company) throws some light on the events of that day. He wrote:

. . . I had been ordered to establish contact with Kampfgruppe Mohnke in Louviers at the Seine on 23 August. Together with my driver, Sturmmann Armbrust, and my messenger, Rottenführer Walter Pomm, I started out immediately after receiving the order. Because of the incessant air attacks we could jump only from one wood to the next, from farm to farm, and arrived after seven hours, at 13.00 hours, at the Mohnke command post in Louviers. Fighting was under way already ten kilometers south of Louviers. The enemy had reached the Seine. After carrying out my orders, I drove back to the north at 15.00 hours, swinging toward Elbeuf. The enemy situation in the area I had to travel through was totally unclear. Under the constant, loathsome attacks by fighter-bombers, frequently sneaking from bush to bush, I reached Elbeuf which was under a massive bombing raid. I drove around the city and came to the arterial road leading to le Neubourg. I drove along that road to the south. Three kilometers south of St. Germain [probably three kilometers north of Amfreville] I encountered a stopped American tank spearhead in front of, and securing the bridge. We made it past the first tank, but the second one blocked us. Armbrust had to stop and we were pulled from the vehicle. They drove us back a few kilometers in a jeep, probably to the forward command post of the division. After a short interrogation we were locked in one of the rooms of the house.

When we were captured, my FN-pistol, thirteen rounds, was clipped to the dashboard of the vehicle. My PKK [Walther Pistol] was stuck in my waistband under the camouflage jacket. Despite being searched it had not been found. The interrogating officer, who was under the influence of alcohol, returned my pay-book and we were left alone. Pomm and Armbrust were in the next room. There was total silence in the house. Pomm told me that a door led from his room into the garden, and that it was unlocked. Since I had not given up the idea of fleeing, I told the men that I would disappear. If they wanted to get out also, they were to wait for some time until everything was quiet. I thought the risk for a group of three would be too great. I was already in the garden when the other two followed. I said no more, but ran ahead across the road. A vehicle turned its lights to high beam and we ran up the opposite slope in full light. Raging rifle fire set in. Half-way up the slope I took a bullet through the left shoulder. It threw me to the ground. I jumped up and ran on, taking three more bullets through both thighs and my right shoulder. Still, I reached the down-slope and threw myself behind a pile of dirt. Looking back, I saw both my men lying immobile half-way up the hill, American soldiers running toward them. Then I ran toward a forest 500 meters away. Fortunately, the bullets in my thighs had not ripped any major arteries or broken any bones. My shoulder-blades had been cleanly shot through. I stuck both my arms into my camouflage jacket to support them. It was hard to believe, but I was not being pursued. I reached the forest. After long pauses, which I spent leaning against trees, I marched on, in the direction of the burning town of Elbeuf. In the early morning hours I spotted, near an entrance to the town—probably la Chapelle—a manned anti-tank gun facing south. I sneaked closer, saw German steel helmets, and was safe with fighting comrades of the 'LAH'.

I was given first aid in the local monastery. A supply vehicle driving back took me to the collection center for the wounded at Elbeuf. Together with twenty other wounded, who were unable to walk, a bus took me from there across the northern Seine railroad bridge to Rouen.

In 1962 I located the grave of SS-Rottenführer Pomm in the war cemetery St. André de l'Eure. My search for my driver Armbrust was without results due to my long period of captivity in the Soviet Union until 1951 . . .[14]

Standartenführer Mohnke reported about 23 August 1944:

. . . In the course of the early morning hours, II./26 [Bataillon Siebken], together with remnants of I./25 -(Bataillon Waldmüller), arrived at the Kampfgruppe.

These weak forces were put into action to secure the right open flank in the sector Amfreville [three kilometers southwest of les Planches]-la Haye-le-Comte [two kilometers southwest of Louviers].

The enemy was held off by the outposts. He managed only in the afternoon to advance on both sides of the Gaillon-Louviers road and to break through. During that operation he lost six Sherman tanks, three of them to close combat weapons.

The enemy assembled more forces facing the right sector. Reconnaissance in the Louviers-Elbeuf-Neubourg determined that the enemy had crossed the Louviers-le Neubourg road with strong forces.

On an unimpeded advance from a southerly direction via Quatremare [seven kilometers southwest of Louviers] were:
40–50 tanks,
50–60 trucks,
5 crane trucks,
ambulances,
mounted infantry and
bridge-building equipment.

Reconnaissance east of the Seine detected weak securing positions of 49. Inf.-Div. in the les Andelys-Mantes sector.

An attack by 18. Luftwaffe-Feld-Division, with the objective of pushing back the bridgehead near Mantes, was unsuccessful.

Inside the bridgehead were the
79. US Regiment,
314. US Regiment,
315 US Regiment,
two heavy and
three light artillery units . . .

Untersturmführer Harro Lübbe of the Feldersatzbataillon described the battle at the Gaillon-Louviers road in an entry in his diary:

. . . My reinforced Zug secured the northeastern edge of the village of Vieux-Villez [four kilometers northwest of Gaillon]. We pulled out from there at approximately 16.00 hours after hearing constant din of battle from the direction of Canappeville, Quatremare and Louviers. On the march, in the vicinity of Fontaine-Bellenger, riding on available vehicles, we came under fire from anti-tank guns or tanks located at Acquigny [five kilometers southwest of Fontaine-B]. My Pak was literally blown away from under my behind. We jumped off the vehicles into the road ditch on the right. Under constant fire, we crawled into foxholes dug by others in a grain field with stacked sheaves at the southwestern edge of the village. Those vehicles which had not been knocked out drove into the village, out of the range of aimed fire. We were approximately ten men, armed with machine pistols, carbines and Panzerfausts. From the cover of my foxhole I observed, at 17.35 hours, a tank assembly some two kilometers away. Reconnaissance planes above our positions directed massive artillery fire on Fontaine-B., and probably on Heudebouville and the Seine crossings.

After violent armor and Pak duels, the enemy started his tank attack, in particular on the crossroads Heudebouville-Venables. Only later did the enemy swing toward my sector. Armored personnel carriers with mounted infantry followed hesitantly. I shouted at my men: 'Let them overrun us and knock them out with Panzerfausts from the rear!' Some of the grain sheaves were on fire. Approximately twenty enemy tanks and armored personnel carriers were rolling toward us, their engines roaring and their tracks squealing. They crossed the Vieux-Villez road and penetrated into our positions. Our own artillery tried to stop the enemy. Next to me in the foxhole, after firing a Panzerfaust, there was a heart-rending moan. The gunner had not lifted the tube high enough and he died soon after from massive burns. Fortunately, a light rain started which later increased in intensity. After we had fired all our Panzerfausts, we waited for darkness in our foxholes. The noises from the tanks and other vehicles could be heard moving in the direction of the village. Around 22.00 hours I ventured to move back through the enemy positions. Like a stalking hunter, I sneaked past farms, stopped American vehicles and guards whom I could hear talking. After a long march through woods and bush, I reached the Seine and crept along its bank. After some considerable time I spotted a flickering light now and then, and thought that I heard German sounds. Carefully, I crept forward. It was a German Panzer, on guard there. The time was 02.35 hours. When I reported back to Hauptsturmführer Urabl at the Bataillon command post in the morning, eight of my ten men had also returned . . .[16]

During the night 23–24 August, LXXXI. A.K. and II. SS-Pz.-Korps were able to move into the "Bernay" position, their fourth position. Because of the strong pressure on that position, 5. Panzerarmee approved at 10 A.M. a withdrawal in the course of the day, or the following night, to an intermediate position along a line Fiquefleur (five kilometers east of Honfleur)-Beuzeville-

St. Georges du V.-Brionne. Through the pull-back of the southern front to a line Brionne-le Gros Thiel (ten kilometers northeast of Brionne)-St. Pierre des Fleurs (five kilometers southwest of Elbeuf)-St. Pierre les Elbeuf (at the southeastern exit from Elbeuf), the gap between LXXXVI. A.K. and II. SS-Panzerkorps had also been closed. Parts of 17. Luftwaffe-Feld-Division and the Mohnke Kampfgruppe were still fighting at that time a strong enemy tank force in the area south of Louviers. Panzergruppe Graf Schwerin had been ordered to break through toward Louviers from the area St. Mesley-St. Pierre [St. Meslin-du-Bosc, twenty-one kilometers west of Louviers?] and to establish contact with the Mohnke Kampfgruppe. However, since the Panzergruppe itself was attacked by a strong tank unit along the line Meslin-Amfreville-la Campagne (twelve and sixteen kilometers east of Brionne, respectively), it was unable to carry out that order.[17]

Standartenführer Mohnke reported to 5. Panzerarmee on 24 August 1944 at 14.00 hours:

> . . . In order to clean up the penetration and because of the considerable out-flanking, the Kampfgruppe withdrew during the night 23–24 August to the line Vironvay-le Hamlet-Southern edge of Louviers-road Louviers-le Neubourg inclusive, leaving behind strong outposts.
>
> Contact exists with the 17. Luftwaffe-Feld-Division. The division secures, with only weak remaining forces, the adjoining right wing of the Kampfgruppe to the road Louviers-Elbeuf through a line of strong points, and by reconnaissance on foot to Tostes [eight kilometers southeast of Elbeuf].
>
> At this time, results of our own reconnaissance forces from the Louviers-Elbeuf area have not arrived. However, enemy spearheads are believed to have reached six kilometers south of Elbeuf during the night 23–24 August. More detailed information will follow.
>
> Enemy pressure continues. Air activity is negligible due to the bad weather.
>
> In cooperation with the 17. Luftwaffe-Feld-Division, it is planned to cross the Seine to the east during the night . . .[18]

That plan was carried out. The war diary of 5. Panzerarmee notes, for 25 August 1944, i.a.:

> . . . The Mohnke Gruppe (formerly Wahl) and 17. Luftwaffe-Feld-Div., which had been able to hold their positions southeast of Elbeuf without contact to our own troops until now, were pushed by the enemy to the north bank during the night. There they moved into defensive positions between St. Aubin (northern bank of the Seine

across from Elbeuf, Author) and Amfreville-s-les-Monts [eight kilometers East of Pont-de-l'Arche] . . .

The 2. SS-Panzerdivision recaptured the city of Elbeuf, occupied in the
meantime, from the enemy before noon. The commander of the Panzergruppe, Graf Schwerin requested permission from the armee to give up the
city again and to block it to the north since the Division was very weak in
numbers. The Armee approved the request and ordered that four Kampfgruppen be formed from 2. and 9. SS-Panzer-divisions, 21. and 116. Panzerdivisions. They were to blockade the bends in the Seine south of Rouen and
south of Duclair.

That war diary states, regarding the crossing operation of the Seine:

> . . . Since 20 August, the remaining parts of 7. Armee are being
> transferred across the Seine under major difficulties. Despite con-
> stant enemy air attacks on bridges and ferry crossings, despite the
> lack of ferries, pontoon bridges and boats, it was possible to trans-
> port approximately 25,000 vehicles of all kind across the river dur-
> ing the period 20 August to the evening of 24 August . . .[19]

The following reports offer an indication of the difficulties during the
crossing.

Oberscharführer August Zinflmeister of the Aufklärungs-abteilung, who
had led the small Kampfgruppe near Vironvay, wrote in his diary for 24–25
August:

> . . . We look, questioningly, across the Seine to the other bank. At
> 23.00 hours, we already packed up again and marched back to St.
> Pierre-du-Vauvray [three kilometers northeast of Louviers on the
> Seine] where we moved into the building of the Kriegsmarine
> [navy]. At 05.00 hours on 25 August we crossed, almost as the last
> group, on a Pionier ferry to the opposite Seine bank. We assembled
> our small band in Andé.
> At dawn, we continued via Daubeuf, Bacqueville, Fleury to les
> Hogues [twenty-two kilometers east of Rouen] . . .[20]

Gunner Paul Baier of 4. Batterie of Flakabteilung 12 noted in his diary:

> . . . 20 August—Continued withdrawal to Louviers/Seine. Assembly
> there. A tractor had arrived from the Falaise encirclement. Took
> cover in the woods. 22 August—crossing the Seine during the night
> by way of pontoon bridge. Crossing was possible only at night
> because of fighter-bombers. When we reached the Seine with our

vehicles, the order came that only the drivers would cross with the vehicles. All others had to dismount to be organized into Kampf- gruppen. Then, suddenly, another order arrived. Complete units would cross with their vehicles and only stragglers would be assem- bled into Kampfgruppen. The drivers were especially reminded to take care when driving onto the pontoon bridge, so as not to miss it. The crossing had to take place quickly and efficiently so that as many vehicles as possible would make it across. Any vehicle which missed the bridge would be pushed into the Seine without hesita- tion since neither time nor equipment were available to pull a vehi- cle, which had missed, back onto the bridge. Drivers of vehicles with trailers had to be hellishly careful. After all, it was dark, the bridge was narrow, and the approach to it not particularly good . . .[21]

Oberscharführer Karl Leitner of Feldersatzbataillon 12 reported:

. . . We stopped at the Seine bridgehead near Louviers until the sup- ply units had crossed via a pontoon bridge. During that period I had a chance to observe the activity. At the bridge stood a general, pistol in his hand, and decided which units would be allowed to cross next. I heard reasoning such as: We, of the Flak, have to set up new positions at the other Seine bank. Further: We, of the artillery, the same. Further: Pak and infantry, the same. We crossed last. The bridge was taken down or blown up, I don't remember. But I do remember that, when we were supposed to move into prepared positions, we were all alone. Not a word had been true of all the rea- soning to let the other units cross. Those had not been single strag- glers, but complete units . . .

With the crossing of the Seine by "Kampfgruppe Mohnke", action by the "HJ" Division south of the Seine had come to an end. The core personnel and the Feldersatzbataillon, which had been pulled out for refitting, had sig- nificantly contributed to preventing the Americans from encircling and destroying the troops located south of the Seine at the Channel coast, or those who had broken out of the encirclement of Falaise. Sturmbannführer Bremer had already fought American troops who had advanced to the Seine near Mantes, on 13 August, by his own individual decision. In recognition of his achievements, and those of his SS-Panzeraufklärungsabteilung 12, he was awarded the Oak Leaves to the Knight's Cross as the 668th soldier.

SECTION 7

Withdrawal from Northern France—Rearguard Fighting in the French-Belgian Border Area— Return to the Reich

During the night of 24–25 August 1944, Kampfgruppe Mohnke was the last part of the "HJ" Division to cross the Seine. On 25 August, the supreme command of 5. Panzerarmee ordered all of its units fighting south of the river, to withdraw behind the Risle during the following night and behind the Seine during the night of 26/27 August. The course of the river was to be defended with all means. At the same time it ordered that two battle groups be formed from the Panzer units: one, under the command of Graf Schwerin, from 1., 2., 12. SS-Panzerdivisions and 116. Panzerdivision in the Beauvais region (seventy kilometers east of Rouen); the other group was to be assembled under the leadership of the general command of II. SS-Panzerkorps from 9., 10. SS-Panzerdivisions and 21. Panzerdivision in the area around la Pommeraye-Boissay (approximately eighteen kilometers northeast of Rouen).[1]

"Kampfgruppe Mohnke" remained in action under the direct command of Pz. AOK 5 (Panzer Armee supreme command). The map "Front Location" of the morning of 26 August shows it behind the Seine in the sector Amfreville sous-les-Monts-Muids, while parts of the Division are indicated west of Beaumont (thirty-five kilometers south of Beauvais). The placing of "12.SS" within the frame of the Schwerin Gruppe west of Elbeuf was probably outdated.

While the mass of the "HJ" Division assembled in the Beauvais area, stragglers arrived daily. They had made their way through enemy-held territory in an adventurous manner. Some had been dressed in farmers' clothes, with milk containers, rakes, pitch-forks. Others were dressed in mourning, carrying wreaths. All had traveled for days on bicycles. Between 24 and 27 August, 17 stragglers arrived at the Divisionsbegleitkompanie in Sarcus near Grandvillers (thirty-two kilometers northwest of Beauvais). [2]

The Pz. AOK 5 ordered the further move to the east of those parts of the Panzerdivision not in action as early as 27 August. It ordered "HJ" Division to move into the area east of Laon. General der Panzertruppen West, General Stumpf, took over the responsibility for refitting all Panzerdivisions. During

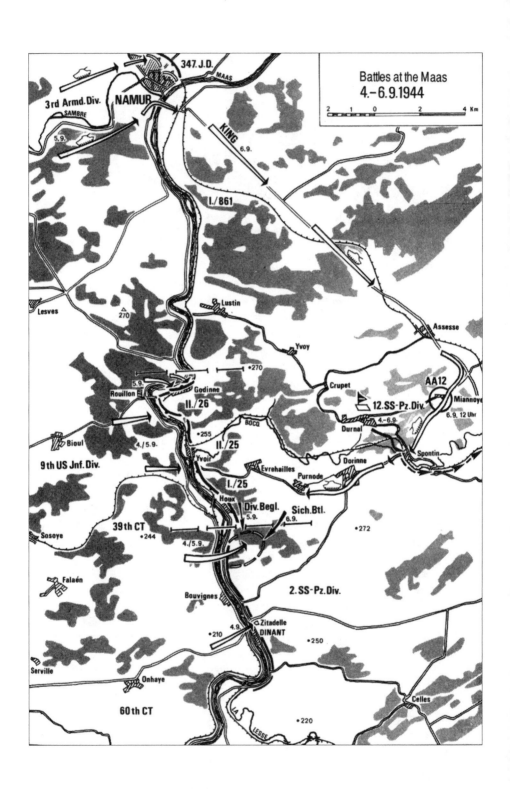

Battles at the Maas
4.–6. 9. 1944

2   1   0   2   4 Km

347. J.D.

3rd Armd. Div.

NAMUR

SAMBRE

MAAS

5.9.

KING
6.9.

I./ 861

Lesves

△ 270

Lustin

Yvoy

•270

Crupet

AA 12

12. SS-Pz. Div.

Miannoye

6.9. 12 Uhr

Godinne

Rouillon

5.9.

II./ 26

BOCQ

•255

Durnal

4.–6.9.

Spontin

Bioul

4./5.9.

II./ 25

Yvoir

Evrehailles

Dorinne

Purnode

9 th US Jnf. Div.

I./ 25

Houx

Div. Begl.
5.9.

Sich. Btl.
6.9.

•272

39 th CT

•244

4./5.9.

Sosoye

2. SS-Pz. Div.

Bouvignes

Falaén

△ Zitadelle
4.9.
DINANT

•210

•250

Serville

Onhaye

Celles

60 th CT

LESSE

•220

the following night, the "HJ" Division marched into the area around Hirson, fifty kilometers northeast of Laon.[3]

The "Front Location" of 29 August showed "Kampfgruppe Mohnke" in the same positions as on 26 August, west of Gournay (approximately fourteen kilometers west of Beauvais).

The defense of the Seine had been unsuccessful. The enemy had crossed the river in the area northwest of Paris in several locations as early as 28 August. In particular to the south of Paris, however, he advanced rapidly to the east and northeast. Thus, on 28 August, Feldmarschall Model ordered the concentration into a combat group of all battle-ready parts of 1., 2., and 12. SS-Panzerdivisions for the same day. They had to be held in readiness so that they could start out at noon on 29 August via Montcornet (twenty-four kilometers south of Hirson), or via Laon, to the south.[4] The "HJ" Division formed two Kampfgruppen from I./25 and III./26.

During his short stay in Hirson, General Stumpf visited the "HJ" Division, which had its Divisional staff quarters there. He brought with him the agreeable news that the Divisional commander, Oberführer Kurt Meyer, had been awarded the Swords to the Oak Leaves of the Knight's Cross on 26 August 1944, as the 91st soldier. There was a joint discussion about which divisional structure was practical and possible for the transitional period.[4a] The results of the discussion were transmitted in detail in a report to the chief of staff of the Panzer forces on 4 September. That plan was never carried out. However, it offers an image of the condition of the Division. The fighting troops were to be approximately halved. Thus, one Panzergrenadierregiment and a mixed Panzerabteilung were foreseen. The exact figures for the personnel required could not be provided since "Kampfgruppe Mohnke" was in action far away. However, 800 Panzergrenadiers and 200 reconnaissance soldiers were considered as necessary. Among others, 37 Panzer IVs, 37 Panthers and 22 Panzerjäger IVs were needed for that structure.[5] The requirement for Panzers and Panzerjägers arose because the Division had been forced to hand over its own battle-ready ones to other units when it was pulled out for refitting.

Even the Panzers on their way to the Division were diverted to the units in action, as Sturmmann Hans Kesper of 4. Panzerkompanie reported:

After the withdrawal from Caen, men of 3. and 4. Kompanie were pulled out and sent to Germany to pick up new Panzers. I drove in a Henschel-Diesel truck, together with forty men under the command of an Untersturm-führer, to Paderborn-Sennelager. I took over from the driver in Cologne and navigated the truck through the badly bombed Ruhr region. I almost lost my way in Dortmund. Hills of rubble from bombed-out houses lined the streets right and left. Around midnight we finally arrived in my home town of Werl, located right on Reichstrafle 1 [Reich road]. We were tired and hungry.

First I woke my mother who was, of course, totally surprised. There was a bucket of raspberry juice to quench our thirst. Then we drove over to my fiancee, my present wife. Again, great surprise, but then there was food for the whole gang. It took all of a ham, and all the neighbors and and my parents-in-law did what they could. Two hours later we arrived at Sennelager. We found ourselves an empty shack and went to sleep right away.

After we had picked up our seventeen Panthers, we set off in a westerly direction at the beginning of August. After five days of rail transport we landed in Ars on the Moselle. I have a field-post letter in front of me, my wife luckily saved all letters, in which I wrote: 'We unloaded our Panzers here and parked them in the old shellproof enclosures dating back to the First World War. The rail line to Paris has been blown up. We cannot use any other since the Panzers are too high and heavy.'

After fourteen days, we continued by rail to Reims. There we unloaded. The town commander used us for propaganda, meaning that we drove around inside and outside of the city for three days. At least, that is what we were told. Then we started out in the direction of the French-Belgian border. During the night drive, a front-end collision occurred. I was driving at the point. At a sharp bend in the road, I had to stop. When the Panzer behind me hit the rear-end of mine, I suffered a cut to my head where it hit the cover of the turret turning mechanism. After first aid had been administered by French nurses in a near-by hospital, we continued our drive. The two Panzers at the very rear of the column had been damaged so badly that there was no thought of driving them any further. I have heard that the crews we left behind suffered losses during a fire exchange with the Americans and were captured.

We continued our drive in the direction of Soissons. There, we were detained by a Flakabteilung. Since we had almost no fuel left, we blocked the entrance and exit roads on our own. Any of the retreating troops who wanted to pass had to hand over fuel to us. The Flak officer did not like that at all. Then we were attached to a Kampfgruppe of the Division. Among others, we escorted the valuable repair companies through French and Belgian villages, and through Charleroi. There, civilians were in the process of plundering the German soldiers' library. In the villages, everyone was waiting for the liberation. Their surprise was all the greater when German Panzers with the Balken crosses still appeared. That caused a hopeless chaos. Later, we formed small Kampfgruppen: one or two Panzers and assorted infantry from all possible branches of the service. We drove to and fro, fighting and guarding. Provisions, ammunition and fuel were available at irregular intervals. The orders were brought to us by motorcycle messengers.

We got caught in the vicinity of Mons. Knocked out by English tanks, hit in the right side. The radio operator was killed, I was wounded in the left knee. I was loaded onto a hospital train leaving for western Germany.[6]

Unterscharführer Heinz Berner of 6. Kompanie was also on his way to pick up Panzers, together with members of II. Abteilung. Under the command of Untersturmführer Pucher, the men drove with two Lancia trucks to the Hermann-Göring works in Linz to receive Panzer IVs there. He reported:

. . . After arriving in Linz, we had to wait a few days before taking over the Panzers. We then set out for France by rail transport. It was planned to unload in Paris. At the Vöklabruck railroad station in Austria we had a bad accident. We had been parked on a siding for a short time. Its overhead electrical contact line was still live. As we camouflaged the vehicles, one of the Panzer drivers came in contact with the wire above and suffered severe burns. In order to get him to a hospital quickly, we stopped a scheduled train and the wounded man was loaded on it. We encountered a further delay of several days in Unna, caused by bombing raids on the railroad installations and a supposed lack of locomotives.

Our transport stopped at Perl on the Moselle. At that time, Paris had already fallen. Untersturmführer Pucher drove to the front line command center at Metz to find out where we should drive. During his absence we were attacked by sixteen fighter-bombers. The majority of the men were just having a swim in the Moselle. It was around noontime. The fighter-bombers suddenly dove out of the sun and attacked the railway station with bombs and on-board weapons. We defended ourselves with the turret MGs which we had used as anti-aircraft MGs during the transport. Unfortunately, an ammunition train was parked next to us. Two Panzers were ripped off the carriers by the explosions, there were wounded and killed. I was blinded for several days and moved to the hospital at Saarburg.

After one week, I ran away from there and got on a train in Saarburg, in a Wehrmacht uniform and without marching orders. When I was taken to hospital I was clad only in my sports trunks and gym shoes. I wanted to travel via Trier to Metz, to get back to my Kompanie as quickly as possible, despite the fact that my vision was still not quite restored. I was convinced that every man was needed there.

The railway station guard in Trier arrested me and I was brought in front of the station commander, an elderly major. I told him the

reason for running away. He believed me and issued me with marching orders to Metz. As we were rolling through Perl—one track had
been restored—I spotted my comrades and jumped off the slow-
moving train. The rest of the unit were repairing the Panzers.

Together with Untersturmführer Pucher I then rode to Metz on
our 750 cc. BMW motorcycle. However, we only got as far as Dieden-
hofen since all German administrative units had already pulled out
of Metz. We almost fell into the hands of an American vanguard
unit. A Wehrmacht general was glad of our presence and we were
sent to guard a bridge in Luxembourg. We did not become involved
in combat. Some time later, an orderly officer of the Regiment
found us. He had been sent to look for us. The civilian population of
the area had been evacuated in the meantime. As ordered, we
handed over our Panzers at the Panzerstützpunkt Mitte (Panzer Base
Center) near Kaiserslautern. From there, we traveled by train into
the Siegen region where I ended up back with 6. Kompanie . . .[7]

During the time the "HJ" Division was located in the area around Hirson, "Kampfgruppe Mohnke" also arrived there. The Regimental staff and
units, as well as I. Bataillon were sent to Kaiserslautern for refitting. The
Panzergrenadier-Ausbildungs-und Ersatzbataillon 12 (training and reserve
battalion), which had previously been stationed in Arnhem, Holland, had
been there for some time. Standartenführer Wilhelm Mohnke was transferred to the "LAH" Division as divisional commander, since Brigadeführer
Wisch had been seriously wounded on 20 August during the breakout from
the Falaise encirclement. Sturmbannführer Bernhard Krause, the commander of I./26, was given—initially on an acting basis—the command of
SS-Panzergrenadierregiment 26. For the time being, II. and III. Bataillon
remained with the Divisional Kampfgruppe.

On 30 August 1944, the Americans broke through unexpectedly via Soissons toward Marle in the direction of Hirson. As had been ordered, the two
Kampfgruppen of 1. and 12. SS-Panzerdivisions were located at the Serre sector: around Marle, that of "LAH" Division, on both sides of Montcornet, the
I./25, and on both sides of Rozoy, the III./26 (25.5 south and twenty-three
kilometers southeast of Hirson respectively). The Kampfgruppen were
assigned to II. SS-Panzerkorps. Scouting parties of III./26 had encountered
the enemy in the Rozoy area as early as 28 August, as indicated in a report on
losses. The enemy, advancing from the direction of Laon on Montcornet on
30 August, was repelled by I./25 and swung off to the east. Near Rozoy,
III./26 took in a company of Fliegerregiment 22 which had guarded an operational airfield near Laon until the arrival of the Americans, enabling a few
ME 262s to take off. The company, led by Major von Boddin, was moved to
Brunehamel (7.5 kilometers northeast of Rozoy). Soon after, an American
tank spearhead attacked the securing positions of the Bataillon and forced it

backward to Brunehamel. The Gefreite (lance corporal) Jarczyk of the Fliegerkompanie watched some of the advancing American tanks being knocked out in Brunehamel by two Tigers and a 8.8 cm Flak. The American troops withdrew. On 31 August, the Americans captured Montcornet, located on the south bank of the Serre, but they were unable to cross the river.

The 2. Panzerdivision had been ordered to connect with the Kampf-gruppen of the "HJ" Division on the left. At the request of the general command of II. SS-Panzerkorps, the chief of staff advised Heeresgruppe B that 2. Panzerdivision ". . . was planning to reach the line Montcornet-Rethel probably by 20.00 hours . . ."[8] Since there was no contact on the left, a scouting party of Aufklärungsabteilung 12 was sent on 1 September to reconnoiter in the direction of Rethel. It consisted of the only still serviceable eight-wheel armored reconnaissance vehicle and a group of Schwimmwagen (amphibious vehicles). On the previous day, Obersturmführer Keue, the chief of 3. (Aufklärungs-) Kompanie, had brought twenty Schwimmwagens from Metz. The scouting party was led by Oberscharführer August Zinflmeister. He reported:

> . . . In a village outside of Château-Porcien (nine kilometers west of Rethel, fifty kilometers southeast of Hirson, Author), we found the first marks made by tracked and wheeled enemy vehicles. The people greeted us with: 'Vivent les Américains!' (Long live the Americans). We waved back and drove on. At the southwestern exit from Château-Porcien we ran into an American tank spearhead. One jeep and seven personnel carriers were taken out by our weapons, as well as, probably, two armored reconnaissance vehicles which stopped under the fire from our 2 cm gun. When a Sherman opened fire on us across the gully, we had to beat it and start the drive back. Delayed by a defective tire, collecting of individual Fallschirmjäger stragglers, 'Ami' tanks at a bridge, obstacles built by the partisans with trees, etc., we arrived back at Hirson only in the late afternoon. The Abteilung has moved into the forest since the Americans were pushing again from the south. We drove to Macquenoise in Belgium (eight kilometers northeast of Hirson, Author) to refuel and then back into the forest. At dusk we returned to Macquenoise, and, around midnight, we drove at the point of the Abteilung, with ripped and smoking tires, to the north. We drove throughout the night by way of Chimay, Rance, and arrived at Hestrud toward morning . . .[9]

While the enemy apparently felt his way forward northwest of Rethel with only tank spearheads and reconnaissance forces, he established a strong point at Montcornet after its capture on 31 August. He succeeded in pushing back the weak forces of I./25 on 1 September. The Bataillon was only able to fight off the pursuing enemy near Origny (5.5 kilometers southwest of Hirson). The III./26, also, was pushed back and moved into new positions behind the Thon on both sides of Aubenton (twelve kilometers southeast of Hirson).

Further to the west the enemy achieved a deep penetration to the north. The "HJ" Division was pulled out of the area around Hirson in order to close a gap which had opened south of the Sambre. It was ordered to move into a blocking position west of Beaumont, adjoining on the left of 116. Panzerdivision. The Kampfgruppen in action disengaged from the enemy in the evening of 1 September. Parts moved into a rear position near Anor (eight kilometers north of Hirson). The Divisionsbegleit-kompanie had been reorganized into an Aufklärungskompanie during the preceding days and equipped with Schwimmwagens. Initially, it consisted of three Aufklärungs squads and a heavy machine gun squad. During the night of 1–2 September, it moved from Fourmiers to Solre-le-Château (twenty-one kilometers north of Hirson) and secured southwest of the village. The I./25 moved into a securing line near Montignies (six kilometers northwest of Beaumont), the II./25 near Trélon (fifteen kilometers north of Hirson), facing west.[10]

The staff of SS-Panzergrenadierregiment 26, the Regimental units and I./26 were already on the march to Kaiserslautern to be refitted. During the night of 1–2 September, III. Bataillon also started out for Kaiserslautern. The following route had been ordered: Aubenton, Rocroi, Couvin, Philippeville, Charleroi, Gembloux, Leez (forty-seven kilometers southeast of Brussels). There, a message center of the Regiment was reportedly located. The major detour to the north was necessary since the American troops in the south had already advanced far to the east. The commander of II./26, Sturmbannführer Erich Olboeter, drove at the head of the column. Major von Boddin rode in the same vehicle, a car of the Kfz. 1 type. His company from Fliegerregiment 22 followed, on trucks, close behind.

During the night the column crossed, driving without lights, a large wooded area. When its point drove through a hollow, there was a sudden deafening explosion and bright flames lit the night. Partisans had pulled a mine onto the road by a wire. It detonated under the vehicle of Sturmbannführer Olboeter. Gefreiter Jarczyk of Fliegerregiment 22 rode on the first truck behind the lead vehicle. The explosion jerked him from his half-sleep. Together with his comrades, he jumped from the vehicle, as did the crews on the other trucks. In the bright glare of the burning car he saw Sturmbannführer Olboeter lying on the ground, his uniform on fire. Major von Boddin ripped off his coat, threw it on the wounded man, and rolled him back and forth on the ground to extinguish the flames. The crews from the vehicles stopped close-by fired their hand-weapons into the woods where they suspected the partisans. These had disappeared without a trace. Thanks to the quick and courageous action by Major von Boddin, Olboeter's burning uniform was soon extinguished. However, his legs were smashed. The Bataillon physician provided the critically wounded man with such care as was possible, and had him put into a vehicle, probably an armored personnel carrier of his Bataillon. Major von Boddin remained unhurt, only his hair had been singed. The driver of the commander's car came away without a scratch.

The column continued its march without further delay so as to bring the wounded quickly to a hospital. After the dangerous forest had been crossed, the armored personnel carrier took Sturmbannführer Olboeter to Charleville while the column continued its march north. The hospital in Charleville was already in the process of moving out since the enemy was approaching the city. Despite that, the critically wounded man was operated on immediately. Both of his legs had to be amputated. It is thought that Sturmbannführer Olboeter died while still on the operating table and was buried next to the hospital. A brave, time-tested soldier, loved by his men, had become the victim of a perfidious assassination attempt. For five years, from the first day of the war on, he had fought in many minor and major battles. As a Zugführer, as company chief and Bataillon commander, he could always be found where the action was hottest and where the need was greatest. The location of Sturmbannführer Olboeter's grave is not known. It is likely that he was moved, as an unknown soldier, to the German war cemetery at Lommel in Belgium after the war. More that 38,000 German soldiers of the First and Second World Wars have found a dignified resting place there.[10a]

The operations staff of the Division crossed the French-Belgian border near Hestrud on 2 September 1944 and set up its command post near Beaumont.[11] Parts of the Aufklärungsabteilung had taken up securing positions five kilometers west of the town. A scouting party with a Schwimmwagen, sent out to the west, did not encounter any enemy forces within several kilometers.[12]

A small and amusing event should be reflected here. The commander of 116. Panzerdivision, Generalleutnant Graf Schwerin, arrived at the Division command post of the "HJ" Division in order to establish contact. After the discussions had been completed, the Ia accompanied him to the armored personnel carrier sitting in front of the building. The general put on his heavy, wool-lined coat—a so-called "Lama coat"—and climbed into the vehicle. Amazed, the Ia asked: "Is that heavy coat not too warm just now?" The general replied, smiling: "Old nobility always feels cold."

On 2 September 1944, the enemy attacked the blocking positions of II. Bataillon of Regiment 25 near Trélon. The orderly officer of the Bataillon, Untersturmführer Hermann Buchmann, reported on that:

> The commander, Hauptsturmführer Schrott, sat in the right front seat of the VW-Kübel. I squatted on the hood of the car, observing the skies above. The driver, the commander and I were hit by a burst of bullets. The vehicle rolled into the road ditch. The commander and I sought cover. Because of the excitement, we did not notice our injuries. The enemy was also surprised and stopped his advance and

the fire. We walked back in the ditch to a Pak gun at the edge of town. Only there did the commander lose consciousness and we determined that he had been shot in the chest. I had been shot through the upper arm and was bleeding profusely, but it caused no problems. A messenger took us to the command post by side-car motorcycle. The field dressing station was also located there. Hauptsturmführer Schrott died on the way there. I was moved on to a field hospital and looked after there. In the evening, I had myself brought back to our combat troops and, together with the supply units, I went back to the German-Belgian border in the Aachen area . . .[13]

On 2 September, the English/Canadian army group continued its attack to break through to the north with superior tank forces. It reached Arras and the area south of Cambrai with strong forces. Spearheads advanced to Lille, Valenciennes and Mons. At the 5. Panzerarmee, the enemy broke through via Avesnes (twenty kilometers southwest of Beaumont)-ahead of the securing line of 116. Panzerdivision and 12. SS-Panzerdivision-to Maubeuge (sixteen kilometers northwest of Beaumont). The divisional Kampfgruppe "HJ", probably in order to close a gap there, was moved north. It was put into action to the right of 116. Pz.-Div., its previous neighbor on the left.

The map "Front Situation" as of noon on 3 September 1944 shows the two divisional Kampfgruppen along a securing line in the area Solre-sur-Sambre to Sivry (eight kilometers northwest and seven kilometers southwest of Beaumont respectively). Securing positions of 1. and 2. SS-Pz.-Divs., facing south, are entered north of Philippeville. Behind the Maas river, from Givet to Charleville, where the boundary between 5. Panzerarmee and 1. Armee ran, securing positions of 2. Panzerdivision are shown along a wide front. These entries were, at least partially, outdated already. The securing line near Beaumont had to be given up under strong enemy pressure during the night 2–3 September. The command post of the "HJ" Division was moved to Florennes (twenty-two kilometers east of Beaumont) early in the morning of 3 September. A blocking front was established along the line Thuin-Philippeville-Givet. To do that, 116. Pz.-Div. was moved to the right wing of I. SS-Panzerkorps which had taken over command. In action along the line mentioned, from right to left, were: 116. Pz.-Div., 12. SS-Pz.-Div. "HJ", parts of 1. SS-Pz.-Div. "LAH", 2. SS-Pz.-Div. "DR", 2. Pz.-Div. The repeated crossing of the two divisional Kampfgruppen 116. and 12.SS had thus ended, but not as yet, the change of command relationships, both of which were the results of the rapid and unplanned withdrawal under the pressure of a superior enemy.

The Divisionsbegleitkompanie had moved to Florennes with the Divisional staff. It received orders, on 3 September at 14.00 hours, to secure the road bridge across the river near Yvoir and the railroad bridge near Houx during the following night in preparation for the withdrawal behind the

Maas river. It was responsible for directing traffic across those bridges and to blow them up when strong enemy pressure was encountered. From there, it decided on its own to scout toward Givet and Marche (fourteen kilometers southwest and thirty kilometers east of Dinant respectively).[14]

The leader of the scouting party sent in the direction of Givet, Unterscharführer Leo Freund, reported:

From Yvoir, we drove west of the Maas through several villages: Falaen [eight kilometers southwest of Yvoir], Serville [three kilometers southwest of Falaen], Morville [four kilometers southwest of Serville] which were all still free of the enemy. Along the route from Morville in the direction of Soulme [nine kilometers northwest of Givet], the road dropped steeply down the hill toward a ravine which was heavily wooded. I had an instinctive feeling that this would be an ideal spot for partisans, and stopped. After some quick consideration I ordered that we would drive through the ravine 200 meters apart and at the highest possible speed. My deputy, Unterscharführer Wilfried Tödter, who had earlier been in the I.G. Zug, wanted to take over the point because of the danger. However, I signaled my driver and he immediately drove off at high speed. We raced downhill and when we reached the woods we came under fire from all sides. Instinctively, we ducked and fired our MPs blindly into the trees. Suddenly, the driver screamed and I saw with horror that the thumb of his right hand was dangling only by the skin. I quickly grabbed the steering wheel with my left hand and we raced on without slowing down. Then, the Rottenführer sitting behind the driver yelled. A bullet had hit the artery in his left forearm, and blood was gushing into the vehicle in a high arch. Quick-witted, he dropped his MP and pressed his arm to close off the artery. Then we had reached the bottom of the valley, went uphill again, and made it out of the woods. We quickly put dressings on our two wounded. Only then did we notice that our other two vehicles had not followed us. We already thought that we had lost them when we heard our MG 42s barking down in the ravine. Despite the wounded, we drove back immediately to help our comrades. To our great amazement, the firing had stopped and we found our two vehicles, lined up one behind the other, sitting on the road. There was no sign of the crews. A terrifying picture offered itself along the road. Partisans were lying everywhere, having dropped out of the trees. Then, reassuringly, we heard our MGs firing deep inside the woods and after some time, our eight men returned unharmed. They were beaming, but I admonished them for having left their vehicles and followed the enemy into the forest regardless of the danger of running into an ambush. Unterscharführer Tödter then reported that they had immediately stopped half-way down when my vehicle had come under fire. The two MGs had opened fire on the trees and the partisans sitting in them with devastating effect. Those who were able to save themselves had fled into the forest while Tödter ordered the men to dismount and started the pursuit. During that, some of the fleeing were hit. On the return drive we traveled along the Maas. I do not remember whether it was in Houx or in Yvoir, but in one of those villages we came across our Divisional commander. He stood in an open square, clad in a leather coat, his head bandaged, and he signaled us to stop. The first we heard from him was a dressing-down for driving too fast inside the village. Only then was I able to report, and 'Panzermeyer' listened intently to every detail of our reconnaissance mission.[15]

The Divisional staff moved to Durnal (7.5 kilometers east of Yvoir) by way of Yvoir. Two reports are indicative of the situation during that withdrawal movement. Sturmmann Hermann Laudenbach noted the following in his diary:

> . . . Florennes, 3.9.1944. We took up position with our radio cars next to the church in the center of the village. We moved into quarters with a Belgian laborer's family.
> They also prepared meals for us. Regrettably, we had to take those meals along in our mess-tins in the late afternoon since there was an unexpected change of positions. The American tanks were already sitting within five kilometers from Florennes. Then, the chase started. We raced back and forth until we finally located the right exit. Everyone was confused, including the population. At a crossroads outside of Florennes I was dropped off, ordered to guard it and to direct vehicles. I continued the trip with the last vehicle. That was Jenkner's vehicle. Unfortunately, we had lost contact with the columns. We roamed about as the only vehicle in the area which, on top of everything else, was heavily infiltrated by partisans. But we were lucky. Near Yvoir, located on the Maas, we crossed the river and then found a part of the staff. Then, the vehicles assembled. During that occasion, we paid a quick visit to the inn and drank, after a long, long time, our first dark beer. Toward the evening, the drive continued to Durnal . . .[16]

And Oberscharführer Zinflmeister wrote in his diary:

> . . . I was ordered to reconnoiter and drove with a group of Schwimmwagen [amphibious cars] past Florennes to the west. I found Regiment 25 [Waldmüller] and Untersturmführer Wienecke

AA [Pz.-Aufklärungsabteilung 12] in contact with the enemy, with small squads as a rear guard. I returned to Philippeville to report. In the evening, the Abteilung continued to roll toward the Maas. With three 'flats' on the armored vehicle we were able to move only slowly. At the fall of darkness, we even had to send off the Mahl Zug, which covered for us, because of the danger in the partisan-infested forest. Alone in the armored vehicle, all hatches locked tight, we made it undamaged through the fireworks thrown at us by the snipers. We fired all around us and dropped hand grenades outside. Thus, we reached the Maas bridge near Yvoir shortly before midnight where our Pioniers were awaiting us impatiently. We crossed over and reached Evrehailles [2.5 kilometers east of Yvoir] . . .[17]

Heeresgruppe B issued orders on 3 September 1944 regarding the refitting of the Panzerdivision:

. . . 2. and 116. Pz.-Divs., 9. and 10. SS-Pz.-Divs, and Sturm-Pz.-Abt. 217 will remain in action with their combat-ready parts. Those parts not in action will be moved by 5. Pz.-Armee to the Venlo-Arnhem-Hertogenbosch area for refitting.

To be moved into the Reich territory for complete refitting with all their elements: 1., 2., 12. SS-Pz.-Divs., SS-Pz.-Abt. 101 and 102, heavy Pz.-Abt. 503 and 654 . . .[18]

For the time being, the situation did not allow the pull-out of the divisions, with the possible exception of 1. SS-Pz.-Div. "LAH" which did not appear anymore in the front lines on the situational maps from 4 September onward.

The Divisional Kampfgruppe prepared for defense during the night of 3/4 September and on 4 September behind the Maas. The II./26 was on the right wing near Godinne (eight kilometers north of Dinant). The sector on both sides of Yvoir was defended by II./25, the adjoining sector up to Houx, by I./25. Attached to it was the Divisionsbegleitkompanie at a strength of twenty-three men which was assembled as a reserve in Evrehailles (two kilometers southeast of Yvoir). The Kampfgruppe, consisting of three weak battalions, was commanded by Obersturmbannführer Milius. The 347. Inf.-Div. was in action to the right of the "HJ" Divisional Kampfgruppe. The sector up to Namur was defended by I./861. Located in Namur was Sicherungsregiment 16 (security regiment), probably attached to 347. Inf.-Div. The 116. Pz.-Div. was adjacent on the right of that division along the Sambre. On 4 September, those two divisions left the attachment to the general command of I. SS-Panzerkorps and moved to LXXIV. A.K. Adjoining the "HJ" Division on the left, the Divisional Kampfgruppe "Das Reich" was in position on both sides of Dinant. Its left neighbor was 2. Pz.-Div.[19]

The Aufklärungsabteilung was situated in Mianoye, a small village approximately three kilometers east of Durnal, where the Divisional command post was located. The commander of II. Artillerieabteilung, Sturmbannführer Günter Neumann, was detailed to the Divisional staff as artillery liaison command officer. During the following days, 4. and 5. Batteries of his Abteilung and 4. Batterie of Werferabteilung 12 were assigned to him. It is uncertain whether they still saw action at the Maas. Since all combat-ready Panzers had already been handed over—including the Jagdpanzer IVs—the only armor-piercing weapons available to the Kampfgruppe were individual Paks and Panzerfausts.[20]

At the time the Divisional Kampfgruppe prepared for defense at the Maas, it had the following strength:

three weak battalions of 150 to 200 men each,

two Pionier Züge, without explosives,

one "Wespe" (light self-propelled field howitzer),

one mixed battery of 3 light field howitzers, 2 heavy field howitzers, and 200 shells,

ten rocket launchers with 251 rounds of ammunition,

one 7.5 cm Pak, and

one 8.8 cm Flak (anti-aircraft gun).[20a]

In the morning of 4 September, the last parts of the rear guard arrived at the bridge near Yvoir and crossed the river. Unterscharführer Eberhard Köpke was among them and wrote in a letter:

> . . . We barely made it across the Maas. Diehl raced up to the bridge at breakneck speed and delayed its demolition at the last moment. When we were on the other side, there was not a second to be lost. The first enemy armored reconnaissance vehicle was almost blown up together with the bridge . . .[21]

The demolition occurred on 4 September at 5 A.M..[22]

The war diary of Heeresgruppe B noted, regarding the progress of the fighting on 4 September, inter alia, that the enemy had established locally limited bridgeheads across the Maas near Dinant and south of Givet. Armored reconnaissance units were advancing on Ciney (eleven kilometers east of Dinant). The map "Frontal Situation" of the evening of 4 September indicates bridgeheads in Dinant, near Fumay (twenty-seven kilometers southwest of Dinant), and north of Charleville.[23]

On that day, 4 September, the other side initiated its decisions regarding the further conduct of the fighting for the longer term. General Montgomery, in person, made the following proposal to General Eisenhower in a radio message:

. . . I would like to submit certain considerations for future operations and convey my intentions to you.

1. I believe that we have reached the stage where a really powerful and bloody thrust toward Berlin would probably end the German war there.
2. We do not have sufficient supplies for two major thrusts.
3. The thrust selected must be provided with all needed supplies without any restrictions. All other operations will have to make do with what is left over.
4. There are only two possible directions of the thrust, one toward the Ruhr district, the other toward Metz and the Saar river.
5. It is my opinion that the northerly thrust to the Ruhr district will provide the best and fastest results.
6. The element of time is vital. The decision on which thrust should be carried out must be made immediately. Point 3. will then become effective.
7. If we attempt a compromise solution and divide our supplies so that neither of the two thrusts is really powerful, we will prolong the war.
8. I believe that the problem, as indicated above, is quite straightforward and clearly outlined.
9. The matter is of such vital importance that I feel you will agree that a decision on the above is required immediately.

Should you be in this area, please look me up and discuss it with me. If possible, I would be glad to see you at lunch tomorrow. I think that, especially now, I cannot leave the battlefield . . .[24]

In the afternoon of that day, British units had reached the port of Antwerp and found the docks undamaged. The docks could have easily been rendered useless through the destruction of the electrical guidance mechanisms of the floodgates. In view of the existing long supply routes, which still relied on Cherbourg and the man-made harbors north of Bayeux, this was an unexpected major success which supported General Montgomery's plan. However, General Eisenhower decided the next day that the attack by the American and British armies would be continued on a wide front despite the existing supply problems. The aim was to overrun the Westwall, cross the Rhine river, and to capture the Saarland and the Ruhr district before the remnants of the German armies had a chance to recover. He did not believe that a re-directing of the supplies would make it possible to drive a successful thrust toward Berlin. Montgomery only received news of that decision on 7 September. Eisenhower still had his headquarters in Granville, on the west coast of the Cotentin.[25] That decision hampered the establishing of bases, and slowed the advance since it could not be sustained with the available fuel supply.

On the German side, a change for the better had unexpectedly occurred during that disastrous situation. On 4 September, Generalfeldmarschall von Rundstedt had again been appointed as Supreme Commander West. That office had previously been held by Feldmarschall Model as an additional responsibility. On the same day, Reichsmarschall Hermann Göring made available six Fallschirm (paratroop) regiments which were in training. In addition, he provided several thousand men, made up of convalescents as well as Luftwaffe air and ground personnel who could no longer be used for air activities because of the shortage of fuel. With the help of these units, the 1. Fallschirmjäger-Armee, under the supreme command of Generaloberst Student, was created. However, those forces were not yet available. Instead, the remnants of 7. Armee and 5. Panzerarmee had to delay the British and American advance in Belgium until the Westwall could be manned.

On 1 September, the VII Corps of the First US Army had attacked from the area south of Hirson to the north. Its objective was Mons. After crossing the line Hirson-Vervins, the 3rd Armored Division attacked in the center. Its flanks to the east were secured by the 9th Infantry Division, to the west by the 1st Infantry Division. On 3 September, when it became clear that the German troops were withdrawing to the north and northeast, the American leadership determined from that, that they would defend themselves behind the Maas and the Sambre. The Corps was thus swung to the east and ordered to form a bridgehead across the Maas. That task was given to the 9th US Infantry Division.

As was usual, that division consisted of three infantry regiments with three battalions each, one reconnaissance unit, one communications company as well as the required supply troops. Attached to it were three heavy artillery units, two companies of a chemical warfare battalion, one tank unit, one self-propelled tank destroyer unit and, from 6 to 7 September, one reinforced tank unit of the 3rd Armored Division. In general, the American divisions formed combat groups from various branches of the forces which were combined into "Combat Teams" (CT) or "Combat Commands" (CC). A "Combat Team" of the infantry divisions was the equivalent of a reinforced infantry regiment.

In the evening of 3 September, the 9th US Infantry Division had reached the area around Philippeville, after encountering variable resistance. The orders for 4 September, issued to the 39th and 60th Combat Teams, were to advance to the Maas as quickly as possible and to establish a bridgehead across the river in their attack sector. The 47th Combat Team was to leave one battalion behind in Beaumont to secure the major crossroads, and to follow, with its bulk, to Philippeville as divisional reserve. The 39th CT reached the western bank of the Maas opposite Dinant and Houx. It came under fire from rifles, machine guns, mortars and artillery so that the assault troops were unable to reach the river bank. The attack was halted at 16.30 hours. The crossing of the river was prepared for the night. The 60th CT had been ordered to establish bridgeheads between Dinant and Givet. One battalion reached the Maas near Agimont (three kilometers north of Givet) and came under weak artillery fire. The other battalion advanced, without encountering any resistance, into the Maurenne district (nine kilometers southwest of Dinant). That CT was ordered to prepare an attack across the river for the coming night.

Reports from Belgian civilians indicated that the German troops wanted to hold the Maas with all available means. Approximately 2,000 infantrymen, a small number of Panzers, Pak and assault guns, as well as six artillery batteries were reported between Namur and Blaimont (eight kilometers southwest of Dinant).

The 9th Division ordered the crossing for 00.01 hours on 5 September. The 39th CT was to cross immediately south of Rivière (one kilometers north of Godinne), also just to the southwest of there, and immediately south of Yvoir. The attempt to cross at the northern crossing point began only at 03.00 hours since the originally available time had been insufficient to scout the condition of the river bank, and to provide boats. The II./26, in action there, sank most of the boats by machine gun fire. A company commander and twenty men of the American battalion attacking there reached the opposite river bank. Contact with them was lost, they were probably captured. Further to the south, between Godinne and Yvoir, the 3rd Battalion of that CT managed to cross without initially encountering any resistance. When it advanced further inland, it came under massive machine gun, mortar, and artillery fire which lasted all day. The 2nd Battalion was able to establish a bridgehead south of Yvoir at 19.00 hours. All attempts to set up an infantry bridge at one of the crossing points were foiled by intensive fire from the east bank of the river. The 60th CT formed two bridgeheads north of Givet. It suffered heavy losses from Panzer and infantry fire.[26]

The preceding accounts from the "Report of Operations" of the 9th US Infantry Division do not confirm the notation in the war diary of 5. Panzerarmee according to which the enemy had been able to cross the Maas with tanks by way of an undamaged bridge near Dinant on 4 September.[27]

Available reports from members of the "HJ" Division indicate that the enemy had, apparently unnoticed, established a bridgehead during the night, southeast of Houx. At approximately 15.00 hours on 5 September, the Divisionsbegleitkompanie received orders from Obersturmbannführer Milius to attack the enemy, of unknown strength, reported in the forest southeast of Houx and to drive him back across the Maas. Unterscharführer Leo Freund reported on that battle:

> On 5.9.1944, the Divisionsbegleitkompanie was given orders by
> Obersturmbannführer Milius to attack the enemy who had crossed

the Maas south of Houx, and to destroy the bridgehead he had established. The enemy had established himself in a large wooded area which extended to the Maas. Our Kompanie counted only twenty-three men. We had no information on the enemy. We drove with our Schwimm-wagens from Purnode (4.5 kilometers southeast of Yvoir) through pastures and grain fields to the edge of the wood, which we reached without encountering any problems. Immediately behind the closest trees, to the right of the lane, was a large farm. To our surprise, it was free of the enemy. At that time I had no premonition that the farm would be of significance to me later.

We continued our drive into the wood. The path led straight ahead. A bend to the right could be spotted some 300 meters ahead. Just before the curve, a small house stood to the left of the lane, in front of it was a grass-covered clearing. We reached that house unchallenged. However, when the first vehicle turned into the curve, all hell broke loose with a bang. The point vehicle was immediately shot to pieces. Even so, the crew, although wounded, was able to leap into the ditch and find cover behind the trees. They even opened fire on the enemy located in front of us. The second car, in which I was riding, came to a halt immediately next to the house. All of us immediately jumped from the vehicles and sought cover. After the first shock, two of us ran over to the wounded. We took over the MG just in time to repel the enemy attacking us from the road. However, all of us continued to be under fire. Suddenly, we realized that the fire came from the small house. We found ourselves in a ticklish situation. However, Unterscharführer Tödter, who had been in the last vehicle, fully understood it. By himself, he crept to the left of the lane in a curve through the woods. Then, he had to cross the clearing, some seventy to eighty meters wide, in order to approach the house from the rear. I spotted him at that very moment! I yelled and simultaneously fired on the house. The others, too, realized what was happening. The house came under concentrated fire. Tödter, however, raced with long leaps toward the house. He hurled several hand grenades through the windows, came around the house, threw more hand grenades into the windows, and then it was quiet inside the house. We then had a pause to catch our breath. It did, however, not last long. The enemy started to cover us with mortar fire. We were forced to pull back to the edge of the wood. After that lengthy mortar attack, the enemy probably did not count on any more resistance and attacked. However, we had expected the attack, and had taken up favorable positions. We opened fire very late and were able to repulse the enemy attack, causing him severe losses.

The farm located at the edge of the wood then became the center of our defense. It was inhabited by approximately twenty people, men and women.

In the late afternoon, a guard battalion of the Wehrmacht (no longer very strong in numbers) joined us. Together with it, we attacked again. They were generally older men. The attack did not move very far so that we had to pull back to the edge of the wood and the farm. Even during the evening hours we realized that we were under extremely well aimed artillery fire, to the point where individual men moving about were fired at. It was obvious to us that an observer was able to look into our positions. Since the farm was under fire, and the civilians were thus endangered, Unterscharführer Tödter received orders from Obersturmführer Fritz Guntrum to collect all civilians and install them in a secure cellar. The farm had a nice cellar, many steps led down to it. There, the civilians were safe from the shells, and we hoped to have overcome the observer by moving there. Still, the fire continued. To us, that was almost inexplicable . . .[28]

On 5 September, the Aufklärungsabteilung scouted in a southerly direction and established contact to 2. SS-Panzerdivision. The leader of the scouting party, Oberscharführer August Zinflmeister, wrote about that in his diary:

. . . I drove south with a Schwimmwagen scouting party. Reconnaissance, and establishing contact were the objectives. In the wood near Celles [seven kilometers southeast of Dinant] we encountered tree obstacles. We fired at them and went around. Carefully, we crept ahead. Everywhere, signs of partisan ambushes on German vehicles. Bent nails on the road caused flats on two cars. We pulled up in a circle, fired on partisan observers, repaired the flats, set fire to a hiding place and made our way via Ciergnon [nine kilometers southeast of Celles] to 'Das Reich' Division located at Javingue [eight kilometers southeast of Givet]. The return drive was without problems. In the afternoon, patrols via Krupet, Dorinne (near Durnal), etc. Other than that, in readiness at the Abteilung command post . . .[29]

On 5 September 1944 the supreme command of 5. Panzerarmee handed over command of the units assigned to it to the supreme command of 7. Armee. It was pulled out and moved to the Strasbourg area for refitting. Based on the available strength reports, Heeresgruppe B recommended that 1. and 12. SS-Panzerdivisions be pulled out if Supreme Command West were able to provide replacements for them. That was not possible, largely because the enemy had pushed back the securing forces of 347. Inf.-Div., 116. Pz.-Div. and 47. Inf.-Div. along the line Namur-Gembloux (fifteen kilometers northwest of Namur) to the northeast. Available reports indicated that he had penetrated into Namur with fifty to sixty tanks.[30]

Because of the unclear situation in the Maas sector between Godinne, where the right wing of the "HJ" Division was located, and Namur and further down-river to Huy, the Divisional commander deployed a scouting party from the Aufklärungsabteilung. The leader of the scouting party, Untersturmführer Theo Flanderka, reported:

> In the evening of 5 September I was ordered to report to the Divisional commander. He briefed me on the situation and specified my mission as follows: While it was still dark, I would drive with a motorized scouting party from the northern border of our sector along the Maas to the north. During that drive I would determine which German units were deployed to secure the sector up to Namur. Further, the condition of the Maas bridges would be determined. Reportedly, they had been blown up, including the bridge in Namur.
>
> From Namur on I would follow the Maas along its southern bank to the east. At Huy, or east of it, I would cross the river by one of the undamaged bridges and scout from there to the west until encountering the enemy. I would attempt to determine the enemy strength and direction of thrust and then return to the Division by the fastest possible route.
>
> With that order, issued by the Divisional commander in person, I returned to the Kompanie in the darkness of night. The men had already gone to sleep. I awakened the three VW crews picked for the scouting party and described our mission to them. Our vehicles were refueled and I went to sleep. Many thoughts raced through my head before I could find some quiet. One factor, in particular, caused me quite a headache: I could not take along a radio transmitter/receiver since none was left in working order. But how would I send a report if I was thirty or even fifty kilometers away from the Division? Should I send back a single vehicle? Or should I wait until the whole scouting party could start the return trip? Depending on circumstances, several hours might be in between. It was decisive that the report should be received as quickly as possible. With those thoughts on my mind I finally fell asleep.
>
> It was still dark when the scouting party was ready to move out. Most of the men were veteran comrades in arms, much tested, whom I could fully trust. I had two Unter-führers with me. I have forgotten the name of one of them, but the other was Unterscharführer Dupiralla. Without much talk, we started out. It was cool at that hour of the morning, but the clear starry sky indicated that we would have a

nice, warm, late summer day ahead. We drove westward, some five kilometers to the Maas. Then our real mission started. The road in the direction of Namur followed the winding river exactly, and quite often ran directly along the bank. The river itself could hardly be seen since it was covered by veils of fog. Other than that, the coming dawn did not yet allow a clear field of vision. It was absolutely quiet. Now and then, we encountered German guards belonging to various units. Even when we approached Namur, the sun had not yet come up far enough to allow clearer visibility. Vehicle noise could be heard from the northern section of the city, but only intermittently since the easterly wind carried the sound away from us. Approaching the Maas bridge, we met a few German soldiers. However, they gave an impression more of being stragglers than a combat-ready unit. Still, we were directed to a command post where a Hauptmann [captain] briefed us on the situation. All appeared quiet on the opposite Maas bank, only occasionally did they hear vehicle noises. The Maas bridge had been blown up. Large pieces of the bridge had collapsed in such a manner, however, that a usable roadway had been maintained below the surface.

Then we turned east, following the course of the Maas. There was no sign of German troops. It was as quiet as inside a church. We carefully approached the city of Huy. There, too, deep silence, not a soul in the streets. At the south side of the Maas bridge sat a German Panzer. When we got closer, we found out that it belonged to a Wehrmacht unit. It had got stuck, with track damage, at the exact spot where it was to take over guarding the bridge. The Panzer commander, an Unteroffizier, told us that the bridge had been prepared to be blown up. There was one group of Pioniers left, right at the entrance to the bridge. We quickly found the Pioniers. They reported that the section of the city north of the bridge was absolutely quiet. Carefully, we crossed the bridge to the north. The streets were deserted. We drove on to the village of Wanze and turned west. In the meantime, daylight had come. We did not want to get too far away from the Maas and moved along the road in the direction of Lavoir-Hingeou. The quiet in the villages was most noticeable. Now and then we merely spotted faces behind the closed windows, but they pulled back as soon as we got closer.

It was my opinion that the enemy spearheads would approach Namur from the north and northwest. Thus, it was important to quickly scout that area. We approached the city from the northeast by way of Gelbressée. The terrain was hilly and partly wooded. I looked for a spot from where I could observe Namur and the Maas. After we had crossed a ridge, that observation spot was found. But, what I saw, caused me great alarm:

A few hundred meters southwest of us lay that destroyed Maas bridge which we had already seen at dawn. We did not believe our eyes: the Americans had made that bridge passable again, making use of the parts of the bridge which had only dropped slightly. While one vehicle after the other slowly crossed the bridge to the south, engineers were setting up a pontoon bridge next to it. We observed ambulances, trucks, self-propelled guns, and then tanks. The stream of vehicles continued. Several spotter aircraft circled over Namur and flew from there into southerly and southeasterly directions.

In a flash I realized what had happened: while we were driving down the Maas to Huy at dawn, enemy spearheads must have crossed the Maas at Namur. If that estimate of time was correct, however, the enemy tank spearhead had to be to the rear of our Divisional command post already. Now the fact that I had no radio with my scouting party came back to haunt us. Because of the confused situation, I decided to drive back immediately with the whole scouting party, by the fastest possible route. The road led slightly downhill, with several curves, toward a small village we had passed two hours previously. Innocently, we approached the village, this time from the other direction. After passing the last curve, the village was some 100 meters in front of us. But how it had changed! White pieces of cloth were hanging from all windows. The whole of the population seemed to have congregated in the village main street. American vehicles, tanks, jeeps and trucks sat in the street. We had no time left to think. There was no way to leave the road. Only one way to proceed was left: Full throttle, and right through it! Fortunately, the American soldiers were involved in fraternizing to the point where they were anything but ready for action. By the time they had figured out what was happening, we had already passed through. Several machine gun salvos, which they sent after us, caused no damage. The next village was only a few kilometers away. I was convinced it would be free of the enemy. We approached the first houses along an uphill road curving to the left, under cover of a man-high embankment on its left side. Only at the end of the curve, at the first houses, could we look down the village main street. We were driving at high speed. When I had almost reached the first houses, a shock ran through all my limbs: Here, too, any number of 'Amis', fraternizing, parking their vehicles. Immediately ahead of me, some thirty meters away, a half-track sat across the street. With the best will in the world, there was no way to get through. So, nothing was left but turning around and getting out of there. The 'Ami' in the armored vehicle had, of course, spotted us and quickly opened fire on the street with his machine gun. He hit our second car and wounded two men. We assembled under cover of the embankment, but one man, Unterscharführer Dupiralla, was missing. He had jumped off the vehicle to the left when the enemy fire started while the rest of the crew had put down their heads and stayed in the car, relying on the cover of the embankment on the side of the street. There, he had found cover in a ditch leading away from the road. He was apparently not wounded. There was no answer to our shouts. In the meantime, the armored car started to follow us. Pushing our VW to the limit, we raced off, back to the woods. At a curve from where we could observe the road in both directions, we called a short halt to determine the situation, study the maps and decide on future action. The two wounded had suffered only minor injuries and we could look after them. One tire had been shot out, other than that the vehicles were serviceable.

We were trapped between two villages in enemy hands. There was no country lane leading away from the road, and a cross-country drive was impossible. Only one course of action was left: to trust the element of surprise once again and drive through the village we had previously passed one more time, coming from the other direction. We approached cautiously. Outside the village, still under cover, we called a short halt and observed with binoculars. The vehicles had been parked, the street was open, no guards could be spotted. The smoke grenades, which I had never needed throughout the war, now came in handy. We passed through the village in no time, without a single shot being fired. A few kilometers later, a narrow lane led from the road to the north. That had to be our salvation. I wanted to pass the enemy spearhead in a wide bend to the north and east and then get back to the Maas. Our orientation was more by compass than map. South of Hingeou we swung to the east. We drove around the village of Héron to the south and gathered the impression that it had not been occupied by the enemy. Based on that, we were hopeful that Huy was still free of the enemy. However, we found out differently when we approached the city. We were almost spotted again. Again, we swung off to the north and drove in the direction of Liège.

Hours had passed in the meantime. One tire was flat and had to be repaired. My driver, who was among the wounded, needed a break. After a short rest we approached Liège in the early hours of the evening. A sense of threat enveloped the city. Hundreds of people were standing in the street, obviously awaiting the arrival of the Americans. How was I to find the Maas bridge in this large, unknown city? I picked up two civilians and sat them on the hood, demanding that they lead us to the bridge by the shortest possible route. It appeared that the German troops had already withdrawn from Liège, there was not a German uniform to be seen anywhere. Occasionally, white pieces of cloth had been hung from windows. Suddenly, in the falling dusk, we spotted a member of the German labor service, who stood guard, in a steel helmet and with a rifle, in an archway. The conversation with him brought out the fact that his administration had pulled out. Quite obviously, he had been forgotten. There was nothing left for him to guard. We took the seventeen-year-old lad on board, making only slow progress through the milling crowd. It felt like Christmas when the undamaged Maas bridge was finally in front of us. There was no sign of a German guard at the bridge. Heaving a sigh of relief, we crossed the bridge. Wildly waving German soldiers awaited us at the southern bank. We had no time to wonder why, since, at that very moment, the bridge behind us blew up with a terrific explosion. We were still sitting in our vehicles when the rocks fell back to the ground all around us.

In the section of Liège south of the Maas, several staffs were still located. Everyone was ready to leave. No-one knew any particulars about the whereabouts of our 12. SS-Panzerdivision. It was late in the night when we finally found our unit again . . . [31]

It is indicative of the circumstances during the rearguard fighting in Northern France and in Belgium that the firm and combat-tested organization of the units was ripped apart. Parts of units were assigned to other units and the command structure of the divisions under general commands was frequently changed. Obviously, the Bataillon of 347. Inf.-Div., located south of the Maas near Namur, did not know what had occurred north of the river in the city in the course of the day. Reports of American tanks penetrating into Namur on 5 September did reach the Heeresgruppe by way of 7. Armee, but not I. SS-Panzerkorps and the "HJ" Division. The reason for that may be found in the elimination of the supreme command of 5. Panzer-armee. The consequences were grave. Into the picture of that day must also be added the inadequate destruction of the Maas bridge in Namur as well as the lack of long-range portable radio equipment for the Flanderka scouting party. The shortage of personnel prevented the scouting party from being reinforced to the point where it could have sent back reports at certain intervals. During that uncertain situation, to which partisans contributed, two vehicles would have had to be sent for each report.

Without any premonition of the threat in its right flank, the "HJ" Division ordered Kampfgruppe Milius on 6 September to eliminate the American bridgehead near Houx. Throughout the rest of the sector of the Divisional Kampfgruppe, the enemy had been unable to gain a foothold on the eastern bank of the Maas. At 04.00 hours, Obersturmbannführer Milius issued an order to the commander of the Divisionsbegleitkompanie, Obersturmführer Guntrum, to attack with the remnants of "Hoppe", "Neumann" and "Braus" companies—probably part of a guard battalion—and another guard company, commanded by Oberleutnant (1st lieutenant) Kraas. The attack on the enemy in the wood near Houx would come from the northeast at first light and he was to be thrown back across the Maas. According to prisoner statements, approximately 800 Americans were located in the wood, equipped with heavy and super-heavy machine guns, mortars and light anti-tank guns. The attack started at 07.20 hours. Kompanie Kraas, 107 men strong, had not yet arrived. After heavy losses to both sides, the attack stalled at 11.30 hours. At 13.00 hours, Obersturmbannführer Milius, based on a directive from the Division, ordered disengagement from the enemy and the formation of a blocking line at the southern edge of Purnode (3.5 kilometers northeast of Houx).[32]

The "Report of Operations" of the 9th Infantry Division confirms that, on 6 September, only one bridgehead each existed north and south of Dinant. In the northern one—near Houx—fought two battalions of the 39th CT. They were able to enlarge the bridgehead only ". . . against determined resistance . . ." It was impossible to construct a bridge across the river. In order to support the attack by the 9th Infantry Division, the VII Corps put into action an armored combat group of the 3rd Armored Division, Task Force "KING", in the flank and rear of Divisional Kampfgruppe "HJ". The mass of the American tank division remained in and near Namur, without fuel. TF "KING" marched from Namur initially along the road Namur-Marche in a southeasterly direction.

Toward noon, a messenger of a scouting party of the Aufklärungs-abteilung burst into the farm house in Durnal where the Divisional command post was located. He reported that a scouting party had encountered an enemy tank column on the road Namur-Marche in the vicinity of Assesse (five kilometers northeast of Durnal). It was approaching from the direction of Namur and was moving in the direction of Marche. That report appeared unbelievable to the Ia. He ordered the messenger to drive back immediately. His scouting party was to maintain contact with the enemy and report on his further activities.

The Aufklärungsabteilung was located in Mianoye, some three kilometers east of Durnal. Oberscharführer August Zinflmeister reported what happened during those minutes:

> . . . While we looked after the equipment and cleaned our weapons, approximately twenty-five 'Ami' tanks rolled past the house. The neighbor next door betrayed us. Soon, single Shermans rolled toward us. After the third hit, the turret of our eight-wheeled recon-naissance vehicle was blown off and the armored vehicle, under which the three of us were still lying, had caught on fire.
>
> As well, one Schwimmwagen after the other caught on fire in the hail of shells. The driver, Buchmeier, had run off into the gardens

before the 'hail' started. We tried, in long jumps, to get through. I landed, right away, exactly in front of a Sherman, whose commander yelled at me: 'Hands up!' The tank pursued me, firing, as I took off. During that 'race for my life', jumping and rolling over, I reached a forest after racing across some 300 meters of pasture, sustaining only two grazing shots. Krüger and Oberstedt, in the meantime, were knocked down, wounded, and were taken prisoner for a time. They were able to escape during the following night.

Crossing the wood, I encountered, one after the other, five or six stragglers from our company. We moved, together, in a northerly direction. We crawled through a potato field, with difficulty, toward a road along which 'Ami' columns were rolling. We jumped up, our weapons ready to fire. In the village square of les Fontaines (two kilometers north-northeast of Mianoye, Author), we avoided the enemy column by running right through the partisan assembly, through gardens, along field and forest lanes. We reached our supply troops, to the north of us, by way of Huy . . .[33]

A messenger of the Aufklärungsabteilung immediately raced from Mianoye to Durnal. He arrived there a few minutes after the messenger from the scouting party had been sent back and reported that an American tank column had turned off the main road from Namur and was approaching Durnal. At that very moment, Oberführer Kurt Meyer arrived at the Divisional command post. He had only just left the Siebken Bataillon. He ordered that the Kampfgruppen, located at the Maas, immediately disengage from the enemy. Then they were to, in delaying fighting, withdraw to the ridge of hills on both sides of Emptinne (four kilometers northeast of Ciney). The Ia sent messengers and orderly officers with the respective orders to the units of the Division. The operations unit of the Divisional staff and all the others present at the command post grabbed their weapons and equipment and jumped into their vehicles. Lunch, ready to eat, remained on the table.

The command post was located at the southern edge of the village. The four or five VWs drove as fast as possible cross-country down the slope to the south and assembled on a country road just outside the northern entrance to the village of Spontin. Inside the village, that road joined the road from Ciney to Yvoir. A choice had to be made of two possibilities. The staff could turn off to the right, make its way to the Kampfgruppe in action near Houx, and then break out together with it. Or it could drive on, turning to the left, in the direction of Ciney and thus escape the threatening encirclement. The Ia and the First Orderly Officer, Hauptsturmführer Ruprecht Heinzelmann thought that the first possibility would be the best solution. The commander decided on the second. Hauptsturmführer Heinzelmann took over the point, the commander and his 04, Untersturmführer Kölln, rode in the second VW. The Ia rode in the third VW, driven by Sturmmann Helmut Schmieding. One or two more cars followed.

The village of Spontin is located in a deeply-cut valley. Most of the houses lie staggered up the steep southern slope to the adjoining high plain. To the north of the street runs a creek. Behind it is a park, enclosed by a wall made of natural rocks. The first car had already driven through the center of the village when a tank gun was fired in the valley. Its shell hit the corner of a house which Hauptsturmführer Heinzelmann was just passing. The vehicles at the point stopped immediately. Their crews jumped out, seeking cover anywhere. For a while, a cloud of dust cut off visibility. Then, a Sherman could be spotted, sitting on a higher road leading down from the hill along the slope, at a right angle. Behind it, another Sherman could be seen. Both tanks stopped, without firing again. The members of the staff tried to find cover in the houses. The doors were barricaded from the inside, as were the passages to the stairways made of rocks, leading up the slope through the gardens. Using all their force, the men were able to push open a few front doors and to make their way through the houses, away from the street, into the upper part of the village. Located above the western exit of the village was a small wooded area which drew the stragglers like a magnet. They had been joined by Sturmbannführer Arnold Jürgensen, who was acting as the commander of the Panzerregiment, and Obersturmführer Rudolf von Ribbentrop, his adjutant. They were on their way from Herbestal, where the Panzerregiment assembled, to report to the Divisional staff and to receive new orders. In Huy, they had met Hauptsturmführer Rolf Möbius with a Tiger of the heavy SS-Panzerabteilung 101. Up to the Divisional command post in Durnal they had encountered neither German nor enemy soldiers. They had arrived there at the moment of departure and joined the column of the staff.[33a] The Divisional commander, his orderly officer, his driver, and Hauptsturmführer Heinzelmann were missing. The Ia and his driver went off to search for them.

They stopped at various spots inside the village, half-way down the hill, and shouted the name of the commander. At the church they encountered a man clad in a blue overall who disappeared quickly when he spotted them. Other than that, the village seemed deserted. There was no answer to their shouts. From the village street below, the noise from the running VW motors could be heard, then the rattle of tank tracks. The two men observed the American tanks rolling into the village, jubilantly greeted by the inhabitants who had come out of their hiding places. Hubert Meyer and Helmut Schmieding had to return to the wood without success. Since none of the missing had answered, it was assumed that they had already left the village and had been able to escape across the hill.

Later, it became known that Hauptsturmführer Heinzelmann had been wounded in the leg by a shrapnel. He had managed to drag himself along

the village street. At the important intersection he found the car of Sturmbannführer Jürgensen. Fortunately, the motor was running. The car was facing west so that Heinzelmann, without having to maneuver it, was able to
drive off. One of the tanks fired its machine gun after him, but missed. Later
the car was found by Sturmbannführer Gerd Bremer, stopped at a crossroads. Heinzelmann had collapsed unconscious behind the steering wheel.
In front of his seat was a large pool of blood. The physician of the Aufklärungsabteilung looked after the seriously wounded man and had him
transported to a hospital by ambulance. The injured lower leg could not be
saved and had to be amputated.

Oberführer Kurt Meyer reported on the events after the fire from the
Sherman as he had experienced them:

> . . . A flying dive took me across a yard gate and a wire fence farther
> back which separated the yard from the garden. But, what a sur-
> prise! I was stuck in a terrible trap! An escape behind the row of
> houses was impossible, the yard had been built deep into the slop-
> ing hill and was bordered by a high wall. Even as I raced toward it, it
> became clear to me that I must not climb over the wall if I did not
> want to be used as a target by the Americans.
>
> First, I had to take full cover. A chicken-coop offered the only
> chance—I jumped inside! A body flew across the wire fence. Max
> Bornhöft joined me just in time. Then, both of us were sitting in the
> trap. In any case, the barn covered us from being spotted by the
> enemy. We were hoping that we would find the way to our comrades
> during darkness.
>
> Loud shouting came from the street—the population cheered
> the Americans. The tanks rolled past. From the house next door I
> heard an agitated exchange of words and picked out the name
> Kölln. I did not see Obersturmführer Kölln again. His name ended
> up on the list of losses.
>
> By then, it was 14.00 hours. Light rain was falling on the roof of
> the barn. I could not take it anymore. I had to know what was hap-
> pening in the street. Hugging the ground, I crawled to the wire
> fence. I had barely reached the corner of the barn when I experi-
> enced some of the most exciting seconds of the war.
>
> Several partisans came over to the fence and interrogated an old
> farmer. They probably wanted to know whether the farmer had seen
> any German soldiers on the farm. The farmer shook his head. With
> clenched teeth, I was lying only a few meters away from the parti-
> sans. They were leaning against the fence, searching the slope with
> their eyes. Would these be my last minutes? My hand firmly held the
> grip of the pistol. They would not get me without a fight. A nettle
> bush was my cover.

Yells and shots drew the men to the neighboring farm. The life of a comrade had found an end. We felt somewhat more secure since the farm had been searched. Also, we hoped that the rain would keep away the curious. Minutes turned into hours. We were glad about the weather. Suddenly, a stupid look crept into our faces. The chickens were gathering outside the barn, wanting to get into the coop. But, they did not want to share their home with us. They wanted us out. That story could not end well, and thus, what had to happen, did. The little old farmer was standing, baffled, at the fence and then tried to chase his feathered flock into the barn. But, the beasts were stubborn, they wanted their domicile all for themselves.

Curious, the farmer poked his head into the barn. He should not have done that. Even before he could open his mouth, he was sitting on an old barrel in a dark corner. He had become the third man in our little community, and stared, frightened, at our pistols. That was a nice mess. The situation had become more complicated. If our luck was really bad, the farmer's wife would join us as well. Surely, she would miss her husband soon and start looking for him.

We decided to let the old man go. He promised to keep quiet and not to make contact with the partisans. With quick steps, he shuffled off.

Of course, we did not take his promises at face value. As soon as the old man was gone, we climbed up the wall, jumped and landed—right in front of the command post of the partisans!

I had really not expected that surprise. It could not be much worse. The partisans lived in the cellar boiler room of the church. A young guy stood in the cellar door, enjoying his first American cigarettes.

Heavily armed partisans were coming up the cellar stairs. Like weasels, we leapt, crawled, sneaked and ran across the cemetery. Old graves and head stones saved us from being spotted.

We ended up near the compost heap in a corner of the cemetery. Since there could be no thought of further escape for the time being, I covered Max with old wreaths and asked him to watch the approach to the church. I was planning to crawl under cover behind a few bushes.

A yell rang out across the cemetery. That kind of yell indicated extreme danger. Even as I turned, I spotted two policemen on the stairs and was facing the muzzles of their weapons. The policemen were baffled for a moment since they had not spotted Max. Like a flash, I pulled up my pistol into their direction and made as if to fire. All that took place in fractions of a second. The policemen took full cover. Get way, quickly! I raced toward the southern edge of the cemetery and was again facing the muzzle of a carbine. The gunman stood in a doorway and took off when I ran directly toward him, threatening with my pistol. We were surrounded. The old man had alerted everybody. I jumped across the cemetery wall and landed on the village street, four meters down. Max was panting behind me.

Unbelievable, how nimble one can be when one's dear life is at stake! The street was climbing up the slope. My lungs seemed about to burst. Bullets whistled past our ears. I turned and fired a few shots down the street. Max was lying on the ground—he had been hit. My shots had forced the brave freedom fighters into cover. I turned toward the exit from the village and spotted, just in time, two more partisans guarding the exit. Where to? I glimpsed a small door, pushed to the wall by a large piece of rock. So that my disappearance would not be noticed by the partisans, I took full cover behind the door.

Completely exhausted, I squatted in a corner of the stable and spied through the cracks in the door. The partisans arrived a few moments later. Excitedly, they ran to and fro. Every bush was searched. They were unable to explain my disappearance and put the blame on each other.

One of the partisans loudly demanded that I leave my hiding place and surrender. At the same time, he promised to respect international law and to hand me over to the Americans. I did not react to his demands.

My pistol grew ever heavier in my fist. There was, once, a time when we had sworn ourselves never to be taken prisoner alive. The terrible experiences in Russia had prompted that. Now, the time had come. One bullet was in the barrel, another in the magazine. Would I now live up to my oath? Or was it valid only for the eastern front? Were the circumstances here not totally different? Minutes passed. Time and again, my eyes glanced at the metal in my hand. For a moment, I though of my family and our unborn child. It was difficult, very difficult, to make a decision. The partisans were standing only a few meters from my hiding place. I could study their faces. Some had grim, brutal features—others, instead, looked like harmless citizens who had, possibly, weapons pushed into their hands only minutes ago.

The leader of the group again demanded my surrender. A boy of some fourteen years stood next to him. Obviously, they were father and son. The rascal held a carbine in his hands. Suddenly, the boy became excited and pointed at my door and the piece of rock which had been rolled away. He had understood the situation. Where the rock had sat, the ground was dry. Thus, the rock must have been moved only a few minutes ago. His father renewed his demand for my surrender.

A shot slammed through the door. Hand grenades were demanded. Two more bullets splintered the wood of the door and forced me further into the corner.

I addressed the father and yelled at him: 'My weapon is pointed at your boy! Will you keep your promise?' Immediately, he pulled his son close to him and repeated his promise to treat me correctly.

It was all over. My only hope was in a counterattack by my comrades. I threw the magazine into one corner, the pistol into another. What a wretched feeling it was being taken prisoner!

Slowly, I opened the door and walked toward the leader of the partisans. Some of the guys immediately wanted to pounce on me. Several pistols and carbines were pointed at me. Not a word was spoken. I paid no heed to the threatening weapons—I searched out the eyes of the father. With a movement of his hand he forced his companions to lower their weapons. Grumbling, they gave in to his demand and escorted us to the church. The leader of the partisans told me that he had been in Germany during the World War as a laborer and had experienced only good things there. Also, he had no desire to lead a gang of murderers. Still, he admitted that it was difficult to prevent the young men from committing murder and manslaughter.

Max Bornhöft was still lying in the street. He had taken a bad hit to the upper leg. We carried him to the police station where he was immediately given a tetanus shot. The village physician displayed a positive readiness to help. He wished us a speedy return home.

The two policemen then brought handcuffs out of their pockets and put them on my wrists. I thought I would sink to my knees from the pain. Those fellows almost cut off my wrists. The chain links cut ever deeper into my flesh. Expectantly, they looked into my face. The chaps must have practiced that torture frequently before, since it was obvious they were waiting for my shouts of pain. Max looked at me and shouted: 'Oh, these bastards!'

The leader returned to the room and ordered me to be led off. We stumbled across the cemetery and ended up in the boiler room, the hiding place of the partisans . . .[34]

For those hiding in the small wooded area, the situation was totally unclear. They could not observe the village street. From the noise of the tanks they concluded that the tanks were moving on to the west. However, it was possible that Americans had remained in the village and that more troops were moving in. Between the houses and the gardens, civilians in blue overall were milling about. Obviously, that was the "uniform" of the partisans. However, they had no badges on their overalls. In the pastures above the small wood, "blue men" also appeared. They were probably looking for stragglers. Suddenly, the stillness which had fallen was ripped apart by a terrible scream. It came from the vicinity of the church, and sounded like a scream of death. Had another straggler been murdered? The hiding men only had pistols and a few rounds of ammunition with them. The machine pistols and hand grenades had been left in the cars. Another search for the missing men was hopeless. A "blue man" approached the wood from the village below and shouted: "Are German soldiers in the wood? Come out!" He received no answer. In the course of the afternoon, a horse-drawn column apparently drove into the village. Some shots were fired, but quiet returned soon, after some loud yelling.

It appeared hopeless to leave the hiding place during the day. It was probably best to wait for the night and to keep still until then. Toward evening, rain set in which would be favorable for the night march ahead.

In the meantime, German troops would have pulled back from the Maas. Thus, the only direction in which to march was east. The maps had remained in the vehicles. Having studied the maps, the Ia remembered that a rail line ran through Spontin in a generally easterly direction. It could be used as guidance. The fully motorized American troops had to use the road and surely did not guard the rail line. The partisans had to be looked after.

The group started out around midnight. They were concerned about the unknown fate of the missing. But, maybe, they had already reached safety. As the men marched in line across the pasture behind their hiding place, the sleeping cows woke up and galloped off. There was no movement in the village. The rail line was soon reached. The march continued on the railroad ties. After some hours, the stragglers approached a brightly lit railroad station. On the way to the station, the railroad tracks led across a bridge over a narrow river, some ten meters below. If they wanted to bypass the station, they had to swim across the river. It seemed more promising to continue marching down the tracks. And, indeed, it worked out. It was certain that railway employees were watching us from behind the windows and reported the event to the next station. But, so far, there were probably no American troops there which could be brought in. After marching further, suddenly a challenge: "Halt! Who goes there? Password?" German soldiers! They were a guard from the Siebken Bataillon, posted at a railway crossing. The Bataillon had been able to withdraw to the east on motorized vehicles when the order reached it at noon. The general command of I. SS-Panzerkorps had ordered the Bataillon to set up a thin network of guard positions in the Ciney area. For the time being, the stragglers were safe. The Aufklärungsabteilung, too, had already arrived in the vicinity. The Ia ordered Sturmbannführer Bremer to reconnoiter toward Spontin and search for the missing. A scouting party, consisting of two VWs, was forced by enemy fire to turn back even before reaching Spontin. Another scouting party managed to make it into the village. They learned from some civilians that a dead officer had been lying in the street. Another one, with a medal around his neck, had been transported away, together with another soldier, by the Americans. The dead man was probably Untersturmführer Kölln, the two others, the Divisional commander and his driver.[35]

The Divisional commander described in his book—*Grenadiere* (*Grenadiers*)—what happened to him and his driver after being captured. The Belgian policemen handed them over to an American unit which took them to Namur. Outside the prison, a civilian shot dead the seriously wounded Rottenführer Max Bornhöft. Thanks to the intervention by an American officer, Oberführer Kurt Meyer was taken to a Catholic hospital and given medical care. The other soldiers of the Waffen-SS and of the Fallschirm unit who had been part of the transport, were, according to a German sergeant in the medical corps, shot dead by partisans.[36]

The 9th Infantry Division attempted to construct a bridge across the Maas in the vicinity of Yvoir. Because of fierce German machine gun fire, the work proceeded only slowly. Toward evening, the "KING" TF of the 3rd Armored Division, part of which had driven through Spontin, established contact with the American bridgehead near Houx. The TF added one battalion of the 39th Infantry Regiment and advanced along the road along the river bank to the outskirts of Dinant. That enabled the parts of the Kampfgruppe Milius located north of Houx to disengage from the enemy and to withdraw to the east.

Shortly after 13.00 hours, the Divisionsbegleitkompanie received a report that strong enemy tank forces were located in Durnal and Dorinne. One half hour later, the way from Purnode to the east was already blocked by twenty tanks and several armored personnel carriers. The Kompanie trickled in small groups through the enemy lines to the east. At noon on 7 September, one officer, three NCOs and seven men assembled in Corbion (4.5 kilometers south of Ciney). Not all members of the Kompanie had managed to make their way through. Unterscharführer Freund reported:

... When we had almost reached the first houses of Purnode, we spotted a large tank column coming from Dorinne in the east, rolling toward the village. At the same time we observed our comrades racing up the slowly rising terrain on the other side of the houses. We also saw the tanks firing at them. The two of us wanted to follow them quickly. We ran toward the northern exit from the village, past the last houses and crossed the street. At that moment, we saw the first tanks coming along that village street. Fortunately, we spotted a foxhole a few meters off the road and jumped into it. The whole tank column rattled past and we were not spotted. Soon after that column, more vehicles showed up, and that continued without interruption for the whole day. Since we had still not been detected, we were hoping for darkness, since it was almost evening. But it turned out differently. A passing column suddenly stopped. The vehicles veered into the pastures to the left and right, probably to keep the narrow road open. An armored personnel carrier drove exactly over our foxhole. It was our bad luck that an 'Ami' sat on the rear of that vehicle, legs dangling, staring at the ground. We sat in our foxhole, looking up, and clearly saw the frightened impression on the American's face. An awful yelling followed, followed by sudden silence. We expected oval hand grenades and concentrated on how to throw them out again immediately. But nothing happened. We even had time to bury our weapons in the sandy soil, and still nothing happened. The situation became downright uncanny. Since darkness was already falling, I risked a glance across the edge. What I saw then bewildered me. Our foxhole was surrounded by a least fifty men, forming a complete circle. All had their weapons at their hips, ready to fire, and were very slowly closing in on our foxhole. I almost felt like laughing. I stood up, raised my hands, almost all of my upper body rising above the edge. Wilfried Tödter also stood up, his hands raised. Then, several 'Amis' came over and helped us out of the foxhole since our limbs had turned stiff. All the others held their positions, ready to fire. Only when they had determined that we were unarmed did they pounce on us. Within seconds, we had nothing left in our pockets, not even a handkerchief. Rings and watches were the first items which were taken from us with a sure and fast snatch. Then, we spotted the armored personnel carrier which had driven over our foxhole and sat a few meters further on. It was an ambulance vehicle. We spent the night with that unit, under close guard. We were all-the-more surprised when an armored personnel carrier took us to the farm at the edge of the wood, which we had left only the previous day, the next morning. We were immediately locked into the pigsty. The door's upper half remained open, and two men were posted in front of it. Next, the civilians of the farm came over, they swore at us, spat at us, and even threw rocks at us. That abuse lasted throughout the morning. Then, a first lieutenant showed up. He addressed us in perfect German. Since, until then, we had been given nothing to eat or drink, and we were on edge from the treatment by the Belgians, which had been silently tolerated by the 'Amis', I immediately asked the first lieutenant forcefully whether this was the American way to treat prisoners. He looked at me startled, and immediately demanded that I go with him. He led me to the farm and inside the room which I remembered, I stood facing a colonel. A conversation between the colonel and the first lieutenant began during which the first lieutenant spoke on our behalf. He then had to ask me several questions regarding the units, the commanders and the actions until then. I was convinced that the colonel understood all my answers. Despite that, he had them all translated. I was led back to the pigsty where Wilfried Tödter welcomed me gladly, since he had already expected the worst. The first lieutenant ordered the guards to keep the Belgians away from us and then asked me whether he could have my SS-insignia. I nodded my head and he removed it with his pocket knife from my uniform jacket. As soon as the first lieutenant had left us, one of the guards set down his rifle, came inside, and removed my second insignia as well as Tödter's two. We could see on their faces that they were happy with that, the other guard was also given his share. We were safe from the Belgians, but were not given anything to eat or drink.

The next morning, we were both picked up and taken to the colonel again. Some of the Belgians were inside the room. They pointed at Tödter, wildly gesticulating. They had recognized him and accused him of having threatened them with a machine pistol and locked them into the cellar. Tödter answered in the affirmative to the colonel's question on that, but we took turns making it clear to him that it had been for their own safety and, of course, ours. Further, that any soldier in the world would have acted the same way. I blurted out that we had sheltered the Belgians from American shells, after all, and could tell from the expression on the colonel's face that he understood each word. After a short gesture from him we were led off again. Still, there was nothing to eat. Altogether, we had not eaten or drunk for three days.

The next morning, I no longer cared at all. I talked at the guards for such a length of time that they went to get the first lieutenant. I explained to him that we had been prisoners for three days, without being fed, and that we had nothing the day before that in our foxhole. If they wanted to starve us, it would be better if they shot us right away. He, again, took me to that colonel and demanded that I repeat everything. I did that in detail and added that we knew that we, the men of the Waffen-SS, could expect nothing from them. The next question to me was: 'Did your officers tell you that?' I answered in the negative and immediately added that we all had learned that already from our own experiences. Addressing the colonel, I continued that our fate was already sealed in any case, and that, maybe, the only thing he was not sure of yet was how he would have us done away with.

The first lieutenant looked at me shocked, while thoughts were obviously racing through the colonel's mind. After a while of silence, the colonel said in perfect German: 'You will see that we are not as you believe.'

Without another word, I was led back to the pigsty. A short time later we were given food and even cigarettes.

Toward evening, we were fetched by fifteen men. The first lieutenant appeared once more and made clear that we were being taken to a camp. The guard surrounded us, and we set off—on foot! We marched down the same path through the wood where a majority of the fighting had taken place previously. Our senses were tensed since we believed that those fellows would finish us off in the woods there. We had quietly agreed that we would try to escape to the left and right into the trees at the first suspicious sound. However, we reached the Maas without anything having happened. An old boat waited for us there, and we were taken across. Those who received us at the other bank enjoyed pushing us into the water a few times. Then, they led us to a quarry were approximately 200 prisoners were located, nicely lined up in rows of three. So we stood the whole night, including the two of us in our wet rags.

The next day, we were taken by truck by way of Fourmies and Paris to a camp at Voves near Chartres, where approximately 9,000 men had been assembled. Wilfried Tödter and I remained together for our period of imprisonment which would last two years for us . . .[37]

Unterscharführer Eberhard Köpke reported in a letter on the events with the Waldmüller Bataillon (I./25):

. . . Suddenly, the report came from the right that we had lost contact with the Bataillon. To the left of us, in any case, we had mounted a counterattack the day before. There, we expected another unit to move into the gap. I had sent several messengers to the Waldmüller command post. The chief was sitting with two messengers in a front line bunker at the Maas, under extremely heavy fire, and could not get out. Finally, Senn returned. The only things he brought with him were a map fragment and Waldmüller's cap. The former command post was already swarming with enemy tanks. It was not long before those machines came rolling up from both sides along the road on the river bank. Still, those positions were to be held to last drop of blood. Well, what should I do? We had no other choice but to beat it once again. Fortunately the chief also came out of his mouse-hole before long. We reached the Maas hills at the last light of day. When we turned into the direction of the village where we had left our vehicles, we spotted a large number of tanks; clouds of dust, as far as we could see. The Bataillon order to pull back had not reached us in time, everything had happened too quickly again. Thus, we moved, using the compass, in groups right through the enemy tanks in the direction of a previously agreed assembly point. Fortunately, it was a pitch-dark night and it was rain-ing furiously. Once we walked within meters of an enemy tank com-pany.

Somewhere, we found the Bataillon again, in a village through which enemy tanks had already rolled the previous day. From there, we continued on horse-drawn carriages in a northeasterly direction. It had already become the general direction of the march . . . [38]

The remnants of the various Kampfgruppen and units of the Division, which had fought at the Maas, assembled in the course of 7 September around Durbuy on the Ourthe. It is indicative that the remaining members of the Divisionsbegleitkompanie reached the Divisional command post on bicycles. They also continued on to Ferrières, located twelve kilometers northeast. [39]

The war diary of Heeresgruppe B contains several entries for 6 September on the events south of the Maas. The following ones are of interest:

. . . 19.05 hours, long distance telephone conversation between the chief of the general staff of AOK 7 and the Ia of the Heeresgruppe:

The situation: The enemy has advanced from Namur along the road on the southern bank of the Maas to the east and has captured Huy. He continues the advance on Liège. The Armee has decided . . . , to fight its way back, in several intervals of a day each, to the line Maastricht—Liège. The line Hasselt—St. Trond—Huy will be reached during the night 6–7 September. The I. SS-Panzerkorps will have to be pulled back to the adjoining line Huy—Rochefort—west of Marche—Bouillon . . .

Further, the chief of the general staff of AOK 7 reports that the Namur bridge has been blown up. The enemy must have achieved the crossing using his own bridging equipment, or broken through the battalion of 347. Inf.-Div. in position south of Namur without that report having reached the Armee . . .

There is contact with I. SS-Panzerkorps. Twenty enemy tanks have appeared to the rear of the 12. SS-Panzer-division south of Namur. An enemy attack took place from the bridgehead south of Lustin [nine kilometers south of Namur] to the north and northeast. No contact to the command post of I. SS-Panzerkorps Werris [northeast of Marche] . . .[40]

The non-combat-ready parts of the "HJ" Division moved to the Reich ter-ritory starting on 8 September 1944. One small Kampfgruppe, led by Ober-sturmbannführer Milius, was assigned to the "Das Reich" Division. Its composition is not known in detail. It can be said with some certainty that

Bataillon Siebken (II./26) and the mixed Artillerieabteilung of Sturmbannführer Neumann belonged to it. The command of the "HJ" Division was
temporarily handed to the First General Staff Officer, Sturmbannführer
Hubert Meyer, while he continued his previous responsibility and duties. On
8 September, the staff moved to Wanne near Stavelot, Belgium, and on 9
September to Adenau. On 11 September, it reached the district to the right
of the Rhine and established its staff headquarters in Plettenberg in the
Sauerland.[41]

During the march back through Belgium, individual members of the
Division were ambushed and murdered by partisans. On 8 September,
Sturmbannführer Hans Waldmüller and Untersturmführer Marquardt rode
on a motorcycle with a side-car from Werbomont to Stavelot. On a stretch of
approximately six kilometers they had to cross through an extensive forest.
At a spot where the road dropped off after crossing a hill down toward Basse-
Bodeux, at a lower elevation, the partisans had positioned a cable across the
road. When the cycle approached, they tightened the cable so that it came
up off the ground. The cycle either stopped or was caught by the cable. The
partisans opened fire. Soon after, several horse-drawn carriages of Sturmbannführer Waldmüller reached that spot. The men observed the traces of
the ambush with horror. Untersturmführer Marquardt sat dead on the rear
seat of the cycle, he had been shot in the head. The driver was found, seriously wounded, in the undergrowth on the left side of the road. After a
lengthy search, Sturmbannführer Waldmüller was discovered in the drainage
pipe of a small lake. His body had been brutally mutilated, his belly had
been slit open, the genitalia cut off. Both dead men and the wounded driver
were taken along on one of the horse carriages.

Within one week, the second Knight's Cross holder of the "HJ" Division
had fallen victim to a perfidious ambush by partisans. Sturmbannführer
Hans Waldmüller had fought bravely for five years, often in action at the hot
spots, and had often escaped grave danger. He was the corner stone of the
defense during the heavy fighting south of Cambes near Caen on 8 July and,
one month later, near Cintheaux, "the tower in the battle". The two dead
men were given their last rest in the cemetery at Düren.

The Milius Kampfgruppe remained in action at the Westwall until the
end of October. It is known that 6. Kompanie of SS-Panzergrenadierregiment 26 was in position near Brand-scheid, eight kilometers northeast of
Prüm in the Eifel. Obersturmbannführer Milius reported that two battalions
were assigned to him. One of them consisted of artillery men who no longer
had any guns. The other was a Volkssturm battalion (militia), with many
Hitler youths. He wrote:

> . . . I can see those boys in front of me even today. Shining, trustful
> eyes; uniforms which did not fit; rifles whose muzzles reached up to
> their shoulders or eyes . . .

Also assigned to him was a Luftwaffe unit which

... gave the impression of total neglect. Those soldiers moved into their sector with some of them wearing slippers, carrying rabbits, cats and other such animals in their arms. They were facing a battle-tested unit opposite. The losses were suffered accordingly. The keys for the bunkers were found only after a long time. The first map of the fortifications showing the communications network, etc., was available to us only after days when we captured an American scouting party. The field of fire in front of the fortifications was grown over with shrubs and bushes. It could not be cleared since the Americans had followed right on our heels . . .[42]

With the move into the Reich territory, the fighting to repel the Allied invasion in Normandy and the ensuing rearguard fighting had found an end. "HJ" Division had stood the test, with excellence, during attack and defense, frequently in situations which seemed hopeless. But, it had also suffered severe losses.

Killed were 55 officers, 229 NCOs, and 1,548 men; wounded were 128 officers, 613 NCOs, and 3,684 men; missing were 56 officers, 182 NCOs, and 2,012 men; 7 officers, 16 NCOs, and 96 men died outside of hospitals. The total losses amounted to 8,626 officers, NCOs and men, as far as the figure can be confirmed by lists of losses.

The lists of losses for the following are incomplete: Divisional staff, III./25, Panzerjägerabteilung 12 (officers), Flakabteilung 12 (officers), Werferabteilung 12, Nachrichtenabteilung 12 (communications), Pionierbataillon 12, Instandsetzungsabteilung 12 (repairs), Sanitätsabteilung 12 (medics), and Feldgendarmerie Kompanie (military police).

The following are missing: Feldpostamt 12 (field post) and Feld-Ersatz-Bataillon 12 (replacements).

The total losses, including those not documented, probably amounted to almost 9,000 officers, NCOs and men.

Details are shown below in the table compiled by Wolfgang Lüdeke, based on the lists of losses available at the Deutsche Dienststelle (German service office).

The Division entered action at the start of the invasion with every confidence that it would be possible, despite the already known enemy air superiority, to destroy the enemy who had landed and to repel the invasion. At the end of that fighting, a defeat of the forces in the west, to an unimaginable extent, was the result. The survivors asked for the causes. Any individual was able to offer answers only from his own point of view at the time. Today, we know more about it, but certainly not everything. However, the major causes can be determined. They are listed below, in order of their importance and impact:

1. A wrong picture of the enemy before the invasion and during the fighting:

The office "Fremde Heere West" (foreign forces west) of the general staff of the Heer provided the Wehrmacht operations staff with an intentionally falsified account of the enemy. On 6 June 1944, the Allies had 37 divisions ready for action in Normandy. Based on the assumptions by "Fremde Heere West", the situational map of Supreme Command West of 6 June 1944 showed, in the summary, 70 divisions and 18 brigades, for a total factor of 79 operational units. That led, even until the middle of July, to the assumption that, in addition to the Normandy landing, a second landing was to be expected at the Channel coast. Thus, two Panzerdivisions of the Heeresgruppenreserve (Heer group reserve) and Infanterie Divisions of 15. Armee were held back for weeks and not moved to the landing front in Normandy.

2. A wrong assumption of the Allied landing sector:

Supreme Command West, Feldmarschall von Rundstedt and Generalleutnant Blumentritt, and the supreme command of Heeresgruppe B, Feldmarschall Rommel and Generalleutnant Speidel, expected the Allied landing at the Pas de Calais. Adolf Hitler and the OKW (supreme command of the Wehrmacht) took the point of view, since February 1944, that it would come at the Normandy coast. Against the expectations and intentions of the supreme command of Heeresgruppe B, they pushed through a reinforcement of the Normandy front.

The minimum strategic aim of the repulsion of the invasion had to be a strike at the enemy, hard enough, that he would need several months before he could dare a new landing. The mass of the Panzerdivisions located in the west could then, possibly after a short period of refitting, be pulled out and moved to the eastern front. There, they were urgently needed. In addition, time could be gained in order to effectively wage the "long range battle" against England which was expected to have a decisive impact.

Above all, there were two operational options to achieve that strategic goal. The concept of field marshals von Rundstedt and Rommel envisaged to ". . . to smash the attacking enemy in the water well before he reached the main line of battle (the coast) and force him to turn back . . ." The General der Panzertruppen, Freiherr Geyr von Schweppenburg represented the viewpoint that the enemy landing would be successful. The enemy would then, outside the range of the ships' artillery, have to be destroyed by a counterattack of all Panzerdivisions. That concept—if achievable—would better realize the strategic goal than that of the field marshals. The basic order No. 37 by Supreme Command West of 27.2.1944, parts of which have been cited above, remained, however, the binding operational directive to repel the invasion. That plan failed for the following reasons:

3. At the start of the invasion, the Panzerdivisions had not been assembled in proximity to western Normandy for the counterattack against the

landing enemy. Of the three Panzerdivisions of Heeresgruppenreserve, the 21. was located in the greater Caen area. However, it was broken up. Parts of it were in the vicinity of the coast and assigned to 716. Inf.-Div. at the start of the invasion. Other parts were located near Caen, separated from each other by the Orne, yet others were near Falaise. Both were assigned to the Divisional command of 21. Pz.-Div. The location and command structure did not allow action by that division as a unit. The 2. and 116. Pz.-Divs. were located north of the Seine whose bridges had been destroyed. They were some distance away from the coast.

Since Feldmarschall von Rundstedt thought a first success of the landing possible, he kept back, as an operational reserve, the general command of I. SS-Panzerkorps, 12. SS-Pz.-Div. and Pz.-Lehr-Div. (all three were, at the same time, OKW reserve), 17. Pz.-Gren.-Div. and 2. SS-Pz.-Div.

4. Heeresgruppe B moved 21. Pz.-Div. on 6 June into the counterattack, too late, and 2. and 116. not at all.

Supreme Command West decided on 6 June, shortly after 5 a.m., without awaiting approval from the OKW, to move the "HJ" Division forward into the line on both sides of Lisieux. However, it was in the wrong spot there and had lost hours when it was turned off into the Caen area. The late release of the OKW reserves was the result of the inadequately determined enemy situation and of the fact that Heeresgruppe B had not sent two Panzerdivisions from its own reserves into action.

The Allied landing was made easier because

5. The Kriegsmarine, during the night of 5/6 June, had not posted forward guards because of ". . . unfavorable tide and weather conditions . . ." and, even after having been given the preliminary alert, did not lay rapid mine obstacles in front of the Normandy coast.

After the enemy had gained a foothold on the mainland and joined the two bridgeheads near Arromanches, it was of urgent importance to separate them by a counterattack of all Panzerdivisions and to destroy the landed troops one after the other. That did not succeed because;

6. The reinforcements were not brought up on a timely basis. Since 21. Pz.-Div., 12. SS-Pz.-Div., Pz.-Lehr-Div. and 17. SS-Pz.-Gren.-Div. were already engaged, -Infanterie Divisions had to be brought in immediately after the landing to relieve them. That occurred too late since a second landing was expected at the Pas de Calais (see Point 1.). Further, it was delayed through the destruction of the railway facilities and the lack of improvised measures (truck columns of the Luftwaffe and the Kriegsmarine).

The Panzerdivisions not yet in action were brought in too late, or not at all, for that mission. The 2. SS-Pz.-Div. was ordered to first combat an uprising by the Résistance in the area around Limoges. The first parts of 2. Pz.-Div. only arrived at the invasion front on 12 June. The 116. Pz.-Div. remained initially still east of the Seine and was moved even closer to the coast there.

The two Panzerdivisions stationed in southern France remained there because of the expected landing on the Mediterranean coast.

7. A—possibly last—favorable circumstance to smash the Allied bridge-head existed around 28 June 1944 when the 21st Army Group of General Montgomery had tied up nearly all forces in the "EPSOM" Operation. The Americans had not regrouped after the fall of Cherbourg. Instead of a coun-terattack into the deep flank of the enemy who had broken through, or even against his man-made ports, from the area around St. Lô, together with 2. Pz.-Div. and 2. SS-Pz.-Div., the II. SS-Panzerkorps, and the parts of 1. SS-Pz.-Div. which had arrived so far, were sent into action against the shoulder of the breakthrough area. The 9. and 116. Pz.-Divs. were located, at that time, idle and distant from the battlefield.

Based on today's knowledge, General von Geyer's concept to destroy the landed enemy outside the range of the ships' artillery through attacks by all Panzerdivisions, was probably not achievable. The reason for that must not so much be seen in the Allied air superiority. Taking account of the safety mentality of the Allied supreme command, the enemy would not have bro-ken out of the bridgehead before he had assembled superior forces. That tendency showed itself already during the first two weeks of the invasion bat-tles. The existing plan for the German counterattack could not be carried out in time because of the lack of forces (delayed arrival). It could have been successful, despite the Allied dominance of the air and the attack within range of the enemy ships' artillery, in particular during night attacks when friend and foe were inextricably intertwined. The thrust to the man-made ports, which had been rendered unusable by the storm of 19 June for some time, could have been decisive.

Without question, the enemy air and sea superiority severely aggravated all German operations, but they were not hopeless because of it.

On the opposite side, in particular, the radio intelligence activity "ULTRA" and the feint action "FORTITUDE" are being credited with deci-sive importance. Frequently, the "ULTRA" findings came too late or were not given sufficient attention. The operational directives issued by teletype, or in writing through couriers, could not be intercepted by that otherwise quite valuable instrument. If "ULTRA" had the importance it is credited with, it would be unexplainable why the Allies did not achieve much greater suc-cesses sooner. No doubt, "FORTITUDE" had deceived the Ic operatives, but not the Supreme Command. The enemy picture of "Fremde Heere West", false for other reasons, was decisive.

The operational decisions taken after 28 June 1944 need not be dealt with in this analysis. The decisive mistakes in judging the situation and deci-sion making already predate that time.

Unit	Report Period	Running no. of loss reports	Wounded			Killed			Missing or captured			Died		
			O	N	M	O	N	M	O	N	M	O	N	M
SS-Pz.-Div.12 "Hj" staff, staff comp., Begleit Komp.	6. 6.44–30. 9.44	1–12	?	12	83	?	7	39	?	13	54	-	-	-
SS-Pz.Rgt.12 "Hj" Rgt. staff, Rgt. unit	6. 6.44–27. 9.44	1–25	9	44	112	3	5	20	5	8	36	-	-	-
SS-Pz.Rgt.12 "Hj" Staff I and units	7. 6.44–31.10.44	1–62	16	75	242	11	12	60	3	16	141	-	2	3
SS-Pz.Rgt.12 "Hj" Staff II and units	7. 6.44–20.10.44	1–58	28	68	296	9	30	115	6	6	144	-	1	1
SS-Pz.Art.-Rgt.12 "Hj" Rgt. staff & Rgt. units	6. 6.44–20. 8.44	1–13	1	3	33	1	4	6	3	6	41	-	-	-

Unit	Report Period	Running no. of loss reports	Wounded			Killed			Missing or captured			Died		
			O	N	M	O	N	M	O	N	M	O	N	M
SS-Pz.Art.-Rgt.12 "HJ" Staff I and units	6. 6.44–10. 9.44	1–27	5	15	127	2	4	38	3	13	105	-	-	-
SS-Pz.Art.-Rgt.12 "HJ" Staff II and units	6. 6.44–22. 9.44	1–22	4	19	118	1	4	36	2	2	98	1	1	1
SS-Pz.Art.-Rgt.12 "HJ" Staff III and units	6. 6.44–10.10.44	1–25	3	26	179	-	4	23	4	10	99	-	1	4
SS-Pz.Gren.-Rgt.25 "HJ" Rgt. staff & Rgt. units	6. 6.44–31. 7.44	1–39	4	19	157	2	15	57	3	9	65	-	-	5
SS-Pz.Gren.-Rgt.25 "HJ" Staff I and units	6. 6.44–20. 9.44	1–79	8	43	299	3	16	140	1	7	157	1	1	10

SS-Pz.Gren.-Rgt.25 "HJ" Staff II and units	6. 6.44–31.10.44	1–42	4	35	208	4	18	105	1	10	92	1	-	6
SS-Pz.Gren.-Rgt.25 "HJ" Staff III and units	6. 6.44–20. 6.44	1–4	6	6	118	?	5	43	-	-	20	1	-	2
SS-Pz.Gren.-Rgt.26 "HJ" Rgt. Staff & Rgt. units	2. 6.44–28. 8.44	1–68	5	21	233	?	11	96	2	3	76	-	2	10
SS-Pz.Gren.-Rgt.26 "HJ" Staff I and units	6. 6.44–17. 8.44	1–48	3	44	258	4	19	93	1	17	135	-	-	-
SS-Pz.Gren.-Rgt.26 "HJ" Staff II and units	6. 6.44–19. 9.44	1–51	5	41	244	5	17	134	5	5	173	1	1	13
SS-Pz.Gren.-Rgt.26 "HJ" Staff III and units	7. 6.44–29. 8.44	1–72	8	43	341	3	15	136	5	7	142	-	-	-
SS-Pz.Aufkl.-Abt.12 "HJ" staff and units	6. 6.44–31.10.44	1–38	9	32	168	?	14	158	5	11	125	-	6	15

Unit	Report Period	Running no. of loss reports	Wounded			Killed			Missing or captured			Died		
			O	N	M	O	N	M	O	N	M	O	N	M
SS-Pz.Jäger-Abt.12 "HJ" staff and units	16. 6.44–31.10.44	1–6	?	4	10	1	5	4	?	5	14	-	-	8
SS-Flak Abt.12 "HJ" staff and units	6. 6.44–8. 9.44	1–9	2	15	71	?	4	51	2	4	50	1	1	3
SS-Werf.Abt.12 "HJ" staff and units	23. 5.44–30. 7.44	1–5	3	9	72	1	1	22	2	4	82	-	-	2
SS-Pz.Na-Abt.12 "HJ" staff and units	6. 6.44–18. 7.44	1–9	2	12	56	2	1	17	-	1	6	-	-	1
SS-Pz.Pi-Abt.12 "HJ" staff and units	3. 6.44–31. 8.44	1–59	2	18	194	3	12	113	3	19	134	1	-	7
SS-Inst.-Abt.12 "HJ" staff and units	7. 6.44–22. 8.44	1–6	-	-	22	-	2	16	-	-	-	-	-	2

Unit	Period													
SS-Pz.Nachschb.-Trp.12 "HJ" staff and units	6.6.44–10.9.44	1–9	–	8	26	–	3	22	–	–	–	–	–	–
SS-Verwltgs.-Trp.-Abt.12 "HJ" staff and units	6.6.44–15.10.44	1–4	1	–	14	–	1	3	1	4	23	–	–	–
SS-San.-Abt.12 "HJ" staff and units	?.?.44–30.6.44	1	?	?	?	?	?	?	?	1	?	–	–	–
SS-Feldgend.-Kp.12 "HJ" Kp.	6.6.44–27.10.44	1	1	1	3	?	?	1	?	1	?	–	–	2
SS-Feldpostamt12 "HJ"	no information													
SS-Feld-Ers.-Btl.12 "HJ" staff and units	no information													
Totals			128	613	3684	55	229	1548	56	182	2012	7	16	96

(Werf.Abt.=Werfer Abteilung, Na-Abt.=Nachrichten [communications], Pi-Abt.=Pionier, Inst.-Abt.=repair Abteilung, Nachschb.Trp.=supply troops, Verwltgs.-Trp.=administration, San.-Abt.=medical Abteilung, Feldgend.-Kp.=military police -Kompanie, Feldpostamt=field post office, Feld-Ers.-Btl.=field replacement Bataillon)

A young grenadier
brings forward an
MG 42 in support.

In the firing position of a battery. On the right, the telephone operator with Field Telephone 33, who can communicate with two or three units at the same time; on the left, the radio operator who has contact with the observation post.

This Panzer IV of the 2nd Battalion has twenty-four "Kill" rings on the gun barrel, indicating twenty-four destroyed enemy tanks. It is rolling out of the maintenance workshop back into battle.

Radio signals detachment with backpack radio equipment b/f with the forward observer sitting (left). It has radio contact with the firing position. The radio man on the right has the microphone, his left thumb on the speak button.

10.5 cm self-propelled light field howitzer "Wespe" of 1st Battalion of SS Panzerartillerieregiment 12 while firing, the barrel has recoiled.

Caen area, June 1944. The 2 cm four-barreled Flak platoon of Artillery Regiment protects the firing positions of the battalion against fighter-bombers.

Heavy howitzer of 3rd Artillery Battalion firing during battle.

A Panther destroyed during a German counterattack in the Cheux area on June 27.

British 7.5 cm (17-pounder) anti-tank gun.

Normandy, summer 1944. A break for the motorcycle messengers.

Machine-gunner
No. 1 with his Light
Machine Gun 42.

British Bren Carrier drives through a village in the Cheux area on June 28. Note the
captured MG 42.

A Panzer IV changes position.

June 1944. Knocked out British Cromwell tanks at Hill 112.

Unterscharführer Willy Kretzschmar with the crew of his Panzer IV of 5th Company after the successful defensive battle on Hill 112. From the left: Sturmmann Schreiner, panzer driver; Sturmmann Stephen, radio operator; Unterscharführer Kretzschmar, panzer commander; Sturmmann Schweinfest, gunner; and Sturmmann Gaude, gun loader.

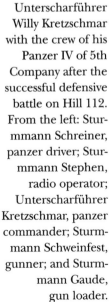

Caen area, June 1944. Men of SS Panzerregiment 12 in front of a knocked out British Cromwell tank.

Panzer IV No. 538 of 5th Company of SS Panzerregiment 12 received a hit between the motor and crew space during the first attack on Hill 112 southwest of Caen. Unterscharführer Kretzschmar, Sturmmann Schweinfest, and Sturmmann Stefan by the tank.

Command post of 3rd Battalion Regiment 25 in Buron.

Unterscharführer Klein, the adjutant of 1st Battalion Regiment 25, in his observation post south of Cambes.

Before the Allied offensive against Caen on July 8 and 9, 1944. The commander of 1st Battalion Regiment 25, Sturmbannführer Waldmüller in his battalion command post in front of Cambes.

Normandy, summer 1944. 7.5 cm anti-tank gun (Pak 40) in its firing position behind a breached wall.

Caen area, June 1944. The panzer Flak platoon of the regimental staff watches over the airspace during the march (2 cm Flak on a panzer chassis 38t).

Caen area, June 1944. Four-barreled Flak panzer in action against fighter-bombers.

July 1944. Panzer-grenadiers in front of their dugout north of Caen.

July 1944. 7.5 cm Pak ready to fire, north of Caen.

Oberscharführer Richard Rudolf, 9th Company Panzer-regiment 12, was awarded the Knight's Cross on November 18, 1944.

NCO and men of 1st Company of SS Panzergrenadierregiment 25. Second from right: staff sergeant Herbert Stengl; fourth, Unterscharführer Eberhard Köpke with four tank destruction badges. On the next page is his document confirming that he destroyed a Sherman tank with a Panzerfaust.

BESITZZEUGNIS

DEM   SS-Unterscharführer
(Dienstgrad)

Eberhard   K ö p k e
(Vor- und Familienname)

1./SS-Pz.Gren.Rgt. 25
(Truppenteil)

VERLEIHE ICH FÜR DIE VERNICHTUNG VON

1 Cherman-Panzer
mit Panzerfaust   IM NAHKAMPF

1 PANZERVERNICHTUNGSABZEICHEN

O.U., den 9.1o.1944 i.V.
(Ort und Datum)

(Unterschrift)

SS-Hauptsturmführer
und Btls.-Kommandeur

(Dienstgrad und Dienststellung)

"La Maison Blanche" in Airan near Caen. Site of divisional command post at the end of July 1944 (photographed in 1976).

August 1944. A rifleman of the Kraderkundungs-Zug of SS-Panzer-regiment 12 installed a sign at a signpost for vehicles of his Regiment "Wünsche" during the withdrawal to the Seine.

Normandy, July 1944. A bunker is built at the divisional command post in Airan. Standing in the middle, from the left: Oberführer Kurt Meyer, divisional commander; General Peltz, commander of a Luftwaffe corps; Sturmbannführer Siegfried Müller, CO SS Panzer Engineers Battalion 12; Sturmbannführer Hubert Meyer, GSO 1.

Awarding of the Knight's Cross to Sturmbannführer Karl-Heinz Prinz by Oberstgruppenführer Sepp Dietrich. On the right: Obersturmbannführer Max Wünsche.

Near Gausmesnil, south of Caen, the knocked out Tiger No. 107 of Heavy SS Panzer Battalion 101. The turret lies upside down after the explosion. It is the Tiger of Michael Wittmann, who was killed here on August 8, 1944.

A Jagdpanzer IV of SS Anti-tank Battalion 12, destroyed during the fighting around Cintheau.

Field Marshal Model at the Battle HQ of 5th Panzer Army, north of the Seine, on August 24 or 25. From left: Oberstgruppenführer Sepp Dietrich; Colonel v. Gersdorff, Chief of Staff of 7th Army; Field Marshal Model, C-in-C West and Army Group B; General Gause, Chief of Staff of 5th Panzer Army; and General of Panzer Troops Eberbach.

Field Marshal Rommel with SS Obergruppenführer and General of the Waffen SS Hausser, C-in-C of 7th Army, July 1944.

PART III

The Division during the Ardennes Offensive

CHAPTER 8.1
Refitting in Reich Territory

The originally planned short-term refitting of parts of the "HJ" Division units in the area around Hirson—in the French-Belgian border district—in September 1944 had not come about because of the rapid enemy advance. The Division was thus moved into Reich territory, since the hope was that a lasting defense would be possible behind the Belgian canals and the Westwall. On 13 September, the Führungshauptamt (senior operations office) communicated, in writing and in the context of a teletype message, the reporting points for the divisions of the Waffen-SS withdrawn, or to be moved from, the west. For the "HJ" Division, Arnsberg in the Sauerland had been chosen. Responsible for the refitting was the General der Panzertruppen West. The provision of equipment would be the responsibility of the chief of staff of the Panzertruppen and the quartermaster general. Personnel assignment would be done by the SS-Führungshauptamt.[1]

On 22 September, the orders issued until then were changed or supplemented. Among other changes, "HJ" Division left the responsibility of the General der Panzertruppen West. It was assigned, for the refitting, to the staff of Panzer-Armee-Oberkommando 6 (Panzer Armee supreme command), whose creation had been ordered under the supreme commander, SS-Oberstgruppenführer and Panzergeneraloberst of the Waffen-SS, Sepp Dietrich.[2]

For the refitting, the units of the Division were scattered across a large area. Its farthest spread was more than 200 kilometers. Panzergrenadierregiment 26 was located in and around Kaiserslautern where the Panzergrenadier-(A. u. E. 12) -Ausbildungs und Ersatzbataillon 12 (training and replacement) was also stationed. The Panzerregiment and Panzerjägerabteilung assembled in the area around Daaden on the Sieg river. The body of the Division was located in the Sauerland, the Divisional headquarters was in Plettenberg. At the end of September, the Division was scheduled to move, by rail transport, to the area around Heilbronn. Parts, such as the Flak-Abteilung and Regiment 26, were already on their way when the order was canceled. The units already on their way would remain in their new locations until further orders. The route taken by 4. Flakbatterie during the period 21 to 24 September is indicative of the traffic conditions of the time: Arnsberg, Neheim-Hüsten, Wickede/Ruhr, Fröndenberg, Langschede, Schwerte, Hohensyburg, Hagen, Obervogelsang, Schwelm, Wuppertal, Leichlingen, Opladen, Cologne—Mühlheim, Brühl, Bonn, Remagen, Koblenz, Mainz, Groß-Gerau, Darmstadt, Weinheim/Bergstraße, Heidelberg, Eberbach, Jagstfeld, Möckmühl, then motorized march to Leibenstadt (near Osterburken).[3] Through these moves, the distances between the locations increased to a maximum of 270 kilometers. The Reichsbahn (Reich railway system) and its personnel deserve the highest recognition for their untiring work under the most difficult circumstances which were caused, primarily, by frequent air attacks on its installations and on the transports.

At the beginning of October, the whole Division was moved into the western Lower Saxony-southern Oldenburg-northern Westphalia area. The 4. Flakbatterie—again by rail transport—took the following route between 8 to 10 October: Seckach, Würzburg, Karlstadt/Main, Gemünden, Jossa, Fulda, Nienburg/Weser, Sulingen, Diepholz, Barnstorf.[4] During that period, the A. u. E. 12 also moved to Nienburg/Weser. The Divisional headquarters was located in Sulingen.

On 14 October, the Führungshauptamt issued further information by teletype on the refitting. Based on a Führer directive, the "HJ" Division would be refitted in the course of October, to be completed by 31 October. Full replacement of personnel had been ordered. At the Panzerregiment, in addition to the Regimental staff, only a mixed Abteilung of two companies of fourteen Panzer IVs each and two companies of fourteen Panzer Vs (Panthers) would be equipped. For the Regimental and Abteilung staffs, only two command Panthers each were assigned. The Regiment received only a mixed Panzer-Flak-Zug with four Flakpanzer IVs (2 cm four-barrel) and four Flakpanzer IVs (3.7 cm). For the time being, both Abteilungen remained in existence as Panzer IV and Panther Abteilung.

Heavy weapons were to be provided at the 100% level. Those which had remained after the withdrawal battles, had been handed over during the pullout to the units which continued in action. Hand- and automatic weapons were to be replaced to the 75% level. The requirements of motorcycles, cars and trucks were also to be filled only to the 75% level of requirement. Tractors would be provided as supply allowed. The Aufklärungsabteilung received sixteen armored reconnaissance vehicles and thirty light armored personnel carriers for one Aufklärungskompanie. The armored Bataillon (III./26) was to be provided with a minimum requirement of up to 135 medium armored personnel carriers.[5]

The greatest difficulties encountered were with personnel. Approximately 9,000 officers, NCOs and men had been killed, wounded or were missing and had to be replaced. The Divisional commander had been taken prisoner, wounded. In his place, and in addition to his own duties, the first general staff officer led the Division. Still fit for action were the following general staff officers: the commander of the Artillerieregiment, Obersturmbannführer Oskar Drexler, the commander of his I. Abteilung, Sturmbannführer Karl Müller, and the commander of II. Abteilung, Sturmbannführer Günter Neumann. The commander of III. Abteilung had been transferred to the staff of the senior artillery commander of 6. Panzerarmee. As well, the commanders of I. Panzerabteilung, Sturm-bannführer Arnold Jürgensen, the Aufklärungsabteilung, Sturmbannführer Gerd Bremer, and of the Werferabteilung, Sturmbannführer Willy Müller, were still in their previous positions. All other command positions had to be newly filled.

Sturmbannführer Willi Hardieck was initially given command of the Panzerregiment. However, he was then transferred to Panzerbrigade 150 Skorzeny. Sturmbannführer Herbert Kuhlmann, previously Abteilung commander in the Panzerregiment of "Leibstandarte", took over the Regiment. The command of II. Abteilung of the Panzerregiment had been handed to Hauptsturmführer Hans Siegel. The previous commander of the Pionierbataillon, Sturmbannführer Siegfried Müller, was given command of Panzergrenadierregiment 25. The I. Bataillon of that Regiment was given to Hauptsturmführer Alfons Ott. Just before the start of the Ardennes offensive, Obersturmbannführer Richard Schulze took over II. Bataillon. The III. Bataillon was initially commanded by Hauptsturmführer Alfred Brückner, later by Hauptsturm-führer Arnold Lammerding. Sturmbannführer Bernhard Krause, who had previously led I./26, took over Panzer-grenadierregiment 26. The I. Bataillon was given to Hauptsturmführer Gerd Hein, II. Bataillon to Hauptsturmführer Karl Hauschild, III. Bataillon to Hauptsturmführer Georg Urabl. At the Artillerie-regiment, Hauptsturmführer Fritsch took over III. Abteilung. The Flakabteilung was taken over by Sturmbannführer Dr. Wolfgang Loenicker, the Pionierbataillon by Hauptsturmführer Johannes Taubert, the Panzerjägerabteilung by Hauptsturmführer Karl-Heinz Brockschmidt, and the Nachrichtenabteilung by Hauptsturmführer Walter Krüger. A majority of these commanders had not held such command previously. Three of the Regimental commanders had previously been successful Bataillons-/Abteilung commanders. The new Bataillon-/Abteilung commanders had proved their worth previously as Kompanie or Batterie chiefs. Even more difficult was the situation with the Kompanie commanders. The only available war-time listing of ranks is that of III./25. According to it, one Kompanie commander was an Obersturmführer, two were Untersturmführers, one a Standartenoberjunker (officer cadet). Of the sixteen Zugführers, one was an Untersturmführer, three were Standartenoberjunkers, the others were Unter-führers.[6] In II./26, of which an activity report is available, all four Kompanieführers were Untersturmführers. One of them was replaced by an Obersturmführer in December.[7]

The replacement of NCOs and men came, partly from the replacement units, among them young volunteers as well as convalescent wounded. More than 2,000 men came from the Luftwaffe and Kriegsmarine; they were not trained for ground combat. Among them were older men who had carried out ground duties. As far as possible, they were exchanged for younger NCOs from the administration services.

The replacements did not arrive as a body in September, but in small groups. Also, there was an initial lack of weapons and equipment for the replacements. Together with the uneven level of previous training, that had a significant negative impact on the training even in small units. In order to show clearly what could be expected from the Division in future actions, the questions of personnel replacement, provision of weapons, equipment and clothing, and of training must be explored in more detail. That will be done using II./26 as example:

1. Personnel replacement:
   The Bataillon was set up in the '23-er Kaserne' in Kaiserslautern from remnants of Feldersatzbataillon 12 which had been in action at the Eure and Seine rivers in the framework of the Mohnke Kampfgruppe, and of I. and II./26, parts of which had still fought at the Maas. From the Panzergrenadier A. u. E. 12 (training and replacement), 450 recruits were added. The formation started on 3 September 1944.

   4.9. Transfer of four Untersturmführers as Zugführers.

   15.9. Transfer of three Untersturmführers to the A. u. E. 12.

   23.9. Transfer of one Untersturmführer from the Divisional combat school as Kompanie chief. One Kompanie chief is transferred to the Führungshauptamt, one let go to A. u. E. 12.

   26.10. Acceptance of 4 NCOs and 19 men from the Nachrichtenzug (communications) of Kampfgruppe Siebken.

   5.11. Release of 100 surplus men to A. u. E. 12.

2. Weapons delivery:
   5.9. 400 rifles and bayonets received, on loan, from A. u. E. 12; 8. Kompanie has available 1 heavy and 1 medium mortar. Significant shortage of gas masks and spades.

   5.10. Received 38 light machine guns, -Modell 34,
   1 heavy mortar 12 cm, and
   1 medium mortar 34.

   1.11. Received 3 Pak 7.5 cm.

   7.11. Exchanged light machine guns Modell 34 for 46 Modell 42;
   Received 7 Gewehre 41 (rifles),
   11 Maschinenkarabiner 43 (automatic carbines), and
   447 bayonets.

   11.11. Received 179 pistols, and
   3 light machine guns Modell 42.

   18.11. Received 800 gas masks.

   21.11. Received 9 "Ofenrohre" (stove pipes=anti-tank rocket launchers) and 141,600 rounds of rifle and machine gun ammunition as basic provision.

   24.11. Received 7 light machine guns Modell 42,
   3 rifle scopes, mark 41, and
   36 signal pistols.

   27.11. Received 160 mortar shells 12 cm,
   60 stick-grenades,
   30 oval hand grenades,
   33 infantry mines, and
   36 Panzerfausts (large).

29.11. Received 36 Panzerfausts.

3. Motor vehicle delivery:

8.11. Transferred from I. and III./26: 18 trucks;
with that, the Bataillon is motorized to the 57% level.
16 motor vehicles are unserviceable due to transmission damage. No fuel available to test and drive the repaired vehicles. The Bataillon has brought back 21 vehicles from the invasion battles.

26.9. Received 6 cars, model "Steyr".

4. Training:

6.9. Start of infantry training for the recruits, special training for the NCOs within the companies.

10.9. Move into the area Enkenbach—Nehlingen-Alsenborn-Sembach (ten kilometers north of Kaiserslautern) due to frequent air raid alarms in Kaiserslautern; furnishing of quarters.

16.9. The training grounds at Kaiserslautern are available for firing of live ammunition. Training focuses on: hand-to-hand combat, firing in groups. Automatic weapons are still missing.

20.9. Short course for stretcher-bearers by -Bataillon physician.

23.9.
–26.9. Move to the area southeast of Heidelberg.

29.9. Start of group training using live ammunition at night. Blank cartridges are not being supplied for training purposes.

7.10.
–9.10. Move to the area southeast of Oldenburg.

12.10. Start of fourth week of training. Time loss due to moves.

16.10.
–11.11. Transfer of 50 men and 2 instructors to NCO course at the -Regiment.

22.10.
–22.11. Transfer of 30 men to NSKK (national socialist vehicle corps) motor school in Mittweida/Saxony for training as drivers. The Kompanies carry out, weekly, one company exercise, two night exercises and Zug combat firing.

1.11. Live firing of Pak and mortars not possible due to lack of fuel.

3.11. Lack of heating material for troop quarters. Kompanies collect wood in the surrounding woods so that uniforms and shoes can be dried after returning from outdoor activities. Available, per man, only 1 set of cloth uniform and 1 pair of laced shoes.

7.11. Bataillon is fully ready for defensive fighting, only conditionally ready for attack. Heavy Kompanies have not yet been able to hold exercises with live ammunition.

10.11.

–23.11. Bataillon moves by rail transport into the area west of Cologne. The 2,000 liters of fuel provided for training have to be used for the move. The vehicles are being pulled to the loading ramps by wood-gas tractors to save fuel.

18.11. During unloading, transport of 5. and 7. Kompanies attacked by low-level aircraft. One aircraft shot down by four-barrel Luftwaffe Flak accompanying the transport, one aircraft shot down by 7. Kompanie with machine guns. Two men of the machine gun crew, Panzergrenadier Otto Jahns and Panzergrenadier Horst -Borkenfels, seriously wounded. Borkenfels dies soon after.

30.11. Map exercise for officers at the Regiment, theme: "Attack against an enemy prepared for defense and switch to defense".

2.12. Discussion of terrain regarding map exercise of 30.11.1944.

4.12. Transfer of a complete squad of 1 NCO and 10 men for a Panzerjäger-Begleit-kompanie being set up. Setting up a supply Kompanie of the Bataillon.

5.12. Move into the area Fühlingen-Esch-Pesch-Volkshoven, northwest of Cologne, since the Grevenbroich area is overused and under air attack because of the heavily used Grevenbroich railway station to the point where training during daylight hours is nearly impossible.[8]

In a similar manner as for II./26, personnel replacement, delivery of weapons, equipment and vehicles took place in all other units of the Division. The Panzerregiment had salvaged several non-combat-ready training Panzers with which the training could be started. Maneuvers in larger units, in particular maneuvers of Panzers and Panzergrenadiers were impossible due to lack of fuel. There was a very disturbing bottle neck in the delivery of batteries for the radio equipment which also had a negative impact on that part of the training. Firing of live ammunition by the artillery was impossible due to lack of nearby firing ranges. Joint exercises of the different branches—infantry, Panzers, Panzerjägers, and artillery—were not possible for the same reason and for lack of fuel. The majority of the Panzergrenadier battalions consisted of new replacements of officers, NCOs and men. Thus, exercises in units would have been essential in order to form the soldiers into a combat unit and weld them together, so that the individual parts could work together smoothly.

Under such unfavorable material conditions, and the constantly deteriorating war situation, an outsider would have felt understandable concern about the fighting spirit of the troops. In fact, that would have been without cause. While everyone was aware that there was hardly a chance for a final victory, the Allied demand for an UNCONDITIONAL SURRENDER left no other avenue than to continue the fight. In particular, as the horrible fate suffered by the civilian population in the German territories captured by the Soviets had become known. To the reader who did not live through that period in Germany it is probably inconceivable that, despite the serious defeats of the last years, the predominant belief of the troops was that the supreme leadership would find a way out in the end. Above all, the esprit de corps which had developed through bitter battles, held the troops together. The wounded tried, by all means and even if they were not completely healed, to return to their division, their old unit, where their surviving comrades were waiting for them, where they were "at home". Excerpts from a letter by an Untersturmführer, below, will serve as an example:

. . . From 25.9.1944 I had been treated in the reserve hospital at Villach for the effects of being wounded, on 22.8.1944, crossing the Seine near Elbeuf. As ordered by the senior physician, I was moved, on 19.11.1944 to the convalescent hospital Badgastein for six months so as to enable the problem-less healing-in of a shrapnel stuck in my heart. Thus, my marching papers indicated Badgastein. Previously, however, I had 'privately' corresponded with comrades in the staff of the '12'. And, I was determined, more or less on my own account—although with the quiet acquiescence of influential people at the '12.'—to attempt a return to "HJ" Division. I was quite tired not only of hospital life but also of being forced to sit for hours, idly, in the air raid shelter any time enemy aircraft were flying overhead. When I was released from the Villach hospital, I was able to convince a young paymaster aspirant to enter in my pay-book— contrary to the other differing papers—'can be used for work in the reserves' [office duties]. Thus, furnished with documents which gave me at least some leeway, I climbed on the train to Badgastein. However, I rode past it (although the Wehrmacht ticket ended there) to the terminus, Munich.

There, I reported to the station commander's office and requested marching papers to my unit, field post number 59 900. Just as the train patrols previously, the officers there were used to dealing mostly with dodgers, 'deserters', picked up by the Feldgendarmes. To them, I was such a 'crazy' case that they sent me to the office responsible for directing soldiers to the front in Stuttgart. From there, I was sent on—quietly or sometimes openly—gazed at in wonder as a 'peculiar special case', by way of several such offices in the west. None of them could offer any information on the location of the desired field post number since the Division was being moved, at the time, from northern Germany to the west. Finally, the

office in Düsseldorf (or was it Cologne?) was able to help. It was
aware that units of our Division had already reached its district and
initially sent me on to Neuß. There, after a violent attack by low-level
aircraft, I encountered a motorcycle messenger who, by chance, was
on his way to one of our regiments, where Harro Lübbe was also at
the time. After various stops, I reached it and, finally, the Divisional
staff.

Celebrating the successful return and the reunion with many old
acquaintances, I spent the time as a guest at various units of the Divisional staff where I was known from way back in the time of the Normandy invasion.

I can no longer clearly remember who ordered me to undergo a
serious examination by Dr. Oborny.

However, before I could be 'sent off' in accordance with the stern
medical findings of 23.11.1944 (the question was only whether to
the reserves or the convalescent hospital Badgastein), a lucky break
came my way: low-level attack aircraft had caught the 0 2 of the time
so that he would be out of action for a long time. I took advantage
of that: I would carry out the 0 2 duties, as a 'guest', only until a
replacement showed up. But, of course, where would a replacement
come from? . . .[9]

Another significant event from the early period of the refitting must be
reported. After having proved its mettle during the invasion battles, the Division had been awarded the sleeve bands with the inscription "Hitlerjugend",
which was, by no means, a matter of course. On 19 September 1944, the first
of the sleeve bands were presented by Reichsjugendführer (Reich youth
leader) Artur Axmann to the members of Panzergrenadierregiment 26 and
the A. u. E. 12. One of the participants reported on the event at the time in
a letter to his family:

> . . . Today, then, was our big day. I am writing these lines still full of
> that experience. The Reichsjugendführer spent long hours with us.
> Quite early in the morning, while fog still covered the ground all
> around, our Kompanies marched to the parade square. There, the
> whole Regiment and the Ausbildungsbataillon stood in formation.
> The square was very nicely decked out with weapons and guns in
> arrays. When the time came, the fog disappeared and marvelous
> sunshine brightened the heath of the exercise grounds. At 10 A.M.,
> our Regimental commander reported to the reichs-jugendführer,
> who arrived accompanied by Gauleiter (district director) Bürckel,
> whose son is an instructor in my Kompanie. The Reichsjugend-
> führer then slowly passed down the ranks. After singing, together,
> the song: 'Nur der Freiheit gehört unser Leben' (Our lives belong

only to liberty), our Regimental commander then spoke very impressively about the previous heroic battles by our Division. Then, the swearing-in took place. After a trumpet call, the Reichs-jugend-führer addressed us and, above all, conveyed to the Division the Führer's highest esteem. The Reichsjugendführer spoke wonderfully, and all the men were enthusiastic. 'With such volunteers as you, we will never lose the war, despite all the hardships!' Following that, the Reichs-jugendführer presented the members of the Regiment and the Ersatzbataillon the sleeve bands, and handed time-tested soldiers of the Division the Iron Crosses they had been awarded.

At lunch, we sat together with the Reichsjugendführer in the officers' mess. Before that, he had greeted all of us with a handshake and personally presented the sleeve band. We then sat together, in comradeship, for quite a while. Tonight, the Reichsjugendführer drove further west to visit the Hitler youths digging entrenchments there. . .

On a day in late October 1944, members of the Panzer-regiment and the Panzerjägerabteilung were presented the Knight's Crosses awarded to them by the acting Divisional commander in front of the lined-up troops: Sturmbannführer Arnold Jürgensen, commander I. Abteilung of Panzerregiment 12; Obersturmführer Georg Hurdelbrink, chief of 1. Kompanie of Panzerjägerabteilung 12; and Oberscharführer Rudolf Roy, Zugführer in 1. Kompanie of Panzerjägerabteilung 12.

In October, while the refitting was still under way, the Division had to release parts for temporary front action. The I./25, located in Steinfeld/Oldenburg, put together a combat-ready company. It was sent into action in the Reichswald near Kleve on the Lower Rhine. The Kompanie was led by Untersturmführer Fehrmann, the Bataillon adjutant, Untersturmführer Willi Klein, also belonged to it. Presumably, another company was put together by Panzergrenadierregiment 26 and attached to the Kampfgruppe. During the action, under the command of a Fallschirmjäger unit, Untersturmführer - Fehrmann was wounded, but remained with the unit.[11]

On 20 October 1944, Supreme Command West ordered the disengagement of the Kampfgruppen in action at the front, belonging to the Panzer-divisions being refitted, to be completed by 25 October.[12] Consequently, the above mentioned Kampfgruppe was withdrawn from the Reichswald and disbanded. Also, II. Artillerieabteilung under Sturmbannführer Neumann returned to the Division. It had been attached, after the end of the battles at the Maas, to 2. SS-Panzerdivision "Das Reich", and had been in action with a Kampfgruppe of that division at the Westwall. As well, Kampfgruppe Milius came back to the Division and was distributed among the core units.

CHAPTER 8.2
Planning and Preparation

The military situation existing in the fall of 1944, and the rapid worsening of the personnel and material conditions which had to be expected in the German Reich, rendered a defense on all fronts, for the long term, hopeless. A marked improvement could only be expected if it was possible to deliver a major blow to the enemy at an important front, and if such blow would prevent the enemy from carrying out offensive advances for a considerable time. Thus freed German forces—Panzerdivisions, in particular—could then have served at another front to establish major points of thrust, with the goal to achieve operational freedom.

For several reasons, the western front offered itself for a first counterblow. There, after a dogged defense, Aachen had capitulated on 21 October and the Ruhr district was seriously threatened. On the other side, the British and Americans at the western front suffered significant supply problems. They could only rely on the man-made ports in western Normandy and on Cherbourg. The port of Antwerp could not be used by them as long as the mouth of the Schelde river was held by 15. Armee. The other efficient ports in France were still being defended as fortresses, or had been effectively destroyed before being abandoned.

As early as August 1944, Adolf Hitler had indicated to Generaloberst Jodl that he wanted to take to the offensive again in the west. The time he had in mind for that was November, since the enemy air force could then not take advantage of its superiority. On 16 September, he made his decision known, within a small circle, to force a breakthrough from the Ardennes to the Channel coast near Antwerp. That operation would be carried out by thirty divisions. During a discussion with Generalfeldmarschall Keitel and Generaloberst Jodl, which took place a few days later, Adolf Hitler had conveyed his judgment of the enemy situation and his plan of attack in broad strokes: He expected that the English-American army group would first clear the Schelde estuary and then continue its attack across the Maas. The Americans would then try to break through the Westwall near Aachen and then force with two armies, in cooperation with the British/Canadian army group, the breakthrough to the Ruhr district. The formation of further strong points aimed against the Saarland and at the Belfort Gap was to be expected. The establishment of a German focused attack point with thirty divisions opposite sixty-two Allied divisions along the full length of the western front would have to change the overall situation in our favor and stabilize the situation in the west. That would then free forces in the west to repel the expected Russian winter offensive. Hitler planned a surprise breakthrough across the only thinly-held American front in the Ardennes where only four

American divisions were located in the Monschau-Echternach sector. In that tree-covered terrain, the German assembly could be well camouflaged. After a rapid breakthrough by Volksgrenadier (militia grenadier) divisions across the not deeply staggered American positions, the Panzer units would push through to the Maas. If possible, they would establish bridgeheads between Liège and Namur as early as the second day, and then capture Antwerp in an attack across the Maas from these bridgeheads. The British-Canadian Montgomery Army Group and the 9th US Army, as well as the mass of the 1st US Army would thus be cut off from their supplies. The destruction of twenty to thirty divisions would then be possible.

Hitler was well aware that this operation carried several risks. He hoped to meet the Allied air superiority by the choice of a period of weather which was unfavorable for air action. There was still the possibility that the enemy would start an offensive before the German preparations were complete, but those risks would have to be taken.[1]

On 9 October 1944, Generalfeldmarschall Keitel and Generaloberst Jodl had reported which troops and which amounts of material could be made available. Keitel indicated a requirement of 17,000 cubic meters of fuel and 50 ammunition trains. That would be provided by the end of November. According to information from Jodl, twelve Panzer and Panzergrenadier divisions would be available. Some of them were still in action and would have to be pulled out for refitting. In addition, 16 Volksgrenadier divisions would be available by the end of November, another four by 10 December. Three more were to be withdrawn from the front and refitted, and one would be brought in from Norway. Added to that would be two Fallschirmjäger divisions which had to be refitted, so that, by 10 December, a total of twenty-six infantry divisions would be ready. Forces available from the Heer, by the end of November, would be twelve Volks-Artillerie-Korps and seven Volks-Werfer brigades, three more by 15 December as well as fourteen Heer Artillerie Abteilungen. Also ready by 1 December would be sixteen heavy Panzerjäger Abteilungen, four Pionier battalions, six to ten bridge construction units, and one bridge construction battalion. The troops, fuel and ammunition thought to be necessary could also be made available by 10 December.[2]

After discussing five different and possible offensive operations in the west, prepared by Generaloberst Jodl and his staff, Hitler decided on the one corresponding to his original plan, and recommended by Jodl as first choice, Operation Antwerp, starting out from the Eifel. On 22 October, the chiefs of staff of Supreme Command West, Generalleutnant Westphal, and of Heeresgruppe B, General der Infanterie Krebs, were briefed on the intentions and on the plan. During that briefing it was promised, supplemental to the troops specified in the previous discussions of the plan, that five Flak regiments would be brought in and that 1,500 fighter aircraft—among them 100 jet fighters—would be available so that local German air superiority would be assured.[3]

On 1 November, the Wehrmacht operations staff informed Supreme Command West of the "basics of Operation 'Watch on the Rhine'", the code name of the planned offensive.[4]

While in basic agreement with the general reasoning, Generalfeldmarschall von Rundstedt made counterproposals. He thought it necessary to attack from the area north of Aachen simultaneously with the attack from the Eifel. Otherwise it would not be possible to smash the strong forces already located in the triangle Sittard-Liège-Monschau. In addition, he doubted whether it would be possible to pull out all the designated fast units. Altogether, he considered the available forces, in view of the size of the operations area and the strength of the enemy, as extremely weak.[5]

Similar reservations regarding the relative strength were also held by Generalfeldmarschall Model, the supreme commander of Heeresgruppe B, which had to carry out the attack. Moreover, he rejected the proposal by Supreme Command West for a second attack from the area north of Aachen since he did not expect it to be successful considering the enemy preparedness for defense and the relative strength.[6]

On 10 November, Hitler issued the "order for assembly and preparation for the attack" as originally planned.[7]

During the following day, Supreme Command West issued the order for the offensive to Heeresgruppe B. From it, the mission of the Heeresgruppe is reproduced below in full, since it provided information on all essential points in a concise and clear manner.

Order for an operation by Heeresgruppe B.
1. The Führer has ordered a surprise offensive operation in the center of the western front.
   The objective of that operation is, through the -destruction of the enemy forces northeast of the line Antwerp-Brussels-Luxembourg, to bring about a decisive turning point in the western campaign and, with that, possibly of the whole war.
2. I charge Heeresgruppe B with carrying out that operation, for which I hold responsibility.
3. On Day X, Heeresgruppe B, taking advantage of a period of bad weather conditions, will break through the front of the 1st American Army between Monschau and Wasserbillig at several tactically favorable points, after intense, short (approximately 1 hour) preparatory fire.
   In a daring and reckless breakthrough, Heeresgruppe B will gain the Maas crossings between Liège and Dinant, securing its flanks by units staggered to the rear.
   A further objective is, by advancing to Antwerp and the western bank of the Schelde estuary, to cut off the entire English forces and the northern wing of the 1st American Army from

their lines of communication to the rear, and to destroy them in cooperation with Heeresgruppe H.[8]

On 16 November 1944, a major American offensive started in the Aachen area. Several of the divisions designated for the Ardennes Offensive had to be sent into action in the Aachen front sector to prevent a breakthrough. On 20 November, Generalfeldmarschall Model issued a report to Supreme Command West regarding the situation which had emerged, the expected further development and its impact on the planned offensive— here called a "defensive battle" for security reasons. Accordingly, the enemy had assembled eleven infantry and three tank divisions in the area around Aachen. Behind them, further forces, among them several tank divisions, were reported in readiness. In Model's opinion, that massing of forces offered the possibility, ". . . immediately after repelling the enemy attacks, which seek to bring about a decisive change, or even during those attacks, to land a destructive blow against the densely crowded enemy forces through a pincer encirclement . . ." He expected that, in order to prevent a breakthrough to the Rhine, ". . . for the short term, four Volksgrenadier divisions and nine fast units . . ." would not be available for other duties. The remaining 6 Panzer- and 6 Volksgrenadier divisions, and the 3. Fallschirmjägerdivision, would not be sufficient for an attack with far-reaching goals. After completion of the defensive battle, however, the American units would be decisively weakened for a short time so that the available German forces would be sufficient for ". . . a promising encircling attack against the 9th American Army and the adjoining wings of the 2nd English and 1st American Armies. . ." According to Model's conception, the 5. Panzerarmee would attack, at a width of approximately twenty kilometers, from the area around and to the west of Heinsberg (approx. thirty kilometers north of Aachen) in a southwesterly direction. It would break through to Maastricht, establish a bridgehead on the western bank of the Maas, and then swing with the fast units (9. Panzerdivision, 15. Panzergrenadierdivision, 10. SS-Panzerdivision) to the south and southeast. The 6. Panzerarmee would have to break through the still thinly held enemy front line, at a width of some twenty-five kilometers, near and south of Monschau. It would push through to the Maas line between Visé-Liège, by way of Eupen and Verviers, and then turn one of its Panzerkorps toward the north. That Armee would consist of 5 Volksgrenadier divisions and the 4 SS-Panzerdivisions of I. and II. SS-Panzerkorps. The 15. Armee would tie down the enemy between Linnich (twenty-six kilometers north of Aachen) and Schmidt (at the northern edge of the Rur reservoir, eighteen kilometers southwest of Düren) through local attacks. It would then prepare to pursue on both sides of Aachen, while 7. Armee, with a strong right wing, would join the attack by 6. Panzerarmee and advance, with its northern wing, via Malmedy to the Amblève sector.

Through that operation, the enemy forces around Aachen were to be destroyed. The fast units would then be available for a continued, or a new, operation. Feldmarschall Model was of the opinion that the, initially limited, operation ". . . would have to be successful . . ." and, in addition, offered the possibility to strive for more distant goals.[9]

Feldmarschall von Rundstedt, in a flash teletype of 21. November, 00.40 hours, to Generaloberst Jodl, accepted that proposal. The OKW replied on 22 November that the Führer had not agreed to the proposal.[10]

The substantiation for that decision, which followed on 25 November, stated that the enemy picture, on which the planning was based, had been confirmed, the supply problems of the enemy were increasing. Thus, the "large-scale solution . . ." would be maintained, despite the very unwelcome tying up of forces, in the Aachen area, designated for the offensive. During a discussion which took place on 2 December, and in which the involved supreme commanders in the west took place, Feldmarschall Model once again presented his point of view forcefully, but was unable to change Hitler's mind. In a subsequent conversation with General von Manteuffel, the supreme commander of 5. Panzerarmee, Hitler also spoke about his political considerations. He regarded the enemy coalition as fragile, he wanted to shake it up through a major military defeat of the Western Allies. He expected that the Western Allies would then be willing to negotiate and to drop their previous demand of an UNCONDITIONAL SURRENDER. He was aware of the big risk, but was determined to now stake everything on one card.[11]

On 28.11.1944, Heeresgruppe B then issued the "Operational order for the attack by Heeresgruppe B across the Maas on Antwerp". The most important points of that order, which provide the required overview, are reproduced below:

   . . . 1. Enemy situation
    a) Enemy forces:
      Facing the front of Heeresgruppe B, the American Army Group 12, including reserves close to the front, has available Two armies and 25 large units, namely
      facing Pz.AOK 6: 5 large units with 300 tanks,
      facing Pz.AOK 5: 3 large units with 150 tanks,
      facing AOK 7: 2 large units with 100 tanks,
      facing AOK 15: 15 large units with 1,450 tanks,
      for a total of 25 large units with 2,000 tanks.
      Of these, 3 or 4 large units are reserves close to the front, of which the enemy can initially withdraw three from the Aachen area for an attack to the south. A further unit is presumably located behind the central sector of the Eifel front. The 1st

American Infantry Division is not yet battle-ready because of its heavy losses. Operational reserves—a maximum of 3 large units—are available to the enemy for action no sooner than at the Maas. The English Army Group 21 in Holland consists of 16 large units, almost all of which are in action at the front.

b) Enemy activity:

The American Army Groups 12 and 6 will continue their attacks from the Aachen area and in the Saarland. Their present focal point is in the Saarland. The quiet Eifel front, located between two focal points, is, at the present, the weakest enemy sector on the whole of the western front . . .

3. On Day O (probably 14.12.1944), Heeresgruppe B will, taking full advantage of the moment of surprise, break through the front line of the 1st American Army, which is at present thinly held, at a width of approximately 100 kilometers. It will, irresistibly, push across the Maas line Liège-Namur toward Antwerp in order to destroy the enemy forces located north of the spearhead later in cooperation with Heeresgruppe H.

The start of the attack depends on a period of bad weather which is being awaited . . .

5. Tasks:

6. Panzerarmee

6. Panzerarmee will break through the enemy front north of the Eifel and recklessly throw its fast units at the enemy's right flank toward the Maas crossings between Liège and Huy in order to capture them undamaged, in cooperation with Operation 'Greif' (griffin). Following that, the Armee will advance to the Albert Canal between Maastricht and Antwerp (inclusive).

The breakthrough by the Volksgrenadiers through the Hohe Venn will be supported by the Fallschirm Operation 'Stößer' (thruster).

Adjoining the Vesdre river on both sides of Eupen and the eastern fortification of Liège, a strong defensive flank, including artillery, must be established toward the north and, initially, defended with utmost determination. As soon as 6. Panzerarmee has forced the crossing of the Maas, that defensive flank will be handed over to 15. Armee.

Operation 'Stößer' will be carried out by 800 Fall-schirm-jägers on Day O at approximately 07.45 hours. Their mission is to capture, with some of their parts, the pass and road fork near Monte Rigi, and, with its mass, the pass and high ground on both sides of Hockey. They will hold on to the captured terrain until ground troops arrive to relieve them. Should it be impossible to carry out the Operation because of weather, it will follow 24 hours later. The mission then will be either to capture the Maas bridges between Liège and Huy undamaged, or, depending on the situation, to capture important objects northwest of the Maas early. Respective proposals to be submitted to the Heeresgruppe on Day O.

5. Panzerarmee

5. Panzerarmee will break through the enemy front on both sides on the northern border of Luxembourg and advance, without halt (especially, using the roads Marche-Namur and Bastogne-Dinant), across the Maas between Andenne and Givet. Parts of the Armee will, in case the situation requires or offers itself, be brought forward via Dinant and the Sambre river into the Brussels area and west of Antwerp. There, the objective of the Armee will be to prevent any activity of enemy reserves against the rear of 6. Panzerarmee along the line Dinant-Givet. To do that, the Armee spearheads will have to keep abreast, at least, with those of 6. Panzerarmee, and, without concern for the deep flanks, gain the Antwerp-Brussels area as quickly as possible.

7. Armee

7. Armee is charged with securing the flanks of the operation to the south and southwest. In order to do that, it will break through the enemy positions between Vianden and Echternach and establish a defensive front along the general lines Godinne-Libramont-Medernach.

With its right wing, using spearheads of the Volksgrenadier divisions, the Armee will maintain contact with 5. Panzerarmee. Through an energetic advance to the south and southwest, making use of any favorable circumstance, territory and time will have to be gained in order to build up a firm defensive front from where extensive destruction and mining will be carried out. The most important precondition for that is the destruction of the enemy artillery forces facing the southern wing in the vicinity of Old-Trier.

Extensive supplies of blockading equipment and units, and anti-tank weapons are required.

15. Armee

15. Armee will initially secure the crossing of the Maas by 6. Panzerarmee at its right flank and rear. The first objective of the Armee is to tie up the strong enemy forces in the area south of Roermond-Liège-east of Eupen through numerous individual attacks from the north, east and south.

As soon as the situation makes it at all possible, a concentrated attack, massing all available forces, will break through these enemy forces and destroy them. In that sector, the enemy must not be warned by minor attacks before the start of the attack . . .

7. Support by flying units.

Luftwaffe-Kommando-West will support the attack by Heeresgruppe B with all available air force units. To do that, strong
fighter- and destroyer units have been readied.

a. Reconnaissance:

During the operation, it is initially important to monitor the
movements by enemy reserves, in particular of the motorized
units, against the spearheads and the flanks of the attacking
armies.

b. Operational action:

The focal point is concentrated on the action by the fighter
squadrons whose main objective is to give cover to the Panzer
spearheads, routes of advance, and assemblies. In addition, a
surprise attack against occupied airfields of the enemy strike
forces close to the front is possible.

Action of direct support to the Heer may only be considered
at focal points in view of the small number of German air
units.

Air attacks against major traffic centers, rail- and road traffic,
will be the main objective of the squadrons in action during
darkness, provided the weather is favorable.

8. Support by the Flak units.

a. The III. Flak-Korps will accompany the advance of the Heeresgruppe. It will support, depending on the situation in the air,
the artillery preparatory fire with all available heavy batteries.
It will take over and concentrate on the air defense of the
spearhead units of the attacking army and will bring up further Flak forces to provide cover to the Heeresgruppe in the
depth of the advance sector.

b. The following are ordered to coordinate their -actions:

2. Flak-Div. with 21 heavy, 23 medium and light batteries with
6. Panzer Armee;

19. Flak-Brigade with 14 heavy, 14 medium and light batteries
with 5. Panzer Armee;

Flak-Regiment 15 with 12 heavy, 14 medium and light batteries
with 7. Armee;

1. Flak-Brigade with 16. heavy, 8 medium and light batteries
with 15. Armee . . .

f. The Flak Abteilungen of the Heer and the Waffen-SS will be
put into action according to the wishes of the Heer commands, with a focus on air defense. They are tactically assigned
to III. Flak-Korps for the coordinated conduct of the air
defense.

9. Command posts.

As of 10.00 hours of 11.12.1944, command of the Heeres-gruppe will be conducted from the advanced battle command post Münstereifel. The remainder of the command posts will operate as already ordered . . .[12]

Appendix 3 to that order determined the:

. . . Details for the start of the attack

   a. The time for the opening of fire is fixed for 05.30 hours for all units.

   b. In order to maintain the element of surprise to the greatest possible extent, the time period for preparatory fire for the attack will be restricted to 5 to 10 minutes depending on the distance of the infantry from the enemy positions. To carry out that preparatory fire, all available barrels of the artillery, mortars and Flak, as well as all heavy weapons of the infantry, will join together to create a hurricane of fire, using the most rapid possible rate of fire, in the narrow breakthrough zones.

      Immediately prior to, and during, the preparatory fire, the infantry must be moved close enough to the enemy positions so that the breakthrough, on the run, can take place as soon as the last shell is fired.

      Advantage must be taken of all points where it is possible to infiltrate through the enemy lines without preparatory fire, in particular where creeks or sectors close to the main line of defense have to be crossed, in order to save time. If enemy resistance is encountered, the fire attack ordered for the other front points must take place, as annihilating fire, on pre-selected fire zones without delay on the request of the infantry.

   c. 05.35 hours is fixed as the time when all headlights will be turned on.

   d. Immediately after the preparatory fire, the artillery, mortars and Flak will carry out the following tasks:

      aa. Suppressing the recognized and suspected enemy command posts within the fire zone in order to paralyze the enemy command and its communications network.

      bb. Suppressing the enemy artillery.

      cc. Concentrating fire on villages, camps, and other troop lodgings.

   e. It is particularly important for the artillery to ensure, through rolling fire, that the forward observers accompanying the advancing infantry will be able to direct fire, based

on their observations, with the arrival of daylight. In order
to maintain contact with the infantry under all circumstances, it is thus required that strong artillery elements follow immediately behind the infantry . . .[12a]

The 6. Panzerarmee was to be divided as follows for the offensive:
Generalkommando LXVII (general command) A.K. with
   272. Volksgrenadierdivision and
   326. Volks-grenadier-division;
Generalkommando I. SS-Panzerkorps with
   277. Volksgrenadierdivision,
   12. Volksgrenadierdivision,
   3. Fallschirmjäger-Division,
   12. SS-Panzerdivision "HJ" and
   1. SS-Panzerdivision "LAH";
Generalkommando II. SS-Panzerkorps with
   2. SS-Panzerdivision "Das Reich" and
   9. SS-Panzerdivision "Hohenstaufen";
further, Volks-Artillerie-Korps 388, 402 and 405 as well as the Volks-Werfer Brigades 4, 9, and 17. Volks-Artillerie-Korps 410 was to move in
later to reinforce the northern flank. Added to that were, from the
Heer, five heavy mortar- and gun batteries and one light reconnaissance Abteilung, three Pionier battalions, two Pionier construction
battalions, nine bridge building squads, one bridge building battalion
and one OT—Brigade (Organisation Todt=labor services) with four
regiments, two assault gun brigades, one assault Panzer ("F")
Abteilung and one Panzerjäger Abteilung (mot.-Zug).
The 5. Panzerarmee would structure itself into one -General-kommando
with two Volksgrenadierdivisions and two Panzerkorps with two Volksgrenadierdivisions and three Panzerdivisions—116., 2., and Panzer-
Lehr-Division. Added to that were two Volks-Artillerie-Korps and
three Volks-Werfer Brigades as well as Heer forces of similar structure
and similar size as with 6. Panzerarmee.[13]

The structure of 15. and 7. Armee with four and three Armeekorps
respectively do not need to be listed here in detail.
    The Heeresgruppe had one Volksgrenadierdivision available as reserve.
It was scheduled to arrive between 13 and 16 December. In addition, the
Heeresgruppe could fall back on the OKW reserve which was to consist of
10. SS-Panzerdivision, 3. Panzer-Grenadier-Division, 6. SS-Gebirgs-Division
(mountain infantry), 11. Panzerdivision, and three Volksgrenadierdivisions.
These divisions were either being refitted, were on the move, or had to, as
11. Panzerdivision, first be pulled out of the front line.[14]

While the supreme commands were planning and preparing for the offensive, the refitting of "HJ" Division continued with all the previously described problems, but also with great zeal. In accordance with an order from OKW of 6 November, the Division moved into the area west of Cologne.[15] The move took until the end of November. Entries in the war diary of III./26, the only one preserved, may serve as an example of the difficulties which had to be overcome during the move. The Bataillon began the move on 17 November from the Diepholz district on two transport trains. On 19 November at 13.10 hours, the second train was attacked by several low-level attack aircraft on the stretch between Paderborn and Soest. The 2 cm Flak Zug attached to the transport fought off the low-level aircraft and was able to prevent serious damage to the unit. Three men were wounded by shrapnel and minor damage to vehicles occurred. However, the transport was stalled since the rail line had been destroyed by bombs and the locomotive had been immobilized by fire from the low-level aircraft. On 22 November, the transport finally arrived in Groß-Königsdorf, west of Cologne, and was unloaded during the night. The staff, supply company, 9. and 10. Kompanies moved into quarters in Gleul, 11. Kompanie in Altstädten, 12. Kompanie in Burbach. The latter only arrived on 24 November.

Personal notes show the route of transport of 4. Batterie of the Flak-Abteilung. It moved between 10 and 13 November by rail transport from Barnstorf by way of Nienburg/Weser, Hannover-Linden, Hameln, Paderborn, Soest, Hagen, Wuppertal, Neuss and Niederaussem near Cologne.[16]

The Divisional staff headquarters was set up in Brauweiler.

In conjunction with the move of the Division, the Panzer-regiment was also restructured. Since it was not possible to fully equip two Panzer Abteilungen, a mixed operations and training Abteilung were each formed prior to the departure. Each Abteilung consisted of two companies of Panzer IVs and two companies of Panthers. The I. Abteilung under the command of Sturmbannführer Arnold Jürgensen moved together with the Division into the area west of Cologne and was provided with seventeen Panzers per company. The II. Abteilung, commanded by Hauptsturmführer Hans Siegel, moved, with several old training Panzers to the training camp Falling-bostel, for refitting there. The OKW order of 17.11.1944 temporarily assigned Schwere Panzerjägerabteilung 559 to the Division as the second operational Abteilung.[15a] It arrived at the Division at the end of November/beginning of December. However, before unloading, it was sent on to the Saar front for immediate action. The members of the Abteilung still believed to be part of "HJ" Division since an American leaflet was delivered to the Divisional staff, stating, i.a., that the strength of the American offensive was already forcing Hitler to throw his last reserves into battle. As an example, the 12. SS Panzerdivision "Hitlerjugend" had already been put into action at the Saar front.

That was unexpected support for the attempt to deceive the enemy. In the place of that Abteilung, the OKW order of 5 December 1944 attached Schwere Panzerjägerabteilung 560 which was equipped with Jagdpanzers (tank destroyers). It was commanded by Major Streger and arrived at the Division a few days before the start of the offensive.[15b]

A Panzerregiment, consisting of a mixed Panzerabteilung and a Panzer-jägerabteilung, could not possibly be fully -operational. The Jagdpanzer Abteilung was not trained for armor- or assault gun-like attack in coopera-tion with Panzergrenadiers, much less did it have any experience in that form of combat. Action as a cohesive unit by the Panzerregiment could thus be hardly expected.

The Schwere SS-Panzerabteilung 501, equipped with Tiger IIs (König-stiger = King Tiger), the Korps Tiger Abteilung, was assigned to the Panzer-regiment of the "LAH" as its II. Abteilung.

On 15 November, Standartenführer Hugo Kraas took over the com-mand of the Division. Immediately previous, he had been commander of the SS-Panzergrenadierregiment 2 of 1. SS-Panzerdivision "LAH". It had initially been intended that Brigadeführer Fritz Kraemer, the chief of staff of I. SS-Panzerkorps during the invasion battles, would take over command of the Division. At the urgent request of Oberst-gruppenführer and Panzergener-aloberst der Waffen-SS Sepp Dietrich, who had been given the command of 6. Panzerarmee, he had declined, and accepted the position of chief of staff of that Armee. In the person of Standartenführer Hugo Kraas, a highly capa-ble commander took over the leadership of "HJ" Division. After the bitter defensive battles in Russia during the fall and winter 1943–44 he had been decorated with the Oak Leaves (the 375th soldier) to the Knight's Cross.

Once established in its new quarters, the Division received orders to pre-vent a breakthrough by the Americans to the Rhine, as OKW reserve. Possi-bilities of action for defense and counterattack were to be determined. The Division was assigned a defensive sector on both sides of Bergheim along the Erft river, which runs half-way between Rur and Rhine, parallel to both rivers. Positions were to be designated and partially reinforced. Units were held in readiness to move into the most important sectors in case of an American breakthrough across the Rur. An armored group, consisting of III./26, I. Panzerabteilung and attached heavy weapons, was assembled in the area around Bedburg. The I./26 was moved forward into the sector Titz-Oberzier (southeast of Jülich). At the same time, training had to continue. It was made difficult by the high density of troops in the area and the radio silence which had been ordered.[17]

On 6 December, the 6. Panzerarmee briefed, in Brühl and with Gener-alfeldmarschall Model present, the divisional commanders and the chiefs of staff in broad outlines on the planned offensive by means of a map exercise. Substituting for the supreme commander, the commanding general of II. SS-Panzerkorps, SS-Oberstgruppenführer and General der Waffen-SS Wilhelm

Bittrich, directed the briefing. After the map exercise, the Feldmarschall said to his escorting officer, Sturm-bannführer Hein Springer, who had been the adjutant of the "HJ" Division during its formation: "Herr Springer, that was a magnificent map exercise tonight, as well prepared and directed as I have seldom seen. I am highly pleased."[17a] On 9 December, the commanding general of I. SS-Panzerkorps, SS-Gruppenführer and Generalleutnant der Waffen-SS Hermann Prieß, informed the divisional commanders and senior general staff officers of the tasks of their divisions.[18]

Regarding the enemy expected in the attack sector of I. SS-Panzerkorps, it was reported that the 99th Infantry Division was in the forward line at a broad front in a loose arrangement, anchored on strong points, from Losheimergraben to the north. The 106th US Infantry Division was reported in position south of Losheimergraben. Several days later, it was reported that the 2nd US Infantry Division was being moved from the south to the exercise grounds at Elsenborn, to be refitted after the losses it had suffered at the Saar front. The 1st US Infantry Division was reported northwest of Verviers for refitting and as reserve.[19] It was known that the two divisions in action at the front line had only recently been moved from the United States to Europe and had no combat experience. Obviously, they had been assigned to the quiet front sector in the Eifel to get acclimatized. It was reported that scouting parties of the forward German infantry divisions had succeeded in penetrating several kilometers deep into the American combat area some time previously. During the last weeks, activity by scouting parties had been stopped in order to create the impression that the Germans considered that sector of the front of no importance.

The chief of staff of I. SS-Panzerkorps, Standartenführer Rudolf Lehmann, requested from the chief of staff of 6. Panzerarmee, Brigadeführer Fritz Kraemer, that the attack sector of I. SS-Panzerkorps be moved south by a distance of the width of one or two divisions. That request was based on the apprehension of an enemy threat from the direction of Elsenborn. The Armee supreme command, in turn, requested it from the Heeresgruppe. It, or the OKW, refused the request.[19a]

On Day X, after short preparatory fire from the massed artillery, I. SS-Panzerkorps was to break through the American positions in the Hollerath-Krewinkel sector with three infantry divisions. It would then, with 12. SS-Panzerdivision on the right and 1. SS-Panzerdivision on the left, ". . . throw itself at the Maas". . . with no regard to any threats to the flanks. In the Liège-Huy sector, it was to establish and hold bridgeheads across the Maas. The Korps had to be prepared to either break through to Antwerp or to move to protect the right flank of 6. Panzerarmee.

Assigned to the Korps for the breakthrough were 277. and 12. Volksgrenadierdivisions as well as 3. Fallschirmjäger-division. The 277. Volksgrenadierdivision had been in position in the attack sector of the Korps since October. It had been assembled in September 1944 from the remnants of 277. Infanteriedivision which had escaped the Falaise encirclement, and 574. Volksgrenadierdivision which was being established in Hungary. On approximately 10 November, it had begun to relieve, as the units arrived, the 347. Infanterie-division. After a four-week period of action at the Westwall, its divisional commander, Generalmajor Wilhelm Viebig judged his troops as being ". . . suitable for defense . . ." A few companies had been trained for offensive tasks (counterattacks), in a limited scope.[19b] The 12. Volksgrenadierdivision had proved itself in many bitter battles, it was well equipped with the latest weapons. Shortly before the start of the attack, it was to be brought in from the Aachen area and replace parts of 277. Volksgrenadierdivision on the left wing of that division. The 3. Fallschirmjügerdivision, as well, had to be moved in from the area east of Aachen. It had suffered significant losses during the battles in the Düren forest. The division was well equipped with weapons but suffered from a shortage of tractors. One assault gun Abteilung had been promised to both the 277. Volksgrenadierdivision and 3. Fallschirmjägerdivision in order to support their attack. However, they did not arrive.[19c]

The attack by the infantry divisions was planned to start, as mentioned, after a five to ten minute period of preparatory fire. The artillery regiments of all divisions, the Korps Artillerie Abteilungen, the Volks-Artillerie-Korps, the Volks-Werfer brigades and the heavy Heer artillery batteries were to take part in the fire attack. The enemy was to be smashed in his positions, and demoralized, so that the attacking infantry could force a breakthrough with relative ease.

In the sector of the Korps, the American positions ran from the right wing at the road bend west of Hollerath to Lanzerath, embedded in a wooded belt some 2–3 kilometers deep. They could thus not be observed directly. Since there were no late reports from scouting sorties either, only assumptions regarding the line of positions could be made. That constituted an impossible situation for a successful preparatory fire attack as ordered. Thus, the general command had repeatedly requested from the Armee to forego the preparatory fire, and only to open fire on confirmed targets simultaneously with the infantry attack, or on certain points in the terrain. That request was rejected. As well, the Korps had suggested to the Armee that it would put parts of the Panzer divisions into action for the breakthrough attack, since the combat effectiveness of 277. Volksgrenadierdivision and of 3. Fallschirmjäger-Division was insufficient for the tasks. The proposal was not accepted.[19d]

Five routes in the depth of the Korps sector were designated for the breakthrough by the two Panzer divisions: A, B, C, D, E. The capacity of those roads varied greatly. Thus, Route A from the road bend west of Hollerath toward Rocherath was an unimproved wood path for the first three kilometers, the continuation to Rocherath was an improved road of some four meters serviceable width, ". . . only conditionally usable by trucks . . ." From

Rocherath, the road continued via Krinkelt and Wirtzfeld to Elsenborn. Krinkelt and Wirtzfeld were connected by an ". . . improved country lane . . ." which was ". . . usable by single vehicles at all times, except during unusual weather conditions . . ." From Wirtzfeld to Elsenborn led an improved lane, for two kilometers. It was followed by three kilometers of lane, less well maintained which connected, in turn, to an improved lane before the village of Elsenborn was reached. The further course of Route A from Lager Elsenborn via Sourbrodt-Ovifat to Hockai (Hockey) followed, for long stretches, improved roads and maintained lanes.

Advance Route B branched off Route C between Weißer Stein and Losheimergraben. It ran from there along forest- and field lanes to Mürringen and then on to Bütgenbach. Then followed a good road to Belair. However, from there again it ran along field lanes via Bruyères to G'doumont, and on via Bèvercè to Bernister, reaching a paved road at Francorchamps.

Advance Route C started near Neuhof, joined the Reichsstraße (paved major road) 1.5 kilometers to the west. It followed the Reichsstraße to Losheimergraben and from there continued along a paved road via Büllingen, Morschheck to west of Hepscheid. Then, along a country lane to Möderscheid, along an improved road via Schoppen and Faymonville, and finally to reach Malmedy along a paved road. The advance route then continued along the same kind of road via Stavelot. The other two advance routes, D and E, also had to use forest lanes for lengthy stretches (Route D between Pont—two kilometers southwest of Engelsdorf—and Logbierme—three kilometers southeast of Wanne; Route E between Herresbach—six kilometers southwest of Manderfeld—and Meyerode). The only good advance route in the whole sector of the Korps, and thus of 6. Panzerarmee, was Route C, with one minor exception which could, if necessary, be avoided by using a stretch of Route B.[20] In addition, the effectiveness of the advance routes was diminished by the winter weather. Those roads and lanes which were not used by the Americans as supply routes could be expected to have only one lane after the snow cover had been packed, and could thus be used only as one-way routes.

In contrast to the deficient east-west roads there were several good roads from north to south which allowed a fast movement of reserves. Among these, above all, were the paved roads Eupen-Sourbrodt-Weismes-St. Vith, the paved road Verviers-Francorchamps-Stavelot-Vielsalm, the paved road Liège-Louveigne-Werbomont-Houffalize, the paved road Liège-Sprimont-Bomal-Amonines-Laroche. There were numerous roads of the same quality connecting them.

Many creeks and rivers, flowing to the Maas, cut through the attack sector of the Korps up to the Maas. In particular, the Amblève and Ourthe might create problems. Up to the Maas, the terrain was very hilly. In the region south and southwest of Malmedy it climbed up to 600 meters, while the highest hills then dropped off to the west to 500 meters, 400 meters to

200 meters immediately east of the Ourthe. In the area between the Ourthe and Maas the high plains were at elevations between 200 meters and 300 meters. Ahead of the front lay a belt of woods, one to four kilometers deep. Behind it in the right sector stretched open terrain up to Weismes, while in the left sector of the Korps more extensive connected wooded areas covered the slopes. West of the Malmedy-St. Vith line then began a large forest which opened up only a few kilometers from the Ourthe. The terrain between the Ourthe and Maas was mainly open and covered only by smaller wooded areas, except in the region immediately southwest of Liège.

From the Amblève northwest of Stavelot, the Hohe Venn stretched into the vicinity of Monschau. That wooded and partly swampy ridge of hills with elevations of 562 meters north of Stoumont, 692 meters near Mont Rigi and 658 meters northwest of Monschau, constituted somewhat of a barrier on the right flank of the Korps. However, as described above, it was crossed by two paved roads from Eupen and Verviers in a north-south direction.

Based on the road and terrain conditions, it was important that the three infantry divisions should speedily break through the American main battle field so that the two spearhead Panzer divisions could quickly reach open terrain. The 12. SS-Panzerdivision "HJ" would be most exposed to the threat from the right flank, in particular as the LXVII. A.K., adjoining on the right, would not advance with immediate contact to I. SS-Panzerkorps. That would create a fifteen-kilometer-wide gap. After achieving the breakthrough, the three infantry divisions were to swing northwest and secure the flank of I. SS-Panzerkorps along the line Arenberg-Elsenborn-Sourbrodt. However, that plan required a time-consuming restructuring after the breakthrough fighting and a troublesome crossing of the advance routes of the Panzerdivisions. Given those circumstances, the focal point of the thrust to the Maas had to be with 1. SS-Panzerdivision which was better equipped with Panzers for that action.

The attack by the three infantry divisions was planned and approved by the Korps as follows:

The 277. Volksgrenadierdivision forms two attack groups and will attack, with the focal point on the left, southwest of Udenbreth.

Grenadierregiment 989, reinforced by one Pionier Kompanie and parts of the Panzerjägerabteilung, assembles in the vicinity of the Westwall bunkers around Hollerath. Following maximum artillery preparation, it will advance on Rocherath from Hollerath across the Jans creek and capture the town.

Grenadierregiment 990, reinforced by one Füsilier Kompanie and one Pionier Kompanie, assembles in the vicinity of the Westwall bunkers near Udenbreth. It will capture Krinkelt.

Grenadierregiment 991 assembles approximately in the center between the two attack groups in the vicinity of Ramscheid. After clearing the Reichsstraße Hollerath-Weißer Stein, it will follow either the right or left group, depending on the development of the situation.

The 12. Volksgrenadierdivision will break through the positions on both sides of Losheim. It will advance with a reinforced Grenadier regiment across the important crossroads Losheimergraben. With a second reinforced Grenadier regiment, it will advance along the rail line, capture Honsfeld, and then advance on Hünningen and Büllingen.

The 3. Fallschirmjäger Division will capture the enemy positions in the Berterath-Manderfeld sector and then push forward toward Hepscheid and Heppenbach.

After the infantry divisions had broken through the American positions, "HJ" Division would start out in the following formation:

along Route A: one reinforced Panzergrenadier Bataillon with attached Panzerjägerabteilung 12;

along Route B: one reinforced Panzergrenadier regiment without one reinforced Bataillon;

along Route C: as the first marching column, the -armored group; as the second column, the Aufklärungs-abteilung; as the third column, one reinforced Panzergrenadier regiment without one Bataillon.

The Division designated the reinforced I. Bataillon of SS-Panzer-grenadierregiment 25 and the Panzerjägerabteilung as the column on Route A. Behind them, the remainder of the reinforced Regiment 25 was to follow, since Route B diverged from Route C, on which the body of the Division would march, between Weißer Stein and Losheimergraben. It could be assumed that the column designated for Route B could switch over from Route A to Route B at Krinkelt.

The armored group designated as the first column on Route C was to consist of Panzerregiment 12, reinforced by the SPW-Bataillon (III./26), the armored Pionier Kompanie, the heavy infantry gun company of Regiment 26, and I. Artillerie-abteilung. As already stated, the Aufklärungsabteilung would follow behind as the second column. The operations staff of the divisional staff would initially join the Aufklärungsabteilung. The third column would be made up of the reinforced Panzergrenadierregiment 26 (without III. Bataillon), Werfer-abteilung 12, and the staffs of the Artillerieregiment, the Flak Abteilung, the Pionierbataillon and the Nachrichtenabteilung (communications). The attached Luftwaffe-Flak-Abteilung and the bridge construction unit of the Heer were to be incorporated depending on situation and requirements.[22]

The "LAH" would march on Routes D and E. On the right route, the first column would be the armored group, behind it as the second column, the reinforced Aufklärungsabteilung. The third column would be a reinforced Panzergrenadier-regiment, with it, the operations group of the general -command of I. SS-Panzerkorps. One reinforced Panzer-grenadier-regiment and the assault gun Abteilung were designated for the left route.[23]

According to that structure, the armored groups and the bulk of 1. and 12. SS-Panzerdivisions would march abreast on Routes C and D. The columns on Routes A and B on the right and on E on the left could, if required, secure their flanks.

Since covering the open right flank was of major importance, action by a Fallschirmjäger combat unit in a parachute drop on the Hohe Venn was planned. Their mission was to block the roads Eupen-Malmedy and Verviers-Malmedy in the vicinity of the road fork Belle Croix (twelve kilometers north of Malmedy). They would later be incorporated into the infantry divisions which had turned north. Oberstleutnant Freiherr von der Heydte was charged with the formation and command of the Fallschirmjäger combat unit. For reasons of secrecy, he had to form up his unit from members of all Fallschirmjäger regiments in the west. They were pulled out of their units under the pretense of being posted to a Fallschirmjäger combat school of the Armee. The structure of the combat unit was one Nachrichten Zug, four rifle companies, one heavy company with twelve heavy machine guns and four medium mortars, and one Pionier company. After a briefing on the overall situation and their own intentions at the Luftwaffe Command West and at the Heeresgruppe B, Oberstleutnant von der Heydte received his orders on 14 december at the headquarters of 6. Panzerarmee. The jump would take place on Day X, immediately before the planned artillery attack, i.e. still during darkness. There was no information on the enemy situation in the jump area. The request for aerial reconnaissance or scouting action by front line squads was refused for reasons of secrecy. Carrier pigeons, which were requested as a reserve means of sending information, could not be provided. Approval was given only for the assignment of a forward observer from a battery. He would jump at the same time and direct fire on identified targets. Maps and photo documentation were inadequate.[24]

The Division provided, as the forward observer for the action which could have great significance for the security of its open right flank, the chief of 7. Batterie, Obersturmführer Harald Etterich, together with a portable radio communications squad. None of these men had ever jumped with a parachute. The paratroop action was given the code name "Stößer" (pouncer).

It was important for the success of the operation that the major bridges across the larger rivers, in particular the Amblève, Ourthe and Maas, fell into German hands undamaged. Thus, they had to be captured, if possible, before they were blown up. It was highly questionable whether it would be possible to throw fast German groups of sufficient strength, with the element of surprise, in time at the decisive points. Adolf Hitler had the idea of sending a combat group into action, disguised as Americans. That task was handed to Obersturmbannführer Otto Skorzeny. He was the commander of the SS-Jagd (rifle) units and had become famous for liberating Mussolini, together with Fallschirmjägers of the Luftwaffe. He was called to the Führerhauptquartier (Führer headquarters) at the end of October and briefed on the plan by Adolf Hitler. He was given orders to set up a tank brigade of volunteers who spoke American English perfectly. It would be equipped with American weapons, vehicles and tanks, and its members would be dressed in American uniforms. Its task was, above all, to capture certain Maas bridges above Liège undamaged and to hold them until the German Panzer spearheads would take them over. The more detailed briefing by Generalfeldmarschall Keitel and Generaloberst Jodl took place at the end of November or beginning of December. Skorzeny structured his unit into two main groups: the "Commando group" and the "Panzerbrigade 150".

The "Commando group" consisted of members from all armed forces branches who spoke American English. These men were issued American uniforms. The top rank was Colonel. The group was given American jeeps. Three different kinds of groups were set up: the "destroyer squads", consisting of five to six men each, to destroy bridges, fuel storages and ammunition dumps; the "Aufklärungs squads" of four to five men, to scout the movements of tank units, artillery units and of other forces south and north of the Maas. They were, to some extent, equipped with radios. In addition to their pure reconnaissance activities, they would also issue wrong orders to American forces, turn around road signs, remove the markings from mine fields or indicate mine fields which did not exist. The "Lead Commandos" had the task, in close cooperation with the attacking divisions, to cut enemy telephone lines, destroy radio communications posts, and issue false orders.

The "Panzerbrigade 150" was formed from the following staffs and units:
Staff and Nachrichten-Kompanie,
2 Panzer groups, 1 infantry group as well as
3 smaller staffs for the combat groups.

The personnel came from various branches:
2 battalions from "Kampfgruppe 200", a Luftwaffe Fallschirm unit (800 men),
1 infantry company from "Jagdverband Mitte" (rifle unit center) (175 men),
2 companies from "SS-Fallschirmjägerbataillon 600", a special infantry battalion (380 men),
2 Panzer companies of the Heer (240 men),
2 Panzergrenadier companies (350 men),
2 companies heavy mortars from the Heer (200 men),
2 Panzerjäger companies from the Heer (200 men),
1 Pionier company (100 men),
2 Nachrichten companies from the Heer (200 men) and
3 vehicle repair units (75 men).

All units were at less than authorized strength. Each Panzer-kompanie had twelve Panzers, half of them Shermans or Panzer IIIs, the other half Panthers. The Panzergrenadier companies had two or three American armored personnel carriers, the other vehicles were of German make.

The combat groups were structured as follows (the infantry group without Panzers):

a small staff,

1 Nachrichtenzug,

1 Panzerkompanie,

3 infantry companies of 120–150 men (e.g. 2 companies "Kampfgruppe 200", 1 company "Jagdverband Mitte" or SS-Fallschirmjägerbataillon 600),

2 Züge heavy mortars (12 cm),

2 Züge Panzerjäger,

2 Züge Panzergrenadiers,

1 Zug Pioniers, as well as 1 vehicle repair Zug.[25]

The 6. Panzerarmee reckoned that the Panzer divisions would reach the southwestern part of the Hohe Venn by midnight of 17 December.[26] It expected that there would already be a high degree of uncertainty and confusion on the enemy side. Then, Panzerbrigade 150 would start its march along three roads in order to capture two Maas bridges near Amay (twenty-four kilometers southwest of Liège), Huy or Ardenne, if possible, undamaged. The shortest road distances from the line Trois-Ponts (twelve kilometers southwest of Malmedy)-Baraque Fraiture (twelve kilometers southwest of Vielsalm) were sixty to seventy kilometers. The groups were scheduled to reach their objectives within six hours. They would detour around resistance and maintain radio contact with each other. The operation was given the code name "Operation Greif" (Operation Griffin).[27]

After the briefing of the Divisional commander and the Ia, the orders for the action had to be developed. A small working group was set up at the Divisional staff. It consisted of the senior general staff officer, the senior orderly officer, Hauptsturmführer Hesselmann, and the director of the Divisional map office, Unterscharführer Kriegge. The two co-workers of the Ia were briefed only to the extent required for their tasks. They were sworn to extra secrecy, at the threat of capital punishment. Except for that circle of people, no other members of the Division were briefed. The units were given the code designator "Baustäbe" (construction squads) and their quarters were designated in the same manner. Quarters for the units of 25. Armee had to be found, determined and marked with signs, as well as the approach routes from the assumed unloading stations, in the already heavily populated area. The troops considered this order as fairly nonsensical. Still, grumbling, they tried to carry it out as well as possible. The 25. Armee existed only on paper, but the troops did not know that. In addition, marches by columns of vehicles in westerly and northwesterly directions were carried out during daylight on 9 December in order to deceive the enemy air reconnaissance. At the same time, fake radio traffic was carried out on the orders of the Armee. Scouting of the advance routes and the assembly area of the Division was prohibited. During the preparatory work at the Divisional staff, the Divisional commander was on his way daily to visit the units of the Division in order to become acquainted with the unit commanders, the state of training, the weapons and equipment. Most of the time, he returned very depressed. He gained the impression that the state of training for an attack by the Division, although its required personnel numbers had been achieved, was inadequate, in particular for such a difficult attack in unfavorable terrain and in winter weather conditions. Also, a portion of the Panzers for I. Abteilung was still undelivered, and, for a long time, II. Abteilung was completely missing. Various other armored vehicles, tractors for parts of the artillery, batteries for the radios, and a portion of the basic supply of ammunition and fuel were still lacking. The Division reported weekly, as requested, in its report on conditions, that it was only "conditionally suited" for an attack.

A listing of personnel strength and supplies of weapons, Panzers, armored and non-armored vehicles of 8 December 1944 is available. The most important figures are reproduced here:

PERSONNEL

	Required	Available	Ill and wounded as on 1.11.1944
Officers	633	484	52
NCOs	4,128	3,174	381
Men	13,787	19,586	2,098
Total	18,548	23,244	2,531

The number of ill and wounded within the eight weeks ending on 8.12.1944 is not known. In order to have a figure to compare to, these numbers from 1.11.1944 were adopted. The number of available personnel includes 2,805 personnel of the Feldersatzbataillon. After subtracting the ill, wounded, and the surplus of the Feldersatzbataillon, one can assume that the Division was fully manned.

WEAPONS

	Required	Available
Machine guns	1,710	1,159
Artillery guns	59	59
Heavy anti-tank guns	25	25

Available, in addition, were

2 cm Flak	45
2 cm four-barrel Flak	5
3.7 cm Flak	35
8.8 cm Flak	18
Heavy infantry guns	13
7.5 cm Pak (mounted)	22

PANZERS AND ARMORED VEHICLES

	Required	Available
Panzer IVs	103	37
Panzer Vs	81	41
Panzerjäger IVs	31	22
Artillery observation Panzers	5	
Light armored personnel carriers	13	
Medium armored personnel carriers	522	118
Armored reconnaissance vehicles	16	
Heavy infantry guns (self-propelled)	6	

The number of Jagdpanthers in the Schwere Panzerjägerabteilung 560 (heavy tank destroyers) is not given. Obviously, the Abteilung had not arrived at the date of the report (8.12.). The large number of missing armored vehicles, in particular of armored personnel carriers (375 armored vehicles short) is conspicuous, as is the lack of almost one-third of the Panzerjäger IVs.

NON-ARMORED VEHICLES

	Required	Available	% of Req.
Motorcycles	615	259	42
Cars	74	504	
Cars (all-terrain)	782	312	95
Trucks	914	1,408	
Trucks (all-terrain)	933	237	88
Half-tracks	147	100	68
Tractors,			
1 to 5 tons	118	35	30
8 to 18 tons	109	68	62

Among the non-armored vehicles, the large shortfalls of motorcycles and towing vehicles, the half-tracks and tractors, are noticeable. That had a negative impact on the transmittal of reports and orders along the expected narrow roads, and, in particular, the movement of towed guns such as the heavy infantry guns, of Pak, Flak, and artillery. It would be especially negative during poor road and weather conditions. Thus, changes of positions could be achieved only in stages.

The number of cars and trucks was insignificantly below required figures, 5 percent and 12 percent respectively. However, many all-terrain vehicles were replaced by road vehicles. That, too, had to be negative under the expected conditions, in particular since a significant portion of the drivers did not possess adequate experience, especially in winter driving.

Differing from the report of 8 December, III./26 (armored personnel carriers) possessed twelve mounted 2 cm three-barrel, which had extraordinary fire power. Instead of Panzerjäger IV/L 48s which Panzerjägerabteilung 12 used during the invasion, it now had Panzerjäger IV/L 70s, as well as Panzers which were armed with the long gun and additional twin-barrel MGs.[29]

These figures differ in some points from those quoted in the reports of Supreme Command West Ia/VO.Pr. of 10.12.1944, and in the summary in Appendix 50 "Operation Martin" to the war diary Supreme Command West/Ia Appendices 29 and 30 by Hermann Jung "Die Ardennenoffensive 1944/45".[29a] In the required figure of Panzers (Appendix 29), the need for command Panzers in Regiments and Abteilungen was overlooked. Also, the required figures for II. Abteilung was not considered. The available figure for Panzer IVs is high by five, the available figure of heavy field howitzers in both reports (Appendices 29 and 30) is 6 low. Altogether, there can be no suggestion of an over-supply compared to the regular structure of a Panzerdivision '43-model. Just the opposite, there was a significant shortage of important weapons, Panzers, and armored vehicles.

A report by the commander of SS-Panzerjägerabteilung 12, Hauptsturmführer Karl H. Brockschmidt, indicates the extraordinary efforts which were undertaken to prepare the Division, as best possible and even outside normal channels, despite all the difficulties, for the future action. He wrote:

> The Abteilung had proved itself as a Panzerjäger-abteilung and received high decorations. The task now was to turn that Panzerjägerabteilung into an assault gun Abteilung. That meant that the tactic of the Panzerjägers: wait in ambush and then knock out tanks, had to be changed to the dynamic tactics of the assault gun Abteilung. It would be the task of the Abteilung to blast free the way for the infantry at focal points and then pull through together. The terrain available to us was unfavorable. It was cultivated and built up and we could rarely drive cross-country. Together with the Divisional

commander, Kraas, we tried to hold a maneuver in the Aachen region, but it was not possible to practice under combat conditions. The Nachrichtenabteilung was kind enough to provide me with radios which were installed in individual vehicles. That was an essential requirement if assault artillery action was to be carried out in an energetic and determined manner. We procured twin MGs from the Luftwaffe. They were short, easy to swing around, with high fire power, and they proved themselves as excellent in later action. Those twin MGs were mounted to the right of the loader's hatch, could be swiveled and easily removed. After the move to the Kirchberg area, we had a discussion with the commanders of 25. and 26. Panzergrenadierregiments and the Divisional commander, Kraas. I suggested to him to establish an infantry escort company for the assault guns. The reasoning was that it would be of benefit to the regiments if the assault guns were properly escorted and could thus move more easily. Further, that the escorting infantry was required to, practically, serve as eyes for the guns during fighting in built-up and wooded areas. The infantry would indicate problems and direct attention, above all, to centers of resistance which the guns could not themselves spot because of the limited visibility in the woods and during combat in built-up areas. Both commanders agreed to provide me with fifty to sixty of their men . . .[30]

The result was totally unsatisfactory since the regiments had too few battle-tested men available. In addition, the time available for training was much too short. The preparations at all other units of the Division proceeded in a similar manner, with a high level of personal commitment.

On 11 December 1944, the Supreme Commander West and the Supreme Commander Heeresgruppe B, the Armee supreme commanders of 6. and 5. Panzerarmee, several of the commanding generals, among them the commanding general of I. SS-Panzerkorps—Gruppenführer Priess—and the divisional commanders of I. SS-Panzerkorps, were called to the Führer headquarters "Adlerhorst" (eagle's nest) at Ziegenberg Estate, eleven kilometers west of Bad Nauheim, for a situational briefing. An identical briefing took place the next day with the supreme commanders, commanding generals and divisional commanders of 15. and 7. Armee and of II. SS-Panzerkorps. Sturmbann-führer Hein Springer, then aide-de-camp of Feldmarschall Model, reported on the situational briefing:

. . . The Feldmarschall requested that I accompany him to this 'situational briefing'. As always, we traveled in two cars. I was in front as decoy and so as not to bet everything on one horse. In a large room at 'Adlerhorst' the supreme commanders and commanders of the western front in the sector of Heeresgruppe B assembled in the

evening hours. Among them: Supreme Commander West, Generalfeldmarschall von Rundstedt, the Supreme Commander Heeresgruppe B, Generalfeldmarschall Model, the Supreme Commander
of 6. Panzerarmee, Oberstgruppenführer Sepp Dietrich, the
Supreme Commander of 5. Panzerarmee, General der Panzertruppen von Manteuffel, and many other high-ranking officers, a total of
approximately fifty to sixty persons. The reason and purpose for this
evening gathering were known to all of us. Hitler wanted to explain
the plan and the objective of this last major offensive in the west
once more, in person, to the responsible supreme commanders and
the other commanders and to implore them to gather and use all
their forces. As far as I can remember today, after thirty-six years,
Hitler spoke, standing up, for almost one hour. The majority of the
listeners stood as well.

It was not a briefing on the situation in the traditional sense, with
lectures and decisions, it was a kind of '. . . address before the battle
of Leuthen on 4.12.1757 . . .' by Frederick the Great.

Adolf Hitler gave a relaxed, quiet impression. His manner of
speech was the same, without pathos. As so often during his
speeches, Hitler went far back into history before getting to the
Ardennes offensive itself. Hitler spoke without notes, easy to understand, without moving his hands. However, Hitler was able to
describe the objective of the operation, the splitting of the American and English forces through a lightening advance via Liège to
Antwerp, the destruction of the English armies in an encirclement
battle west of Aachen, in a vivid and convincing manner. I can well
remember Hitler's final words. He said in closing:

'Gentlemen, if our breakthrough via Liège to Antwerp is not successful, we will be approaching an end to the war which will be
extremely bloody. Time is not working for us, but against us. This is
really the last opportunity to turn the fate of this war in our favor. I
thank you, gentlemen.'[31]

The Divisional commander told the Ia on the following day that, after a
break, there was an opportunity for individual conversations. Since Adolf
Hitler's address spoke of the great responsibility which "HJ" Division held for
the right flank of I. SS-Panzerkorps and of the special trust placed upon it, he
had thought it necessary to voice his concerns. He had reported that his Division was not ready for action. Oberstgruppen-führer Sepp Dietrich, sitting to
his right, had kicked him in the shin in order to stop him. Hitler had then,
very quietly, asked which reasons he had for his judgment. The Divisional
commander then spoke about the personnel situation, the inadequate level
of training, the lack of certain weapons, vehicles and equipment—such as batteries for the radios. He stated that, in order to overcome the training short-

ages, a four-week stay at a major training area was required. The Führer had then asked the responsible officers of the OKW, the chief of staff of the Panzer forces and other branches regarding the provision of the missing supplies. It had either been explained that they were already on their way, or it was determined where they could be secured. There had not been any strong words. Rather, the discussions had been carried out with great seriousness and a readiness to help. After the material questions had been clarified, Adolf Hitler stated that a delay of the attack deadline was impossible, based on several known reasons. "HJ" Division could not be replaced by another. He regretted not to be of more help. Everything had to be done by the Division in order to achieve the established goals, using the available forces.[32]

The first part of the address Adolf Hitler gave the following day survived in short-hand. It is reproduced in "Lagebesprechungen im Führerhauptquartier" (situational briefings in the Führer headquarters), published by Helmut Heiber.[33]

After the commander had briefed the Ia, they deliberated on what could still be done to overcome or lessen the reported shortcomings. There was practically no time left to do anything. The weapons and equipment reported to be on their way indeed arrived before the start of the attack, despite the existing skepticism.

CHAPTER 8.3
The Assembly

The Artillerieregiment of "HJ" Division was also scheduled to take part in the fire attack by the artillery to prepare the offensive. After scouting and measuring the fire positions, it was to move initially into its assembly areas. It would then strengthen the positions, establish the communications network and stockpile the ammunition in the fire positions. To do that, it had to march into the assembly areas one day prior to the bulk of the Division.

The commander of the Artillerieregiment, Obersturmbannführer Oskar Drexler, was ordered to report to the HARKO (senior artillery commander) of 6. Panzerarmee on 9 December at 14.00 hours and briefed on his mission. The Division was not informed of that. It briefed the adjutant of the Artillerieregiment on 10 December to the extent required. At that time, the commanders of the other Regiments had no knowledge of the planned operation.[1]

The troops marched into their assembly areas at night, without using any vehicle lights. Even the brake lights were covered. The march was made even more difficult by the wintry weather and partially iced-over, narrow and hilly roads. In order to move quickly and, if necessary, to be able to stop the columns and re-direct them, the advance routes had been divided into blocks. The general command had established block directors who had available to them traffic control services, clearing squads and towing vehicles. They were connected to each other and the Korps command post by telephone. Depending on the traffic situation, the block directors would approve or stop the continuation of the march.[2]

The Artillerieregiment began its march on 12 December at 19.00 hours. It reached its assembly area in the Schmid-theimer Wald (forest), after two nights of marching. The Regimental command post was set up in Unter-wolfert, 9.5 kilometers southeast of Hollerath.[3]

During the nights of 13–14 and 14–15 December, the bulk of the Division marched into their assembly area. Two routes were available for that move: one for wheeled vehicles and another one for tracked vehicles. The war diary of III./25 contains details on the march. It is stated there for

12 December: Gleuel. Commander and adjutant discussion. Regimental commander determines structure for the march in case of action. Regimental commander orders final preparations.

13 December: Gleuel. Orderly officer arrives at Regiment. He carries orders for the move, orally and in person to Kompanie officers and . . . (illegible) Reserve -Kompanie. The orderly officer drove ahead to reconnoiter. 21.30 hours: Bataillon departs. Sequence of the march: 9., 10., operations staff, 11., 12., supply company. Route: Euskirchen-Ülpenich-Emmenich. [Ülpenich is located on B 56 (Federal Road) between Euskirchen and Zülpich, four kilometers southeast of Zülpich.]

14 December: 4.30 P.M.: Bataillon arrives in Ülpenich area. Command post at Prols mill, 9. Kompanie, supply company, 10. Kompanie are in Emmenich, 11. and 12. Kompanie in Ülpenich. During the day, servicing vehicles and resting. Commander is at the Regiment. Incidents during the march: 3 vehicles broke down, moved to repair unit at Gleuel. 14.00 hours: order to repair unit—continue work, move forward when ordered. 19.00 hours: orally and personally to Kompanie commanders—march to be continued -tonight. Assembly to be completed along main road by 20.00 hours. Sequence of march: 10., 9., staff, 11., 12. Kompanies, supply company. Route of march: Zülpich-Kommern-Strempf. (two kilometers southwest of Kommern, fourteen kilometers southwest of Euskirchen, Author) From there, direction by orderly officer. Departure: 20.00 hours.

15 December: Bataillon will arrive in the new area at 4 o'clock. Bataillon command post will be in Strempf (church), 9., 10., 11., 12.

Kompanie see sketch [missing]. Incidents: parts of 12. Kompanie stranded without fuel. A total of 7 vehicles of the Bataillon have not yet arrived. To be towed in.[4]

An example of the marching orders issued on 13 December to 4. Batterie Flakabteilung 12 has survived. It reads as follows:

March objective: Billig [position one kilometer north of Billig]. Route of march: Stommeln [sixteen kilometers northwest of Cologne]-Pulheim-Braunweiler-Königsdorf-Horrem-Mödrath-Türenich-Kirdorf-Liblar-Lechenich-Friesheim-Niederberg-Mühlheim-Wichterich-Fraue nberg-Dürscheren-Elsig-Euenheim-Billig [four kilometers south of Euskirchen].
    Lighting level: Totally blacked out.
    Marching speed: 15 kilometers;
    Maximum speed: 15 kilometers;
    Spacing: 20–30 meters.[5]

The difficulties which the troops had to overcome during the move are shown in a report of 3. Panzerkompanie. It is stated there:

The night drive led via Neurath, Bergheim/Erft, Blatzheim, Zülpich to Schwerfen where the Kompanie took up quarters. Even on that relatively short marching route, the Kompanie had left behind distinct traces. Just after passing Frimmersdorf, the vehicle of Unterscharführer Lorkowski stalled. The radiator water hose had burst. The crew moved into an isolated farm close-by and waited for a squad of the repair unit. Of all places, that isolated farm was hit by an emergency bomb drop from an English aircraft. The Panzer driver Theo Wieczorek, much liked by all, was killed.

A few kilometers farther, the Panzer of Unterscharführer Zwangsleitner had pushed aside a whole section of garden fence and also knocked down several telegraph posts, leaving them dangling from the wires as if blown down by the wind. In Bergheim/Erft, a Panzer had got stuck at a column of the city gate. The Panzer was only able to move after the historic structure had been propped up.[6]

The commanders of the Regiments and independent Bataillons/ Abteilungen received the orders for action in the billet area which had been reached after the first night march, i.e. on 14 December. The Divisional commander gave a broad synopsis of the situation and of the German intentions. He stressed the importance of the offensive which could be decisive for the outcome of the war, and called upon the commanders to give their utmost and to demand the same from their troops. Then, the Divisional order for the pursuit by the infantry divisions, after breaking through the American positions, was issued. All participants clearly understood the importance of the plan and the difficulties of its execution. On the other hand, they all understood that only a daring venture could bring about a change in the critical war situation.

The Division arrived in the assembly area northeast of Sistig (six kilometers east of Hellenthal) in the morning of 15 December. The last parts arrived only after daybreak. The falling snow, there had been blowing snow in some areas, allowed the move to be completed without enemy detection. Because of a shortage of fuel, accidents or mechanical problems, some vehicles had to be towed, moved to repair squads, or repaired by them on the spot, if possible. Despite the unfavorable roads and weather which, however, helped to conceal the move, the Division managed it quite well. The Divisional command post was established in Benenberg, 2.5 kilometers south of Sistig.

After the orders had been issued on 14 December, the commanders prepared the orders for their battalions or companies/batteries. Once the troops had arrived in the assembly area, the orders were handed out. The war diary of III. Bataillon of SS-Panzergrenadierregiment 25 states:

15 December, 13.00 hours. The Bataillon commander is ordered to report to the Regiment. He returns at 18.00 hours. Briefing of the Kompanie chiefs. The commander issues preparatory orders for the major offensive. Briefing on the situation, expected departure time and sequence of the march. Fuel is still missing. The Regimental adjutant arrives at 21.00 hours with a fuel allocation. Motor vehicles depart.[7]

The first parts of the Division scheduled for action were reinforced Panzer scouting parties which would march ahead even of the spearheads. One of the scouting party leaders, Oberscharführer August Zinßmeister, noted in his diary on their planned action:

15 December, Friday. In the evening we receive an order and are briefed in a neighboring village held by units of Skorzeny, by one 'Dr. Wolf'. The overall order reads: The reinforced Panzer scouting party with 3 'Pumas' and two rifle squads in Schwimmwagen will drive ahead of the spearheads of the advance unit. It will capture an Ourthe bridge in a surprise raid, or reinforce paratroop units present there. It will hold that bridge as well as one Maas bridge south of Liège, in each case until our own spearhead arrives. We are enthusiastic, although we have some inkling of the difficulty of the mission.

Eagerly and with great care we prepare for all possibilities and await the order to move out.[8]

Even during the move there had been some shortage of fuel. At the start of the attack, four consumption units were to be available to the Division. One part was planned to be with the troops, the other part in storage west of the Rhine or in transport. It was expected that another consumption unit would arrive each day (one consumption unit was the amount of fuel required under "normal" circumstances for a marching distance of 100 kilometers). Given the road and weather conditions, it had to be expected that the amount would be sufficient for only half of the distance. The supreme command assumed that the troops would be able to satisfy their requirements with the available amounts. However, in case the weather situation allowed effective action by the US air force and thus cause supply problems, an attempt would have to be made to fall back on captured fuel. The troops had been supplied with enough ammunition for eight days. The amount required for another eight days was in storage or in rail transport.[9] This information, provided by the chief of staff of 6. Panzerarmee, Brigadeführer Fritz Kraemer, during an interview in captivity on 14 and 15 August 1945, differs from the figures quoted by the chief of staff of I. SS-Panzerkorps, Standartenführer Rudolf Lehmann, in his study. According to him, the following had been promised: three consumption units with the troops and two with the supply units. At the start of the attack, "HJ" Division had available 1.3 consumption units, sufficient for a march and combat in high terrain of 60-70 kilometers. Two units of ammunition had been promised, however, only one was available. The artillery required half of that for its preparatory fire.[10] A verification of the available amounts of fuel and ammunition, which were either with the troops or in storage within range, is no longer possible.

Feldmarschall Model was aware of the shortages in the supply of fuel and ammunition, and of the delay in the relief and the arrival of individual units. Thus, he advocated a postponement of the start of the attack. However, a postponement appeared impossible to Feldmarschall von Rundstedt, based on the development of the enemy situation. The war diary of Supreme Command West notes for 13 December: "The move of a tank destroyer unit from Malmedy to Büllingen is notable. Its possible connection to our own strong moves into the Eifel would be very disquieting."—"The intention of the enemy to capture initially the west bank of the Rur and, if possible, the dams, is becoming more and more obvious."[11]

For the following day, 14 December, it is noted there: "The Supreme Commander West has fought particularly hard for the earliest possible start of the attack and the provision of the requirements for it, since the danger of a breakthrough in Palatinate is moving closer by the hour. It would threaten to put the whole operation into jeopardy. In addition, a renewed enemy attempt to break through across the Rur must be expected."[12]

On 15 December, the war diary of Supreme Command West notes: "Against the wish of Heeresgruppe B to postpone Day-0 once again, the Supreme Commander West resolutely advocates the standpoint that 16 December must be maintained as Day-0. This, in particular, since the development at the left wing of Heeresgruppe G urgently demands the earliest possible start of the attack."—"At any rate, the grouping of enemy forces, as far as the attack sector is concerned, is essentially unchanged. No pull-out of enemy forces from other Front sectors has been detected."[14]

The general assessment of the enemy situation proved to be correct. However, one change, which would have a significant negative impact on the attack by I. SS-Panzerkorps in the sector of 277. Volksgrenadierdivision and on the action by "HJ" Division, remained unnoticed in its full extent. The map "Front Situation" of 13.12.1944, as well as those of 14 and 15 December show the 2nd American Infantry Division on the move from the south to the Hohe Venn near Hill 692 (694) with a question mark at the tip of the arrow.[14] The map "Enemy Situation" of 15.12.1944, as of 20.00 hours, surprisingly does not mark the 2nd US Infantry Division at all.[15]

"HJ" Division continued to proceed on the assumption that the 2nd US Division was located in the Elsenborn camp for refitting. In fact, not only a tank destroyer unit had been moved from Malmedy to Büllingen, as determined on 13 December.

The 2nd US ("Indian Head") Infantry Division had, indeed, moved initially to Elsenborn. However, the move was not for refitting but for a special operation. The American leadership feared that the Germans would, one day, blow up the dams on the upper run of the Rur and flood the American positions on both sides of Düren with the waters from the Rur and Urft reservoirs. Thus, the Americans had ordered that the Rur could be crossed in the endangered area only on the specific order of the Army. On the other hand, they saw the opportunity to cut off the supply of the German troops fighting in the Hürtgenwald, i.e. west of the Rur, if they, themselves, were in possession of the reservoir drainages.

The expectation that it would be possible to capture the reservoirs quickly in the process of the November offensive had been disappointed. Thereafter, the Americans had tried to destroy them by aerial bombardment. During the period from 30 November to 11 December, the dams had been attacked three times by some 200 aircraft each without any noticeable success. Several more planned actions had been canceled because of unfavorable weather.[16]

In the meantime, preparations for a ground attack had also been made. It was to start on 13 December. While the 78th Infantry Division would advance from Vossenack via Schmidt to the Rur reservoir from the northwest, the 2nd Infantry Division would attack from the Rocherath/Krinkelt district. It would initially push through the Westwall to Wahlerscheid, and then via Dreiborn from the southwest to the dams. The 395th Infantry Regiment of the 99th Infantry Division was attached to the division to cover its right flank during an attack with a limited objective. In the evening of 12 December, the 2nd Division arrived in its assembly area near Lager (camp) Elsenborn.[17]

By the evening of 15 December, the attack by the 78th Division had made only minor progress. Initial successes were largely reversed by German counterattacks.[18]

The "Indian Heads" had to attack on both sides of the road Rocherath-Wahlerscheid-Dreiborn. No other roadways were available. The two infantry regiments scheduled for the breakthrough thus had to start out one behind the other. The 9th Infantry Regiment, at the point, had orders to break through the Westwall positions to the forester's house at Wahlerscheid. It would then swing to the northwest in order to take the German positions near Höfen. The mission of the 38th Infantry Regiment, following behind, was to advance via Wahlerscheid and Dreiborn to the dams. The 23rd Infantry Regiment remained behind in Elsenborn as reserve. Two battalions of the 395th Infantry Regiment and the attached 2nd Battalion of the 393rd Infantry Regiment were given the task to capture and hold the high terrain west of the confluence of the Olef creek and Wies creek, approximately two kilometers south-southeast of Wahlerscheid. That would secure the right flank and thus the only supply route from Rocherath to Wahlerscheid. For the attack, one unit of 10.5 cm howitzers, one unit of 11.6 cm rocket launchers, one battery of 15.5 cm self-propelled guns, one company heavy mortars, and two units of tank destroyers, one of them self-propelled, were also attached to the 2nd Division. The 406th Field Artillery Group with four units of 155 mm guns, and larger caliber, was instructed to cooperate. The Combat Command B of the 9th Armored Division was assigned for a possible enlargement of a successful attack. The artillery of the 99th had also been reinforced by one battery 155 mm guns.[19]

On 13 December at 08.30 hours, the 9th Infantry Regiment started its attack without preparatory artillery fire in order to surprise the enemy. In addition, the German positions had not sufficiently been scouted in the broken terrain to allow effective shelling. On the first day of the attack, neither the 9th nor the 395th Regiment succeeded to penetrate into the German positions. The attacks were without success on 14 December as well. Although the artillery had laid preparatory fire in the morning, the terrain conditions, poor visibility and insufficient reconnaissance made its action virtually ineffective. No progress was achieved on 15 December either. Moreover, the 9th Regiment had suffered 737 casualties within three days of which, however, 400 had not been caused by enemy action. After the fall of darkness, one battalion of the 9th Infantry undertook the attempt to penetrate into the German Westwall position through a narrow gap which had been cut, unnoticed, through the barbed wire obstacles on 14 December.

Unfortunately—for the German side—the parts of 277. Volksgrenadierdivision in action near Wahlerscheid were being relieved in order to be available for the attack farther to the south, in the framework of the Reserveregiment of 277. V.G.D. The Americans initially succeeded in sending forward two companies through the gap before midnight. Then, with two battalions, to capture several bunkers, one after the other, together with their respective field positions. Finally, they took the customhouse at Wahlerscheid and the road junctions into Reichsstraße 258. The two spearhead battalions of the 9th Infantry prepared for defense. The attack by the Division would then be continued from the captured "bridgehead" as previously planned.[20]

The German side did not recognize the importance of the attack by the 2nd US Infantry Division near Wahlerscheid, and it did thus not receive proper attention. The war diary of Supreme Command West notes for 15 December, inter alia: ". . . The penetration at the boundary between 15. and 6. Panzerarmee is not severe enough that it cannot be repelled using local forces without negative impact on the right attack wing . . ."[21] The above mentioned boundary between the two Armees ran approximately just north of the reservoirs via Schmidt-Rötgen. Thus, the penetration by the 78th US Division near Simmerath and Kesternich in the sector of 272. V.G.D. was addressed, but not the penetration near Wahlerscheid which only took place during the night 15–16 December. That penetration could be known to the responsible LXVII. Korps several hours after midnight, at the earliest, and to I. SS-Panzerkorps, adjoining on the left, and to 6. Panzerarmee not before morning. It is likely that no prisoners were captured by the German side, preventing the action by the 2nd US Division from being recognized. There was also no clear picture of the strength of the forces taking part. It is thus not surprising that, from I. SS-Panzerkorps through 6. Panzerarmee and Heeresgruppe B to Supreme Command West, all command authorities believed that these "fringe events" would incidentally be taken care of by the German offensive which was to start in a few hours.

There was great concern on the German side that the assembly of such a large number of troops might not go unnoticed by the enemy after all. What had the other side, in fact, noticed? The 28th and 106th US Infantry Divisions, located north of Luxembourg and adjoining north from there up to Losheim respectively, had reported increased vehicular traffic at night since 13 December. The 28th Division considered that to be a normal occurrence during relief activities at the front, such as had already been observed three weeks previously. On 14 December, a woman refugee had reported to the 28th Division that the woods near Bitburg were bursting with German equipment. That information was considered to be of such importance that the woman was sent to the headquarters of the First Army. She arrived there only on 16 December—too late. Toward the evening of 15 December, the 4th and 106th Infantry Division (the 4th adjoined to the 28th on the south) had taken two prisoners each. All four had stated that fresh troops were arriving in the forward lines and that a major offensive was in the offing. It could start on 16 or 17 December, but certainly before Christmas. Two of the prisoners were deserters who were not taken very seriously, this offensive had been promised to the German troops before. The other two prisoners were wounded. One of them, who had seemed of interest to the interrogator, had been under the influence of morphine. Thus, another interrogation was planned for later. The information in the statements was not sufficient to base effective measures upon them. If anything, they might have suggested that more information could be gained through reconnaissance. Any results would probably have arrived too late to still be of impact, which could, however, not be predicted then. The 67th Tactical Reconnaissance Group of the US Air Force had flown seventy-one sorties between 10 and 15 December. They had spotted a large number of hospital trains on the west bank of the Rhine, several sections of flatbeds, loaded with Tigers, near Euskirchen and fifty searchlights at a locale near Kaiserslautern. Usable reports were thus available, but they were interpreted wrongly. It was assumed that the material was to reinforce the sectors in which the Third and First Armies were on the attack themselves: at the Rur and in Palatinate. It can be assumed that a combined consideration of the reports from the Army and the Air Force would have made a better evaluation possible. The crucial reason for inadequate reconnaissance and wrong interpretation of the information received can, however, probably be found in the underestimation of the German capability for a major offensive operation.[22]

CHAPTER 8.4
The Attack on 16 December 1944—Fighting to Break through the American Front Line

In the morning of 16 December, shortly before the start of the attack, the following Order of the Day from Generalfeldmarschall von Rundstedt announced to the troops:

> Soldiers of the Western Front!
> Your decisive hour has arrived! Strong offensive armies are assembled today against the Anglo-Americans. I need tell you no more.
> You all feel it:
> It's now or never!

May you feel inside yourselves the sacred obligation to give your all, and to perform superhuman feats for our Fatherland and our Führer!
The Supreme Commander West
signed: von Rundstedt
Generalfeldmarschall[1]

The book on 3. Panzerkompanie states on this: ". . . We knew that the time had come. Finally, this was an order of the day as in the best of times. But, based on intuition, there was something so absolutely final in it, as if it was an irrevocably last opportunity to bring about a positive change to the war in the west . . ."[2]

The I. SS-Panzerkorps had reported completion of its assembly at 2 A.M. At 277. Volksgrenadierdivision, a reinforced battalion in the new sector of LXVII. A. K. had not been relieved. It did not join action at the start of the attack. As planned, 12. Volksgrenadierdivision had relieved parts of 277. V.G.D. and taken over the responsibility in their sector. The 3. Fallschirmjägerdivision had arrived in its attack sector with only two regiments. The third regiment did not arrive during the night 16–17 December.[3]

The Ardennes offensive began at 05.35 hours with a mighty and concentrated fire attack from the artillery and rocket launchers. There are contradictory accounts of its duration. The Heeresgruppe had ordered a uniform duration of five to ten minutes. In the interview of Brigadeführer Kraemer, the chief of staff of 6. Panzerarmee, and in the study by Standarten-führer Lehmann, a preparatory shelling of one-half hour duration is mentioned.[4] In a study, the commander of 277. V.G.D., Generalmajor Viebig, indicates a short artillery preparation. Generalleutnant Engel, the commander of 12. V.G.D. reports a ". . . short fire attack, but carried out with an immense expenditure of ammunition . . ."[5] The Ia of 6. Panzerarmee's HARKO, Sturm-bannführer Karl Bartling, also indicates that only a short fire attack took place. There would not have been enough ammunition available for a preparatory shelling lasting half-an-hour.[6] The war diary of Supreme Command West states: "05.35 hours. The 6. and 5. Panzerarmee, as well as the spearhead units of 7. Armee, start the attack after a ten-minute artillery preparation.[7]

Whether the preparatory fire was of short or long duration, it did, in any case, not achieve the hoped-for impact. So say, unanimously, the commanders of 277. and 12. V.G.Ds. Generalmajor Viebig wrote for 277. V.G.D. that the artillery fire had not hit the breakthrough spots and had been mostly wide. Further, the planned amount of ammunition had not been available. Generalleutnant Engel, commander of 12. V.G.D., reported: ". . . The fire attack by the artillery and launchers on identified positions, traffic junctions, town entrances and exits remained virtually without impact due to inade-

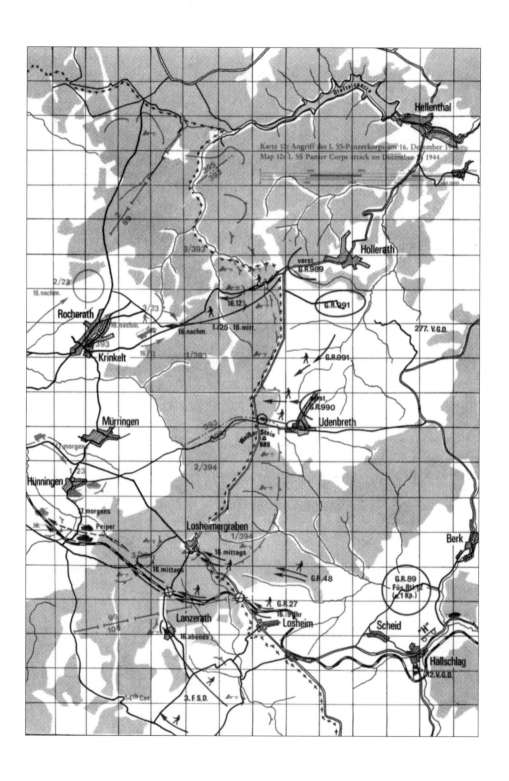

Karte 10: Angriff des I. SS-Panzerkorps am 16. Dezember 1944
Map 10: I. SS Panzer Corps attack on December 16 1944

quate reconnaissance and thinly manned bases . . ."[8] The 'After Action Report' of the American 393rd Infantry Regiment stated on the matter: ". . . At 05.30 hours, the Germans shelled with terrifically concentrated artillery. That fire, to which was added that of their mortars and six-barrel rocket launchers, practically covered the whole battalion front line [meaning the 1st Battalion] . . ."[9]

The fire attack destroyed the American telephone connections between the battalions and the regiments. Some of the radio connections were also knocked out.[9a]

The assault groups of the Infanteriedivision started the charge after the completion of the fire attack. Generalmajor Viebig did not provide an exact time for 277. V.G.D., he wrote that the Regimental groups assembled while it was still dark. The right attack group consisted of Grenadierregiment 989, reinforced by one Pionier company and parts of the Panzerjägerabteilung. It had assembled in the Westwall bunkers near Hollerath. Its task was to break through along Advance Route A from the road bend west of Hollerath to Rocherath and capture the village.

While the bright light from the searchlights in the Hollerath area and north of it illuminated the low clouds overhead, partially blinding the enemy and partially outlining the dark silhouettes of the German troops, making them easy to spot, the reinforced Grenadierregiment 989 attacked, with the Sturmkompanie (assault company) in the lead. It probably encountered the right wing of the 3rd Battalion 393rd Infantry Regiment which defended the left sector of the regiment. Two platoons of "K"-Company, in position on the right, were immediately overrun, and almost all its men were killed, wounded or captured. The remaining platoon, located in favorable positions, inflicted heavy losses on the attackers. "L"-Company, in action in the center of the 3rd Battalion, was attacked at the same time. It was able to hold its position until the afternoon. "I"-Company, in position at the left wing, was not exposed to any attacks at the beginning. On orders of the Battalion, it prepared for defense to all sides. The assault wedges of Grenadierregiment 989 pushed trough the gap ripped open between the 3rd and 1st Battalions to the west and cut off the only supply route in that sector. The 3rd Battalion was almost completely encircled. The Regiment probably reached the point where the forest lane crossed the Jans creek, from the road bend near Hollerath. After suffering heavy losses, and in the face of stiffening American resistance, it was unable to continue its attack.[10]

The 277. Division had located its focal point to the left. The 12. V.G.D., abutting on the left, had as its task, among others, to open up the Panzer advance route Losheimergraben-Büllingen-Malmedy. There, Grenadierregiment 990, reinforced by one Füsilier company and one Pionier company, attacked after assembling in the Westwall bunkers around Udenbreth. On the left, the Füsilier company advanced from the southern section of the town (Neuhof) along both sides of the road leading in a westerly direction to the Reichsstraße, and along the forest lane running from there toward Krinkelt. It probably encountered "C"-Company of the 1st Battalion 393rd Infantry Regiment there, at the extreme right wing of the regiment along the boundary with the 394th Infantry Regiment. The two platoons in position at the right wing were overrun, the one on the left was able to hold on with great difficulty. Fighting was under way for the company command post. It was approximately ten o'clock by then. Grenadierregiment 990, its Sturmkompanie at the point, attacked to the right of the Füsilier company from the western section of Udenbreth. It succeeded in breaking into the positions of "B"-Company, in the left portion of the sector of the 1st Battalion. Two platoons were overrun, the third was encircled. The battalion commander ordered his reserve, the "A"-Company, to clean up the situation at the left ("B") company and asked the regimental commander for help for the company on the right. In the meantime, the left company had been bypassed and almost encircled, but it was still fighting. The reserve company, attacking with determination, was able to almost re-establish the previous situation. In the face of a counterattack—probably by the reserves of Grenadierregiment 990—it was forced to retreat some 300 meters. However, it was able to dig in and bring the attack by Regiment 990, which had suffered severe losses, to a halt. The regimental commander did not have any rifle units available to reinforce "C"-Company since his 2nd Battalion had been assigned to the 395th Regiment. He made do by sending the mine-laying platoon of the Anti-Tank Company to the hard-pressed "C"-Company. It arrived at the 1st Battalion at approximately 10.30 hours and subsequently attacked, together with the engineer platoon and members of the staff, who could be spared, in order to relieve "C"-Company which was by then encircled. The attack succeeded in clearing the company command post and establishing contact with the platoon which had remained in its positions.[11]

In order to re-start the attack which had stalled at the point of main effort, 277. V.G.D. sent Grenadierregiment 991, which had been held in reserve, into action from the area south of Remscheid, in a southwesterly direction. It was expected that the right wing of Grenadierregiment 990 would be swept along. However, that attack soon stalled under the fire at the flanks from the American positions at the edge of the woods immediately west of the Reichsstraße, or it was broken up. In the course of the morning hours, the American artillery fire increased again. Attempts by Grenadierregiments 990 and 991 to restart the attack from out of the rear were prevented by concentrated fire in front of the Westwall.[12]

At noon of 16 December, the following situation existed in the sector of 277. V.G.D.: Both assault groups had been able to penetrate into the American positions and smash gaps into the forward positions. At the two forward battalions of the 393rd Infantry Regiment, a disintegration of the defenses had been barely prevented only with great effort and use of the last immediately available reserves. the assault groups of 277. V.G.D. had suffered heavy losses, in particular of officers and NCOs. They no longer possessed the strength to continue the attack. Surely, the non-arrival of the promised assault gun brigade played a significant role under the circumstances, at least during the first phase of the attack. The right assault group of the Division had reached the Jans creek, having penetrated to a depth of two kilometers into the forest sector, but had stalled 3.5 kilometers short of its attack objective. The left assault group, which had started out from the Udenbreth area, had been able to push only an even shorter distance into the enemy's main battle area which, by the way, was not very deeply staggered in that sector. That assault group was still at least five kilometers away from its attack objective. Even the action by the Reserveregiment had not succeeded in restarting the attack. From the study by the Divisional commander, one gains the impression that the successes achieved and the critical situation of the enemy had not been fully understood to their real extent. One factor, surely, had to be the fact that reports arrived late or in insufficient numbers due to the inadequate communications system. The Divisional commander considered the plan of breaking through the forest area unexpectedly and quickly, in order to open the roads for the Panzer units, to have failed.[13]

What impact had the attacks by the two infantry divisions in action on the left made by noon? The 12. V.G.D. had been given the task of breaking through the American positions on both sides of Losheim, seizing the important crossroads at Losheimergraben with a reinforced regiment, and attacking along the rail line with another reinforced regiment, capturing Honsfeld, and then advancing on Hünningen and Büllingen. In the further course of the attack, it would swing to the north near Malmedy and block the roads leading up from Verviers, thus securing the right flanks of the Panzer units. The assembly had taken place, in the main, in the Westwall district. It had encountered no difficulties during that, relief and assembly had not been detected by the enemy. The Division attacked at six o'clock. The reinforced Grenadierregiment 48 on the right, on the left was the reinforced Füsilierregiment 27. Grenadierregiment 89 and Füsilierbataillon 12 initially remained in the area around Frauenkron as Divisional reserve. The Panzerjägers and assault guns (six of which were combat-ready) with Pioniers and a mounted company of Füsilierbataillon 12 had been assembled as a spearhead unit and stood ready on the Kronenburg-Hallschlag road in order to start out, depending on the situation, in the direction of Büllingen via Losheimergraben. Regiment 48 attacked along both sides of the path from Scheid to Losheimergraben, Regiment 27 along both sides of the rail line leading from Losheim to Honsfeld. The first attack objective was the western edge of the Staatsforst (national forest) Schleiden and the Staatsforst Buchholz. Both assault groups initially advanced rapidly. Regiment 48 had pushed into the forest without encountering resistance. Then, however, violent fighting broke out for individual consolidated positions which had been reinforced with barbed wire obstacles, tree barriers and mines. Heavy losses occurred. During the noon hours, the Regiment was stalled in front of Losheimergraben which had been built up as a strong point and was being doggedly defended by the enemy. At nine o'clock, Regiment 27 reported the capture of Losheim, and it continued to advance along both sides of the rail line. It encountered increased resistance at noon at the Buchholz railroad station (also called Losheimergraben station).[14]

The 3. Fallschirmjägerdivision, in action to the left of 12. Volksgrenadierdivision, was stuck with both assault groups in mine fields west of Ormont, approximately in line with the Reichsstraße. Two companies of the Pionierbataillon of 1. SS-Panzerdivision were assigned to the Division, and moved in to clear the mines.[14a]

Thus, around noon, no breakthrough across the American positions in all of the sector of the Korps had been achieved, and not even one of the advance routes for the Panzerdivisions had been opened. Of the three advance routes planned for "HJ" Division, only that leading from Losheimergraben via Büllingen, Büttgenbach to Malmedy was really good. How-ever, it could only be reached by way of Rocherath-Krinkelt or via Losheimergraben. It has to be assumed that it would be possible to open the road near Losheimergraben earlier than the one leading via Rocherath-Krinkelt to Büllingen. In order to take the route via Losheimergraben, "HJ" Division had to use either the Reichsstraße from Hollerath or the road from Sistig via Hallschlag and Losheim. However, since the road Hallschlag-Losheim was part of the advance route of 1. SS-Panzerdivision, it was not available to "HJ" Division. In addition, the bridge across the rail line along the road Losheim-Losheimergraben had been blown up since the fighting during the withdrawal in the autumn of 1944, as was the bridge across the rail line one kilometer north of Lanzerath. Large sections of the Reichsstraße from Hollerath to Losheimergraben were still in American hands, or under the control of the fire from their light infantry weapons, and partially mined, thus unusable. Hence, the Korps issued orders around noon, to pull the forward reinforced Panzergrenadierbataillon ahead of the right marching column and assigned it to 277. V.G.D. in order to enlarge the breach along Advance Route A (Hollerath, Rocherath-Krinkelt) into a breakthrough. The war diary of Supreme Command West notes for 12.45 hours:" . . . spearhead units of 12.SS in Hollerath. Will start out in one-half hour to complete the breakthrough . . ."[15]

That task was given to the reinforced I./SS-Panzergrenadierregiment 25 which had one Pak Zug and one Zug of heavy infantry guns attached to it.

The marching column on the right had been pulled out of the assembly area already in the morning and made ready to move out immediately after the successful breakthrough by the Volksgrenadiers. The following times were noted in the war diary of III./25, which was the last battalion within the marching column:

16.12.1944: Orderly officer brings orders

07.00 hours: for assembly, line-up, and attack;

07.10 hours: Verbal order to Kompanie commanders:

Bataillon will march to the road Roggendorf-Kall (9.5 kilometers northeast of Hollerath, Author), spearhead in line with Strempt (six kilometers northeast of Kall, Author); initial sequence of march: 10. Kompanie, operations staff, 12. Kompanie, 9. Kompanie, 11. Kompanie. After assembly, advance to Kall and stop, await further orders. Our Bataillon is the last in the marching -sequence of the Regiment. Attached are:

1. one Zug Panzerjäger (motorized),

2. one Zug anti-aircraft guns,

3. for the march, 1. Kompanie Pionier-bataillon 12.

. . .

07.25hours: Arrival of fuel and distribution to the -companies.

07.45 hours: Bataillon assembles.

. . .

08.20 hours: Bataillon reaches northern entrance to Kall, commander reports in person to -Regiment.

. . .

10.30 hours: Bataillon continues its march.

. . .

Marching sequence now:

10.Kompanie:

Panzerjägerzug (motorized),

operations staff,

anti-aircraft Zug;

12.Kompanie (Panzerjäger and heavy mortar Zug);

9.Kompanie:

Pionierkompanie;

11.Kompanie;

11.30 hours: Bataillon reaches entrance to Sistig [8.5 kilometers northeast of Hollerath].

12.30 hours: Continuation of march delayed. Units rolling ahead of us in line are merging. Bataillon stops on advance route, point is in Sistig. On orders from the Division (liaison officer at departure point), III./25 stays put."[16]

Shortly after noon, the reinforced I./25 under the command of Hauptsturmführer Alfons Ott started out for the attack after a short assembly in the vicinity of the road bend west of Hollerath. The first losses occurred during the assembly from harassing fire which fell in the area of the road bend. The Bataillon advanced on Rocherath through the gap opened by Grenadierregiment 989 south of the forest path from the road bend (Advance Route A). At that time, the spearhead units of the Grenadierregiment had already reached the Jans creek. The Bataillon advanced in wedge formation: one company in the lead, the other two companies staggered to the right and left rear, the Bataillon staff behind the lead company, the heavy company behind the Bataillon staff. The heavy weapons, the Pak Zug and the attached heavy infantry gun Zug followed. They were delayed since the track plates which were required to climb over the Westwall obstructions of concrete humps were not available in time. While the Grenadier companies advanced in the forest, the heavy weapons had to be pulled along the forest path. After a short time, they were stuck in the mud. The same fate awaited the communications, ambulance and supply vehicles.

The Bataillon encountered its first contact with the enemy after crossing the Olef creek south of the forest path (approximately 500 meters west of the Reichsstraße). It was a guard consisting of three men. They were taken prisoner and sent to the rear. During its further advance, the Bataillon encountered almost no resistance. In the late afternoon, it reached Point 634 at the exit from the Forêt Communale de Rocherath, approximately 500 m west of the junction (on map 1 : 25,000 of 1949 this forest is designated "Büllinger Wald").

The spearhead of the Bataillon initially came under weak rifle and machine gun fire from the direction of Rocherath, probably from guards which the 393rd Infantry Regiment had pushed forward between the forest and the villages of Rocherath and Krinkelt where its command post and all its supply facilities were located. Hauptsturmführer Ott reported:

> . . . We were within shouting distance of the enemy. I ordered one of my men, who spoke English well, to shout at the Americans, who were surprised by our sudden appearance, that they should surrender since they had already been encircled. I even sent one man to the high spot in front of us, with the same invitation. He got there unharmed, but did not make it back . . .[16a]

Those demands remained without result. In the meantime, a small column of vehicles approached the junction near Point 634 along the field lane from Krinkelt. They were probably supply vehicles transporting ammunition to the American troops still in the forward line. The column was stopped, the men were taken prisoner and taken to the rear.

During its advance through the Dreiherrenwald and the Forêt Communale de Rocherath, the Bataillon had no contact with the units of Grenadierregiment 989. It had also been unable to establish radio communications with its own regiments. The Americans, by the way, also had such problems in the extensive wooded area. Because of the unclear situation, Hauptsturmführer Ott initially switched over to defense. He sent his adjutant, Untersturmführer

Willi Klein, to the rear with a scouting party to report to G.R.989 and to obtain further orders. The Bataillon was under heavy American artillery fire. At the same time, the enemy was probing the two open flanks of the Bataillon during the night. Hauptsturmführer Ott was gaining the impression that the enemy was trying to outflank and encircle him. Since it had still not been possible to establish contact, Hauptsturmführer Ott decided during the course of the night to withdraw to the most forward German positions. It is not clear when that took place, the Bataillon probably pulled back in the early hours of the morning.

While the reinforced I./25, under the command of 277. V.G.D. assembled on 16 December at noon and advanced through the Dreiherrenwald, 12. V.G.D. had continued its attack. At 16.00 hours, Füsilierregiment 27 stood at the Buchholz station (Losheimergraben station). Grenadierregiment 48, in action to the right, was stalled at the heavily fortified strong point Losheimergraben, doggedly defended by the Americans.[17]

In the meantime, 3. Fallschirmjäger division had captured Lanzerath. With that, the road Losheim-Lanzerath-Buchholz station (Losheimergraben station) was open, and the blown bridges could be by-passed.[18]

The 12. V.G.D. moved up Grenadierregiment 89, waiting as reserve, into the Schleiden forest in order to have it available in case Grenadierregiment 48 did not succeed in breaking through near Losheimergraben during the next day.[19]

The evening report of Supreme Command West of 16 December 1944 stated: ". . . Spearhead of the 12. SS-Panzerdivision started the attack at 16.00 hours by way of Losheimergraben in the direction of Honsfeld. Langerath and Merlscheid (South-Langerath) captured . . ." That report contains several mistakes. The spearhead was actually 1. SS-Panzerdivision "LAH". It did not attack via Losheimergraben, rather via Losheimergraben station (Buchholz station), after Lanzerath (not Langerath) and Merlscheid had been taken. The daily report of 16 December corrected that to some extent.[20] While in the attack sector of 277. V.G.D. no decisive headway had been achieved in the course of the afternoon and the early evening hours and 12. V.G.D. was still stuck near Losheimergraben, the preconditions for a breakthrough existed at the boundary between 12. V.G.D. and 3. Fallschirmjägerdivision.

The enemy recognized that danger. The 99th Infantry Division asked the 2nd Infantry Division for a rifle battalion to man a prepared rear position along the line Hünningen-Mürringen. The 2nd Division provided the 1st Battalion 23rd Infantry Regiment and one company each of tanks and tank destroyers which had been kept in reserve in Lager (camp) Elsenborn. They arrived in the intended district during the course of the night 16–17 December and moved into defensive positions south and southwest of Hünningen. They were ready for defense before sunrise on 17 December. The 3rd Battalion 23rd Infantry Regiment set up for defense on a hill northeast

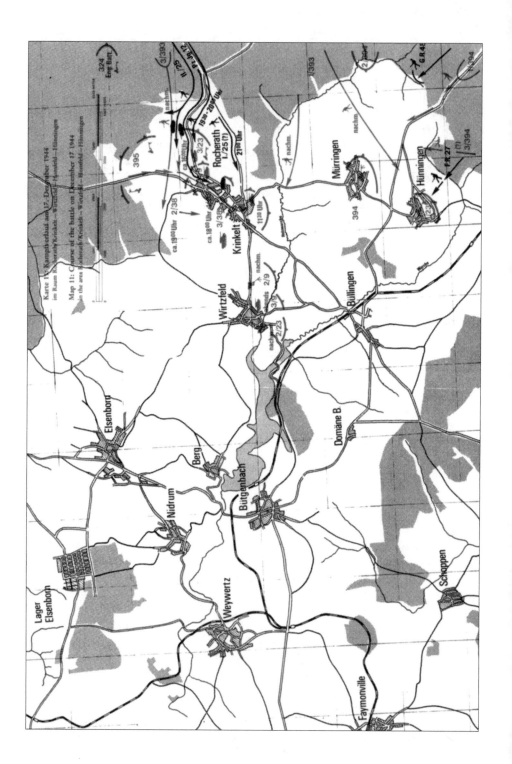

Karte 1: Kampfverlauf am 17. Dezember 1944
im Raum Rocherath/Krinkelt – Wirtzfeld – Hünsfeld – Hünningen

Map 11: Course of the battle on December 17 1944
in the area Rocherath–Wirtzfeld–Hünsfeld–Hünningen

of Rocherath in order to prevent a threatening breakthrough between the 1st and 3rd Battalions of the 393rd Infantry Regiment. The 2nd Battalion of the 23rd Regiment had already advanced to approximately two kilometers north of Rocherath in the late afternoon of 16 December and was held in readiness there. At that time, a stop to the 2nd Infantry Division's attack against the reservoir dams had not yet been ordered. Around midnight, the 26th Infantry Regiment of the 1st Infantry Division was moved from the area north of Verviers to the exercise grounds in Elsenborn.[21]

For 17 December, I. SS-Panzerkorps ordered the continuation of the attack with the objective of forcing the breakthrough on a wide front. The 277. V.G.D., after reorganizing its forces, was only able to restart the attack around noon. Hence, the whole reinforced SS-Panzergrenadierregiment 25 was assigned to it in order to enlarge the deep penetration in the Dreiher-renwald for a breakthrough to Rocherath. The fact that the attachment of the Panzergrenadierregiment to the V.G.D. took place can be gathered from the studies by Generalmajor Viebig and by the Author, and the notes of the Divisional commander, Standartenführer Kraas, while the then-chief of staff of I. SS-Panzerkorps indicates in his study that Grenadierregiment 991 was attached to "HJ" Division. It appears plausible that the command should remain in the hands of 277. since it knew the battle ground and had at its disposal the telephone network of the Westwall, and since the staff of "HJ" Division was intended to remain free to lead the armored group which stood ready to enlarge the expected breakthrough. Along these lines, the Korps had ordered that the Division be prepared to by-pass the not-yet opened and unsuitable Advance Route A by using the Reichsstraße between the road bend west of Hollerath and Losheimergraben after the obstacles and barri-ers had been removed. The Division was not pleased with that order since a whole reinforced regiment was put under the command of another com-mand authority which, in addition, had no experience leading a motorized unit, and which had yet been unable—for whatever reasons—to achieve the objective it had been given.

The mission given to 12. V.G.D. for 17 December was to capture Losheimergraben with a systematic attack, and to continue the attack on Honsfeld and Büllingen during the night. The 3. Fallschirmjägerdivision was to continue its attack in accordance with the orders, which meant advancing on Hepscheid and Heppenbach. The armored Kampfgruppe of 1. SS-Panz-erdivision under the command of Obersturmbannführer Jochen Peiper had been moved up along the road from Hallschlag to Lanzerath in the evening of 16 December. It would break through as soon as possible to Honsfeld and then advance in the direction of the Maas.[22]

Around midnight, Panzergruppe Peiper attacked the American posi-tions near Buchholz station (Losheimergraben station). It destroyed the two platoons of "K"-Company of the 3rd Battalion 394th Infantry Regiment in position there and advanced to Honsfeld. The town was taken while it was still dark, the tank destroyers and 90 mm anti-aircraft guns which had been hastily moved there were unable to prevent it.

The 99th Infantry Division wanted to regain the old positions in the sector of the 3rd/394th Infantry, after two battalions had moved into prepared rear positions north and northeast of Rocherath in the afternoon of 16 December to prevent a breakthrough. That was of major importance in order to prevent a threat to, or even a break in the supply route of the 2nd Division which was fighting in the Wahlerscheid district.

In the afternoon of 16 December, "I"-Company of the 394th Infantry Regiment, which had obviously been attached to the 393rd Regiment for that purpose, had succeeded in temporarily fighting open the supply route from Rocherath in the direction of the Hollerath road bend at the Jans creek. It broke through, bringing ammunition, to the cut-off 3rd/393rd. The Battalion was then ordered to first capture the high terrain to its rear in the morning of 17 December. Then, to open the supply route, and to transport the wounded and prisoners back to the regimental command post in Krinkelt. Subsequently, it was to recapture its previous positions in an attack to the east. The Battalion started its attack on 17 December at 08.00 hours and was, in fact, able to open the supply route.[23]

In the meantime, the reinforced Panzergrenadierregiment 25 had assembled in the area north of the Hollerath road bend during the night. At that time, I. Bataillon had not yet returned. It was known, however, that it had reached the western edge of the forest near Point 634 in the evening of 16 December and set up for temporary defense there.[24] The morning report of 17 December of Supreme Command West stated: ". . . Spearhead of the Kampfgruppe of 12. SS-Panzer-division has crossed Hill 639, two kilometers northeast of Krinkelt. Forward reconnaissance west of Wetthau (one kilometer east of Krinkelt) . . ."[27]

Sturmbannführer Siegfried Müller, commander of Regiment 25, started out II. Bataillon to the right of the forest lane (Advance Route A) since the forest lane was not passable and plugged with stuck vehicles. That attack would also eliminate the threat to the flanks of the spearheads of Grenadierregiment 989, which were located at the Jans creek. Panzerjägerabteilung 12 was ordered to cooperate with II./25. The II. Artillerieabteilung and one Pionier company were assigned to the Regiment. Nothing definite can be said regarding the tasks of I. and III. Bataillons. It is probable that III. was initially held back as reserve, while I. could be expected to still be located at the western edge of the forest, near the junction, which was an intermediate objective of the attack by II. Bataillon and the Panzerjägers who had to move along forest lanes.

Obersturmbannführer Richard Schulze commanded II./25. As a company commander in Russia, he had been awarded the German Cross in Gold. After being wounded, he was transferred to the Führer headquarters to replace his killed brother Hans-Georg (called Frettchen = ferret). He served there as the personal adjutant of the commander-in-chief, Adolf Hitler, until the beginning of 1944. He had received approval to take part in the Ardennes offensive within the framework of 6. Panzerarmee. He did not want to remain in the staff and had requested Oberstgruppenführer Sepp Dietrich to assign him the command of a unit. Since no regiment was available, he was offered to take over II./25. Richard Schulze was glad to take on that assignment even though it meant he would report to an officer junior in service time. The Panzerjägerabteilung was led by Hauptsturmführer Brockschmidt who was already reported on earlier. Sturmbannführer Neumann commanded II. Artillerieabteilung which took up positions in the vicinity of the Hollerath road bend.

The Bataillon attacked, with 7. Kompanie at the point. It was structured as an assault company, and additionally equipped with explosives and flame throwers. The Kompanie was followed by 1. and 2. Kompanies of the Panzerjäger-abteilung, and the staffs of II. Bataillon and Panzerjäger-abteilung. The other two Panzergrenadier companies and the heavy companies followed staggered to the right and left rear. The men had been sitting in their vehicles since noon of 16 December. Without winter clothing, they had been freezing and were glad when they could move around and warm up.

The II./25 and the Panzerjägerabteilung had turned onto a logging road, running into a northwesterly direction, at the Olef creek. They pushed into the attack by 3rd/393rd to regain its old main line of defense. Untersturmführer Ernst Stuhr led a Zug of 7. Kompanie and reported on the attack:

. . .The Kompanie moved forward, widely dispersed. To the left of the country lane was I. Zug, to the right II. Zug. I spotted Bataillon commander Schulze standing upright at the side of the lane. He was looking through his binoculars. An armored reconnaissance vehicle had taken up position in front of him. Its commander, a holder of the Knight's Cross, stood in the turret, observing the terrain ahead through his binoculars. [He was probably Sturmbannführer Gerd Bremer, commander of the Aufklärungsabteilung, holder of the Oak Leaves.] When we entered the woods there was a loud bang. A mine had exploded. An Unterscharführer lost his right lower leg. The woods were mined, the mines were connected by above-ground wires. After moving into the woods, we encountered stragglers from the Heer. They were asked to join us. Our attack initially progressed well. The fighting spirit of the men was excellent. Enemy resistance increased constantly. All sorts of shells exploded around us, not only on the ground, but also in the treetops. A messenger brought me the order to take over the Kompanie since Untersturmführer Hirsch had been wounded. The same was true for the leader of II. Zug . . .[28]
[presumably Untersturmführer Lützel, Author].[28a]

Soon after, Untersturmführer Stuhr was also wounded several times, first in his right armpit so that the arm became largely useless. Thereafter, he was hit by shrapnel in his back to the right of the spine, then he was wounded in the right upper leg, and a few moments later he took a salvo from a sub-machine gun in the right leg. He lost consciousness and only regained it on the hospital train. His right leg had to be amputated later.[29]

During the continuation of the attack, II./25 came across the command post of the 3rd Battalion. In its vicinity was a fire position of 81 mm mortars which can still be recognized today, and mined obstacles made of trees blocked the forest path.[30] Well dug-in anti-tank guns dominated the path to that point. Hauptsturmführer Brockschmidt moved to the point when he noticed that the attack stalled. He directed Obersturmführer Helmut Zeiner, the leader of 1. Kompanie, to pull his Panzerjägers into the woods, spread out, by-pass the trees, and smash the pockets of resistance. That action brought the attack back to life.[31] Obersturmführer Helmut Zeiner reported on the details of that fight:

> . . . We followed a narrow, occasionally winding forest lane to a spot where it split and dropped off. There, all hell broke loose. The enemy had armor-piercing weapons, snipers in the trees, and a few Shermans (or tank destroyers, Author) in ambush positions. Ober-scharführer Roy, who had taken over I. Zug in my place, was driving behind me. He was killed by a shot to the head. Roy had been awarded the Knight's Cross during the invasion. He was a likable young lad with a lot of skill and courage. None of that helped! The death of our comrade surely provoked great rage in us all, and I drove ahead recklessly. I overtook an American two-barrel anti-tank gun, and we fired explosive shells as well as our twin-machine gun to the left and right on the fleeing enemy. The forest path led down-hill, there was a valley to the right (probably the Jans creek, Author). On the slope opposite, there was a clearing with a fleeing Sherman. It escaped during the rush of the pursuit . . .[32]

The Grenadiers were tied down by the snipers in the trees for some length of time. Finally, the enemy was overcome. When the command post was seized, the men found hot drinks, chocolate, and various provisions. Inevitably, a short stop ensued. Then, the Bataillon commander restarted the attack. Hauptsturmführer Brockschmidt's further report is indicative of the manner in which combat, and command, was carried out there:

> . . . Obersturmführer Schulze put a pouch on the ground and said: 'The Bataillon command post is located here!' We discussed for a short time how to restart the attack and where to apply the heavy

pressure. A few minutes later there was an explosion and I was wounded in the left knee joint by shrapnel . . .[33]

Under the fire from snipers in the trees, the Panzer-grenadiers were able to advance only slowly, in particular since contact to the Panzerjägers, who had broken through, had partly been lost. Obersturmbannführer Richard Schulze remembered the progress of the fighting in this manner:

> . . . Since the men were largely without combat experience, only the deployment of the officers in the front lines could help. In the first hours, all Kompanie chiefs were lost, either killed or wounded. That included the Bataillon adjutant, Untersturmführer Buchmann, and the technical officer. Oberscharführers took over the companies. I remember the very difficult crossing of the Jans creek so well because, almost at the creek, I came under fire from snipers in the trees. I pretended to have been killed and, after some considerable time, I suddenly leaped up and into cover. The continuation of the attack, swinging further south after assembling the Bataillon, then led to success. During the fighting in the woods, a considerable number of prisoners were taken. They were immediately led to the rear . . .[34]

Obersturmführer Helmut Zeiner had been ordered by his Abteilung commander to continue the attack across the Jans creek toward Rocherath with his 1. Panzerjägerkompanie. The 2. Panzerjägerkompanie and II./25 would follow. In the meantime, darkness had set in. Obersturmführer Zeiner reported on the course of his attack:

> . . . My trusty men and I drove off into the night and the snowstorm, slowly, so that the infantry could keep pace. It was a narrow road. We could make it out, despite the blowing snow. Then we arrived at a road fork. We drove to the left and, after approximately one kilome-ter, landed at the edge of the village of Rocherath. Silence! We strained our ears, listening into the night, the engines turned off. Nothing! I sent a few men from the infantry ahead as a scouting party. They were to determine whether the village was occupied by the enemy or had been abandoned. In the meantime, I attempted to establish radio contact with the guns following behind, and with the commander. The result: the village was occupied by the enemy and I only had three Panzerjäger IVs behind me. The others had probably turned to the right at the road fork in the snowstorm. The important thing was to engage the (as the scouting party reported) unsuspecting enemy and to capture the village. From the map, I

gained the impression of a small village with a church, cemetery, and a few houses. Not until we approached the church did we see anything of the enemy.—Infantry fire.—I pulled ahead to the church, the remaining guns right behind me. I had directed the infantry Zug to comb all the houses and to bring the soldiers they found, disarmed, to the street. However, a dramatic event occurred right then. I stopped my Panzerjäger at the intersection after the church and ordered the motor turned off so that I could determine the situation by listening. Now and then I heard shots behind me, but, suddenly, to the right of me and apparently behind the church, the roar of a heavy engine. The only thing I could see was the corner of the church standing out from the snow-covered square. I suspected an enemy tank starting to move behind the church. I had our own engine started and pivoted my Panzerjäger around by ninety degrees to the right. In that position, I spotted a Sherman pushing out from behind the church, in reverse gear, some 8-10 meters away. I ordered "anti-tank shell", had the barrel lowered and when the giant was right in front of my gun I disappeared into my hatch, and we knocked out the tank. It was in flames immediately and lit up the battle ground and the church square for a long time. Two men were able, limping from the tank, to flee into the church. We left them alone. In the meantime, I again heard tank noises and we caught another Sherman at the far end of the square. A third Sherman was knocked out by a Panzerjäger following behind us and which had swung to the right. Now, there was silence. I dismounted and saw approximately 100 meters behind a large number of freezing negroes, some of them in nightshirts or some such garments, huddled in the street between the two Panzerjägers following me, and guarded by our infantry. I felt really sorry for those fellows and ordered all prisoners taken into a house, and then to secure the house from the outside. That saved me additional guards, who would probably not have been necessary in any case, since the prisoners were totally demoralized, shaken by the events of the night. A white American officer assured me that none of his men had any weapons left and would do anything I demanded. He, too, remained in the house mentioned.

After a short discussion of the situation with the leader of the infantry and my gun commanders, I wanted to know how much fuel and ammunition we had left. As I returned to my fighting vehicle, we came under sudden and unexpected fire from a house. It was an armor-piercing weapon, probably a bazooka. I turned my barrel back into the direction of the fire and it took about half-an-hour before there was no more movement in that spot. Aiming explosive shells at the muzzle flashes, we had obviously brought about silence.

The reports from the gun commanders arrived then and, based on the disastrous situation they indicated, I radioed to request fuel and ammunition.[34a]

The bulk of II./25 and Panzerjägerabteilung 12 had followed Obersturmführer Zeiner after they had dislodged the enemy from the Krinkelt forest. They followed him closely along the country lane leading to Rocherath. Soon after leaving the forest they came upon the enemy, ready for defense, in the darkness. After a bitter fight, they were able to throw him back, effectively supported by their own artillery. Immediately east of Rocherath they again encountered superior enemy troops. The attack stalled there under very heavy artillery fire. An attempt to by-pass the enemy by swinging to the north also faltered in the face of his superior forces, with the loss of several Panzerjägers. It is probable that the chief of 2. Panzerjägerkompanie, Obersturmführer Wachter, and the leader of his III. Zug, Oberscharführer Bitau, were killed during these battles.

The course of these battles was described by the American side in a detailed and, at the same time, confusing manner. Thus, Cole wrote:

> . . . The first tank coming along the forest path from Hollerath rolled into firing range of the American machine guns. It stopped and fired its machine guns systematically for twenty minutes. Attempts by the artillery to hit it were in vain, although the American fire momentarily scattered the accompanying infantry and allowed a tank-hunter squad to destroy one track. But even after it had been immobilized, the tank was still able to pin down the American infantry. Four more tanks appeared. One was knocked out by a bazooka, the others worked their way forward along the network of firebreaks and paths. The collaboration of tanks and numerous infantry finally threatened to smash the whole position of the 3rd Battalion. Ammunition was running out, and the wounded could not be transported to the rear . . .[37]

In the After Action Report of the 393rd Infantry Regiment it was stated that the Regiment had ordered the 3rd Battalion in the afternoon to withdraw as a reserve into an area to the rear of the 3rd Battalion 23rd Infantry Regiment which had moved into a prepared rear position in the area of the Lausdell crossroads, 1.5 kilometers east-northeast of Rocherath. It was stated as follows:

> . . . The withdrawal was carried out under constant enemy pressure, including enemy tanks. Almost all vehicles and equipment in the front district of the 3rd Battalion had been destroyed by enemy action. In the afternoon of 17 December an attack by strong Ger-

man forces with accompanying tanks hit the 3rd Battalion 23rd
Regiment and forced it into a disorderly retreat. That Battalion did
not inform the commander of the 3rd Battalion 393rd Infantry
Regiment of its retreat and left its flanks unsecured. The Battalion
was again encircled and had to fight to all sides. Vehicles and equipment, which had been saved from its original positions, were again
hit by artillery and tank fire. Most of the men had not eaten anything for two days, but their spirit and determination were high.
Since they could not withdraw to Krinkelt, the Battalion commander
ordered that they fight open their way to 395th Infantry Regiment
during the night of 17 December, and they joined it in Elsenborn
on 18 December. During the cross-country march, more vehicles
were lost. As far as possible, they were destroyed before they could
fall into enemy hands . . .[38]

Cole states that the order to withdraw was issued to the 3rd and the 1st
Battalion 393rd Regiment, abutting on the right, at approximately 10.30
hours. The whole 3rd Battalion was able to disengage around noon without
major problems and arrived in its new positions two hours later. Fifteen
wounded, who could not be transported, were left behind with the Battalion
physician and a few men. The Battalion was only 475 men strong, and had
lost all its machine guns except two.[39]

The After Action Report of the Regiment notes, concerning the 1st Battalion 393rd Infantry Regiment, that the Battalion commander ordered the
withdrawal in the late afternoon when he realized that he was unable to hold
his position. The Battalion made its way cross-country—in particular through
dense forest—and thus had to destroy and leave behind, its vehicles. The
Battalion was only a little more than 200 strong. It succeeded in joining up
with a battalion of the 394th Infantry Regiment, and, together, they fought
their way back to Elsenborn. It arrived there around midnight of 18 December, after having been encircled once more.[40] Cole reported that this Battalion received the order to withdraw at approximately 11.00 hours and that it
had moved into a narrow position east of Rocherath-Krinkelt next to the 3rd
Battalion 23rd Infantry Regiment at approximately 14.00 hours. A unit of
medium tanks from the 174th Tank Battalion had been moved to the
3rd/23rd during the previous night. Two tanks had been sent to guard an
intersection of forest paths. Reportedly, they knocked out two Panzers in a
short-distance duel, but were themselves knocked out. After occasionally
determined resistance, the Battalion finally had to retreat and was scattered,
in open terrain, by artillery and rocket launcher fire. Thus, the 1st Battalion
393rd Infantry Regiment was then completely isolated. It found itself forced,
in cooperation with the 2nd Battalion 394th Infantry Regiment, to withdraw
to Wirtzfeld. The rearguard had remained in Krinkelt.[41]

The 2nd Division, in the process of attacking the reservoir dams, was not informed of the developments at the 99th Division and its neighbor to the right on the evening of 16 December. General Gerow, the commanding general of V Corps, had gained the impression in the afternoon of 16 December that the 2nd Division could soon be in a difficult situation. He had requested approval from the First Army to break off the attack near Wahlerscheid and to pull back the division to the range of hills on both sides of Elsenborn. The request was denied. He repeated his request the next morning, 17 December, at 09.30 hours. The Army still did not want to order the withdrawal of the 2nd Division, but empowered the V Corps to act according to its own judgment. General Gerow then ordered the "Indian Heads" to break off the attack near Wahlerscheid, to withdraw from that sector, and to move into defensive positions on the range of hills on both sides of Elsenborn. It was only at that moment that Major General Robertson, the commander of the 2nd Infantry Division, learned what had happened in his rear. It now became important to keep the only route of withdrawal through Rocherath-Krinkelt open. The 3rd Battalion 38th Infantry Regiment, which had not been in action so far, was immediately moved up from the district southwest of Wahlerscheid in order to take up defensive positions at the southern fringe of Krinkelt since, at that moment, the area north of Büllingen was threatened by armored Gruppe Peiper. At 11.30 hours, the Battalion was dug in at the intended spot. The 9th Infantry Regiment was to be the first to disengage from the enemy near Wahlerscheid. It would march through Rocherath-Krinkelt and establish defenses with the bulk of its troops around Wirtzfeld in order to keep the route of withdrawal to Elsenborn open. The 38th Infantry Regiment was directed, together with its two battalions still in action and as these arrived, to build up a defensive position near Rocherath-Krinkelt. The 1st/9th Infantry was pulled out from near Wahlerscheid in the early afternoon. When Major General Robertson learned that the front line of the 393rd Regiment had been breached and that the defenses east of Rocherath-Krinkelt threatened to disintegrate, he immediately sent the 1st/9th Infantry into action to block the road from Hollerath to Rocherath. By dusk, the battalion, reinforced by three guns of the Tank Destroyer Battalion 644, was in position atop an elevation in the terrain east of the village of Rocherath. From there, it was able to observe the edge of the woods. At approximately 19.30 hours, three Panzers (no doubt, Panzerjägers) with approximately one Zug accompanying infantry unexpectedly broke through the position of the 1st Battalion at the road. That was the small Kampfgruppe of Obersturmführer Zeiner. Half-an hour later, more "Panzers" (Panzerjägers) appeared from out of the darkness. Two "Panzers" were taken out of action by mines, two more by bazookas. In the end, the remaining five or six "Panzers", together with their accompanying infantry, managed to break into the positions of the 1st Battalion. The attack was then, however, stopped by the concentrated fire from seven artillery units firing from Lager Elsenborn. Those were the parts of Panzerjägerabteilung and of II./25 following behind, after having waited, in vain, in Rocherath for Obersturmführer Zeiner. He had assumed that they had turned off in the wrong direction.[42]

The Unit Journal of the 9th Infantry Regiment recorded for 17 December, 21.00 hours:

> . . . Artillery radio unit monitored a message that tanks have broken through our Red Battalion, in a westerly direction toward Rocherath . . . [At 22.40 hours:] . . . Colonel Graham says 'Kraut' is in Rocherath and Krinkelt with strong forces . . . [Then, at 22.45 hours:] . . . One enemy tank spotted in the village, others heard outside the village to the east and northeast . . . Some 'Kraut' forces in the village. 'C'-Company of the Tank Destroyers tries to determine where they are, in order to destroy them . . .[43]

After the 9th Regiment of the 2nd Division had withdrawn from the combat area near Wahlerscheid under the cover of artillery fire and smoke, the 1st Battalion 38th Infantry Regiment was also pulled out and assembled, while the 2nd Battalion covered the retreat. At the road fork "Rocherather Baracken" (Rocherath barracks), approximately one kilometer north of the town, the battalion came under heavy artillery and rocket launcher fire as soon as the point company had passed. It was ". . . the heaviest fire this old, battle-hardened battalion had ever encountered . . ." "C"-Company suffered the most losses and was scattered. "Panzers" (Panzerjägers) in the vicinity were held off with difficulty through hastily laid mines. The lead, "A"-Company, withdrew through Rocherath to Krinkelt. It was forced to turn around twice by rifle fire before an officer from the battalion led it into its intended positions. "B"-Company, which arrived at approximately 21.30 hours, was sent into action on the left. Before they could dig in, the two companies were hit by an attack by "Panzers" (Panzerjägers) and infantry from a northeasterly direction. "A"-Company let the Panzerjägers roll by and opened fire on the infantry following behind which it was able to repulse. "B"-Company was smashed and only one platoon was able to escape. The survivors retreated, together with the remnants of "C"-Company, to the regimental command post in Rocherath and joined the anti-tank company in the combat inside the town. ". . . The battle for Krinkelt seesawed back and forth, house by house, hedge by hedge . . ."[44]

The 2nd Battalion had followed the 1st/38th. At approximately 19.00 hours it moved into positions some 400 meters north of Rocherath, abutting the 2nd/9th Infantry to the left. There, it came under brisk artillery and machine gun fire. It handed over "G"-Company for the defense of the regimental command post.[45]

The Journal of the 38th Infantry yields the following details: 16.30 hours ". . . Tiger tanks leaving the woods in the direction of the Service Company. The 23rd withdraws from the forest. Our tanks have pulled out . . ." Then, 16.33 hours: ". . . Two of our tanks reported knocked-out by the 'Jerries' . . ." And, 16.50 hours: ". . . The enemy has broken through Tuttle's battalion. Tuttle's battalion is very disorganized. A platoon of tank destroyers is on its way to us . . ." 21.45 hours: "The 'B'- and 'C'-Company are still trying to reach their intended positions. They are under fire. Enemy tanks and infantry have penetrated into the town from the east. They have advanced to the command post. Members of the staff have killed numerous infantrymen. They forced a tank to withdraw after it had fired three 88 mm shells into the command post building. Before that, it had rammed into the building . . ." That was not an 8.8 cm gun of a Tiger, but the 7.5 cm gun of a Panzerjäger. Finally, at 23.15 hours: ". . . Sergeant Buckenby observed three Tiger tanks and five groups of enemy infantry of 150, 20, 20, 20, 18, and 20 men respectively, advancing into Rocherath to the vicinity of the church while he was hiding in a foxhole along the north-south route through Rocherath. He also observed twenty-seven US prisoners marching into the direction of the church . . ."[46] In the course of the evening, the staff of the 38th Infantry Regiment had also reached Rocherath. The houses intended for the command post were occupied by German Grenadiers. The houses had first to be fought free.[47]

At 21.00 hours, a German attack on Krinkelt from the east was reported. It was repulsed in one sector by the fire from artillery, mortars and small-arms. In another sector, three "Panzers" and one Grenadier company made their way as far as the rear positions before they were forced back by units of the 3rd Battalion.[48] It is conceivable that the attack farther south against Krinkelt was carried out by parts of I./25. The three "tanks" and the accompanying Grenadiers were, without question, the small Kampfgruppe of Obersturmführer Zeiner.

In the late evening, the following picture developed in the combat area of the village of Rocherath-Krinkelt: The 1st and 3rd Battalions 393rd Infantry had been smashed by the attacks of 16 and 17 December. Their remnants retreated in a disorderly fashion, leaving their material behind. They were collected and moved back to Elsenborn for reorganization and its defense. Smaller parts were initially incorporated into the, only weak, defensive front line east of Rocherath-Krinkelt. The 3rd/23rd Infantry, deployed in a prepared rear position northeast of Rocherath, was overrun. The 395th Infantry Regiment with the attached 2nd/393rd Infantry, adjacent to 3rd/393rd Infantry in the north, had been given the task of securing the withdrawal of the 9th and 38th Infantry from the attack sector near Wahlerscheid. To do that, it moved into positions, facing north and northeast, along both sides of the two roads, which joined at the Rocherather Baracken. The 324th Engineer Battalion was left behind on the Rath-Berg (hill) as a guard. In order to secure its threatened southern flank, the Division moved its reserve battalion (3rd/38th Infantry) back to the southern and eastern edge of Krinkelt and Rocherath, respectively. It sent the 2nd/23rd, the 2nd/9th and the 3rd/9th Infantry into action to defend its route of retreat south of Wirtzfeld. In the evening of 17 December, the defense of Rocherath and Krinkelt was in the hands of the four infantry battalions: 3rd/38th, 1st/9th, 1st/38th and 2nd/38th. They were reinforced by tanks and tank destroyers, the number of which cannot be given with any certainty. In the course of the day, the 3rd/393rd and the 3rd/23rd as well as the 1st/393rd, which had already been badly mauled on 16 December, were smashed or scattered, and thrown back.

In the face of the vastly superior enemy—seven battalions with tanks and tank destroyers—Regiment 25, with two companies of Panzerjägerabteilung 12, had forced the breakthrough to Rocherath-Krinkelt after heavy fighting, with high losses. However, only three Panzerjägers and approximately one Grenadier Zug had penetrated into the village. Thanks to their bold attack, the superior enemy assumed them to be much stronger. The II./25, together with 2. Kompanie of the Panzerjägerabteilung, was stalled east and northeast of Rocherath. Parts of the Bataillon and a few Panzerjägers had pushed into the northern sector of Rocherath for some time, but were unable to hold on. The I. Bataillon was located east of Krinkelt. No reliable information can be provided on the whereabouts of III./25. The reinforced Regiment 25 had achieved a massive initial success against an enemy growing constantly stronger in numbers, who was, in the end, vastly superior. The enemy defended his well fortified positions in Dreiherrenwald with valor and, finally, was able to stop the attack which came from out of the forest across open, rising terrain, from his elevated positions northeast and east of Rocherath and Krinkelt only with the greatest of effort. The successes achieved were primarily thanks to II./25,and 1. and 2. Kompanie of the Panzerjägerabteilung. They were paid for with high losses. For instance, two officers and eight men of 7./25 were killed; one officer, four NCOs and forty men wounded; one NCO and forty-two men missing, of whom a majority were to find their way back to the unit, others were probably killed. In the evening of 17 December, the fighting strength amounted to one NCO and twenty-six men. There are no reports concerning the other units of the Bataillon.[49]

The breakthrough along Advance Route A had not yet been achieved on 17 December either.

To conclude the reports on that bloody and bitter day of combat, the Kompanietruppführer of 2. Kompanie of the Panzerjägerabteilung, Unterscharführer Alfred Schulz, should have his say here. He wrote:

> . . . The wooded terrain had been shredded by shells. The paths were in the condition described already. Bad news awaited us. The attack was not progressing, the losses were high. There had been a

number of wounded and losses of Panzers. Thank God, no total losses, the Panzers could be repaired later.

The leader of 3. Zug, Oberscharführer Bietau, had been killed. We took him with us, bedded in our VW, and drove him to the supply unit. He had been shot in the head. Just after leaving the front, we were slowed down. New units of the Heer were pushing forward, and Pioniers had to work on the muddied stretches of the road time and again to prevent the Panzers from sinking in further. At one of those bottlenecks in the Krinkelt forest we had to wait for about two hours before we got through. We were sitting to the right of the path under the treetops. We were frozen through and through and moved around a bit. The -Kompanie squad vehicle of 1. Kompanie appeared behind us. It was being pushed by several of our comrades. The motor had some kind of damage which could only be fixed by the repair unit. We took the VW under tow.

But, in that vehicle, too, lay a killed comrade. He was Oberscharführer Roy, also shot in the head. They had bedded him down so that the Knight's Cross was clearly visible. He and his comrades of 1. Kompanie had been so proud of it. It had been awarded to him in October, together with his gunner, Rottenführer Eckstein, and the Kompanie chief, Obersturmführer Hurdelbrink. The two Panzers had knocked out thirty-six enemy tanks each in Normandy.—After that, only such a short span was left to him. Another promotion, to Oberscharführer, and then, very quickly, the soldier's fate had come to a conclusion.

Those pushing forward gazed at our dead comrade with reverence. I made a sort of reconnaissance sortie approximately fifty meters deep into the woods to look for another possible way through. Suddenly, I spotted two American infantrymen in the undergrowth. Immediately, I leveled the machine-pistol, which I carried with me, at them and motioned them to surrender to me. I took them both prisoner and brought them to our vehicles. They were young men, around twenty, just as we were. They were shaking with fear of the Waffen-SS, something with which they had probably been indoctrinated. I searched them for weapons, they had none left. Then I asked them in English whether they had cigarettes or chocolate, regrettably they did not have those either!

They looked at our killed comrades with great sincerity. What may have been their thoughts, what tales did they later tell at home? Both our Oberscharführers wore the Iron Cross I on their chests, as well as the wounded badge, the Panzer combat badge, in addition to the bar with several ribbons of other decorations. I had told the two prisoners to sit on the hood of the vehicle in front. We still felt cold, it was damp and chilly in the wintry woods, our boots were wet. The Americans, too, seemed to be cold. For the time being, we could not move on. We were hungry. I cut a thick slice from the slightly frozen loaf of army bread and put on a thick layer of canned meat. I offered some to the Americans, but they did not feel like it. They watched us, astonished, as if to say: How can they possibly eat like that in view of the dead? But one learns that after a lengthy period of time in action. Finally, there was a break in the opposite traffic, and we could move on. Carefully, our twin-unit found its tortured way through the dirt and mud. After leaving the wooded area we finally regained a firm road and were able to move somewhat faster. We passed a column of some 200–300 American prisoners who were being led to the rear by soldiers of the Wehrmacht. I ordered a short halt at one of the guards and had my two prisoners join the column. We were glad that they no longer obstructed our visibility during the drive. And they were probably glad to be with their comrades. Time and again, we met opposite traffic. New units moving to the front, as well as individual supply vehicles with fuel and ammunition. The winter sun threw sparse rays through the leaf-less treetops onto the snowy Eifel landscape. We transported our dead comrades safely to the supply unit at Hellenthal. We arrived there around noon. A short rest, reports delivered, then we loaded the vehicle with the articles which were needed at the front as well as provisions for the crew. Soon, we started out again in the opposite direction, to our Panzers at the front. Sleep had been abolished. Our killed comrades were then buried with military honors in the war cemetery in Schleiden . . .[49a]

While Regiment 25 and the Panzerjägerabteilung attacked, under the command of 277. V.G.D., fighting also continued at their neighbors. On the morning of 17 December, while it was still dark, the spearhead of Kampfgruppe Peiper of 1. SS-Panzerdivision captured Honsfeld. Reconnaissance indicated that stretches of the intended advance route between Honsfeld and Schoppen were impassable. Hence, Obersturmbannführer Jochen Peiper turned onto the road to Büllingen. Since the road Losheimergraben-Büllingen was not available to "HJ" Division, he was able to use its Advance Route C without misgivings. After overcoming the resistance from the 254th Engineer Battalion and a reconnaissance platoon of the 644th Tank Destroyer Battalion, which had been put into action to secure Büllingen, that town was taken in the morning shortly after 7 A.M. The majority of the tank destroyers were knocked out. The engineers withdrew to Schwarzenbüchel, immediately north of the town, and set up defenses, together with two companies which had avoided enemy contact. They were reinforced by four anti-tank and anti-aircraft batteries. The Peiper spearhead rolled through Büllingen at 10.30

hours and continued to the southwest in order to regain its advance route near Möderscheid.[50]

The Americans were surprised that neither their positions south of Wirtzfeld nor those northwest of Büllingen came under attack. They still had no idea of the far-reaching objective and the extent of the German offensive. Obersturm-bannführer Jochen Peiper's Kampfgruppe was on the advance into the depth of the undefended terrain. At noon, it was already driving through Engelsdorf (Ligneuville). It was approximately eighty kilometers away from the Maas near Huy. By dusk, the spearhead reached Stavelot but deferred an attack across the Amblève river for the time, after one of the three Panthers at the point had driven onto a mine and been taken out of action.[51]

At Losheimergraben, an attack by Grenadierregiment 48 and Füsilier-regiment 27, with the support of a few Panzers, finally broke the last resistance at nightfall. The 395th Regiment received orders from the 99th Division, in the afternoon, to withdraw to Mürringen.[52]

To the left of 12. V.G.D., the 3. Fallschirmjäger division took advantage of the gap opened by Kampfgruppe Peiper, and continued to advance in a northwesterly direction.

The withdrawal of the 2nd Infantry Division was noted by the parts of 326. V.G.D. fighting near Wahlerscheid. The Volksgrenadiers followed the retreating Americans after some period of time, without seriously pressing them.

Another action took place on 17 December 1944 which had already been scheduled for the first day of the attack: "Operation Stößer". In the evening of 15 December, the Kampfgruppe was to be transported after dark to the Paderborn and Lippspringe airfields. Because of fuel shortages, the transport column was able to move only about one-third of the Kampf-gruppe there on time. The action had to be postponed by one day. In the afternoon of 16 December, the 6. Panzerarmee ordered Oberstleutnant von der Heydte to jump during the night of 16–17 December. The Armee had not been able to reach its attack objectives for the first day. The enemy had been observed moving reinforcements to Elsenborn from the north. The Kampfgruppe was to prevent or delay that by blocking the pass across the Hohe Venn to the south, or at least significantly disrupt the movement of troops from the north to the south. Shortly before midnight of 16 December, the first Ju 52s departed. The Fallschirmjägers once more sang their song "Red glows the sun" in the aircraft on their way to their last jump of the war. Not all the aircraft reached the jump area. Some were shot down, others dispersed, by anti-aircraft fire. Unexpectedly strong surface winds of 12–15 meters per second, practically a storm, together with light blowing snow additionally contributed to the failure of the Kampfgruppe to land in its landing zone as a unit. In the morning, the commander of the Kampfgruppe had collected only some 125 men of the approximately 400 at the road fork which had been designated as the landing zone. Among them were the artillery observer, Obersturmführer Etterich, and his two radio operators, Sturmmann Leonhart and Sturmmann Rosenauer, who had survived their first jump, without any training, unharmed. At daybreak, the Fallschirmjägers observed American columns on the move south. Scouting parties located artillery positions and assemblies. It was impossible to establish radio contact with the respective German units. The reports had to be sent blind. There was no way of determining whether they arrived. In any case, "HJ" Division could gather from its radio intelligence of American radio traffic that the Kampfgruppe had landed in the operations area.

In the afternoon, Oberstleutnant von der Heydte pulled back into the forest to the northeast. There, he found another group from his unit of about 150 men. The Kampfgruppe had only few heavy weapons available since most of the weapons containers, which had been dropped, had not been found. In the evening, a scouting party brought in the first prisoners. Together with two Fallschirmjägers, who were no longer fit for action, and an accompanying letter, they were sent to the main road and picked up by passing American troops. Their reports created an exaggerated image of the strength of the Kampfgruppe.[53]

A first warning had already been issued to all American units in the morning. The following entry was recorded in the Journal of the 9th Infantry for 17 December, 07.20 hours: ". . . Paratroopers reported near 08167520 and 81149699. All battalions informed . . ."[54]

The After Action Report of the 18th Infantry Regiment of the 1st US Infantry Division contains more detailed information concerning the American countermeasures. There, it reads:

> . . . In conjunction with their strong ground attack, the Germans also dropped paratroopers at a number of points in the vicinity of Eupen, Malmedy, Monschau and the large wooded districts in that area. At 15.30 hours on 17 December, the 18th Combat Team started its march into the Eupen district by truck. Its mission was to deploy at the eastern fringe of the city and to coordinate the defense of the important major crossroads, and to block the roads to Monschau and Malmedy . . . An estimated number of 500 paratroopers was reported at various points in the extensive forests which stretched several miles south of -Monschau. Part of our mission was to comb those woods and to destroy the enemy there. On 17 December, at 24.00 hours, the order was issued to send a task force into the vicinity of V-8116, a section of the forested area where, according to reports, the paratroopers had blocked the Eupen-Malmedy road by harassing fire from automatic weapons . . .

One company of the 3rd/18th Infantry Regiment was sent out from the north, and a reinforced platoon of the 16th Infantry Regiment from the south, at 07.30 hours in order to jointly destroy the enemy. Toward the evening, another company of the 3rd Battalion was brought in. The task forces ". . . carried out their missions with minimal enemy contact. Either, the paratroop unit had been numerically overestimated, or it had changed its operations area. Only small enemy groups were encountered most of whom withdrew into the woods when we approached. Four were captured. They stated that they belonged to the von Heydte Kampfgruppe . . ." Before nightfall, the two companies of the 3rd Battalion took up a blocking position on both sides of the road.[54a]

Since the Kampfgruppe was unable to exert major influence on the progress of the fighting, the further development of the events is reported here in anticipation. Slowly, the ammunition supply ran out, the jump provisions were soon used up, and a supply container drop by a Ju 88 was observed only once. One container was found, inside was drinking water and cigarettes which had got wet. On 18 December, the Kampfgruppe "was handed" the operational orders of the XVIII US Corps by American messengers. It was unable to evaluate the orders and Fallschirmjägers, who volunteered, were given the task to carry them through the enemy lines to the German troops which were some fifteen kilometers distant (Monschau or Büllingen). Two of the messengers, sent off at different times, reached the German units. The noon report of Supreme Command West of 19. December 1944 states: ". . . Two men of Gruppe 'Stößer' have made their way here and reported that 200 men under the command of Oberstleutnant von der Heydte are located in the forest 5–6 kilometers south of Eupen. They have blocked the road from Eupen south at several spots. There are no reports from the other parts of Gruppe 'Stößer' available . . ."[54b]

On 20 December, the Kampfgruppe initially tried to break through in a body. However, it soon encountered American securing forces which were of superior strength and had tanks available. The Kampfgruppe withdrew. On the following day, Oberstleutnant von der Heydte disbanded his Kampfgruppe and ordered that the men make their way east in small groups.[55]

The American leadership recognized that the situation in the sector of V Corps had taken a dangerous turn. The defenses in the sector of the 99th US Division had broken down. The 2nd US Division had been forced to break off its attack near Wahlerscheid, and to retreat, in order not to be cut off. So far, it had managed, only with the greatest of effort, to prevent a German breakthrough near Rocherath-Krinkelt. A large gap had been smashed into the pulled-back defensive front between Holzheim and Büllingen. Through it, the armored group (Peiper) had advanced a considerable distance. The badly damaged forces of the divisions in action so far were unable to prevent a widening of the breakthrough. Only weak infantry forces and anti-aircraft

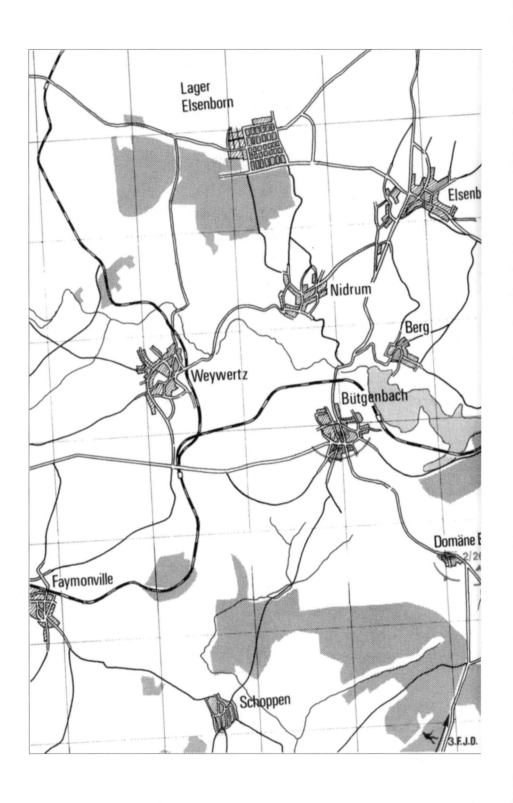

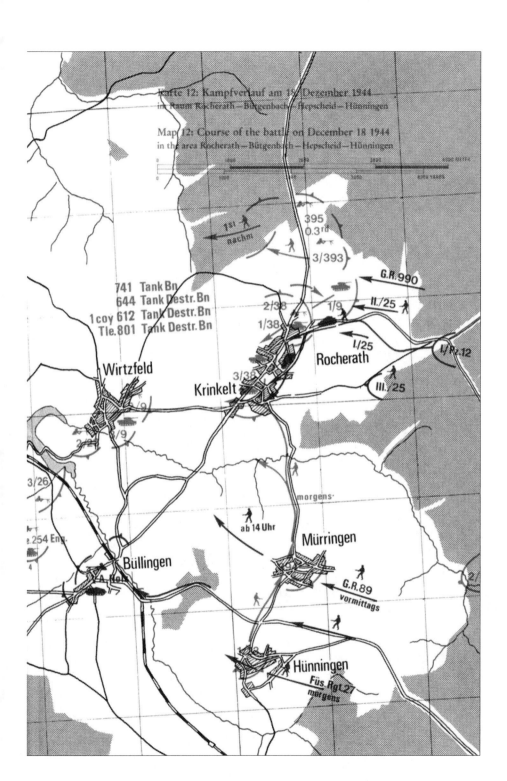

Karte 12: Kampfverlauf am 18. Dezember 1944
im Raum Rocherath–Bütgenbach–Hepscheid–Hünningen

Map 12: Course of the battle on December 18 1944
in the area Rocherath–Bütgenbach–Hepscheid–Hünningen

1st
nachm.

395
0.3rd

3/393

G.R. 990

741   Tank Bn
644   Tank Destr. Bn
1 coy 612 Tank Destr. Bn
Tle. 801 Tank Destr. Bn

2/38
1/38
3/38

1/9
II./25

Wirtzfeld

Krinkelt

Rocherath

I./25

I./Pz.12

III./25

/9

3/26

.254 Eng.

ab 14 Uhr

morgens

Büllingen

Mürringen

G.R. 89
vormittags

Hünningen

Füs. Rgt. 27
morgens

batteries near Schwarzenbüchel, northwest of Büllingen, and one company of the 612th Tank Destroyer Battalion near the Bütgenbach estate initially blocked the important road to Malmedy. Reinforcements had to be brought in. At first, only the 1st US Infantry Division was available. It had been relieved during the first days of December in the sector east of Aachen by the 9th and parts of the 78th US Infantry Division. Since the evening of 6 December, it was located, together with the 26th Infantry Regiment, in the district around Aubel (thirteen kilometers north of Verviers), and, since the morning of 8 December, together with the 18th Infantry Regiment, in the Plombiers area (sixteen kilometers north of Verviers). After bitter fighting and high losses, the division was scheduled to rest for some time, and to refit.

As early as 21.15 hours on 16 December, the 26th Regiment was put on a one-hour alert. Soon after midnight it received orders to start out together with the 3rd Battalion at 02.30 hours. The two others would follow. At 04.00 hours, the column was stopped since paratroops were reported dropped behind the American front lines. They continued their drive after some time, without lights, and arrived at Lager Elsenborn at 07.00 hours. At 14.00 hours, they marched to Bütgenbach. The 2nd Battalion had also reached Bütgenbach in the meantime. At 18.30 hours on 17 December, both battalions were ready for defensive action. They were attached to the 99th Infantry Division. The 18th Regiment had been alerted on 17 December at 14.00 hours, to march into the Weismes district (six kilometers west of Bütgenbach). Finally, the 16th Regiment was also alerted and ordered to move into the Robertville area (four kilometers north of Weismes) on 18 December.[55a]

Two entries in the Journal of the 9th Infantry mention the 26th Infantry Regiment: 19.20 hours: ". . . 1st Division located immediately south of the lake [Bütgenbach reservoir] . . ."; and 19.45 hours: ". . . 26th Infantry located immediately south of the lake. All battalions advised . . ."[56] The 26th Infantry had taken up positions in the following manner: 3rd Battalion southwest of Wirtzfeld—probably adjoining the 2nd/23rd Infantry of the 2nd US Division to its right the 2nd Battalion around the Bütgenbach estate, its front facing east, southeast and south, while the 1st Battalion was located in the vicinity of Bütgenbach as a reserve. That defensive position was supported by tank destroyers and strong artillery which were in position in Lager Elsenborn. They could call on an ammunition depot near Robertville (six kilometers northwest of Bütgenbach) which contained 6,000 tons.[57]

The I. SS-Panzerkorps ordered the continuation of the attack on Rocherath-Krinkelt for 18 December 1944, with action by I. Panzerabteilung under the command of 12. SS-Panzerdivision. The Reichsstraße between Neuhof and Losheimer-graben was to be cleared as quickly as possible of mines and other obstructions so that Advance Route C could be used. The 12. Volksgrenadierdivision was ordered to seize -Mürringen and Hünningen, then to attack toward Wirtzfeld, and to advance from Büllingen toward Bütgenbach. To its left, 3. Fallschirmjägerdivision was to advance into the Faymonville district. The 1. SS-Panzerdivision was ordered to follow Panzergruppe Peiper along two advance routes, to close up to it, while the Panzergruppe captured Stavelot and continued the breakthrough to the Maas.

During the night, I. Panzerabteilung, consisting of 1. and 3. Pantherkompanie, and of 5. and 6. Panzer IV-Kompanie, moved forward along the Reichsstraße from the Blumenthal area (two kilometers northeast of Hellenthal) by way of Hellenthal, Hollerath, Miescheider Heide to the road fork west of Udenbreth or via the road bend at Hollerath. Then, along the forest lane swinging off to the northwest, it advanced into the assembly area in the Forêt Communale de Rocherath. The Abteilung received orders, together with the reinforced Regiment 25 and Panzerjägerabteilung 12, in action with it, to destroy the enemy still defending Rocherath and Krinkelt and then to advance further on Elsenborn. The Aufklärungsabteilung would support the attack on Krinkelt from the south, as soon as Mürringen was captured by 12. V.G.D. Schwere (heavy) Panzerjägerabteilung 560, SPW-Bataillon III./26 (armored personnel carriers), and the marching column of the bulk of Regiment 26 were to be in readiness to move forward along Advance Route C as soon as the obstructions had been cleared away and Mürringen and Hünningen had been captured. Artillerieregiment 12 and Werferabteilung 12 were to support the attack from their existing fire positions. The Division established a forward command post in a Westwall bunker immediately north of the road bend west of Hollerath.

The situation of the weak forces which had broken through to Rocherath and Krinkelt had deteriorated during the night of 17–18 December. In view of the immense superiority of the enemy who had concentrated three battalions of infantry, anti-tank guns, tanks and tank destroyers there, that was not surprising. Obersturmführer Zeiner reported about it:

. . . It was about two o'clock at night (18.12.1944). We tried, time and again, to establish radio contact with our own Panzerjägerabteilung. Suddenly, we had a very short period of contact with a Panzerregiment radio unit of the Waffen-SS. The conversation was inconclusive since there was constant interference. Ammunition, fuel and hot coffee would have been just what we needed. We set up a hedgehog defensive position. The small village was larger, according to infantry reconnaissance, than we had originally thought. Enemy infantry was still sitting in its western section; at dawn we heard track and engine noises. It was about six o'clock in the morning when I arrived at a very difficult decision. I still had no radio contact with the Abteilung, did not have a motorcycle messenger available, did not know where my Abteilung was located, probably

2–3 kilometers behind us in the woods we had broken through the previous day. I only had some forty infantry men, and my Panzer-jägers had only some ten high explosive shells each left. Also, our fuel supply was very low. As well, we had taken approximately eighty prisoners. Tactically, our situation in the village center was hopeless in case of an enemy infantry attack. Why should I lose my men, the Panzerjägers—all of them were combat-ready—and the prisoners when the enemy determined the real strength, ridiculous for him, of his foe?

Answer—dissolve the hedgehog position! Set up another hedge-hog, but with the prisoners in the center, Panzerjägers in the front and rear. In the meantime, visibility was good. My hope was to estab-lish, based on the map, visual contact with German units at the edge of the forest. So we left the old positions in Rocherath and set up new positions approximately 300 m east of the edge of the village.

We had barely arrived there when a thick hail of enemy shells set in. But, another sensation was also in the making. Watching the edge of the forest, we saw Panzer after Panzer leaving it in wide for-mation. They were German Panzers. We waved pieces of cloth so as not to be fired at by our own people, forgetting to watch out for the phosphorous shells exploding next to us. Our prisoners had crawled under the Panzerjägers for cover. Our infantry did the same . . ."[58]

The confused situation in Rocherath-Krinkelt is also illustrated by the report of the Kompanie medic of the Panzerjägerkompanie, Sturmmann Benno Zoll. He wrote:

. . . Part of the village was still occupied by the Americans. At the fringe of the village was a house ruin with a large Red Cross flag. I thought that the cellar would be empty and walked down into it. To my surprise, I saw that five Americans were still there. One of them spoke perfect German. He questioned me on what being a prisoner of war of the Germans would be like. They gave me cigarettes, chocolate and their first aid supplies since all that would surely be taken away from them in captivity. They told me that all five had been conscientious objectors. Still, they had been trained as medics and sent to the front line to prove themselves. I returned to the street to look for our men. I was shocked to find out that the village was still full of Americans, there was fire from all the cellar windows. Our Panzerjägers had gone. Luckily, I found some men from the accompanying infantry and asked them what was going on. They said: 'Get away quickly before the Amis catch you!' I joined them. After some time, we reached our own troops. I still wonder what the American medics may have thought? . . .[58a]

Obersturmführer Zeiner's small Kampfgruppe was unable to join the attack by the Panzerabteilung. It had to refuel, pick up ammunition, and the men needed to get some sleep first. For that, the Gruppe had been pulled back. The prisoners it brought along were sent to the prisoner assembly area.[58b]

The attack by I. Panzerabteilung commenced shortly before daybreak. The Abteilung had to use the country lane from Point 634 to Rocherath since mine obstructions had been reported on both sides of the lane. Travel was in file. In the lead was 1. Kompanie, behind it, 3. Kompanie, followed by 5. and 6. Kompanie. Hauptsturmführer Götz Großjohann, the chief of 6. Kompanie, reported:

> . . . After the fog had lifted in the morning, we started the attack. The Panther companies penetrated into the village of Rocherath ahead of us. My Kompanie was driving at the end of the Abteilung. I thought I had spotted a movement at the edge of the forest, located half-right from us, and suspected an enemy anti-tank gun. In order to improve my visibility, I opened my turret hatch for a moment and pointed my binoculars toward the edge of the forest. That very instant, I was hit by an infantry bullet. By radio I handed over command of the Kompanie to Untersturmführer Pucher . . .[59]

Approximately in the vicinity of Lausdell, II./25, which had been stalled there the previous evening, joined the attack. Presumably, I./25 was advancing to the left of the country lane. In the fog, the attack first smashed into the 1st Battalion 9th Infantry which was dug-in near Lausdell, facing east and south. The spearhead Panzers were able to roll into the village of Rocherath. While the American artillery was furiously shelling the country lane, the Grenadiers attacked and broke into the American positions. There was bitter hand-to-hand combat. The Grenadiers were unable to achieve a breakthrough for the time being. When the fog lifted around 08.30 hours, more Panzers advanced along the country lane, firing their machine guns at the American foxholes along the path. The Grenadiers rushed forward. "A"-Company was overrun. It requested artillery support. An artillery unit shelled that sector for half-an-hour. "G"-Company, attached to the 1st/9th, was also decimated. Of the two companies, only one officer and twenty-two men escaped. The other two companies were able to hold on to their positions. The 2nd Battalion of the 38th Infantry was pulled out of its positions north of Rocherath and moved to the east in order to take up a rear position behind the 1st/9th to enable it to withdraw. An unexpectedly approaching platoon of Shermans of the 741st Tank Battalion was able to knock out two Panzers but did not manage to push its way through to the cut-off company. Under cover from its fire, the remnants of the company retreated, pursued closely by the Grenadiers. The Panzers and Grenadiers who had penetrated into the northern part of Rocherath became involved in bitter fighting with the 1st and 2nd Battalion 38th Infantry which lasted the whole of the morning.[60]

A Panzer commander in II. Zug of 3. Kompanie, Willi Fischer, reported on the battle in Rocherath:

> . . . The fatal attack on Rocherath-Krinkelt got under way on 18.12.1944. A perfect 'Panzer grave'. The Panzers of 1. Kompanie drove at the point, then followed our Kompanie, with Brödel as Kompanie chief. Myself, I was slotted in behind Beutelhauser, my Zugführer. When I reached the vicinity of the church, a gruesome picture was waiting for me. Beutelhauser was knocked out in front of me. We had both already crossed the second intersection. When Beutelhauser was hit, I was able to spot the approximate location of the enemy twin anti-tank gun.
>
> Beutelhauser was able to bail out and reach safety. His loader was killed by rifle bullets as he bailed out. I moved my Panzer into position behind a house, which provided visual and fire cover, without knowing, right then, what to do next. Brödel's vehicle stood next to me, burning lightly. Brödel sat lifeless in the turret, he had been killed. Along the course of the street ahead of me, all of the Panzers had been knocked out, some were still on fire. One Panzer was still moving, I believe it was Freier's. It was able to pull back in the direction of the eventual Abteilung command post under my covering fire. Some of the crews from the knocked-out Panzers who had been hiding in a shed took advantage of that opportunity. They also went back using the Panzer as cover. They barely escaped being taken prisoner by the encircling American infantry. Behind me, Jürgensen in his Panzer appeared. I realized that it was time to give up my untenable position and I wanted to pull back to the other side of the intersection. It was clear to me that the American anti-tank gun had seen through my plan and would fire at the intersection. That, it did. The first shell was wide, the second hit the track and the hull from the side, fortunately, there were no human losses. The radio equipment was destroyed, the track almost ripped off. I just managed to follow Jürgensen's directions before the track dropped off. The running wheels on that side sat in the mud which later froze hard as a rock. The whole attack had stalled. Next to our new position we found approximately 20 Americans in a hole in the ground covered by a tarpaulin. They surrendered. Still, there were more Americans in several of the houses in the sector of the village we were already occupying. It was they who killed our comrade Bandow from an ambush with a bullet in the heart as he, unsuspectingly, was about to camouflage Jauch's Panzer with some slabs of wood. That happened in my immediate vicinity, right before my eyes . . .[61]

After Hauptsturmführer Großjohann had been wounded, the crew of the command Panzer of 6. Kompanie continued the report. Here, the gunner, Sturmmann Max Söllner:

> . . . After the chief had been wounded, we continued to roll into the attack with our Panzer. That was very difficult for us since, without the commander, our visibility was restricted. Despite repeated requests, none of the Zugführers came forward to climb aboard. So I just relayed all the orders which came from the Abteilung to our Panzer. Despite all, that worked out fairly well, since our Kompanie arrived at Krinkelt without losses and took up positions there. I met Untersturmführer Pucher there who wanted to join us . . .[62]

Now follows the report of the loader, Sturmmann Hannes Simon:

> . . . Soon after, we were in a Panzer attack in the direction of the church. We fired approximately ten high explosive shells, two of which turned out to be shells which did not fire immediately. I exchanged views with Untersturmführer Pucher. He said I should open the gun breech early after the second such shell. While we were talking, the shell fired. The casing of the last high explosive shell welded itself in the gun. Under the cover from the wall of a house we managed, under fire, to loosen the case from the outside, using the barrel cleaner . . .[63]

The Panthers of 1. and 3. Kompanie were fighting in the village of Krinkelt, located to the south. Several attempts to penetrate deeper into the village faltered in the fire of the enemy artillery. Still, a number of Panzers managed to advance to the road leading to Wirtzfeld from the southern village exit. However, they were put out of action by tanks, tank destroyers and bazookas. In Rocherath, Panzers and Grenadiers pushed ahead to the command post of the 38th Regiment, but were unable to hold on there. In the afternoon, the 2nd/38th Infantry was pushed back into the northern section of the village.[64]

Untersturmführer Willi Engel, Zugführer in 3. Panzerkompanie, had suffered a stroke of bad luck during the march to the assembly area. His Panther had driven onto a mine and was rendered unserviceable because of damage to the track.

In the afternoon, he was able take over the leader-less Zugführer vehicle of II. Zug, coming from the repair company, and follow his Kompanie together with another Panther. He reported:

> . . . After a rapid drive we reached the village of Rocherath. Even the first houses showed the marks of the previous fighting. Battle noise

could be heard from the center of the village. Untersturmführer Jungbluth, orderly officer at the Regimental staff, stood at the point and signaled us to maintain our direction. Somehow, however, I sensed disaster since I was expected to act counter to the elementary rules of armor combat: that a built-up settlement, without having securing infantry available, should be by-passed if at all possible. Hence, in a fraction of a second, I pulled out to the left and ordered the Panzer accompanying me, to follow. Barely half-an hour later I received proof that I acted correctly. Driving along the rear slope, along the backside of the line of houses, swinging our turrets towards cellars and windows, we reached an open square at the church. I let Bellmer pass me, and we drove both Panzers into the '3-o'clock position', so that the nose faced toward the enemy, and one side was under cover from a house. Our open flanks were facing each other. Two streets leading straight-ahead into the sector occupied by the Americans were located within range of our weapons. Directly in front of us lay the main street along which the Kompanie had attacked and which we had avoided. Opposite, inside some kind of administration building, I spotted the Abteilung command post. Next to its entrance sat the command Panzer of Sturmbannführer Jürgensen. Close to it stood the commander, in discussion with a few officers and men of the Abteilung staff. I reported to him. His face mirrored dejection and resignation. The failed attack and the painful losses, in particular of 1. and 3. Kompanie, obviously depressed him severely. He directed me not to change positions for the time being since I could best join the action from there. From where he stood, I could survey the main street. The knocked-out Panzers of the Kompanie offered a distressing picture. At that moment, a single Panzer approached the Abteilung command post. Suddenly, only about 100 meters away, it turned into a flaming torch. Soon after, the commander of that vehicle, Unterscharführer Freiberg, showed up at the command post, his head wrapped in a bandage. He reported: 'In the doorway of a house I spotted a woman waving a white piece of cloth. As I directed my attention there, wondering what that was all about, I was hit. My Panzer was immediately in flames.'

It was later determined that an immobile, but otherwise serviceable and manned Sherman had scored the hit. Surely, I would have suffered the same fate if I had followed the directions at the village entrance. The fighting in Krinkelt flared up time and again. Both sides fought with bitter determination. During the night 18–19 December, the American artillery fire increased. The explosions went off surprisingly close to our Panzers. Since I could hear directions and corrections to the fire on my receiver, it was probable that the American artillery radio was, coincidentally, using the same frequency we were transmitting on, or that a well-hidden forward observer could observe us directly and guide the shelling.

Based on his experience, Hauptscharführer Bellmer distrusted his new surroundings. He felt closed-in inside his steel box. His visibility was limited. The watchful eyes of the infantryman, used to darkness, did not seem to work properly as shadows, resembling tanks, moved in the reflection from the burning houses. Unknown noises played tricks on his ears. Suddenly, the motor of his Panzer roared, the vehicle jumped on its tense tracks, and he raced backward down the slope. When I asked by radio where he was going he replied that an American tank had just pointed its gun at him. I was able to convince him that it had been an optical illusion. He returned to his previous position. Since he could not see any of our own infantry, he had the turret MG removed and ordered the loader to use it to secure to the rear from the open hatch, just in case, as the loader told us afterwards. Later, we laughed together about that novel idea quite a few times . . .[65]

In the evening it was confirmed that Panzers and Panzergrenadiers had penetrated into both villages—Rocherath and Krinkelt—and were pushing hard against the vastly superior enemy. However, they were unable to completely capture the villages. The attack cost high losses in Panzer crews, Panzers and Grenadiers. The I./25 and II./25 of the infantry carried the main load of the fighting. The III./25 had probably been stopped by the American artillery fire after leaving the forest east of Krinkelt. Grenadierregiment 990 threw the 3rd/393rd Infantry back behind the Rocherath-Wahlerscheid road, but was unable to break through its front line. Two battalions of the 395th Infantry Regiment still stood on its right flank.

The enemy, too, suffered significant losses. A tank unit (741st), a tank destroyer unit (644th) and a company of tank hunters (801st) provided strong support to the valiantly fighting infantry. During the fighting in the village, they provided effective support from the rear. It must be stressed that, contrary to reports from American units and Cole's statements based on them, no "Tigers" were in action on the German side, nor were there two, but only one Panzer-abteilung. [66] In the face of the American tanks and tank destroyers, the lack of Grenadiers was particularly noticeable on the German side since they are indispensable for armor combat within built-up areas. The two Panzergrenadier-bataillons I./25 and II./25 faced more than four American infantry battalions.

The situation in the sector of the southern neighbors had developed in a more positive manner. Contributing to that, in part, was surely that "HJ" Division had tied down strong American forces and threatened the flanks of others. The 394th Infantry Regiment, which only had left a route of withdrawal through Krinkelt, abandoned its positions in Mürringen on 18 December at 02.00 hours, as did the 1st/23rd Infantry in Hünningen. They believed themselves justified in doing that based on a radio message from the 99th Division. They formed one motorized and one foot column. When the motorized column approached Krinkelt, they heard battle noise and the din of tanks. That was the small Kampfgruppe Zeiner. The column dismounted since the commander believed that the road to Wirtzfeld, which led through Krinkelt, could not be used. The troops continued their march on foot toward Elsenborn. The foot column, which arrived somewhat later, found the abandoned vehicles. It confirmed that a part of Krinkelt was still in American hands and manned the vehicles. It reached Elsenborn without any problems. In the vicinity of Mürringen, an American artillery unit was in position, the 371st Field Artillery Battalion. When it had to withdraw, it left the bulk of its guns behind. [67] At 07.40 hours, the 3rd/38th Infantry reported that parts of the 394th Infantry Regiment were moving through.[68] Approximately one hour previously, the Zeiner Kampfgruppe had withdrawn from Krinkelt. The I. Panzerabteilung had not yet advanced that far.

While the 1st/23rd Infantry in Hünningen prepared for withdrawal, parts of Füsilierregiment 27 of 12. Volksgrenadierdivision penetrated into the village at several spots. The American battalion had to fight its way out. The Füsiliers took Hünningen, Grenadierregiment 48 of 12. V.G.D. occupied the abandoned village of Mürringen. The road from Losheimergraben to Büllingen was open. Presumably, it was only then that the spearhead of 12. V.G.D. started its drive toward Büllingen. It consisted of the Panzerjägerabteilung, the assault gun Abteilung with six operational assault guns, one Füsilier company, and Pioniers. Generalleutnant Engel, in his study, erroneously mentioned the evening of 17 December, the commander of the spearhead, Major Holz, in his recollections, the evening of 16 December.[69] After the breakthrough by Panzergruppe Peiper, the Americans had re-occupied Büllingen with weak forces. It was captured again and cleared. The 12. V.G.D. disallowed a further advance on Bütgenbach since its right flank was completely open. The Holz spearhead established defenses at the northwestern and western edges of Büllingen.[70] That is confirmed by the daily report of Supreme Command West of 18 December 1944 which states: ". . . 12. V.G.D. took Büllingen and captured, among others, sixteen aircraft and seven anti-tank guns. Since 14.00 hours it is on the advance toward Wirtzfeld and Bütgenbach . . ." The report by Major Holz indicates that the order to attack Bütgenbach estate was ". . . called off at the last minute . . ."[72]

Kampfgruppe Peiper captured Stavelot at 10.00 hours. According to a monitored report, it was southwest of the city at 15.00 hours. By evening, it had reached the Stoumont district. Other parts of "LAH" Division took Recht (four kilometers south of Engelsdorf-Ligneuville) at 14.30 hours. The 3. Fallschirmjägerdivision pushed to the north from the area northeast of Heppenbach.[73]

It had become of decisive importance for 6. Panzerarmee to open the road via Malmedy to Spa in order to secure the right flank of Kampfgruppe Peiper and to create some room to bring up supplies of ammunition and fuel. Hence, it ordered the attack by "HJ" Division in Rocherath-Krinkelt to be broken off. The 3. Panzergrenadierdivision was scheduled to take over that combat area on 19 December. The elements of "HJ" Division not in action were ordered to move forward into the Büllingen district as quickly as possible, to secure the road to Bütgenbach from there. Those parts which were in action in Rocherath-Krinkelt had to follow later. The units designated to carry out the attack on Bütgenbach were assigned to II. SS-Panzerkorps.

The V US Corps had decided to abandon the protruding position in Rocherath-Krinkelt, threatened in its southern flank, as soon as the last parts of the 99th Infantry Division, which were still retreating east of the line Mürringen-Rocherath, had moved through. The positions around Wirtzfeld were also to be abandoned immediately after the troops coming from Rocherath-Krinkelt had passed through the town. It was planned to have the 2nd Infantry Division and the remnants of the 99th Infantry Division establish a new defensive front line northwest of Wirtzfeld. The withdrawal movement was to be camouflaged and secured by the 741st Tank Battalion, the 644th Tank Destroyer Battalion and the engineers of the division. The withdrawal movement began on the left wing so that the road from Krinkelt to Wirtzfeld could be used.[73a]

One preparatory measure for the withdrawal was the destruction of all their own material which was no longer operational or could not be transported, and of the knocked-out German Panzers. The Journal of the 38th Infantry Regiment notes for 08.50 hours on 19 December: ". . . Set fire to all enemy tanks in your sector . . ." An entry for 09.47 hours states: ". . . The German are trying to salvage tanks in front of the 2nd Battalion . . ." (The 2nd was located in the northern sector of Rocherath.) Entered at 10.13 hours: ". . . Will set fire to the tanks as soon as possible . . ."[74] The Americans began to disengage slowly and withdrew to the western section of the village. Untersturmführer Engel of 3. Panzerkompanie remembers:

> . . . Under the threat of a court martial, Jürgensen had delegated to me the responsibility to defend my Panzer, another Panzer of 1. Kompanie with a crew of three men, and an unmanned Panzer IV. That was some pleasant feeling, the Americans in one half of the village and the eight of us on the other side with three inoperable Panzers. Luckily, the Americans had no idea of that. Even before daybreak, and before the assault guns of 3. Panzergrenadierdivision occupied the town, they had withdrawn far beyond the edge of town . . .[75]

Still, there were losses among the remaining Panzers, securing the section of town captured during the previous days, until relief arrived. In order to camouflage and secure the preparations for withdrawal, the American artillery fiercely shelled the section of town time and again. Sturmmann Max Söllner, gunner in the chief's Panzer of 6. Kompanie, wrote about it:

> During a fire attack on Krinkelt we took a direct hit in front of the turret. It ripped a hole of about 1 m into the armor. The explosion virtually tore our driver, Sturmmann Karl-Heinz von Elm, into pieces. Our radio operator, Sturmmann Gottfried Opitz, lost his left arm. The radio equipment had provided him with some protection. The legs of Sturmmann Hannes Simon ended up full of shrapnel. I was sitting in the cupola, my legs pulled up, so I got away with just a fright. I was able to get Hannes and Gottfried onto an armored personnel carrier which was on its way to the dressing station. Our Panzer was towed to the repair company at Losheimergraben. There, we buried Karl-Heinz . . .[76]

On 19 December, 3. Panzergrenadierdivision attacked Krinkelt from the south and southeast, together with Panzerabteilung 103 which was equipped exclusively with assault guns. At the same time, a Panzergrenadier battalion (II./8), attacked Wirtzfeld together with Grenadierregiment 89 of 12. V.G.D. After assembling in the Rocherath forest, I./8 was scheduled to by-pass Rocherath to the north and capture the high terrain immediately north of Rocherath.[77] The noon report of Supreme Command West notes:

> . . . A Kampfgruppe of 277. I.D. started an attack to the north by way of Rocherather Baracken. The 3. Pz.Gren.-Div. (slowed down by mud-choked lanes) started out toward Elsenborn. Its spearhead, at present, is southwest of Hollerath. Probable start of attack is 13.00 hours . . .

Regarding the course of the fighting at the 38th Infantry Regiment, its Journal noted:

> . . . 11.50 hours: 'tanks near 983051 behind the anti-aircraft tower. 'Jerries' are in the anti-aircraft tower.'; 12.37 hours: 'Approximately one hour ago, two tanks showed up and fired at the vicinity of the command post (possibly P IVs)'; 13.05 hours: 'Another tank on the road, where five have been knocked out, on the left flank of A-Company, fires directly at A-Company.' 13.16 hours: 'German tanks brought men forward and dropped them at the knocked-out tanks from where they fired machine guns into the vicinity of the church.' 13.45 hours: 'Colonel Stokes orders: At 17.30 hours, withdrawal to the position indicated on the map. The 395th, together with the attached 2nd Battalion 393rd will move on the road. . . . All other

units under the command of 38th Infantry . . . road to Wirtzfeld . . . destroy all German and American equipment at the same time. Do not leave any equipment behind which could be used by the Germans!' 13.40 hours: 'tank activity near 987052. Concentrate artillery fire there. One tank hit, crew bails out.' 13.45 hours: 'Are we firing at the church tower? Yes.' 13.55 hours: 'Start withdrawal now, important vehicles immediately.' 16.10 hours: '12 tanks coming up the road where others tanks have also been reported' (at the 3rd/38th in the Krinkelt sector of the town) 16.50 hours: '1st Battalion reports that the artillery has knocked out 3 tanks, damaged two more, the others scattered . . . ; one tank knocked out by tank destroyer.' 17.37 hours: 'Use own covering forces to mask the withdrawal.' 18.35 hours: 'J-Company reports enemy tanks rolling into the village.' 19.30 hours: 'Ready to move out.' 22.15 hours: 'All units here at 22.00 hours' . . .[78]

During the night 19/20 December 1944, the Panzers, Panzerjägers and Grenadiers remaining in Rocherath/Krinkelt were pulled out. Sturmmann Heinz Nußbaumer of 6. Kompanie reported on that:

. . . We were relieved during the night of 19 to 20 December. We drove back along the same route via Rocherath. We carried as many wounded as possible in each Panzer. The creek crossing was under constant artillery harassing fire. Our Panzer had a broken brake belt, in order to steer we had to always use the reverse gear. The repair squad organized another brake belt for us the same night from a knocked-out P IV in Krinkelt and installed it right away . . . [79]

There is only sketchy information regarding the German losses of personnel and material. Available information has previously been noted. However, the losses on the American side are also indicative of the ferocity of the fighting. The 393rd Infantry Regiment of the 99th Division reported for the period 1–31 December, where the heavy fighting took place only during the time from 16 to 20 December: 173 killed, 606 wounded as well as 141 missing.

The 38th Infantry Regiment of the 2nd US Infantry Division recorded, for December 1944 alone: 49 killed, 321 wounded as well as 409 missing; of whom, according to Cole's research, 625 losses took place alone during the three days of battles for Rocherath/Krinkelt.

Cole lists the losses of tanks, Panzers, tank destroyers and anti-tank guns for both sides as follows: ". . . The 741st Tank Battalion lost eleven Shermans and knocked out twenty-seven tanks, five of which were 'Tigers'. Two 7.62 cm tank destroyers of the 644th Tank Destroyer Battalions were destroyed, it reported knocking out seventeen tanks and two assault guns/tank destroyers. The 801st Tank Destroyer Battalion suffered very heavy losses without being able to report any successes of its own. Of its own 7.62 cm anti-tank guns, seventeen were destroyed, as were sixteen of its armored tractors. The 5.7 cm anti-tank guns of the infantry battalions had proven themselves ineffective and the majority of them were destroyed . . ."[80]

The figure of forty-four destroyed Panzers and two Panzerjägers of "HJ" Division appears significantly too high. However, no reports on losses are available from the German side. Only the information contained on the map "Lage Frankreich" (situation in France) of the OKW can be used as a basis. For 17 December 1944. "Lage 3" (situation 3) indicates as combat-ready: thirty-nine Panzer IVs, thirty-eight Panzer Vs and fifty-three Jagdpanzers. The numbers for 18, 19, and 20 December remained unchanged: thirty (9) Panzer IVs, thirty-four (4) Panzer Vs, and fifty-seven (4) Jagdpanzers (figures in parentheses indicate the number of vehicles under short-term repair). Hence, they reflect an earlier level—probably after the completed assembly in the morning of 16 December—while the numbers stated on 17 December reflect available vehicles before departure for the assembly area in the Eifel. On the situation maps 22–23 and 24 December, the following identical figures of combat-ready vehicles appear: twenty-six Panzer IVs, twenty-one Panzer Vs, and thirty-three Jagdpanzer. The figures in brackets have to include repairable and destroyed Panzers and Jagdpanzers. The numbers probably reflect the Panzer situation on 20 December when the magnitude of total losses could not yet be realized. The losses of Schwere Panzerjäger-abteilung 560 near Bütgenbach estate from the attack on that estate during the night of 19 to 20 December are likely contained in the Jagdpanzer figures. Since Cole states that almost all reported twenty-seven destroyed Panzers had been examined, that number can be assumed to represent the total losses of Panzers and Panzerjägers. Reported successes beyond those numbers are probably duplicate reports or destruction of repairable Panzers and Jagdpanzers. The report of five knocked-out "Tigers" is an error. The Division did not have any available. The Tigerabteilung of I. SS-Panzerkorps was part of Kampfgruppe Peiper of the "LAH" and in combat southwest of Malmedy.

For the Division, the battle for Rocherath-Krinkelt was over. Despite high losses of Panzergrenadiers, Panzerjägers, Panzers and their crews, it had not achieved a breakthrough along Advance Route A. The forces of 277. V.G.D., which had been given that task, were insufficient for it. Even sending I./25 into action in the afternoon of 16 December under the command of 277. V.G.D. did not bring about the breakthrough to Rocherath. Hindsight shows that immediate action by the whole reinforced Regiment 25 and Panzer-jägerabteilung 12—instead of only one battalion—under the command of the "HJ" Division would very likely have made that breakthrough possible.

Thereafter, the Kampfgruppe would certainly have been tied down for some time by combat with the retreating 2nd Infantry Division. Since Advance Route A was completely unusable, the armored group and the marching column of Regiment 26 could not have been brought up along that route. They could advance only along the road Hollerath via Losheimergraben to Hünningen, as soon as it had been opened up and the obstructions cleared. That could have happened at the earliest in the morning of 18 December, unless the armored group had been sent into action in the evening of 17 December to force, by itself, the breakthrough between -Mürringen and Hünningen to Büllingen and Bütgenbach. In case its breakthrough near Hünningen had been successful, the Kampfgruppe would have encountered the ready-for-defense 2nd/26th Infantry toward the evening of 17 December. The success of a night attack—and only such attack had any hope for success—was uncertain. To swing farther south in order to by-pass Bütgenbach estate and Bütgenbach village was impossible since the Büllingen-Mödersscheid road was under directed fire from Bütgenbach estate and the artillery at Elsenborn. Later, the 3. Fallschirmjägerdivision was already on the advance in that area. It follows that favorable prospects for a breakthrough via Büllingen, Bütgenbach to Malmedy existed only on 16 December, or at the latest, in the morning of 17 December. However, Losheimergraben was captured by 12. V.G.D. only on 17 December around nightfall.

There were three major reasons which prevented a deep breakthrough of the "HJ" Division: In the first place, the uselessness of Advance Routes A and B, secondly, the unexpected presence of the 2nd US Division, whose importance was realized too late, in the Wahlerscheid-Wirtzfeld-Rocherath district and, thirdly, the failure of the attack by 277. V.G.D. and the delay in the capture of Losheimergraben by 12. V.G.D., for whatever reasons. Also, the consequences of inadequate training in units, caused by lack of time, had become obvious.

It then becomes an important question whether, by shifting the focal point to the inner wings of the two Panzer armies and by opening the only good advance route in the sector of 6. Panzerarmee (the road Büllingen-Bütgenbach-Malmedy) the ultimate objective could still have been achieved.

CHAPTER 8.5
Attacks on the Bütgenbach Estate and on Bütgenbach from 19 to 22 December 1944

The previous chapter reported on the course of the offensive operations of I. SS-Panzerkorps until 19 December 1944. The present chapter will initially illustrate the developments at the neighbor units in order to provide an overall view of the general situation.

To the right of I. SS-Panzerkorps, the LXVII. A.K. was in action with the 272. and 326. Volksgrenadierdivisions, in the framework of 6. Panzerarmee. Its mission was to break through the American front on both sides of Monschau and then turn to the northwest in order to cover the right flank of the Panzer units pushing toward the Maas, along the line Simmerath-Eupen. With its attacks on 16 and 18 December 1944, the Korps achieved initial successes but was unable to hold on. The main line of resistance in the whole sector remained in American hands.

Connecting to the left of 6. Panzerarmee was the 5. Panzerarmee. The breakthrough of "LAH" Division near Krewinkel and of 3. Fallschirmjägerdivision near Manderfeld pulled its extreme right wing along. The divisions of the Korps in action there, LXVI. A.K. and LVIII. Panzerkorps, had initially encountered significant difficulties. To the left, XXXXVII. Panzerkorps crossed the Our river between Dasburg and Gemünd and broke through the American front line on 16 December. The 7. Armee crossed the Our to the left of 5. Panzerarmee, encountering only minor resistance, and established a bridgehead near Vianden. Even farther to the left, the Sauer river was crossed between Wallendorf and Echternach.

On 17 December, the right wing of 5. Panzerarmee -advanced only slowly in the direction of St. Vith. The LVIII. Panzerkorps achieved no progress either. In contrast, XXXXVII. Panzerkorps pushed forward, with 2. Panzerdivision, across the Clerf and took Clerveaux. The 26. Volksgrenadierdivision set up a bridgehead near Drauffelt through which the Panzer-Lehr-Division advanced. At 7. Armee, 5. Fallschirmjäger formed a bridgehead across the Clerf near Kautenbach, in the vicinity of the confluence into the Wiltz. The divisions adjoining on the left gained only little ground.

On 18 December, significant successes were achieved in the sector of 5. Panzerarmee. The LXVI. A.K. advanced further in the direction of St. Vith. At XXXXVII. Panzerkorps, the Panzer-Lehr-Division reached Mageret (four kilometers northeast of Bastogne) during the night. That town would later be of considerable importance to "HJ" Division. To the right, 2. Panzerdivision reached Noville (seven kilometers northeast of Bastogne). The right wing of 7. Armee advanced toward Wiltz. The left wing made only slow progress, Echternach was not taken.

In the evening of 18 December, two spearheads had penetrated deeply: at the 6. Panzerarmee, Panzerkampfgruppe Peiper's point was located near Stoumont (sixteen kilometers west of Malmedy) and, thus, forty kilometers west of the old front line. At 5. Panzerarmee, the points of two divisions of XXXXVII. Panzer-korps were outside Bastogne, having advanced thirty kilometers. It was now important to provide more forces to those spearheads, to widen them, to advance farther, and to secure their flanks.

Kampfgruppe Peiper was stalled in the La Gleize district with small fuel reserves, a primary reason that it was unable to continue its attack in the direction of the Maas. The marching columns following behind were unable

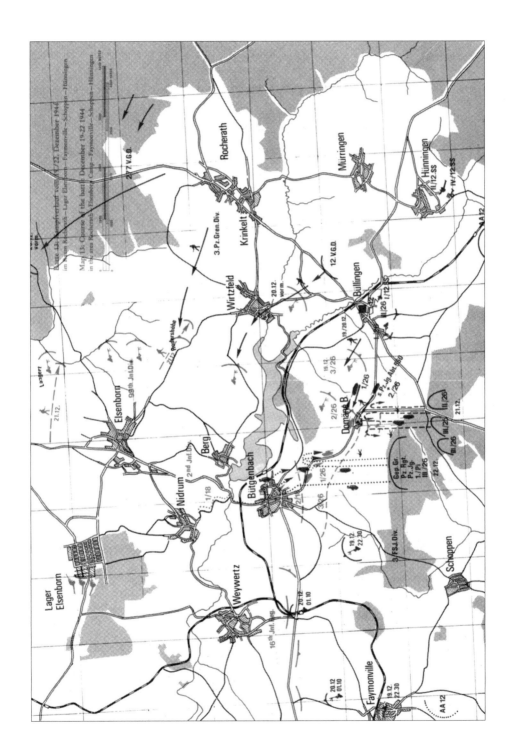

Skizze 13: Kampfverlauf vom 19./20.–21./22. Dezember 1944
im Raum Rocherath–Lager Elsenborn–Faymonville–Schoppen–Hünningen

Map 13: Course of the battle December 19–22 1944
in the area Rocherath–Elsenborn Camp–Faymonville–Schoppen–Hünningen

to establish contact. The supply routes were cut at several locations. The "LAH" Division had been assigned Routes D and E. Because of impassable stretches of Route D, the Panzerkampfgruppe used Advance Route C which had been assigned to the "HJ" Division. Obersturmbannführer Jochen Peiper could not cross the Amblève at Trois-Ponts as he had planned, since the bridge across the river had been blown up. Instead of using the road via Werbomont, he had to take the one via La Gleize to Stoumont. That was also the reason that the marching columns following behind could only use that route. However, the stretch Losheimergraben-Büllingen-Morschheck was no longer available since fairly strong enemy forces had occupied the Schwarzenbüchel hill northwest of Büllingen and, since, in addition, 12. Volksgrenadierdivision required that road. Route E, between Herresbach and Meyerode, could not be used at all. Although the road Manderfeld-Schönberg-St. Vith-Vielsam had many bends, it could be fairly well traveled at least by wheeled vehicles. However, most of it was located in the sector of 5. Panzerarmee. The major road junction of St. Vith was still occupied by the enemy. It was obviously negative for 6. Panzerarmee that its left boundary ran five kilometers north of the city and that Vielsam was also located outside its attack sector. Its narrow width did not allow the Panzerarmee, considering the mostly poor or impassable roads, any room to deploy its forces. The marching columns of the "HJ" Division thus had to struggle forward with difficulty along muddy narrow roads or even country lanes. On top of that, the right flanks of Panzerkampfgruppe Peiper and the marching columns behind were threatened. Thus, it became important to open up the Advance Routes Büllingen-Morschheck-Faymonville-Malmedy and Bütgen-bach-Bruyères-Bévercé-Francorchamps. That would allow the securing of the right flank of Panzerkampfgruppe Peiper and provide a shorter route for the marching columns following behind it. At the same time, the right flank of the "HJ" Division also had to be covered. To do that, it was necessary to clear Advance Route A via Wirtzfeld-Elsenborn-Sourbrodt. Since the element of surprise no longer existed, and the enemy was moving in reinforcements from the north, that became a very difficult mission. The "HJ" Division was given the task of concentrating on opening up the road in the Büllingen-Bütgenbach-Malmedy sector. Available for that were, initially, Panzergrenadierregiment 26 and Schwere Panzerjägerabteilung 560, which were still located, on 18 December, in their assembly area behind the Westwall. Adjoining on the right, 12. Volksgrenadierdivision, 3. Panzergrenadierdivision and 277. Volksgrenadierdivision were to attack toward Wirtzfeld and Elsenborn. Between the "HJ" and "LAH" Divisions, the 3. Fallschirmjägerdivision was on the advance to the west. Only a single road was available for the assembly and supply of the three divisions in action next to each other-12. V.G.D., "HJ" Division, and 3. Fallschirmjägerdivision. That imposed a significant handicap. For that attack, they were assigned to the general command of II. SS-Panzerkorps whose divisions (9. and 2. SS-Panzerdivisions) had not been able to join action in any case. The war diary of Supreme Command West noted, inter alia, for 19 December 1944:

> . . . A further reason for the stalling of 6. Panzerarmee can be found in the shortage of available space to deploy the Armee. Thus, another attempt must be made to speedily open up the Elsenborn area. In addition to the three divisions assigned to II. SS-Panzerkorps, the action will be carried out by: 277. V.G.D. to the northeast of Elsenborn and 12. SS-Panzerdivision which is being moved toward Bütgenbach. Thus, five divisions (3 infantry and 2 fast units) are available for that attack. Given adequate leadership, the objective must be achieved with that . . .[1]

That entry creates the impression that the German forces were greatly superior to the American in that combat theater. An analysis provides a different picture. On the American side, in a curve around Lager Elsenborn, to the east, southeast and south, stood the 2nd Infantry Division which had suffered considerable losses during the fighting for Rocherath-Krinkelt, the 99th Infantry Division which had also suffered severe losses, and, initially, parts of the 1st Infantry Division with the 26th Infantry Regiment and parts of its artillery. The 2nd and 99th Divisions had only lost a few of their guns. The artillery group was in position around Lager Elsenborn. Of the 300 barrels, 150 each could be concentrated in a firing area, set up in clearings cut into the forest. The artillery had available large ammunition depots. It formed the backbone of the American defenses in the Elsenborn-Bütgenbach-Weismes sector, the so-called "Elsenborn Ridge". In addition to the anti-tank guns of the divisions, three tank destroyer units, Tank Destroyer Battalions 612, 613 and 614, were in action, or combat-ready, for anti-tank duties in the few pieces of terrain which were usable by armor.[1a]

On the German side, 277. Volksgrenadierdivision was deployed on the right wing. It was only conditionally fit for offensive action, as had already shown itself during the first day of the offensive. Parts of 3. Panzergrenadierdivision were still on the march forward. The 12. Volksgrenadierdivision had suffered significant losses during the first days of the offensive, but was combat-ready for the continuation of the attack. Of "HJ" Division, on 18 December, Panzergrenadierregiment 26 together with Schwere Panzerjägerabteilung 560 was approaching along partly clogged roads. Elements of the artillery and the Flakabteilung were changing positions, other ones were still in action. In addition, the Aufklärungsabteilung and the Pionierbataillon were available; however, the Pioniers were still a long way back. Panzergrenadierregiment 25, I. Panzerabteilung and Panzerjägerabteilung 12 were relieved in the area around Rocherath-Krinkelt in the course of 19 December, meaning that they were not quickly available. The 3. Fallschirmjägerdivision, which was on the advance to the west in the district south of

Büllingen, was needed to secure the southern flank and could not be taken into consideration for the attack on Bütgenbach. The divisions assigned to the attack were short of Panzers and assault guns, fire-ready artillery and, because of the poor road conditions, artillery ammunition.

The village of Elsenborn is located at an elevation of 630 meters. From there, the terrain drops toward Wirtzfeld to 570 meters, Büllingen is at about the same lower elevation. The Schwarzenbüchel hill, located immediately west of Büllingen, reaches an elevation of 603 meters. From the Schwarzenbach creek, at approximately 560 meters, the terrain climbs to 602 meters north of the Bütgenbach estate, drops initially again to 570 meters in the direction of Bütgenbach and then climbs to 597 meters at the town. The terrain north of the line Rocherath-Elsenborn is wet and crossed by numerous creeks which flow in a generally northerly direction. South of that line, which is a local watershed, a number of creeks run southwest toward the Bütgenbach reservoir. Apart from the creeks and a few areas bordering the reservoir, the rolling terrain there is dry and interspersed with small wooded areas. South of the reservoir, the open terrain narrows in an east-west direction on both sides of the Bütgenbach estate to an approximately one kilometer wide strip. To the north, behind the Schwarzbach creek, are wet meadows and, behind that to the west, a forest (Plättscheid or Platzheid). To the south is a deep strip of forest, called "Bütgenbacher Heck" or "Bütgenbacher Nock". The narrow spots on both sides of the estate, with a forward position on the Schwarzenbüchel hill, offered themselves to the defenders.

The Americans had clearly recognized that; in particular since the V Corps and the 99th Infantry Division which were fighting there, had known the terrain in detail for months. The 26th Infantry Regiment of the 1st Infantry Division was responsible for the Bütgenbach-Weismes sector. The regiment departed its refitting area around Aubel, south of Verviers, on 17 December at 02.30 hours. The lead battalion, the 3rd, was stopped by the jump of German paratroopers behind the American lines. The column then drove on without headlights and arrived at Lager Elsenborn on 18 December at 07.00 hours. At 14.00 hours, the battalion continued to drive to Bütgenbach and set itself up for defense northwest of Büllingen. The 2nd Battalion was sent into action to defend the narrow spot east of the Bütgenbach estate. Both battalions were in their sectors at 18.30 hours. The regiment was assigned to the 99th Division.[2]

The notes in the Report of the 26th Regiment regarding the course of the positions are of a very general nature and differ from those in Cole's war history. He wrote that the 2nd Battalion had set up defenses on a ridge near the Bütgenbach estate.[3] Based on the information from both sources, it can be concluded that the 3rd Battalion had occupied the Schwarzenbüchel hill, while the 2nd Battalion was in position on both sides of the Büllingen-Bütgenbach road at Bütgenbach estate, facing east and south.

The directive to II. SS-Panzerkorps, to open the road to Malmedy, demanded greatest possible acceleration of all measures. The success of the attack by the five divisions, so confidently expected, was, on the other hand, only achievable if they attacked together. Above all, the enemy artillery had to be forced into simultaneous action on a wide front. To reconcile both requirements was the overwhelming problem, considering the narrow width of the deployment area and the poor roads.

During the night of 18–19 December 1944, the troops assigned for the attack near Bütgenbach advanced in several marching columns from the assembly area into the operations area. The marching and timing sequences cannot be reliably stated because of the lack of documentation. In the war diary of II./26, which was drawn up by the adjutant, Obersturmführer Lübbe, and the operations recorder, Unterscharführer Fuhrmann, after the end of combat activities and based on the reports from the companies, the following route can be found: Harzheim (five kilometers west of Bad Münstereifel)-Zingsheim-Nettersheim-Marmagen-Schmidtheim-Dahlem-Hallschlag-Scheid-Losheim-Losheimergraben.[3a]

Driving as the first marching group were probably SPW-Bataillon III./26, the staff of Panzerregiment 12 and Schwere Panzerjägerabteilung 560, i.e. the second "Pursuit Group" without I. Panzerabteilung. They were presumably followed by the operations staff of the Divisional staff without the commander and his escort, who were at the forward Divisional command post at the Hollerath road bend, directing the units in action at Rocherath-Krinkelt from there. The second "Pursuit Group" was followed by the third, consisting of SS-Panzergrenadierregiment 26 (less III. Bataillon) and the Pionier-bataillon. The parts of the Artillerieregiment and of the Flakabteilung, attached for the march, had to be incorporated depending on when they were available and on how they were able to change positions.

Some information regarding action by the Aufklärungs-abteilung must be inserted here. Regrettably, information on it is quite sparse. The planned course of the breakthrough fighting envisaged that one scouting party would reconnoitre along each of the advance routes of the Division. That requirement was not there, thus the operation was eliminated. In addition, it would have been a mission of the Abteilung to scout in the open right flank and to take on, if required, securing and blocking tasks. That, too, had so far not happened. Information on the action of the Abteilung is available from both the war diary of Supreme Command West and the map "Lage Frankreich" of the OKW. On the map, which obviously shows the situation at different times on 18 December 1944, the attack by I. Panzerabteilung on Rocherath is indicated by an arrow. Above another arrow, pointing from Rocherath in the direction of Elsenborn, "A.A. 12.SS" is written. On the same day, the war diary of Supreme Command West notes: ". . . A.A. of 12. SS-Panzerdivision was turned toward Krinkelt . . ."[4] No confirmation or explanation for either

notation can be found. On 19 December, the scouting party of Oberscharführer August Zinßmeister was ordered to establish contact with the Panzerregiment from the Honsfeld area where he had arrived after ". . . a tough,
slow march along clogged and muddy lanes . . ." and to reconnoiter to the
north. He made his way via Mürringen where he ". . . established contact
with Fallschirmjägers in field positions . . ." to just outside of Krinkelt. The
report by the scouting party leader continued:

> . . . Driving through the valley after crossing a wooden bridge (prob-
> ably across the Holzwarche creek, Author) we caught an 'Ami' col-
> umn of eight trucks, four cars and one armored personnel carrier
> whose crews obviously bolted when they spotted us. We pulled past
> and up the gully, at the end of which our 2 cm barely beat an 'Ami'
> Pak in firing first. In view of Krinkelt, we drove under heavy mortar
> fire into the gully. A VW in the middle of the scouting party took a
> direct hit, caught on fire, the driver killed, another rifleman
> wounded. We turned back. Under more mortar fire we climbed up
> the slope, back to Mürringen. The armored cars and VWs all have
> several flat tires. I reported to the Abteilung, the Division, and com-
> mander Prieß . . .[5]

That report confirms the American information quoted in the previous
chapter.

In the course of the night from 18 to 19 December, III./26 arrived in
Büllingen which was occupied by parts of 12. Volksgrenadierdivision, assembling in the Hohe Berg area, immediately east of Büllingen, for the attack on
Wirtzfeld. The Bataillon took over securing the town to the west, southwest
and south. The Bataillon command post was located next to the post office.
The noon report of Supreme Command West reads: . . . 12. SS-Panzerdivision
has reached the district immediately southeast of Bütgenbach at 06.30 hours
. . ."[6] That notation surely refers to III./26. The Bataillon sent out reconnaissance toward the Schwarzenbüchel, Bütgenbach estate, to Morschheck and
Riechels-Busch. The scouting part sent to the west reported that the
Schwarzenbüchel hill was occupied by strong enemy forces. A scouting party
on armored personnel carriers sent in the direction of the estate came under
fire in the vicinity of the crossroads immediately east of the estate. Two
armored personnel carriers were knocked out to the right of the main road
from Büllingen to Bütgenbach. [7] The scouting parties sent to the southwest
and south encountered units of 3. Fallschirmjägerdivision which could not yet
provide any information on further intentions. American artillery was fero-
ciously shelling the village of Büllingen. The armored personnel carriers had
to be pulled out of their securing positions and driven into cover behind the
houses of the village. [8] Together with a report from III./26, the other halves
of the identification tags of four men killed on 19.12.1944, who could not be

recovered, were sent to the Wehrmacht information office: Oberscharführer Emil Löbert (born 1919), Sturmmann Hermann Geisler (1926), Panzergrenadier Heinz Zietlow (1927) and Panzergrenadier Herbert Seidl (1927). They had been killed at Büllingen, and south of it, respectively. That report confirms various other information on the action of the Bataillon on 19 December 1944.[9]

The other marching columns followed behind the III./26 as previously listed. The march was significantly slowed down by clogged roads. Under those circumstances, the assembly of the full Regiment 26 and the move into positions of all Abteilungen of the Artillerieregiment could not be awaited. All senior command authorities, with justification, pushed for an early attack in order to pre-empt the further reinforcement of the enemy. Under the command of the commander of the Panzerregiment, the Division formed the "Kampfgruppe Kuhlmann". It consisted of the staff of Panzerregiment 12, I. Bataillon of Panzergrenadierregiment 26 under the leadership of the holder of the Oak Leaves, Sturmbannführer Gerd Hein, Schwere Panzer-jägerabteilung 560, led by Major Streger, and II. -Abteilung of the Artillerieregiment under the command of Sturmbannführer Günter Neumann. While III./26 secured the assembly area and scouted, I./26 and Schwere Panzerjägerabteilung 560 prepared for attack along both sides of the Büllingen-Bütgenbach road. The II. Artillerieabteilung received orders to support the attack from positions near -Hünningen. The chief of 6. Batterie, Obersturmführer Dieter Kilchling, was to direct the fire from a Panzer IV which had been borrowed from the Panzerregiment.[10]

Scouting by the advance unit Holz of 12. V.G.D. and of III./26 had determined that strong enemy forces were ready for defense in the attack sector of "Kampfgruppe Kuhlmann". The forward terrain was under constant directed fire from the American artillery. Hence, the attack could be carried out only at night.

Concerning the planned attack on the right wing of 6. Panzerarmee, the situation briefing of Heeresgruppe B on 19.12.1944 contains the following information:

. . . 1) Krinkelt district: 272. V.G.D. [must read 277. V.G.D.] attacks from Rocherather Baracken, obviously still in enemy hands, toward the north.

3. Pz.Gren.-Div. is advancing along the road from Hollerath by way of Rocherath to Elsenborn. Present situation not known.

12. V.G.D attacks from the Hohe Berg area in the direction of Wirtzfeld, flanked by artillery fire coming from the southwestern section of Krinkelt.

12. SS-Pz.-Div. attacks from the Büllingen district in the direction of Weywertz-Bütgenbach. 3. Fallschirmjäger-division attacks from the line Morschheck-Moderscheid in the direction of Weywertz . . .[11]

The daily report of Supreme Command West states:

. . . The muddied lanes significantly slow down the movements of
12. SS-Pz.-Div. and of 3. Pz.Gren.-Div . . . Clearing the forest southeast of Rocherather Baracken resulted in 260 prisoners (among
them 22 officers) from 2nd American Infantry Division . . . II. SS-
Panzerkorps: 3. Pz.Gren.-Div. is on the attack on the southwest section of Krinkelt and Rocherath.
    12. V.G.D. at present stalled in front of enemy anti-tank gun line,
one kilometer southeast of Bütgenbach. Enemy reinforcements continually being brought in from the northwest.
    12. SS-Pz.-Div. on the attack since 19.00 hours via Büllingen on
Bütgenbach.
    3. Fallschirmjägerdivision with two regiment groups two kilome-
ters north of Schoppen. One regimental group seized the area
immediately south of Roymonville (must read Faymonville, Author).
    I. SS-Korps: Panzer-Gruppe 1. SS-Pz.-Div. seized the district twenty-
five kilometers west of Stavelot in the early afternoon.
    9. SS-Pz.-Div.'s spearhead reached the Recht area around 14.00
hours. Roads other than the paved roads muddied, motorized traffic
greatly impeded.
    10. SS-Pz.-Div. on the march in the Euskirchen-Schwerfen-Mün-
stereifel-Rheinbach area (towns exclusive) . . .[12]

Some details in that report probably do not quite accurately reflect the
situation in the evening of 19 December. At that time, Rocherath-Krinkelt
had already been captured. If anything, parts of 3. Pz.Gren.-Div. were still
clearing out the villages. It is quite certainly incorrect that 12. Volksgrenadierdivision was stalled in the face of an enemy anti-tank gun front one
kilometer southeast of Bütgenbach. The positions of the 2nd Battalion 26th
Infantry Regiment ran barely two kilometers southeast of Bütgenbach, in
front of them were still the positions of the 3rd Battalion on the Schwarzenbüchel hill. Parts of 12. Volksgrenadierdivision were located at the northern
fringe of Büllingen, the front of the Division faced north toward Wirtzfeld,
not toward Bütgenbach. The actual attack by "Kampfgruppe Kuhlmann" had
surely not yet started at 19.00 hours. On the other hand, the report indicates
that a simultaneous attack by 3. Pz.Gren.-Div. with 12. Volksgrenadierdivision
and "Kampfgruppe Kuhlmann can likely not be assumed. At the most, the
two '12's-divisions attacked at the same time, however into different directions.
    "Kampfgruppe Kuhlmann" presumably started its attack at approxi-
mately 22.00 hours. Before anything else, the threat to the right flank from
the 3rd/26th from the Schwarzenbüchel had to be eliminated. During that
action, at least the southern portion of the hill was captured. That alerted

the 2nd/26th, located in positions on both sides of Bütgenbach estate, and it expected an attack along the road from Büllingen. The commander of the point Jagdpanther advancing on the road was shot in the head when the American positions were approached. The driver pulled his vehicle back to escape the fire, but rammed the vehicle behind. Still, the attack gathered speed again quickly. Against the ferocious defensive fire from anti-tank guns, tank destroyers, artillery and light and heavy infantry weapons, a company of Jagdpanthers and parts of I./26, with the support of II. Artillerieabteilung, succeeded in breaking into the American positions and penetrating into the estate. Some anti-tank guns were destroyed, prisoners were brought back and identified as members of the 26th Regiment of the 1st US Infantry Division. The resistance inside the estate already seemed to slacken when the Jagdpanther company in action on the right made use of the early morning fog, disengaged from the enemy and pulled back. The company on the left, fighting inside the estate, was unable to hold on and also withdrew, with it the bulk of the Grenadiers. A part of 1. Kompanie, with its chief, was still holding out and was encircled. Those men fought their way back to their own lines after about two days. The II./26 had penetrated the deepest into the American positions, but it, too, had to withdraw. The Division ordered a suspension of the attack and a move to more favorable defensive positions, as far as possible to the west, in order to resume the attack later.

There are no reports available from the German side on the course of the battle which were prepared immediately after the fighting was over. Also, no survivors could be reached. Hence, the progress of the fighting cannot be dependably described from the German point of view. However, the battle report of the 26th Infantry Regiment is very illuminating and follows here unabridged:

> . . . On 20 December at approximately 01.30 hours, machine gun and tank fire in the sector of 'E'-Company alerted the 2nd. Battalion. The 33rd Field Artillery provided blocking fire in the front of the company's positions. At 01.45 hours, everything was quiet; it was the calm before the storm. At 03.30 hours, approximately 20 tanks and one infantry battalion attacked the positions of the 2nd Battalion. The focal point of their attack was located at the 'E'- and 'F'-Companies. Lt. Colonel Daniel requested fire support from all available artillery. The 33rd Field Artillery combined its fire with that of the 955th and 15th Field Artillery units. The fire from enemy artillery and rocket launchers on the positions of the 2nd Battalion increased tremendously, as the enemy tanks and infantry broke into the positions of the 2nd Battalion. They overran the forward lines of 'E'- and 'F'-Companies but the men remained in their positions. They trusted that their own tanks, tank destroyers and anti-tank guns would eliminate the threat to their rear. The enemy infantry,

trying to follow behind the tanks, was unable to break through our positions. The companies withstood the heaviest pressure they had ever experienced. In the haze and smoke of the early morning, a fire fight at short distance broke out. The anti-tank guns waited until the tanks had come very close before they fired. The German tank hunting teams following behind the tanks fired their bazookas at the anti-tank guns.

The reserve of the 2nd Battalion, a platoon of 'G'-Company, was thrown into action as quickly as possible, and a company of the 1st Battalion was called for. 'C'-Company was removed from its position and thrown into the sector of the 2nd Battalion. Two of its platoons were sent to reinforce 'F'-Company, two others kept at the Battalion as reserve.

Five German tanks approached to within ninety meters of the command post of the 2nd Battalion and opened heavy fire on it. Lt. Colonel Daniel repeated his order: 'Hold on!' Anti-tank guns were moved forward and fired at the tanks. Two of them were knocked out, the other three pulled back a short distance.

At approximately 05.30 hours, there was a lull. The battalion established radio contact with the regiment. The commander of the 2nd Battalion requested mines and tank destroyers. At 10.00 hours, three anti-tank guns were sent forward. An engineer platoon was also requested to help place 1,000 anti-tank mines in front of the positions of the battalion. The mines only arrived in the late afternoon.

After the tanks and infantry had withdrawn, German artillery concentrated heavy fire on the sector of the battalion. The Germans had pulled back only temporarily. From the morning until night, the enemy mounted three separate attacks in order to break the contact between 'E'- and 'F'-Companies. They were primarily repelled thanks to the immensely effective fire from our artillery.

A new, massive, attack by six tanks and two infantry companies advanced close to the Battalion command post, but was then fought off. Thereafter, the enemy ceased his attacks . . .[13]

Various reports provide an overall insight on the attack by "Kampfgruppe Kuhlmann" and its neighboring units on 19 and 20 December 1944.

Supreme Command West, morning report of 20.12.1944: ". . . LXVII. A.K. . . . 277. Div. in the process of clearing out the woods northeast of Krinkelt.

II. SS-Pz.-Korps: 3. Pz.Gren.-Div. attacking Elsenborn. Artillery and rocket launcher fire from 12. V.G.D. on Höngen (probably meant Hünningen, Author), Mürringen and Büllingen. Our own attack has not advanced farther. 3. Fallschirmjägerdivision, at 22.30 hours, reached Bütgenbacher

Haus (house)—1.5 kilometers southwest of Bütgenbach (presumably Büt-genbacher Hock, Author) and Faymonville. Enemy tanks of unknown strength in Weismes and to the west. 01.10 hours, Oberweywertz railroad station and Ruthier (one kilometer north of Faymonville) captured.

I. SS-Pz.-Korps: 22.30 hours, Stavelot recaptured by enemy from the north. Counterattack started.

9. SS-Pz.-Div. advancing on Vielsam . . ."

Noon report of 20.12.1944: ". . . 3. Pz.Gren.-Div. has taken Krinkelt and has encountered strong enemy resistance during the attack on Bütgenbach . . ."

Daily report of 20.12.1944: ". . . LXVII. A.K.: 277. V.G.D. has captured, with the Kampfgruppe on the right, in rapid advance the area one kilometer southeast of Hohe Mark (southeast of Kalterherberg) at 19.00 hours.

II. SS-Pz.-Korps: 3. Pz.Gren.-Div., approximately 23.00 hours, again swinging north of Elsenborn, started an attack on Lager Elsenborn.

12. V.G.D., after capture of Wirtzfeld (high enemy losses), at present advancing along the Wirtzfeld-Borg (must red Berg, Author); 3. Fallschirm-mjägerdivision is covering the flank of II. SS-Pz.-Korps along the existing line.

I. SS-Pz.-Korps: 12.SS-Pz.-Div. ready to renew the attack on Bütgenbach.

1. SS-Pz.-Div. is involved in defensive fighting at Stavelot railroad station against attacking enemy tank forces from the north and west, supported by artillery. Wanne is clear of the enemy.

9. SS-Pz.-Div. at 13.00 hours near Poteau advancing on Vielsam. Successes from 16 to 20 December (at 6. Panzerarmee, Author): prisoners: 94 officers and about 5,000 men. Captured and destroyed, respectively: 40 tanks, 17 anti-tank guns, 30 guns 100 motor vehicles, 1 tractor, 16 aircraft . . ."[14]

The first attack to open up the road to Malmedy, with the simultaneous elimination of the threat to the flank from Lager Elsenborn, had not succeeded. The 12. Volksgrenadierdivision merely captured Wirtzfeld which the enemy held only until his troops withdrawing from Rocherath-Krinkelt had passed through the village. At the time, it was no more than a forward position. "Kampfgruppe Kuhlmann" captured most of Schwarzenbüchel hill, but the breakthrough through the narrow passage at Bütgenbach estate failed. After the attack had been broken off, the chief of the Jagdpanzer company, which had pushed its way into the estate, reported that, in his judgment, the withdrawal of the Jagdpanzer company in action on the right, had not been necessary and that, otherwise, the attack could have been continued successfully. It must be appreciated, however, that the offensive mission was particularly difficult to achieve by Jagdpanzers. Without rotating turrets, they were less flexible during fire fights, especially at close distance, than Panzers. The Abteilung had not been trained for action as assault guns. Their accomplishments must be valued all the higher! From that Abteilung, as the only element of the Division, a report on losses exists. During that battle it lost:

killed, two men; wounded three officers, thirteen NCOs and six men; missing, two men.[14a] Success had been on the razor's edge. In the final analysis, with a numerical infantry ratio of better than 1:1 in favor of the Americans, their artillery superiority of 10:1 was the decisive factor.

As before, it was imperative to open up the road to Malmedy. A new attack had to be started from another direction and with stronger forces. It was necessary to carry it out simultaneously with the attack by other forces on Lager Elsenborn in order, above all else, to break up the artillery defense. The enemy had a strong anti-tank defense available which made it necessary to concentrate all German Panzer forces at "HJ" Division for its attack. The attack would, again, take place at night.

For several reasons, an attack on Bütgenbach from the south was out of the question. Numerous marshy sections and extensive forests prevented Panzers from being put into action there. In addition, "HJ" Division would have had to assemble in the attack sector of the 3. Fallschirmjägerdivision. Hence, it decided on a concentrated breakthrough from the district south of the estate, by-passing it, on Bütgenbach. The estate itself would then be captured by elements attacking from the east and west. The attack was planned as follows:

> Panzergrenadierregiment 26, with attached III./25 and without III./26, will assemble one battalion each for the attack in Richelsbusch and in Morschheck, two forested areas 1.5 kilometers south of the Bütgenbach estate. It will attack on both sides of the line crossroads Morschheck-path to Hill 575 (one kilometer west of "Zum Grünen Jäger" = The Green Huntsman)-path from Hill 575 to Bütgenbach-western edge of Bütgenbach. It will take Bütgenbach and block the road coming from the north. Blocking forces will advance to the rail line north of Bütgenbach. The attack of the battalion on the right will be supported by Panzerjägerabteilung 12, that of the battalion on the left by Panzerregiment 12 without a company of Schwere Panzerjägerabteilung 560. The III./26 will assemble in Bütgenbacher Hock in such a manner that it can quickly follow the breakthrough by the Panzergrenadier battalion, in action in the forward lines, and push through to Bütgenbach with the Panzerregiment. The I./26, with the attached company of Schwere Panzerjägerabteilung 560, will join the attack on the express order of the Regiment.
>
> The Artillerieregiment and Werferabteilung 12 will support the attack from positions near Hünningen, Büllingen and Honsfeld. At the start, they will concentrate a barrage on the enemy positions located near the Bütgenbach estate. Start of the attack is 21 December 1944 at 03.40 hours.[14b]

The march into the assembly areas was delayed by blocked roads and fighter-bomber attacks. Flakabteilung 12 shot down four enemy aircraft from positions in the Losheimergraben district within a period of ten minutes.[14c] The war diary of II./26 notes that, at times, three vehicles were sitting abreast in Honsfeld. Harassing enemy artillery fire lay on Hünningen, Büllingen and the area in-between. The Bataillon departed on foot from the Hünningen area at approximately 23.00 hours via Point 596 (two kilometers west of Hünningen on the road Honsfeld-Büllingen)-Point 628 (one kilometer southwest of Büllingen) toward the Richelsbusch forest.[15]

Since the attack by "Kampfgruppe Kuhlmann" on 19-20 December, the enemy had boosted his forces in the area around Bütgenbach. The 18th Infantry Regiment of the 1st Infantry Division was alerted in the morning of 20 December and moved forward into the district around Sourbrodt (7.5 kilometers northwest of Bütgenbach). It was assembled there at 16.55 hours. Its 2nd Battalion was sent to support the 1st and 2nd Battalions of the 26th Regiment ". . . along a wide front . . .", apparently in a prepared rear position behind their sectors.[16] On 18 December, the 16th Regiment of the 1st Division had been moved forward to Robertville (six kilometers northwest of Bütgenbach) in order to defend that sector to the southwest. There is no information on the course of the positions. On 20 December, it fought off attacks by the 3. Fallschirmjägerdivision and moved its own front line ahead in a counterattack.[17]

The III./25, the Panzerregiment, the Panzerjägerabteilung 12 and the III./26 reached their assembly areas in time. The Artillerieregiment was in position and ready to fire with the I. Abteilung near Büllingen, II. Abteilung and Werferabteilung near Hünningen, and III. Abteilung at the southern edge of Honsfeld.[18] Punctually, on 21 December at 03.30 hours, the Artillerieregiment opened the preparatory fire. The start of the attack had to be postponed since the II./26 had not yet reported its assembly. Radio contact with the companies had not been achieved. The adjutant and the orderly officer were looking for the companies but could not find them. The Divisional commander, Standartenführer Hugo Kraas, located at the Morschheck crossroads, postponed the start of the attack to 04.30 hours. Even at that time, the companies had not been found. It was expected that the attack could start, at the best, just before dawn. The danger existed that the Regiment, during daylight, would have to pass by the American positions at the Bütgenbach estate and would be decimated by fire from the flank. Hence, Standartenführer Kraas changed the plan of attack. He ordered, after the assembly was complete, an attack on the estate from the south and east as the first attack objective, and only to advance on Bütgenbach after the estate had been neutralized.

At 05.30 hours, the Bataillon adjutant of II./26 established contact with the 6. Kompanie. It turned out that the Kompanie had assembled approximately one kilometer west of the designated area. It was immediately moved into its assembly area and briefed on the changed situation.

At 06.00 hours, the companies were assembled in the designated area. At 06.45 hours, the artillery and rocket launchers again laid a fire attack on the American positions. Cole reported on the effects:

> . . . The shelling of the village lasted until the first light of dawn. It caused many losses, destroyed weapons by direct hits and ripped wide gaps in the main line of defense. There was intensive fire from the American artillery on the German fire positions, but it did not diminish the enemy shelling . . .[19]

With the start of the effective artillery shelling, the Panzers, Panzerjägers and Panzergrenadiers mounted their attack. They were only able to deploy after passing the northeastern corner of the Bütgenbacher Heck. Hence, they were forced to drive, for a while, parallel to the front line in a westerly direction. A member of 3. Panzerkompanie reported on the progress of the attack:

> . . . To the right of us, approximately 100 to 150 meters away, stood a line of tall spruce trees. They were located at the apex of the pasture which rose slowly to that point but was out of sight beyond it. The estate, our attack objective, had to be located in that dead ground. Some veils of fog were still spreading across the pasture, but they were dissolving quickly. Instinctively, as if by order, all turrets swung toward the row of trees on our right flank. No shot had yet been fired, but we felt that conspicuous silence to be depressing and threatening. On the drive, we fired a few salvos from our turret MGs between those trees, opening the battle against an imagined enemy, in the knowledge that he was hiding somewhere, well camouflaged, his eye pressed to the sight of his anti-tank gun. The marching sequence had not yet been changed. The spearhead Panzer was commanded by Untersturmführer Schittenhelm, followed by Hauptmann Hils, Untersturmführer Engel, an Unterscharführer of the staff company, behind him the Panzer IVs of the 5. and 6. Kompanies, then Jagdpanzers and self-propelled infantry guns. Untersturmführer Schittenhelm had just reached a protrusion of the forest, when a flash of flame, as if ignited by the hand of a ghost, shot up from the rear of his Panzer. A thick, heavy mushroom cloud of smoke covered the vehicle, two men bailed out. Hauptmann Hils issued orders to take up position toward three o'clock. He stood in the turret of his Panzer, studying the map once again, to make sure of his exact location. Then he fired a signal flare to mark the final

direction of the march. It died away on the terrain sloping downward to the estate. We awaited the 'March, march!' for the attack. Since nothing happened, I looked again toward his Panzer. The turret was burning! Hauptmann Hils could no longer be seen. The hull crew was leaving the Panzer. I recognized the driver, Unterscharführer Bunke, as well as the radio operator whose name I did not know. It had to be assumed that the turret crew, made up, in addition to Hauptmann Hils, by the gunner, Lorentzen, and the loader, Krieg, had been killed.

Abruptly, an almost indescribably devastating fire from the American artillery set in. The pasture turned into a plowed field, a number of Panzers took direct hits. Renewed and well-aimed anti-tank fire was directed at Untersturmführer Engel's Panzer. He pulled back about twenty meters so that the rear of the Panzer stood in the woods. From there, he was hoping to have a better field of observation. At the same time, he reported on the situation by radio. In the line of trees, suspect from the start of the attack, he assumed at least two American anti-tank guns. Since he could not land any effective hits by direct fire, he fired explosive shells in rapid sequence into the tree tops in order to neutralize the American gun crews by shrapnel. He was successful, several Americans fled into the close-by forest. Immediately, he rolled his Panzer forward to the row of trees. For the first time, the view to the estate was clear and he opened fire on it immediately. The artillery fire had continued at unabated strength. Finally, Untersturmführer Engel was also knocked out. The crew was able to bail out. Only the radio operator, Sturmmann Fitz, lost a finger. Chased by the artillery fire, the crew still managed to carry a seriously wounded infantryman out of the zone of fire. After reaching the road, they handed him over to an ambulance . . .[20]

The other Panzers and Panzerjägers continued their attack on the estate. Sturmmann Heinz Müller of 5. Panzerkompanie (Panzer IVs) remembered:

. . . We mounted the attack to the left of the road [Heppenbach-Bütgenbach estate] and closed in on the first houses of the estate. The Grenadiers, however, were stalled and unable to keep pace with us because of the heavy artillery fire. During that attack, one of Oberscharführer Kretzschmar's tracks was blown off. We took one of his crew into our vehicle, and continued the attack with six men in the Panzer. We were knocked out close to the first houses of the estate. Then, we tried to reach our own lines along the road, without success. After moving back toward the spot at the estate where we had been knocked out, we managed to be spotted by our Kompanie, and split up into the remaining vehicles. Since we were in front of the estate without Grenadiers, the order came to pull back . . .[21]

Oberscharführer Willy Kretzschmar supplemented that report:

. . . Half of the right driving sprocket of our Panzer was blown away and we rolled off the track. We were immobile. A row of trees and hedges located approximately 150 meters away was still occupied by American infantry. Using our turret and hull MGs, as well as explosive shells, we were able to keep them at bay for the time being. For two hours, we played 'dead' because of the intense artillery fire. The previously white, snow-covered pasture had turned black. When there was a break in the fire, I ran over to the closest Panzer IV, to ask that it pull mine back on the track. Regrettably, it had been knocked out. The other Panzer IVs and the self-propelled gun had suffered the same fate, most were knocked out by artillery and heavy mortar hits. At about 14.00 hours, a Panzer from the neighbor company came back. I waved, it came over, and pulled us back onto the track. We then fixed it in a makeshift manner and mounted it, under constant American artillery attacks. Thereafter, we drove at walking speed, using half of the driving sprocket left, in the direction of the main road. On the way, I picked up the crew of Otto Knoof's knocked-out vehicle. His driver was Heinz Müller. I dropped Otto Knoof at the main dressing station, he had shrapnel in the left leg and ankle . . .[22]

Oberscharführer Karl Leitner, Zugführer in the 6. Kompanie of Panzergrenadierregiment 26, experienced the attack in this manner:

. . . It was our first day of action after refitting. Only the NCOs had any front experience. On the advance, we crossed through a very sparsely wooded area, in slowly rising terrain. Suddenly, a barrage set in. We heard the incessant discharges and sought cover immediately. My Unterscharführer and I jumped into a ditch, ahead and to our right, running in the direction of the enemy, and a good meter deep. We were lying next to each other. Shells exploded on the forest ground and in the trees. Just the spearhead of our Zug had been caught by the barrage which was very concentrated and lasted for about one hour. After approximately ten minutes, a shell hit to the right of us, probably the trunk of a tree. We were hit by shrapnel in our ditch. My Unterscharführer must have been badly wounded in the lung, he only gasped and died after a short time. I had taken a piece of shrapnel in my right hip. Then, a shell exploded in a tree behind me. A piece of shrapnel hit me in the left ankle and pierced it. Other fragments slashed my right foot and ankle. I pushed myself half under my dead comrade. Soon after, fragments from another shell hit me in the left upper arm. That was at about 9 o'clock in the morning. In the afternoon, an armored ambulance vehicle (armored personnel carrier, Author) arrived and collected us, while the barrage was still going on. All three Unterscharführers and I had been taken out of battle . . .[23]

Despite the terrific defensive fire, especially from the artillery, several Panzers managed to penetrate into the estate. The following American reports describe the combat there. First, the 26th Infantry Regiment:

. . . Six German tanks had been destroyed by the artillery fire which fell just ahead of our front line positions. Their flames lit the battle-ground. Then, enemy tanks succeeded in breaking through the lines of 'G'-Company. When anti-tank fire was aimed at them, the German tanks sought cover behind some buildings in the vicinity of the Battalion command post. They fired on the crews of the Battalion's rocket launchers who were trying to move within firing range. In order to drive off the enemy tanks, mortar fire on the positions of the Battalion was requested. As soon as the tanks left the cover of the buildings, the anti-tank gun crews opened fire on them. It was a lengthy job since the tanks were moving from building to building and had to be overcome systematically by mortar fire. By 16.00 hours, all enemy tanks—later determined to be five—had been knocked out. In the meantime, the infantry held its positions, withstanding one enemy infantry attack wave after the other, advancing steadily through our terrible barrages and engaging our infantry in close combat. Our infantry fought the enemy tanks with hand grenades, rocket launchers, automatic rifles and rifle-grenades. Machine guns were in constant action, the crews of the tanks, tank destroyers and anti-tank guns remained in their positions until they had either destroyed the enemy or had been wiped out themselves . . .[25]

Cole writes:

. . . When the Germans crossed the fields in attack formation, the forward American observers requested barrages on their own forward lines. At least ten light artillery units were finally involved (in addition, the batteries of the 2nd and 99th Divisions were incorpo-rated in the fire control system of the 1st Division); they succeeded in discouraging the German infantry.

Several tanks and tank destroyers rolled through the hail of exploding shells against the right wing of the 2nd Battalion. During the previous night, two platoons of the tank destroyer company of the Regiment had moved into positions in line with the anti-tank foxholes. They surprised the tanks with fire from a distance of no more than ninety meters. The 1st Platoon counted two or three vic-tories, but the other tanks very quickly annihilated the crews of the 57 mm guns and overran the guns of the 2nd Platoon. In that sector the main line of resistance, the positions ran along an extensive hedgerow. After they had broken through and destroyed our anti-tank guns, the German tanks rolled down that hedge, searching for the automatic weapons which had previously helped to stall the infantry attack. Unprotected against the rolling steel, the automatic weapons and machine gun crews were wiped out.

More tanks moved through that gap in the right sector of the 2nd Battalion during the course of the morning and rolled down the slope toward the Bütgenbach estate. A tank destroyer of the 634th Tank Destroyer Battalion reported seven victories when the tanks came into view, one after the other, after crossing a depression in the ground. Two Shermans sitting close to a barn hit two German tanks before they were knocked out themselves. Three German tanks reached the buildings and fired right into the houses and barns which were defended by Lt. Colonel Daniel and his blocking forces. Every opportunity was used to get the tanks, but that remained without success except for two which obviously felt it was getting too hot. They rolled into the open terrain and were stopped by a group of 90 mm tank destroyers which had just arrived. The last German tank was chased out from behind a barn by a 81 mm mor-tar, but was able to escape . . .

Cole's report continues, stating that the concentrated artillery had fired approximately 10,000 shells within eight hours to defend the Bütgenbach estate sector.[26]

The Divisional commander had remained near Morschheck, to 'keep his finger on the pulse'. His greatest concern was caused by the effects of the immense enemy artillery fire. When the high losses of Panzergrenadiers, Panzers, and their crews became known, and when it became obvious that the Grenadiers were unable to support the penetration by a few tanks into the estate, and to take advantage of it, and that there was also no progress of I./26 along the Büllingen-Bütgenbach road, he ordered the attack broken off, and a return to the starting positions. In January 1990—only a few weeks before his sudden death—when he inspected the old battlegrounds together with several participants in the fighting, he said that it had been the darkest day of his military life.

Only one report on losses is available for that day. It cannot give an indication of the total losses. The Schwere Panzerjägerabteilung 560 lost one officer, wounded, Oberleutnant Gerhard, one NCO and one man killed. The I. Panzerabteilung, as indicated in the participants' reports reproduced here, suffered considerable casualties and losses of Panzers. The figure of thirty destroyed Panzers (report of 23 December), given in the After Action Report of the 26th Infantry Regiment, is, without doubt, significantly too high. The II./26 suffered the heaviest losses, but, here, too, numbers are missing.

The evening report of Supreme Command West was noted for 21 December:

. . . Enemy counterattack with massive artillery support caused the loss of Hohe Mark (4.5 kilometers north-northeast of Elsenborn, Author), Langert (1.5 kilometers northeast of Elsenborn, Author) and Roderhügel (also, Roderhöhe, 1.5 kilometers southeast of Elsenborn, Author). An attack by the 3. Pz.Gren.-Div. on Schörren (Point 580, north of Elsenborn, Author) did not break through.

12. SS-Pz.Div. captured Bütgenbach estate and is on the attack on Bütgenbach, together with 12. V.G.D.

The 3. Fallschirmjägerdivision is securing the flank along the existing line . . . The 1. SS-Pz.Div. is, at present, involved in heavy defensive fighting along the line La Gleize-Stoumont-Cheneux against enemy armor attacking from the north and west. The enemy has broken into Cheneux and Stoumont. Counterattack is under way. One Kampfgruppe of 9. SS-Pz.Div. is on the attack via Wanne on Trois-Ponts, another Kampfgruppe, on the attack toward Vielsam, embroiled in heavy fighting south of Poteau . . .[27]

The daily report negated the hope which had grown. It stated:

. . . The planned attack by all Volksgrenadierdivisions against the strong block of enemy forces around and south of Elsenborn will be continued. The 12. SS-Pz.Div. will disengage from the attack in order to establish the basis for the northern flank and the breakthrough to Malmedy. The further attack by I. SS-Pz.Korps will be pushed forward again by the combined thrust of 9. SS-Pz.Div. and 2. SS-Pz.Div. across the Salm creek on Durbuy (on the Ourthe, Author).

Elements of 9. SS-Pz.Div. will attack toward Vielsam by way of St. Vith which was captured at 21.30 hours. Parts of 2. SS-Pz.Div. will attack toward Salmchateau in order to seize the Salm sector and the crossings. According to dependable documents, the enemy is attempting to set up a prepared rear position at the Ourthe . . .

Among the details reported:

> . . . The attack by 12. SS-Pz.Div. and 12. V.G.D. on Bütgenbach did not break through . . .[28]

The reason for the failure of the attack by "HJ" Division was thought to be that the attack could not be started until daybreak because of the delay in the assembly of one battalion. The terrain did not allow to swing wide to the west in order to avoid being outflanked from the estate. Hence, the general command of II. SS-Panzerkorps, or its superior command authority, ordered, for the next day, a renewed, last effort to capture Bütgenbach. Some element of surprise was to be achieved by starting the attack during darkness and by-passing the focal point of the American defense, the estate. Of the "HJ" Division, only the armored group was to attack. It consisted of the Panzerregiment of I. Abteilung and Schwere Panzerjägerabteilung 12, both of which, however, had only a small number of Panzers and Panzerjägers left; probably also Panzerjägerabteilung 12, Schützenpanzerbataillon III./26 (armored personnel carriers), and 1. (armored) Kompanie of Pionierbataillon 12. The 12. Volksgrenadierdivision was to attack simultaneously with the armored group.

On the American side, while the 2nd/26 continued to defend the Büt-genbach estate, the 1st and 3rd Battalions were in action to the west of it. The 2nd Battalion of the 18th Infantry Regiment was located in a widely curved prepared rear position. It was attached to the 26th Regiment. As on the previous day, large numbers of tanks and tank destroyers were available. The losses of the previous day had been partly replaced.

The attack by the armored group started on 22 December 1944 at 06.30 hours. From six o'clock on, the 2nd Battalion noted and reported tank noises ahead of its front. "A"-Company of the 1st Battalion heard the approach of tanks and infantry at 06.40 hours. The battalion raked the field ahead of its position with machine gun fire. ". . . It sounds as if there are more behind . . .", reads the Journal of the 26th Regiment. At 07.50 hours, it was reported that German infantry and Panzers had broken through at "A"-Company. One of the Panzers was one fire. An American tank destroyer was also knocked out. At approximately the same time, Panzers and infantry broke through at the position of "K"-Company of the 3rd/26. The German infantry was part of III./26. At 08.35 hours, the positions of the American mortars under Colonel Williamson were encircled. The regiment sent several tanks to block the road to Bütgenbach and to free the mortars. At approximately nine o'clock, Panzers and infantry broke through the position of "G"-Company of the 2nd/18 south of Bütgenbach and pushed into the town. "B"- and "K"-Companies retreated, inside the town there was fighting close to the command post of the 2nd/18. At 09.20 hours, General Taylor requested a report on the situation from the 26th Regiment. It was difficult to provide exact information. Four Panzers had overrun "A"-Company and broken through at "G"-Company of the 18th Regiment. Three Panzers were stuck in the mud and being fired at. The General asked how further developments were being judged. The answer was: ". . . It could get serious, but that is not yet certain . . ." In view of the uncertain situation, the 1st Battalion of the 18th Regiment was alerted to, if required, clear up the situation in and around Bütgenbach by a counterattack. The Battalion arrived in the sector of the 3rd Battalion at 12.48 hours and attacked in order to re-establish the positions. The 2nd/26 was concerned that its supply route had been cut. The Regiment had been ordered to shorten its front although it was not in favor of that. It appeared easier to the 2nd Battalion to hold its position rather than to pull back and move into a new position. The Americans made an effort to push the German troops who had broken through, farther and farther back. At 17.42 hours they had the impression that the bulk of the Germans had withdrawn. One German company with approximately 150 men was still holding a key position. By 19.00 hours, the 1st/18th Regiment had taken over the positions of the 1st/26, and "A"- and "B"-Companies were attached to it. It was scheduled to attack the next morning in order to regain the old line. Four-hundred men had arrived at the 26th Regiment as replacements. On 21 December, twenty-nine German Panzers were reported knocked out, five more on 22 December.[29]

Only limited information on that attack is available from the German side, and they are somewhat contradictory. For that reason, the reports from the Journal of the 26th Regiment and the After Action Report of the 18th Regiment were provided above. During the attack, the Panther of Sturmbannführer Arnold Jürgensen, the commander of I. Panzerabteilung, was hit and burned. Together with the commander of the Panzerabteilung, the commander of the III./26, Hauptsturmführer Georg Urabl, who sat in the same Panzer, was seriously wounded. Both wounded men were taken to the rear and arrived at a field hospital by way of the main dressing station. Sturmbannführer Arnold Jürgensen, a brave and esteemed soldier, died in hospital the following day. He was given a resting place in the German war cemetery at Recogne near Bastogne where many members of his Abteilung and "HJ" Division are also buried.[30]

Unterscharführer Günther Burdack of the 9. Kompanie of the Schützenpanzerbataillon remembers as follows:

> . . . Taking advantage of the heavy snowfall, the attack moved ahead at a good pace, but it stalled just outside of Bütgenbach. Several armored personnel carriers penetrated into the village but had to retreat again since the Volksgrenadiers were unable to advance. The

Bataillon was pulled back to the starting position and given a blocking function . . .[30a]

In his study, the commander of the 12. Volksgrenadier-division, Generalleutnant Engel, wrote about the attack on Bütgenbach:

> . . . Joint attack on Bütgenbach estate and Bütgenbach. Both attacks initially advanced well. The Panzers of 'HJ' again pushed into Bütgenbach and took the village, but it was impossible to clear the village of the enemy . . . In the evening hours, the remaining Panzers broke through to the south into their starting positions. The attack on Bütgenbach estate also stalled right before reaching the objective. The Korps ordered that the line, which was reached, be held . . .[30b]

In error, Generalleutnant Engel mentions 20 December as the date of that attack. Without doubt, his description refers to 22 December 1944. However, the Journal of the 26th Regiment does not provide any reference to an attack on the positions of the 2nd/26 near the Bütgenbach estate on 22 December. It is probable that the armored group of "HJ" Division was attached to the 12. Volksgrenadierdivision for the attack on 22 December, since the "HJ" Division's command had already been ordered to pull out all elements not engaged and hold them ready for a move to a different front sector. That assumption is supported by the Generalleutnant Engel's remark regarding a "joint attack'.

The result of that attack was disappointing. Although the armored group broke through two positions, one behind the other, and entered Bütgenbach, its strength had been weakened by the heavy artillery fire, by tanks and tank destroyers, to the point where it could not clear the enemy from the village. By evening, since no reinforcements had come forward, it was forced to withdraw under the pressure from the counterattacks. The enemy, who had been hard pressed, was able to retake his previous positions with reserves brought up. The 1st Infantry Division had to use all its reserves, except one battalion, for that. The attack by the armored group could have had a lasting success if further forces had been brought into action. The order by Supreme Command West, to pull out "HJ" Division and hold it ready for action in another location, made that impossible. It would have been better not to attack with insufficient forces.

Known losses:

Schwere Panzerjägerabteilung 560: one officer killed (Hauptmann Heinz Wewers, who had penetrated into the Bütgenbach estate on 19/20 December), three NCOs wounded, one man killed and five wounded. Of the III./26, killed were 1 officer (Untersturmführer Helmut Richter), three NCOs (Oberscharführer Gerhard Gellert and Unterscharführers Hans Dörr and Horst Ibihs) and six men (Sturmmann Adolf Nörenberg and Panzer-grenadiers Franz Glasel, Ewald Knappheide, Horst Mertins, Max Summer, Herbert Tenner—all Panzergrenadiers born in 1927). It is questionable that this reflects the losses of the whole Bataillon.[31]

The daily report of the Supreme Command West of 22 December 1944 states, concerning the situation at the 6. Panzerarmee:

> . . . A heavy battle rages along the whole front of the 6. Panzer-armee. While the 3. Pz.Gren.-Div., on the right wing, succeeded in slowly gaining ground through a persistent attack and to capture the Langertberg (hill) and the Schnörresberg [three kilometers north of Elsenborn], the attack to open up the Bütgenbach-Weismes road had to be discontinued because of our own high losses. Disengage-ment of the first elements of 12. SS-Pz.Div. to the east and south is now under way. The Aufklärungsabteilung of the Division has reached the district south of Faymonville. The bravely fighting 1. SS-Pz.Div. 'LAH' successfully repelled 14 strong enemy attacks, sup-ported by tanks, near Stavelot and La Gleize on 22 December. The fighting for the Salm crossings and to establish contact with the parts of 1. SS-Pz.Div. encircled near La Gleize are still ongoing, as further forces are being brought in. The Aufklärungsabteilung of 2. SS-Pz.Div. has captured the Salm sector south of Vielsam, by way of Joubieval, and is on the attack from the southwest toward Vielsam. The LXVI A.K. is on the attack with all its elements from the St. Vith area to the west, up to the Salm sector. The march of the 2. SS-Pz.Div. was delayed by problems in the fuel delivery . . .[32]

The noon report of Supreme Command West of 23.12.1944 indicates as having been pulled out until then: the bulk of the Aufklärungsabteilung, Panzergrenadierregiment 25, Panzerregiment, Panzerjägerabteilung 12. The evening report mentions that movements would only be possible at dusk. The daily report states that all elements had been disengaged and were on the march into the assembly area. On the other hand, the noon report of 24 December states that the bulk—not all parts—had been pulled out and would be moved after the 9. SS-Pz.Div. had overcome the Salm sector.[33]

For the elements approaching from the east, that was a torturous drudg-ery along clogged roads and snowed-in lanes. Regiment 26 secured the posi-tions reached until it was relieved by the Volksgrenadiers, collected its wounded, transported them to the rear, searched for, and buried, its killed men. The Panzerregiment and the Panzerjägerabteilung towed knocked-out Panzers which could be reached and had not burned out. The repair shops worked feverishly to bring them back into combat-ready state. The road con-ditions greatly inhibited those activities.

The Division was catching its breath for the forthcoming new action.

CHAPTER 8.6
Attacks Against the Ourthe Sector—Battles near Sadzot from 27 to 29 December 1944

While the "HJ" Division, in cooperation with the 12. Volksgrenadierdivision, attempted to open up the road to Malmedy near Bütgenbach, the situation on other sectors of the front developed in different ways. The right wing of the 6. Panzerarmee was stalled and the Armee tried to establish contact to the far-advanced Kampfgruppe Peiper in order to re-start Peiper's attack. The 5. Panzerarmee, its flanks covered by 6. Panzerarmee and 7. Armee, achieved major successes. It was able to take advantage of a dense network of roads with several good routes for advance which ran in a northwesterly direction toward the Maas river. On the right wing of the 5. Panzerarmee, the Führer-Begleit-Brigade (Führer escort brigade) and the 18. Volks-grenadierdivision captured the important road traffic center of St. Vith on 21 December 1944 at 21.30 hours, after bitter combat against the 7th US Armored Division.

In the meantime, the 560. Volksgrenadierdivision, the 116. and the 2. Panzerdivisions pushed past Bastogne to the north and drove forward a wedge to the west. A spearhead Abteilung of the 560. V.G.D. reached Dochamps (6.5 kilometers northeast of Laroche) on 20 December. To its left, simultaneously, the 116. Panzerdivision attacked from Samrée (five kilo-meters north-northeast of Laroche) toward Marcourt on the Ourthe. The 2. Panzerdivision crossed the Ourthe near Ortheuville (twelve kilometers south of Laroche).

The stalling of 6. Panzerarmee and the progress of the 5. Panzerarmee in the center caused the Supreme Commander West, on 20 December 1944, to modify the existing plan and move its focal point to the 5. Panzerarmee. He ordered, as a first priority, the seizure of the Maas crossings near Huy or Dinant, or, if required, even farther south, near Givet. By 23 December, the Aufklärungsabteilung of the2. Panzerdivision had succeeded in by-passing Marche to the south and in advancing to Achne (9.5 kilometers east of Dinant), thus reaching an area immediately before the Maas. Adjacent on the right, elements of the 116. Panzerdivision fought their way forward, by noon, into the area north of Grimbiémont (eleven kilometers northwest of Laroche) before strong enemy tank forces brought them to a halt.

In the meantime, the 2. SS-Panzerdivision "Das Reich" and the 9. SS-Panzerdivision "Hohenstaufen" also advanced and were again assigned to the chief command of II. SS-Panzer-korps. The "Hohenstaufen" Division attacked against the Salm sector near Grand-Halleux on 23 December. "Das Reich" Division captured Salmchateau, the Kampfgruppe "Der Führer" reached, on the attack, Baraque de Fraiture (fifteen kilometers west-south-

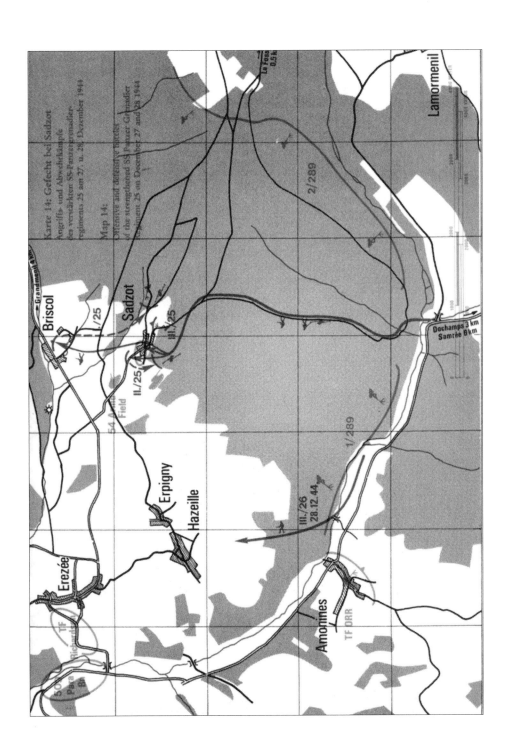

Karte 14: Gefecht bei Sadzot
Angriffs- und Abwehrkämpfe
des verstärkten SS-Panzergrenadier-
regiments 25 am 27. u. 28. Dezember 1944

Map 14:
Offensive and defensive battles
of the strengthened SS Panzer Grenadier
Regiment 25 on December 27 and 28 1944

La Fosse
0.5 km

Lamormenil

Briscol

Grandmenil 4 km

I./25

Sadzot

III./25

II./25

2/289

54 Field

Field

Dochamps 3 km
Samrée 8 km

1/289

Erpigny

Hazeille

III./26
28.12.44

Erezée

TF

Amonines

TF DRR

509 para
Richard

8th para

Bn

west of Salmchateau). Adjoining on the left, the 560. Volksgrenadierdivision managed, on its further advance to the northwest, to reach the Briscol-Erézée road. In order to free up the Panzerdivisions tied down on the northern wing of the 6. Panzerarmee for the attack farther to the west, the LXVI. Armeekorps, in action on the right wing of 5. Panzerarmee, together with 18. and 62. Volksgrenadierdivisions, were assigned to the 6. Panzerarmee on 23 December. The boundary of the Armee was correspondingly moved to the south.

The assessment of the situation by the Supreme Commander West, and his own intentions, emerges from the following entries of 24 December in the war diary:

> . . . The development shows more and more clearly that the enemy is moving, or has moved, strong forces from the north to the south in order to stop our own advance still east of the Maas. That intention can only be prevented by the speed of our advance. Accordingly, Heeresgruppe B, on the direction of Supreme Command West of 22 December, orders the continuation of the attack by the 6. and 5. Panzerarmee with the focus on the inner wings, and the objective to destroy the enemy still on this side of the Maas; with, at the same time, sufficient cover to the south and assured seizure of the Salm bridges and of Bastogne . . .[1]

The war diary states, for the same day, regarding the enemy situation:

> . . . The ongoing identification of individual regiments being brought up indicates that the enemy leadership is moving all reserves available into combat. Brought up, altogether, until now: Against our own northern wing, four tank and seven infantry divisions; against the southern wing, two tank and five infantry divisions . . .[2]

On the morning of 24 December, the "HJ" Division, starting out from its assembly area, was to move forward either via Recht (eight kilometers northwest of St. Vith) or behind the 9. SS-Panzerdivision. It was to, together with other Panzer divisions, reinforce the attack against the Maas. However, the first elements were only able to start out in the evening since the attack by 9. SS-Panzerdivision made only slow progress.

On 24 December, the 2. SS-Panzerdivision continued to attack to the northwest from the area around Baraque de Fraiture. The 116. Panzerdivision renewed its attack to the northwest via Marche. The spearhead of the 2. Panzerdivision continued its advance toward Dinant, the bulk of the Division followed approximately twenty kilometers behind. The Panzer-Lehr—Division captured Rochefort (eleven kilometers south of Marche). Because of fuel shortages, the spearheads of the Panzer divisions had to advance on foot. It became more and more crucial to strengthen the northern flank of the 5. Panzerarmee.

In the evening of 24 December, at 22.00 hours, the first elements of "HJ" Division started out. An armored scouting party of the Aufklärungsabteilung was sent to reconnoiter the route of advance from Eibertingen (Ebertange), where the Divisional command post was located, via Amel/Amblève-St. Vith-Maldingen/Maldange-Bowies/Bovigny-Mont le Ban (seven kilometers north-east of Houffalize)-Les Tailles (two kilometers south of Baraque de Fraiture) to Samrée (five kilometers northeast of Laroche). The leader of the scouting party, Oberscharführer August Zinßmeister, noted in his diary:

> . . . My scouting party drove through the snow and cold toward St. Vith on which, immediately before we reached it, a heavy bombard-ment rained down. As we by-passed it, we lost radio contact. But we had to press on, ahead of the Abteilung following behind one hour later. The moon-lit, snowy landscape lay dead as we felt our way for-ward via Bowies to the west. After crossing through a village, we found ourselves among a destroyed, still glowing, column of 'Ami' tanks. We were threading our way through, had already passed more than a dozen tanks, when two gun shots whipped across the valley, at an angle and in rapid succession. The shells landed in the wrecks. 'Ami' twin anti-tank gun? We pushed back as quickly as possible, without being hit by further shells. Suddenly, outside the village, the road was clogged with the vehicles of Heeresartillerie-abteilung 504 [?] with its 8.8 Flak guns. When we tried to squeeze past, the com-mander, Hauptmann Littmann, had me arrested for insubordina-tion. However, I was soon able to 'bolt', reach the Panzers which had pushed their way through under Oberscharführer Dittrich, and join them until we reached Bowies. The forward Abteilung was located there. We reported, and camped there until dawn . . .[3]

Flakabteilung 12 moved from the Losheimergraben district to Deiden-berg (two kilometers southwest of Amel-Amblève) on 24 December and took up positions there. During the night of 24–25 December, one enemy aircraft was shot down, another was hit and caught fire. There is no information con-cerning the aircraft types.[4] During the night, until the morning hours, the Divisional staff, Panzergrenadierregiment 25, the Flakabteilung and, proba-bly at least a part of the Artillerie-regiment, moved by way of St. Vith-Maldin-gen/Maldange into the vicinity of Bochholz/Beho. During the following night-25 to 26 December-those units continued their march via Bowies/Bovi-gny-Mont le Ban-Les Tailles into the area around Samrée (five kilometers northeast of Laroche). The first elements arrived there during the morning. The Divisionsbegleitkompanie (escort company) reached that town at approximately 10 A.M. and made camp in a forest close-by. The Kompanie lost one man killed and six wounded from the artillery shelling.[5] The Aufklärungsabteilung, as well, likely arrived near Samrée on 26 December. The leader of the armored scouting party, which set out at the point during the night of 24–25 December, reported as follows on 25 and 26 December:

> . . . 25.12., Monday. I started out early with the order to establish contact and exchange information with 'Das Reich' Division. After some effort, we found it in a castle in the St. Hubert district. Commander Lammerding was full of the spirit of victory after a very successful armor battle during the previous day. The return drive to Bowies took place under strong harassment by fighter-bombers. But we arrived unscathed in the afternoon, into warm quarters, in time to receive the Christmas mail.—26.12., Tuesday. Early in the morning we rolled via Salmchateau-Baraque de Fraiture and stopped outside of Dochamps (2.5 kilometers northwest of Samrée, Author) among knocked-out Sherman tanks and Panthers which had repulsed the 'Ami' counterattack not long before. I was able to easily get the first Sherman (latest model with a 7.6 cm gun) going again. I sent my armored vehicles up to the edge of the forest and drove that 'Ami-crate' behind them to increase our fire power. However, the artillery started shelling our forest edge. During the afternoon we had to move into the forest close to Laroche . . .[6]

The Aufklärungsabteilung, following behind, installed its command post four kilometers northwest of Samrée as indicated in the diary, written into a notebook, of Oberscharführer Heinz Thomas, half-Zug leader in I. Zug of the Fernsprechkompanie (telephone communications company).[7] The Division set up its command post in Samrée, where the command post of the Artillerieregiment was also located. It is known that the Flakabteilung arrived in Samrée during the morning of 27 December and took up positions around that village.[8] As well, the bulk of Regiment 25 and of the Artillerieregiment likely arrived in the assembly area in the morning and forenoon of 27 December.

The first element of Regiment 26 to arrive was Schützen-panzerbataillon III./26. The bulk of the Regiment was able to follow only later. One can read in the war diary of II./26:

> 23.12. . . . At the fall of darkness the Bataillon disengages, by companies, leaving behind blocking forces . . . The remaining parts only pull out when the relieving Volksgrenadierdivision arrive . . . The Bataillon makes camp in Hünningen.—24.12.: 00.10 hours, the remaining elements of the Bataillon arrive at the camp area. Combat vehicles are brought in and refueled . . . 18.25 hours: a fire

attack on the quarters in town kills eleven men and wounds six (at the field kitchen, being issued bread).—25.12.: During the night from 25 to 26.12.44, the Bataillon moves into the Maldingen district. Route of march: Hünningen-Honsfeld-Holzheim-Medendorf-Andler-Schönberg-St. Vith-Neuendorf-Maldingen [approximate road distance thirty kilometers].—26.12.: 08.30 hours, Bataillon arrives in Maldingen . . . Bataillon remains in M. since no fuel is available. Is scheduled to follow in the course of 27.12.44.—27.12.: 13.05 hours, orders from the Regiment: Bataillon will march on foot and move to its new quarters. Only those vehicles absolutely necessary for the leadership . . . will be brought along at the fall of darkness. 16.00 hours: enemy fighter-bombers attack the quarters in town with bombs and on-board weapons. Approximately twenty bombs were dropped. During the attack, the commander, the physician, as well as one NCO and three men were wounded. SS-Obersturmführer Brinkmann, chief of 8. Kompanie, takes over command of the Bataillon. 18.30 hours: the Bataillon starts out on foot for the march from Maldingen to Chabrehez, about thirty-eight kilometers to the west (six kilometers northeast of Samrée, Author).—28.12.: 0.55 hours, arrival in Chabrehez. The young men, for whom the march on foot with weapons and equipment was the first longer one, definitely need a rest, since 75 percent of them have chafed feet due to poor footgear. The footgear is worn down to the point where it cannot withstand any further distance marching . . .[9]

No information can be provided on time and location of the arrival of the Panzerregiment and Panzerjägerabteilung 12.

In the meantime, the overall situation changed considerably compared to that on 24 December. The "LAH" was unable to break through to the encircled Kampfgruppe Peiper in La Gleize and establish contact. The I. SS-Panzerkorps ordered the Kampfgruppe to break out, after it had reported that it only had minor supplies of infantry ammunition left; the towns of Stoumont and Cheneux had been given up. In the morning of 25 December, the Kampfgruppe succeeded in reaching the German lines southwest of Wanne on foot. Having left behind 250 American prisoners of war as well as 200 wounded Germans and Americans, together with the required medical personnel, the Kampfgruppe had broken out with approximately 800 men. Of them, 770 men managed to get through: thirty-five Panzers, sixty armored personnel carriers and two artillery batteries, of which, at the end, three Panzers, a few armored personnel carriers and two guns were still combat-ready, had to be left behind. A return of the wounded, in consideration of releasing the prisoners, had been agreed on.[10] During the course of the day, II. SS-Panzerkorps advanced farther to the northwest. The 9. SS-Panzerdivision captured Arbrefontaine and Lierneux (seventeen and fourteen kilometers northeast of Samrée, respectively). The 2. SS-Panzerdivision took Grandmenil (nine kilometers north-northeast of Samrée), but was unable to advance further. At the 560. Volksgrenadierdivision, adjacent on the left, the enemy managed to break through near Hotton. Eventful fighting took place at the 116. Panzerdivision, Verdenne (four kilometers northeast of Marche) was lost. The spearhead of the 2. Panzerdivision, located near Foy-Notre-Dame (six kilometers from Dinant), was cut-off. Contact with the bulk of the 2. Panzerdivision was cut near Buissonville (ten kilometers west-southwest of Marche).

At 03.00 hours on 25 December, the 5. Panzerarmee started a major attack on Bastogne which had been encircled since 22 December, ". . . since that bulge has to be cleared out before it can become, in conjunction with the enemy attacks from the south, a serious threat to the southern front . . ."[11] By evening, the German troops had approached within two kilometers on the west and 500 meters to the south of Bastogne, while the enemy continued his attempts to break through to Bastogne from the south.

Field Marshals Model and von Rundstedt, on 26.12.1944, judged the situation as follows, first FM Model:

> . . . despite the fact that the 6. Panzerarmee had partly lost contact and that the combat strength of all attack units had been weakened, it had been possible to break through the new enemy defensive front line ahead of the spearheads while fighting off the relief attack into the flank of 7. Armee. Consequently, there is the prospect of destroying the strong enemy forces east of the Maas in cooperation with 6. and 5. Panzerarmees. In order to achieve that, 6. Panzerarmee would have to continue its advance with all possible vigor. The 5. Panzerarmee would turn northeast after reaching the Maas, and 7. Armee would continue to repulse all enemy relief attacks and destroy enemy forces in the Bastogne area with its rear elements. At the same time, it was possible and necessary to attack the greatly weakened enemy in the Aachen bend. Such an attack from the Düren district is being prepared by Heeresgruppe B for 29 December.—The supreme commander of Heeresgruppe B considers it imperative that, in order to achieve that goal, not only must all available reserves in its sector be brought into action, including OKW reserves, but also that three to four Panzer divisions be brought up from other theaters of war to form a battle reserve.—As a further prerequisite for the success of that operation, not only are adequate supplies required, in particular of fuel, but it also needs weather conditions which preclude unlimited enemy air force action.—The Supreme Commander West is in agreement with the reported intentions for 6. and 5. Panzerarmees, as well as for the 7. Armee. Nevertheless, he emphatically points out the danger that 5. Panzerarmee,

when it swings to the northeast, could possibly be caught from the rear . . . The offensive operation, planned by Heeresgruppe B from the Düren district, is being rejected by the Supreme Commander West since the losses would probably be too high, given the forces available . . .[12]

The development of the fighting had forced the abandonment of the "Big Solution" with Antwerp as the objective. Under certain circumstances, Feldmarschall Model still considered the realization of the "Small Solution" possible, i.e. the encirclement and destruction of the enemy forces located east of the Maas.

In contrast, Feldmarschall von Rundstedt was convinced that a success even of the "Small Solution" could not be expected in view of the increasing supply problems and he requested the OKW to stop the offensive. The OKW ordered the continuation of the attack. The 5. Panzerarmee was to capture the high terrain at Marche and, after receiving two Panzer divisions from 6. Panzerarmee, continue the attack.[13]

The fear of Supreme Commander West that the 5. Panzerarmee, when swinging to the northeast, ". . . could be caught from the rear . . ." appeared confirmed when Heeresgruppe B reported at noon of 26 December: ". . . The Aufklärungsabteilung of 2. Panzerdivision, which had advanced farthest to the west, was smashed. The enemy appears to be bringing up further forces from the south against the southern front of 5. Panzerarmee . . ."[14] Reports by Ic emphasized those suppositions and informed on the transport of the 17th US Airborne Division from England and the approach of the 51st British Infantry Division.

At the I. SS-Panzerkorps, the relief of the "LAH" Division by the 18. Volksgrenadierdivision was under way. On the left—west of the Salm—the 62. Volksgrenadierdivision was advancing toward the Trois-Ponts-Basse Bodeux road. At the II. SS-Panzerkorps, adjacent to the left, the 9. SS-Panzerdivision attacked on the right toward the section of the road Basse Bodeux-Bra-Vaux Chavanne. Vilettes (six kilometers northeast of Vaux Chavanne) was captured. The villages of Bra and Vaux Chavanne, which had already partly been taken, were lost again to American counterattacks. The Division temporarily changed over to defense south of those villages. To the left of 9. SS-Panzerdivision, the 2. SS-Panzerdivision attacked from Grandmenil to the northwest. After initial successes, the Division was forced to pull back and give up Grandmenil and Manhay. It changed over to defense along a line Hill 455 (south of Manhay)-Oster-Freyneux.[15]

The LVIII. Panzerkorps of the 5. Panzerarmee adjoined to the left of II. SS-Panzerkorps. On its right wing, the 560. Volksgrenadierdivision defended the line from north of Dochamps-east of Amonines-western edge of Trinal-edges of the woods south of Trinal-Werpin against massive American counterattacks. Attacks by the Führer-Begleit-Brigade and 116. Panzerdivision on

Menil (two kilometers south of Hotton) and Verdenne (3.5 kilometers east of Marche) stalled. The Führer-Begleit-Brigade was pulled out and moved into the Bastogne district. The 116. Panzerdivision changed over to defense. Attacks by the 9. Panzerdivision on Buissonville and by the Panzer-Lehr-Division on Ciergnon (ten kilometers west of Rochefort) were without success. The 2. Panzerdivision pulled back to Rochefort after an attempt to relieve its Aufklärungsabteilung outside of Dinant had failed. The Panzer-Lehr-Division took over the securing of the southwestern flank of 5. Panzerarmee between Rochefort and Bastogne. The attack on Bastogne made no progress. Toward the evening, the 4th US Armored Division succeeded in breaking the encircling ring and break through to the city. An attempt to close the encirclement again through a counterattack was unsuccessful.

"HJ" Division, assembling around Samrée, was attached to II. SS-Panzerkorps in order to get the attack in a northwesterly direction going again, together with the 9. and 2. SS-Panzerdivisions, to cross the Ourthe in the vicinity of Durbuy, and then to continue the attack toward the Maas. The distance from Durbuy to the Maas near Huy is only twenty-five kilometers. The 1. SS-Panzerdivision, which was assembling in the St. Vith and Vielsalm districts, was to follow later. The "HJ" Division would then again come under the command of I. SS-Panzerkorps.

At this point, a look should be taken at the other side. The enemy threw quickly alerted reserves against the rapid advance of 5. Panzerarmee in a northwesterly direction, closing in on the Maas near Dinant. Those reserves were initially unable to form a cohesive defensive front. Enemy units blocked the German spearheads wherever they were encountered. Even on 27 December, the front line between Trois-Ponts—the confluence of the Salm into the Amblève river—and Dinant, where the Maas runs from south to north, was not yet manned without gaps. It ran from Trois-Ponts via Grandmenil-Hampteau into the area south and west of Marche. Farther to the west, the front line was in violent movement. The 30th US Infantry Division was located behind the Amblève from Trois-Ponts to the east. Adjacent to the west, up to Vaux Chavanne (exclusive), the 82nd US Airborne Division linked up. Farther to the west stood the 7th US Armored Division which had suffered heavy losses near St. Vith. Its narrow sector extended east only to Grandmenil. From there to the Ourthe near Hampteau, the 3rd US Armored Division and the 75th US Infantry Division were in action along a width, as the crow flies, of only thirteen kilometers. The 84th US Infantry Division linked up near Hampteau. Farther to the west, up to the Maas, the 2nd US Armored Division and the 29th British Armoured Division were in combat against elements of the Panzer-Lehr-Division and of 2. Panzerdivision.

The fighting at II. SS-Panzerkorps, and the LVIII. and XXXXVII. Panzerkorps adjacent to the left, took place in those days in the Ardennes. They stretch, a wooded range of hills, from the Maas between Givet and Fumay in a shallow bend in an east-northeasterly direction to the Salm on both sides of

Vielsalm. The ridge runs, from approximately 350 meters in the west to 422 meters, 550 meters near St. Hubert, 652 meters near Baraque de Fraiture, to 400 meters near Vielsalm in the east. Coming from Bastogne, one main road leads via Baraque de Fraiture and Manhay on to Liège; another from Bastogne via Laroche, mostly along the Ourthe valley, by way of Hotton-Bomal, also to Liège; a third, again from Bastogne, via Barrière de Champlon-Marche to Liège, Huy and Namur. Those three roads were of the greatest importance for the further operations. An important connecting road leads from Manhay via Grandmenil-Erézée-Soy-Hotton to Marche. Parallel to it, an east-west connecting road runs approximately along the crest of the Ardennes from Baraque de Fraiture via Samrée-Laroche to Barrière de Champlon. The southern connecting road was in German hands, the northern one, on 27 December 1944, in those of the enemy. In the first instance, it was important to seize that road in order to cut the enemy cross-connection, and use the road for German movements. Between the northern and southern connecting roads stretches an extensive wooded area; in it cohesive forests of three to five kilometers depth. In that area, Panzers and armored personnel carriers could not operate. Only behind the line Werbomont-Mormont-Durbuy-Baillonville did armored units again have the possibility to move and deploy. As the second step, that area had also to be taken. At first, the "HJ" Division was probably given the mission—this could not be dependably clarified—of attacking from the Dochamps (three kilometers north of Samrée) district in the direction of Grandmenil and of getting the attack by 2. SS-Panzerdivision going again. Obviously, however, that plan was altered again.

The "HJ" Division, which had only available, so far, Panzergrenadierregiment 25, the III./26 (Schützenpanzerwagenbataillon), the Aufklärungsabteilung, the Flakabteilung and parts of the artillery, captured Freyneux and Lamormenil (five kilometers north of Samrée) before noon on 27 December. It continued its attack toward Oster and La Fosse (seven kilometers north-northeast of Samrée), which it captured during the course of the day in the face of tenacious enemy resistance. Then, the attack stalled.[15a]

The 560. Volksgrenadierdivision was located along a general line from south of Amonines-Magoster-Hampteau. It is unclear whether Hampteau was still in German hands.[16] It is probable that it had already been seized by the Americans. The Division prepared an attack on Amonines.[17] Since the "Das Reich" Division had not succeeded in overcoming the enemy near Grandmenil and breaking through to the northwest, the "HJ" Division was ordered to push through the Bois (forest) du Pays and via Sadzot to the Grandmenil-Erézée and, initially, to cut if off. At the same time, the 560. Volks-grenadierdivision was to take Amonines and advance on Erézée and Fisenne.[18] The 2. SS-Panzerdivision was given orders to attack, simultaneously, toward Mormont (six kilometers northwest of Grandmenil). The "HJ" Division expressed to II. SS-Panzerkorps its serious concerns against that order. Because of the aerial situation, the attack would have to be carried out through broken forested terrain at night. (An illustration of the aerial situation is the fact that the Ia, on his way from the Korps command post to the Division on 27 December, needed three-quarters of an hour to travel two kilometers along an open two-kilometer stretch of road.) Panzers, armored personnel carriers, and wheeled vehicles could not be taken along or brought up later. On leaving the forest, at the best, medium mortars and only Panzerfausts to fight tanks would be available. Effective artillery support would be close to impossible because of the uncertain communications connection through the hilly terrain. The Korps indicated that the Armee was insisting on the attack being carried out, despite of those known difficulties.

Since the bulk of Panzergrenadierregiment 26 had not yet arrived, because of fuel shortages, the Aufklärungsabteilung was assigned to the 2. SS-Panzerdivision.

In the course of 27 December, the units in the sector of the 3rd US Armored Division had also been re-grouped. The 289th Infantry Regiment of the 75th US Infantry Division had prepared for defense from Grandmenil to Amonines (exclusive). Amonines was defended by Task Force Orr of the 3rd Armored Division. Adjacent, to the west, was the 290th Infantry Regiment of the 75th Division, whose right wing was located at the Ourthe near Hampteau. Between the 1st Battalion 289th Infantry, whose left wing was located at the deeply-cut Sous l'Eau creek and the 2nd/289th Infantry which was in position to the east, a gap of several hundred meters width had remained. The 2nd Battalion, with its left wing, extended to Grandmenil. To the west of Erézée, "along the main road", the 509th Parachute Infantry Battalion had assembled, the remnants of Task Force "Richardson" were located between it and Erézée. The 54th Armored Field Artillery Battalion stood north of Sadzot, its forward parts in positions inside the town. "C"-Company of the 87th Chemical Battalion and one platoon of tank destroyers were also located there.[19]

The evening report of Supreme Command West of 27 December 1944 states: ". . . 2. and 12. SS-Panzerdivisions are at present in the process of re-grouping for the attack on Sadzot and Erézée, planned for 19.00 hours . . ." The daily report of Supreme Command West reads: ". . . 2. and 12. SS-Panzer-divisions. Massive enemy artillery fire on the main line of resistance and the artillery fire positions. Approximately 7 to 8 enemy batteries in the Mormont-Erézée district. At 19.30 hours, 12. SS-Panzerdivision started the attack on Erézée . . ."[20]

Panzergrenadierregiment 25 had been moved forward to Dochamps on vehicles. It reconnoitered to the north. Fortunately, the scouting parties found the gap between the 1/289 Infantry and the 2/289 Infantry immediately north of the road bend three kilometers north of Dochamps. The forward enemy elements were in position in the vicinity of the Sous l'Eau creek, which flows into the Aine (Aisne) at the road bend mentioned, and along the Aine to Amonines and into the woods located north of it. Hence, the

Regiment was forced to reach its assembly area south of the road bend on foot. Engine noise would have alerted the enemy to the move. Regiment 25 was given the task of pushing through the forest to the north and, via Sadzot, to the Grandmenil-Erézée road, and of blocking it. To the left, and under the command of Regiment 25, the reinforced Panzeraufklärungsabteilung 2 of the "Das Reich" Division was put into action. Assigned to it were the 9. (armored) Kompanie of the "DF" Regiment, the Divisionssturmkompanie (assault company), and III. Abteilung of the Artillerieregiment "Das Reich". It was to break through the forest belt, a maximum of one kilometer deep there, from the area east of Amonines, by way of Erpigny and Hazeille, to the Erézée-Grandmenil road.[20a] The batteries of the "HJ" Division, which had arrived, were moved into positions so that they could provide the farthest possible support for the attack. In order to keep the preparations for the attack a secret, there could be no question of ranging the guns by firing them.

After an exhausting march on foot, during which Panzerfausts, mortars and ammunition had to be carried, Regiment 25 reached the assembly area at the road bend in the early evening hours. A pause to rest and eat followed. The Regiment started out at 19.30 hours. Only a narrow, unimproved forest trail was available for the advance. It was a clear, cold night, lit by a full moon, which made orientation inside the forest easier. The spearhead of the Regiment was formed by II. Bataillon, led by Hauptsturmführer Werner Damsch. The III. Bataillon marched at the rear. It had been taken over by Hauptsturmführer Wilhelm Dehne a few days ago. At the end of the column traveled three 7.5 cm Pak with the crews.

The forest trail starts out at an elevation of 340 meters. It climbs to 460 meters in the middle of the forest and then drops toward Sadzot to an elevation of 360 meters. The troops advanced in file along the snowed-in forest trail, avoiding any noise. After some time, the point of II. Bataillon came upon an enemy scouting party. There was a short exchange of fire, the Americans were captured and sent back to the command post of Regiment 25. When they arrived—surely hours later—at the Divisional command post, they were identified as members of the 75th US Infantry Division which had so far not been encountered in that area. It is likely that it was a scouting party which was to establish contact between the 1/289 Infantry and the 2/289 Infantry. The spearhead elements of II./25 reached the exit from the forest near Sadzot around midnight. The Bataillon staff set up its command post in a hunting cottage near the St. Jean wayside shrine, which stands some 400 to 500 meters south of the exit from the forest. The troops, tired by another exhausting march on foot, closed up and rested for some time.

Soon after midnight, the I. and II. Bataillons started the attack. The III. followed behind and moved into a prepared rear position close to the edge of the forest. The I. Bataillon advanced through the right section of the village, then through the valley of a creek, and its spearhead reached the

Grandmenil-Erézée road near the chapel. The II. Bataillon, advancing on the left, encountered the enemy, in the larger, left, section of town. Both Bataillon commanders reported on the action, first Hauptsturmführer Damsch:

> . . . Through the bitter cold and bright moonlight, the I. Bataillon advancing on the right, II. Bataillon on the left, the attack against the totally surprised and initially confused enemy progressed well. The first prisoners were made and an abandoned light tank was captured. The I. Bataillon advance, without exchanging fire, through the eastern section of Sadzot and continued the attack rapidly along a creek valley running in the direction of Briscol. After contact had been lost with the II. Bataillon on the left, and reconnaissance had determined enemy armor in Briscol and on the Grandmenil-Erézée road, the attack was stopped before dawn in consideration of the open terrain and our own shortage of heavy weapons . . .[21]

Obersturmbannführer Richard Schulze reported on the action by II. Bataillon:

> . . . I especially remember that mission during a beastly cold, moonlit night because I had to, first of all, reconnoiter and then form the spearhead of the Regiment. I tried to make it clear to the men how important it was to advance through the forest without any noise and unnoticed. We crept through the night, without encountering the enemy, to the northern edge of the forest. From there, anti-aircraft or anti-tank positions, or, at least outposts, could be spotted. They, however, did not detect the approach of the Bataillon. As ordered, we managed to penetrate into the village of Sadzot under complete silence, and surprise the enemy inside the houses. The enemy fled, some of them only incompletely dressed. However, enemy tanks on the move were spotted during the clearing of the village and the advance toward the road near Briscol . . . [22]

The II. Bataillon took a few prisoners who were identified as members of the 75th US Infantry Division. In the course of the night it had been possible, with great effort, to pull two or three Pak forward through the forest. They took up ambush positions close to the edge of the forest and at a crossroads in the woods south of the village.

At approximately two o'clock, the 54th Armored Field Artillery Battalion (armored self-propelled artillery), which was in position north of Sadzot and had a spearhead inside the village, reported that the enemy had penetrated into Sadzot and was located in the forest south of the village. Until then, the American infantry battalions in the front lines had reported no contact with the enemy. General Hickey, commander of Combat Command A of the 3rd Us Armored Division, immediately alerted the 509th Parachute Infantry Battalion. He sent it south, with the task of occupying Sadzot and securing the artillery positions. One company moved into a rear position north of the village while the other two by-passed it on the left and the right in order to encircle the German troops. A smaller force advanced on the village. Task Force "Richardson", which consisted of two infantry platoons, one company of medium tanks at half strength, and one company of light tanks at full strength, marched off toward Briscol. It was to support the 509th Battalion.[23] Inside Sadzot, bitter close combat broke out during darkness, it lasted into the morning. It caused high losses. After daybreak, the Americans were effectively supported by their artillery which was vastly superior to the German artillery support. At 11 o'clock, the parachute infantry had encircled Sadzot.[24] The last elements of II. Bataillon reached the cover of the forest and the rear positions of the III. Bataillon at that time. There, Regiment 25 initially changed over to defense with II. and III. Bataillons. After reaching the Grandmenil-Erézée road, the I. Bataillon had sought to establish contact with II. Bataillon on the left, but had not succeeded. Toward daybreak, when the enemy attacked with infantry and tanks from the Briscol-Erézée road, the I. Bataillon which, except for Panzerfausts, had no armor-piercing weapons, pulled back from the road. It found cover in a protruding piece of forest which juts out into the area north of Sadzot. At a fork in the path leading to La Fosse, it came upon a German Pak which fought off the pursuing tanks.[25] The last elements of the reinforced Panzeraufklärungsabteilung 2 reached the assembly area only by 23.30 hours. It started its attack at 24.00 hours. Contact within the units and to the Abteilung was lost, so that the attack stalled after a short time.[25a]

The noon report of 28 December 1944 in the war diary of Supreme Command West states:

> . . . During the attack on Erézée, Oster was captured again. The Kampfgruppe of the 560. V.G.D. is on the attack on Wy [2.5 kilometers west-northwest of Amonines]. The attack by 12. SS-Panzerdivision from Sadzot was thrown back by an enemy counterattack with tanks. The enemy pushed into the northwestern section of Sadzot . . .

The evening report of 28.12. reads:

> . . . The 9. SS-Panzerdivision has taken over the sector of 2. SS-Panzerdivision. The 2. SS-Panzerdivision has assembled for the attack along a line Frennex [must read Freyneux]—south of Amonines. The 12. SS-Panzerdivision is re-grouping for a further attack to the north . . .

The daily report states:

> . . . The attack on the left wing of the 6. Panzerarmee on Mormont-
> Erézée is under way since 18.00 hours . . . The attack by the 12. SS-
> Panzerdivision via Sadzot on Briscol pushed, as confirmed by
> prisoner statements, into the assembly of the 75th US Infantry Divi-
> sion and the 3rd US Tank Division. Sadzot was lost to an enemy
> counterattack. The 2. SS-Panzerdivision started its attack on Erézée
> at 22.30 hours. The 560 V.G.D. has been attached to 6. Panzerarmee
> (I. SS-Panzerkorps) . . .[26]

Since the attack by Regiment 25 did not achieve the blocking of the
Grandmenil-Erézée road, and the enemy started a counterattack with tanks
there, the attack along both sides of the Dochamps-Amonines road was to be
re-started. While Regiment 25 was defending the positions south of Sadzot,
Regiment 26 was to attack in the evening of 28 December from the
Dochamps-Amonines road to the north and capture Erpigny and Hazeille
(1.5 kilometers southeast of Erézée). On its left, along both sides of the main
road, the "Das Reich" Division, to which the reinforced SS-Panzeraufklärungsabteilung 2 was attached again, was to attack.

Initially, only the III./26 was sent into the attack. The other two battalions of the Regiment were to follow a successful attack. For that reason, the
III. Bataillon assembled toward the evening of 28 December in the woods
two kilometers north of Samrée. Unterscharführer Günther Burdack
reported on the action by III./26:

> . . . The armored personnel carriers were left behind in a ravine
> south of Samrée. The crews, except for the drivers, assembled in
> Samrée and marched via Dochamps in the direction of Erézée. The
> road was totally clogged by abandoned and destroyed enemy vehi-
> cles, mostly artillery, and was under constant heavy enemy shelling.
> After approximately six kilometers, the Bataillon was directed by a
> liaison officer of the 'DF' Regiment to leave the road in a northerly
> direction and to advance along a field lane toward the twin-village of
> Hazeille-Erpigny. After some 1.5 kilometers we reached the desig-
> nated position at the edge of the forest. The village could not be
> observed from the edge of the forest. It was located at a higher eleva-
> tion than our own position. Reconnaissance in the direction of
> Erézée, to the west past H-E. The deeply-frozen ground did not allow
> us to dig in. The III./26 did not have any heavy weapons with it, only
> rifles and light MGs. Harassing fire covered the whole sector . . .[27]

The attack by the "Das Reich" Division along the Amonines-Erézée road
did not break through. In the morning of 29 December, the III./26 pulled

back the bulk of its Bataillon from the line it had reached, leaving behind only blocking forces, since the enemy artillery and mortar fire was increasing. The I. and II./26 remained in their assembly areas.

Simultaneously, the Americans attempted to close off the gap which had allowed Regiment 25 to push through to Sadzot. To do that, the 2nd Battalion 112th Infantry (28th US Infantry Division) was assigned to Combat Command "A" under General Hickey. It was moved forward still during the night of 28 to 29 December, but lost its orientation in the forest. In the morning of 29 December its left wing established contact with paratroop elements south of Sadzot. However, General Hickey assumed the withdrawal route of Regiment 25 had been blocked. He ordered an attack by the 509th Paratroopers, with the support from six light tanks, on the German positions at the edge of the forest south of Sadzot in the early morning hours of 29 December. During that battle, three American tanks were knocked out by the 7.5 cm Pak and the paratroopers were repelled.[28]

For 29 December, the war diary of Supreme Command West, morning report 29.12.1944, states:

> . . . The 12. SS-Panzerdivision on the attack since 22.30 hours. It has broken through the forested area west of Amonines under heavy enemy artillery fire, advancing to the north. Individual enemy thrusts southwest of Amonines were fought off . . .

The evening report reads:

> . . . Attacks by 2. and 12. SS-Panzerdivision on Mormont are stalled . . .

And the daily report reads:

> . . . The attack by II. SS-Panzerkorps on Mormont did not break through the tenaciously fighting enemy who was supported by strong artillery . . . Enemy reconnaissance advances from the Sadzot area as well as enemy armor attacks against 560. V.G.D. were repulsed. Five tanks knocked out.—On 28.12., 12. SS-Panzerdivision destroyed twenty-five armored vehicles, twenty-four trucks, four tanks in close combat, eight heavy mortars . . .[29]

The diary of II./26 notes for 29 December that enemy artillery and mortars were shelling the assembly area, but that it suffered only minor losses. The attack on Erézée had been postponed and reconnaissance had again been sent out. The study by Generalmajor Langhäuser, the commander of the 560. Volksgrenadierdivision, states, for 29 December, that the "HJ" Division had taken over the sector of "Gruppe Schmitt"—the middle one of the three Volksgrenadier regiments—southeast of Amonines. "Gruppe Schmitt" was to have been pulled out in the evening and joined, by way of Dochamps, "Gruppe Schuhmann", the regimental unit on the left.[30] No clear picture on the developments on 29 December outside the sector of Regiment 25 can be obtained from the various documents. In any case, the overall situation there did not change much. The enemy had brought up too many reinforcements. Action by the German Panzerdivisions—of which the "HJ" Division was not yet fully assembled—was enormously hampered by the difficult terrain. Hence, the German attack in that sector of the front was discontinued. Panzer units were to be disengaged in order to clear up the situation near Bastogne through the concentration of all forces.

The relieving of the "HJ" Division by elements of the 560. Volksgrenadierdivision began on 30 December 1944. The 560. V.G.D. had itself just been relieved by the 2. SS-Panzerdivision and moved into temporary quarters in the Dochamps-Samrée-Odeigne district. The daily report stated on that:

. . . Repeated enemy attacks northwest of Lamormenil were repelled. Temporary breakthroughs were cleared out through counterattacks.—Relief of 12. SS-Panzerdivision and parts of 9. SS-Panzerdivision by 560. V.G.D. has begun.—Assembly of the 12. SS-Panzerdivision under the chief command of I. SS-Panzerkorps planned for the area northwest of Laroche, with a possible move into the Bastogne combat theater . . .[31]

The battles in the Sadzot area have entered the American war history under the name "The Sad Sack Affair", where a part of the name of the village was used in a play on words. It had really been a battle in the dark. With it, the last attempt to break through to the Maas, in line with the "small solution", had also failed.

During an inspection of the battlefield on 5 September 1981, in which the three former Bataillon commanders and Helmut Hacker, then a telephone operator in the Nachrichtenstaffel of the II./25, took part, together with the Ia, they found a commemorative plaque next to the Briscol chapel. The Touring Club of Belgium had set it up there. Next to a Panzer, depicted in relief, these words are carved: "Ici fût arrêté l'envahisseur hiver 1944–45" ("Here, the enemy who had broken through was brought to a halt in the winter of 1944–45"). That location had been the first attack objective reached by the I. Bataillon of Regiment 25 on 28 December 1944.

The first elements of the "HJ" Division were moved into the Bastogne district even on 31 December 1944. The Divisionsbegleitkompanie started its march to Wigny (eleven kilometers northwest of Bastogne) at 17.00 hours. It arrived there at 23.30 hours and received scouting and reconnaissance tasks from the Ia who was already there. Another, probably even more difficult action, awaited the Division.[32]

CHAPTER 8.7
The Attacks near Bastogne from 2 to 7 January 1945—Change-over to Defense from 7 to 10 January 1945

During the winter of 1944–45, Bastogne was—as it is today—a more important crossing point of major roads than either Malmedy or St. Vith. These roads cross here:

Echternach-Diekirch-Marche-Huy and Namur,
Luxembourg-Arlon-la Roche-Huy and Liège, and
Florenville-Montmédy-Neufchateau-Houffalize-Liége.

Around the turn of the year 1944/45, the area around Bastogne became the focus of the fighting. The 5. Panzerarmee and 7. Armee were taking part in those battles. The development until then must be quickly recalled.

The mission of the 5. Panzerarmee read:

> . . . The 5. Panzerarmee will break through the enemy front line in the northern section of Luxembourg. It will advance, taking advantage of the Bastogne-Namur road, across the Maas between Amay and Namur. Parts of the Armee will, if the situation requires or the opportunity arises, be pulled forward via Dinant or across the Sambre into the Brussels area and to the west of Antwerp. The task of the Armee in that eventuality will be to prevent action by enemy reserves across the line Antwerp-Brussels-Dinant against the rear of the 6. Panzerarmee. In order to achieve that, the Armee's spearheads will have to keep pace with those of the 6. Panzerarmee and, without regard to its deep flank, capture the Antwerp-Brussels area as quickly as possible . . .[1]

The 7. Armee, adjacent on the left, had to provide cover to the southern and southwestern flanks of the 5. Panzerarmee. On 16 December, the XXXXVII. Panzerkorps of General der Panzertruppen Freiherr von Lüttwitz broke through the positions held by elements of the 28th US Infantry Division between Dasburg and Gemünd. On 17 December, the 2. Pz.-Div., led by Oberst von Lauchert, advanced across the Clerf and occupied Clervaux. The 26. Volksgrenadierdivision, which was also part of that Korps, established a bridgehead across the Clerf near Drauffelt through which the Panzer-Lehr-Division advanced. The LVIII. Panzerkorps, adjoining on the right, did not achieve any progress. Consequently, the VIII US Corps threw its reserves to the front in order to prevent a breakthrough into its rear. The CCR (Combat Command R) of the 9th US Armored Division was put into action in the area east and northeast of Bastogne to block the National Route 12 near Lul-

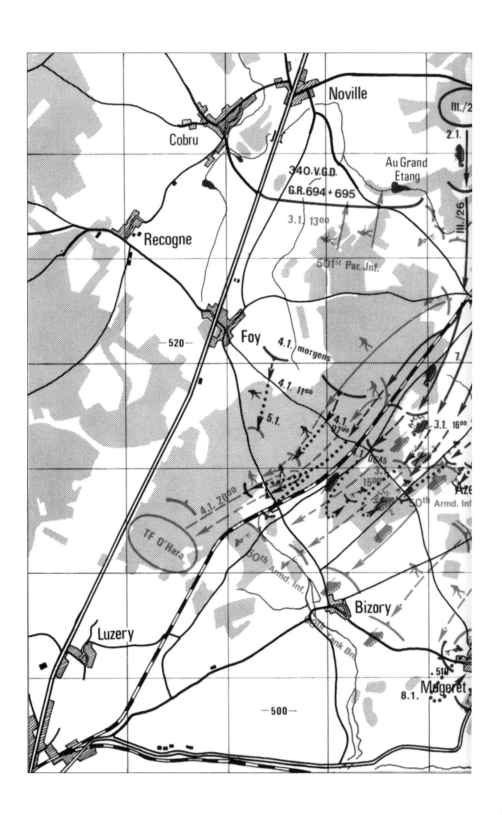

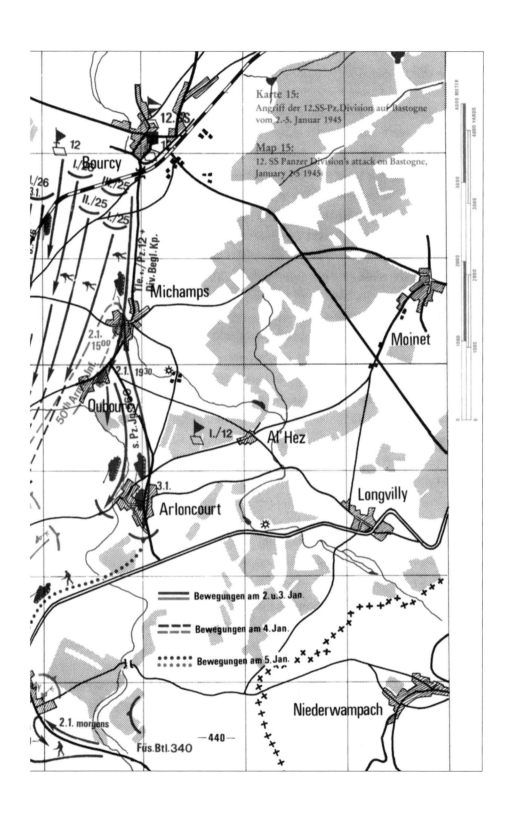

Karte 15:
Angriff der 12.SS-Pz.Division auf Bastogne
vom 2.-5. Januar 1945

Map 15:
12. SS Panzer Division's attack on Bastogne,
January 2-5 1945

12. SS

12

I./26
3.1.

I./Bourcy

II./25

II./25

I./25

Tle.+v./Pz.12 +
Div.Begl.Kp.

Michamps

2.1.
15⁰⁰

Moinet

2.1. 19³⁰

50th Arm. Inf.

Oubourcy

s.Pz.Jg.c.

I./12

Al'Hez

3.1.

Longvilly

Arloncourt

Bewegungen am 2. u.3. Jan.

Bewegungen am 4.Jan.

Bewegungen am 5.Jan.

Niederwampach

2.1. morgens

—440—

Füs.Btl.340

lange and Allerborn (17.5 and 11 kilometers northeast of Bastogne, respectively). The 2. Pz.-Div. overran both positions. The remnants of the CCR retreated to Longvilly (8.5 kilometers northeast of Bastogne) and prepared for defense there. On 18 December, the Panzer-Lehr-Division, under the leadership of Generalleutnant Bayerlein, reached Mageret (four kilometers east-northeast of Bastogne). To the right, the 2. Pz.-Div. advanced to Noville (seven kilometers northeast of Bastogne).

In order to reinforce the CCR of the 9th Armored Division, situated near Longvilly between the two German attack spearheads, and to block the approach to Bastogne from the east—from Mageret—the VIII Corps moved a part of the CCB of the 10th US Armored Division, Team Cherry, forward to Neffe (three kilometers east of Bastogne) and to Longvilly on 19 December. In the morning of 19 December, the 101st US Airborne Division arrived in Bastogne as further reinforcements. The first element to arrive was the 501st Parachute Infantry Regiment. It moved into a prepared rear position northwest of Bizory (3.5 kilometers northeast of Bastogne) in the evening of 19 December.

On 20 December, the 560. Volksgrenadierdivision, which belonged to LVIII. Panzerkorps, reached Dochamps (6.5 kilometers northeast of Laroche). The 116. Pz.-Div. attacked from Samrée on Marcourt. In the afternoon of that day, Oberst von Lauchert requested permission from his superiors for a thrust into Bastogne. He was ordered to by-pass the city to the north and advance on the Maas. The vanguard of his Division had already crossed the Ourthe near Ortheuville (twelve kilometers south of Laroche) on that day. On their thrust to the west, the Panzer-Lehr-Division and the 26. Volksgrenadierdivision blocked the roads leading to Bastogne from the south. With that, a wide ring around the city was closed. During the following day, the 26. Volksgrenadierdivision relieved the elements of the 2. Pz.-Div. and of the Panzer-Lehr-Div. still in action near Bastogne, except for one Panzergrenadierregiment, in order to free them up for the further advance to the west.

For the encircled Americans, artillery ammunition ran short on 22 December and medical care was suffering. Because of the poor weather, the attempt to supply the troops from the air was without success. Around noon, German envoys called upon the encircled Americans to surrender honorably, otherwise the city would be demolished. General McAuliffe refused.

On 23 December, the 5. Panzerarmee achieved a deep breakthrough in the direction of the Maas. The Aufklärungs-abteilung reached the vicinity of Achne, barely ten kilometers from the Maas, the bulk of the Division was five kilometers away from Rochefort. The 26. Volksgrenadierdivision was able to shrink the encircling ring somewhat.

While the attack spearheads of 2. Panzerdivision were able to advance to within five kilometers of Dinant and the Maas on 24 December, the situation in the surrounded city of Bastogne was becoming very critical.

Ammunition was running short despite the fact that 241 aircraft had brought in supplies during the previous day. The 101st Airborne Division managed to make contact with the VIII Corps, using the civilian telephone system, and requested that the relief by the 4th US Armored Division be expedited by all means. However, a quick decision was also imperative for the "besiegers". Heeresgruppe B reported the following intentions for the Bastogne district:

> . . . In consideration of the enemy attack expected today to relieve Bastogne, the vanguard Kampfgruppe of the 15. Panzerdivision has been moved into the area south of Bastogne during the night.—The remaining units of the 9. Panzerdivision (two battalions, artillery, Panzerjägers), originally scheduled to follow the vanguard Kampf-gruppe, were temporarily stopped in the region southeast of Bastogne. They will recommence their march in the evening of 24 December. The remaining units of the 15. Panzergrenadierdivision are located northeast of Bastogne. They are to be used in the capture of Bastogne. The 26. V.G.D. remains, as was, in position around Bastogne. The 5. Panzerarmee has orders to take Bastogne from the northeast and to be ready for action south of Bastogne if the situation requires. After the capture of Bastogne, the 15. Panzer-grenadierdivision will follow the attack divisions of the 5. Panzerarmee, while the 26. V.G.D. is to join AOK 7 . . .[2]

The attack on Bastogne started at 03.00 hours on 25 December 1944. By the evening, the attacking troops advanced to within two kilometers to the west, and 500 meters south of the city. The enemy tried to break the encir-cling ring from the south with strong forces, initially, however, without suc-cess.[3]

The attack against the encircled forces did not move ahead on the fol-lowing day. In contrast, the 4th Armored Division succeeded in breaking through the encircling ring from the south and establishing contact with the 101st Airborne Division. German counterattacks were unable to cut off the narrow corridor. At the same time, the situation at the Maas also took a turn for the worse. The Aufklärungsabteilung of the 2 Panzerdivision, which had been cut off outside Dinant since the previous day, was destroyed. Ic reports gave rise to the assumption that the Americans had pulled out forces from opposite the Heeresgruppe G and the 19. Armee in the south, and that troops from the sector of the British army group and from England were being brought up.[4]

The Americans continued their attacks against the German encircling ring on 27 December. The 5. Fallschirmjägerdivision lost Assenois (five kilo-meters southwest of Bastogne), the 26. Volksgrenadierdivision lost Sibret (seven kilometers southwest of Bastogne). The Führer-Begleit-Brigade, led by

Oberst Remer, coming from the district south of Hotton, arrived west of Bastogne in the evening. It started an attack against the American corridor but was unable to cut it. In order to make possible a unified conduct of combat in the area around Bastogne (units of the 5. Panzerarmee and of the 7. Armee were taking part in the fighting) command was transferred to XXXIX. Pz.-Korps. The commanding general was General der Panzertruppen Decker.[5]

Bastogne could only be taken if it was first possible to cut the corridor through which the city, as well the troops defending it, were being supplied. Further reinforcements were brought up for that attack. However, the 3. Panzergrenadierdivision and the 167. Volksgrenadierdivision did not arrive in time so that, on 28 December, the Führer-Begleit-Brigade and elements of the 15. Panzergrenadierdivision had to attack toward Villeroux and Sibret (six and seven kilometers southwest of Bastogne, respectively) by themselves. Simultaneously, the Americans attacked also, from Villeroux toward Senonchamps. They were brought to a halt by artillery fire. Clearing of the forest southwest of Senonchamps was still going on in the evening. In order to further strengthen the attacking forces, the 1. SS-Pz.-Div. "LAH" was attached to the 5. Panzerarmee and, toward evening, it started its march into the region of Arloncourt-Harzy-Schimpach-Longvilly, east of Bastogne.[6]

The Supreme Commander West ordered Heeresgruppe B in the afternoon of 28 December 1944:

> . . . 1) it is of decisive importance that the enemy attack wedge toward Bastogne and . . . (unreadable) be smashed within the shortest possible time and with sufficient effective forces and material.— 2) On that score I am in agreement that 1. SS-Panzerdivision 'LAH' be moved expeditiously, and today, into the Bastogne area in order to provide the required support at the focal points of the concentric attack by the 3. Panzergrenadierdivision and the 167. V.G.D. against the deep flanks.—I take for granted that strongest possible artillery firepower through participation by the Volks-Artilleriekorps and rocket launchers is assured. There must be no doubt that the attack has to take place on 29.12. at the latest in order to prevent a further continuation of enemy reinforcement . . .[7]

Since most of the reinforcements were still on the move, the concentric attack on Bastogne could not start on 29 December. The bulk of the "HJ" Division arrived in the region east of Bastogne in the evening and advanced into its assembly area southeast of the city. The last battalion of the 167. Volksgrenadierdivision was still on the march from its unloading area around Neuenahr to the assembly area of its Division. The 3. Panzergrenadierdivision marched into its assembly area west of Bastogne, one regiment was still on the move. In the course of the day, the enemy managed a breakthrough into the forest southeast of Chenogne (7.5 kilometers south-west of Bastogne). Individual tanks advanced to Senonchamps (4.5 kilometers west of Bastogne). A counterattack was started.[8]

The attack against the Bastogne corridor from the east and west started on 30 December 1944 at 04.00 hours after a short, massive, artillery preparation. The Führer-Begleit-Brigade, elements of the 3. and 15. Panzer-grenadierdivisions attacked from the west, the 167. Volksgrenadierdivision and the "LAH" Division from the east, toward the Bastogne-Martel-lingen/Martellange road. The 3. Pz.Gren.-Div. reached the area immediately north of Villeroux, but was unable to advance farther in the face of strong enemy artillery fire. The attack by the 167. V.G.D. and the "LAH" Division reached the road from Bastogne to Martellingen/Martellange between Sai-wet/Sainlez (nine kilometers south of Bastogne) and Point 535 south of the city. The "LAH" Division captured Losange castle (6.5 kilometers south of Bastogne) and continued to advance farther to the west. At noon, the enemy mounted an attack between Hatrival (three kilometers west of St. Hubert) and Morhet (eleven kilometers southwest of Bastogne) with strong infantry and tank forces of the 87th US Infantry Division and the 11th US Armored Division. At Hatrival, the Americans were repulsed, however, Moircy (eight kilometers southeast of St. Hubert) was lost after bitter fighting. Enemy tanks which had penetrated into Remange (two kilometers southeast of Moircy) were thrown back in a counterattack. Approximately fifty enemy tanks which had broken through to Rechrival (five kilometers north of Morhet) were intercepted by a regiment of the 15. Panzergrenadierdivision north of the village. A counterattack by the Führer-Begleit-Brigade was starting there; fif-teen tanks were knocked out.[9] The Supreme Commander West expected that the Americans would continue to meet the German attack on Bastogne with attacks on a broad front between Hatrival and Sibret. Through those, they sought to gain freedom of action in the area around Bastogne and to capture the region around Houffalize. Since the focal point of the fighting at Heeresgruppe B was clearly in the Bastogne area, the Supreme Commander West intended to move the "HJ" Division there as well.[10]

The following day, 31 December 1944, plainly showed that the forces available for the attack on Bastogne were insufficient. The group in the east gained only little ground. Thus, the group in the west could not start its attack again until noon since it required, as a precondition, the progressing of the attack from the east. In order to support the further attack, the 340. Volksgrenadierdivision and the "HJ" Division were speedily brought up. The Volksgrenadierdivision was to attack along the road from Noville to Bas-togne—i.e. from the northeast—while the "HJ" Division was designated to protect the flanks in the area southwest of Bastogne.[11]

In the war diary of Supreme Command West, the situation was judged as follows:

. . . The decision on the future fate of our own attack rests with this battle. If the enemy forces can be destroyed, the 6. and 5. Panzer-armees will again be freed up and strong enough to continue the attack. If it is unsuccessful, it will mean the end of the offensive operation and the change-over to defensive and attrition fighting. In any case, the most important first result remains that the threat of an enemy offensive on the Rhine and the Palatinate is lifted for the near future.—Heeresgruppe B judges the developments in a similar manner . . .[12]

The first elements of the "HJ" Division departed the area around Sam-rée at 17.00 hours on 31 December 1944. At 23.30 hours, the Divisionsbe-gleitkompanie reached Wigny (11.5 kilometers northwest of Bastogne). The Divisional commander drove ahead to the command post of the Führer-Begleit-Brigade for a briefing on the situation by Oberst Remer. His Brigade was to be relieved by the "HJ" Division and sent into action to help close the ring around Bastogne. The 12. SS-Pz.-Div. was scheduled to reach its assembly area by way of Houffalize.[14]

In reality, only a part of the Division used the road via Houffalize, another part marched via Laroche-Ortho (seven kilometers south-southeast of Laroche)-Beaulieu (three kilometers southwest of Ortho)-Wimbay (five kilometers southwest of Ortho)-Wyompont (on the Ourthe, two kilometers southeast of Wimbay)-Roumont (two kilometers southwest of Wyompont)-Herbaimont (two kilometers southeast of Roumont, on National Route 4, Bastogne-Marche-Namur) into the district northwest of Bastogne.[15] The move caused considerable problems which are shown here with the example of the II./26. The entry in its war diary for 31.12.1944 reads:

. . . 17.00 hours, order from the Regiment concerning the departure and move into the area of Berhain estate, two kilometers southwest of Wigny. The empty vehicles of the Bataillon are, at present, still located in Maldingen (four kilometers southwest of St. Vith, Author) because of lack of fuel. Two vehicles for each rifle company are on the move to Chabrehez [six kilometers northeast of Samrée] for refuelling. The Regiment has issued a total of 1.0 cubic meters of fuel to the Bataillon. Of that, 500 liters are at the present located in Maboge [four kilometers southeast of Laroche] since no empty space for transport is available. The Regiment is providing four trucks [Stabskompanie—staff company] to make the Bataillon ready for the march. Two of these already broke down on the move here. On orders of the Regiment, one Kompanie [7. Kompanie] is being loaded with the SPW-Bataillon [armored personnel carriers]. The remaining rifle companies are loaded on 6 vehicles. At the 8. Kompanie, three rocket launchers and three Pak guns are operational. According to orders, the Bataillon was to be at the departure point of Samrée at 18.15 hours. However, at that time the vehicles have not yet been refuelled and are located in Chabrehez. The Bataillon is awaiting the vehicles at the Honnet estate, three kilometers west of Samrée. The vehicles arrive there at 22.45 hours . . .

The Bataillon reached the destination of its march, Herbaimont, on 1 January at 07.00 hours.[16]

Other elements of the Division marched via Nadrin (six kilometers northeast of Ortho), the Panzerregiment via Houffalize. The Americans intended indeed, as Feldmarschall von Rundstedt assumed, to cut off the German divisions located to the west and northwest of Bastogne through attacks from the south and northwest in the direction of St. Vith. To achieve that, in accordance with an order of 28 December 1944, the III US Corps was to mount an attack on 31 December 1944 from the area southeast and east of Bastogne. Namely, it was planned that the 6th US Armored Division, newly brought in from the district around Arlon, would attack in the direction of St. Vith. The 4th US Armored Division—later replaced by the 11th US Armored Division—would attack toward Houffalize. That plan was altered on 29 and 30 December so that only the 6th Armored Division was to attack from Bastogne in a northeasterly direction, while the 11th Armored was designated for action, under the VIII Corps, southwest of Bastogne. The attack by the 6th Armored was to be joined by only one regiment of the 101st Airborne, to the left of the 6th Armored, for an attack with a limited objective.[17] It was planned that the 35th US Infantry Division and the 26th US Infantry Division would attack to the right of the 6th Armored.

For its mission, the 6th Armored set up Combat Commands "A" and "B". CCA was ordered to attack from Bastogne in an easterly direction, to take Neffe, to clear out the forests to the east and south of the town, and to capture the hill northeast of Wardin. Action by CCB was planned adjacent on the left. It consisted of three Combat Teams (CT). They were constituted as follows:

CT 68 (Davall)
    68th Tank Battalion (without "B"-Company),
    "B"-Company 50th Armored Infantry Battalion,
    1st Platoon "C"-Company 603rd Tank Destroyer -Battalion, and
    3rd Platoon "A"-Company 25th Armored Engineer Battalion;
CT 50 (Wall)
    50th Armored Infantry Battalion (without "B"-Company),
    "B"-Company 68th Tank Battalion,
    2nd Platoon "C"-Company 603rd Tank Destroyer Battalion, and
    1st Platoon "A"-Company 25th Armored Engineer Battalion;

Reserves
>   Headquarters CCB,
>   Battery B 777th Anti Aircraft Artillery Battalion (without elements),
>   "A"-Company 25th Armored Engineer Battalion (remains), and
>   "C"-Company 603rd Tank Destroyer Battalion (remains).[18]

CCA reached its assembly area on schedule. The movements of CCB crossed the route of the 11th Armored Division so that its first elements only reached its assembly area in the evening. CCA postponed the start of the attack because of the delays at CCB and only mounted the attack at noon. Neffe was captured, then the attack was stopped at dusk by German attacks into the flanks. Harassing artillery fire halted the counterattacks. Available for that were, in addition to the three artillery units of the 6th Armored, four more from the 193rd Field Artillery Group which had arrived in Bastogne during the course of the day.[19]

On New Year's Day 1945, the attack, as ordered, by CCA and CCB was resumed at 08.00 hours. CCA was to reach the attack objectives designated for the previous day. A German counterattack stopped the CCA along the line Neffe-Wardin. CCB was able to take Bizory at 10.30 hours, Mageret and Hill 510 immediately west of the village in the afternoon. During the continued attack, the 68th Tank Battalion pushed past to the left of Mageret and into Arloncourt. However, since the 50th Armored Infantry Battalion, adjacent to the left, was unable to advance against determined resistance in the forest areas north of Mageret, the tanks withdrew from Arloncourt during darkness. The 50th Armored Infantry also pulled back to its starting position after it had been hit by a counterattack by elements of Grenadierregiment 78 of the 26. Volksgrenadierdivision, finally brought to a halt by massive artillery fire. The neighbor on the right of the 6th Armored, the 35th Division, was unable to support the attack. Hence, the 6th Armored extended its attack sector up to Bras, so that it reached from Bras to Bourcy. The division sent out all its reserves to reinforce the two Combat Commands.[20]

With justification, the 5. Panzerarmee feared the continuation of the American attack and expected a breakthrough to the east and northeast, since the front of the 26. V.G.D., in action there, was overextended. Hence, it ordered, at approximately noon on 1 January 1945, the move of the "HJ" Division and the hand-over of the sector of the 26. Volksgrenadier-division north and east of Bastogne to the I. SS-Panzer-Korps. Further, it ordered a joint counterattack by 12. SS-Panzer-division, as well as the 26. and 340. Volksgrenadierdivisions in order to push the 6th Armored Division back to Bastogne. Later, the 9. SS-Panzerdivision was also to be brought up.[21]

On 1 January 1945, still, at 16.00 hours, the Divisionsbegleit-kompanie marched off from Wigny to Bourcy in order to take up a prepared rear position south of the village along the railroad line.

Returning units reported that twenty-five tanks were located approximately two kilometers south of the village. All armor piercing weapons were brought into position. During twilight, the first Panzer unit arrived in Bourcy. It consisted of eleven Panzer IVs and Vs which had been readied for action again by the repair company. They had moved during the night of 1 January via Houffalize to Noville and remained there; guarded and under cover.[22]

Part of the reason for the delay in the march by the bulk of the Division was the fact that units, which had already moved into positions west of Bastogne, remained tied down there. Thus, the war diary of the II./26 states:

> . . . 19.05 hours, Bataillon remains in billet area, except for 7. Kompanie, since no fuel has arrived. As on the previous day, 7. Kompanie is being transported by the SPW-Bataillon.—At approximately 16.00 hours, enemy tank spearheads broke through our own main line of resistance in the Cerimont-Hubermont (12.5 and 9.5 kilometers west of Bastogne, respectively) area. For that reason, those parts of the II. Bataillon which are to be left behind, will be sent to take up blocking positions at the crossroads Point 460—Bastogne and Salle—Sprimont (on the National Route, twelve kilometers west of Bastogne), as well as into local securing positions around Herbaimont . . .[23]

During the night of 1 to 2 January 1945, the first elements of the 340. V.G.D. reached the battlefield. They opened that day's fighting. The history of the 68th Tank Battalion relates:

> . . . We prepared to spend the night in Mageret. Parts of it were still burning from our shelling during the day. At 2 A.M., 'Jerry' mounted a ferocious attack on foot from Benonchamps along the Benonchamps-Mageret road. At the same time, a single aircraft dropped bombs into the defensive positions and around them, and helped us by dropping them right between the attackers. After we had fought off that attempt, the enemy swung to the west and approached Mageret along the creek bed from the south. The attack was finally stopped at 04.00 hours after some of the 'Krauts' had penetrated into the village and come within 75 yards of the command post . . .[24]

According to statements by a prisoner, it was the 1. Kompanie of Füsilierbataillon 340 of the 340. V.D.G.[25]

The 6th Armored Division re-organized during the course of the night from 1 to 2 January. CCB was reinforced by the 69th Tank Battalion, bringing it up to two tank units. CCA received two new units from CCR. Around 13.00

hours, the 68th Tank Battalion attacked toward Arloncourt from the Mageret district. The icy slopes hampered the advance. Engineers had to make them passable by spreading straw on them. When the tanks approached Arloncourt, they came under fire from rocket launchers and assault guns. Eight of them were knocked out. The remainder was able to retreat under cover of smoke fired by the artillery. Adjacent to the left, the 50th Armored Infantry Battalion had been attacking since 09.25 hours. It encountered only minor resistance in Oubourcy and took the village at eleven o'clock. However, it came under heavy fire from machine guns and field howitzers from the area of Bourcy. Its attack was supported by twelve artillery units. Thus, it managed to push into Michamps around 15.00 hours against the determined resistance of Grenadierregiment 78 of the 26. Volksgrenadierdivision. In order to restore the situation there, the Panzers of the I. Abteilung, located near Bourcy, together with the attached Divisionsbegleitkompanie, were sent into a counterattack under the command of Obersturmführer Rudolf von Ribbentrop. As they approached, the 50th Armored Infantry abandoned Michamps and Oubourcy which were occupied by Kampfgruppe von Ribbentrop at 19.30 hours. The Divisionsbegleitkompanie, led by Untersturmführer Erwin Stier, who had only returned from hospital in the morning, reconnoitered throughout the night to the west, south and east. The 50th Armored Infantry moved into a defensive position east of the Bois Jacques, approximately along the line of the starting position in the morning of that same day.[26]

Task Force Davall attacked toward Arloncourt from the west at 13.00 hours. While one tank company seized the village under heavy fire cover from the other, a company of the 50th Armored Infantry took the wooded area south of the village. The tanks came under massive fire from Pak and, possibly, PanzerJägers inside the village and its vicinity. Except for one, all tanks of "B"-Company were knocked out. The accompanying infantry suffered severe losses from fire by infantry weapons and was pinned down. The attackers were forced to retreat under cover from artificial smoke. The remnants of "B"-Company and one platoon of infantry pulled back to Mageret. Task Force Kennedy (69th Tank Battalion), adjacent on the right, had to take over a section of TF Davall's (68th Tank Battalion) attack sector and to enlarge its own attack sector to the north in order to establish contact at Mageret.[27] During the previous day, TF Kennedy had attacked the forest east of Mageret and captured it at 12.30 hours. It established its command post in Mageret.[28]

CCA did not gain any ground on 2 January 1945 either. Its attack on Wardin was repulsed, with the loss of 7 tanks of the 15th Tank Battalion and serious losses to the 9th Armored Infantry Battalion.[29]

At noon on 2 January, the chief command of I. SS-Panzer-korps took over command in the sector of XXXXVII. Panzer-korps, designated as the location for the attack. It submitted its plan of attack to the 5. Panzerarmee: The 26.

Volks-grenadier-division was to attack west of the Houffalize-Bastogne road, the 340. Volksgrenadierdivision along both sides of the railroad line Bourcy-Bastogne, the 12. SS-Panzer-division from the area around Michamps on Bastogne. In addition, the 9. SS-Panzerdivision was to be brought up and attached after its arrival. It was then to attack from the forest south of Compogne/Rastadt on Longchamps and Monaville. The attack was scheduled to start on 3 January 1945. The Korps requested a postponement to 4 January. It reported that the bulk of the "HJ" Division would only arrive during the night of 2–3 January, the artillery, except for one light Abteilung, even later. Also, not all elements of the 340. Volksgrenadierdivision could be assembled in the morning. However, the Heeresgruppe insisted on the earlier target date, while agreeing to the overall plan, as did the 5. Panzerarmee.[30] It is probable that the Heeresgruppe pushed for the earlier target date in particular because it expected daily the attack by the Allied northern group, under the command of General Montgomery, with Houffalize as the objective.

On 2 January 1945 at 18.30 hours, the VIII US Corps issued orders for 3 January:

. . .1.b. Third US Army continues the attack to seize Houffalize;

. . .3.c. 101st Airborne

attached: 705th Tank Destroyer Battalion;

CCB, 10th Armored Division;

755th Field Artillery Battalion (155 mm);

969th Field Artillery Battalion (155 H);

(1) Continuation of the defense of the connections center Houffalize;

(2) Attack to the north on orders of the Corps and capture of Noville;

(3) Maintaining contact with the 6th Armored Division and the 17th Airborne Division . . .[31]

Those intentions were thwarted by the attack of the I. SS-Panzerkorps, or already demolished in their initial stages. On the right wing, the so far not completely assembled Division "Hohenstaufen" attacked on 3 January 1945 at 13.00 hours from the Compogne/Rastadt district on Longchamps and Monaville with Panzergrenadierregiment 19 and Panzerregiment 9, which had thirty operational Panzers. Panzergrenadierregiment 20, which arrived later, joined the fighting in progress. The attack stalled under the fire from enemy artillery in front of Hill 497 and the two villages.[32] the After Action report of the VIII Corps reads:

. . . A strong attack by tanks and infantry was repelled by Task Force Higgins in the area of Monaville between 13.30 and 22.00 hours. In the meantime, the 2nd Battalion 327th Glider Infantry of the 502nd Parachute Infantry Regiment was assigned to re-establish the main line of resistance which had been broken by that attack . . .[33]

Feldmarschall Model pressed for the continuation of the attack. However, he finally agreed with the suggestion of the commander of the "Hohenstaufen", Oberführer Silvester Stadler, to capture Longchamps and Monaville in a night attack since a continuation of the attack during the day would cause too high losses.[34]

Avoiding the extensive forests between the Longchamps-Bastogne and Noville-Bastogne roads, the 340. Volksgrenadierdivision and the 12. SS-Panzerdivision were to attack east of the Noville-Bastogne road. For that reason, the 340. V.G.D. assembled Grenadierregiments 694 and 695 in the northern section of the Bois Jacques for the attack. At the same time, the 501st Parachute Infantry Regiment attacked inside the Bois Jacques to the northeast in order to, initially, capture the northeastern section of the forest. That attack pushed into the assembly of the 340. V.G.D. after the forward blocking positions had been overrun. The only available reserve, the Pionierbataillon, (the Füsilierbataillon was located east of Mageret) was sent to mount a counterattack and was able to stop the American attack.[35]

The 12. SS-Panzerdivision was to attack from the area south and southwest of Bourcy, its right wing touching on the rail line Bourcy-Bastogne. The objective of the attack was the northeastern entrance of Bastogne. The following positioning was planned for that: to the right, Panzergrenadierregiment 26 with attached Panzerjägerabteilung 12; to the left, Panzergrenadierregiment 25 and Panzerregiment 12, which had been ordered to cooperate. Obersturmführer von Ribbentrop, as the successor of the killed Sturmbannführer Jürgensen, led I. Abteilung. The artillery was to move into positions in the area north of Bourcy so that it could support the attack by the two regiments. At the time, the Flak-Abteilung was still on the march from Samrée to the Hardigny district where the Divisional command post was located. A forward Divisional command post was established in Bourcy, where the command post of the Artillerieregiment was located. The Flak-Abteilung had been ordered to set up positions in such a manner that it could support the attack with its heavy (8.8 cm) batteries, indirectly trained, while the 3.7 cm battery took over the air defense. A Volks-Artilleriekorps was to be provided to support the attack by the 340. Volksgrenadierdivision and "HJ" Division. No information can be offered on which unit that was, and when and where it took up position.

The move of the "HJ" Division into the assembly area had begun on 1 January. Marching as one of the first elements of Regiment 26 was the SPW-Bataillon, the III./26, during the night of 1 to 2 January, from Rastadt via Mabompre and Vaux to Noville. Vaux was under concentrated shelling, forcing the armored personnel carriers to drive through the village one at a time, and at high speed. At seven o'clock, the Bataillon arrived in Noville together with a company of the II./26 it had brought along. The Bataillon command post was established there, while the 9.–12. Kompanies continued to march approximately another two kilometers in the direction of Bourcy and took up positions in the wooded parcels south of the road. Because of the uncertain enemy situation, the blocking positions were pushed ahead to the south. The 9. Kompanie sent out a scouting party of two NCOs to the south toward the rail line. The first enemy positions were made out approximately 200 meters south of a creek valley which runs in the direction of Au Grand Etang and on to Noville. However, it was not a connected line of positions, rather, they were individual strong points. The scouting party was able to pass through them undetected and reach the country lane leading from Foy to Michamps about one kilometer west of the rail line before noon. Numerous small snow mounds were spotted in the fields and woods. They were killed comrades of the Heer. Their automatic rifles and identification tags were still with them. A sketch of the terrain was drawn up at the field lane mentioned, then the scouting party started its return trip. As it crossed a snow-covered field, the party came under rifle fire from approximately 150 meters away, but was not hit. Subsequently, it even came under artillery fire which seemed to be directed by an aerial observer. Consequently, the leader of 9. Kompanie, Untersturmführer Schmidt, sent forward a Zug of armored personnel carriers to pick up the scouting party. Fortunately, they found each other. The uniforms of the two scouts were frozen solid, they had to be cut from their bodies. The companies advanced into the forest, which reconnaissance had reported to be clear of the enemy, approximately 1.5 kilometers south of the road. Immediately south of the Noville-Bourcy road, a horse-drawn artillery unit—presumably from the 340. Volksgrenadierdivision—had taken up positions. It quickly drew the fire of the enemy artillery on itself.

On 2 January, the II./26, less one company, also moved from the Herbaimont district into the area around Vaux. At 20.45 hours, 1,200 liters of fuel arrived. The vehicles were refuelled and incorporated into the blocking positions. The Bataillon marched off at 22.15 hours and arrived in Vaux, by way of Salle-Gives-Compogne around midnight. One truck took a direct artillery hit on the way, killing three men. From Vaux, the Bataillon advanced to the Noville-Bastogne road. There it dismounted and made camp in Rachamps. The empty vehicles were sent back to Wicourt.[37]

During the morning of 3 January 1945, the Division assembled for the attack, grouped as ordered: the II./26 to the left of the III./26 in a wooded area approximately two kilometers south of the Noville-Bourcy road and adjoining on the rail line to the left; to its left, the I./26. During the attack, the III. Bataillon was to follow the II. Bataillon to the right rear and cover the right flank. The mortar Zug of the III./26 was attached to II. Bataillon. The assembly was completed by 12 noon.[38]

It is not known when the other Bataillons and Abteilungen were assembled. The start of the attack, which had initially been scheduled for 10 A.M., had to be delayed until 14.00 hours because of the late arrival of the II./26 for the reasons mentioned.

The war diary of the II./26 notes: ". . . 13.00 hours, loud battle noise at the right neighbor (enemy pushes into the assembly) . . ."[39] Evidently, the neighbor in question was the 340. V.G.D. The previously given information from both sides concerning the developments there was confirmed by that.

As ordered, the attack by Regiment 26 started at 14.00 hours. In a rapid advance, the III./26 reached the rail line at the crossing of the Foy-Michamps country lane, without having contact to the neighbor on the right. The II. Bataillon, advancing after having dismounted, fell behind but reached the rail crossing at 14.50 hours as well. Weak enemy resistance from the Bois Jacques was quickly overcome. The fire from that forest increased more and more during the further advance to the southwest. It could not be eliminated by the III. Bataillon either, despite the fact that a part of it moved over to the west side of the rail line again. At approximately 16.00 hours, the II. Bataillon encountered determined resistance north of the Azette forest and was attacked by three Shermans. Two of them were knocked out by the 7. Kompanie using Panzerfausts, the other by Panzerjägerabteilung 12 and the gun Zug of the III./26. The 5. and 6. Kompanies, located immediately east of the woods north of the Azette forest, received violent fire from the flanks. They suffered high losses in the open snow-covered field and were forced to stop the attack. The 7. Kompanie, in action on the right, came under heavy fire from the Bois Jacques, to the right and ahead. It also took high losses and stalled. The III./26 lost several armored personnel carriers to fire from anti-tank guns and bazookas—six at the 9. Kompanie alone—but suffered only minor losses of personnel. The enemy was out of range of the 2 cm three-barreled guns of the SPW-Bataillon. The attack was halted there also. After the fall of darkness, 4 of the 6 knocked-out armored personnel carriers of the 9. Kompanie were towed away by the repair Zug of the Bataillon despite the artillery fire. Their crews, who had bailed out, secured at the edge of the woods in the direction of the hill south of Oubourcy and the Azette forest.[40]

Oberscharführer Ewald Rien reported on the situation at the 7. Kompanie:

. . . Any movement was answered by heavy fire from the right flank as well as from the hills in front of the Kompanie. Obersturmführer Werner Löbzien, the chief of the 7. Kompanie, was among the many men already killed or wounded. However, they could not be rescued or cared for because of the heavy fire. Any attempt ended with being wounded or killed. There was no choice but to wait for darkness and then to assemble the Kompanie and send it into action again. After it had turned dark, we collected our wounded as best possible and pulled our forward line back by about 300–400 meters. Orders arrived from the Bataillon to dig in there. Of the IV. Zug, led by Oberscharführer Müller, which had remained behind at the corner of the woods, no-one was found again. They were all missing. Since all of the Kompanie leaders had been lost, I ordered the Kompanietruppführer (company squad leader) of 7. Kompanie, Oberscharführer Kowalski, to determine the strength of the three companies: At approximately 20.00 hours, the II. Bataillon was only about sixty NCOs and men strong . . .[41]

It is noted in the war diary of the II./26 that most of the wounded had to be carried to the rear by members of the Bataillon since the ambulance armored vehicle was inoperative, and the four-wheeled ambulance car could only transport one wounded bedded down or three sitting up.

Panzergrenadierregiment 25 assembled to the left of Regiment 26, together with the Panzerregiment, in the open terrain northwest of Michamps: on the right, the II.; on the left, the I.; behind, as reserve, the III. Bataillon. Despite support by the Panzers, the attack by the Regiment stalled, under the concentrated fire from artillery and mortars, northeast of the Azette forest. Serious losses were suffered there again. The Panzers of I. Abteilung were able to advance along the Michamps-Arloncourt road to that village. They managed to drive back the Americans, located west and northwest of it, in collaboration with the Schwere Panzerjäger-Abteilung 560, attacking via Oubourcy. The I. Abteilung set up its command post in the forester's house in the La Hez forest, one kilometer northeast of Arloncourt.

As the other side saw it, the day progressed as follows (the sequence from west to east was chosen also): The attack by the III. and II./26 threatened the flank of the right wing of the 501st Parachute Infantry Regiment which had attacked to the northeast at noon. In order to maintain, or re-establish, contact with the 6th Armored Division adjacent to the east, the Regiment withdrew to a prepared rear position farther to the south in the course of the afternoon. Together with it was "A"-Company of the 50th Armored Infantry which was to maintain the contact. The After Action Report of that battalion states:

. . . That was a battle between ground troops. Only men and tanks were in combat since the aircraft from both sides could not take off because of the bad weather, and the observation by the artillery deteriorated all the time. Finally, when the visibility was down to zero, the Germans played their trump card: They sent their reserves into battle. These exerted such pressure that the much weakened battalion had to withdraw to its starting line west (should probably read: east, Author) of the Bois Jacques to avoid being encircled. The extended line could not be held. In order to overcome the now critical situation, all available troops were thrown into the front lines, without regard to their original tasks . . . Everything seemed to work, as in a giant conspiracy, in favor of the 'Nazis'. The heavy cold, the extremely poor visibility, the lack of contact and organization helped the enemy who was, already, numerically superior . . .[42]

At the 69th Tank Battalion, adjacent to the east, 4 tanks were knocked out. At 15.00 hours, it was forced to retreat to a more favorable position north and east of Bizory. The history of the Battalion states:

. . . As far as we knew, that was the first time we had to retreat because of enemy pressure. It was a bitter pill to swallow, to give up terrain for which we had fought so doggedly, but it had to be . . .

The new position ran from the Bizory-Foy lane in a curve around the northern and eastern sections of Bizory, along the Bizory-Mageret road to half-way to Mageret. There, a link-up existed to TF Kennedy (among others, the 69th Tank Battalion and "A"-Company of the 44th Armored Infantry Battalion).[43] The After Action Report of CCB also indicates that, from 16.00 hours onwards, the fire from German artillery and rocket launchers increased extraordinarily, while the 6th Armored Division recorded that its artillery concentrated heavy shelling on Michamps, Arloncourt and Bourcy.[44]

The "HJ" Division ordered the attack to be continued on 4 January 1945. The II./26 was to attack along the rail line—on its eastern side—to a point 1.5 kilometers northwest of Bizory and then turn toward the village. Panzerjägerabteilung 12 was to advance along the eastern edge of the forest and provide flanking fire into the wood ahead of the Bataillon, to which the 13. (heavy infantry gun) Kompanie had also be attached. The III./26 was given the task of advancing on foot to the west of the rail line, covering the open right flank of the Regiment, since the 340. V.G.D. had not caught up. The I. Bataillon was to follow to the left rear of the II./26. Adjoining on the left of Regiment 26, Regiment 25, together with the Panzerregiment, was to continue the attack, its focal point on the left, and with Mageret as the attack objective. The start of the attack was ordered for 04.00 hours, with a surprise attack by artillery and rocket launchers. [45]

The attack began, as scheduled, at 04.00 hours. The III./26 and the II./26 initially encountered only weak resistance since the enemy had pulled back his forward line during the night. Between 06.30 and 07.00 hours, they reached the railroad bridge across the country road from Foy to Mageret. Oberscharführer Ewald Rien of the 7. Kompanie reported on the progress of that attack:

. . . After some 800 meters, the spearhead came under machine gun fire. Oberscharführer Kowalski and I went forward and determined that the fire came from tanks. We had no more Panzerfausts, so we fired a rifle-grenade at the tank. That was apparently enough to make the crew bail out. A closer look showed that we had captured two operational Shermans. The companies continued to advance and reached the lane and railroad bridge Foy-Mageret at first light of day . . .[46]

The III./26 also started out as ordered and reached the railroad bridge across the Foy-Mageret lane around 07.00 hours. There, it established its Bataillon command post and a field dressing station with one ambulance armored personnel carrier and one ambulance vehicle under the command of Oberleutnant Dr. Rathmann.[47]

Regiment 25, to the left of Regiment 26, had stalled under heavy enemy fire, in particular from artillery which, at times, fired phosphorus shells, in a line with the Azette forest. Hence, the commander of Regiment 26, Sturmbannführer Krause ordered that the attack be stopped at the line it had reached. In the meantime, a battalion of the 340. V.G.D., in action to the right of the rail line, had also arrived at the Foy-Mageret lane. It took over guarding the railroad bridge. The II./26 made contact on the left in order to close the gap to the I./26., which had been created by the falling behind of Regiment 25. At 16.00 hours on 4 January, the combat strength of the II./26, without the operational staff and without 8. Kompanie, totaled: one NCO and twenty-eight men.[48]

The 340. Volksgrenadierdivision, in action to the right of the "HJ" Division, had started its attack soon after midnight. By eleven o'clock, it had reached a line from Foy along the path to the southeast to the railway crossing. It then cleared the forest north of that line in bitter fighting.[49]

As already mentioned, Regiment 25 and the Panzerregiment were only able to gain little ground. With the coming of daylight, they were hit and pinned down, time and again by concentrated enemy artillery shelling. Because of the high losses suffered by the I. and II. Bataillons, their remnants were consolidated. Hauptsturmführer Werner Damsch took over the command, while Obersturmbannführer Richard Schulze was transferred to the officer reserve. When he reported to the Divisional command post, it was noted that his overcoat had countless burn holes from the phosphorus shells. On 19 January 1945, the order reached the Division that Obersturmbannführer Richard Schulze had been transferred to the officer cadet school at Tölz as its commander and that he was to leave immediately.

The daily report of Supreme Command West states:

. . . A Kampfgruppe of the 12. SS-Panzerdivision was able to advance to one kilometer north of Bizory against strong enemy pressure. East of that, our own attacks stalled in consequence of heavy fire from the flank and strong artillery and anti-tank fire . . .[50]

On the American side, the 501st Parachute Infantry Regiment was scheduled to attack again on 4 January. It was able to advance only slowly. Because of the attack by Regiment 26, contact to the neighbor on the east, the 50th Armored Infantry, was lost. At approximately 16.30 hours, members of "A"-Company of that battalion were retreating in groups of four and five men each. The leader of that unit reported that he could not hold his position. Around 20.00 hours, the 501st Regiment sent a part of its reserve, Task Force O'Hara, into a counterattack. Opposing it, an attack by an infantry company with eight Panzers (presumably Panzerjägers, Author) developed along the rail line and brought the counterattack to a halt. The gap could not be closed. As proposed by the 501st Regiment, the 101st Airborne Division allowed both battalions to be pulled back.[51] The After Action report of the 50th Armored Infantry reads:

> . . . By the night of 4 January, so many officers and NCOs in key positions had been lost that the battalion was completely confused. There was another retreat, to a line which ran from the railway northeast of La Hez to the road junction northwest of Bizory. There, a mixed company from the remains of the infantry was set up. All officers of "A"-Company had become casualties . . .[52]

According to the report from the 6th Armored Division, strong pressure also developed on the right wing during the second half of the day to the point where it had to be pulled back into a more "favorable position". Emphasis is put, in particular, on the extremely heavy fire from artillery, mortars and rocket launchers which lasted, as did the fire from light weapons, throughout the whole day. However, the American artillery also supported the defense throughout the day and covered the withdrawal. from 16.00 hours onwards, the 69th Tank Battalion was also forced to withdraw.[53]

On 4 January 1945, the OKW issued an order concerning the continued conduct of the fighting. The passages, which concerned Heeresgruppe B, read:

> . . . The Supreme Commander West was ordered to smash the Anglo-American armies through a series of attacks in quick succession in order to hold on to the initiative under any circumstances. The attack sectors would be determined by the Führer . . .
>
> The first objective of Heeresgruppe B was to tie down the enemy concentrated in front of its line and to annihilate the enemy near Bastogne so as to firm up its position. Subsequently, it would have to establish a strong southern front . . .[53a]

For 5 January 1945, the I. SS-Panzerkorps ordered the continuation of the attack. The 340. Volksgrenadierdivision and Panzergrenadierregiment 26, with Panzerjägerabteilung 12, were to continue the attack to the southwest along both sides of the Bourcy-Bastogne rail line. Panzergrenadierregiment 25 and the Panzerregiment were given the task of breaking through between the Azette forest and the wooded area north of Mageret to Bizory.[54]

In the morning of 5 January, reconnaissance by the 340. Volksgrenadierdivision determined that the enemy had abandoned the positions he had held the previous evening. Weapons and equipment laying about indicated a hasty departure. The Division pursued immediately in order to gain the attack objective: the lane from Foy to the railroad station. Just before reaching the lane, it encountered determined resistance from well-fortified strongholds. It was forced to stop the attack and change over to defense.[55]

Combat reconnaissance sent out by the II./26 during the night of 4 to 5 January determined that the enemy had abandoned the Azette forest east of the rail line and the woods north of Bizory, and that the rail line up to the station was clear of the enemy. In the early morning hours, the III./26 advanced on the west side of the rail line to the crossing near the station. It then continued on to the forest lane, which ran to the northwest, 200 meters west of the station. Since the attack objective had been reached, and since forces to continue the attack were lacking, the Bataillon prepared for defense. While the men were digging in, they were surprised by mortar fire which lasted for a lengthy period of time. The shells exploding in the tops of the trees had a devastating effect, they caused high losses. The 9. Kompanie lost almost 80% of its fighting strength, more than half of that number were killed. Additional men were wounded during the transport of their wounded comrades. Two NCOs and six men of the Kompanie remained in the position and continued to strengthen it. A scouting party sent out during the next days came upon the enemy mortar position which had by then been abandoned. It was equipped with captured German 8 cm mortars.[55a]

Simultaneously with the III. Bataillon, the II./26 advanced to the southern edges of the woods north of Bizory. To the left of the II./26, the I./26 connected south of the crossroads, 1.3 kilometers northeast of Bizory. Elements of Regiment 25 and of the Panzerregiment succeeded in capturing Mageret and Hill 510 immediately west of it. The hill could not be held because of the heavy fire from tanks in Bizory and the American artillery. However, the town remained in German hands. The daily report of Supreme Command West states, inter alia:

> . . . Our assault troops mounted an attack on Bastogne from the north and northeast. They were able to gain much ground against bitter enemy resistance. The wood northeast of Bizory was reached. Mageret was captured. The battles are continuing . . .[56]

The commander of the Kampfgruppe consisting of the remnants of I. and II./25, Hauptsturmführer Werner Damsch, remembers that day as follows:

> . . . After the assembly in the wooded area in front of us during the evening twilight, and after orders for the further advance had been issued, I wanted to make contact with our neighbor on the left to discuss the course of the attack. On my way there, at around 19.00 hours, an enemy artillery salvo caught me and both my legs were wounded, leaving me lying, unable to move, in the open terrain of the no man's land. I then had the almost unimaginable good fortune that a crew on a tracked motorcycle from our Panzer-Abteilung spotted me at about 1 A.M. They transported me through the violent artillery fire on a wild drive to the dressing station . . .[57]

The forces of the "HJ" Division had been used up to the point where an attack on a broad front could not be continued. Its heavy losses were caused, in particular, by the enemy artillery, tanks and tank destroyers. However, the situation on the American side was also critical. The history of the 68th Tank Battalion of the 6th Armored Division recorded on that:

> . . . The strain was terrible, the men were dog-tired, their faces mask-like, not showing any emotions. While the previously mentioned activity (attacks by tanks and infantry, artillery shelling) lasted throughout the day, Bastogne and its surroundings lay under constant fire from heavy guns. The whole city resembled a slaughterhouse. It will probably never be known how desperate our situation was. One can only now imagine what von Rundstedt's troops could have done, had they been able to break through our positions. We were at the focal point of the events. If 'Jerry' had succeeded in taking Bastogne, he would have had in his possession a major route with an excellent road net to all points. Then, he could have revitalized his assault and no-one can say how far he could have gone, or how much time we would have lost . . .[58]

The relief of the 9. SS-Panzerdivision "Hohenstaufen" by the 26. V.G.D. in the Longchamps-Monaville sector had begun in the course of 5 January 1945. The 9. SS-Panzerdivision was to be moved to the threatened northern sector of the 6. Panzerarmee. On orders of the 5. Panzerarmee, the "HJ" Division was also to be relieved, by the 340. V.G.D., in order to be available as a Korps reserve. At 03.45 on 6. January, a battalion of the 340. V.G.D. began relieving the II./26. It assembled at the railroad underpass, one kilometer north of the station, as battle reserve of Regiment 26. During the night, at

23.30 hours, a preliminary order for the relief of Regiment 26 by the 340.
V.G.D. arrived.[59]

There is almost no information available from the German side regarding its offensive actions on 6 and 7 January.

However, a report from Unterscharführer Alfred Schulz of Panzerjäger-abteilung 12, who was wounded on that day, is quite illuminating. He wrote:

> . . . After several night battles we had cleared, together with our infantry, the wooded terrain up to Bastogne [meant are the forests between the rail line Bourcy-Bastogne and the Bourcy-Mageret road]. The Panzers of Obersturmführer Hurdelbrink (chief of 1. Kompanie), Untersturmführer Rehn (2. Kompanie) and Unterscharführer Schulz (2. Kompanie) had advanced the farthest. In the morning of 6 January, we were firing on enemy targets immediately north of Bastogne [presumably in the vicinity of Bizory]. Suddenly, the edge of the forest came under violent artillery fire. Untersturmführer Rehn was wounded, his Panzer was hit [damage to the track]. We pulled back into the woods out of range of the artillery shelling. I was removing telephone wires which had wound themselves around the axle of the drive sprocket when I was wounded by a sudden artillery attack.
>
> The crew of Untersturmführer Rehn's Panzer sought cover with us since their vehicle was no longer operational. I did not want to give up that Panzer and attempted, on my own, to salvage it. I drove my Panzer forward, the accompanying infantry and Rehn's crew came along. The terrain had been plowed by shells. Under the infernal shelling, we managed to hook up the tow ropes. However, I was unable to move the Panzer even one centimeter. It was able to operate only on one track and dug itself into the soft ground. The Panzer sat with its hull stuck to the ground. I had the tow ropes unhooked again and ordered to go back. When Schütze [rifleman] Fuchs was disengaging the tow rope, he was seriously wounded by the constant artillery fire. A shell fragment hit him in the back, his ripped belt dropped to the ground. We bedded him on the front of my Panzer, his comrades were holding him gently. By the time we were out of shelling range, he was already dead. Obersturmführer Hurdelbrink enquired about my wound. I had a shell fragment in my left thigh. Obersturmführer Hurdelbrink directed that I be transported back to the dressing station immediately. I handed my Panzer over to the gunner, left my belt and pistol behind, since I wanted to return right away. The Kompanie squad vehicle was delivering mail and provisions, and it took me along to the physician. He ordered an immediate transfer to a hospital . . .[60]

It is reported for 7 January in the history of the 68th Tank Battalion that, at four o'clock, "Jerry" had attacked toward Bizory along the path which leads from Bizory to the northeast (presumably the Bizory—Arloncourt path):

> . . . We held him off, but the pressure continued until the break of day. 'Jerry' swung off to the west, several fanatical enemies penetrated into the village. At about nine o'clock several riflemen were firing. Our infantry and engineers then cleared the village.

German Panzers and artillery had also fired at the positions of the tank unit throughout the day, but they had been held.[61]

The relief of Regiment 26 commenced on 7 January 1945. Oberscharführer Ewald Rien of the II./26 reported on its progress:

> . . . On 7 January at 03.00 hours, the combat strength of the Bataillon amounted to 16 NCOs and men. Around that time, we heard a unit approaching through a glade which ran approximately 300 meters northeast of the rail station. A battalion of a Volksgrenadierdivision was looking for the II./26 in order to relieve us. After we had briefed the relieving unit, we walked along the rail line back into the Bourcy area. From there, we were taken by a troop transport vehicle to Wicourt (3.5 kilometers north of Noville, Author). As I recall, the losses of 7. Kompanie in the period from 3 to 7 January 1945 amounted to tweny-three killed, approximately fifty wounded and twenty-one missing. The missing never reappeared again, even after the war it was impossible to locate them through the tracing service . . .

The attack by the "HJ" Division had brought its spearheads at the rail station to within 3.5 kilometers of the city center of Bastogne. However, from that location there was no possibility to observe into the city. The Heeresgruppe wanted to have at least the capability of shelling the city and its vicinity by artillery, under observation. Hence, it ordered the Division to capture Hill 510 immediately west of Mageret. Pointing out the losses suffered so far, and the exhaustion of the troops, the Division tried to have the order lifted. However, Feldmarschall Model insisted on his order. Thus, the Division handed the task of carrying it out to the commander of the Pionierbataillon, Hauptsturmführer Hannes Taubert. Of his own Bataillon, only the 2. Kompanie under Obersturmführer Hans Richter was available to him. The 1. and 3. Kompanies had been assigned to the two Panzergrenadierregiments, the 4. Kompanie was located behind Regiment 25 as air defense and to cover the flanks.

At noon on 7 January, Hauptsturmführer Taubert and Obersturmführer Richter were briefed at the Division command post on the situation and the mission. Obersturmführer Richter reported on that:

> . . . The Divisional commander insisted on personally showing Hauptsturmführer Taubert and me the terrain. We climbed onto an armored personnel carrier and were made, as best possible, familiar with the area. It had snowed, the weather was misty, the visibility was poor.
>
> During the scouting drive we encountered several Panzers of the von Ribbentrop Kompanie which were securing in the direction of Bizory. The commanders briefed us on their observations.
>
> After returning to the Divisional command post, the Divisional commander gave orders to provide snow suits to camouflage the attackers.
>
> Around noon, the 2. Kompanie reached Mageret. The vehicles were left outside the village and camouflaged. The required preparations, such as putting together concentrated and elongated charges, readying the flame throwers, etc., were carried out.
>
> As far as I know, the Divisional command post was located in a building next to the church. The Bataillon physician, Stabsarzt [staff physician] Dr. Zöberlein also set up the dressing station in a cellar there. My command post was situated before the attack in a house at the western edge of Mageret, located directly by a road leading to Bizory. A communications squad had already moved into the house. There was a telephone connection to the Divisional command post. Contact was quickly established with the leader of the Volksgrenadierdivision unit which was to relieve the 2. Kompanie after the seizure of Hill 510. He was a Hauptmann, already in Mageret. The village was under constant enemy shelling . . .[63]

Since the inspection of the area had revealed that the 2. Pionierkompanie was not strong enough for its scheduled task, the Divisionsbegleitkompanie was assigned to Hauptsturmführer Taubert. It was transported to Mageret during the night of 7 to 8 January.[64] In addition, the Panzers sitting in positions around Mageret were available to Hauptsturmführer Taubert. The attack was to be supported by all of the Divisional artillery, Korpsartillerieabteilung 501 and by rocket launchers. The attack plan envisaged that an artillery fire attack be concentrated on Hill 510 just before daybreak on 8 January. The 2. Pionierkompanie had the task of attacking from its assembly area, in the western section of Mageret, south of the road to Bizory and to take the Hill.

It was the mission of the Divisionsbegleitkompanie, under the command of Untersturmführer Erwin Stier, to attack to the left of the 2. Pionierkompanie in the direction of Hill 510, and to secure its open left flank.

As planned, the attack started on 8 January 1945 at approximately 07.30 hours. Obersturmführer Richter described its course as follows:

> . . . The 2. Kompanie was assembled for the attack after the camouflage clothing had been provided in time. The strength of the 2. Kompanie amounted to barely eighty men. The fire attack by our artillery on Hill 510 lasted for about five minutes. The enemy returned the fire. His artillery salvos mostly hit the western edge of Mageret. Some houses were set on fire. At 07.30 hours, the 2. Kompanie attacked: On the right, II. Zug under Hauptscharführer Hofmann, I. Zug under Untersturmführer Rehme in the middle, III. Zug under Hauptscharführer Waltring on the left. I was with I. Zug, together with the Kompanie squad. Because the reconnaissance and the reports from von Ribbentrop's Panzer commander had indicated that enemy tanks were located in the Bizory area, II. Zug was purposely sent into action on the right. Hauptscharführer Hofmann—he was the holder of three or four tank destruction badges—and some of his men were especially experienced in fighting tanks. It was remarkable that the enemy artillery fire hardly touched the attack sector of the Kompanie. However, the fire from enemy infantry weapons was all-the-stronger. Despite their snow suits, the attackers made good targets since their bodies were silhouetted against the burning village. Thus, most casualties were caused by rifle and machine gun fire. Next to me, one of my messengers, Sturmmann Schwui, was killed by a shot to the head, and Sturmmann Gude by a bullet in the chest.
>
> The enemy resistance strongholds were overcome. Several tanks, which had been dug in there, were put out of action with explosives and flame-throwers. It also turned out that our artillery had performed good preparatory work.
>
> Around 09.39 hours, the Hill was in our hands. By field telephone I reported to the Ia of the Division that Hill 510 had been captured and occupied. He congratulated me and the Kompanie on that success. I explained to the Ia that the losses of the Kompanie had been significant and that, because of them, it would be impossible to hold the Hill in case of a counterattack. He told me that he would immediately arrange for a unit of the Volksgrenadierdivision to move up. The Kompanie would be reinforced or relieved. Regrettably, a lengthy delay occurred since that unit was not assigned to the 'HJ' Division. The reinforcement or relief did not take place in time. In the meantime, the enemy mounted a counter-thrust with

tanks from the direction of Bizory and Harzy (two kilometers southeast of Mageret). The pressure from those tanks—there were about
ten—attacking from the Bizory area kept increasing. The considerable number of casualties, the loss of most squad leaders and the
lack of Panzerfausts made it impossible to hold the Hill. The Kompanie was forced to withdraw, fighting, to Mageret. The leader of III.
Zug, Hauptscharführer Hofmann, reported the destruction of two
tanks. The reports of losses from the various units indicated that
approximately 35 NCOs and men were killed, wounded or missing.
Several men, among them Unterscharführer Giermann, died at the
dressing station from their serious wounds. One of those missing
was the leader of III. Zug, Hauptscharführer Waltring . . .[65]

The Divisionsbegleitkompanie attacked together with the 2. Pionierkompanie. Its diary stated:

. . . The Kompanie was only able to advance 400–500 meters before
it was forced to a halt by overwhelming enemy fire from heavy
machine guns and tanks. Enemy tanks were moving in. The Kompanie suffered some losses. The I. Zug, under the command of
Untersturmführer Horstmann, was sent into action as a reserve Zug
by the Kompanie commander, Untersturmführer Stier. Based on the
situation, the Zug had to by-pass the Kompanie, swinging left, in
order to support the attack on the flank. It ended up in a hollow
which was dominated by strong fire from heavy machine guns and
tanks, and suffered high losses. On orders from Hauptsturmführer
Taubert, the Kompanie was to pull back unnoticed. However, since
the terrain was completely open and easily observed, and since the
newly fallen snow offered no chance of camouflage, the enemy spotted the move to disengage. The men crawling back came under
heavy fire from sharpshooters, tank machine guns and heavy
machine guns which, again, caused many losses. At approximately
11.00 hours, the Kompanie reached the village exit from Mageret
again. Our own Panzers had knocked out seven enemy tanks . . .[66]

The 8.8 cm batteries of the Flakabteilung fired, aiming indirectly, at
ground targets in Bizory and Bastogne.
The history of the 68th Tank Battalion reports on that day:

. . . On 8 January, the enemy again mounted a joint attack by tanks
and infantry against our right flank and along the Bizory-Mageret
road. Six tanks of 'A'-Company were knocked out like clay pigeons,
their fire could not effectively hit 'Jerry' in his positions. Finally,
there was fire support from the adjacent 69th (Tank Battalion,

Author), but it also was without effect. The enemy then concentrated on the hill south of the road and southwest of Mageret. In the end, before he could inflict major damage, 'Jerry' was driven off by our tank destroyers and artillery . . .[67]

The Unit History of the 68th Tank Battalion recorded, as the start time for the German attack: ". . . 8 January, at dawn . . ."[68]

In the course of the morning, Feldmarschall Model telephoned the Division, just when the report on the capture of Hill 510 had been received. He congratulated the Division and ordered the continuation of the attack on Bizory. Later, it had to be reported that the important Hill had been lost again and that no forces were available to restart the attack.

In the evening hours, Untersturmführer Stier sent out a scouting party from Mageret in order to search and bring back the wounded and killed left behind on the Hill. The scouting party, consisting of volunteers—one NCO and six men—came under rifle fire during its first advance, according to the report from Unterscharführer Gerd Rittner, and was forced to wait for darkness. More newly fallen snow and snow drifts hampered the search. They managed to bring back Unterscharführers Schlender and Becher, as well Sturmmann Nydza, alive but wounded. They had waited out the day in the snow. Killed men brought back were: Untersturmführer Horstmann, the leader of I. Zug; Sturmmänner Semran, Schmidtke, Kokemüller, König, Oberschütze (Pfc) Krüger, the Schützen (privates) Kalies, Schroeder and Kessel. The missing Schütze Rind had been able to get back on his own after the fall of darkness. Before that attack, the Zug had a combat strength of one officer, two NCOs and nineteen men. Of them, one officer and nine men had been killed.[69]

The daily report of Supreme Command West of 8 January 1945 states: ". . . Our attack, mounted east of Bastogne, did not advance further after initial success. . ."[70]

The order from the 5. Panzerarmee for the I. SS-Panzerkorps had been to throw back the enemy, engaged in attacking from Bastogne to the north, northeast and east, to Bastogne. The "HJ" Division, although badly weakened itself, had succeeded in initially halting the attack by Combat Command B of the 6th Armored Division, after bitter and bloody fighting, near Michamps. In the course of several days of pursuing attacks, the enemy had been thrown back to a line railroad station-Bizory-Mageret, and, finally, Mageret had been captured. A breakthrough by weak—too weak—elements into Bizory could no longer be taken advantage of because of a lack of forces. The dominating Hill 510 west of Mageret had been captured in a final effort, but could not be held. Hence, at the end of the attack operation, the Division was situated along the line railroad station-edges of the woods 500 meterse north of Bizory-Mageret. It had advanced to within 3.5 kilometers of the center of Bastogne. The enemy, vastly superior in tanks and tank destroyers, had suffered considerable losses in troops and equipment. The backbone of his defense were tanks and tank destroyers, in particular, however, his artillery which obviously had a plentiful supply of ammunition available. Despite that, the Americans had been forced back to their starting positions of 1 January.

The "HJ" Division had also suffered heavy losses. They could only be illustrated with a few examples since there are no surviving reports on losses. They are available only from the Schwere Panzerjägerabteilung 560. During the period from 2 to 10 January 1945, that Abteilung lost in the Bastogne combat theater: killed, three NCOs and two men; wounded, three NCOs and eight men; missing, three men. No information can be provided on the losses of Panzers and Jagdpanzers. The figures occasionally mentioned in enemy reports are, with certainty, too high.

With the attack on Hill 510, the offensive action by the "HJ" Division in the Ardennes came to an end. Starting on 7 January, it began to be relieved by elements of the 340. Volksgrenadierdivision. After fuel had arrived, it moved into an assembly area near Deyfeldt, 15.5 kilometers southwest of St. Vith. The departure was delayed since the fuel had, partially, to be transported in from the region around Cologne. The chief of the 5. Kraftfahrkompanie (motor vehicle company) of the Divisionsnachschubtruppen 12 (supply troops), Untersturmführer Walter Bald, reported on that:

> . . . Snow and ice covered the roads. Feldmarschall Model ordered: 'Sand into the sacks!'. Each vehicle had to carry a sack with sand in order to scatter it on the roads as required.
>
> The march back began. Fuel was urgently required. Ten Ford trucks were carrying fuel for the troops. Because of the urgency, the commander of the Divisionsnachschubtruppen, Sturmbannführer Rolf Kolitz, supervised the rapid servicing in the fuel depot. We were supposed to be loading at 10 P.M., but no fuel was there. So we had to wait until the tankers arrived. Then we had to pour the fuel into barrels which were loaded onto the vehicles. We set out at dawn. The roads were icy but, after a short drive, the sun was bright in the sky. We sought cover from an air attack in a forest clearing. Two vehicles did not manage to get under cover in time, American aircraft fired at them and they burned out.
>
> As we continued the march, two vehicles became unserviceable due to transmission damage, and then we had only six left. During the day individual vehicles were only able to travel short distances before having to look for cover. At the fall of darkness, the speed increased again. Another vehicle was lost to a damaged transmission. Around 22.00 hours we reached the Divisional staff. We were immediately greeted with the question: 'Do you have any juice?— We've got to get out of here!' We supplied several units with the

smallest possible amounts. Three trucks drove over to the Flakabteilung which was still firing at ground targets. The direct path
there was under enemy fire, hence we had to follow a detour. The
snow was deep, we could not see any trail to follow. We moved a
pace at-a-time, the co-driver sat on the fender or walked a few steps
ahead of the vehicle. That was the only way we could advance slowly.
Suddenly, the front vehicle lost the road and drove into the ditch.
The other two could not get by, but we were also unable to open up
the way. Two men walked off to locate the German position. When
we arrived there, the troops were overjoyed. A big Flak tractor
pulled the trucks free, and then we unloaded.

We made better time on the way back. Some men had suffered
frostbite sitting on the fenders, but we had carried out our task . . .[70a]

The combat-ready elements of the I. Panzerabteilung and of Panzerjägerabteilung 12 remained in the Michamps region until approximately 10
January 1945 as a battle reserve of the Korps.

During those days, probably on 9 January, parts of the I. Panzerabteilung
were sent into action with the 26. V.G.D. west of the Noville-Bastogne road.
In the course of an attack, enemy elements had advanced to outside of
Noville. The enemy was to be repelled by a night counterattack. Obersturmführer von Ribbentrop, together with the remaining Panthers of I.
Abteilung, was attached to the 26. V.G.D. for that counterattack. A night
attack by the Panzers in the forest could not be considered, they were able
only to watch the attack by the Grenadiers. Their attack was repulsed.[71]

Probably on 10 January, Untersturmführer Engel, with 3 Panthers which
had just become operational and several Panzerjäger IVs of Panzerjägerabteilung 12, was sent into action near Arloncourt in order to strengthen the
anti-tank capabilities of the Volksgrenadiers in position there. However, during the night that group received orders to move out of the positions and
join their Abteilungen.[72]

In the meantime, Hauptsturmführer Hans Siegel who, as the commander of the II. (mixed) Abteilung of Panzerregiment 12, had been posted
to Fallingbostel together with his unit's Panzer-less crews, had arrived at the
Division. He was ordered to locate all damaged Panzers of the I. Abteilung in
the whole combat theater, to expedite their repair and then to assemble
them. Panzers which could not be repaired were to be blown up.

The units of the Division arrived in the area around Deyfeldt one after
the other. The Aufklärungsabteilung was given a securing task, but had contact with the enemy.

Damaged vehicles were towed in and repaired. The troops were busy
cleaning and maintaining their weapons, equipment and clothing. Frostbite,
other illnesses and minor wounds were treated. As much as possible, they
enjoyed a rest. The first replacements arrived. On 12 January 1945, the fol-

lowing were assigned to the II./26: one officer (Untersturmführer Sprotte), four NCOs and twenty-four men. On 14 January, the commissioned positions in the Bataillon were manned as follows:

Position	Rank	Name	Rank Since	Born
Commander	SS-Hstuf.(active)	Ott, Alfons	9.11.43	1917
Adjutant	SS-Ostuf.(reserve)	Lübbe, Harro	9.11.44	1920
Orderly Off.	manned by NCOs			
Admin. Off.	SS-Ostuf.(res.)	Paierl, Walter	9.11.44	1911
Tech. Off.	SS-Ustuf.(res.)	Ribbert, Karl	21.6.44	1910
Motor Vehicles I				
Physician	Unt.Arzt (res.)	Löffler, Hermann	1.11.44	1920
5. Kompanie				
Kompanie cmdr.	SS-Ustuf.(res.)	Gruber, Fritz	1.9.44	1914
Zugführers	manned by NCOs			
6. Kompanie				
Kompanie cmdr.	SS-Ustuf.(res.) (since 12.1.45)	Sprotte, Georg	9.11.44	1916
Zugführers	manned by NCOs			
7. Kompanie				
Kompanie cmdr.	SS-Ostuf.(res.)	Löbzien, Werner	1.10.42	1914
Zugführers	manned by NCOs			
8. Kompanie				
Kompanie cmdr.	SS-Ostuf.(act.)	Brinkmann, Werner	21.6.42	1916
Zugführers	manned by NCOs			
Supply company	SS-Ustuf.(res.)	Kaiser, Bruno	15.7.44	1914
Wounded:				
	SS-Hstuf.(act.)	Hauschild, Karl	30.1.44	1919
	SS-St.O.Jk.(res.)	Dr. Reiss, Ernst	1.9.44	1919
	SS-Ustuf.(act.)	Bütschek, Herbert	10.3.43	1920
	SS-Ustuf.(res.)	Lehmann, Walter	1.4.41	1905
	SS-Ustuf.(res.)	Scheib, Karl	9.11.44	1910
	SS-Ustuf.(res.)	Börner, Berthold	21.6.44	1916 [73]

Note: SS-Hstuf. = SS-Hauptsturmführer; SS-Ostuf. = SS-Obersturmführer; SS-Ustuf. = SS-Untersturmführer; SS-St.O.Jk. = SS-Standartenoberjunker.

The Bataillon was scheduled to have twenty-seven officers. However, after action in the Ardennes offensive, it had only ten. Of the four chiefs of the combat Kompanies, two were Obersturmführers who had held that rank for two-and-a-quarter and two-and-a-half years respectively. They had a significant amount of front experience which qualified them for their responsibilities. The other two Kompanie chiefs were Untersturmführers who had held that rank for three months, and, hence, had no experience in leading a Kompanie. Their high fighting morale and real-life experience—they were twenty-eight and thirty year old reservists—could not compensate for that. The orderly officer and all sixteen Zugführers of the combat companies were NCOs. The manning of the officer positions thus did not fulfill the requirements or even the norm by any means. It was self-evident, however, that every-one gave his best in the position to which he had been assigned.

The vehicle situation of the II./26 can be viewed as indicative for the two Panzergrenadierregiments and, hence, for the whole Division. The Bataillon entered the Ardennes offensive with 105 motor vehicles. Of that number, 38 were lost. At the end of January, 34 of the remaining 67 vehicles, i.e. 32 percent, of the initial number were still operational. The composition of the inventory of vehicles (without tractors) is informative: 13 Ford V8s, 10 Opel-Blitz, 1 Prag, 14 Fiats, 2 Studebakers, 1 Bedford; that meant 6 different makes, among them 3 captured vehicles. The difficulties in providing spare parts and doing repairs can easily be imagined.[74]

The Division marched in several stages from the Deyfeldt district into the area west of Cologne where it had been located prior to the start of the Ardennes offensive. From there, it was to be moved by rail transport to the eastern front. The stages of that march were also burdened with great difficulties and delays caused by lack of fuel, inoperable vehicles and over-crowded roads. The individual stages are shown here, using the war diary of the II./26 for that Bataillon, and notes of the commander of the Flak-abteilung, for that Abteilung, representative for the whole Division.

From the area around Braunlauf (6.5 kilometers southwest of St. Vith), the Bataillon moved to Bleialf (12.5 kilometers southeast of St. Vith) on 17–18 January 1945.

. . .

18 January: March on foot to Holzheim (twelve kilometers north of Bleialf), departure twelve noon, arrival 17.30 hours. Wheeled elements to follow after fuel arrives. Heavy snow fall and drifting snow. During the night, harassing artillery fire on Holzheim.

19 January: 8. (heavy) Kompanie and vehicle squad take up quarters in Manderfeld (four kilometers southeast of Holzheim); move to Holzheim made impossible by heavy snow drifts. Empty vehicles not yet arrived. Bataillon sent out to shovel snow.

20 January: Bataillon marches to Nereth (four kilometers west of Holzheim) and moves into a blocking line from Point 516 south of Valendar-northern edge of Valendar-eastern edge of Valendar-south-

ern bank of the Amel/Amblêve. 6. Kompanie in reserve in Halenfeld-Heppenbach.

21 January: Securing along the designated line, contact with III./Fallschirmjägerregiment 5 in Heppenbach and to the III./25 on the left. Forward observer of the II. Artillerieabteilung is at the 5. Kompanie. Heavy harassing artillery fire on the whole sector.

22 January: Harassing artillery fire on the whole sector. The Division relays an order from the 6. Panzerarmee regarding traffic regulations, issued by Feldjägerkommando (mot) III (military police command, motorized) of 13.1.45. It designates 4 one-way routes for west-east, and 3 one-way routes for east-west traffic.

23 January: Disengagement from the blocking line. March on foot to the area around Manderfeld (ten kilometers east of Valendar). Departure at 7 A.M., arrival in Berterath (two kilometers northeast of Manderfeld) at 15.00 hours, without 8. (heavy) Kompanie since no fuel available.

24 January: Rest. Repairing of motor vehicles by the repair squad still in Bleialf. The vehicles of 8. Kompanie are partly in Andler (five kilometers southwest of Manderfeld), partly on the march from Braunlauf to Bleialf.

25 January: No changes.

26 January: 8. Kompanie moves from Andler to Hulscheid (1.2 kilometers southwest of Losheim).

27 January: Ordered to move via Losheimergraben, Hollerath, Hellenthal, Blumenthal, Reifferscheid, Sistig to Nettersheim (twelve kilometers southeast of Schleiden). At 22.00 hours, still no fuel available, empty vehicles have to be brought in from Bleialf after refueling.

28 January: 5., 6., and 7. Kompanies march, 'hitch-hiking'; 40 percent of combat vehicles run out of fuel on the way. Fuel tanker loaded fuel on 27 January at 15.00 hours in Hellenthal. It did not arrive at the unit and could not be found despite intensive searching.

29 January: Fuel provided is insufficient. As soon as more fuel arrives, the vehicles left behind will be brought up. They are sitting along the leg from Berterath (two kilometers south of Losheim) to Nettersheim.

30 January: The Bataillon received 1.3 cubic meters of fuel in order to bring up its stalled vehicles. Two officers charged with that task. Bataillon is standing ready to continue the march.

31 January: Not all vehicles have arrived. The 8. (heavy) Kompanie reaches Nettersheim. Extremely bad road conditions caused by a thaw.

1 February: At 10.30 hours, a truck is sent out to bring back 2.6 cubic meters of fuel, only 2.4 cubic meters are issued.

At 17.30 hours, departure from Nettersheim to Bergheim (twenty-two kilometers west of Cologne). Route of march: Nettersheim-Zingsheim-Weyer-Mechernich-Obergartzen-Enzen-Wichternich-Lechenich-Diemerzheim-Bergheim.

2 February: 01.30 hours: arrival in Diemerzheim (sixteen kilometers southeast of Bergheim);

09.30 hours: more fuel arrives, refueling. Since the weather is clear and enemy air activity is brisk, the Bataillon departs only at the fall of dusk. New destination is freight rail station Bedburg (six kilometers southeast of Bergheim).

Reinforcements for the Bataillon are located in Frimmersdorf (five kilometers north of Bedburg) and are ordered to march on foot from there to Bedburg.

18.00 hours: Departure of the Bataillon from Diemerzheim, without 8. Kompanie whose vehicles are not yet all there.

20.45 hours: arrival at the freight -station . . .[75]

Similar difficulties existed in supplying Flakabteilung 12. Added to that were considerable losses through enemy action. The following account is taken from the notes of the Abteilung commander, Sturmbannführer Dr. Wolfgang Loenicker:

. . .

13 January: The Abteilung receives order to move, but cannot depart because of lack of fuel.

16 January: 23.00 hours, departure from the district around Hardigny via St. Vith-Bleialf to Auw (nine kilometers southwest of Hallschlag).

17 January: Arrival in Auw at noon.

18 January: In Auw. Heavy snowstorm setting in.

19 January: Everything is snowed and drifted in. The Abteilung is kept as a reserve and brings in the guns which got stuck in the snow, one after the other.

23 January: Massive bombing raid. There are losses.

29 January: Fuel arrives in the early morning. At 09.45 hours, Hauptsturmführer Fischer killed, Obersturmführer Grimm wounded. 10.45 hours, departure via Hellenthal (rest) to Oberhausen (two kilometers south of Schleiden). First parts arrive at 19.00 hours.

30 January: March to Sistig (five kilometers southeast of Schleiden). Batteries got stuck in a heavy snowstorm. Many losses to fighter—bombers.

31 January–1 February: In Sistig. Thawing temperatures and rain. Losses to enemy artillery fire.

2 February: The Abteilung is pulled out and moves to Krekelkirch (2.5 kilometers southeast of Sistig). The artillery follows there also.

3 February: Fuel arrives. Departure at noon via Lechnich to Gymnich (fourteen kilometers southeast of Bergheim), arrival in the evening.

4 February: Drive to Quadrath-Ichendorf (four kilometers southeast of Bergheim) for loading on rail transport . . .[76]

On 31 December 1944, Heeresgruppe B had changed over to defense on almost all sectors of the front. It depended on the outcome of the battles for Bastogne whether offensive fighting, in a limited extent, could be resumed. If not, an ultimate change to defense had to take place in a more favorable position.

On 1 January 1945, the German Luftwaffe carried out an attempt to neutralize the Allied tactical air forces for a period of time through a major action by fighter aircraft, among them a squadron of jet fighters Me 262 A. A total of 1,035 aircraft attacked airfields in southern Holland and in Belgium. During that "Unternehmen Bodenplatte" (operation bed-plate), a large number of British and American aircraft were destroyed or damaged on the ground. Reported figures vary from 156 to approximately 500 craft. During the action, 277 German aircraft were lost. It achieved only a short-term impediment of the Allied tactical air forces. The high German losses precluded a repeat of the operation.

On 3 January 1945, an attack by the First US Army and the XXX British Corps started under the command of General Montgomery against the northern flank of the German breakthrough area in the Ardennes. The operation saw little success on the first day. It was hampered by heavy snowfall on the second day. Then, the enemy succeeded in deep penetration, forcing the German front to be pulled back, a pace at the time, to the southeast.

On 9 January, the enemy continued his attacks with infantry and tanks in the sector from Vielsalm to west of Laroche, but was repulsed with high losses on both sides. Since the enemy attempts to break through to Houffalize from the northwest and the south had been fought off, the XXXXVII. Panzerkorps was able to disengage to the line Nadrin (seven kilometers northwest of Houffalize)-Bertogne-Longchamps (eleven kilometers northwest of Bastogne). Mageret was lost on 13 January.

On 12 January 1945, the Soviet winter offensive started on the eastern front. The enemy succeeded in breaking through the German front and advancing to the former Reich border. Troops from the western front had to be moved to the eastern front. That required a shortening of the front in the west. The new forward line ran from Cherain (fifteen kilometers northeast of Houffalize) via Houffalize (exclusive) to Longvilly (seventeen kilometers north-northeast of Bastogne).

On 16 January 1945, the spearheads of the Third US Army, attacking from the south, met the First US Army, coming from the north, near Houffalize. The German divisions located to the west of the attack wedge had been able to withdraw in time so as to elude the planned encirclement. From 18 January on, the units of the 6. and 5. Panzerarmees pulled back, in sections, to the Westwall which they reached by the end of the month. Except for a few bridgeheads across the Our near Dasburg and near Vianden, the starting positions for the Ardennes offensive were thus occupied again.

CHAPTER 8.8
Final Observations on the Ardennes Offensive 1944-45

It was the aim of the German Ardennes offensive in December 1944–January 1945, after breaking through the front line of the First US Army along a width of approximately 100 kilometers, to push through the Maas sector Liège-Namur to Antwerp, and then to destroy the Allied forces north of the attack wedge in cooperation between Heeresgruppe H and Heeresgruppe B.

Thereafter, the Panzerdivisions taking part in the operation and, presumably, further forces were to be thrown to the eastern front in order to participate in the defense against the expected major Soviet offensive.

All available forces had been brought up for the Ardennes offensive. The resulting weakening of other sectors had been accepted. At the start of the operation, the Panzerdivisions had been extensively replenished with personnel and material. The personnel and material conditions reflected the limited facilities of the sixth year of war.

The offensive failed. Both sides suffered losses. Those on the German side could be replaced only partially at that time. Questions remain regarding the causes of the failure of the operation. Only the most important ones will be mentioned here.

In the majority, the enemy forces had been correctly judged regarding their numbers and fighting strength. One significant change had not been recognized; together with other factors it would be of decisive importance. The 2nd US Infantry Division, assumed to be on the march to the north, had been mounting an attack since 13 December 1944 on the Westwall sector at Wahlerscheid, with the Rur river dam as the objective. Its starting point was the twin village of Rocherath-Krinkelt, immediately behind the forward lines of the 99th US Infantry Division, along Advance Route A of the "HJ" Division. That led to a massing of enemy forces in dominating terrain at a decisive breakthrough point.

With regard to the enemy, the German plan of attack was based on a further assumption: That the move of reserves from the Aachen area would require a lengthy period of time. Elements of the 7th US Armored Division, located as a reserve in the Heerlen district (fifteen kilometers northwest of Aachen), reached St. Vith as early as 08.00 hours, its Combat Command B reached Vielsalm at 11.00 hours. Around noon on 18 December, the bulk of its Combat Command A marched through St. Vith. CCA and the bulk of the artillery of the Division crossed the path of Kampfgruppe Peiper near Stavelot. Two battalions of the 26th Infantry Regiment of the 1st US Infantry Division were in positions northwest of Büllingen and near Bütgenbach estate at 18.30 hours on 17 December. Thus, the enemy had succeeded in moving strong forces forward into the right flank of the attacking Panzerarmee.

A third important precondition for the success of the offensive was absolute secrecy. It was totally achieved. However, significant disadvantages had to be accepted in return.

The fourth—extremely important—prerequisite for success was the elimination of the Allied (tactical) air forces for a lengthy period of time by poor winter weather. That expectation was only partly fulfilled. As early as 18 december, the Flakabteilung of the "HJ" Division shot down four aircraft in the Losheimergraben area. The weather cleared on 23 December. Concentrated Allied air attacks on the combat area and the rear sectors began immediately. St. Vith was heavily bombarded on 25 December. Because of the clear visibility, the "HJ" Division could move only at night into the district around Samrée. The flying units and Flak of the Luftwaffe were unable to provide cover for the main routes of advance. The situation was similar or the same at all the other units.

Causes for the failure can also be found in the planning and decisions for the action by the German leadership. Of the five routes of advance for the 6. Panzerarmee, only one was usable to Panzer units, two of them were merely unpaved forest paths in the breakthrough sector. The Panzerdivision scheduled for the first wave had available only one good road into the area of Malmedy: Losheimergraben-Büllingen-Bütgenbach-Weismes. The 5. Panzerarmee had a better network of roads available. The important road junction town of St. Vith in the northern attack sector of the 5. Panzerarmee would have been better assigned to the 6. Panzerarmee, of course, together with the respective roads there and back. Even if the infantry had succeeded in breaking through to Rocherath-Krinkelt during the first day of the attack along Routes A and B, the road situation would not have allowed taking advantage of that achievement.

Since the road situation in the first phase did not allow the 6. Panzerarmee to deploy, the lack of cover on the right flank had extremely unfavorable results, in particular since numerous American divisions were massed in the area west of Aachen, constituting a threat. The less endangered left flank of the 5. Panzerarmee was secured by the 7. Armee with four divisions which joined its attack. Only the LXVII. A.K. with two Volksgrenadierdivisionen had been assigned for the corresponding task at the 6. Panzerarmee. The attack by the 78th and 2nd US Infantry Divisions on the Rur dams had blocked those two German divisions since 13 December 1944, preventing them from taking over covering the flank of the 6. Panzerarmee. The 15. Armee did not succeed in tying down strong enemy forces ". . . through numerous individual attacks from the north, east and south".

Operation "Stößer"—the action by paratroopers at the Hohe Venn—was planned to be another measure to guard the right flank of the 6. Panzerarmee. It was delayed when fuel for the transport column was not available in time. Lack of training of the flight crews caused a wide-spread landing of the paratroopers during unfavorable wind conditions. They were unable to mount a unified action.

The large delay in capturing St. Vith had a very negative impact on the progress of the overall operation. Additionally, that Bastogne was only encircled and not taken.

When comparing the forces on both sides, one must not overlook the fact that German divisions—even if refitted—were not nearly of the standard as during the spring battle of Charkow 1943, or at the start of the invasion of Normandy on 6 June 1944. That led to incorrect estimates of the time required for moves, assemblies, attacks and supply. Still, the fighting spirit of the troops was excellent. However, even a higher standard could not have overcome the disadvantages of the road situation in the Ardennes battlefield.

In addition to the reasons which had a basic impact on the progress of the operation, there were also unfavorable events in the tactical sector. These have been illustrated in detail in the reports on the combat of the 6. Panzerarmee. Four of them appear to be of particular importance:

1. The artillery fire attack at the opening of the attack on 16 December 1944 did not have the intended impact. Because of the lack of reconnaissance against the enemy, the important targets were not hit. Instead, the enemy was alerted prematurely.

2. Sending into action only one reinforced Bataillon of the "HJ" Division after the attack of the 277. Volksgrenadierdivision had stalled, proved to be insufficient in light of later knowledge of the real enemy situation.

3. The failure of the first attack by the 12. Volksgrenadierdivision on the heavily fortified positions at Losheimergraben led to a decisive delay in the action by Panzergruppe Peiper. The causes may be sought in inadequate reconnaissance, the non-arrival of the assault gun brigade and a lack of artillery support.

4. The delayed start of the attack by the "HJ" Division on the Bütgenbach estate on 21 December 1944 robbed that action of the planned

element of surprise. That disadvantage was increased by the fact that the three divisions participating attacked at different times.

Above all others, three facts probably contributed decisively to the failure of the offensive:

a) Four of five of the advance routes of the 6. Panzerarmee into the Malmedy district were totally unsuited for Panzer units.

b) Action by the 2nd US Infantry Division, one of the best, battle-hardened American divisions, was recognized too late. It tied down a Panzergrenadier-regiment, the Panzerjägerabteilung and the I. Panzerabteilung of the "HJ" Division for three days in bloody combat. The attacks of the two US divisions on the Rur dams tied down the LXVII. A.K. and robbed the 6. Panzerarmee of the cover for its right flank.

c) The movements of the fighting troops and the supply with fuel and ammunition was significantly hampered by Allied air attacks while adequate German air support was lacking.

Other observers have cited other reasons, or have distributed the weights differently. If ever the histories of other divisions become available which illustrate that period of time based on detailed personal knowledge of the authors—in particular, one must think here of the 1. SS-Panzerdivision "LAH" and the 116 Panzerdivision—then new and noteworthy aspects may possibly come to light.

After the outstanding achievements during the invasion battles in Normandy, the Supreme Command settled extraordinary expectations on the "HJ" Division. Standartenführer Hugo Kraas, the Divisional commander, had dampened them during the Führer situational briefing in Bad Nauheim. The Division made the best of its orders for action and the resulting situations it faced. The troops gave their all and repeatedly achieved remarkable successes against a superior enemy. However, it could not carry out its real mission: A deep advance after the 277. Volksgrenadierdivision had broken through the American positions. Instead, it was forced to fight its way forward with difficulty in bitter fighting against a vastly superior enemy, facing the most unfavorable terrain conditions, without being able to bring all of its strength into play in a concentrated manner. Outside of Bastogne, its target was within reach when it was forced to give up its attacks, totally bled and on its own.

The 12. SS-Panzerdivision "Hitlerjugend" had fought with honor and valor. Veterans of the battle-tested 2nd US Infantry Division (Indian Head) assured the Author during a comradely get-together after the war: The "Hitlerjugend" Division had been their first enemy in the face of whom they were forced to retreat.

Another action lay ahead in February 1945. A move to the eastern front was expected, the destination remained unknown for the time. Surely, difficult times were awaiting the worn-out Division.

Kaiserlautern, September 19, 1944. Reichsjugendführer Artur Axmann presenting the "Hitlerjugend" cuff-title. In the center, Obersturmführer Alois Hartung, commander of 4th Company Regiment 26; next to him on the right is Oberscharführer Heinz Förster.

The Knight's Cross holder Sturmbannführer Arnold Jürgensen, CO 1st Panzer Battalion; Obersturmführer Georg Hurdelbrink, acting CO Anti-Tank Battalion; and Oberscharführer Rudolf Roy, platoon leader of the Anti-Tank Battalion walk down the front of the paraded Panzer Regiment after the award ceremony, together with acting divisional commander Sturmbannführer Hubert Meyer.

Standartenführer
Hugo Kraas takes over
command of the Division
on November 15, 1944.

Presentation of the award of the Knight's Cross to Obersturmbannführer Bernhard Krause, CO Panzergrenadierregiment 26, and Rottenführer Fritz Eckstein, gunner in 1st Company, Anti-Tank Battalion 12. First and second rows from left: Rottenführer Eckstein; Brigadeführer Fritz Kraemer, Chief of Staff 6th Panzer Army; Oberstgruppenführer Sepp Dietrich, C-in-C 6th SS Panzer Army; Obersturmbannführer Krause; and Standartenführer Hugo Kraas, commanding 12th SS Panzerdivision "HJ," November 1944.

Hauptsturmführer Gerd Hein, here a Gebietsführer (area leader) in the Hitler Youth. He led the 1st Battalion of SS Panzer-grenadierregiment 26.

From December 25, 1944, Hauptsturm-führer Werner Damsch led the 1st Battalion of SS Panzergrenadier-regiment 25. He received the Knight's Cross at the beginning of May 1945.

Bad Oeynhausen, October 1944. Personnel of SS Corps Field Hospital 501. In the middle of the front row from left: two German Red Cross sisters, Obersturmbannführer Dr. Libau, Hauptsturmführer Dr. Scharfe, Hauptsturmführer Dr. Hugendubel, two German Red Cross sisters, and a French Red Cross sister. In the second row: twelve Russian sisters who were handed over to the Soviets by the Americans after they had taken them prisoner.

The church of Rocherath after the fighting of December 16 to 19, 1944.

During the Ardennes Offensive, Obersturmbann-führer Richard Schulze led 2nd Battalion of SS Panzergrenadierregiment 25.

Knocked out US "Stuart" reconnaissance tanks in the Ardennes.

Armored personnel carrier of 3rd Battalion of SS Panzergrenadierregiment 26 with 2 cm three-barreled gun (aircraft cannon).

Two-ton "Maultier" half-track truck, Model Ford, used as a tractor for 3.7 Flak of 4th Battery of SS Flak Battalion 12, in place of the unavailable self-propelled chassis.

Hungary, March 1945. Jagdpanzer IV of SS Anti-Tank Battalion 12 retreating from Lake Balaton. The supply vehicles are out of action so the field kitchen and a field canister are carried on the panzer.

Hungary, March 1945. Hungarian and German military columns come together.

Hungarian refugees leave the battle area. On the house gable, instructions for "Baustab 18".

Military police control military personnel and civilians in rear areas and collect soldiers who have lost contact with their units.

Hungary, March 1945. Panther of SS Panzerregiment 12 on the march in Hungary.

Columns of the Division on the march to the offensive at Lake Balaton, beginning of March 1945.

Many of our comrades who were killed in action during the Ardennes Offensive have found a final and worthy resting place in the German military cemetery at Recogne, near Bastogne. In the chapel, these words in the hall commemorating the dead have a message for the living: "We all should read what is written / In the silent stone: / You have been loyal and true / May we be the same."

American POW camp Auerbach in the Grafenwöhr military training area. Accommodation was in wooden huts and stables.

American POW camp Haid bei Linz in Austria, summer 1945. Men of 4th Battery: from left, Friedel Hustet, Fritz Voigt, Horst Megow, Unterscharführer Heinz Scharrer, Horst Busch, Willi Döring, and Rudolf Aschentrup.

February 2, 1980. For the preparation of this divisional history, former members of the Division met together for a battlefield visit at Rocherath/Krinkelt. From left: Hermann Buchmann, Richard Schulze-Kossens, Kurt Goericke, Hubert Meyer, Rudolf v. Ribbentrop, Hugo Kraas (died February 20, 1980), and Dr. Willi Kändler.

In front of the "Tiger of Vimouthiers" in Normandy during a Battlefield Study of the National Defence Headquarters of Canada in 1990: Obersturmbannführer der Waffen-SS A.D. Hubert Meyer, former chief of staff 12th SS Panzerdivision "Hitlerjugend," and Major-General, rtd., George Kitching, former CO 4th Canadian Armoured.

The Division during the Battles in Slovakia, Hungary and Austria During Winter and Spring 1945

SECTION 9

Move of the Division to Hungary—Action during the Offensive Operations in February and March 1945

CHAPTER 9.0
Systematic Account

Through the Ardennes offensive, the German Supreme Command had planned to destroy strong enemy forces in Holland and Belgium, to take away the important supply base of Antwerp from the enemy, and to stabilize the situation on the whole western front for a considerable period of time. The mobile troops, which would then be freed up, were to be rushed to the eastern front in order to throw back or destroy the Soviet armies which had pushed into Reich terrain. The Ardennes offensive had not achieved its objective. At the price of heavy German losses, in particular of the mobile troops, the initiative had, temporarily, moved to the German side. The enemy had also suffered considerable losses and had to give up terrain. His further advance had been delayed for some time.

The situation in the east deteriorated quickly at the beginning of 1945. The progress of the Soviets and their new allies in Hungary threatened the only natural petroleum deposit in the German-controlled territories, the crude oil deposit area around Nagykanizsa, as well as productive refineries. The battle could not be continued without the Hungarian crude oil production, in particular since the German synthetic gasoline production sites were neutralized, time and again, by air attacks for shorter or longer periods of time.

On orders of Adolf Hitler, the 6. SS-Panzerarmee was pulled out of the western front and moved to Hungary in order to remove the threat to the petroleum deposits there in the framework of an offensive. Sturmbannführer Otto Günsche, the personal adjutant of Adolf Hitler, verbally carried the order, to commence the disengagement and the move of the Armee, to Oberstgruppenführer Dietrich at the beginning of January 1945.[1]

On 16 January 1945, the Führungshauptamt (supreme operations authority) issued an order by flash-priority teletype. It read, inter alia:

> ...1) On orders of the Führer, the Supreme Commander West will pull the following out of the front and immediately refit them in the district of Supreme Command West between 20.1.45 and 30.1.45:
>   a) Chief command I. SS-Pz.Korps with
>   1. SS-Pz.Div. 'LAH',
>   12. SS-Pz.Div. 'HJ';
>   b) Chief command II. SS-Pz.Korps with
>   2. SS-Pz.Div. 'Das Reich',
>   9. SS-Pz.Div. 'Hohenstaufen'. . .
> 2) c) Last day of refitting 30.1.45
> 3) a) Provision of personnel takes place by SS-FHA (SS supreme operations authority), Amt -(office) V/IIa and Amt II./Or.Abt. E . . .
> 4) Refitting with material takes place exclusively through OQu West (chief quarter master west) or Gen.Insp.d.Pz.Tru. (chief of staff of the Panzer troops) . . .[2]

A refitting in the normal fashion was out of the question. The replacements of personnel and material mostly arrived at the railroad stations at the time of loading, partly during the transport, and partly in the assembly area in Hungary.

CHAPTER 9.1
Move from the Cologne Area to Hungary into the Area Southeast of Raab

From the end of January 1945 onward, the "HJ" Division moved by rail transport from the Cologne area to Hungary into the area southeast of Raab (Györ in Hungarian). Reliable data on loading times, departure and arrival are only available from the II. Bataillon of SS-Panzergrenadierregiment 26 (II./26) and from the Divisionsbegleitkompanie. The II./26 departed from Bergheim (twenty-two kilometers west of Cologne) on 3 February at 06.45 hours, the Divisionsbegleitkompanie from Groß-Königsdorf (thirteen kilometers west of Cologne) on 5 February at 03.00 hours. Panzerjägerabteilung 12 loaded in Brühl (twelve kilometers southwest of Cologne), Flakabteilung 12 in Quadrath-Ichendorf (nineteen kilometers west of Cologne). The rail transports ran via Dortmund-Hamm-Bielefeld-Leipzig-Altenburg-Crimmitschau-Reichenbach-Plauen-Hof-Eger-Pilsen-Gmünd-Vienna-Bruck-Raab (for II./26), or Essen-Bielefeld-Halle-Meißen-Leipzig-Dresden-Kolin-Brünn-Preßburg-Raab (for Div.Begl.Kp., and 4. Flakbatterie).

The transports of the II./26 arrived in Raab on 7 February 1945 at 15.30 hours. The Divisionsbegleitkompanie reached the city on 9 February at 06.00 hours. The Flakabteilung also arrived in Raab on 9 February. It is very likely that all the rail transports ended there. The wheeled elements of the Division marched from Raab into an assembly area approximately 20-40 kilometers southeast of that city. The Divisional staff headquarters was located in Gicz, twenty-nine kilometers southeast of Raab. In its vicinity, in Hathalom, the Divisionsbegleitkompanie took up quarters, the II./26 around Merges (twenty kilometers southwest of Raab). It moved into the Rede district (thirty-six kilometers southeast of Raab) on 11 February. The tracked elements were probably transported by rail from Raab into the proximity of the planned area of action near Neuhäusl north of the Danube.[1]

In order to keep the preparations for the attack secret, all members of the 6. SS-Panzerarmee removed their sleeve bands before the start of the move from the Cologne area. In addition, the designations of the branches were replaced by code names. They read as follows:

6. SS-Panzerarmee	Höherer Pionierführer Ungarn
	(senior commander, engineers, Hungary)
I. SS-Panzerkorps	SS-Abschnittsstab Süd
	(SS sector staff south)
1. SS-Panzerdivision "LAH"	Ersatzstaffel "Totenkopf"
	(Death's Head replacement squadron)
12. SS-Panzerdivision "HJ"	Ersatzstaffel "Wiking"
	(Viking replacement squadron)
II. SS-Panzerkorps	SS-Ausbildungsstab Süd
	(SS training staff south)
2. SS-Panzerdivision "DR"	Ausbildungsgruppe Nord
	(training group north)
9. SS-Panzerdivision "H"	Ausbildungsgruppe Süd (south).

The regiments of the "HJ" Division were designated "Baustäbe" (construction staffs). Thus, the SS-Panzer-grenadierregiment 26 was named "SS-Baustab 22". The battalions were given the names I., II., and III. Abteilung, the companies retained their numbers.

While the troops and the staff of the "Höherer Pionierführer Ungarn" moved to Hungary, the Ia of the 6. SS-Panzerarmee, Obersturmbannführer Georg Maier, with parts of the operations staff as advance personnel, faked an unloading of the Armee in Bad Sarow near Berlin, destined for the area Cottbus-Forst-Frankfurt/Oder. The Armee staff assembled in a small Hungarian town at the end of February. The Supreme Commander, Oberstgruppenführer Sepp Dietrich, was allowed to arrive there only just before the start of operation "Frühlingserwachen" (spring awakening).[2]

It has already been mentioned that personnel and material replacements partly arrived just prior to loading, partly during the rail transport of the troops. The activity report of the II./26 noted on that:

> . . . 2.2.1945, 20.25 hours: Arrival at the loading station. The Bataillon immediately began loading the vehicles.
>
> 21.30 hours: Replacements report, 2 officers, 17 NCOs and 140 men.

Distribution to the companies:

> 5. Kompanie: 8 NCOs and 32 men;
> 6. Kompanie: 4 NCOs and 31 men;
> 7. Kompanie: 5 NCOs and 28 men;
> 8. Kompanie: — NCOs and 3 men . . .[3]

Unterscharführer Günther Burdack reported on the replacement of personnel and material at the III./26:

> . . . During the rail transport, men from the Ausbildungs und Ersatzbataillon 1 (training and replacement) in Spreenhagen, as well as NCOs and men—mostly recuperated wounded of the invasion battles and the Ardennes offensive—of the Ausbildungs-und Ersatzbataillon 12 in Nienburg/Weser were added. Near Dresden, NCOs from the technical personnel of the Luftwaffe also joined. The 9. Kompanie received two armorers who had an excellent knowledge of the 2 cm triplet guns. Armored personnel carriers arrived in two sections so that the full required strength was reached. The 9. Kompanie again had 22 armored personnel carriers . . .[4]

CHAPTER 9.2
Organization and Condition of the Division at the Start of the Action in Slovakia

At the time of arrival of the Division in the assembly area around 10 February 1945, it had not been completely refitted with personnel. Following below are combined figures, given in the report on the conditions of 1. February 1945, as well as those from the notes of the Divisional commander, Brigadeführer Hugo Kraas:

	Condition Report 1.2.45				Notes H. Kraas		
	1 Requ'd Strength	2 Effect. Strength	3 Ill and Wounded by week 6	4 Col. 2 Minus Col. 3	5 Effect. Strength	6 Fighting Strength	7 Combat Strength
Officers	633	471	99	372	428	292	142
NCOs	4,128	2,753	544	2,209	2,175	1,643	684
Men	13,787	16,878	3,623	13,255	14,242	10,422	8,232
Total	18,548	20,102	4,266	15,836	16,845	12,377	9,058

The difference between columns 4 and 5 can probably be explained by the additions during the rail transport. At the start of the operation in Hungary, the "HJ" Division had a shortfall of 1,703 men. Particular attention is to be given to the fact that a shortage of 205 officers (32 percent) meant that their positions had to be filled by NCOs. Hence, the shortfall of 1,953 NCOs was increased by another 205 so that, in reality, 2,158 NCO positions (52 percent) were filled by men.

In regard to the personnel situation, the "Brief Value Judgment by the Commander" in the condition report states:

As a consequence of the late addition of the replacements, they have not yet been incorporated into the units.

Numerous losses of motor vehicles can be explained by the fact that the young drivers are inadequately trained and not independent enough. An exchange for 500 experienced drivers is urgently required.

The combat strength of the Panzergrenadierregiments is not very high since the positions of Bataillon commander and Kompanie chiefs are, in the majority, filled by new officers, and since maneuvers by the troops with the new replacements are not possible.[1]

The staffing of the commander positions—except for those at the Panzergrenadier Bataillons—changed only little. Obersturmbannführer Martin Gross was transferred to the Division to command the Panzerregiment. He took over his new position at the beginning of March 1945. The I. (mixed) Panzerabteilung had been led, until he was mortally wounded on 21 or 22 December 1944 during the Ardennes offensive, by Sturmbannführer Arnold Jürgensen, then by Obersturmführer Rudolf von Ribbentrop.

It was exchanged for the mixed II. Abteilung under the command of Hauptsturmführer Hans Siegel. During that process, the personnel of the 2., 4., 7., and 8. Kompanie, which had been refitted during the Ardennes offensive at the Fallingbostel training grounds, took over the remaining Panthers and Panzer IVs of the mixed I. Abteilung in the middle of January in Sistig, Eifel. Obersturmführer von Ribbentrop, together with the personnel of 1., 3., 5., and 6. Kompanie, which had been in action, and the staff of the I. Abteilung, moved to Fallingbostel for refitting.

The II. Panzerabteilung was provided with Panzers as follows:

Panthers	taken over from I. Abteilung	6
	newly arrived at time of loading	22
	from Fallingbostel	4
	from Panzer AOK 6	12
	Available on 10.2.1945	44
Panzer IVs	taken over from I. Abteilung	14
	allocation January 1945	12
	from Fallingbostel	4
	from General d. Panzertruppen West	4
	from Vienna arsenal	4
	Total	38

The Artillerieregiment had lost one light field howitzer (10.5 cm), 2 heavy field howitzers (15 cm) and one 10 cm gun. On 10.2.1945 it recorded the following available equipment:

    34 light field howitzers 10.5 cm, mot. Z,
    2 light field howitzers, self-propelled "Wespe" (wasp),
    9 heavy field howitzers 15 cm, mot. Z,
    3 10 cm guns, as well as
    24 15 cm rocket launchers.

The Panzerjägerabteilung had available, on 1.2.1945, in the 1. and 2. Kompanie, 6 and 7 Jagdpanzer IVs respectively, and in the 3. Kompanie, eight 7.5 cm Pak 40 mot. Z.

On 1.2.1945, the Flakabteilung reported as available: three batteries of 8.8 cm with eighteen guns, and seven guns 3.7 cm mot. Z, as well as two batteries of 3.7 cm mot. Z, with fifteen guns. In addition, there were two 2 cm self-propelled four barrel guns.

It is amazing that, after five and a half years of war and despite years of the heaviest bombing raids, the German armament industry was still able to compensate to such an extent for the Panzer losses suffered in a major offensive. That was not possible for motor vehicles. The supply of motor vehicles, including those in short-term repair, on 1.2.1945 consisted of:

Motorcycles	34.4 percent of required strength,
Cars	63.8 percent of required strength,
Trucks	78.2 percent of required strength,
Tractors	44.5 percent of required strength.

Regarding the material situation, the "Brief Value Judgment by the Commander" in the condition report of 1.2.1945 stated:

> . . . Extensive shortage of tractors for the artillery. Eleven light field
> howitzers, six heavy, and one gun cannot be moved.
>   Lack of spare parts for motor vehicles and Panzers.
>   Lack of command vehicles . . .

The overall judgment read:

The Division is conditionally ready for offensive action tasks.[2]

The Division had been refitted with personnel to the 90.8 percent mark, and almost totally in material with Panzers, armored personnel carriers and guns. Despite that, the same achievements shown during the Ardennes offensive or even during the invasion battles, could not be expected from it. In addition, the overall situation had deteriorated considerably. A change for the better could not be foreseen. Into the place of hope for a German victory had moved the conviction that one could not unconditionally surrender, especially not to the enemy in the east. On the contrary, it was paramount to guard the homeland from that in particular. Above all, the spirit of comradeship and esprit de corps held the troops together. Even the replacements, which had come from the Luftwaffe and Kriegsmarine before and after the Ardennes offensive, were, in the majority, caught up in that spirit. The wounded members of the Division found amazing ways to get back to their units where they were "at home". Their place was there during the final phase of the war: at the side of their comrades with whom they had fought during the invasion battles or in the Ardennes.

CHAPTER 9.3
The Development of the Military Situation in Southern Slovakia and in Central Hungary around the Turn of the Year 1944-45

By the beginning of December 1944, the Red Army had occupied all of eastern Hungary. In the course of further operations it succeeded in crossing the Danube to the west on 3 December near Ercsi (thirty kilometers south of Budapest) and, subsequently, to establish a large bridgehead. In the face of the attack by the superior Soviet forces toward the north and northwest, the German troops pulled back to the not-yet completely fortified Margarethen positions. Those ran along the approximate line Lake Balaton-Stuhlweißen-burg-Lake Velence-Budapest.

On 20 December 1944, the two Soviet army groups, 2. and 3. Ukrainian Front, started a major offensive. Their aim was the encirclement of Budapest and the destruction of all German troops in action in the area around the Hungarian capital. The Soviet 6. Guards Tank Army and the 7. Guards Army which belonged to the 2. Ukrainian Front, reached the left bank of the Danube at the confluence of the Gran river on 26 December 1944. At the same time, the city of Gran was taken by troops of the 3. Ukrainian Front which attacked from the south. As early as 24 December, the Soviet 18. Tank Corps had cut off the major connecting road from Budapest to Vienna; the city was then completely surrounded and any provision of supplies by ground transport had become impossible.

The Hungarian capital, designated as a fortress, was being defended by the IX. SS-Gebirgskorps (mountain infantry) under the command of SS-Obergruppenführer (3-star general) Karl Pfeffer von Wildenbruch. Waffen-SS units assigned to him were: the 8. SS-Kavalleriedivision (cavalry) "Florian Geyer" and the 22. Freiwilligen-Kavalleriedivision (volunteer cavalry) "Maria Theresia". Additionally, he had available various units of the Heer and the police, among them the 13. Panzerdivision, the Panzergrenadierdivision "Feldherrnhalle", a Kampf-gruppe of the 271. Infanteriedivision, Flakregiment 12 and Polizeiregiment Nr. 6 (police regiment no. 6). The Hungarian I. Army Corps, which was also assigned to Pfeffer von Wildenbruch, comprised the remnants of different Hungarian elements. the total number of defenders of the fortress was reported to have amounted to between 40,000 and 70,000 men.[1]

In order to liberate Budapest, the OKH (Army Supreme Command) set in march from the area around Warsaw to Hungary, on 25 December 1944, the IV. SS-Panzerkorps, under the command of Obergruppenführer Herbert Gille, with the 3. SS-Panzerdivision "Totenkopf" and the 5. SS-Panzer-division "Wiking". In addition, the 96. Infanteriedivision was brought up from Galicia. The attack by the three divisions during the night of 1 January 1945 from the region southeast of Komorn/Komarom surprised the Soviets. They had not thought it possible that the German leadership would be able to mount a counterattack with appreciable forces. The IV. SS-Panzerkorps pushed through the Vertes mountains to within 2one kilometer of Budapest. However, it came to a halt in the face of a quickly established Russian defensive line on 6 January 1945 due to lack of forces. The 711. Infanteriedivision succeeded in recapturing the city of Gran on that day.

The 6. Soviet Guards Tank Army and the 7. Guard Tank Army attacked the German front behind the Gran river on 6 January. They reached Köbelkut on 7 January. In the evening of the next day they already stood outside Neuhäusel/-Ersekujvar and Komorn. German counterattacks pushed the enemy back at several points. After heavy losses, the Soviet units halted their attacks, but they were able to hold on to an extensive bridgehead across the Gran river.

In the meantime, Obergruppenführer Gille had reorganized his Korps in order to break through from the area south of Gran through the Pilis mountains to Budapest. The attack started on 10 January 1944. Two days later, the spearhead of the "Wiking" Division reached Pilisszentkereszt, thus standing only twenty kilometers from Budapest. The chief command and the troops were confident that they could reach Budapest. In that situation, the attack was stopped on orders of the OKH. The plan was to break through, with stronger forces, from the region north of Lake Balaton, by-passing Stuhlweißenburg to the south, to the Danube and then—swinging to the northeast—to Budapest. The result of that "large solution" was to be the destruction of the Russian forces north of the Margarethen positions.

Sent into that action, code-named "Konrad 3", were the following:

the IV. SS-Panzerkorps with its two SS-Panzerdivisions and the 1. Panzerdivision of the Heer, as well as several Panzer-Aufklärungsabteilungen, one Volks-Artillerie-Korps and one Volks-Werfer-Brigade,

the III. Panzerkorps with the 3. and 23. Panzerdivisions—without their Aufklärungsabteilungen—one heavy Panzerabteilung, the VIII. Hungarian Army Corps and

the I. Kavalleriekorps with the 6. Panzerdivision, the 3. Kavalleriebrigade, the 96. and 711. Infanterie-divisions and supporting artillery.[2]

The attack started on the morning of 18 January 1945. The positions of the surprised Soviets were overrun. On 19 January, the 3. Panzerdivision reached the Danube near Dunapentele (forty-five kilometers southeast of Stuhlweißenburg). After bitter fighting, Stuhlweißenburg was taken on 22 January. During the next day, the "Wiking" Division reached the Danube near Adony (thirty-six kilometers east of Stuhlweißenburg). The bulk of the IV. SS-Panzerkorps swung to the northeast and reached the southern bank of the Vali river, running from the northwest into the Danube five kilometers north of Adony, on the same day. On 24 January, elements of the "Wiking" Division penetrated into Baracska (twenty-nine kilometers northeast of Stuhlweißenburg). Parts of the "Wiking" Division crossed the Vali river at two points, but were unable to advance farther. Hence, Armeegruppe (army group) Balck ordered an initial attack between Vali and Lake Velence to the northwest and the destruction of the enemy located north of the lake, before the attack on Budapest would be continued.

On the attack to the northwest, the "Totenkopf" Division and the 1. Panzerdivision broke through the enemy positions on 26 January 1945, reached the line Val-Vereb (ten kilometers northwest of Baracska) and turned to the west. During the following day, the enemy mounted a counterattack with hastily brought-up forces from the south against the sector of the 3. Panzerdivision, and north of the Velence Lake from the northeast with a tank corps. However, he was unable to achieve a breakthrough. The attack to relieve

Budapest came to a halt, and it could not be started again in the subsequent time period.

On the proposal of Armeegruppe Balck, approved by the OKH, the III. Panzerkorps was to overcome the enemy attacking in the south through a counterattack. The 1. Panzerdivision was attached to it for that purpose. The northern and eastern fronts of the Armeegruppe were forced to change over to defense in the meantime. The attack by the III. Panzerkorps did not get under way. Instead, the Soviet attacks west of the Danube from the north and south made progress. The two attack spearheads met near Adony on 2 February. -Stuhlweißenburg was held.

On 11 February 1945, the defenders of Budapest tried to break out of the fortress to the west, after the ammunition, except for a small amount, had been used up. The attempt failed. Only 785 men reached the German lines near Zsambek in the evening of 13 February. The vast majority of the German and Hungarian soldiers, and the civilians accompanying them, who had attempted the breakout, were killed in the Russian fire or taken prisoner. The defenders had withstood the attacks by superior forces, and tied them down, for fifty-one days. Thus, they enabled the establishment of a continuous German front west of the Danube.

CHAPTER 9.4

The Division in the Offensive against the Soviet Bridgehead at Gran from 17 to 24 February 1945

In order to clear up the situation west of the Danube, south of Lake Balaton and north of the Drau river, a German offensive by units of Heeresgruppe Süd (south) and Heeresgruppe Südost (southeast) was being planned. There existed, however, the danger of a simultaneous attack by the Soviets from their Gran bridgehead north of the Danube in the direction of Preßburg and Vienna. Hence, prior to the start of the Balaton offensive, the bridgehead was to be eliminated. In order to do that, the 8. Armee received, from the Heeresgruppe Süd, the

> ... order to attack, concentrating all available infantry and armored forces, and accepting the consequent weakening of other front sectors, with the newly brought-up I. SS-Panzer-korps, on Day-X at 05.00 hours. After a short artillery preparation, to thrust from the north, to destroy the enemy in the Gran bridgehead, and to capture the bridgeheads across the Gran river near Garamkövesd, Köhidg-yarmat, Kemend and Beny to the east . . .[1]

Karte 16: Angriff gegen den Gran-Brückenkopf 17.-24.2.1945

Map 16: Attack against the Gran Bridgehead February 17-24 1945

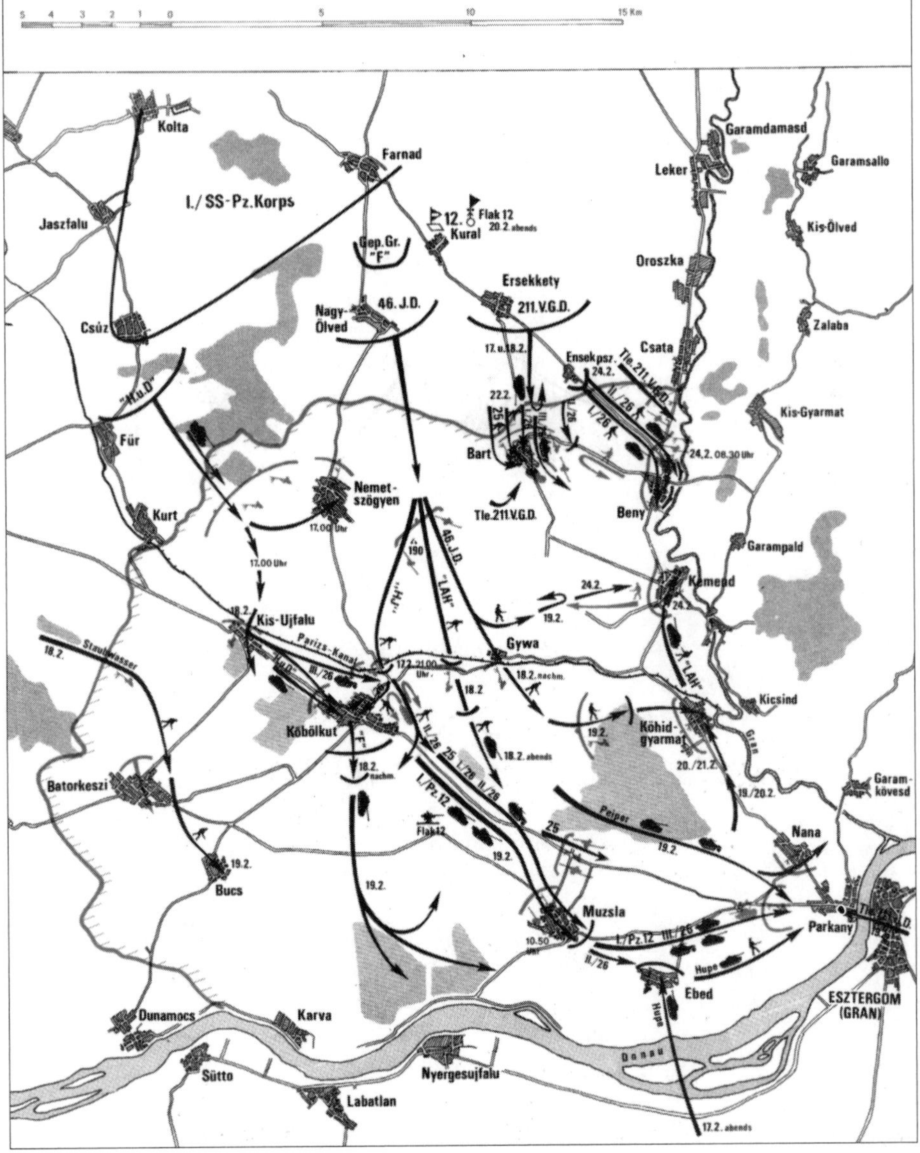

The Russian bridgehead ran from the Gran river immediately south of Csata (eighteen kilometers northwest of the city of Gran/Esztergom) in a westerly direction to two kilometers north of Nemetszögyen, from there in a flat curve to two kilometers west of Batorkeszi and farther to the southeast to two kilometers west of Karva on the Danube. It was approximately twenty kilometers deep. There were four river crossings: Kemend, Beny, and two at Garamkövesd.

The operational order for the attack contained no information of the strength of the enemy, the individual elements, and their theaters of action. It stated, concerning the enemy:

> . . . According to aerial photography and ground observation, the enemy inside the Gran bridgehead has organized himself for defense. It can be assumed that the armored forces of the IV. Guards Mechanized Corps are still assembled in the interior of the bridgehead. The IX. Guards Mechanized Corps and the V. Guards Tank Corps with the attached 6. Guards Tank Army are probably located in the refitting area east of the Gran. It must be expected that those units as well as elements of the Plijew Group will be moved into the Gran bridgehead in the course of the combat . . ."[2]

The evaluation of aerial reconnaissance on 15.2.1945 read as follows:

> . . . Aerial photography confirms that enemy defenses are strongly staggered into the interior. Important individual results:
> 1.) Infantry positions northwest of Bart have been further fortified. Anti-tank blocking position west of Bart reinforced by mortars.
> 2.) Parizs-Vgy. (Parizs canal, Author) forms considerable obstruction because of flooding (up to 100 meters wide). According to aerial reconnaissance on 15.2., crossings are usable.
> 3.) Continuous fighting trench from Ebed via Muzsla to one kilometer south of Bart, facing west.
> 4.) One bridge each near Beny and Kemend, and two bridges near Garamkövesd (vicinity of Gran confluence, Author) are usable.
> 5.) Judging by truck traffic, the roads and paths are thawed but not yet soft . . .[3]

The following German and Hungarian units were in action around the Soviet bridgehead on 11 February 1945:
> the 46. Infanteriedivision with several attached elements of the 13. Pz.-Div., of the Hungarian 20. Inf.-Div. and of the machine gun battalion "Sachsen" from the Danube to west of Batorkeszi;

from west of Batorkeszi to northwest of Nemetszögyen, the 44. Reichsgrenadier-Division "Hoch-und Deutschmeister";
from northwest of Nemetszögyen to the Gran river near Csata, the 211.
Volksgrenadierdivision with attached elements of the Hungarian 23
Infanteriedivision.

The supreme command of the 8. Armee judged the terrain for the
attack operation as follows:

    ... 1.) The wooded and broken terrain in the right section of the
        attack sector is favorable for the assembly of the infantry and
        the setting-up of artillery positions close-by. The assembly in
        the left (eastern) sector must take place somewhat more
        removed from the main line of resistance, north of the line
        from the southern edge of Nagy Ölved-Ersekkety.
    2.) Favorable observation possibilities in the right sector will
        enable an effective support of the attack by heavy weapons.
        Observation possibilities in the left sector, due to the open
        and not elevated terrain, are less promising for the first phase
        of the attack.
    3.) The broken terrain in the western portion offers the possibil-
        ity of advance under cover for the infantry. Terrain usable by
        Panzers is restricted to individual higher ridges. In the eastern
        section, the infantry will find less cover. Instead, the terrain is
        favorable for support by assault guns and armored vehicles up
        to the Parizs sector. The villages of Nem.Szögyen and Bart are
        heavily fortified strong points and must be taken by infantry
        forces from the rear.
    4.) After overcoming the anti-tank barricade near Point 190 [3.5
        kilometers southeast of Nemetszögyen], the Panzer attack will
        have to cross the Parizs-Vgy. as the first major terrain obstruc-
        tion. It is important to establish bridgeheads south of Parizs-
        Psz. and near Gyiva through a rapid advance. The wide road
        from Köbölkut to Parkany offers itself for the continuation of
        the Panzer attack, despite the anti-tank blocking position near
        Muzsla. An advance via Gyiva, through the narrow spot at
        Köhidgyarmat, to the bridge south of Garamkövest does not
        offer any success because of the flanking hills west and east of
        Köhidgyarmat.
    5.) The surface of the ground has already thawed to a depth of
        10 cm and large amounts of water have collected in the val-
        leys. Hence, severe difficulties must be expected for each
        Panzer action. It cannot be predicted whether the conditions
        will have worsened by the time the attack starts. The provision

of artillery has become of decisive importance if the fighting
has to be carried out largely by infantry.

6.) This assessment may be changed in several points since the
results of the aerial reconnaissance, which is under way, are
not available at this time . . .[4]

Available to the 8. Armee for that offensive operation, which was given
the code name "Südwind" (south wind) were:
Panzerkorps "Feldherrnhalle" with the
46. Infanteriedivision, the
44. Reichsgrenadier-Division "Hoch-und Deutschmeister", the
211. Volksgrenadierdivision, the
armored group of the Panzerkorps "Feldherrnhalle", the
I. SS-Panzerkorps with the
1. SS-Panzerdivision "LAH" and the
12. SS-Panzerdivision "HJ".
The supreme command of the 8. Armee issued the following missions:

a) The "Feldherrnhalle" Panzerkorps will disengage the bulk of the elements of the 46. Inf.-Div., the "H.u.D." Division, and the 211. V.G.D.
now in action around the Russian bridgehead. They will be assembled
in the area Für-Csuz-Nagy Ölved-Ersekkety, the armored group
around Farnad.

The Korps will by-pass the villages of Nemetszögyen and Bart, neu-
tralizing the flanking positions in the process, and will capture the
hills south of Nemetszögyen, Point 190, the creek section Sar-Völgy
south of Bart. Focus will be on Point 190. The Panzerkorps will later
enable the armored forces of the I. SS-Panzerkorps to attack to the
south. The villages of Nemetszögyen and Bart will be taken from the
rear. The attack will be driven forward regardless of the progress of
the attack on the two villages.

b) The I. SS-Panzerkorps will follow closely behind the infantry units of
Pz.-Korps "F". It will start its attack when ordered by the Armee and
will capture the hills south of the Parizs canal east of KöKölkut and
the main route south of the village. It will create the precondition for
a further attack in the direction of Gran. House-to-house fighting for
KöKölkut is to be avoided.

c) Thereafter, the I. SS-Panzerkorps will attack, together with the infantry
forces of Pz.-Korps "F", the narrow passage Muzsla-Bela. The infantry
will capture the high terrain east and southeast of Libad and Bela.

d) As soon as the attack becomes effective, the divisions in position will
join it on the orders of Pz.-Korps "F".

e) A reinforced Regimental Group of the 6. Armee (General der Panzertruppen Balck) will establish a bridgehead across the Danube from

the south during the first day of fighting and will cooperate with the units attacking from the north.

f) In order to deceive the enemy, Pz.-Korps "F" will set up a small bridge-head across the Gran during the night before the attack in the sector of the 271. V.G.D.

Among others, the operational order contained the following instructions regarding the assembly:

During the night of Day-X minus 1 to Day-X, the divisions of the I. SS-Panzerkorps will advance from their assembly areas around neuhäusel into the region northwest of Farnad.

Regarding the support of the attack, the order stated:

The artillery of the I. SS-Panzerkorps will support the infantry attack by Pz.-Korps "F". It must, however, be ready to be pulled out at any time in order to be available to the I. SS-Panzerkorps for its attack.

Pioniers of the attacking divisions will remove barricades, obstructions and mines immediately. Such will also have to be expected in the depth of the main theater of combat. The Armee Pionier commander will provide forces to construct bridges and tracks, in particular at the Parizs canal, in order to enable the assault guns and Panzers to cross. The Luftwaffe will destroy recognized anti-tank gun emplacements southeast of Nemetszögyen, near Bart, in the area around Kölkut and in the Muzsla-Bela area. It will delay the arrival of reserves, in particular of tanks, from the rear across the Gran river.[5]

During the nights between 14 and 16 February 1945, the "HJ" Division moved into the assembly area around Neuhäusel. The wheeled units marched on the road, the tracked elements were transported by rail. The II./26 received the required fuel at 19.45 hours on 14 February. At 20.30 hours, it was located at the merging point and it set out at 23.00 hours. It arrived in its quartering region around Kiskeszi-Ban (six kilometers north of Neuhäusel) on 15 February. The Divisions-begleitkompanie started its move to Udvard as early as 15.00 hours on 14 February. The Divisional staff headquarters were set up there. During the following day, it scouted the assembly area for the Division: Farnad-Kolta-Csuz (twenty-five kilometers and eighteen kilometers east, respectively, and eighteen kilometers southeast of Neuhäusel).[6]

The Division moved into the assembly area during the night of 16 to 17 February 1945. Together with the operations squad of the Divisional staff, the Divisionsbegleitkompanie departed for Kolta at 17.45 hours. The II./26 was scheduled to move out at 17.00 hours. Since the fuel only arrived at 18.00 hours, that was not possible before 18.30 hours. It arrived in Kolta at 23.55 hours. At 06.00 hours the next morning, the companies marched into their assembly areas two kilometers north of Nagy-Ölved which they reached by 10.00 hours. The operations squad of the Bataillon was able to depart only around 07.30 hours since it had to wait for fuel. All other units of the "HJ" Division moved into their assembly areas in a similar fashion.

A special event is noted in the activity report of the II./26. The leader of the 7. Kompanie, Obersturmführer Werner Löbzien, handed over to the Bataillon staff a sum of 4,005 Reichsmarks in the evening before the Kompanie's first action on the eastern front. The Kompanie had collected that money for the German Red Cross. Many of its men hailed from East Prussia and Upper Silesia. With that collection, they wanted to help refugees from their homeland, among whom were probably also many members of their families.

The attack by Pz.-Korps "Feldherrnhalle" began in the early morning of 17 February. The Reichsgrenadier Division "Hoch-und Deutschmeister" ("H.u.D"), in action on the right, encountered a dug-in enemy west of Nemetszögyen, who resisted tenaciously. Adjacent on the left, the 46. Inf.-Div. came upon a surprised enemy and penetrated deeply into the enemy positions between Nemetszögyen and Bart. The armored group of Panzergrenadierdivision "Feldherrnhalle" (the bulk of the division was encircled inside Budapest) stood in readiness south of Farnad. It joined the battle. With several Tigers, it supported the attack by the "H.u.D." Division which succeeded in advancing past the square wooded area northwest of Nemetszögyen. At approximately 09.00 hours, the 46. Inf.-Div. had pushed forward to within 600 meters north of Hill 190 (three kilometers southwest of Nemetszögyen and encountered the expected anti-tank gun position there. A few individual enemy tanks were also spotted. The 1. SS-Panzerdivision "LAH" was brought up and, together with the 46. Inf.-Div., mounted an attack on the Russian anti-tank gun position as early as 11.40 hours. The 12. SS-Panzerdivision "HJ" followed behind it. At that time, its spearheads reached the former main line of resistance. The 211. V.G.D. made only minor progress in its attack on Bart. Enemy assemblies and movement into a westerly direction were spotted east of the Gran river. The German Luftwaffe attacked the Gran crossings, concentrating on Beny.

By 17.00 hours, the "H.u.D." Division, supported by the Tigers, had captured Nemetszögyen and the western section of the forest south of the town. It continued to advance in the direction of Arad-Puszta and the Parizs canal. Elements of the 46. Inf.-Div. and the "LAH" Division had already reached the canal. The bridges had been blown up.[7]

In the afternoon, the "HJ" Division was sent into action adjacent to the right of the "LAH" Division. Panzergrenadierregiment 25 advanced on the right, Panzergrenadierregiment 26 adjacent on its left. The I./26, under the command of Sturmbannführer Kostenbader, succeeded in establishing a small bridgehead across the canal immediately southeast of Parizs-Puszta by approximately 21.00 hours. The II./26 followed and enlarged it in cooperation with the I. Bataillon. By 00.45 hours on 18 February, the II./26, led by Hauptsturmführer Ott, reached the crossroads 800 m southeast of Parizs-

Puszta. Both battalions prepared for defense in the bridgehead they had gained. While they were reorganizing for that, the Soviets attacked the German positions with forces of approximately one battalion strong, supported by two T-34 tanks and several anti-tank guns. The enemy was thrown back after bitter fighting. He suffered heavy losses. The II./26 moved into a position in high terrain 350 m south of the crossroads. Although the bridge across the Parizs canal had been destroyed, a ford, usable by wheeled vehicles, had been found in the vicinity.[8]

Approximately three kilometers farther to the east, the "LAH" Division established a small bridgehead across the canal near Gyiva. No possibility for vehicles to cross existed there.

The supreme command of the 8. Armee urged that further forces be brought up immediately in order to mount an attack from out of the bridgeheads in the direction of the confluence of the Gran. It wanted to pre-empt the attempt by the enemy to set up a new line of resistance south of the canal. In support of that intention, it requested from the Heeresgruppe that the assembled Regimentsgruppe (regimental group) Hupe of Armeegruppe Balck establish the bridgehead across the Danube near Ebed even during the night. That was achieved, still, in the late evening without enemy resistance.[9]

The "H.u.D." Division forced the crossing of the canal near Kis-Ujfalu on 18 February 1945. From 12.50 hours on, Panzers could cross the canal there. In the course of the afternoon, elements of the "H.u.D." Division, together with the SS-Panzergrenadierregiment 26, captured Köbölkut and the high terrain north of the town. The "H.u.D." penetrated into the western section of Köbölkut with Panzers and infantry. Adjoining the "H.u.D." on the left, the III./26 attacked. It had already reconnoitered toward the industrial area north of the town. Russian anti-tank guns and mortars were overcome by the German artillery fire and concentrated fire from machine guns, the 2 cm triplet guns and the mortars of the 12./26. The industrial area and the hills north of it were captured. One of the two armored personnel carriers which had scouted during the night, and had not returned, was found. It had got stuck in a road ditch. Inside and next to their armored personnel carrier lay the crew, shot and butchered.

The I./26 took the eastern section of the town, while the II./26 attacked toward the south. It captured Hill 186 and then advanced to the road and the rail line from Köbölkut to Parkany. There, it took up blocking positions toward the south and southeast. Elements of the "H.u.D." and of the "Feldherrn-halle" Panzerabteilung took the high terrain around Point 129 (2.5 kilometers south of Köbölkut) in the afternoon. Adjacent to the west on the "H.u.D.", "Gruppe Staubwasser" captured the Orias-Puszta and advanced farther toward Batorkeszi (7.5 kilometers southwest of Köbölkut).

The "LAH" Division expanded its Gyiva bridgehead in the early morning hours of 18 February. One temporary bridge was built, and the Panzers of the "LAH" started rolling across it from 12.50 hours on. In the afternoon, they mounted an attack toward the south and captured Sarkanyfalva. Toward the evening, they were fighting northwest of Muzsla.

The 46. Inf.-Div. pulled its heavy weapons forward and was reinforced by elements of the Pz.-Gren.-Div. "Feldherrnhalle". It started an attack from the area around Gyiva to the east in the afternoon. One assault group penetrated, south of the canal, into Libad (three kilometers southeast of Gyiva). The other attacked north of the canal in the direction of Kemend (Gran crossing 6.5 kilometers northeast of Gyiva). The enemy had apparently set up a blocking position from Bart to Libad.

Due to the heavy losses suffered during the previous day, the attack by the 211. V.G.D. on Bart made no progress. The supreme commands of the 8. Armee and Heeresgruppe Süd expected a Soviet counterattack from the area around Bart and Beny as soon as the enemy had brought up reinforcements across the Gran. In order to reinforce the 211. V.G.D., AOK 8 planned to withdraw the bridgehead across the Gran, established northwest of Leva to deceive the enemy. In addition, it intended to pull out the "HJ" Division for an attack on Bart as soon as the developments in the narrow passage of Muzsla would allow that.[11]

The German Luftwaffe did not observe any unusual traffic across the Gran in the course of 18 February. It attacked the bridge near Beny and reported hitting it. It also supported the attack of the German ground troops by approximately 140 sorties of combat and fighter aircraft. Enemy combat and fighter aircraft concentrated their actions on both sides of the Danube.

During the night of 19 February, as on the previous day, the temperature was below freezing. During the day it climbed to six degrees celsius. The weather was mostly sunny, the soft and muddy lanes began to dry.

"Gruppe Staubwasser" occupied Bucs and Batorkeszi in the morning. The enemy had retreated to the east during the night. Elements of the "H.u.D." Division cleared the wooded terrain northeast of Karva (ten kilometers south of Köbölkut on the Danube). They were scheduled to be ready, later, to relieve parts of the I. SS-Panzerkorps.

The I. SS-Panzerkorps had been charged, in cooperation with "Regimentsgruppe Hupe", to break open the narrow passage near Muzsla, as well as to take Parkany and Nana near the Gran confluence. Toward that objective, the "LAH" Division attacked north of the road Köbölkut-Parkany from the area south of Gyiva in the morning of 19 February. The armored group of the "HJ" Division assembled southwest of Köbölkut in the course of the night, while the enemy attempted to recapture the terrain south of the Muzsla-Köbölkut road which he had lost the previous day. The Panzergrenadier-regiments 25 and 26 cleared out local breakthroughs. At approximately 05.30 hours, the armored group, with the III./26 at the point, started an attack, past the positions of the Panzergrenadierregiments. The Schützenpanzerbataillon (armored personnel carriers) advanced along both sides of the Köbölkut-Muzsla road. The II. Panzerabteilung followed behind on the road because of suspected mine barriers. The III./26 came under fire from anti-tank guns and artillery from the direction of Muzsla. Consequently, the Panzerabteilung under the command of Hauptsturmführer Hans Siegel moved forward to the point, with the 2. Kompanie under Obersturmführer Helmut Gaede in the lead. The enemy was overrun before daybreak and the village was secured by the armored group. The dismounted Panzergrenadiers of the I. and II./26 followed and cleared the terrain. At 10.50 hours, the II./26 reached Muzsla. It was charged with advancing on Parkany by way of Ebed in the further progress of the attack, and to establish contact with the Regimentsgruppe Hupe. Regiment 25, attacking north of the Köbölkut-Muzsla road, had to overcome strong enemy resistance. Several Panthers supported its attack from Muzsla, so that the Regiment was able to close up by noon. Flakabteilung 12 took up positions at 17.00 hours near Kismuzsla-Puszta, five kilometers north of Muzsla, and battled attacking bombers.

The armored group reorganized for the attack on Parkany. During a surprise fire attack by "Stalinorgeln" (Stalin organs = rocket launchers) on the road from Muzsla to Ebed, the commander of SS-Panzergrenadierregiment 26, Obersturm-bann-führer Bernhard Krause, was mortally wounded. "Papa Krause", holder of the Knights' Cross and the German Cross in Gold, of the Iron Cross I and II, a leader revered by his officers, NCOs and men, and beloved by the "old men" of the Normandy action, was mourned by all who knew him. Sturmbannführer Kostenbader, the commander of the I./26, took over the leadership of the Regiment. His place was filled by Hauptmann Schmidt.

The attack of the armored group started at around twelve noon. The Panzers of the II. Abteilung knocked out several Russian T-34s and T-43s outside Parkany and during fighting inside the town. The 9. Kompanie lost two armored personnel carriers, those of Unterscharführer Haak and Unterscharführer Kosel. Obersturmbannführer Jochen Peiper with the Panzerregiment of the "LAH" pushed into Parkany from the northwest. The Regimentsgruppe Hupe of the 96. Inf.-Div. effectively supported the attack on Parkany from the southwest with twenty assault guns and mounted infantry. An assault squad of the 711. Inf.-Div. crossed the Danube from the town of Gran and took part in the capture of Parkany.

In the course of its attack, the "LAH" Division also seized the village of Nana (1.5 kilometers north of Parkany). After capturing Libad during the previous day, the 46. Inf.-Div., reinforced by elements of the armored group "F", pushed its way farther to the east. It reached the eastern edge of the wooded high terrain immediately west of Köhidgyarmat, located right on the Gran river, and scouted toward the village. "Gruppe Schöneich", together with parts of the 46. Inf.-Div., attacked north of the Parizs canal toward Kemend. It reached Kemend-Puszta—two kilometers west of Kemend—but was pushed back by a Russian counterattack.

The 19 February 1945 did not bring any clarification of the enemy situation. Elements of the IV. Guards motorized mechanized Corps, belonging to the Soviet 6. Guards Tank Army, were spotted in the northern part of the Russian bridgehead. The location of the bulk of the Army was uncertain. The office of Fremde-Heere-Ost (foreign armies, east) assumed that it was refitting south of Lake Balaton. Heeresgruppe Süd suspected that the Army was situated north of the Danube, and that its refitted elements were being moved to the Gran river in order to be inserted into the northern remainder of the Gran bridgehead. The OKH, in any case, thought it required, with regard to the overall situation, that the remnants of the Soviet bridgehead be smashed as quickly as possible. When asked, Adolf Hitler rejected the planned establishment of bridgeheads across the Gran and an attack up to the Eipel river (8–10 kilometers east of the Gran). He wanted to have the I. SS-Panzerkorps freed up as quickly as possible for the operation at Lake Balaton.[13]

Aerial reconnaissance during the night determined brisk enemy movements from the south toward Balassagyarmat (approximately seventy kilometers northeast of Gran) and toward Ipolysag (not shown on available maps). A total of 3,600 vehicles were observed driving from the Budapest area to the north. It remained uncertain whether the enemy was moving forces into the remainder of the Gran bridgehead, or whether he was planning an attack farther to the north. The determined resistance inside the compressed Gran bridgehead appeared to indicate that he wanted to hold and reinforce it, under all circumstances, as a departure position for further actions toward the west. AOK 8 reported that six to eight enemy divisions had been weakened or destroyed inside the bridgehead.

In order to quickly clear up the situation west of the Gran, three Kampfgruppen attacked the southern portion of the bridgehead still during the night of 19 to 20 February 1945. A Kampfgruppe of the "LAH" Division attacked from the south toward Köhidgyarmat, one from the 46. Inf.-Div. from the west. Gruppe Schöneich attacked north of the Parizs canal toward Kemend. The Kampfgruppen gained some ground, but then stalled. Because of the strong enemy air superiority, the attacks could not be continued during daylight. The Armee planned to capture Köhidgyarmat during the first phase, the bridgehead Bart-Kemend-Beny during the second. The "HJ" Division was to be moved into the area north of Bart for the second attack. It was relieved by the "H.u.D." Division on 20 February, as were elements of the "LAH" Division and Regimentsgruppe Hupe of the 96. Inf.-Div.

In the course of 20 and 21 February, the "HJ" Division moved into the district south and southeast of Farnad. Because of the brisk enemy air activity, the columns marched with large spacing between vehicles. The Flakabteilung moved to Kural (approximately three kilometers southeast of Farnad) on 20 February. It arrived there at 20.00 hours and took up positions to provide air defense for the assembly area. The Führungs-abteilung (operations) of the Divisional staff marched from Kismuzsla-Puszta to Kural on 20 February.[14]

During the night of 20 to 21 February, the "LAH" Division and the 46. Inf.-Div. pushed into the southern and western sectors of Köhidgyarmat, suffering high losses, and captured the town after the fall of darkness.

On 21 February, aerial reconnaissance indicated that enemy movements had slowed down. The Soviet IV. Guards motorized mechanized Corps had apparently been pulled out of the bridgehead and then moved farther to the rear. From those two observations, the Heeresgruppe concluded that the enemy was expecting a strategic assault across the Gran, and was preparing for defense on the eastern bank of the river with quickly brought-up forces. The assumption that he had reinforced the troops inside the bridgehead for that reason also, was not substantiated in any detail. It could only make sense in order to gain time. There was consideration of the possibility that the enemy might want to hold the bridgehead as a starting position for his own attack. According to data from Heeresgruppe Söd, the following were in action inside the bridgehead, from north to south: 81. Guards Division, 72. Guards Division, 6. Guards Paratroop Division, 93. Guards Infantry Division, for a total of four Soviet divisions.[15]

In the preparation of its attack on Bart, the "HJ" Division was dependent mostly on aerial reconnaissance, as well as ground reconnaissance from the 211. Volksgrenadierdivision which had attacked there, without success, on 17 and 18 February. On 20 February, the "HJ" Division sent an armored scouting party from the Aufklärungsabteilung ahead to Nagy-Ölved (six kilometers northwest of Bart), with the task of reconnoitering toward Bart. The leader of the scouting party, Oberscharführer August Zinßmeister, noted in his diary:

> . . . Mission: Reconnaissance and scouting the terrain around Bart. Together with Fritz Dittrich, I crawled the whole day through the mostly marshy terrain. We observed the enemy in his positions. In the evening, we reported. Then we drove with the Panzers (armored reconnaissance vehicles, Author) to Farnad where we took up quarters for several days . . .[16]

The reconnaissance of the various positions resulted in the following picture: The village of Bart was heavily fortified. To the north of the town was a deeply staggered system of positions, ahead of it a mine field. Large numbers of light and heavy machine guns, mortars and anti-tank guns were in position. The terrain for the attack undulated lightly, crossed by individual creeks which flow into the Gran, and completely without cover, except for shocks of corn.

Hence, only a night attack had any prospect of success. The "HJ" Division sent into the attack from the north, Regiment 25 on the right and Regiment 26 on the left. The armored group was initially to follow behind Regiment 26. The Regiment put the I. Bataillon into action on the right; the II. was ordered to follow it to the left rear and cover the left flank toward Beny. With the fall of darkness, the battalions moved from their assembly areas into their readiness areas which were located only a few hundred meters in front of the enemy positions.

To ensure that the Panzers following behind would be able to maintain contact with the Panzergrenadiers advancing on foot, the men in the rear of the companies of the I./26 had flashlights, showing red light, attached to their backs. There was a light frost, the night was dark, the ground was soft, some of the low spots in the terrain were still filled with snow. The soft ground muffled the sounds. During the advance into the readiness areas, contact was lost between the Grenadiers of the I./26 and the Panzers following them. When the Panzers caught up, they took the Grenadiers in front of them to be the enemy since they could not see any red lights, and opened fire on them with machine guns. The leader of the 2. Kompanie, Untersturmführer Schulte, and four men were killed, eight more members of the Kompanie were wounded. The orderly officer of Regiment 26, Obersturmführer Hans-Jürgen Ross, was ordered by Sturmbannführer Kostenbader to determine the reason for the premature opening of fire. He succeeded, from a "Wespe" of a Wehrmacht unit, to have the fire stopped through a clear-text radio message. In the meantime, the Russians had been alerted and, in return, opened fire with machine guns and mortars.

At approximately 04.45 hours, the II. Panzerabteilung started its attack on Bart after having assembled in a valley north of the town. German artillery, rocket launchers and mortars concentrated heavy fire on the identified enemy positions. Just before the Panzers reached the first positions, they drove into a Soviet mine field. Several Panzers, among them also that of Hauptsturmführer Siegel, were stopped with damage to the tracks. The damage was repaired under enemy fire. The Panzers rolled back to the rear slope. A number of Soviet anti-tank guns were fired at from those positions and destroyed. The grenadiers in particular those of Regiment 25—suffered considerable losses from the fire of enemy artillery, Stalinorgeln, and mortars.

The 9. Kompanie of Schützenpanzerbataillon III./26, in action farthest to the left (east), was able to roll forward outside of the Soviet mine field. It came under heavy anti-tank fire from the left flank. It pinned the enemy down with its 2 cm triple and single barrel guns and overran the anti-tank gun positions. The other armored personnel carriers continued to advance on Bart, led by Obersturmführer Dieter Schmidt. A number of the vehicles got stuck in a creek bed. Three armored personnel carriers with the Unterscharführers Hans-Günther Drost, E. Franke, O. Schnittke and Günther Burdack broke into the village from the north. They were effectively supported by fire from German Panzers. The armored personnel carriers pushed past the church and on to the southern edge of the village. The report of Günther Burdack stated, inter alia:

> . . . The village was choked with enemy vehicles. The tracer shells from the 2 cm guns had a devastating effect. The loaders and radio operators could not insert the belts into the belt boxes of the triple barrel guns quickly enough. Several T-34s and T-43s, still inside the town, forced the armored personnel carriers into cover. Günther Drost tried, driving backward, to push down the door of a barn in order to get out of firing range of a T-34. He was surprised to find that another T-34 was sitting inside. The driver had been wounded in the leg, the rest of the crew had disappeared. The Russian tanks, without securing infantry fire, left the town in the direction of Beny . . .[17]

Regiment 25, scheduled for action on the right, had not reached its readiness area in time. After reorganizing, it joined the attack by the Panzerabteilung and by the I. and III./26, and took the western section of the town.

Obersturmführer Ross, who took part in the latter phase of the attack in the armored personnel carrier of the commander of the III./26, Sturmbannführer Hermann Brand, reported on it:

> . . . We advanced, firing, on the first houses of Bart. The battle was still in full swing. Fire from our heavy weapons had badly damaged most of the buildings. Roofs had been stripped off, walls had crumbled. I will never forget the sight: During the pitched battle, civilians came out of the ruins of their houses, men, women, children and waved scarves or even their hands at us, unconcerned with what was going on around them. They were obviously happy beyond measure to be liberated again from their 'liberators'. How much those people must have had to suffer! . . .[18]

In order to relieve the defenders of Bart, the Soviets attacked the II./26 in the morning from Beny along the road to Bart and laid heavy mortar fire on the Bataillon. The attack was repulsed.[19]

Elements of the 211. Volksgrenadierdivision attacked Bart from the south. In the course of the morning, the town was completely cleared of the enemy and occupied by Regiment 25. The I. and III./26 were pulled out. The enemy left a large number of anti-tank guns, mortars and vehicles behind in Bart. Two undamaged T-34s and six 17.2 cm howitzers were captured; eighty prisoners were taken, among them a -colonel.[20]

During 22 February 1945, the chief of staff of the 6. SS-Panzerarmee, Brigadeführer Kraemer, repeatedly pushed Heeresgruppe Süd for a quick disengagement of the I. SS-Panzerkorps. The commanding general, Gruppenführer Priess, had reported that, if he were to carry out the present mission inside the Gran bridgehead, he would not be ready, with men and material, for further action in less than fourteen days. In Brigadeführer Kraemer's opinion, that could be very detrimental for the attack at Lake Balaton. He asked to consider whether the capture of Kemend and Beny could not be abandoned. The supreme commands of Heeresgruppe Süd and the 8. Armee did not want to waive the complete destruction of the Russian bridgehead under any circumstances, in particular since Bart had fallen ". . . more quickly than estimated by the 8. Armee . . .". The acting chief of the operations group in the general staff of the Heer commented that ". . . the present success against the enemy Gran bridgehead was amazing, since the relative strength, compared to the rest of the eastern front, was most unfavorable within the sector of Heeresgruppe Süd . . .". The 8. Armee expected that, after the reorganization, which had started, the attack on Beny and Kemend could begin on 24 February and would be completed during the night of 25 to 26 February. In the most unfavorable circumstances, it would take two more nights.[21]

The attacks on Kemend and Beny were prepared on 23 February. The "LAH" Division was to attack Kemend together with elements of the 46. Inf.-Div. from the south and southwest. The "HJ" Division, together with the 211. Volks-grenadier-division, was to attack Beny from the west and north, respectively. The start of the attack was ordered for 02.00 hours on 24 February 1945. Aerial reconnaissance indicated that the enemy had particularly concentrated his artillery at the lower Gran and that it was less strong near Kemend and Beny. Elements of two motorized mechanized brigades were assumed to be inside the bridgehead.

The attack on Beny was to be carried out with a focus from the northwest along both sides of the Ersekkety-Beny road. There, too, the terrain offered no cover, as during the attack on Bart. Hence, the attack could take place only during darkness. Aerial photos showed that the enemy had dug positions from the rear into the railroad embankment, which ran in a general north-south direction. Based on the experiences of the 211. Volksgrenadier-division during its attacks on 17 and 18 February, light and heavy machine guns and anti-tank guns would be in position at the railroad embankment. They were extremely well camouflaged toward the German side. As well, the flood dikes—also called " Turkish walls—had been fortified into positions. A mine obstacle was reportedly located ahead of the railway crossing along the Ersekkety-Beny road. The terrain dropped from Ersekkety-Puszta to Beny by about thirty meters. The terrain to the left (north) of the road was dominated from Leand-Puszta. The somewhat elevated road provided cover to the infantry advancing to its right.

Regiment 26 (without III. Bataillon) and the armored group were sent into action for the attack. Regiment 25 secured around Bart. According to the war diary of Heeresgruppe Süd, parts of the 46. Inf.-Div. were scheduled for the attack from the west. Both battalions of Regiment 25 assembled in Ersekkety-Puszta: to the right of the road the I., to the left, the II. The armored group assembled east of Ersekkety-Puszta. In order to camouflage the engine and track sounds, the German artillery laid harassing fire on recognized enemy positions during the forward move.

Before the start of the attack, a mine clearing squad of the Pionierbataillon was to remove the mine obstacle ahead of the railway crossing. However, it was spotted by the Soviets and fired on. The II./26 picked up the squad during its advance. In order to safeguard the planned element of surprise and the clearing of mines, the attack started without a fire attack from the artillery and the heavy weapons. Since the Soviets had been alerted, they immediately fired barrages. The 1. and 3./26 suffered significant losses during the advance, the 2./26 found sufficient cover in the road ditch. It was only about half a meter deep and partly filled with water from melted snow, but that had to be accepted. The II./26 came under concentra-ted rifle fire from the left flank and fell somewhat behind. Others moved over into the right road ditch behind 2. Kompanie. In the meantime, the II. Panzerabteilung was pulled forward. Two Panzers each rolled ahead to the right and left of the road and opened fire, in the light of dawn, at the anti-tank guns spotted at the railway embankment. Simultaneously, the 2./26 had advanced to within 200 meters of the railroad crossing. It took advantage of an attack by artillery and heavy infantry weapons to get to the other side of the crossing and rolled up the close-by Soviet positions with machine pistol fire and hand grenades. In the meantime, the II. Bataillon also moved in and broke into the Russian positions. The Panzers eliminated several anti-tank guns at the railway embankment and knocked out several T-34s. Under covering fire from the 2 cm guns of the SPW-Bataillon, the Grenadiers of the I. and II. Bataillons and the armored personnel carriers, taking turns in attacking, battled their way forward. By approximately 08.30 hours, the town was taken. Some of the Soviets fled across the Gran bridge. It was blown up by the enemy when the Grenadiers approached. The I. and II. Bataillons cleared the town and then secured from its eastern edge toward the Gran.[22]

The 211. Volksgrenadierdivision took advantage of the success of the "HJ" Division and captured Leand-Puszta in the course of the morning.[23]

After eventful fighting, the 46. Inf.-Div. took Kemendi-Puszta and continued its push to the east. The "LAH" Division broke through a strong anti-tank blocking position with 37 guns and then, with support from the "H.u.D." Division, captured Kemend after bitter house-to-house fighting.

The battle for the Gran bridgehead was evaluated in the war diary of Heeresgruppe Süd as follows:

> . . . After eight days of fighting, with high losses to both sides, operation 'Südwind' resulted in the total elimination of the enemy Gran

bridgehead. During the first three days (17–19.2.) it led to quick successes against the surprised enemy and took away from the enemy the western and southern sections of the bridgehead up to the mouth of the Gran. In the remaining northeastern sector which included the villages of Kam-Darmoty (Köhidgyarmat, Author), Bart, Kemend, and Bina (Beny), the enemy dug in, supported by heavy defensive fire from the heavy weapons located on the eastern bank, and offered determined resistance. Starting from the night of 20 to 21 February, and reorgani-zing repeatedly, the German attack groups broke stronghold after stronghold from the remainder of the bridgehead. They used the darkness in order to avoid the well-aimed enemy fire from the eastern bank. After the difficult capture of the towns of Kemend (must read Köhidgyarmat, Author) and Bart in the evening of 21 February, and after another regrouping, the attack again gathered speed in the morning of 24 February while it was still dark. During the noon hours, it led to the seizure of Kemend and Bina [Beny] and, in the afternoon, to the complete clearing of the bridgehead. Remnants of the enemy held on only at the Kemend road bridge . . .[24]

During the period of 17–22 February 1945, the following enemy losses in the Gran Bridgehead were noted:

Prisoners	537
Enemy dead, counted	2,069
Enemy dead, estimated	850
Tanks destroyed	71
Guns destroyed or captured	45
Pak destroyed or captured	134
Aircraft shot down	3 [25]

The German forces also suffered high losses, figures are not known. According to documents from Heeresgruppe Süd, of 102 armored vehicles (meant are probably Panzers and Panzerjägers), 43 were still combat-ready on 23 February.[26]

Despite the poor conditions, the "HJ" Division had fought excellently and very successfully. For the first time, it had been able to send its armored group into the attack as a solid unit. Success did not fail to show. In spite of the painful losses, it gave confidence and encouragement to the troops.

CHAPTER 9.5
The Division in the Lake Balaton Offensive from 6 to 18 March 1945

PLANNING AND ASSEMBLY FOR THE OFFENSIVE

At the start of the year 1945—as already reported—the Soviets had succeeded in crossing the Danube south of Buda-pest and advanced far to the west south of Lake Balaton. They had been brought to a halt only approximately thirty kilometers east of Nagykanizsa, the major city in the Hungarian petroleum region. Further to the south, the front ran along the lower course of the Drau river. In the north, the Soviets stood at the line: southeastern corner of Lake Balaton-southwestern corner of Lake Velence-eastern edge of the Vertes mountain-Gran.

Heeresgruppe Süd was given the task, in cooperation with Heeresgruppe Südost (E), of destroying the Soviet forces in the region between the Danube, Lake Balaton and the Drau. Further, of capturing the Danube between the mouth of the Drau and east of Lake Velence and of establishing bridgeheads near Dunapentele, Dunaföldvar and Baja. German reconnaissance had identified in that area (in sequence from north to south): the 4. Guards Army, the 26. Army, the 57. Army and the 1. Bulgarian Army. The enemy did not expect any major German operation for the time being. He was refitting the units which had suffered significant losses during the fighting in December and January, and assembled further forces for the planned operation which had Vienna as its objective.

During the German offensive against the Gran bridgehead, the Soviets had taken a few prisoners and, to their surprise, determined that the captured men were members of the I. SS-Panzerkorps. That was interpreted as a definitive indication of a major German offensive operation.[1]

The Soviets expected a German offensive from the region around Stuhlweißenburg in the direction of the Danube. Hence, they reinforced the 4. Guards Army and the 26. Army, which had eight and ten divisions, respectively, with artillery and anti-tank guns. Behind their sectors, the 27. Army was installed in a second defensive position. The 3. Ukrainian Front had as reserves the 18. and 23. Tank Corps, the 5. Cavalry Corps, one rifle division, and army artillery. The Soviets fortified their positions energetically. In that, they were masters.[2]

Available for the German offensive, code-named "Frühlingserwachen" (spring awakening), were:

the 3. Hungarian Army south of the Danube, with the left wing of the VIII. Hungarian Army Corps near Gran/Estergom, while its II. Hungarian Army Corps was in action behind Lake Balaton,

the IV. SS-Panzerkorps on both sides of Stuhlweißenburg,
the III. Panzerkorps with the 1. and 3. Panzerdivisions
as the northern attack group;
these units formed Armeegruppe Balck;
the 6. SS-Panzerarmee with
the II. SS-Panzerkorps (2. and 9. SS-Panzerdivisions)
the I. SS-Panzerkorps (1. and 12. SS-Panzerdivisions) and
the I. Kavalleriekorps (3. and 4. Kavalleriedivisions)
as the major assault group;
the 2. Panzerarmee with the LXVIII. Armeekorps and the XXII.
  Gebirgskorps (mountain infantry), with it the 16. SS-Panzer-
  grenadierdivision "RFSS" (Reichsführer SS) and the 13. Waffen-
  Gebirgs-Division SS-"Handschar" (Croatian No. 1) between the
  southwestern corner of Lake Balaton and the Drau;
four divisions of Heeresgruppe E;
as reserves of Heeresgruppe Süd:
the 44. Reichsgrenadierdivision "Hoch und Deutschmeister",
the 25. Hungarian Infantry Division,
the 23. Panzerdivision, the armored elements of the 6. Panzerdivision
  and Brigade 92 (mot.).[3]

The two divisions of the I. SS-Panzerkorps had suffered considerable
losses during the offensive to smash the Soviet Gran bridgehead. Those were
approximately replaced in numbers. "HJ" Division received 23 officers, 60
NCOs and 1,040 men. Among them were numerous former members of the
Kriegsmarine.[4] The two divisions had the following strengths on 3 March
1945:
    1. SS-Panzerdivision "LAH":
        3 strong, 1 medium-strong, 3 average battalions;
        21 heavy Pak, 15 assault guns, 14 Panzer IVs, 26 Panzer Vs;
        4 light, 3 heavy batteries, 2 medium, 1 heavy launcher batteries.
    The level of motorization stood at 72 percent, the combat readiness
    was judged as 'II'.
    12. SS-Panzerdivision "HJ":
        1 strong, 1 medium-strong, 5 average battalions;
        12 heavy Pak, 13 Jagdpanzer IVs, 12 Panzer IVs, 9 Panzer Vs;
        attached Schwere Panzerjägerabteilung 560: 6 Jagd-panthers, 8 Panz-
        erjäger IVs;
        6 light, 1 heavy batteries, 4 launcher batteries.
    The level of motorization stood at 50 percent, the combat readiness was
judged as 'II'.[5]
    In that report on strength, seven battalions are shown for "HJ" Division.
Each of the two Panzergrenadierregiments consisted of three battalions.
Regiment 25 integrated the Regimental companies into a heavy battalion

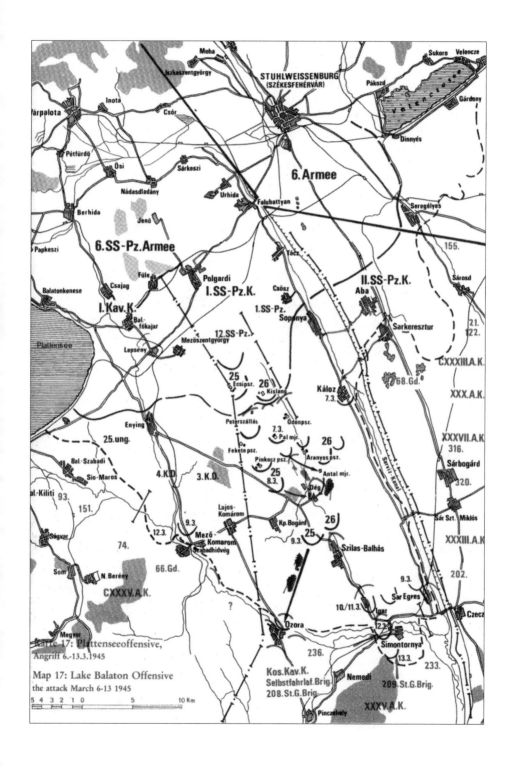

Karte 17: Plattenseeoffensive,
Angriff 6.-13.3.1945

Map 17: Lake Balaton Offensive
the attack March 6-13 1945

5 4 3 2 1 0   5   10 Km

under the command of Oberleutnant Kaminski. The light infantry guns of the Panzergrenadier battalions were added to the heavy infantry guns in the 13. Kompanie. It was led by Untersturmführer Voith. As before, the 14. continued to be the 2 cm Flak-Kompanie. The Pak-Züge of the Panzergrenadier battalions were combined into the 15. Kompanie, led by Untersturm-führer Wunderlich. The 16. Kompanie consisted of its launcher platoons. The Aufklärungskompanie and the Pionierkompanie were dissolved.[6] The seventh battalion mentioned above was probably not the heavy battalion of Regiment 25, but the Feldersatzbataillon 12 (field replacement battalion), on which no information is available.- Obersturmbannführer Martin Gross took over the command of Panzerregiment 12. The mixed II. Abteilung was led by Hauptsturmführer Hans Siegel, the heavy Panzerjägerabteilung by Major Goldammer.

The divisions of the II. SS-Panzerkorps , which had not taken part in the attack on the Gran bridgehead, were stronger in Panzers, Panzerjägers, and Panzergrenadiers than the I. SS-Panzerkorps.[7]

In preparation for operation "Frühlingserwachen", the "HJ" Division moved from the area east of Neuhäusel initially into the Varoslöd-Papa district (3 March) and subsequently into the assembly area southeast of Polgardi. The tracked elements of the Division reached Papa by rail transport. Only few details are known. The II./26 marched on

26 February 1945 from Ersekkety (thirty kilometers east of -Neuhäusel) via Kolta to Caszfalu, on

28 February by way of Neuhäusel to Kiskessiban -(Bankesi), on

1 March to Bankesi, on

3 March to Polgardi, on

4 March into the assembly area north of Kislang.[7a]

Flakabteilung 12 marched on

28 February ". . . through the deepest mud . . ." from Palpuszta (near Udvard, 8 kilometers east of Neuhäusel) via Neuhäusel, Komorn, Raab, Papa to Deka (6 kilometers southwest of Papa), on

4 March from Deka via Devecser, Varoslöd, -Veszprem, Balatonkenese to Polgardi.[8]

The road conditions were bad and hampered the initial assembly of the numerous motorized and armored units. Not all units of the Division reached their assembly areas in time.

The Offensive

The task given to Heeresgruppe Süd has already been noted. The Armies and Armeegruppe Balck were issued the following objectives:

On the attack will be

the 2. Panzerarmee with two attack groups from the line on both sides of Nagybajom in the direction of Kaposvar, the 6. SS-Panzerarmee, with the attached I. Kavallerie-korps, along both sides of the Sarviz canal across the line Csarda mjr.-Seregelyes in a southerly direction.

Armeegruppe Balck, with the III. Panzerkorps, across the line Seregelyes-Lake Velence in easterly and southeasterly directions.

The 6. SS-Panzerarmee was scheduled to break through rapidly to the south, concentrating on the left, in order to cut off the enemy's rear connections across the Danube. In cooperation with the 2. Panzerarmee and the elements of Heeresgruppe E attacking south of Fünfkirchen across the Drau river, it was then to destroy the enemy forces located between Lake Balaton and Drau.

The 6. SS-Panzerarmee brought into action: on the right, the I. Kavalleriekorps, in the center, the I. SS-Panzerkorps, on the left, the II. SS-Panzerkorps. The Sarviz canal formed the dividing line between the two Panzerkorps. The I. SS-Panzerkorps shifted its focal point with the stronger 1. SS-Panzerdivision "LAH" to the left, its neighbor on the right was the 12. SS-Panzerdivision "HJ". As their first attack objective, I. SS-Panzerkorps and the I. Kavalleriekorps were to reach the Sio canal and establish several bridgeheads.[1]

The terrain for the attack between Lake Balaton and the Sarviz canal climbs from a shallow basin to the southwest, south and southeast of Polgardi from an elevation of 138 to 133 meters (Lake Balaton is at an elevation of 106 meters) in one step to an undulating high plain with an average elevation of 150 meters. Along the direction of the attack, at the time, runs a creek (Bozot) past Janosmjr. and Ödönpuszta, through Deg, past Szilas-Balhas (Mezescilas), flowing into the Sio canal west of Simontornya. Several other creeks empty into the Bozot from both sides in Deg. Another creek runs in the same direction from the area west of Lepseny past Enying to the Sio canal west of Mezö-Komarom. During the spring melting of snow, water collects in many depressions in the terrain so that they become marshy and unusable for vehicles. The highest points are 167 (eight kilometers southeast of Enying), 171 (six kilometers southeast of Deg), 176 and 178 (six and two kilometers southeast of Lajos-Komarom, respectively). Immediately south of the Sio canal, the terrain rises to 220 meters near Ozora and Simontornya, and to 253 and 275 meters (five kilometers and fourteen kilometers southwest of Simontornya, respectively). Small forests are located west of Deg and around Hill 167 (eight kilometers southeast of Enying). Noteworthy, in addition to the already mentioned towns, were Mezöszentgyörgy (seven kilometers southwest of Polgardi), Csösz, Soponya and Kaloz (nine, twelve, and fifteen kilometers southeast of Polgardi). In addition to the few villages, there was a large number of larger and smaller Pusztas (farms, ranches). Only two hard-surface roads were available in the direction of the attack: from Balatonkenese via Enying to Mezö-Komarom, and from Falubattyan via

Soponya and Kaloz to Simontornya. On the 1:200,000 map available at the time, the second road was shown in its last section for a stretch of 5 kilometers as only a "non-improved track". In the sector of the "HJ" Division, no roads existed in the direction of the attack. Available were only a "non-improved track" from Mezöszentgyörgy via Deg, and an "improved track" from Deg to Szilas-Balhas.

In general, the terrain for the attack by the I. SS-Panzer-korps would have been quite usable for tracked vehicles during dry weather or heavy frost. However, the winter weather changed unexpectedly at the end of February. It became sunny, the temperatures climbed to eleven degrees Celsius, bringing a thaw. The terrain could hardly be used by vehicles off the roads and tracks.

Inside the attack sector of the "HJ" Division, the Soviet positions were located approximately 500 meters south of Kislang (nine kilometers southeast of Mezöszentgyörgy) and ran in a generally west-east direction. In order to keep its own intentions secret, the Division did not reconnoiter with scouting parties. Rather, it made use of the results of reconnaissance and observations by the 23. Panzerdivision which defended the southern section of the German front between Lake Balaton and the Sarviz canal, adjoining to the east on the 25. Hungarian Division. The Heeresgruppe ordered the attack to begin on 6 March at 04.00 hours, after a short artillery preparation.

The plan of attack for the "HJ" Division envisaged:

Panzergrenadierregiment 25, reinforced by 1. Kompanie of Pionierbataillon 12, will assemble near Ecsi-Puszta, break through the Soviet network of positions in front of it, and will capture Fekete-Puszta (five kilometers south-southeast of Ecsi-Puszta) as its first attack objective;

Panzergrenadierregiment 26 (without III. Bataillon), reinforced by 2. Kompanie of Pionierbataillon 12, will assemble in the vicinity of Kislang, break through the Soviet network of positions located south of the village, and will capture Ödön-Puszta (three kilometers southeast of Kislang) as its first attack objective;

the armored group will assemble north of Ecsi-Puszta in order to penetrate into the rear, with the Sio canal as its objective, after the Panzergrenadierregiments have broken through the Soviet network of positions;

Artillerieregiment 12, Werferabteilung 12, and the heavy batteries of Flakabteilung 12 will concentrate a short fire attack on the recognized enemy positions at the start of the attack, and then support the attack of the two Panzergrenadierregiments;

Panzerjägerabteilung 12 will follow the Panzer-grenadierregiments at daybreak and will combat enemy tanks, anti-tank guns and strongholds;

Panzerpionierbataillon 12 will hold the 3. Kompanie in readiness as support for the crossing of the Sio canal and subsequent bridge construction, the 4. Kompanie remains in reserve and will be available for ant-tank and anti-aircraft duties;

Panzeraufklärungsabteilung 12 will be available to the Division as required;

Panzernachrichtenabteilung 12 (communications) will set up a telephone link from the Divisional -command post in Mezöszentgyörgy (6 kilometers southwest of Polgardi) to the forward Divisional command post in Kislang, to the Panzergrenadierregiment 26 in Kislang, to the Panzergrenadierregiment 25 in Ecsi Puszta, to the armored group, to the Artillerie-regiment 12, and to the Flakabteilung 12; back-up by radio; radio silence until the start of the attack.[2]

Day-time temperatures on 6 March 1945 were around zero degrees Celsius. Snow was falling from a low cloud cover, visibility was poor, the trails totally muddied. The attack by the "HJ" Division started, as ordered, at 04.00 hours. It encountered a deeply staggered and very well fortified network of enemy positions which was being tenaciously defended. The Panzergrenadiers were able to overcome the forward positions, but then stalled. The II./26 was forced to stop its attack at 04.45 hours approximately 500 meters outside of the Ödön-Puszta. Its reconnaissance determined the existence of five well-fortified systems of trenches, one behind the other. Contrary to expectations, the enemy was apparently waiting for the attack and was thoroughly prepared. When the day dawned, the Bataillon came under violent enemy artillery fire. Those troops outside the captured Soviet positions suffered considerable losses. During the night, the ground had frozen again on top, making it almost impossible to dig in. Enemy combat aircraft attacked Kislang and Ecsi-Puszta. The Flakabteilung 12 shot down a IL2. At 16.00 hours, the II./26 again attacked the Ödön Puszta, with support by fire from Werferabteilung 12. However, before reaching its objective, it was stopped by fire from Stalin organs and mortars. It suffered heavy losses, among others, the chief of the 5. Kompanie, Untersturmführer Deutsch, was killed. At 17.45 hours, skillfully taking advantage of an attack by German fighters, Untersturmführer Rechers managed to penetrate into the system of trenches outside the Puszta with a few men. The forward Soviet positions were abandoned.[3]

The attack by the I. Bataillon of Regiment 26 initially also made little progress. After daybreak, the Bataillon suffered considerable losses from enemy artillery fire. With the help of two Panzerjäger IVs led by Obersturmführer Georg Hurdelbrink, the 2. Kompanie, under the leadership of Untersturmführer Hans-Jürgen Ross, managed to drive the Soviets from their positions at approximately 13.30 hours. They retreated headlong to the Ödön-Puszta, leaving their heavy weapons, such as anti-tank guns, mortars and heavy machine guns, behind in the positions.[4]

Because of the high losses, Sturmbannführer Kostenbader ordered Regiment 26 to stop its attack. It was to be continued the following morning with Panzer support.[5]

In bitter fighting, Panzergrenadierregiment 25 broke through the forward Soviet positions. When daylight broke, the Regiment was stopped by artillery and mortar fire for some time. The SPW-Bataillon was brought forward and it overran the second network of positions under heavy Soviet fire. Sturmmann Nolte of the 9. Kompanie shot down a IL2 with his single-barrel 2 cm gun out of a formation of attacking Soviet combat aircraft. Peterszallas was captured, but the attack came to a stop north of Fekete-Puszta in the heavy enemy defensive fire. Because of the difficult terrain conditions, the attack of the III./26 could not be supported by Panzers.[6]

The cavalry divisions attacking on the right of the "HJ" Division were also stalled after initial successes. The 4. Kavalleriedivision, attacking on the southern shore of Lake Balaton toward Siofok, was forced back to its line of departure around the evening hours by enemy counterattacks. The 3. Kavallerie-division came under heavy fire to the flank, from out of the attack sector of Panzergrenadierregiment 25.[7]

The "LAH" Division took Hill 149 (4 kilometers northeast of Kislang). A Panzer attack, from the area northeast of Kislang, into the rear of the enemy south of Hill 149 stalled in difficult terrain after two kilometers. Toward the evening, elements of the Division pushed into Soponya.[8]

The II. SS-Panzerkorps had been forced to move into its assembly area mostly on foot and did not reach them in time. The Korps was only able to start its attack at 18.30 hours. The III. Panzerkorps, adjacent in action on the left, succeeded in advancing approximately 4 kilometers to the north via Seregelyes.[9]

After initial successes, the 2. Panzerarmee was stalled south of Lake Balaton. One Kampfgruppe was able to gain six kilometers by the evening.[10] Units of the 297. Infanteriedivision and the 104. Jägerdivision advanced during the night of 5 to 6 March across the Drau south of Fünfkirchen. They threw back the 2. Bulgarian Infantry Division and were able to construct a pontoon bridge across the river.[11]

The results of the first day of the attack were generally unsatisfactory, except at Heeresgruppe E which succeeded in establishing two bridgeheads across the Drau. The decisive reasons for this were that it had been impossible to surprise the enemy, and that the deeply thawed terrain delayed the assembly, and made Panzer attacks almost impossible.

The sky on 7 March was variably cloudy, the daytime temperatures climbed to four degrees Celsius. Some snow was falling, but it cleared toward the evening and turned colder. The terrain conditions allowed only individual and limited action by Panzers.

Panzergrenadierregiment 25, in its attack against Fekete-Puszta, gained only little ground and was stopped north of the Puszta by extremely tenacious resistance. Panzergrenadierregiment 26 made better progress. The II. Bataillon started an attack on Ödön-Puszta at 04.40 hours. It was supported by a Panzer company and parts of the SPW-Bataillon. The attached 2. Pionierkompanie cleared away a mine barrier to make way for the Panzers and armored personnel carriers. In a rapidly moving attack, Ödön-Puszta was captured soon after 5 A.M. by the II./26, the Panzers and armored personnel carriers. During the continued attack, the I./26 took Pal-Major (two kilometers southwest of Ödön-Puszta). The II./26, together with the Panzers and armored personnel carriers, advanced to just north of Aranyos-Puszta (3.5 kilometers south of Ödön-Puszta), but stalled there. Regiment 26 had to fight off counterattacks, especially from the right flank. The attached Panzers and three "Grillen" (crickets = heavy self-propelled 15 cm infantry guns) effectively supported the defense. On 7 March, the II./26 captured two heavy machine guns and three 7.62 cm anti-tank guns.[12]

The Kavalleriekorps gained only little ground in the direction of Enying. The "LAH" Division attacked to the east from the district northeast of Ödön-Puszta. It blocked the Kaloz-Simontornya road and took Kaloz from the south. During the attack from three sides, Saponya was captured soon after. That made the only improved road in the combat sector of the I. SS-Panzerkorps available for the further attack to the southeast.

The day of 8 March 1945 did not bring a drastic improvement in the weather although the temperatures remained below freezing. Variable cloudiness brought light snowfalls. Reconnaissance against the enemy indicated that the Soviets had pulled out at least three divisions from the area around Budapest and their Drau bridgehead in order to send them into action against the German offensive.

The "HJ" Division continued its attack on Deg on 8 March 1945. Regiment 25, supported by Panzers and the SPW-Bataillon, captured Pinkocz-Puszta (six kilometers northwest of Deg). With the SPW-Bataillon and the Panzers at the point, it advanced to the Deg-Enying road by the evening and blocked it approximately 3 kilometers west of the village.[13] Regiment 26 mounted its attack at 05.15 hours. It overran an enemy anti-tank gun. One of the Panzerjäger IVs became unserviceable. By the evening, the Bataillon reached a group of farms 4 kilometers northeast of Deg. Soviet counterattacks were repulsed. Fire from the "Grillen" was concentrated on enemy positions at the northern entrance to Deg. During an attack by Soviet combat aircraft, the commander of Panzergrenadierregiment 26, Sturm-bannführer Kostenbader, was mortally wounded. He was an outstanding and brave leader, had come from the Ellwangen Bataillon, and was trained by the then-Obersturm-bannführer Felix Steiner. The command of the Regiment was transferred to Obersturmbannführer Braun.[14]

A strong enemy position, equipped with several anti-tank guns, was holding on around the road junction two kilometers east of Pinkocz-Puszta. It was located at the joint between the two Panzergrenadierregiments and presented a significant obstacle to the attack on Deg which was planned for the following day. The Division sent out an armored group under the command of Hauptsturmführer Hans Siegel to eliminate the threat to the flank in a night attack. The group consisted of the two companies of the Schwere Panzerjägerabteilung 560 with Jagdpanthers and Panzerjäger IVs, several Panzer IVs of the II. Panzerabteilung, several Flakpanzers and parts of Panzeraufklärungsabteilung 12. Altogether, they were some forty armored vehicles. After eliminating the flanking position at the road junction, the armored group was to break through to the Puszta Antal Major (two kilometers north of Deg) and from there support the attack on Deg in the morning of 8 March.

The armored group started out just after midnight on 8 March. Hauptsturmführer Hans Siegel reported on the attack:

> . . . During the deployment of the unit into a wide wedge formation, our own artillery shelled the detected blocking position, mostly dug-in anti-tank guns. The concentrated force of fire and movement, added to which was the din of motors and the rattle of the tracked vehicles firing tracers in front of them, explosions from mortar shells hurled from armored personnel carriers on the move, all that happening during otherwise total darkness, discouraged probably even the most hardened Red Army man . . . We overran the anti-tank barrier and the fortified positions without losses.
>
> After overcoming the enemy position we stopped firing. It was important to stay on the right direction and to keep moving so as not to fall victim to tank hunting teams. At first, our Panzers were still under fire, but that was only dangerous to anyone standing in the turret with his head outside the cover of the armor. During such a situation it is not possible to stop and wait for stragglers. In an armored group at night, the only way for a man to orient himself is by the glowing exhaust of the Panzer driving in front of him. The radio, too, is useless since no-one can determine the exact position during darkness in open terrain. I oriented myself by using rows of widely spaced trees, from one Puszta to the next.
>
> It was still dark when I spotted, on a flat hill top and behind the tops of trees, silhouettes of buildings hard to the right of me. A large farm! Let's get in there! Right away, a man showed up, the swineherd of the Puszta Antal Major, as he introduced himself to us in good German. His son had also 'joined' the German forces. Inside the farm, a Russian communications officer was still hiding. The swineherd asked us to get him right away. He also said that he had immediately told the servants of the Puszta when they were forced to construct tank traps with mines at the bottom of the traps: 'The Germans aren't that stupid, they'll just drive around them'. While others were looking after the Russian and silenced the radio, I sent

back a motorcycle messenger with the report: 'Spearhead has reached Antal Major around five o'clock. Request further orders'. One of the men came back to my Panzer and reported: 'The radio has been eliminated. We are all invited to breakfast by the lady of the manor. It is just being prepared.' The breakfast remained untouched. We stayed mounted in the vehicles. Nine Panzers and several armored personnel carriers had come along, the others had lost contact. From the open square farmyard between the buildings I was able to see a village to the south, with a church steeple, in the haze of the morning. Distance 2000. Deg! . . .[15]

While the I. Kavalleriekorps gained very little ground on 8 March 1945, the possibility of a major breakthrough was taking on shape at the I. SS-Panzerkorps. The "HJ" Division had been occupied all day with clearing the area around Saponya. Some of its elements were able to capture Nagyhörcsök-Puszta (five kilometers northwest of Deg) in the evening. The armored group followed into the area north of it. The I. SS-Panzerkorps received orders from the 6. SS-Panzerarmee to continue the attack with concentrated forces and to cross the Sio canal between Ozora and Simontornya. The 23. Panzerdivision was to follow behind.

The temperature in the night of 8 to 9 March dropped below freezing, during the day it climbed above zero degrees Celsius. It was variably cloudy and windy, with some localized snowfall. The unimproved lanes were better to drive on than during the previous days.

The "HJ" Division attacked Deg in the morning with parts of the two Panzergrenadierregiments and the armored group. Hauptsturmführer Hans Siegel had refused the breakfast offered by the lady of the manor of Antal Major in order to take advantage of the morning haze for a surprise attack on Deg. His report continues:

> . . . Commanders, report to me—we're attacking!—Flakpanzers will swing wide to the right, then turn in and attack the village from the north when the frontally attacking Panzers have reached the edge of the village. All others, spread out wide and, then, at the village and into it at full speed. There will be no firing, no stops to fire on the way! Assemble at the church. I will watch the attack from here in the Jagdpanther and, if required, will provide fire cover. I'll follow when the edge of the village has been reached. Panzers—March!
> I stood in the turret of the combat-ready Jagdpanther and followed, through the binoculars, the progress which was almost like a drill. Everything went well—then, just outside the village, an explosion. One Panzer stopped. Anti-tank gun or mine? Down into the Panzer and at the scissor telescope! The gunner had already taken aim at the target, was waiting only for the order to fire. An explo-

sion, a hit to our own Jadgpanther's front armor plate! The scissor telescope was gone, rivet heads popped off, ricocheting—criss-cross—through the fighting compartment. 'Back into cover!' Right away, the second hit to the right drive sprocket. The Panzer swung its front to the left, but rolled into a depression in the terrain. Luckily, it was not burning. Out! Our own Panzers were inside the village—out of sight—and without leadership!—'Motorcycle messenger, over here!' Onto the back of the cycle, no seat—only a carrier to sit on—into the village at full speed, following in the Panzer track so as not to be blown up by mines! Through the dawn, we arrived unscathed in Deg. My Panzers had their hot moments behind them already. They had encountered Russian assault guns, 10 cm, about a dozen of them. The Soviets were surprised, some of them were knocked out, others were able to escape from the opposite edge of the village to the south and southeast. Two were sitting in the creek bed next to the bridge, the others rolled across it. The highlight was that one of the Flakpanzers had knocked out such a behemoth with its 2 cm or 3.7 cm gun, from behind, in the engine compartment. As ordered, the Flakpanzer had driven into the village toward the road fork from the northwest. Barely fifty meters ahead of it rolled a Russian assault gun, its barrel facing forward. The Flakpanzer hammered its rear, the assault gun blew up and burned out . . .[16]

At approximately the same time as the small armored group of Haupt-sturmführer Siegel, parts of Regiment 25 and Regiment 26 also attacked toward Deg. They cleared the intermediate terrain and the village of Deg. The armored group assembled and, after clearing extensive mine fields, started an attack toward the south. Obersturmführer Gaede spotted a with-drawing Soviet vehicle column and pursued it with his Pantherkompanie. The Panzers got stuck in the marshy terrain. It was almost evening before they were mobile again. By the evening, Panzergrenadierregiment 25 and the SPW-Bataillon had reached the area northwest of Szilas-Balhas. The II./26 mounted the attached Panzerjäger IVs of Panzerjägerabteilung 12 and reached the area immediately north of Szilas-Balhas, as did, probably, the I./26.[17]

The "LAH" Division concentrated its advance along the Kaloz-Simon-tornya road to the hills immediately north of the city. The left attack group was stopped by an anti-tank position near Sar Egres (four kilometers north-east of Simontornya). Through the gap, smashed open by the "HJ" Division, the Kavalleriekorps was able to push forward and reach the Kaboka sector between Enying and west of Mezö-Komarom.

On 10 March 1945, the daytime temperature again climbed to above freezing. It was raining and snowing from an overcast sky. The lanes and fields were soft and muddy. The Kavalleriekorps and the I. SS-Panzerkorps continued to push closer to the Sio canal. By 21.00 hours, Panzergrenadier-regiment 26 had captured the heavily fortified Szilas-Balhas and they advanced, even during the night, into the district immediately north of Igar (three kilometers northwest of Simontornya). There, the chief of the 14. (Flak) Kompanie of the SS-Panzergrenadier-regiment 26, Hauptsturmführer Martin Stolze, was seriously wounded. He died on 14 March 1945 at the main dressing station in Deg.[19]

The open right flank badly impeded the advance of Panzergrenadier-regiment 25. The "HJ" Division sought to establish contact with the neighbor on the right through scouting parties. One of the scouting parties was led by Untersturmführer Elmar Lochbihler, the leader of the Pionierzug of Panzer-aufklärungsabteilung 12. He reported:

> . . . I remember a scouting sortie from Deg via -Közebogard and Lajos-Komarom. Both villages were free of the enemy. We were driv-ing along an open road up the rear slope in the direction of Mező-Komarom. There, we spotted, at the opposite slope, Russians in battalion strength digging in. Suddenly, seven Russian combat air-craft were overhead. The first looped to the right, the others follow-ing nicely behind. In line with the Russian position they swung left again and, when they were right overhead their friends, they unloaded. The Russian were firing signal flares, but all was in vain. After the aircraft had disappeared, two of our armored personnel carrier crews fired into the disarray . . .[20]

The enemy had brought up the V. Guards Cavalry Corps and reinforced his bridgeheads across the Sio canal near Ozora, Simontornya and Sar-Egres. In part, he switched over to counterattacks in order to keep the Simon-tornya-Czecze road open. The 23. Panzerdivision was pulled forward to strengthen the I. SS-Panzerkorps, its forward elements moved into the area north of Sar-Egres in the evening.[21]

Heeresgruppe Süd reported its strength as on 10 March 1945 to the OKH. Shown for the "HJ" Division were:

5 weak, 1 average battalions;

12 heavy Pak, 6 Jagdpanzer IVs, 6 Panzer IVs, 9 Panzer Vs,

assigned (Schwere Panzerjägerabteilung 560): 4 Jagdpanthers, 1 Jagdpanzer IV;

6 light, 1 heavy batteries, 3 launcher batteries (16 light field howitzers, 6 heavy field howitzers, 3 guns immobile);

level of motorization: 50 percent,

combat level II.

Compared to the report of 3 March 1945, one strong, one medium-strong, and three average battalions had been turned into five weak battalions in the course of the fighting. The Feldersatzbataillon (replacement), which had been reported as the seventh battalion on 3 March, had probably been disbanded by 10 March to provide replacements for the fighting battalions and was no longer counted. Seven Jagdpanzer IVs of the Panzerjäger-abteilung and six Panzer IVs had been lost. At the Schwere Panzerjäger-abteilung 560, two Jagdpanthers and seven Panzerjäger IVs had been destroyed or were not combat-ready; one launcher battery had been lost.[22]

The condition of the lanes and trails improved only little on 11 March 1945. The night had been cloudy and very stormy. The temperature climbed to four degrees Celsius above zero. Because of the strong wind, the ground started to dry up.

It is likely that Panzergrenadierregiment 26 captured Igar during the night of 10 to 11 March and cleared it of the enemy. To the south of the village, the Soviets were resisting tenaciously in order to secure the Simon-tornya bridgehead. Several Soviet counterattacks were repelled. While the II./26 defended Igar, which was repeatedly attacked by combat aircraft, the I./26, in action adjacent to the right, pushed the enemy back. In the course of the day, elements of the "LAH" Division, in cooperation with Regiment 26 and Panzerjägerabteilung 12 captured the road fork 1.2 kilometers south of Igar and a hill 2 kilometers north of Simontornya. Regiment 26 (without III. Bataillon) was assigned to the "LAH" Division for the attack on the city planned for the next day, and for the establishment of bridgeheads.[22a]

Panzergrenadierregiment 25 had been given the task to set up a bridge-head across the Sio canal near Ozora. Two companies of the SPW-Bataillon and the combat-ready Panzers and Jagdpanzers of the Schwere Panzerjäger-abteilung 560 were attached to the Regiment. According to the report on strength of 10 March, they were six Panzer IVs, nine Panzer Vs, four Jagdpan-thers and one Jagdpanzer IV. The assembly was delayed since the Jagdpanz-ers had not yet been refueled and loaded with ammunition, and since parts of Panzergrenadierregiment 25 had not arrived. The two armored personnel carrier companies were sitting, well camouflaged, in a corn field when Soviet combat aircraft attacked. The Jagdpanzers suffered losses.[23]

After a well-placed fire strike by the German artillery, Panzers and armored personnel carriers mounted their attack in the course of the morn-ing. The first wave was made up of the Panzers and the two armored person-nel carrier companies. One or two armored personnel carriers each drove between two Panzers, staggered to the rear. Unterscharführer Günther Bur-dack of the 9./26 wrote on the progress of the attack:

> . . . Taking advantage of depressions in the terrain and of our own artillery fire, we reached a hill approximately 400 meters from the canal. Our rapid speed had moved us ahead of the starting enemy artillery fire. One armored personnel carrier and the Panzer IVs tried to reach the bridge through a ravine dropping down to the Sio

canal but were prevented from doing that by heavy anti-tank fire. Now it became obvious why the enemy had withdrawn in our attack sector. On the opposite slope—south of the canal—he had set up an anti-tank position in the brush. It resembled a volcano. Three Panzer IVs were knocked out immediately before the entrance to the bridge, another took a hit on the bridge, lost its track and blocked the bridge. Attempts to tow it away under the cover of artificial smoke failed in the anti-tank fire. The III./26 moved into a rear-slope position on the north bank. the Panzergrenadiers of Regiment 25 arrived and took over securing of our sector . . .[23a]

Oberscharführer Willy Kretzschmar, Zugführer in the 5. Panzerkompanie, experienced the attack as follows:

. . . The Panzer at the point was Oberscharführer Auinger's. Then came Unterscharführer Jürgen, Ober-scharführer Kretzschmar and the Kompanie leader, Untersturmführer Peitsch. When we reached the crossroads before the Sio canal, Untersturmführer Peitsch ordered the second Panzer to pull ahead and provide cover to the Pioniers clearing mines. I pulled my vehicle ahead as well since, I said to myself, three guns were better than two. Everything had been quiet until then, even the Russian infantry, dug-in on the hill, did not move. Peitsch, who was sitting approximately eighty meters behind us, raked the hill with machine gun fire. The Pioniers had just cleared the first mines when there were ten to fifteen flashes from the rising terrain behind the Sio canal. That made it clear to me that we were facing a strong anti-tank position. I was just about to indicate the target to the gunner when there were two or three bangs on the Panzer. I shouted at the driver: 'Back up—Let's go!' He replied: 'I can't, the gas pedal is ripped. The sun is shining in here'. I gave orders to bail out. Except for the radio operator, we all got out and assembled behind the Panzer. Finally, the radio operator's hatch opened and Stefan came out, white as chalk. Because of the hit to the transmission he had probably inhaled fumes from the oil. We sprinted into cover behind Peitsch's Panzer. The Russian infantry saw their chance, came out of their trenches and foxholes and made it hot for us. Peitsch pinned them down with explosive shells and machine gun fire. The armored personnel carriers immediately pulled back into the ravine after the first shells from the anti-tank guns. We assembled in the ravine. The other two crews arrived in the ravine, some of them crawling through the mud. Several comrades had been wounded by infantry fire. The armored personnel carriers took us back to the starting position . . .[24]

Sturmmann Heinz Müller of the 5. Panzerkompanie reported about that day:

> . . . The first Russian barrage knocked out the three Panzers at the point. The attack stalled. I had the company chief, Peitsch, in my vehicle. We advanced further in order to provide fire cover for the withdrawing armored personnel carriers. Between the ravine and the bushes, providing cover, stood a shock of straw. There lay our killed Kompanie squad leader. We put him on the engine compartment and continued on. A Panther, which provided us fire cover, reportedly got knocked out later. When we reached safety, we determined that we had received four hits from anti-tank guns . . .[25]

The attempt to quickly grab the bridge across the Sio canal and to establish a bridgehead near Ozora had failed. The enemy had turned the hills south of the canal (191, 208 and 195 meters elevation, the canal's is 100 meters) into strong defensive positions, using reinforcements brought up, and had only left weak forces on the north bank. The German attack came too late. Difficult terrain and attacks from the flanks had delayed it. The war diary of the Heeresgruppe noted:

> . . . An attack by the 12. SS-Pz.Div. on Ozora stalls outside the group of houses at Kula under heavy flanking fire from the west. Reconnaissance sent out along the long open flank. To eliminate the threat to the flank, the Kavallerie Korps will make contact with the right wing of the 12. SS-Pz.Div. on the next day . . .[26]

The daytime temperatures on 12 March 1945 were above freezing. It was cloudy, with scattered rain. Unimproved lanes and the terrain were almost impassable for tracked vehicles.

The 6. SS-Panzerarmee had ordered the I. Kavallerie Korps and the I. SS-Panzerkorps to establish bridgeheads across the Sio canal. At 04.30 hours, Panzergrenadierregiment 25 attacked near Ozora. It was repelled, with high losses. Several further attempts also failed.[27] Simultaneously, Panzergrenadierregiment 26, attached to the 'LAH" Division and Panzeraufklärungsabteilung 1 mounted an attack across the canal to the west and inside Simontornya. The war diary of Heeresgruppe Süd noted, regarding the results

> . . . The railroad bridge is blown. The heights south of the canal are taken in an assault operation. By the evening, the bridgehead has been expanded to a width of 2 kilometers and a depth of 1.5 kilometers. Simultaneously, elements of SS-Pz.Rgt. 1 and of SS-Pz.Gren.Rgt

l attack Simontornya from the west and fight their way to the eastern edge of Simontornya in bloody house-to-house combat . . .[28]

Panzergrenadierregiment 26 had the task of attacking across the canal west of the village, with the two battalions at the front, and of forming bridgeheads. The I. Bataillon attacked on the right, the II. Bataillon on the left. The attack was supported by the attached Panzerjägerabteilung 12, the heavy weapons of the Regiment, and by artillery. Untersturmführer Hans-Jürgen Ross, leader of the 2./26, experienced the attack as follows:

> . . . In the cover of the Panzerjägers, the 2./26 advanced with them, deeply staggered. The 1. and 3. Kompanies took over the cover on the flanks. At approximately 250 meters distance from the enemy positions we came under increasing anti-tank fire. The Panzerjägers fired smoke grenades and pulled back into the cover of the houses in Igar. The Panzergrenadiers continued the attack. The I. Zug managed to break into the enemy positions, taking advantage of the drifting smoke. The Kompanie squad and the II. Zug, in a completely open spot, came under fire from heavy enemy machine guns and mortars from the left flank. The Kompanie leader was seriously wounded, two men received minor wounds. The bulk of the I./26 was only able to cross the terrain, watched and dominated by the enemy, after the fall of darkness. Until then, the I. Zug formed a hedgehog defense in the captured enemy positions . . .[29]

At 14.30 hours, the II./26 reached the Sio canal. The enemy fired mortars at the bank of the canal. German fighter aircraft attacked the enemy with continuous sorties. The German heavy weapons and Panzerjägers laid fire on the enemy positions at the opposite bank and in the vineyards. Soviet artillery shelled the supply route and the attack sector. The Bataillon was unable to cross the canal since the bank was under constant enemy fire from the flanks. It suffered considerable losses. Several rubber dinghies were damaged by the fire and had to be patched. There was a shortage of repair kits. After darkness had fallen, at approximately 18.30 hours, the Regiment started the crossing. In its attack sector, only one spot at the I. Bataillon could be used for that. After a small bridgehead had successfully been set up there, the II. Bataillon followed. Together, the two battalions expanded it to 300 by 100 meters. The enemy defended himself with determination behind the rail line and at the signal man's cottage. In the course of the evening and during the night, several Soviet counterattacks were repelled with difficulty. The Aufklärungs-abteilung of the "LAH" Division was stuck in Simontornya. A company chief of the Abteilung established contact with the II./26. He had orders to use the crossing point of Regiment 26.[30]

In the morning of 12 March, the Kavallerie Korps surprisingly succeeded in setting up a bridgehead west of the mouth of the Kaböka creek into the Sio canal—west of Mezö-Komarom—across the Sio canal. In the course of the day, despite Soviet counterattacks, it was enlarged to a width of three kilometers and a depth of two kilometers.[31] The attachment of Regiment 26 to the "LAH" Division was probably discontinued.

On 13 March 1945, the temperatures climbed to six degrees Celsius. It was partly cloudy, partly sunny. The lanes began to dry off.

Regiment 26 had orders to take Hill 220 (two kilometers south of Simontornya). The attack started at 06.25 hours. Panzers and 2 cm triplet barrel guns of the SPW-Bataillon, and the German artillery, pinned down the enemy in the vineyard by well-targeted fire. By twelve noon, the II./26 had reached Hill 220. At the same time, elements of the "LAH" Division also attacked the hill on the east of Regiment 26. On the right, the Bataillon had contact with the I./26. In the course of the day, the enemy repeatedly attacked the positions on Hill 220 with infantry, tanks and self-propelled anti-aircraft guns. Contact with the neighbor on the left was temporarily lost. The lack of forces meant that the hill could be occupied only by establishing strongholds. In the course of the night, the enemy penetrated into the positions of II./26 once, but he was thrown back.[32] The Divisionsbegleitkompanie was moved and attached to Regiment 26 during the night of 13 to 14 March. The Kompanie crossed the canal between 02.00 and 03.00 hours. One man fell into the water. He could not be rescued, nor was he even found later. At the crossing point, only a small rubber boat with a three-man crew was available. The Kompanie prepared for defense along both sides of the railroad embankment, with its front to the west.[33]

Inside Simontornya, the "LAH" Division managed to reach the southern edge of the city cemetery. The construction of a bridge across the thirty meters wide and four meters deep canal was prepared. The location for the bridge was under Soviet fire. Mustering all its strength, the Kavallerie Korps held its bridgehead against repeated tank attacks.[34] It seemed important to Heeresgruppe Süd to provide some breathing space to the bitterly fighting II. SS-Panzerkorps. In order to do that, the I. SS-Panzerkorps was to establish a bridgehead across the Sarviz canal near Czecze. Preconditions for that were the building of the bridge near Simontornya and the seizure of Sar Egres by the 23. Panzerdivision.[35]

On 14 March 1945, the temperatures climbed to thirteen degrees Celsius above zero. It was mostly sunny. The lanes and the terrain continued to dry off. The terrain became more passable for Panzers.

The enemy succeeded in setting up a small bridgehead across the Sio canal near Ozora. However, it was firmly encircled by parts of Regiment 25. Several Soviet attacks were repulsed in the Simontornya bridgehead. The "LAH" Division continued to attack from inside the bridgehead and captured Hill 115 (two kilometers southeast of Simontornya). Construction of the temporary bridge was commenced farther to the west. Without a bridge, no Panzers and no heavy weapons, except launchers and heavy machine guns, could be transported across the canal. A report by Sturmmann Martin Glade of the 1. Kompanie of Regiment 26 illustrates the difficulties in supplying the troops inside the bridgehead:

> . . . At the time, I belonged to the Kompanie squad of the 1./26. We had crossed the canal, thrown the Russians out of their positions, and had two platoons inside the long trenches the Russians had dug. The other two platoons were situated in a tank trench to our left.
>
> In the course of the night, I was ordered to go back with three comrades and to wait for Oberscharführer Tesch—our top sergeant—at a road fork outside of Igar, to receive warm food for the Kompanie, and to bring it to the front line.
>
> We did not have to wait, Oberscharführer Tesch was already there. In the light of his flashlight we saw two thermal containers and a forty liter can sitting on a truck. Oberscharführer Tesch told us that they contained tea and bean soup for the Kompanie.
>
> My comrade Werner Lange and another, whose name I no longer remember, each took one container immediately and hove it onto their shoulders. Uli Fäustel and I lifted the hot can from the vehicle. It seemed to us that it was filled with lead rather than tea. How to transport the thing? After some extensive searching in the darkness we found a fairly strong branch next to the road. We stuck it through the handle of the can and hauled it onto our shoulders. Our march back began. It took some one-and-one half hours to the canal. First, along a firm path, it went fairly well, apart from the soup container swinging to and fro. But then we had to cross some marshy terrain. A corduroy road had been constructed across it. In the flickering light from the flares and the muzzle flashes of the Russian artillery across and ahead of the positions at the canal, we were able to make out the road as a light-colored band in the otherwise totally dark night. But, the corduroy road was under Russian artillery shelling. I do not remember how often we hit the ground. I do not remember, either, how often Uli and I cursed that heavy can. But curse it, we did!
>
> I had the impression that the damned can, the longer we carried it, was getting heavier all the time. I do recall that I suddenly felt the desire to just stay lying down, not to get up again. But, our comrades were waiting for a hearty meal, so we forced ourselves to get back on our feet, pick up the branch with its dangling load, and to hurry on. Then, when the shells came howling at us and we hit the ground, we were careful to make sure that the can stood upright, that its pre-

cious contents were not spilled. The two comrades with the containers cursed no less than we did, since, every time they hit the ground,
the slopping containers slid up and slammed in the back of their
necks.

Finally, we were at the canal, totally exhausted. Two comrades in
a rubber dinghy were waiting to ferry us across. And then, the can
almost slid into the water on us, never to be seen again. Boy, did we
curse!

When we finally arrived at the Kompanie again, we soup carriers
had no skin left on our shoulders, but the comrades received their
still-lukewarm bean soup and the steaming, delicious, hot tea.[35a]

In the evening of 14 March 1945, a major threat to Heeresgruppe Süd,
in particular to the 6. SS-Panzerarmee, became apparent. The war diary of
the Heeresgruppe noted:

> On the ninth day of our own attack, the enemy uncovered his inten-
> tions for a tactical counterattack. Movements had been spotted dur-
> ing the previous day, for the first time, in the direction of the front
> from the east toward Stuhlweißenburg-Zamoly. They could still be
> interpreted as local reinforcements. However, today's movements
> leave no doubt of the enemy intentions. Based on the results from
> aerial observation, motorized columns of at least 3,000 vehicles are
> moving out of the rear area from Budapest via Budaörs, Bicske,
> Csakvar, and via Bia, Alcsut, to the southwest, most of them in the
> direction of Zamoly. Parts are turning off in the direction of the
> Vertes mountains . . . Accordingly, the enemy will carry out his major
> thrust against the front to the southwest and west of Zamoly (ten
> kilometers north of Stuhlweißenburg). His objective will be to cut
> the rear connections of the German forces which have advanced
> from the narrow passage of Stuhlweißenburg by an attack in the
> direction of Lake Balaton.[35a]

The Heeresgruppe planned to try everything imaginable to pre-empt
the major enemy offensive through a decisive success.

On 15 March 1945, the temperature climbed to nine degrees above
zero. It was overcast and hazy. The lanes and terrain continued to dry off.

The enemy attacked the positions of Regiment 26 in the bridgehead in
the morning between eight and nine o'clock and broke through, between
the first and second hill, 300 meters south of the canal. However, he was
thrown back after a short time. The German artillery was providing harassing
fire, occasionally concentrated shelling. The mortars of the Divisionsbegleitkompanie effectively battled the enemy inside a village on the rail line
one kilometer west of Simontornya.[36]

The Kavallerie Korps expanded its bridgehead near Adand to a minor extent. The "LAH" Division was able, against bitter resistance, to enlarge the Simontornya bridgehead somewhat toward the south and east. No decisive progress was achieved.

The supreme commander of Heeresgruppe Süd, General der Infanterie Wöhler, considered a regrouping of the 6. SS-Panzerarmee as necessary. In a letter on 15 March 1945, 15.10 hours, to the operations section of the general staff of the Heer in the OKH, he offered an evaluation of the situation and provided suggestions for solutions. A continuation of the attack by the I. SS-Panzerkorps to the south appeared inexpedient, because of the hilly terrain, unfavorable to Panzer operations, and because of the constantly moving eastern flank. An attack across the Sarviz canal to the east would probably incur very high losses. The enemy would be able to bring up reinforcements quickly from Dunaföldvar. It was important to eliminate the strong enemy forces situated between the Sarviz canal and the Danube, and to thus create the preconditions for a further attack to the south.

Hence, his intentions were:

> . . . a) Attack by the 6. Pz.Armee with the I. and II. SS-Pz.Korps as well as the III. Pz.Korps across the line Sarkeresztur-Gardony (22 kilometers southeast and 16 kilometers east of Stuhlweißenburg, respectively, Author) with an initial thrust to the Danube, and then a turn, later, to break through to the south.
> b) Regrouping of the I. SS-Panzerkorps, thus
> c) temporary defense of the Sio and Sarviz sectors by I. Kav. Korps, 23. Pz.Div., and 25. Hungarian Inf.-Div. so that these forces will be pulled along across the Sio canal in case of a successful concentrated thrust east of the Sarviz canal . . .[37]

At the same day, the Heeresgruppe reported the Panzer situation. Accordingly, the "HJ" Division had:

- 16 combat-ready Panzers,
- 25 under short-term repair,
- 13 under long-term repair,
- 5 total losses;
- 28 combat-ready Jagdpanzers,
- 21 under short-term repair,
- 20 under long-term repair,
- 2 total losses;
- 96 combat-ready armored personnel carriers and armored reconnaissance vehicles,
- 54 under short-term repair,
- 44 under long-term repair,
- 0 total losses.[38]

The situation at the 1. and 9. SS-Panzerdivisions was more favorable, worse at the 2. SS-Panzerdivision. In the face of the enemy concentration, the available forces were by no means sufficient. Since the regrouping was to last four nights, the enemy would have increased his strength in the designated attack area even further before the German attack could be started. The supreme commander of Armeegruppe Balck judged the situation in his sector in the north very favorably. Oberstgruppenführer Sepp Dietrich considered operation "Frühlingserwachen" as having failed and advocated an immediate change-over to defense.[39]

The OKH approved the regrouping suggested by Heeresgruppe Süd but demanded that it be completed within three days. ". . . Judging by the overall situation, the I. SS-Pz.Korps will be required in other spots as well . . ." The Heeresgruppe ordered the 6. SS-Panzerarmee to move the I. SS-Panzerkorps to the eastern wing with the greatest possible speed. The Adand and Simontornya bridgeheads were to be held and the intention of further attacks to the south was to be faked. If the 23. Panzerdivision was successful in setting up a bridgehead across the Sarviz canal near Örs-Puszta (ten kilometers north of Simontornya) during the night of 15 to 16 March, the I. SS-Panzerkorps was to follow behind immediately.[40]

The "HJ" Division was the first in line for possible relief, since the "LAH" Division was situated in the eastern sector and was tied up in Simontornya. That step was begun as early as 15 March. After the fall of darkness, the first units of the "LAH" Division reported to Regiment 26.[41]

On 16 March 1945, the daytime temperatures hovered around ten degrees above zero. The morning was foggy, the day was occasionally hazy, but mostly sunny.

The relief at Regiment 26 began in the early morning hours, one Zug at the time. The last Zug of II./26 was relieved at 09.10 hours. The Bataillon assembled in Igar. Replacements were taken on there. The supply company handed out winter clothing. Regiment 25 prepared an attack to eliminate the Soviet bridgehead near Ozora. That may have been one of the planned deceptions.[42] The Divisionsbegleitkompanie was not relieved for the time being. The enemy attacked it in the morning, but was repelled. German artillery fired briskly throughout the day.[43]

The attack by the 23. Panzerdivision across the Sarviz canal foundered. A small bridgehead, which had been established, had to be given up in the morning due to strong pressure from the enemy.[44]

At 14.30 hours in the afternoon, the Soviet major offensive of the 2. and 3. Ukrainian Front started in the sector of Armeegruppe Balck after an intensive artillery preparation. In the sector of the 1. Hungarian Hussar Division, which had to defend all of the Vertes mountains along a width of twenty kilometers, the 46. Army attacked. Its major direction of thrust was toward Tata (19 kilometers southeast of Komorn/Komarom), Komorn, and Raab/Györ. The sector of the IV. SS-Panzerkorps, with the attached 2. Hungarian Tank Division, between Stuhlweißenburg and the Vertes mountains was attacked by the 4. and 9. Guards Armies. In addition, the 6. Guards Tank Army stood in readiness there. The attack objectives were Varpalota and Veszprem (ten kilometers northwest and eighteen kilometers northeast of the northern tip of Lake Balaton, respectively). The southern assault group had the task of cutting off the 6. SS-Panzerarmee to the south of the narrow passage between Lake Balaton and Lake Velence, and then destroying it in cooperation with the two armies (26. and 27.) attacking from the south and east. The objective of the overall operation was Vienna.[45]

The 1. Hungarian Hussar Division was unable to withstand the overwhelming onslaught. The threat of a breakthrough was becoming apparent. The IV. SS-Panzerkorps stood its ground. Breakthroughs at the 2. Hungarian Tank Division and the 3. SS-Panzerdivision "Totenkopf" were contained. As late as 23.00 hours, the supreme commander of Heeresgruppe Süd, General der Infantry Wöhler, believed that he would be able to carry out his plan of continuing operation -"Frühlingserwachen" after regrouping. At 01.20 hours, the chief of the general staff of the Heer, Generaloberst Guderian, telephoned the chief of staff of Heeresgruppe Süd, Generalleutnant von Grolmann. He expressed his concern on the situation north of Stuhlweißenburg and recommended, in addition to other measures, to prepare for action by the I. SS-Panzerkorps in a northerly instead of an easterly direction. At 02.40, the Heeresgruppe received a message from the Führer headquarters ". . . that the Führer did not consider action by the I. SS-Panzerkorps to the north as critical for the time being . . ."[46]

On 17 March 1945, the daytime temperature was around ten degrees Celsius above zero. The sky was overcast, the condition of the lanes deteriorated again.

Regiment 25 cleared up the Soviet bridgehead near Ozora.[47] From 02.00 hours on, the Divisionsbegleitkompanie was being relieved by parts of a battalion of the 23. Panzerdivision. It arrived in Szilas-Balhas at 06.30 hours. At twelve noon, an advance party departed for the newly designated assembly area of the Division. At 16.30 hours, the Kompanie followed by way of Deg-Enying-Lepseny-Polgardi-Szadbadbattyan (nine kilometers northeast of Polgardi) to Föveny-Puszta where it arrived at 19.30 hours. The II./26 marched off at 23.15 hours from Szilas-Balhas to Seregelyes (fifteen kilometers southeast of Stuhlweißenburg). During the course of 18 March 1945, the "HJ" Division assembled in the district around Falubattyan (nine kilometers southwest of Stuhlweißenburg).

The last action by the 12. SS-Panzerdivision "Hitlerjugend" in the framework of an offensive operation had come to an end. After great difficulties in the beginning, caused by a strong enemy, ready for defense, and terrain which was almost impassable to tracked vehicles, a breakthrough near Deg by an unconventional night attack of an armored group succeeded. Difficult terrain and a tenaciously fighting enemy delayed the exploitation of that success. Despite that, the breakthrough to the Sio canal and the establishing of a bridgehead near Simontornya was achieved, against the reserves which had been brought up in the meantime to the dominating hills south of the canal. After the seizure of Hill 220 south of Simontornya, the most forward elements of the Division were situated twenty-seven kilometers distant from their assembly area, six days after the start of the attack. The unfavorable development in the situation to the rear of the 6. SS-Panzerarmee and the difficulties in other sectors of the front, prevented an exploitation of that success which had been achieved together with the 1. SS-Panzerdivision "LAH".

The Division in Rearguard Action from Lake Balaton to the Reich Borders from 19 to 31 March 1945

On 17 and 18 March 1945, the Soviet offensive made further progress between Lake Velence and the Danube north of the Vertes mountains. The enemy reached the road Stuhlweißenburg-Söred (seventeen kilometers northwest of Stuhlweißenburg) on 17 March and made further advances in the Vertes mountains. On 18 March, he achieved a deep breakthrough up to the eastern edge of the high terrain northeast of Varpalota. West of the Vertes mountains, enemy forces advanced in the direction of Csaszar (thirty-four kilometers north of Varpalota) and captured Dad (seven kilometers northeast of Csaszar). Elements of the 3. SS-Panzerdivision "Totenkopf" held their ground in Mor (twenty-six kilometers northwest of Stuhlweißenburg) despite heavy losses, against attacks from several directions.[1]

As late as the evening of 17 March, the supreme commander of Heeresgruppe Süd, General Wöhler, clung to his intention of capturing the Danube line in an attack. Prerequisite for that, however, was the crushing of the Soviet offensive forces between Lake Velence and the Vertes mountains. In order to achieve that, the I. SS-Panzerkorps was to attack, together with the 356. Infanteriedivision, from the Fehervarcsurgo (six kilometers northwest of Stuhlweißenburg)-Mor region toward Zamoly (thirteen kilometers north of Stuhlweißenburg). The plan was to straighten the front east of the Sarviz canal and then have the freed-up II. SS-Panzerkorps follow the I. SS-Panzerkorps. Hence, it was of decisive importance that the 5. SS-Panzerdivision "Wiking" would continue to hold Stuhlweißenburg against the assault by the superior enemy. Brigadeführer Kraemer, the chief of staff of the 6. SS-Panzerarmee, hoped on 18 March to be able to push back the enemy to the Vali sector, approximately twenty-seven kilometers to the northeast, through a joint counterattack by the two SS-Panzerkorps from the area between Varpalota and Mor. General Balck, the supreme commander of the Armeegruppe named after him, considered that action questionable since there were only few and narrow crossing points across the watercourses running from the northwest toward Stuhlweißenburg. He proposed to carry out the attack from the region northeast of the Vertes mountains from Bicske into the rear of the attackers.[2]

That recommendation disregarded the fact that the enemy was already located, with considerable forces, to the west of the Vertes mountains and that, moreover, utmost speed was required. At the same time, General Balck voiced the thought that, if required, the ". . . battle of annihilation would have to be fought to the west of the Vertes mountains . . ."[3]

On 18 March, Heeresgruppe Süd reorganized the command structure in the northern sector of its operational area, effective from 19 March. The command of the sector from the southwestern tip of Lake Velence to the Danube north of the Vertes mountains was transferred to the 6. SS-Panzerarmee. Attached to it were the I., II. and IV. SS-Panzerkorps (the II. after it had started its march), the XXXXIII. Armeekorps and the 3. Hungarian Army. The 6. Armee (until then Armeegruppe Balck) took over the command between Lake Balaton and Lake Velence. Attached to it were the II. Hungarian Army Corps, the I. Kavallerie Korps, the III. Panzerkorps and, until its disengagement, the II. SS-Panzerkorps.[4]

In the evening of 18 March, the "HJ" Division began to move from its assembly area around Falubattyan into the district south of Mor, to be in readiness there for the planned counterattack. The columns made only slow progress at night and along poor, occasionally muddy, roads. In the morning of 19 March, the troops were attacked by Soviet aircraft. Stragglers of the "Totenkopf" Division arrived at the forward command post in Balinka (seven kilometers southwest of Mor) around noon. German reconnaissance reported that the enemy had broken through the positions of the "Totenkopf" Division south of Mor. The II./26, which had been forced by the muddy road to dismount and march on foot, was quickly brought up in a shuttle operation. Its first elements arrived in Balinka during the late afternoon and prepared for defense at the eastern edge of the town. The stragglers from the "Totenkopf" Division were integrated. In Bodajk, the Aufklärungsabteilung blocked the Sarviz-Morer canal crossings.[5]

In the afternoon of 19 March, the Divisional command post moved from the Sikator-Puszta (5 kilometers west of Balinka) to Szapar (eleven kilometers west of Balinka). The Flakabteilung took up positions there. The Panzerregiment probably assembled in Bakonycsernye (4 kilometers east of Szapar). For reasons unknown, Panzergrenadierregiment 25 was attached to the "LAH" Division. It is likely that the Panzerjägerabteilung 12 was also with it.[6] In the course of the afternoon, enemy forces broke through to the west at and south of Bodajk. Balinka was held, with 6 Soviet tanks knocked out. Isztimer (four kilometers south of Balinka) was occupied by the enemy. Thus, the enemy was located inside the readiness area of the I. SS-Panzerkorps. The chief command of the I. SS-Panzerkorps ordered the "HJ" Division to attack on 20 March at 05.00 hours from the region southeast of Bakonycsernye and to drive back the enemy from Isztimer.[7]

On 20 March 1945, the daytime temperatures climbed to nine degrees
Celsius. It was sunny, the visibility was fair, the lanes were drying up. As
ordered, Panzergrenadierregiment 26 started its attack on Isztimer and, initially, made good progress. At approximately the same time, the Soviets
attacked along the Bodajk-Balinka-Bakonycsernye road and thrust into the
flank of Regiment 26. It was forced to break off its attack.[8] The Panzerregiment was ordered to bring the enemy attack toward Balinka to a halt,
making it possible for Regiment 26 to withdraw to the starting positions.
Hauptsturm-führer Hans Siegel was given the order and reported on its execution:

> . . . With four or five Panzers, I rolled along a narrow path toward
> our objective. To the right of the path ran a muddy creek with a lot
> of water from the snow melt, its banks lined by poplars. Then the
> valley widened. To the right was a wooded hill, on our left, first, a
> somewhat steeper slope covered with grass. Then we spotted ahead
> of us the outlines of one or more large buildings; a mill? Caution
> was necessary before we approached! No guidance, nothing to be
> seen anywhere, neither friend nor foe.
>
> The point vehicle slowly approached the huge building. Sud-
> denly, it stopped and immediately fired. 'Let's go, closer—full throt-
> tle', I ordered my driver. 'Anti-tank shell loaded?'—'Yes, sir, anti-tank
> shell loaded!', the loader reported from below.—'Attention! Some-
> thing is happening there—Gunner, open fire when target is deter-
> mined—Distance 400!' The vehicle at the point fired. Through my
> headphones, scratchy, the message: 'Attention! Attention!—Enemy
> tanks ahead! Out!'
>
> It took my breath away, and the cigar probably dropped from my
> mouth, when I recognized the situation: enemy tanks, some eight to
> ten T-34s were sitting, close together, on the path along which we
> were rolling. Behind the building—dismounted—stood the com-
> manders during the stop for orientation, probably in a briefing with
> their chief. The luck of war was on our side once again! I immedi-
> ately ordered the two rear-most tanks knocked out, the two at the
> point of the column were already burning. The crews fled, under
> fire from our Grenadiers—who knows where they may have come
> from? In no time, all the tanks were ours. The radios were still on,
> and one of us, who spoke Russian, took over the radio of a T-34,
> together with an 'Ivan'. He reported what he heard: 'Hold on, com-
> rades, two mechanized corps are on the way to support you!' I
> immediately sent back a comrade with that report. The Grenadiers
> were assembling, more were approaching. Our Panzers secured all
> around. The T-34s were totally destroyed. The Grenadiers occupied
> the hills, we waited, covering the area . . .[9]

In the afternoon, a shell from a Soviet tank killed Hauptsturm-führer Fritz Guntrum, who was leading the 10. Kompanie of the SPW-Bataillon, near Tarnok-Puszta (two kilometers northeast of Balinka). Since its inception, and during the invasion battles, he had led the Divisionsbegleitkompanie with much circumspection and great personal valor.[10]

The war diary of Heeresgruppe Süd noted on the progress of combat on 20 March:

> . . . In cooperation with attached elements of 3. SS-Pz.Div., eight Russian tanks are knocked out in the battle for Mecser-Puszta. The left wing of the 12. SS.-Pz.Div. is involved in fighting for Nagy-Veleg in the evening. The village is abandoned during the night . . .[11]

Around midnight on 19 March, the "LAH" Division repulsed strong enemy attacks east of Inota (three kilometers east of Varpalota). It started an attack on the hill three kilometers northeast of Inota at 04.00 hours. The attack stalled in the face of strong enemy resistance. The units of the Soviet 6. Guard Tank Army, attacking in that area, continued their advance toward Varpalota. Thirty-nine Soviet tanks were knocked out.

Toward the evening, superior enemy infantry and tank forces penetrated into Varpalota from the northeast and southeast. In a counterattack, they were thrown back to the hills north of the city.[12] From the "HJ" Division, Panzerjägerabteilung 12 was in action near Inota, and Panzergrenadierregiment 25 near Bakonykuti (six kilometers northeast of Varpalota) and Öslü-Puszta.[13] The I. SS-Panzerkorps destroyed a total of 66 Soviet tanks on 20 March 1945.[14]

The enemy had already penetrated into Stuhlweißenburg on 19 March. On 20 March, the 1. Panzerdivision, in a counterattack, drove back a strong enemy force attacking between Lake Velence and Stuhlweißenburg. It established contact from the southeast with units of the "Wiking" Division which were still tenaciously defending parts of Stuhlweißenburg and which recaptured one district of the city in a counterattack. The 6. Panzerdivision and the 2. SS-Panzerdivision "DR" were on the march to the north in order to attack and drive back the enemy who was advancing out of the Vertes mountains to the west.

The Heeresgruppe Süd demanded that the 6. SS-Panzerarmee rapidly return the situation at and around Stuhlweißenburg to the previous conditions through an attack by the IV SS-Panzerkorps and the forward thrust of the southern wing of the I. SS-Panzerkorps. That demand did not take into consideration the relative strength and the changed situation. The Soviets were not satisfied with the successes of their attacks during the first three days of their offensive and sent the 6. Guards Tank Army into action earlier than had been planned. The attack, which had the northeastern corner of Lake Balaton as its objective, was designed to cut off the 6. SS-Panzerarmee, whose bulk the Soviet believed to be still south of the narrow passage between the lakes. The Russian 6. Guards Tank Army was able to send 425 tanks and assault guns into action. The 6. SS-Panzerarmee had available, at the time, in the I. SS-Panzerkorps against which the attack was initially directed exclusively, only eighty-two operational Panzers, Panzerjägers and assault guns. In addition, it must be taken into account that the bulk of the "HJ" Division was also facing elements of the Soviet 9. Guards Army which had large numbers of tanks and assault guns available as well. Given that relative strength situation of armor, a counterattack by the I. SS-Panzerkorps to regain the previous main line of resistance of Armeegruppe Balck was out of the question. A lasting defense of the area designated for assembly for the attack could not be expected either. The battalions of the two divisions arrived on the battlefield at various times throughout a whole day. Individually, they had to clear their assembly areas and defend them. Thus, there was no continuous defensive front. The 6. SS-Panzerarmee requested from the Heeresgruppe that the Kavallerie Korps be assigned to it for the fighting in the hilly wooded terrain. Above all, infantry was needed there, Panzers were of little use. General Balck felt that he was unable to do without the Kavallerie Korps. Instead, he requested support from the I. and IV. SS-Panzerkorps.[15] It became obvious that the Soviet preparations for "Operation Vienna" in the last phase had not been correctly assessed, and that the attack on the Sio canal had, thus, been broken off too late. The consequences of that error could not be corrected again.

On 21 March 1945, the temperatures climbed to twelve degrees Celsius. It was partly sunny, partly cloudy. The previously muddy lanes were, mostly, dry. The Soviets continued their attack, with the same objective, sending all available forces into action. On the German side it was important, above all, to keep the rear of the 6. Armee open. In order to do that, the 6. SS-Panzerarmee had to prevent an enemy breakthrough via Varpalota to Veszprem and north of it. At the same time, there was the danger that the I. SS-Panzerkorps would be outflanked on the left.

The Soviets renewed their attack along, and on both sides of, the Bodajk-Balinka-Mecser-Bakonycsernye-Szapar-Cseteny-Dudar-Zirc road. Shortly after midnight—at 01.15 hours—the Divisionsbegleitkompanie moved from Szapar via Cseteny, Dudar to Bakonycsernye (eight kilometers east-northeast of Zirc) in order to secure the Zirc-Bakonycsernye road against the unexpected enemy attack from the east. It arrived there at 04.15 hours and made contact with a Heer company which abutted on the right. As a further protection, the Korpssicherungskompanie (corps guard company) was located in Kistes-Puszta (one kilometer west of Tes).

Regiment 26, which defended the hills south and north of the town together with the Panzerregiment, came under attack from superior tank and infantry forces. The war diary of Heeresgruppe Süd noted on those battles:

... In the sector of the 12. SS-Pz.Div., violent fighting rages in the Mecser-Puszta district. During the fighting, nineteen Russian tanks were knocked out and two were captured ...[16]

The positions near Mecser could not be held against renewed attacks, in particular since the enemy was pushing back the III./26 toward Tes (ten kilometers southwest of Mecser). The II./26 withdrew along both sides of the road from Mecser via Sikator-Puszta to Bakonycsernye.

Hauptsturmführer Hans Siegel, whose small number of Panzers constituted the backbone of the defensive fighting near Mecser, reported:

... I ordered the motor started when, suddenly, I spotted a column coming down a wooded hill to my right, in an extended skirmish line. Through the binoculars I determined that they were our own men. I ordered the Oberjunker [officer cadet]: 'Take the Panzer back. I will walk ahead on foot and find out what orders that column has.' The company chief told me that they were withdrawing as ordered. The Grenadiers were all dead-tired, ammunition belts slung around the neck, machine guns over the shoulder, nose to the ground, they were shuffling without looking up—sleepy, an observer might have thought—worn-out, the initiated knew. Together with the chief I marched at the point, behind us two Panzers, about to catch up with us.

Then, a shout: 'Ivan from the right!' As did the others, I jerked my head around and thought I would freeze. Soviet soldiers, their coats fluttering, came hurtling down from the hill, supported by machine guns which had been moved into position up there and were hammering the road. Bullets were whistling, ripping up the road, and along a wide front the hair-raising 'Urraah' could be heard. There seemed to be no salvation, the ambush had succeeded. Frozen by terror, we would be an easy prey. But it turned out differently, thanks to those unbelievably brave young Grenadiers of our Division. That shout 'Ivan from the right' was like an order to attack. None of them hesitated: up came the rifles, firing from the hip, hand grenades being thrown. A concentrated fire strike from all barrels, including the pistols, slammed into the attackers. They wanted to turn back and run up the hill again—in vain! Our boys had taken hold of them and would not let go again. The nightmare lasted only minutes ...[16a]

The bridge near the mill at Sikator-Puszta was blown up. The Panzers, which had accompanied the battalion until then and secured its withdrawal, had previously swung off to the southwest. They crossed the Gaja creek near Nagygyon, destroyed the bridge there and drove on to Bakonynana. The

II./26 took up defensive positions at the edge of Bakonycsernye and on the hill south of the town, the I./26 on the hills north of it.[17]

At approximately the same time as the attack on Mecser took place, the Soviets also pushed westward from the Isztimer district. A gap existed there between the "HJ" and "LAH" Divisions. It could not be closed by either. While the III./26 fought off the attackers south of Mecser, they pushed ahead farther south in the direction of Tes where the command post of the I. SS-Panzerkorps was located. The 2. Batterie of the heavy SS-Artillerieabteilung 501 with its 21 cm mortars was in position near the Csösz-Puszta (2 kilometers northeast of Tes). Reports from members of the 2. Batterie combine to offer the following picture of the events of that day:

> The Batterie chief, Obersturmführer Hinrich Garbade, learned from individually retreating infantrymen that no more German troops were behind them. Hinrich Garbade reported that to the artillery commander of the I. SS-Panzerkorps, Oberstleutnant Knabe, and requested permission to change position. That request was denied and the Batterie chief was ordered to defend the position in order to allow the Korps staff to withdraw to Olaszfalu (sixteen kilometers north of Veszprem). When the first enemy tanks appeared in the morning in front of the position, the two 21 cm mortars fired at them directly. It was the first time that the heavy guns had encountered such a situation. Some tanks were hit and exploded. Others, however, opened fire on the mortars which could not swing around quickly enough. The Batterie had to give up the unequal fight. The guns were rendered inoperable, the crews withdrew. They were sent into infantry action during the subsequent fighting as "Kampfgruppe Garbade".[17a]

In the afternoon, the enemy captured Tes. The III./26 was pushed back to the hill west of the town. To the south of Tes, the Soviets advanced farther to the west and took the Kistes-Puszta. The Korpssicherungskompanie, in action there, withdrew to the forest three kilometers south of Bakonynana. There was danger that the enemy would cut the important connecting road from Veszprem via Zirc to Kisber. It was necessary to throw him back there, and Tes had to be recaptured. For the counterattack, four Jagdpanthers, ten armored personnel carriers of the III./26, the Divisionsbegleitkompanie 12, the Korpssicherungskompanie 501, and another Grenadier company were sent into action. The Grenadiers of the numerically weak companies mounted the Jagdpanthers and the armored personnel carriers. With explosive shells from their guns and the 2 cm triplet guns, the armored vehicles fired, at 17.00 hours, at the hill 600 meters west of Tes until it was ripe for an assault, and then rolled up the slope. The Grenadiers dismounted below the top of the hill and deployed for the attack on the town. Just outside the positions they were stopped by the enemy fire. During a renewed attack at 19.00 hours, the III. Zug of the Divisionsbegleitkompanie managed to break into the enemy positions. However, it was pushed back a short time later by a counterattack from superior enemy forces. A third attack at 20.30 hours was repelled. Three Jagdpanthers were lost to fire from bazookas. The Kampfgruppe was ordered to withdraw to the hill 600 meters west of Tes and to prepare for defense there. One Jagdpanther and one armored personnel carrier remained immediately behind the positions of the Grenadiers as support.[18]

The Soviets followed Regiment 26 along both sides of the road from Mecser to Szapar. At the left neighbor of the Regiment, the 2. Hungarian Tank Division, the elements securing near Acs-Teszer (ten kilometers northwest of Szapar) were pushed back to the southwest in the course of the day. In the evening they abandoned Csatka (eight kilometers northwest of Szapar). With that, the enemy was situated in the deep flank of the "HJ" Division. An attack by superior enemy forces from the northeast on the position of the I./26, and from the east against the II./26, forced the Regiment to abandon Bakonycsernye toward the evening. A Soviet unit advanced from the area northeast of Tes to the northwest. It was stopped near Szapar. Flakabteilung 12 played a decisive part in that success.

The Abteilung commander, Sturmbannführer Dr. Wolfgang Loenicker, noted in his diary:

> . . . Szapar. A major day of combat for the Flakabteilung. Massive attack by the Russians on our positions, 1. and 4. Batteries firing directly at attacking infantry. We fired explosive and percussion shells, and stopped the attack. We came under concentrated fire from rocket launchers. Obersturmführer Ritscher [chief of 4. Batterie] captured, with a few men, an important hill in a counterattack. A few days later he was awarded the German Cross in Gold for that action. The Abteilung was mentioned in the front report for its action. In the evening, to Dudar . . .[19]

The Abteilung adjutant, Untersturmführer Karl Kolb, noted, complementarily:

> . . . Attack by Russian cavalry on 1. Batterie [near Dudar]. Defense with direct fire . . .[20]

The shortage of German forces did not allow the establishment of an unbroken defensive front. The superior enemy, time and again, found gaps or sectors held by weak blocking forces through which he was able to thrust into the flanks of the main Hungarian and German forces. Consequently, even successfully defended positions—such as near Balinka, near Mecser and Bakonycsernye—had to be finally abandoned. In the evening of 21 March

1945, the "HJ" Division, without Regiment 25 and Panzerjägerabteilung 12, defended a line from immediately west of Tes via Szapar to Koromla Te (six kilometers north of Dudar). The Divisional command post was moved to Dudar (four kilometers west of Cseteny).[21]

During the night of 20 to 21 March, the "Wiking" Division had still cleared several enemy breakthroughs in Stuhlweißenburg. In the evening of 21 March it was forced to abandon the city which it had defended for five days against a superior enemy. At the "LAH" Division, Varpalota was lost. Together with elements of the "Totenkopf" Division, it held a blocking line south of Varpalota against the attacks of three Soviet divisions.[22] Panzergrenadierregiment 25 and Panzerjägerabteilung 12, under the command of the "LAH" Division, were also fighting in the Varpalota district—probably north and northwest of the city. No details are known.[23]

During the night from 21 to 22 March 1945, Regiment 26, and the elements of the "Totenkopf" Division adjacent on the left, moved into new positions between Bakonycsernye and Szapar, and to the northwest of it. Pionierbataillon 12 assembled near Jasd (three kilometers northwest of Tes). Parts of the Bataillon took part in constructing the temporary bridge in Simontornya and only withdrew with the last units of the "LAH" Division. The Bataillon assembled near Kislang and became involved in defensive action there. It returned to the Division, delayed, by way of Veszprem. Detailed and reliable accounts cannot be provided.[24]

On 22 March 1945, the daytime temperatures climbed to twelve degrees Celsius. It was sunny and clear, the lanes had dried almost completely. In the early morning, already, the Soviets attacked the blocking line of the "HJ" Division along a wide front. The following report by Sturmmann Martin Glade offers an account of the condition of the troops and the progress of the fighting in the sector of the 1. Kompanie of Panzergrenadierregiment 26. He first described the withdrawal from Bakonycsernye to a new blocking line:

> . . . After a march, which seemed endless, we stumbled, tired and totally exhausted, through the pitch-dark night. We were at the end of our physical strength. At each orientation stop, comrades dropped to the ground where they stood. A few moments later, we heard them snore, more or less loudly. When we went on, it was a pain to us from the Kompanie squad to bring that gang back to their feet and on their way. Time and again, we let the 1. Kompanie move past us, counted them, to make sure none were left behind in the darkness. Our chief, Obersturm-führer Ludwig, continuously tried to cheer us up with some stale jokes. Hardly any-one reacted anymore. The gang trotted along behind him, apathetic.
>
> Suddenly, there were houses. Our Bataillon command post was located right at the entrance to the village, in a mill. Maybe we

would, finally, find ourselves with a roof over our heads again? Maybe we could, finally, get enough sleep again? The chief disappeared into the mill. I, too, crumbled to the floor. To sleep, to sleep! Rudely, I was shaken awake again. The comrades from the Kompanie squad pulled me to my feet. The chief was back: 'Let's go on! But we're almost there!' It took a particularly long time before the Kompanie was back on its feet. A messenger from the bataillon guided us. He was to lead us to our defensive sector. We walked uphill across unplowed fields. Then, gently downhill and up, once again. The messenger had carried out his task and disappeared into the darkness.

"Form a semicircle!', the Obersturmführer ordered. Then he briefed us: 'The hill on our left is reported occupied by Pioniers. Anything coming out of the valley ahead of us can only be 'Ivan'. So, watch out! We will dig in up here and hold the position. The Russians will try to break through to the road on which we marched. That must be prevented under all circumstances, since many vehicles and heavy weapons have to be brought back on it.' He distributed the Kompanie along the ridge in the darkness. 'Dig in! Dig in!', I heard him shout from the darkness, time and again. We, from the Kompanie squad, dug shallow holes for ourselves. Mine was the depth of a spade. Then, fatigue overcame me. The chief tried once again to wake us up. In vain! Half asleep, I still heard him say, in a resigned manner, to Rottenführer [corporal] Schulz: 'Well, let them sleep! But, come daylight, they'll dig. Take over the watch here. I'll go over to the left wing and watch there.' When I woke up again, I was hardly able to get to my feet: I was frozen right through. The sky was turning red in the east. We were going to have a beautiful day. With my stiff, frozen fingers I dug in my haversack for a dry bread crust and a piece of sausage. I began to chew, savoring the taste. Then, I walked along the ridge. It stretched approximately 150 meters in a north-south direction. Not a tree, not a bush to offer cover. Like dark spots, the comrades lie in small groups in the terrain. They were all still asleep. Hardly any of them had still had the will or the energy to dig in during the night.

I chewed faster. A bad sensation came over me. I grabbed my spade, woke the comrades next to me, and tried to deepen my hole. The ground was hard, it was tough labor. Now and then, I looked down into the valley, lying in front of us in the morning fog. Down there it was still almost dark. I could not make out anything. Up on our hill, daylight was coming fast. Even the last of the comrades woke, got up, and tried to get their numb, stiff limbs warm by moving around. Some were eating, others tried, as I did, to dig holes for cover. Like a bolt of lightning out of a clear sky, a short Russian fire attack hit us. It was coming from the left, from the hill where the Pioniers were supposed to be. The effect of the enemy fire was devastating. The Kompanie was in front of the Russians as on a tray, in full view. Only those who had dug down the depth of one or two spades survived unscathed. Hardly a shot was fired from our side. The Russian positions could not be spotted. They did not sleep the night away as we did, I thought miserably. Despite that, I was glad to lie in my hole—barely two spade blades deep. The bitter cup passed me by—more accurately, overhead of me.

Then, silence. I glanced above my cover and was terrified: To the right and left of me, comrades were lying, motionless, silent, strangely curled up, more than half of the Kompanie, I thought. At night, when we moved onto that damned hill, we had been forty-eight. Then, I heard my name called and answered. Someone shouted at me that the chief had been wounded. He had to be brought to the rear since he was losing a lot of blood. Of all places, he was hit again in the lower right arm where he had been wounded before. I was to accompany him. I grabbed my stuff and, seeing that he jumped up and ran down the hill, I followed him. The Russians were firing again. We noticed very quickly that they were concentrating on us. When we reached the bottom of the valley, it turned ugly: The way led uphill again. Those were difficult 150 to 200 meters for us. Somehow, we managed them. Behind the hill, we were finally in safety. Completely exhausted, we sat on the ground. I looked after the chief's dressing and then took him to the field dressing station . . .[25]

Despite strong pressure from the enemy and some high losses, Regiment 25 was able to hold on to its positions for the time being.

The Soviets also attacked in the sector to both sides of Tes. The 1. and 2. Kompanie of Pionierbataillon 12 had taken up quarters in a mill near Jasd. They obviously assumed adequate blocking forces between them and the enemy. They were completely surprised by the Soviet attack at dawn. The bulk of the 2. Kompanie, located in buildings of the mill at the east bank of the Gaja creek was almost totally destroyed. The men of the 1. (armored) Kompanie had slept in their armored personnel carriers during the night. They were alerted by the din of battle. The bulk of the Kompanie managed to reach the west bank of the creek across the bridge and to set up defenses there. Pionier Herbert Pospich was among them. He reported, in a reply to a request concerning a missing man:

. . . Woken up by the shooting, we managed to get across the bridge with our armored personnel carrier. I watched the armored personnel carrier of Unterscharführer Dick try that as well, but it remained behind, stopped by the enemy fire. Wilhelm Werner contributed with his machine gun in preventing the Russians from getting across the creek. He received a minor wound to the head, I believe from rocket launchers. For his action, Wilhelm Werner was awarded the Iron Cross II by the Bataillon commander. Some days later I was at the field kitchen. In an open field, next to the road, three graves had been dug and crosses for them were prepared. One of the killed was Wilhelm Werner. I recognized him by the dressing on his head and the Iron Cross II, and I also remember his name on one of the crosses . . .[26]

After that surprise attack, 120 men of 2. Kompanie were missing. There has been no sign of life from any of them since. During the course of the day, the Pionierbataillon withdrew to the southeastern edge of Dudar.

During the night, the Soviets reconnoitered against the sector of the III./26 and the Divisionsbegleitkompanie west of Tes. They were fought off by brisk infantry fire. Obviously, they found a gap or a weak spot farther south. They broke through there and tried to capture the German positions west of Tes from the rear. The men on the right wing of the Divisionsbegleit-kompanie observed the enemy and recognized his intentions. At the same time, the Soviets also attacked the German positions head-on. At 08.00 hours, the small Kampfgruppe was forced to withdraw to the west. The Begleitkompanie moved into a new position at the edge of the forest 3 kilometers south of Bakonynana. After bitter combat, during which the Bataillon command post was defended in hand-to-hand fighting, the III./26 had to pull back to Bakonynana. There, it moved into the previous positions of the Begleitkom-panie. At 10.00 hours, on orders of the Division, the III./26 and the Jagdpan-ther were withdrawn. The Begleitkompanie took over the defense of the village by itself. A vastly superior enemy attacked the positions of the Kom-panie. At 13.30 hours, it started to withdraw, as ordered by the Division, in the direction of Zirc. It reached Nagyesztergar (three kilometers northeast of Zirc) at 16.00 hours. At 21.00 hours, the III. Zug and parts of the I. Zug marched off to Lokut (six kilometers south of Zirc). Their task was to set up defenses there to secure the right flank of the Division. They arrived in Lokut at 03.20 hours on 23 March.[27]

At 13.15 hours, the II./26 had to fight its way to Dudar under strong enemy pressure after the neighbor on the right, the Pionierbataillon, and the left neighbor, the I./26, had been pushed back so far that the II./26 was already cut off. The I. and II. Bataillon of Regiment 26 moved into positions east of Dudar. During the breakthrough to Dudar, the leader of 5. Kompanie, Standartenoberjunker Kunze, was killed. The 5. and 7. Kompanie consisted of only five men each, the 6. Kompanie of forty, when they reached Dudar.[28]

From noon on, the enemy attacked the positions near Dudar with tanks and infantry, concentrating on the attack from the north. He was supported by combat aircraft. Flakabteilung 12, which was in position around the town, shot down an IL-2. The 2. Batterie destroyed six Soviet tanks. Two 8.8 cm Flak and two 3.7 cm Flak received direct hits from Russian anti-tank shells. In the afternoon, the Abteilung was pulled out and sent on the march, via Zirc, to Putri-Major (four kilometers southwest of Zirc). It was to secure the town in an infantry role.[29]

The batteries of Artillerieregiment 12, in action near Dudar, also changed positions to the west. Toward the evening, the Soviets also attacked the town from the northwest with infantry and tanks. Regiment 26 received orders to withdraw to Najorimont. Elements of the "Totenkopf" Division had already set up defensive positions there. Farther to the south, the Soviets advanced in the course of the day with 40–50 tanks and with infantry from Hajmasker (ten kilometers northeast of Veszprem) toward Veszprem, the important road traffic center at the northwestern edge of Lake Balaton. A wide gap existed between the "LAH" Division, still fighting south and southwest of Varpalota, and the "HJ" Division. In order to secure the open right flank, the "HJ" Division moved Regiment 26 (without III. Bataillon) to Lokut. The II./26 drove there by way of Zirc, mounted on Panzers. The march was delayed by the clogged Zirc-Akli Puszta road. The Panzers, with the mounted Grenadiers, reached Lokut on 23 March at 07.15 hours. The elements of the Divisionsbegleitkompanie which had already arrived in Lokut previously, and taken up blocking positions on the hills southeast of the town, were attached to the II./26.[30]

On the left wing of the Division, the attached elements of the "Totenkopf" Division lost Koromla Te (thirteen kilometers northeast of Zirc) in the course of the day. It was recaptured by the Panzeraufklärungsabteilung 12.[31] The "HJ" Division, with the attached elements of the "Totenkopf" Division, had moved into the "Klara" position by the evening of 22 March 1945. It was located in the vicinity of Zirc, running east of the town, without taking in, however, the Kampfgruppe in action near Lokut and without Regiment 25 and Panzerjägerabteilung 12. The Divisional command post was situated in the Zirc monastery. To the south of the Divisional sector, the enemy had already reached, or crossed, sections of the Klara position.[32]

To the southwest of Stuhlweißenburg, several German Kampfgruppen were fighting their way to the west. The Soviets thrust into the withdrawal movements time and again. The I. Kavallerie Korps intercepted the enemy along the line Balatonkenese-Küngös (sixteen and twenty kilometers southeast of Veszprem, respectively). It was important to keep the way to Veszprem open at that spot for the divisions fighting their way back from the east. The situation was extremely critical. In the northern section, however, between Kisber and the Danube east of Komorn, the German front was firming up. The 2. SS-Panzerdivision "Das Reich" and the 6. Panzerdivision fought successfully there under the leadership of the chief command of the II. SS-Panzerkorps.[33]

On 23 March 1945, the temperatures climbed to twelve degrees Celsius. The sky was cloudless. The morning was quiet in Lokut for Regiment 26 and the II. Panzerabteilung, which had only few operational Panzers left. In contrast, enemy forces were reported around three o'clock in the Olaszfalu area (four kilometers southeast of Zirc). The Kompanie squad and parts of the I. Zug of the Divisionsbegleitkompanie were ordered, at 03.00 hours, to secure the village to the east. As they approached it, they came under fire from machine guns and bazookas. They received orders to drive to Lokut where the bulk of the Kompanie was located.[34]

In the course of the day, the Soviets captured Zirc against the resistance of the III./26 which was withdrawing, in delaying fighting, via Putri-Major to Penzeskut. The Flakabteilung held Putri-Major into the night against the enemy attacking from Olaszfalu. The 2. and 4 Batteries fought as infantry while the 1. Batterie fulfilled an anti-tank role and knocked out 5 tanks. During the night from 23 to 24 March, the Abteilung moved to Penzeskut in order to take up a prepared rear position there.[35]

In the early afternoon, Soviet scouting parties approached the positions of Regiment 26 near Lokut. An enemy armored personnel carrier was knocked out. At 19.30 hours, the enemy attacked Lokut from the east. The German artillery fired barrages whereupon the Soviets withdrew to their starting positions. At 20.15 hours, enemy artillery, which had probably just arrived, shelled the positions of Regiment 26. Several enemy tanks felt their way forward, one of them was knocked out by German Panzers. Because of the shortage of ammunition, the German artillery barrages were not concentrated enough so that enemy tanks were able to overrun the positions of the Grenadiers. German Panzers knocked out two more Soviet tanks. The Kampfgruppe of Regiment 26 fought in Lokut until just before midnight. At 23.50 hours, the Regimental commander issued the order to withdraw toward Penzeskut by way of Akli-Puszta. The Grenadiers mounted the Panzers of the II. Abteilung and abandoned Lokut at 00.15 hours. The attacked Flak Kampfgruppe took the wounded along. The II./26 arrived in Penzeskut at 03.20 hours on 24 March.[36]

On the left wing of the Division, the enemy broke through the weak blocking positions near Csesznek, ten kilometers north of Zirc. It is probable that elements of Panzeraufklärungs-abteilung 12 were in action there, which had recaptured Koromla Te in the evening of 22 March.[37]

The enemy attack with superior forces had broken through the blocking line of the Division, held only by strong points, in several locations. The worn-out "HJ" Division, without Panzer-grenadierregiment 25 and Panzer-jägerabteilung 12, had been ordered to hold, together with elements of the "Totenkopf" Division, of unknown strength, a sector of sixteen kilometers width (linear distance). That was an impossible task for a Panzerdivision in wooded mountain terrain. Only a few narrow sectors at important roads and villages could be defended. In between them, enemy infantry infiltrated unhindered through the woods. The enemy attacked the German position simultaneously head-on and from the flanks and the rear. While the "HJ" Division was fighting in the Klara positions, it was cut off from its supply stores in Veszprem on 22 March. The enemy had already broken into the Klara positions south of its sector. Within its own combat sector, the "HJ" Division had only one road to the rear areas available: Zirc-Penzeskut-Bakonybel-Koppany-Papa. From Zirc to Bakonybel, it was an "improved lane" which did not allow any opposite traffic and, in addition, was partly muddy. From Bakonybel to Papa, the supply route was a country road.

A report by H. Sall is indicative of the conditions at the supply troops. He wrote:

> . . . The ammunition dump at Veszprem was located outside the city, at a forest road. At the end of that road, the Veszprem power station was located. The Russians approached very quickly from Varpalota. The guard crew and five ammunition technicians remained in the dump. The ammunition piles were prepared to be blown up. Suddenly, the 1. Kraftfahrkompanie (motor vehicle company) showed up with 20-25 vehicles. It had orders to clear as much ammunition as possible from the dump. Only a few trucks could be loaded since the Russians were closing in rapidly and the only road was already under machine gun fire. Along country lanes, the Kraftfahrkompanie and the guards were able to reach the road to the west. A few men from the guard crew and the technicians then immediately blew up the dump and came, on foot, to the spot where we were waiting for them . . .[38]

On 23 March, the focal point of the Soviet attack was concentrated between the northern shore of Lake Balaton and the southern edge of the Bakony forest. The enemy attacked from three directions: along the northeastern shore of Lake Balaton, from the Soly-Vilonya area (eleven kilometers east of Veszprem) and from the area around Hajmasker (ten kilometers northeast of Veszprem). The important road traffic center of Veszprem was lost. The enemy could only be stopped near Marko, seven kilometers west-northwest of the city, after twenty of his tanks had been knocked out. The II. SS-Panzerkorps successfully repulsed Soviet attacks in the north.[39]

On 24 March, under a cloudless sky, it was unusually warm. During the night from 23 to 24 March, the Flak-abteilung had moved from Putri-Major to Penzeskut-Puszta. It moved into a prepared rear position, with the remaining guns (and majority of its personnel in an infantry role), approximately 1,000 meters east of the village. During the further course of the night, the Kampfgruppe of Regiment 26 pulled back to that position from Lokut. It arrived there at 03.20 hours. It was ordered, together with the Flakabteilung, to hold Penzeskut-Puszta under all circumstances until the early morning of

25 March since the road to the rear through the Bakony forest was totally muddy and the vehicle columns of the "HJ" Division were able to move off only slowly. Corduroy roads had been constructed at particularly bad stretches of road. Heavy vehicles had already mangled them. Tractors had to pull vehicles through there one at a time. Opposite traffic to supply the fighting front troops with ammunition, fuel and provisions was not possible.

At 10.30 hours, the Soviets attacked Flakabteilung 12. Its mission was to provide combat outposts for the Kampfgruppe of Regiment 26 and to withdraw to the Kampfgruppe's positions, 700 meters east of the town, when facing an attack by a superior enemy. As the Abteilung pulled back, the Soviets followed it, but advanced mostly south of the lane through the forest to the west. One hour later, the enemy attacked the position at Penzeskut-Puszta with tanks and infantry. Immobile German Panzers in reinforced positions knocked out two enemy tanks. A four-barrel Flak Panzer, in action on the right wing of the Kampfgruppe, fired effectively at the Soviet infantry. The enemy withdrew into the forest. At 12.15 hours, the Soviets renewed their attack on the German positions, along both sides of the lane and with stronger forces, after heavy fire from their rocket launchers. The Grenadiers suffered considerable losses from the launcher fire. They had only arrived in the early morning after bitter fighting near Lokut. Because of their physical and mental exhaustion, they had not, or only insufficiently, dug in. Panic broke out among the elements in position to the left of the road. A number of the men retreated and were mowed down by Soviet fire. The officers and NCOs, together with a few combat-experienced men, held on for a while but then had to also withdraw to the village of Penzeskut-Puszta.[40] Standartenoberjunker Wolfgang Lincke, orderly officer at the II. Panzerabteilung, reported on the Soviet attack at noon:

> . . . Suddenly, around noon, a signal flare climbed into the sky from the forest. Right away, concentrated rocket fire was directed at our positions and the rear slope. At the same time, whole hordes of Russian infantry stormed out of the forest. The enemy fire was damnably well aimed. While we were under that effective fire, the Soviets, there may have been a battalion, raced toward us across the open field. The first of our Grenadiers retreated. Next to me, a shell exploded. When I regained consciousness, it became clear to me that I was wounded. Anything but to fall into Soviet hands! I had got it in the legs. My left lower leg was bleeding profusely. With difficulty, I limped in the direction of the edge of the village. The rear slope there was also under concentrated fire from rocket launchers. My strength diminished at a fast rate. More and more often I dropped to the ground. The Abteilung command post was my first safety objective. The staff was also in combat and preparing to move out.

Hauptsturmführer Siegel had problems in bringing his small staff under way in a somewhat orderly fashion. Despite the extremely critical situation he issued his orders in a calm manner. For all his concern about the overall situation, he recognized my poor condition and had me quickly carried into his command Panzer.

The Panzer was not yet ready to move out. There were difficulties getting it started. However miserable I felt, I was still able to register the problems: No juice in the battery, centrifugal starter jammed. The auxiliary generator got the Panzer started at the last moment. The motor howled, Hauptsturmführer Siegel climbed into the turret. We got under way with the engine racing. I do not know how long or how far we drove. Later, I was loaded into a VW-Kübel and transported to the field dressing station. Somewhere on the way, at a crossroads—probably in Bakonybel—stood our Divisional commander, Hugo Kraas. Glancing at my 'wound badge', he said: "Well, so soon again, my boy? It will be all-right, after all'. That, despite the depressing situation which our Division was facing. Those reassuring words I have always remembered . . .[41]

Hauptsturmführer Hans Siegel reported on the withdrawal from Penzeskut-Puszta to Somhegy (four kilometers northwest of Penzeskut-Puszta):

. . . We drove through the village and, halfway up the saving hill—along the road to the north—the crate stopped. The engine seized since the radiator had been shot through and was leaking. I had known that. Dismount, bring out the wounded, and blow up the Panzer! Hauptsturmführer Bert Gasch, the chief of 7. Kompanie looked after that. He was shot through the neck doing it. Marching on foot in the direction of Somhegy, I spotted, up at the edge of the forest where the path turns ninety degrees to the west, the 'Grillen' (heavy self-propelled infantry guns) of Regiment 26. There, I grabbed another Panzer IV for myself and drove as rearguard until the evening. With two Panzer IVs and a handful of mounted Grenadiers each, we drove from one bend in the road to the next, taking turns providing cover for each other. We always took up position and kept the pursuing Soviet at a distance. Our poor Grenadiers were forced to get off the Panzer every time, and into the bushes to the right and left of the road. The reason was, first, so that they would not be endangered by anti-tank fire aimed at us and, second, to prevent enemy infantry outflanking us. Those boys fought bravely.

When darkness fell, we finally reached the position near Bakony-bel. Two Panzer IVs from my bunch were already sitting there, ready to fire . . .[42]

The Divisionsbegleitkompanie moved into a prepared rear position 300 meters east of Somhegy at approximately 14.00 hours. In the afternoon, the II./26 took up positions adjacent on the left. In the meantime, after the high losses of the previous days, it had been reorganized into "Kampfgruppe Ott". In addition to the remnants of the Bataillon, it included infantry combat groups which had been formed from members of the Artillerieregiment and the medical unit. At 18.10 hours, eight Soviet tanks with mounted infantry attacked Somhegy and demolished the village with their fire. As ordered, "Kampfgruppe Ott" withdrew to Bakonybel (two kilometers west of Somhegy) at 19.15 hours. "Kampfgruppe Hauschild" had prepared a position there. It consisted mostly of new, young replacements. "Kampfgruppe Ott" reached Bakonybel shortly after 20.00 hours and moved into a rear slope position. At 22.00 hours, the Divisionsbegleitkompanie received orders to withdraw to Bakonybel.

The report by Hauptsturmführer Siegel illustrates how insufficient the forces, and how inadequate the equipment, were with which the fighting had to be carried out in those days, He wrote:

> . . . To my great joy, my own Panzer crew, with my Panzer, reported back from the workshop. I could have embraced my boys. One extra Panzer, and my own, on top of that. I quickly prepared the anti-tank defenses inside the position. A network of trenches ran across the road and into the field to the left and right. I posted two men with Panzerfausts in the trench and put an anti-tank gun in position a little farther back. On the left wing, we sat with four Panzer IVs, Grenadiers in the trenches in-between. We were ready for 'Ivan'.
>
> A feeling of misgiving made me put on my leather gloves and button my leather jacket to the neck. It was cooling off, and leather protects from fire if one was knocked out. I climbed inside, just as the gunner reported to me that the night illumination of the gun sight did not work. That meant, with increasing darkness we would be unable to make out the cross hairs, to aim the gun at the target. 'For heaven's sake—that's the way they send it back from the workshop?'—'How could we drive back and leave the infantry by themselves?'—In the last light of day, I ordered the gun aimed at the closest tree along the road, distance 200, to my half-right. I was planning to fire when an enemy tank approached the tree. It only took a few minutes before the enemy spearhead appeared in front of us, at the point three tanks, surrounded by a group of infantry. In the meantime, darkness had fallen. The Soviets were feeling their way forward slowly. Then, they were level with the trench, the 'tank busters' should be firing; it remained quiet. A quick communication with my gunner, he understood the situation. 'Anti-tank shell in the barrel'—'Can you still make out the cross hairs?'—'No'—'Then the

tree will be the target'. The Russians kept advancing, they must have passed the anti-tank gun already, and still, there was no movement. The lead tank was stopping right at the tree. Very soon, it would move on and roll past us. Therefore, we had to fire. 'Open fire!' The first shell raced out of the barrel—the flash of fire at the muzzle brake blinded me. The Russian also woke up and one exchange of fire relentlessly followed the other. We had no way of aiming and I could not observe the shells at such short distance in the darkness. Suddenly, an explosion inside our crate, and we were engulfed by flames. Next to me, the signal flares went off, there were orange-colored sparks and smoke. I wanted to get out but was caught between the seat and the cartridge guard. The rivet heads, which had popped off, were ricocheting through the Panzer. One of them caught me in the knee, but I only noticed that later. Using all my strength, I freed myself from the burning prison, finally made it outside and immediately heard the sinister 'Urraahh' from the figures rushing at me. They were firing and racing toward the Panzer which was burning like a torch. I rolled off to the rear, fell on wet grass behind my Panzer, wanted to jump up and disappear, but could not do it. My wounded knee refused to work. But, here also, the courage of a desperate man, who wanted to survive, helped and I managed it somehow. Barely fifty meters to the rear of my Panzer I dropped into a depression in the ground and was safe. My crew had bailed out, but instead of running into the meadow for cover they ran to the road. I heard an unearthly cry, then dead silence. After a short rest to catch my breath, I crept toward Bakonybel. I did not know the password, but I was lucky. I spotted a figure at the edge of the town and was able to identify myself. I had probably ended up at the Divisionsbegleitkompanie. I was taken to the Divisional command post where the Divisional commander, his Ia and the Divisional physician were keeping watch. The physician administered a pain-killing injection and then the Ia took me along in his radio communications armored personnel carrier. I spent the drive through the gorge in the Bakony forest to Koppany in endlessly comforting safety,'submerged', resting on a bench.[43]

The enemy had broken through to the south of the combat sector of "HJ" Division in the direction of Papa to the northwestern edge of the Bakony forest. Thus, at 21.30 hours, the Division issued the order to withdraw from Bakonybel to Koppany (also called Bakony-Koppany). First to depart was "Kampfgruppe Ott". It could only move very slowly down the more than ten kilometers long road which was clogged with vehicles. Its first elements reached Koppany at 02.00 hours on 25 March. "Kampfgruppe Hauschild" formed the rearguard. The Divisionsbegleitkompanie was ordered to disengage from the enemy at 02.00 hours, together with Pioniers as a demolition team, and as the last combat group.

On 25 March 1945, at 05.30 hours, the rearguard was blocking the road for retreat at the bridge two kilometers north of Gerenczei-Puszta (three kilometers north of Bakonybel) when Soviet armored reconnaissance vehicles and approximately 300 infantrymen approached. Under fire cover from a Panther, the explosives team of the Divisionsbegleitkompanie blew up the bridge. Behind it, "Kampfgruppe Hauschild" blocked the narrow valley in order to allow the last vehicles of the withdrawing troops to retreat. Some of the vehicles were being towed, those which were not operational had to be destroyed. The rearguard pulled back one sector at the time. Altogether, four bridges were blown up.[45]

Even before the last vehicles had reached Koppany, the Soviets attacked the town from the west. They had obviously advanced farther south through the woods and had found the gap between Ugod—where the left wing of the "LAH" Division was located—and Koppany. The Divisional commander, who was in Koppany, personally joined parts of the Schützenpanzer-Bataillon III./26 and repulsed the enemy. The last vehicles of "Kampfgruppe Ott" reached Koppany on 25 March at 07.15 hours. All of the still available heavy weapons made their way through "the gorge", three trucks had to be blown up because of engine damage. The Kampfgruppe moved into a prepared rear position on the Koppany-Beb (seven kilometers west of Koppany) road in order to wait there for "Kampfgruppe Hauschild". At 10.00 hours, the Divisionsbegleitkompanie exited the "gorge" as the last unit. It came under fire from the right and from Koppany. Under fire cover from their machine guns, the Kompanie was able to withdraw to Beb. It assembled at noon at the Divisional command post in Vanyola (four kilometers north of Beb).

That night, from 24 to 25 March 1945, remained in the memory of all survivors as the "wild night", as the Divisional commander called it. The fact that the Division was successfully brought out of the Bakony forest along a single country road, destroyed in many spots, despite being outflanked by the enemy, can be regarded as an extraordinary achievement. The drivers had accomplished indescribable feats during the day and pitch-dark night, expecting the enemy close behind and on the flanks. "Kampfgruppe Hauschild" is worthy of particular recognition. The Divisionsbegleitkompanie proved itself once again during a most difficult situation with unshakable valor.[46]

The "LAH" Division withdrew, under fighting, on 24 March along the Veszprem-Herend-Varoslöd-Papa road. Elements of Regiment 25 of the "HJ" Division and, probably Panzerjägerabteilung 12, which had been assigned to the "LAH" Division since 19 March, as well, fought near Herend (seven kilometers southeast of Varoslöd).[47] A Kampfgruppe of the "LAH" Division, with it the Divisional staff, was in combat in the late afternoon near Bakonyjako (nine kilometers northwest of Varoslöd on the road to Papa). It was pushed back to Tapolcafö (seven kilometers southeast of Papa) and took up a blocking position from Tapolcafö to Ugod (three kilometers south of Beb). Adjacent on the left of the "HJ" Division (without Regiment. 25 and Panzerjäger-abteilung 12) stood elements of the "Totenkopf" Division near Papateszer (six kilometers northeast of Koppany).[48] The II. SS-Panzerkorps, with elements of the 6. Panzerdivision, was in action in Gicz and Sikator (12.5 and 17 kilometers northeast of Koppany, respectively) on the Papa-Kisber road. The 2. SS-Panzerdivision "Das Reich" was holding a line from Rede (twelve kilometers northeast of Kisber)-Kisber-Ete (five kilometers northeast of -Kisber). To the south, the 6. Armee and the IV SS-Panzerkorps were in combat between Lake Balaton and the Veszprem-Varoslöd road. Between their left wing and the right wing of the "LAH" Division existed a wide gap. The supreme command of the 6. SS-Panzerarmee expected that the enemy planned to break through, by way of Papa, to the Raab river near Marcaltö, in order to cross it before a new defensive front had been set up. An attack by strong enemy forces on the sector on both sides of Kisber was expected for 25 March.[48]

The day of 25 March 1945 was again warm and sunny. The "HJ" Division had fought its way back through the Bakony forest whose hills rise from around 500 to 653 meters (1.5 kilometers east of Somhegy), and 713 meters (four kilometers north of Somhegy). The terrain just outside the Bakony forest which drops slowly to the northwest toward the Marcal canal, or Eisenburger canal, and the Raab, offered freedom of movement again. The Panzers and armored personnel carriers, which had been lost during the combat in the mountainous forest to enemy action or mechanical problems, were sorely missed. Their lack precluded, to a great extent, the establishing of strongholds at tactically important points, to control the terrain in-between with armored groups, and to quickly move armored strike forces to any threatened strong points. In addition, the decimated Grenadier battalions, which had only just come out of bloody combat in the Bakony forest, were much too exhausted to defend non-prepared positions for an extended period of time without support from Panzers. The situation was similar at the adjacent units, in particular at the "LAH" Division. Hence, the 6. SS-Panzerarmee proposed in the afternoon to withdraw to the bridgeheads of Marcaltö (seventeen kilometers northwest of Papa) and Raab/Györ and, other than that, to set up defenses behind the Eisenburg canal and the Raab. The 6. Armee was then to make contact by way of Devecser and a bridgehead near Janoshaza (twenty kilometers west of Devecser). It was impossible to hold the present positions. The supreme commander of Heeresgruppe Süd refused the proposal, since the length of the front line would be tripled.[49]

As already mentioned, "Kampfgruppe Ott" had moved into a prepared rear position one to two kilometers west of Koppany in the morning of 25 March in order to take in "Kampfgruppe Hauschild". At approximately 11.00 hours, the Soviets attacked along the Koppany-Beb road to the west. "Kampfgruppe Ott" caught the enemy in an ambush, the Artillerieabteilung con-

centrated on fighting enemy assemblies in Koppany. After it had used up all
its ammunition supplies, it changed position. The Soviet attack was repulsed,
but the Kampfgruppe was almost completely out of ammunition. Around
noon, the Kampfgruppe observed that the enemy was bypassing it to the left
in a westerly direction. There, he attacked from a line Koppany-Papateszer,
took Szücs and Zsöck (two and five kilometers north of Koppany, respectively), and later captured Csot (four kilometers west of Beb). In the afternoon, the Soviets attacked, in battalion strength, from Csot to Vanyola where
the command post of the "HJ" Division was located. However, they were
repelled at the southern edge of the town and at the hills southwest of it, in
some cases in the artillery positions. Subsequently, the Soviets swung to the
south and captured Beb. "Kampfgruppe Ott" was cut off and fought its
way—almost out of ammunition—to Nagygymot (four kilometers west of
Beb). There, it was taken in by a Kampfgruppe of the "Totenkopf" Division.
The "Ott" and "Hauschild" Kampfgruppen continued to withdraw farther to
the northwest and reached the Divisional command post in the early morning hours of 26 March.[50]

In the evening, the "HJ" Division moved its command post from Vanyola
to Takacsi (7.5 kilometers north of Papa). The Divisionsbegleitkompanie
covered it from the south near Antalhaza-Puszta. The defense of Papa was to
be handed over to the Division during the night, but that was turned down.
Instead, it was given the task of defending a sector north of Papa, its front
facing east.

In the sector adjacent to the right, the Soviets broke through into the
vineyard district southeast of Papa in the late afternoon. Along the Veszprem-
Janoshaza road, the enemy penetrated into Devecser. The elements of the
"Totenkopf" Division, in position to the left of the "HJ" Division, repulsed
most of the enemy on both sides of Szt.-Ivan (two kilometers northwest of -
Papateszer). As expected, the II. SS-Panzerkorps was attacked by strong
enemy forces. They captured Gicz and Sikator and penetrated into Bakony
Tamasi (four kilometers northeast of Papateszer). The positions on both
sides of Kisber were held. The enemy, attacking from the area of Ete and
Csep, where he had broken through, was brought to a halt along the rail line
from Kisber to Komorn. Most threatened was the Devecser-Papa sector where
the inner wings of the 6. Armee and the 6. SS-Panzerarmee were being
pushed back farther and farther. That threat could not be eliminated even by
the—too late—move of the 1. Volksgebirgsdivision (mountain infantry militia) into that area.

On 26 March 1945, the sky began to cloud over, visibility was only fair.
The daytime temperature climbed to twelve degrees Celsius. The Pionier-
bataillon moved behind the Raab river, southeast of Szany. The Organization
Todt had already prepared the bridges across the Eisenburger canal and the
Raab along the Papa-Marcaltö-Szany road to be blown up. The 232. Panzer-

division was located in the Marcaltö bridgehead. It had been hastily created from reserve units.[51]

In the morning, the Soviets attacked on the right wing of the "HJ" Division, at Regiment 26, and broke through the positions. A counterattack was mounted with weak forces. It was unable to return the situation to its previous state. Around noon, the left wing was also attacked near Takacsi. The Divisional command post was situated there. In the afternoon, the Soviets broke into Takacsi, the village was abandoned. The Divisional staff moved into the Marcaltö bridgehead. The enemy pursued with all his strength, in an attempt to take the bridgehead. Toward the evening, the bulk of the Division moved through the bridgehead to the west bank of the Raab and set up a blocking line north of the bridgehead. The rearguard, consisting of the Divisionsbegleitkompanie, Pioniers, one of the last combat-ready Panzers, and one Flak, remained behind in the bridgehead to provide cover. The Divisional command post was moved to Szany (six kilometers northwest of Marcaltö). The Flakabteilung was located in Szil (six kilometers northwest of Szany). The last straggling elements from Papa were incorporated. During the night of 26 to 27 March, the enemy pushed into the bridgehead. Parts of the Pionierbataillon returned the situation to normal through a counterattack. The Divisional commander, Oberführer Hugo Kraas, and the commander of Regiment 26 were in the bridgehead, in person, once more. The Divisionsbegleitkompanie moved from the bridgehead to Szany at 22.00 hours.[52]

At the 1. Volksgebirgsdivision, the enemy advanced from Devecser to the west. He was stopped at the Eisenburger canal east of Janoshaza. According to an unconfirmed report, the enemy had penetrated into Czelldömölk (fifteen kilometers north of Janoshaza) and had, thus, crossed the Eisenburger canal already. In the northern sector of the 6. SS-Panzerarmee, the Soviets advanced from the region around Papateszer-Romand (nine kilometers northeast of Papateszer) to the northwest and captured the area around Tet (twenty kilometers north-northeast of Papateszer). From there, they moved ahead toward the Raab bridgeheads west and northwest of Tet. The German positions in the Kisber-Komorn sector could, in most cases, be held, against massive attacks.[53]

The temperature on 27 March climbed to sixteen degrees Celsius, it was cloudy and some sporadic rain fell. A commanders' briefing took place in the morning at the headquarters of I. SS-Panzerkorps. Because of the threat to the Morichida bridgehead (nine kilometers northeast of Marcaltö), which was being defended by the 1. Hungarian Mountain Infantry Brigade, the "HJ" Division was given the task of reinforcing the bridgehead with a combat group. That mission was handed to Oberstleutnant i.G. Waizenegger, who had been transferred from the Führer Headquarters to the "HJ" Division. Regiment 25, which had been attached to the "LAH" Division since 19 March, and Panzerjägerabteilung 12 returned to the "HJ" Division. They prepared for defense (without "Kampfgruppe Waizenegger") behind the Raab in the sector from south of Szil to Niczk (twenty kilometers southwest of Szany). The Divisional command post was moved from Szany to Denesfa (twenty kilometers west of Szany), a forward Divisional command post was set up in Repcelak (four kilometers south of Denesfa).

"Kampfgruppe Waizenegger consisted probably of the staff of Panzergrenadierregiment 26, the regimental units, the I. Bataillon (until then "Kampfgruppe Hauschild") and several Panzers. The II./26 was assigned to Panzergrenadierregiment 25. It had prepared for defense in previously set-up positions behind the Raab, approximately south of Repcelak. Adjacent on the right was Panzeraufklärungsabteilung 12, on the left, Panzergrenadierregiment 25. Regiment 25 had elements of the "Totenkopf" Division as its neighbor on the left. For the time being, the 232. Panzerdivision remained in the Marcaltö bridgehead. There was probably no contact to the left.[54]

During the course of the night from 26 to 27 March 1945, the Soviets reached the Eisenburger canal on a wide front. Starting in the morning of 17 March, they attacked across the canal with strong forces. They drove back the combat troops of the "LAH" Division, which put up determined resistance along the Czelldömölk-Kenyeri (twenty-four kilometers southwest and twenty-one kilometers west-southwest of Marcaltö, respectively), to the Raab sector during the noon hours. In the sectors of the "HJ" Division and of the "Totenkopf" Division, the enemy also reached the Raab everywhere. He brought up further forces into the bend of the Raab.[55]

During the morning, the Soviets penetrated into the Marcaltö bridgehead, but were thrown back in a counterattack. In the late hours of the afternoon, the bridgehead had to be abandoned, with the loss of one battalion of the 232. Panzerdivision.[56] The bridges across the Eisenburger canal and the Raab were blown up, but were not destroyed by that. The commander of Panzerpionierbataillon 12, Hauptsturmführer Hannes Taubert, reported on that:

> . . . I was called to the Divisional commander who gave me orders to destroy the bridges personally, effectively, and immediately. Darkness was already falling. Together with Hauptscharführer Gauglitz, I immediately went to the bridge. The retreating men of the 232. Panzerdivision came running toward us. I called upon a major to immediately take up position at the Raab with his men. They all went back to the front again. Two meters above our heads, a four-barrel Flak fired in the direction of the bridge on which three T-34s were already sitting, waiting. With our flashlights, we started to search for the break in the fuse, and fortunately, found the problem after a short time. The fuse had been ripped, it looked quite like sabotage. Then, we blew up the bridge across the Raab, the three

T-34s dropped into the river. Subsequently, I reported to the Divisional commander that the operation was successful . . .[57]

From 16.30 hours on, the Soviets continuously attacked the Kleinzell/Savar bridgehead, adjacent on the right to the "LAH" Division. They were able to cross the river north of the town at several spots. Near Niczk (three kilometers southeast of Repcelak), the enemy also attacked across the river and gained a foothold on the west bank. A counterattack by Panzers of the "LAH" Division and armored personnel carriers brought the enemy attack to a halt. The II./26 was pulled out and sent into action at the eastern and northern edge of Repcelak to guard the ford across the Repce creek. Several Panzer IVs and two armored personnel carriers were moved in to provide support.[58]

At the 1. Volksgebirgsdivision, the enemy crossed the Eisenburger canal on both sides of Janoshaza on 27 March. The Division set up a new defensive front near Bögöte, half-way between the Eisenburger canal and the Raab. At the II. SS-Panzerkorps, adjacent to the I. SS-Panzerkorps on the left, the 1. Hungarian Mountain Infantry Brigade was forced to give up the Morichida bridgehead (eleven kilometers northeast of Marcaltö). Arpas, on the west bank of the Raab, was captured by enemy tanks. A German counterattack—probably "Kampfgruppe Waizenegger"—was still under way in the evening. Contrary to the decision of the previous day, the taking back of the front on the northern wing of the 6. SS-Panzerarmee to a smaller bridgehead around the city of Raab/Györ was approved by a Führer order. The regrouping was under way.

On 28 March 1945, with daytime temperatures of up to sixteen degrees Celsius, it was partly cloudy. The "HJ" Division held its positions behind the Raab against several enemy attacks. The focal points were at Niczk and Vag (two kilometers southwest of Szil). Farther to the south, the Soviets had established a bridgehead across the Raab, north of Savar, during the night of 27 to 28 March. From there, they pushed west on 28 March with cavalry and infantry, and into the deep right flank of the "LAH" Division, which they drove back toward the rail line between Ivanegereszeg and Vamos Csalad (four and two kilometers southwest of Niczk, respectively) through a simultaneous frontal attack. The right wing of the "HJ" Division was pushed back to the southern edge of Niczk. The counterattack on Arpas, mounted the previous evening, reached the southern and northern edge of the town, but then did not gain any further ground. From his bridgehead near Arpas, the enemy attacked with tanks and infantry to the northwest and west. Toward noon, he broke into Csorna (thirty kilometers southwest of Raab). Elements of the 2. SS-Panzerdivision "Das Reich", while successful in gaining ground during a counter thrust, were unable to reach Csorna. During the afternoon, the enemy further advanced southwest of the city and captured Magyar-

Keresztur. Enemy tank forces, attacking from the region around Egyed, caught the 232. Panzerdivision in the flank and the rear, and partly scattered it. The situation near Szany and Szil remained unclear. The "HJ" Division and the elements of the "Totenkopf" Division, in action on the north bank of the Raab, were thus threatened from the rear. The left wing of the 6. SS-Panzerarmee was thrown back to the north bank of the Raab, the enemy captured the southern section of Raab.[59]

In the afternoon and evening, intensive traffic by enemy columns was observed on the right wing of the "LAH" Division from Hegyfalu (sixteen kilometers southwest of Denesfa) in a northwesterly direction. A threat to the deep flank of the I. SS-Panzer-korps began to become obvious. On 29 March at three o'clock, the "HJ" Division moved the Divisionsbegleitkompanie to Czapod (ten kilometers northwest of Denesfa) and established the Divisional command post there.

It was also sunny on 29 March 1945. During the day, the temperature reached fourteen degrees Celsius. Reconnaissance by the "LAH" Division determined that enemy forces were located on the right open flank in Acsad (twenty-seven kilometers southwest of Denesfa). Superior enemy forces attacked the "LAH" Division sector from Ivanegereszeg (twelve kilometers southwest of Denesfa) to the north and northwest. A wide gap was created which could not be closed again. Repeated enemy attacks were repulsed along the line from Felsöag to Ivan (fifteen kilometers southwest of Denesfa) by supreme effort.

At 06.45 hours, the Soviets attacked the positions of the II./26 near Repcelak. The first attack was repelled, but the second forced the Bataillon to withdraw to a small forest 4 kilometers west of the town. During a renewed enemy attack at 08.55 hours, several Panzers attached to the Bataillon effectively fought Soviet anti-tank guns and horse-drawn vehicles. A German armored personnel carrier was hit and lost. After a fourth enemy attack, the II./26 was forced to withdraw to Ivan. There, the Bataillon was attacked at 20.10 hours. Barrages from the artillery initially brought the attack to a stop. New Soviet waves attacked without pause, they were able to penetrate to the Bataillon command post. There was violent close combat. At 22.45 hours, the Bataillon had to pull back to a position one kilometer farther west. There, it waited for parts of the Bataillon which were able to disengage from the enemy only later.[60] To the east of Ivan, a Soviet unit with 14 tanks by-passed Denesfa and captured Cirak and Gyoro (2.6 and 4 kilometers north of Denesfa, respectively). Parts of Regiment 25, which were holding their position near Denesfa, were encircled.[61] In the evening, the enemy broke through to the Divisional command post in Csapod, the command post was moved to Pityer-Major (five kilometers west of Csapod), to where the Divisions-begleitkompanie and the Aufklärungsabteilung had already marched ahead.[62] At the II.SS-Panzerkorps, after the enemy had advanced to Kapuvar (seventeen kilometers west of Csorna) during the previous night from the breakthrough region near Csorna, the positions of Regiment 25 on the north bank of the Raab could no longer be held. The Regiment moved back into the area west of Csapod.

Between Lake Balaton and the Raab, vastly superior Soviet tank forces broke through, by way of Zalaegerszeg (forty kilometers southwest of Janoshaza), deeply in a southwesterly direction and separated the 6. Armee and the 6. SS-Panzerarmee. To the west of the Raab, the enemy advanced with fast troops via Steinamanger (23.5 kilometers west of Klein Zell/Savar) toward the Reich border.[63]

The weather on 30 March 1945 was partly overcast, with some rain. The daytime temperature climbed to sixteen degrees Celsius. While the "HJ" Division was holding the front to the northeast, its right wing located approximately near Csapod, the enemy already stood at its back farther to the south. In the morning, Regiment 25 was in position eight kilometers east of Lövö, on its right was Regiment 26. The right wing, the II./26, prepared for defense immediately south of Lövö. Its front was facing south since no contact with the "LAH" Division existed. The "Totenkopf" Division continued to be the left neighbor of the "HJ" Division, but there, as well, no contact existed.

The weakly manned positions of the decimated battalions came under attack from the east and south in the course of the day. Under strong pressure from the enemy, the Aufklärungsabteilung, together with the Divisionsbegleitkompanie and the operations staff of the Division, moved from Pityer-Major initially to Lövö at 08.00 hours. During the course of the morning, they continued to Sopronkövesd/Gissing, located five kilometers northwest of Lövö. In the morning, replacements for the worn-out Panzergrenadierregiments arrived in Lövö. They were members of the Kriegsmarine (predominantly from the coastal artillery) who had very little infantry training and no combat experience. It became immediately obvious that it was pointless to incorporate such men into the fighting units while combat was under way. However, because of the catastrophically low combat strengths, the supreme command insisted that the replacements be sent into action immediately. The positions of the II./26 at the southern edge of Lövö were attacked from the south by Soviet infantry and tanks at 14.15 hours. Panic broke out among the newly arrived replacements. It spread to the whole Bataillon. Four T-34s overran the Bataillon. It was stopped approximately three kilometers northwest of Lövö along both sides of the road to Nagycenk and set up a blocking position there. German artillery shelled the enemy in Lövö and to the east of it.[64]

Aerial reconnaissance had reported that approximately 100 enemy tanks were situated near Kapuvar, and forty near Csapod. Their attack had to be expected at any moment.[64] Regiment 25 came under attack near Puszta Csapod (nine kilometers southeast of Lövö). Hand-to-hand combat broke out. The Regiment had to fight its way through to the northwest. In the afternoon, the Soviets attacked the blocking positions of the II./26 southeast of Sopronkövesd from the east. When enemy tanks broke through there, the Divisional command post was moved to Nagycenk/Gross Zinkendorf—seven kilometers farther to the northwest. The II./26 followed behind.[66]

Strong enemy forces attacked along the Kapuvar-Ödenburg road. Fertö-Szt. Miklos/St. Niklas and Röjtök (five kilometers to the southwest) were lost by the neighboring division on the left (2. or 3. SS-Panzerdivision). The enemy broke through to Pinnye (six kilometers southeast of Nagycenk). By evening, Soviet spearheads reached the line Oberpullendorf-Nikitsch, approximately ten kilometers southwest of Nagycenk. During the evening and in the course of the night, the I. SS-Panzerkorps withdrew to the line Nikitsch-Pinnye-Hegykö (on the south shore of Neusiedler lake). The 6. SS-Panzerarmee was ordered to pull back its right wing, and to move into the so-called "Reich guard position" near Ödenburg, together with the remnants of the 1. and 12. SS-Panzerdivisions. The 2. SS-Panzerdivision was to prepare for defense behind the Einser canal, which runs from the southern tip of Neusiedler lake to the Raab river near Papa.[67] In order to keep the roads from Nagycenk to Ödenburg open, Obersturmführer Erwin Stier, the chief of the Divisionsbegleitkompanie, was given the task of setting up a blocking position at the southern and eastern exits of Harka/Magyarfalva (five kilometers south of Ödenburg/Sopron). Assigned to him were: the Stabswache (staff guard) of the Division, elements of the Divisionsbegleitkompanie, two 8.8 cm Pak, and eight 8.8 cm Flak. The positions were fully manned by 24.00 hours.[68]

Since several days, in discussions between General der Panzertruppen Balck (the supreme commander of the 6. Armee), General der Infanterie Wöhler (the supreme commander of Heeresgruppe Süd) and the chief of the general staff of the Heer, Generaloberst Guderian, the deteriorating combat morale of the troops had been repeatedly addressed. Above all, complaints were directed at the divisions of the Waffen-SS. Without doubt, that was in order to cover or excuse shortcomings in other areas, since, when one considers the situation at those divisions, what could then be expected from the others? Those discussions created the impression at the Führer Headquarters that the Waffen-SS was failing. Adolf Hitler ordered (probably remembering an example set by Frederick the Great) that the Waffen-SS divisions remove their sleeve bands. A corresponding order with the signature "H. H." (Heinrich Himmler) arrived in the form of a teletype at the command post of the 6. SS-Panzerarmee on 27 March 1945. Oberstgruppenführer Sepp Dietrich and his closest staff were distressed and furious. The order was not passed on to the troops. For reasons of camouflage, the divisions were not wearing the sleeve bands in any case after the move to Hungary. The Ia of the Armee at the time, Obersturmbannführer Georg Maier, will report on the course of events in detail in a book which describes the progress of the combat in Hungary.[69]

There can be no doubt that the fighting strength of the "HJ" Division during the fighting in Hungary was not at the same level which had distinguished it during the invasion battles in 1944. It has been shown that, to make up for the high losses after the bitterest fighting during the invasion and the Ardennes offensive, the majority of the replacements provided had come from the Luftwaffe, the Kriegsmarine and the police. They were predominantly soldiers who had hardly been provided with infantry training and had never been part of a fighting force. That was certainly not their fault. They were thrown abruptly into the whirlpool of bloody rearguard fighting which demanded the utmost physical and mental resistance. That had to reach beyond their strength. In addition, the officers and NCOs of the companies were mostly inexperienced in their positions. Many companies were led by NCOs after the chiefs had been killed or wounded. They all gave their best, but were overtaxed by the tasks given to them. Despite that, together with the constantly shrinking core of combat-experienced members of the Division, they were the soul of the resistance and they formed the assault parties which cleared up the situation through counterattacks or made the withdrawal possible. A number of the replacements joined that core, at the pace in which they gained experience, in the course of the fighting. In the same way as the old cores of the Panzergrenadierregiments, the combat groups did battle, consisting of Panzer-less crews, artillery men and Flak artillery men without guns, and of the supply troops.

Until then, it had distinguished the troops that they would do anything to bring their wounded to safety and to retrieve their dead without regard of their own lives. During the rearguard battles—in particular during night fighting—that was no longer possible at all times. The troops knew that wounded men, who fell into the hands of the Soviet, were mostly brutally massacred. That reduced the powers of mental resistance, in particular at units which had not been welded together by combat, where troops did not know each other. The following report from Sturmmann E. of Panzerregiment 12 vividly illustrates the fate of wounded men during the rearguard fighting in Hungary. He had been wounded during the fighting at the Raab river. He wrote:

> . . . It was barely daylight when our Panzer was knocked out by a hit from a bazooka. We abandoned our exposed position and moved into the gardens around the small farms at the edge of the village. Our ammunition was getting scarce and, on my way to the command post to fetch more supplies, I was caught in a rocket launcher salvo. Wounded! Comrades from a Panzer crew took me to the command post where I was given make-shift first aid. The war was probably over for me—and when they lifted me onto the truck I spotted the gray, exhausted face of Untersturmführer F. who had suffered the same fate. The vehicle rolled off, I fell asleep. Next, there was a

large yellow building with tall chestnut trees in front. Then, doctors and nurses. During the dressing of the wounds, the anxious question was repeated: Are the Russians coming? . . . Hours of lying on a stretcher in the hallway of the hospital, waiting, dozing, trying not to think. A doctor was bending down to Untersturmführer F. . . . It was late and there were no ambulances available for further transport. We were to be given beds; sleep first, tomorrow, we would see further. Tomorrow was far away—we accepted everything. Sleep first.

When I woke up, the large hospital room was filled with daylight. Next to me, Untersturmführer F.; other than ourselves, there were approximately twelve more men, Hungarian soldiers, but also civilians. Everything was very quiet—until vehicles rattled past outside, the first shots were fired, hand grenades exploded. Infantry fire was closing in rapidly, shots fired outside the building, then inside. The door to our room flew open, a doctor entered, his face terrified: 'They're here already—the Russians!' I could already hear them shout hoarsely in the hallway outside; and then, more shots. Our uniforms were hanging next to our beds, and we knew the practice of those enemies. It was all over!—There was no way out anymore. F., whom I had woken with the news: 'Untersturmführer, the Russians are here!'—had the same thought.—'To have to die in this manner!' 'Do you still have your pistol?' It was no longer with me, luckily for us.

However, there were guardian angels. At first, we did not recognize them at all, did not notice them. I believe that both of us were too preoccupied preparing for death in as decent a way as possible. So we did not notice that others were risking their lives for ours. In our situation, and at that moment, we could probably act no different. A nun suddenly appeared, stowed our uniforms under her wide habit and left—past the Russians chattering outside. A Hungarian jumped from his bed and gave us directions in broken German: 'No speak, no hear, no see-or you kaput, Bomba, you no German—I do, you no speak!'

And then they came inside. Pistol in front, a Kazakhstani, behind him, another, rifle in his arm. 'German soldat? German soldat?' (soldier) But only our Hungarian friend gave his explanations, assuring that only good people were there. The Russians, however, went from bed to bed, examining the types in detail. First, at Unterführer F., the one in front lifted his hand with the pistol. 'German!'—No reaction. Well now, the next one could also be one. I had my eyes closed except for a narrow slit. He stood in front of me. 'German?' Nothing else. The Hungarian in the next bed, red hair, freckles and blue eyes, was also classified that way. As if bitten by a tarantula, he was out of bed, protesting his innocence. Unbelievable—they left. Then, others came in, new groups all the time, and always the question for 'Germans' first. They must have found alcohol, every time they came in, they were more tight. And, no one had betrayed us until then! So, there was some small hope of getting through. Untersturmführer F. still had his service watch on his wrist. A Russian came over and took it away, with many polite words and, he paid with a small pack of Pengö notes! Just not to be noticed! We probably lay, unmoving, for hours, exhausted, in any case, by all the preceding events.

The main hospital building was given over to the Russians on the same day still. We were lying in a building to the rear, three men in two beds pushed together, with an old, critically wounded Hungarian. For days, we had to make do in our original dressings, since, of course, the whole routine was derailed. It normalized slowly during the following weeks, but, for us, the danger was still very imminent. The female doctor, who looked after us occasionally, whispered only a few words in German to us (to be quiet, for God's sake) 'the Russians are still searching for you' . . . The two of us were lying close to each other, in the evenings we deliberated quietly. Where was the front, in the meantime—would they be coming back, would we have a chance to get out of there? What illusions they were! We realized that very soon ourselves . . ."[70]

There will be further reports on the fate of the wounded men.

March 1945 came to an end with a cloudless sky and daytime temperatures of up to eighteen degrees Celsius. In the morning of 31 March, the Soviets attacked with approximately sixty tanks and infantry along the Fertö Szt. Miklos/St. Niklas-Ödenburg road, and along the shore road of Neusiedler lake. They took Fertöboz, on the lake shore. At approximately six o'clock, sixteen Soviet tanks drove from Hidegseg, in the northeast, into Nagycenk. They first encountered the command post of the Pionierbataillon which was blocking the southeastern and southern entrance to the town with approximately 150 men. The armored personnel carrier of the Bataillon commander was knocked out, then the Russians rolled on in the direction of the Divisional command post. The close-by din of battle had been heard there as well. The Ia went out into the village street to find out what was going on. He spotted the first enemy tanks approaching already. At lightning speed, the small operations staff abandoned the farm house where the command post was located. While they assembled in the garden between two houses, sitting right next to the wide village street, the first T-34 approached and stopped next to the neighboring house. A Russian auxiliary soldier was the only one in possession of a Panzerfaust. He fired it at the tank from a distance of approximately ten meters, and hit it so that it caught on fire and could no longer move. The Divisional commander, Ia, and a handful of the members of the operations staff gained enough time to run cross-country and reach Deutschkreutz where elements of Regiment 25 had prepared for defense. Of the sixteen Soviet tanks which had broken through in Nagycenk, fifteen were knocked out by German Panzers. In the course of the morning, the Soviets also attacked Deutschkreutz with tanks and infantry and seized it. The Division operations staff moved from there, via Harka, into the forest south of Ödenburg and set up the command post approximately three kilo-meters south of the city on the terrain of a rifle range.[71]

The Soviets attacked from the district around Güns/Köszeg (thirty-two kilometers southwest of Ödenburg) to the north and northwest, and drove into the rear of the elements of the I. SS-Panzerkorps located south of Ödenburg. At 09.15 hours, they attacked the II./26 which had prepared for defense approximately five kilometers south of Harka in the so-called "Reich guard position". Flak of the Heer and German artillery effectively fired at the enemy and brought his attack to a stop. At 11.45 hours, the Soviets renewed their attack and penetrated into the village (Haschendorf?) The Bataillon withdrew to Harka and moved into positions south of that town. At 15.30 hours, the enemy attacked Harka from the west and, immediately after, from the south as well. The town and the road to Ödenburg were under enemy artillery shelling. The Heer Flak pinned down the attackers until approxi-mately 18.00 hours. When all of the ammunition had been fired, the 8.8 cm guns were blown up. At 18.30 hours, the Soviets broke into Harka. The II./26 abandoned the town and withdrew, under enemy artillery fire, along the road to Ödenburg. The commander of the II./26, Hauptsturmführer Alfons Ott, and the commander of the I./25 were seriously wounded. The Bataillon adjutant, Obersturmführer Harro Lübbe, took over the command of the II./26. Elements of Regiment 25 and the Pionierbataillon, fighting near Deutschkreutz, were surrounded and fought their way to Ödenburg.[72]

The Soviets, who had broken through near Nagycenk and Fertöboz in the morning, advanced to Ödenburg in the course of the day. In the evening, they pushed into the city, and elements reached Mörbisch (nine kilometers north of Ödenburg) on the western shore of Neusiedler lake. Throughout the night, the small combat groups of Panzergrenadierregiments 25 and 26 and the few remaining Panzers set out for Ödenburg. They opened their path through the enemy by force, at times in hand-to-hand combat. The operations staff of the Divisional staff was scattered. It finally reached Baum-garten (nine kilometers northwest of Ödenburg). On 1 April 1945, Easter morning, the Kampfgruppe of Regiment 25 moved into a blocking position on the Ödenburg-Vienna road. Farther to the west, the enemy had already advanced past that sector and was only brought to a halt north of Matters-burg (fourteen kilometers southeast of Wiener Neustadt), with the loss of sev-enteen of his tanks.[73]

With the crossing of the Reich border, the fighting in southern Slovakia and western Hungary came to an end. In final, spirited attacks, the "HJ" Division had decisively contributed to the smashing of the Soviet Gran bridgehead. It had established the bridgehead across the Sio canal near Simontornya during the Lake Balaton offensive. It had advanced, together with the "LAH" Division, farther to the south than any other, to the hills south of the city. Facing the most unfavorable tactical and terrain conditions, it then dwindled down to small combat groups during the bloody rearguard fighting. They maintained, or re-established, contact, time and again. The hope for a lasting defense in the so-called "Reich guard position" was dashed. The enemy reached it, and had already crossed it earlier at other spots. There was the danger that the Division would be encircled and destroyed west of Neusiedler lake.

The Division in Rearguard and Defensive Fighting in Austria from 1 April to 8 May 1945

CHAPTER 11.1

Rearguard Action in Burgenland, Rearguard and Defensive Fighting in Lower Austria from 1 April to 2 May 1945

The crossing of the Reich border near Ödenburg/Sopron during the night from 31 March to 1 April 1945 did not bring the rearguard action by the "HJ" Division to an end. The supreme command did not have any reserves available which could have taken in the retreating and exhausted troops at the "Reich guard position" and provided them with a pause to catch their breath. Hence, the enemy had succeeded in crossing that position farther to the south without a fight while the I. SS-Panzerkorps was in combat immediately south of the Neusiedler lake in the most forward line of positions. That line ran, for instance, in the sector of the "HJ" Division near Nagycenk and Deutschkreutz, but could hardly be recognized as such.

During the night from 31 March to 1 April 1945, the "HJ" Division had only been able to fight its way through Ödenburg, occupied by the enemy, with difficulty and with considerable losses. It had thus avoided encirclement and destruction. From 1 April onward, at the latest, one could only speak of a Divisional Kampfgruppe which, in reality, had the strength of two medium-strength battalions. There were, at the most, two to three combat-ready Panzers and Jagdpanzers available. Damaged Panzers were towed into the rear area around St. Pölten for repairs. For the Panzergrenadiers, Pioniers, and members of the reconnaissance, the rearguard fighting continued without a break. The remnants of the German heavy weapons, the artillery, and the Flak, supported the troops to the extent that the meager ammunition allowed.

It has already been reported that the scattered combat groups assembled around Baumgarten (nine kilometers northwest of Ödenburg) and then moved into blocking positions on the Ödenburg-Wiener Neustadt and Ödenburg-Vienna roads. The Kampfgruppe of Regiment 25 took up position in the last line of the "Reich guard position" near Zagersdorf (ten kilometers northwest of Ödenburg). "Kampfgruppe Lübbe", which was formed from the remnants of the II./26, stood in the front line. It had been the last to leave Ödenburg after the vehicle columns had driven through the city. Immediately south of Wulkaprodersdorf (four kilometers northwest of Zagersdorf), the III./26 occupied a prepared rear position. The Kampfgruppe of Regiment 25 blocked the Ödenburg-Wiener Neustadt road, probably near Draßburg (2.5 kilometers southwest of Zagersdorf).[1]

In the morning, the Soviets attacked from the area around Ödenburg with strong tank forces and infantry, concentrated along the road to Vienna. Another spearhead advanced along the western shore of Neusiedler lake to the north. There, the Divisional Kampfgruppe "Totenkopf" was pushed back to the north. Without appreciable anti-tank capability, the combat groups of the II./26 and III./26 were unable to hold their positions on the road to Vienna. They were initially thrown back to the Wulka sector near Wulkaprodersdorf. The 8.8 cm Flak in position there was knocked out by a direct hit from an anti-tank shell, the German forces withdrew behind the creek. The Soviet tanks were looking for opportunities to cross in other spots. Around noon, the Soviets attacked the blocking positions near Wulkaprodersdorf on both flanks. The combat groups withdrew to Müllendorf where the Divisional command post was situated. Oberführer Hugo Kraas noted later:

> . . . Kampfgruppe 26 and the Divisional staff hung on with their last remaining strength. In the afternoon, another attack; breakthrough and counterattack. Regiment 25 joined the Division. In the evening, another breakthrough. Remnants of the Division crossed the Leitha river in the evening and set up individual strongholds behind the Leitha during the night from 1 to 2 April. Late at night, the Divisional command post moved on to Blumau, explosives factory (twelve kilometers northeast of Wiener Neustadt, Author), since the enemy had already established a bridgehead across the Leitha near Pottendorf . . .[2]

The Divisional Kampfgruppe had taken up blocking positions again near Hornstein (seventeen kilometers northeast of Wiener Neustadt), located at the edge of the Leitha mountains, at around 15.00 hours. The Divisional command post was also located there. The Divisional commander charged Oberstleutnant i.G. Waizenegger with the leadership of Panzergrenadierregiment 26. In the course of the afternoon, Soviet tanks with mounted infantry attacked the blocking positions near Hornstein. German Panzers, armored personnel carriers and infantry guns opened fire. Two T-34s and two Soviet armored personnel carriers were knocked out. The enemy infantry, which attacked under cover from its artillery and rocket launchers, penetrated into the gardens at the entrance to the town, but was stopped. The enemy outflanked the positions of the Kampfgruppe. The Panzers were out of ammunition. In the evening, the Kampfgruppe withdrew behind the Leitha. It incorporated the remnants of "Kampfgruppe Lübbe"; the II./26 was disbanded.

The I./26 had been smashed during a counterattack on Rohrbach on 31 March 1945. Only a few men managed to make their way back under adventurous circumstances. Sturmmann Martin Glade reported on that:

> . . . We left the cover of the forest. About 300 meters ahead of us lay the village, our attack objective. We advanced without a sound, our hearts beating faster. The first houses appeared from out of the darkness. Still approximately twenty meters to the closest house: 'Stoj!' (Halt!) Untersturmführer Degenhard jerked up his pistol, fired. The red bundle of rays exploded in the air. The Kompanie spread to the left and right, raced toward the village, into it. Shots whipped past us, yells could be heard. In a rapid assault, we raced through the village. Any resistance was quickly overcome. The Red Army men were too surprised; they fled.
>
> By the time full daylight arrived, the village was clear of the enemy. The population brought us hot coffee, sandwiches, colored Easter eggs. Then, we realized that the next day was Easter Sunday. The village was quiet. We fetched several boxes of German ammunition from some of the captured supply carriages, ammunition which fit the carbines and assault rifles. The boxes were quickly emptied. Suddenly, at noon, a report arrived that the Russians had broken through in the direction of Vienna. Hence, the order to abandon the village did not come unexpected. Two comrades and I were ordered by Untersturmführer Degenhard to cover the withdrawal of the companies until the last man had reached the safety of the forest. We put an MG 42 into position in the road ditch in front of the last house. The Russians had spotted our withdrawal movement, several groups were approaching the village. At a distance of about 250 meters, we opened fire. The Russians were forced into cover. Some fifty meters to the left of us sat a haystack, it suddenly caught on fire. When the Russians were approximately 150 meters away from us, we had run out of ammunition. The village behind us was deserted. Not one human could be seen. We jumped back a few meters. Under cover of the houses, we pulled back. The Russians did not seem to trust the quiet situation, they did not pursue us. What luck!

We managed to leave the village at the other end and run back to the forest, about 300 meters, without any danger.

Inside the forest, our comrades were waiting for us in a clearing. We were cut off. The march, which was to take us to our own troops, began. The companies moved, in complete and exemplary order, 1. Kompanie at the rear. First, farther into the forest. We wanted to disengage completely from the Russians. After several hours, we reached a road along which Russian columns were moving: tanks, supply vehicles, infantry on trucks. We were lying in the underbrush some fifty meters away from the road, waiting for a break in the columns, to jump across. Time was passing, how long had we been lying there? We had lost any conception of time. Finally, an end to the vehicle columns. We raced to the road and crossed it, running since we heard more engine noise coming from the right. The forest swallowed us up again. We moved on, quickly. Then, we reached the edge of the forest. A path led for about 200 meters through the field to a road which also would have to be crossed. No traffic there. Approximately 100 meters on the other side of the road, more forest. We waited. Dusk was setting in. Those at the point got up, moved out of the cover of the forest, toward the road. We, the last, also left the forest. The first men had almost reached the road when two cars came racing up, at high speed. We dropped to the ground. A voice, ordering: 'Don't shoot! Let them through!'

Apparently, someone lost his nerve. Shots were fired. The cars stopped, tried to turn back. Everyone understood that the Russians must not be allowed to get away. It happened very quickly. The cars stalled in our fire. There was no movement anymore. Next to the cars lay three dead Russian officers and two dead Russian women in uniform. We all raced into the forest, assembled again. We hastened onward: through woods, across fields, a fairly wide creek bed had to be jumped across. Not all made that, some slid into the knee-deep water. Helpful comrades pulled the unlucky ones out. Brightly lit villages on the left and right passed by. Toward midnight we found ourselves in a tall forest. In the moonlight, we spotted a road, glimmering through the trees. We approached it silently. Suddenly, a branch snapped. At the same instance, ahead of us: 'Stoj! Stoj!'

We all stopped, frozen. Silence! Then, the voice of the Hauptsturmführer: 'With Hurra across the road!' His own Hurra sounded almost embarrassed through the night. Some other voices joined in. We started to move, shouting. The following was a matter of only a few moments: We raced to the road. Shots barked! In the shadow of the trees along the side of the road, vehicles were parked: cars, trucks, and wheeled vehicles. I even spotted a Stalinorgel.

Red Army men, who had been lying in their vehicles, sleeping, jumped up, grabbed their weapons. We fired among them, leapt across the road, and disappeared again into the woods. On the road, all hell had broken loose! Russians were yelling wildly, motors were started. Bullets whistled after us. We paid it no mind but moved deeper into the forest. When we assembled again, our bunch had shrunk noticeably. The Russians did not pursue us. We found a spot where we planned to spend the day which was beginning to dawn. It was a fairly deep depression in heavy forest. Our rest lasted only a few hours. Around noon we heard the Russians. They were combing the woods in order to catch us. We were lying flat, weapons ready to fire. When the first shots echoed through the forest, some of us cracked up and ran off. Suddenly, the Hauptsturmführer and Untersturmführer Degenhard showed up at our group: 'Get out of here! Otherwise, they've got us!' So, we, too, jumped up and to the rear. That was when I was wounded.

Behind us, the Russians roared: 'German soldier, stand still! Stand!' There was no stopping us. The enemy followed slowly. We reached the edge of the forest. Approximately 150 meters ahead of us was a strip covered with thick, low brush, in a field. We raced toward it, disappeared into the bushes, took up position, waited. The first Russians appeared, yelling, firing, at the edge of the forest. They looked at our brush terrain in which we were lying, awaiting our last battle. But, the Russians turned back and did not return. We heard them shout in the woods for a while—then silence. We stayed under cover for the rest of the day. The sun warmed us, comfortably. We dozed, slept. Gradually, hunger set in.

In the darkness, we stumbled on, across fields and pastures. For how long? Where to? I did not know. Then, a brightly lit city on our right. Someone said: 'That must be Eisenstadt.' Again, we had to cross a road. We had lost count of how many we had crossed already. On the other side, an anti-tank trench. We searched for a spot where to cross it. When a column of vehicles with full headlights approached, we had no choice: We had to get into the trench. All of us slid down into it. Finally, we made our way out at a spot where the side was lower. Inside the anti-tank trench, the Hauptsturmführer had informed us: 'We will shake off the Russians tonight for good. We'll go into the lake.'

Between Rust and Oggau, the terrain became very wet. More and more often, we had to wade through knee-deep water. Finally, the water came up to the waist, then up to the chest: We were marching in Neusiedler lake. That was the start of a terrible night. There was a full moon in the sky, not a breath of wind, the water ice-cold. Time and again, loud splashes, echoing audibly across the surface of the water. Then, the first signal flares were fired in our direction. The Russians had spotted us again. We were physically so exhausted that we no longer cared. Hunger and thirst were torturing us. Above all, the thirst! Who could have drunk that brackish water in which cut reeds were floating, rotting. And, always the signal flares fired in our direction. At last, the moon disappeared. A new day was dawning in the east. We got out of the water and dropped to the dry ground, exhausted. We had marched in the water for almost the whole night and were at the end of our strength. When daylight came, we found ourselves in a vineyard.

We did not get a chance to rest: Suddenly, left and right of us, yelling from the Russians. They were coming from Purbach and Breitenbrunn. They had us cornered. Since we did not want to go back into the water, we had to get through the Russians. We stumbled onto a road. On the other side, a steep slope. Opposite us, it was insurmountable. We, 13 men altogether, ran to the right. Many were undecided, maybe did not have the strength left, stayed where they were. Another group ran to the left. It all went so quickly! Machine pistols rattled. Shouts. We ran towards the Russians, firing, found a spot where we could climb up the steep slope. We shouted, yelled at the others to follow us. In vain. We ran along the ridge, signaling. The comrades were worn out, unable to carry on. They were lying in the road ditch or among the vines. And then, the Russians got there. They massacred everybody. We were terrified. Some of us were completely out of ammunition. I had three bullets left in the magazine. We moved back into the brush. While we were still discussing what to do next, it turned quiet on the road. I crawled back, saw comrades lying on the road—dead. Russians were emptying their pockets, taking their watches.

We withdrew through an orchard. Again, Russians were pursuing us. A forest took us in. Helmut Henn and I were falling farther and farther behind. The others waited, wanted to haul us along. We reached a fire tower. At its base stood a shed. Our comrades ripped up the floorboards. Helmut and I crawled below. The comrades stomped the floorboards back into place. Then, we were alone. It did not take long before the Russians reached the shed, turning everything upside down, smashing it. There were a few more shots fired in the forest. The Russians disappeared. We spent the day in our hiding place. During the night, we set out to cross the front line one more time, to make contact with a German unit. After eight night marches (in the meantime we had reached the Vienna Woods) we gave up. The front had moved too far to the west already. It was in the Vienna Woods where we also found ourselves on 8 May 1945 . . .[3]

In the evening hours of 1 April, the Soviets captured Lanzenkirchen and Neudörfl (eight kilometers south and 5 kilometers southeast of Wiener Neustadt, respectively) on the right wing of the I. SS-Panzerkorps. Enemy forces, swinging to the northeast, penetrated into Neufeld (twelve kilometers northeast of Wiener Neustadt). Attacking enemy tank forces were stopped south of Wiener Neustadt at the slopes of the mountains. Enemy forces, advancing by way of Wiener Neustadt to the north, pushed into Felixdorf and Sollenau (eight and nine kilometers north of Wiener Neustadt, respectively).

Under the pressure of the superior enemy tank forces, the blocking positions behind the Leitha near Wampersdorf and Pottendorf could not be held either. They withdrew, in stages, to Blumau, then to the Wiener Neustadt-Vienna road, and, by the evening of 2 April 1945, to the entrance to the Vienna Woods on both sides of the Triesting valley. The Divisional command post was moved, in the afternoon, from Blumau to Hirtenberg (thirteen kilometers northwest of wi). The Kampfgruppe of Regiment 26 was incorporated into a Kampfgruppe of the Sanitätsabteilung (medical service), which had a few Flak guns of the Heer with it, in Großau (one kilometer northwest of Hirtenberg). The enemy pursued, but was repelled by the blocking positions.[3a]

The enemy broke through the thinly held blocking line between Ebenfurth and Hornstein as early as during the night from 1 to 2 April, and advanced from Eisenstadt into the region north of the Leitha mountains. The 2. SS-Panzerdivision "DR" attacked that enemy during the night from the area north of Mannersdorf (sixteen kilometers northwest of Hornstein). It was able to bring him to a halt in the course of 2 April along the line Münchendorf-Gramatneusiedl (ten and eighteen kilometers northeast of Baden, respectively). It attacked in the direction of Trumau (seven kilometers east of Baden) in the morning of 3 April.[4]

On 3 April, the Soviets tried to force an entry to the Triesting valley. The III./26 fought them off for some time near Leobersdorf, but was then pushed back. The leader of the Bataillon, Hauptsturmführer Joseph Riede, was killed by sharpshooters. The Bataillon lost a brave and able leader. He had joined the Ellwanger Bataillon of the SS-Verfügungstruppe in 1934.

Kampfgruppe Regiment 25 was able to hold Hirtenberg, during bloody combat, until the evening, but was then forced to withdraw to the eastern and southern edge of St. Veit (two kilometers west of Hirtenberg). The enemy tried to outflank Kampfgruppe 26 near Großau by moving north through the woods, but was repulsed at positions located near Haidlhof in the Rohrbach valley (two kilometers northwest of Großau). Oberstleutnant i.G. Waizenegger was wounded by shell fragments but remained with the troops. German artillery shelled enemy targets from firing positions in the area around Berndorf and Pottenstein. The Divisional command post was located in Berndorf.

At the neighbor to the right, the Soviets captured Bad Fischau and Wöllersdorf (six and eight kilometers northwest of Wiener Neustadt, respectively) after eventful fighting. To the left, at the II. SS-Panzerkorps, the enemy took Bad Vöslau and the eastern section of Baden with newly brought-up forces. The counterattack by the 2. SS-Panzerdivision "DR" did not succeed in the face of the strong defenses. The Division changed over to defense and was pushed back to the north after bloody combat.[5]

The Soviets continued their attempts to penetrate farther into the Triesting valley also on 4 April 1945. Kampfgruppe Regiment 25 attacked, with support from one Jagdpanzer and a 3.7 cm self-propelled Flak, the enemy who had penetrated into St. Veit in the evening of 3 April or the following night, and drove him back. The Kampfgruppe prepared for defense east of St. Veit. Enzesfeld, located immediately southeast of Hirtenberg at the edge of the Vienna Woods, had to be given up. Kampfgruppe Regiment 26 was also unable to hold Großau against a superior enemy. It was pushed back into the forest west of the town.[6]

In the sector of the II. SS-Panzerkorps, the enemy captured Gumpoldskirchen and then mounted an attack from the area around Baden (six kilometers southwest of Gumpoldskirchen) to the northwest. The Soviet XXXVIII. Guards Rifle Corps, the IX. Guards Mechanized Corps, and the V. Guards Tank Corps began outflanking Vienna from the southwest and west. The Kampfgruppe of Panzeraufklärungsabteilung 12 was rapidly moved to Alland (thirteen kilometers north of Baden) and blocked the road leading in the direction of St. Pölten between Heiligenkreuz and Alland. Superior Soviet forces prevented a farther advance by the Kampfgruppe to the east. The Soviets were able to push to the north, through the fifteen kilometers wide gap between Gumpoldskirchen and Alland, almost unhindered.[7]

Kampfgruppe Regiment 25 continued to hold St. Veit against attacks by strong Soviet infantry forces, supported by a few tanks, on 5 April. In the sector of Kampfgruppe Regiment 26, the enemy was obviously able to outflank the left wing near Haidlhof. He attacked Pottenstein (1.8 kilometers northwest of Berndorf) from the northeast and reached the northern section of the town. "Kampfgruppe Taubert" (Pionierbataillon) threw back the enemy with support from the artillery, Flak and a few Panzers or Panzerjägers and cleared the wooded terrain of the enemy. At Kampfgruppe Regiment 26, another Kampfgruppe arrived in the afternoon. It had been formed by the Regimental adjutant from members of the supply troops of the I./26, the II./26, the Artillerieregiment and the Flak-abteilung. "Kampf-gruppe Möbius" (commander: Leutnant Möbius), created previously already from members of the Sanitäts-abteilung, was reinforced by NCOs and men from the motorized ambulance company under the command of Oberscharführer Haas. The command post of Divisional Kampfgruppe "HJ" continued to remain in Berndorf. There, too, was the only still operational main dressing station of Sturmbannführer Dr. App.[8]

During the previous days, because of the lack of forces, the gap between Haidlhof and Mayerling (two kilometers southeast of Alland) had been controlled only by scouting parties of the Divisionsbegleitkompanie. Since the extreme left wing of the I. SS-Panzerkorps was under strong pressure, and since the enemy had caught a foothold in the gap, a new sector was assigned to Divisional Kampfgruppe "HJ". The dividing line between Divisional Kampfgruppe "HJ" and Divisional Kampfgruppe "LAH" was established approximately as Haidlhof-Weißenbach a.d. Triesting (both towns to the "HJ"). On 6 April 1945 at 06.00 hours, the operations staff of the "HJ" Divisional staff, together with the Divisionsbegleitkompanie, moved from Berndorf to Neuhaus (7.5 kilometers northwest of Berndorf). A scouting party of the Divisionsbegleitkompanie was moved forward to Gadenweith (two kilometers southeast of Neuhaus) to cover to the east and southeast. In the afternoon, a scouting party was sent to the Neuhaus-Schwarzensee road (two kilometers northeast of Neuhaus), since the enemy had been reported in the wooded terrain between the two towns. Combat reconnaissance established, however, that the area was clear of the enemy. The main dressing station of Sturmbannführer Dr. App moved, with the wounded, on the last possible rail transport from Berndorf to the west, to the foot of the Schneeberg mountain, thirty-three kilometers west-southwest of Wiener Neustadt.[9]

In order to close the gap between Haidlhof and Mayerling, the Kampfgruppe Regiment 26 attacked from Pottenstein to the north and won the road from Großau via Raisenmarkt to Alland against frequently bitter enemy resistance. Schloß (castle) Merkenstein (1.7 kilometers northwest of Haidlhof) was seized by the Kampfgruppe of the Sanitätsabteilung. The blocking forces of "Kampfgruppe Bremer" (remnants of Panzer Aufklärungsabteilung 12 and operational units), located west of Heiligenkreuz and near Mayerling, were pushed back to the eastern edge of Alland by superior enemy forces.[10]

Kampfgruppe Regiment 25, advancing from the district around Schwarzensee, captured the Hohenlindkogel hill (elevation 847 meters, 5.5 kilometers east of Schwarzensee). Untersturm-führer R. Richter reported on that attack:

> . . . Before we started out, we received brand-new assault rifles which were heavily greased. The night was very cold and we could not test those new rifles because of the proximity of the enemy. We climbed uphill in a ravine, with extreme caution and silence, deeply staggered to the rear and, regrettably, the MG too far in the back. To the right of us, in a low spot, we found a whole 'nest' of 15–20 Russians, sleeping on the ground, close together. We dropped to the ground, along the side of the ravine, and had excellent cover and field of fire. It turned out to be our doom that we had not been able to test the new weapons. We yelled 'Ruki werch' and 'Stoj'. The Russians jerked

awake and grabbed their machine pistols, upon which I shouted 'Open fire'. However, only one bullet would be fired from each of our new weapons—they jammed. The grease was obviously so cold that it became stiff and prevented the automatic from working. Most of the Russian had put up their arms, but when they noticed that we were fumbling at our weapons and were obviously unable to fire, they sought cover behind the trees and fired back at us with their machine pistols. The whole forest was humming and whistling with ricochets. In the meantime, our machine gun had made it to the front and the Russians fled uphill. Suddenly, we heard in our rear, namely to the left of the ravine, forceful shouts of 'Urraa'. Obviously, all the shooting had woken up another 'nest' of Russians there. We were under fire from two sides then, but we were able to keep the Russians at bay since our rifles, after a hasty cleaning, fired wonderfully. Fortunately, we suffered no losses except one wounded man. We continued to pursue our objective: the top of the mountain, the 'Iron Gate'. When we arrived up there, we found a massive shelter building. We just made out a few fleeing Russians. On the gate we found a hand-written sign, stuck to the wood with a bayonet, which was later translated at the Regiment. It read: 'We have Vienna, we are fighting for Berlin, and we are on our way to Munich'. We quickly set up a blocking position around the shelter building and sent off two men with the report: 'Iron Gate clear of the enemy . . .[11]

On both sides of the dividing line between the Divisional Kampfgruppen "HJ" and "LAH", the Soviets attacked, toward the evening, to the west across the line Hirtenberg-Gainfarn (3 kilometers northeast of Hirtenberg) with thirty-nine tanks and infantry. In the Großau sector the enemy was repulsed, suffering high losses, by Regimental Kampfgruppe 26. Unterscharführer Ziems of the Kampfgruppe Sanitätsabteilung knocked out a Soviet tank with a Panzerfaust. Leutnant Möbius cleared up a breakthrough with a counterattack of his Kampfgruppe. Divisional Kampfgruppe "LAH" essentially fought off a Soviet attack in its sector, knocking out eleven tanks. In the wooded terrain south of the Triesting valley, the enemy advanced westward from the area to the west of Hirtenberg. He was brought to a halt east of Kleinfeld (two kilometers south of Berndorf) with a counterattack. Another enemy attack, of regimental strength, led to a breakthrough southeast of Kleinfeld.[12]

In the evening of 6 April and in the course of the night, the enemy attacked Alland. He captured the town and advanced along the road to Klausen-Leopoldsdorf, with forces of at least one regiment's strength. "Kampfgruppe Bremer" withdrew, in delaying fighting, in the direction of Laaben (ten kilometers northwest of Klausen-Leopoldsdorf).[13]

On 7 April 1945, Divisional Kampfgruppe "HJ" held its blocking line Haidlhof-Schloß Merkenstein-Schwarzensee. It is probable that a forward guard was located on the Hohe Lindkogel hill. At the right neighbor, the strongly pushing enemy was repelled. The greatest danger existed in the Alland-Klausen-Leopoldsdorf-Laaben sector. A Kampfgruppe, of battalion strength, was formed from members of the supply troops of the "LAH Division". In the course of the morning it was sent out to close the gap between Alland and Forsthof (eight kilometers northwest of Klausen-Leopoldsdorf). SS-Panzeraufklärungsabteilung 1 was pulled out of the right wing of the I. SS-Panzerkorps and moved into the gap which existed north of Laaben. Near Altlengbach and Neulengbach (ten and fourteen kilometers northwest of Klausen-Leopoldsdorf, respectively), bridgeheads across the Große Tulln river were established. In the evening, combat-ready reconnaissance of Divisionsbegleitkompanie "HJ" was sent toward Glashütten (three kilometers west of Alland) and Dörfl (immediately south of Klausen-Leopoldsdorf). It reported at 24.00 hours, at the Divisional command post, that both villages were clear of the enemy.[14]

On 8 April 1945, elements of Divisional Kampfgruppe "HJ" captured the hills of Kleiner and Großer Marchberg, immediately southeast of Raisenmarkt (2.5 kilometers northeast of Schwarzensee), as well as the high terrain immediately south (Buchberg) and one kilometer west of Alland. Five enemy tanks were knocked out. A Kampfgruppe, which also included Panzer-less crews, attacked toward Klausen-Leopoldsdorf from the southwest and relieved the Kampfgruppe of an operations unit which had held on for the whole day near Schöpflgitter (2.2 kilometers northwest of Klausen-Leopoldsdorf).[15]

At 17.00 hours, the enemy attacked the blocking positions of Kampfgruppe Regiment 25 near Steiner/Hofstätten, 1.5 kilometers south of Rohrbach, on the Haidlhof-Schwarzensee road, from the southeast and captured Steiner. Kampfgruppe Regiment 26, which was attached to Divisional Kampfgruppe "LAH" at that time, bent its left wing to the rear. Contact between Regimental Kampfgruppen 25 and 26 was lost.

During the night from 8 to 9 April 1945, the Soviets continued their attacks on the right sector of the Division. At dawn, they advanced from Steinfeld (7.5 kilometers east of Altenmarkt) with three tanks and infantry mounted on trucks toward the hill north of Schwarzensee (5.7 kilometers east of Altenmarkt). Two enemy tanks were knocked out. In the further course of the attack, the strong enemy forces succeeded in penetrating into Schwarzensee. At 06.00 hours, he had already reached the church. Regimental Kampfgruppe 25 pulled its front line back to Bettsteighof, 700 m south of Schwarzensee. At 11.00 hours, the chief command of the I. SS-Panzer-korps ordered Schwarzensee to be recaptured. For a counterattack, only "Kampfgruppe Taubert" (Pionier-bataillon 12) and an element of the III./26

(Schützenpanzer-Bataillon) were available. Since the fighting spilled over into the sector of Divisional Kampfgruppe "LAH", it provided the Begleit-kompanie of its Panzerregiment. The counterattack started at 18.00 hours. "Kampfgruppe Taubert", together with elements of the III./26, advanced from the area south of the Peilstein hill toward Schwarzensee. The Panzer-Begleitkompanie pushed, south of it, toward Seehof, immediately southeast of Schwarzen-see. German artillery effectively supported the attack. Elements of Regimental Kampfgruppe 25, which had been freed up, followed between the two Kampfgruppen. By the following morning, Schwarzensee was again firmly in German hands. In particular, the well-placed artillery fire had shaken the enemy's will to resist, so that he was unable to withstand the swiftly advancing attack by the Pioniers and Grenadiers.[17]

In the left sector of the Divisional Kampfgruppe, at "Kampfgruppe Groß" (Panzerregiment), the front line was pushed east in the region around Klausen-Leopoldsdorf. As well, on both sides of Brand/Laaben, the front line could be pushed ahead by a few kilometers during the attack. At the left neighbor, an enemy attack was repulsed east of Neulengbach. The gap in the front, north of there, was closed by freshly brought-up forces.[18]

After the recapture of Schwarzensee, Regimental Kampfgruppe 25 covered to the north of the village on 10 April 1945. The daily report of Heeres-gruppe Süd stated that Groisbach (2.5 kilometers southwest of Alland) and the hill one kilometer east of there had been seized by Divisional Kampf-gruppe "HJ" in a counterattack. Unterscharführer Günther Burdack of 9. Kompanie of the III./26 reported on the action:

> . . . In the light of dawn, the III./26, supported by Panzerjägers of the Heer, attacked the village of Groisbach and pushed the enemy back to his starting position at Alland. Some 300 meters from the crossroads, Hauptsturmführer Ernst was wounded. Three armored personnel carriers took a hit from anti-tank guns or bazookas and were towed away. The attack was broken off and positions were taken up east of Groisbach. In the course of the day, attacks by strong Russian infantry units were repulsed. Massive noise from engines indicated during the night that the enemy planned to cap-ture the village under all circumstances in order to break through to Altenmarkt . . .[18a]

Several enemy attacks in the sector of "Kampfgruppe Groß" were repelled. At the neighbor on the right, Divisional Kampfgruppe "LAH", the enemy attacked again on a wide front in the Berndorf-Pottenstein sector, and north of there. Among others, he achieved a breakthrough into the area southeast of Fahrafeld (eight kilometers southeast of Altenmarkt). The 4. Batterie (3.7 cm) of Flakabteilung 12, in action there, was pulled out and took up position near Laaben, together with several 8.8 cm Flak guns. One

Zug moved into a blocking position north of the town, probably near Hinterholz, 700 meters north of Laaben. In the sector of the "Schulz chief command", the Soviets attacked the operations units in position there, between Altlengbach and the Danube with infantry and tanks. They succeeded in several deep penetrations along the main road to St. Pölten.[19]

The day of 11 April 1945 passed generally quiet in the sector of Divisional Kampfgruppe "HJ". In the sector of "Kampfgruppe Groß", the enemy trickled into the Brandwald forest (locality indication unclear). The infiltration gap was closed off. The positions of the Flak Kampfgruppe north of Laaben came under fire from enemy anti-tank guns. The enemy was overcome. In the further course of the day, the 8.8 cm Flak fired at a Soviet rifle battalion, advancing on the flank, at a distance of 7.5 kilometers with considerable effect. For the first time in weeks, a German fighter aircraft of the type FW 190 was observed. It flew across the positions at an altitude of approximately thirty meters. Around 16.00 hours, the 8.8 cm Flak fired at a Soviet battery, taking up positions to the side, at 6,500 meters distance. The enemy battery was destroyed in a very short period of time.[20] Farther to the north, in the sector of the "Schulz chief command", several attacks along the Neulengbach-Böheimkirchen road were repulsed. Massive movements in the enemy assembly area indicated reinforcements and a regrouping of his forces. The positions of the neighbor on the right, in the Berndorf-Pottenstein-Neuhaus sector, came under concentrated fire from heavy enemy weapons. In the region around Fahrafeld, localized fighting occurred.[21]

During the night from 11 to 12 April 1945, strong enemy movements were observed on the Heiligenkreuz-Alland road. In conjunction with increased enemy reconnaissance activity in the area around Klausen-Leopoldsdorf, they were interpreted as preparation for on attack on the left wing of Divisional Kampfgruppe "HJ". In the morning, the Soviets attacked the positions of "Kampfgruppe Bremer" (Aufklärungsabteilung and SPW-Bataillon III./26) around Groisbach. The attack was supported by artillery and combat aircraft. Several attacks were fought off. Finally, the violent enemy artillery fire forced the Kampfgruppe to withdraw to prepared positions between Groisbach and Dörfl, on the road to Altenmarkt. The enemy did not occupy Groisbach, since the 2 cm triplet guns and the 7.5 cm guns of the Schützenpanzerbataillon controlled the town and prevented any approach with their fire. To the north of Groisbach, the enemy took the Alland sanatorium. In the afternoon, the Soviets attacked Heiderberg hill from Untermeierhof (1.8 kilometers east of Groisbach). They took the hill and advanced in the direction of Kranleiten. Regimental Kampfgruppe 25 reported enemy troop assemblies at 18.00 hours along the Raisenmarkt-Schwarzensee road near Point 405, as well as south of there (not shown on map 1:50,000). The enemy attacked Schwarzensee at dusk. The blocking forces withdrew. When the Soviets came under fire from the hills east of the road, they retreated hastily.

In order to recapture Groisbach, "Kampfgruppe Bremer" attacked along both sides of the Nöstach-Groisbach road, supported by some Panzers. Hill 489, east of the road, was taken by the Grenadiers but the Soviets recaptured it in a counterattack. In the sector of Regimental Kampfgruppe 25, the assault company under the command of Obersturmführer Hans Bäder fought off an enemy attack on its position at the slope of the Peilstein hill (elevation 716 meters). Elements of Regimental Kampfgruppe 26 reoccupied Hill 537 north of Schwarzensee. With that, an uninterrupted front line in the right sector had been re-established.[22]

In the left sector, the enemy attacked from Dörfl, immediately south of Klausen-Leopoldsdorf, along the Großkrottenbach creek to the southwest. The Kompanie of Leutnant Wemper, in position there, was dispersed, as reported by a scouting party of the Divisionsbegleitkompanie at 11.45 hours. Numerous heavy weapons had been spotted in Dörfl. Enemy infantry was located in the woods approximately 1.5 kilometers southwest of the village. At the left neighbor of Kompanie Wemper, a Kompanie led by Untersturmführer Amboss, the enemy had broken through with infantry. At 15.00 hours, the Divisional commander sent orders to Leutnant Wemper, through the scouting party of the Divisionsbegleitkompanie, to move back into the previous position immediately and to establish contact with Untersturmführer Amboss. A combat-ready scouting party of the Divisionsbegleitkompanie reconnoitered toward Glashütten (3.5 kilometers west of Alland). It encountered Russians who had the same objective and fought them off. Glashütten was still clear of the enemy. A third scouting party of the Divisionsbegleitkompanie had the task of making contact with the Korpssicherungskompanie (corps guard company) which was in action near Schöpflgitter (2.5 kilometers northwest of Klausen-Leopoldsdorf). The scouting party reported at the Divisional command post at 18.00 hours that the company had withdrawn 3 kilometers to the southeast in the face of pressure from an enemy attack, and was blocking the valley there to the northeast.[23]

On the left wing of Divisional Kampfgruppe "HJ", "Kampfgruppe Goldammer" was in action within "Kampfgruppe Groß" (Panzerregiment in primarily infantry action). "Kampfgruppe Goldammer" consisted of the heavy Panzerabteilung 560, led by Major Goldammer, and a few quick-response units. It had available only a few operational Jagdpanzers. For that reason the Armee had provided it with several Panzers. The bulk of the Panzerjägerabteilung was in action as infantry. Major Goldammer reported that the enemy had reached, in an attack, the line Waldhof-Kienberg-Edhof (4.2, 3.2 and 2.5 kilometers northeast of Laaben, respectively). An assembly of two battalions had been observed three kilometers east of Neustift (3.7 kilometers northeast of Laaben).[24]

The weak covering positions in the hilly Vienna Woods, with few through-roads, enabled the enemy to trickle through between the blocking positions and the guards with infantry, and to attack them from the rear.

Quick reporting and countermeasures were difficult. Hence, the Divisional command ordered the Pionierbataillon to hand over its position near Schwarzensee to a Kampfgruppe of the Sanitätsabteilung, and to move to Gsteiner (3.4 kilometers northwest of Altenmarkt) on the Reutelgraben. It was ordered to lay anti-personnel mines across a sector of four to five kilometers width at the approaches from the enemy's attack sector in order to prevent his dangerous infiltration. The Bataillon was to block the St. Corona-Altenmarkt road and reconnoiter toward the east, north and northwest. It set up its command post in Kleinmariazell (2.5 kilometers northwest of Altenmarkt).[25]

Because of the critical situation at the Schulz Korps, adjacent on the left, the chief command of I. SS-Panzerkorps ordered the Division Kampfgruppe on 12 April to relieve the heavy Panzerjägerabteilung on both sides of Laaben. In addition, the Korpssicherungskompanie, attached to it, was to be relieved southwest of Schöpflgitter and assigned to the chief command.

Hauptsturmführer Gerd Freiherr von Reitzenstein of the Aufklärungsabteilung was given orders to take over the sector of Major Goldammer. He had available (compared to Major Goldammer) totally inadequate means. In order to relieve the Korpssicherungskompanie, Untersturmführer Jungbluth of the Divisionsbegleitkompanie, with two NCOs and twenty men was attached. His Kampfgruppe had two light machine guns. Among others from "Kampfgruppe Goldammer", the Flak Kampfgruppe remained behind in its position north of Laaben. It had the only heavy weapons in "Kampfgruppe von Reitzenstein". The commander of the Kampfgruppe reported on how he assumed command:

. . . At the time, the Kampfgruppe command post was located in Kogelhof, approximately 500 meters north of Glashütten [3.2 kilometers southwest of Laaben]. I took over the Kampfgruppe in the afternoon. When we arrived, the staff (Major Goldammer, Author) was fully ready to depart. There was a short briefing. The previous Kampfgruppe commander had a complete Bataillon staff with all personnel and communications equipment. All communications links had already been dismantled. My predecessor departed. My so-called Kampfgruppe staff consisted of the adjutant (an Untersturmführer, assigned to me by the Division) two VW-Kübelwagen and one driver. Everything required to lead was missing: personnel, communications equipment, supplies, and a physician. Until nightfall, I walked down the right sector (from the Reutelgraben, Author) to the Schöpfl hill (3.5 kilometers southeast of Laaben, Author) and established contact with the companies in action there. Each company provided a messenger. The companies on the western slope of the Schöpfl hill had a few armored personnel carriers and were relatively well equipped for defense. A direct cross-connection on roads behind the main line of defense did not exist. In order to reach the positions near St. Corona, I had to drive via Glashütten, Klammhöhe, Neuwald, St. Corona. The companies in position from the Schöpfl hill to the right boundary were inadequately equipped. No heavy infantry weapons of any kind. They were remnants of Artillerieregiment 12 and a company of Luftwaffe personnel, in infantry action, and another Grenadier company. No Pak, no rocket launchers, altogether only two heavy machine guns . . .[26]

The Panzer-less crews of the mixed I. Abteilung, led by Hauptsturm-führer von Ribbentrop, had been moved to Fallingbostel after the Ardennes offensive. During the rearguard battles north of Lake Balaton, 5. Kompanie under the command of Obersturmführer Gasch had already moved to the Panzerregiment in Hungary. The 6. Kompanie, led by Hauptsturmführer Götz Großjohann, followed somewhat later. It reached the Laaben district by truck transport on 12 April, after a detour through Vienna. It was attached to "Kampfgruppe von Reitzenstein". On the attack, it partly regained the previous main line of resistance of the heavy Panzerjäger-abteilung 560 and prepared for defense along the line Pamet-Höfer (2.5 kilometers north-northeast and 2.2 kilometers northeast of Laaben respectively). Reconnaissance toward Innerfurth (2.8 kilometers northeast of Laaben) reported the village occupied by the enemy.[27]

The staff of the I. Panzerabteilung, with the staff company, 1. and 3. Kompanie, had been loaded on rail transport in Fallingbostel on 1 April. They reached Wilhelmsburg, eleven kilometers south of St. Pölten, on 8 April. After unloading, the Panzer companies without Panzers were reorganized into infantry companies. The supply troops were equipped with Hungarian teams of horses and horse-drawn carriages since, apart from the kitchen truck, no trucks were available. The Abteilung had few MG 42s, several MG 34s of the Panzer type, with center support, and K ninety-eight rifles, the old, long model. Only the Zug-führers and a few of the group leaders still had their machine pistols. During the night from 12 to 13 April, the Abteilung was loaded onto trucks and driven to Laaben. Near Forsthof (2.5 kilometers east-southeast of Laaben, 3. Kompanie, led by Hauptsturm-führer Minow, relieved a unit made up of ethnic Germans. Its affiliation is not known. During the night, the Kompanie initially blocked along both sides of the Forsthof-Klausen-Leopoldsdorf road, approximately 500 meters east of the town, facing east and north, since the situation was unclear. A scouting party sent out to the east along the road had contact with the enemy after a short time. Its leader was wounded. The staff company took over a sector to the left of Kompanie Großjohann. It was led by Obersturmführer Jauch. The 1. Kompanie, commanded by Untersturmführer Schulz, was sent into action in the sector northeast of St. Corona. It took over the sector of the Kampf-gruppe of the Divisionsbegleit-kompanie, which had previously relieved the

Korpssicherungs-kompanie, before noon on 13 April.[28] Either still during the night, or in the course of the next day, Hauptsturmführer von Ribbentrop took over command in the Forsthof-Audorf sector. He was in charge of companies Schulz, Minow, Großjohann and Jauch, as well as the Flak Kampfgruppe near Hinterholz.

On 12 or 13 April, the news of the death of US President Franklin Delano Roosevelt was broadcast on the radio. It was the cause for many considerations. The man who had been the first to demand Germany's "Unconditional Surrender" and who had pushed it through as an imperative basic requirement, the promoter of the Morgenthau plan, which would turn Germany into a potato field, he no longer directed the policies of the strongest world power. Many hoped, many convinced themselves to believe, that the USA would now pursue less rigid goals, possibly even put a stop to the further advance by the Soviets. Had the USA not gone to war in order to re-establish freedom and democracy in Poland, in Czechoslovakia, in southeastern Europe? During one of the sleepless nights, the Ia found in the house in Altenmarkt, in which the Divisional command post was located, a highly interesting book. The name of the author had drawn his attention: Major General J. F. C. Fuller. The title read: "The First of the Wars by the League of Nations". In that study of the global political situation, written in 1936 and focussing on Central Europe, the highly respected British military historian and commander of the first tank unit in the First World War, and thus within all of military history, arrived at alarming conclusions. The value systems of the National-Socialist German Reich and of Fascist Italy were in totally irreconcilable contrast to those of the League of Nations. The League's objective was, in the interest of the victors in the World War, to maintain the order imposed by them at Versailles. Germany and Italy had rebelled against it. That would not be tolerated by the victors of the World War. The policy of sanctions against Italy because of the Abyssinian war was only ". . . the first of the wars of the League of Nations . . ." Others would follow, until one of the parties was destroyed. There was no hope for a change in the policies of the Western Allies. There was no way around the "Unconditional Surrender". The only important aspect left was to safeguard as much German land and as many German people as possible from the Soviets, and to save them for a distant future when the unconditional hatred had been replaced by reason. The Divisional command arrived at the conviction that this had to be their guiding principle for the near future.

Soviet attacks, with increased forces, were expected along the whole front line of the Divisional Kampfgruppe for 13 April 1945. Particularly threatened was the left sector, especially the left wing, which had only loose contact with the Schulz Korps, and in front of which the Soviets assembled strong forces. The removal of heavy Panzerjägerabteilung 560 and the Korpssicherungskompanie had weakened it significantly. The relief operation by the Großjohann Kompanie, which had to capture its positions in an

attack, and by the Minow Kompanie during the night (in an unclear situation), as well as that of the Korpssicherungskompanie by a small Kampfgruppe of only twenty-three men, indicated how weak the German position
was. Oberführer Hugo Kraas was with "Kampfgruppe Groß" during the night
in order to oversee the relief action himself. All available forces were in
action, he could provide no further forces.

The enemy, assembled in the area east of Neustift (3.7 kilometers northeast of Laaben), who had been spotted by the heavy Panzerjägerabteilung,
and the enemy forces assembled further east around Hochstraß, mounted
an attack to the west, southwest and south in the morning of 13 April. With
the break of dawn, the Minow Kompanie was attacked by a strong enemy
from the east and north. It became obvious that the positions taken up during the night were unfavorable and did not offer an adequate field of fire.
The I. and II. Zug were thrown back to Forsthof, which was under concentrated rocket launcher fire. The enemy succeeded in pushing forward into
the town. Hauptsturmführer von Ribbentrop came to assist with a four-barrel
Flak Panzer. After a short fire fight, it was knocked out by an anti-tank gun
and burned out. With the support of two Panthers of the Eingreifzug (strike
Zug) of the Regiment, the small reserve of the Kompanie carried out a counterattack and cleared the town by force. The Soviets fled up the slope into
the close-by woods.[29]

Farther to the east, the enemy advanced, in regimental strength,
through the broken wooded terrain from the Hochstraß district (six kilometers southwest of Klausen-Leopoldsdorf) to the southwest. The blocking
forces to the southwest of Schöpflgitter were pushed back to the southwest
by the vastly superior enemy. The Kampfgruppe of the Divisionsbegleitkompanie moved into a blocking position at the northeastern exit of Neuwald
(1.8 kilometers southwest of St. Corona) in order to bar the attackers from
entering the Triesting valley. The Altenmarkt-St. Corona road was already
blocked by a Flak combat squad one kilometer southeast of St. Corona. The
Kompanie of Oberleutnant Stephan (unit unknown), whose task it was to
guard the town, was unable to hold it. The enemy succeeded, around noon,
in capturing the town. Immediately after he had received the report on the
loss of St. Corona, Hauptsturmführer von Reitzenstein drove to Neuwald
and prepared for a counter-attack.[30]

The Flak Kampfgruppe near Hinterholz repelled an enemy attack during the course of the day. However, farther north near Oberkühberg (two
kilometers north of Laaben), the enemy achieved a breakthrough. That
town belonged to the sector of "Kampfgruppe Groß" which had its command post in Wöllersdorf (1.5 kilometers south of Laaben). The exact
course of its left boundary, which was, at the same time, that of Divisional
Kampfgruppe "HJ", is not known.[31]

In the right sector of Divisional Kampfgruppe "HJ" the enemy also
attacked with strong forces. At 08.30 hours, Sturmbannführer Gerd Bremer

reported that he was unable to hold Hill 489, south of Groisbach. It was under concentrated enemy anti-tank fire. He was moving his line of resistance to the ravine near Point 501 (500), immediately northeast of Dörfl, on the road to Altenmarkt. From the area around Groisbach-Alland sanatorium, the enemy advanced to the west on both sides of the Höherberg hill, and threatened Glashütten. In the evening, the enemy took Ruine Arnstein, a German counterattack failed. The sector of Regimental Kampf-gruppe 26 remained quiet.[32]

It had become apparent that Divisional Kampfgruppe "HJ" was able to hold the wide sector from Neuhaus to west of Brand/Laaben only with difficulty, in particular since the left wing had to be extended again. With an attack on 13 April across a line from west of Neustift-west of Ottersbach (3.7 kilometers northeast and 9 kilometers north-northwest of Laaben respectively), the enemy had pushed back the front of Korps Schulz to the approximate line Kasten-Kirchstetten (9 and 9.5 kilometers northwest of Laaben, respectively). The contact with the left wing of "Kampfgruppe Groß" was thus lost. Hence, the chief command of the I. SS-Panzerkorps moved the left boundary of Divisional Kampfgruppe "HJ" farther to the east during the night of 13 to 14 April, to a line: Gerichtsberg (10.6 kilometers west of Altenmarkt on the road to Hainfeld)-Neuwald (1.8 kilometers southwest of St. Corona)-Schaid (one kilometer northwest of Hochstraß). The troops in action to the west of the new boundary were assigned to Obersturmbann-führer Jochen Peiper, the commander of the Panzerregiment of the "LAH Division".[33]

In the evening of 13 April, the remaining bridgehead south of the Danube in Vienna was given up, as ordered, by the last regiment there, "Der Führer" of the 2. SS-Panzerdivision "Das Reich". It crossed over to the north bank of the Danube. Just before 24.00 hours, Vienna's military commander, General der Infanterie von Bünau, crossed the Florisdorfer bridge. It was blown up thereafter.[34]

During the night from 13 to 14 April, the Soviets attacked near Schwarzensee with strong forces. They broke through the blocking positions and pushed into the village. The German artillery shelled the enemy approaches, but despite that, he managed to advance to Bettsteighof, 700 m south of Schwarzensee, during the morning. A counterattack by elements of the Regimental Kampfgruppe 26 was stopped in the late afternoon by concentrated enemy fire, a German Panzer was knocked out. The forward line was pulled back to the group of houses at Kienberg (one kilometer east of Neuhaus). In the sector of "Kampfgruppe Bremer", the enemy attacked in the morning from Groisbach via Pöllerhof (2.5 kilometers west of Groisbach). He captured Hill 672 (674?), 700 meters to the west of Pöllerhof, and advanced farther to the west. Sturmbannführer Bremer took his right wing back to Pankrazi, immediately northwest of Dörfl. The breakthrough was sealed off with support from two armored personnel carriers and one

Jagdpanzer. Prisoners were taken. At noon, elements of Regimental Kampfgruppe 25 attacked toward Hill 622, but were stopped near the roadside
shrine east of Holzschlag (1.5 kilometers northwest of Schwarzensee) where
they encountered attacking Russians. Simultaneously, the Soviets attacked
toward the Kienberg hill (immediately northwest of Holzschlag) and captured it.[35]

The counterattack near St. Corona, prepared by Hauptsturm-führer von
Reitzenstein on the previous day, started at 10.30 hours. After a short
infantry fire fight, St. Corona and Hill 648, one kilometer northeast of the
town, were captured. With the fall of darkness, the previous positions were
again taken. The attackers had suffered no losses. The Kampfgruppe command post was set up in Neuwald. The Korpssicherungskompanie was
returned to the Kampfgruppe.[36]

In the sector adjacent on the left, the Minow Kompanie, in the framework of "Kampfgruppe von Ribbentrop", held the positions near Forsthof
against an enemy attack. The Groß-johann Kompanie cleared up an enemy
breakthrough near Stephof through a counterattack. Its front line ran from
Pamet via Stephof to Griessmühle. From the area north of St. Corona, the
enemy attacked to the west, south of the Schöpfl hill, and captured a hill east
of the Wöllersdorf-Klammhöhe-Hainfeld road, presumably Hill 766, 1.3 kilometers southeast of Glashütten. Caused by the pull-back of the front in the
right sector of Korps Schulz to the line Pyrha (seven kilometers southeast of
St. Pölten)-three kilometers northeast of St. Pölten, in the face of violent
attacks by Soviet forces, the gap between the I. SS-Panzerkorps and Korps
Schulz was widened. The Panzerkorps, i.e. "Kampfgruppe Peiper", set up a
weak line of blocking positions from Brand/Laaben to Stößing (5.3 kilometers northwest of Laaben).[37]

On 15 April 1945, the enemy kept generally quiet in the sector of
Divisional Kampfgruppe "HJ". A few thrusts in the sectors of Regimental
Kampfgruppe 26 and "Kampfgruppe Bremer" were repelled. The Divisionsbegleitkompanie reconnoitered in the morning in the Nöstach area (three
kilometers northeast of Altenmarkt). Nöstach was clear of the enemy, Hill
686 (presumably Kienberg, 681) was occupied by fairly strong enemy
infantry. In the early evening hours, Regimental Kampfgruppe 25 recaptured Hill 686. There, it came under massive fire from rocket launchers.[38]

The neighbor on the right, Divisional Kampfgruppe "LAH", had
mounted a counterattack against the enemy who had broken through northwest of Berndorf up to the Pottenstein-Pernitz road. On 14 April, it cleared
cut-off enemy forces from the forested area west of Pöllau; on 15 April it
cleared the area west of Pottenstein of the enemy encircled there. The old
main line of resistance in the sector west of Berndorf-Pottenstein had been
regained. The focal point of the Soviet attacks was directed at the sector of
Korps Schulz. The Soviets captured their most important attack objective in
the sector between the Vienna Forest and the Danube: St. Pölten.[39]

In the morning of 16 April 1945, the Soviets attacked from the area around Schwarzensee to the south. They broke through between the Dernberg hill (Hill 260, two kilometers east-northeast of Neuhaus) and the group of houses at Kienberg (one kilometer east of Neuhaus). They then advanced via Gadenweith (two kilometers southeast of Neuhaus) to the road fork at the eastern entrance to Weißenbach on the Triesting river. Regimental Kampfgruppe 26 succeeded in closing off the narrow passage between the Dernberg hill and the group of houses at Kienberg and in cutting off the enemy forces situated on Hill 526 near Gadenweith and south of there. Leutnant Möbius and his Kampfgruppe, which consisted of members of the I./26, the medical Abteilung, and the band, held Hill 638 (Dernberg hill, 604?) despite threats to his flank and the rear. Thus, he contributed significantly to stabilizing the situation. In order to completely clear up the situation, elements of Divisional Kampfgruppe "LAH" were to recapture Schreihof and Seehof (between Schwarzensee and Dernberg hill) in an attack from the east. In the course of that fighting, the enemy took Hills 686 (Kienberg hill, 681?) and Hill 718 (Peilstein hill, 716?).[40]

At "Kampfgruppe Bremer", the enemy took Hill 602 north of Pankrazi, and attempted to break through via Pankrazi to Seidl (immediately northwest of Dörfl and Nöstach, respectively) in battalion strength. A small assault party made up of Sturmmann Ivo Dane, Sturmmann Dreger, and a machine gun squad succeeded in breaking into the enemy gun position on the hill while the enemy was being pinned down by a few rounds from heavy infantry guns. Untersturmführer Lauterbach attacked the position on the hill on the flank with support from an armored personnel carrier. The enemy was dislodged, the hill was taken and held. The German troops lost three killed. The enemy suffered high losses.[41]

At the left boundary of the Division, the enemy broke through the blocking positions, in battalion strength, to the west of Obergrödl (3.5 kilometers east of Wöllersdorf). Countermeasures were begun. At 20.00 hours, the enemy mounted an attack on the Schöpfl hill (elevation 893 meters, 2.5 kilometers north of St. Corona) and captured it. Hauptsturmführer von Reitzenstein pulled men out of the positions of his Kampfgruppe to form an assault squad, and took the hill in a counterattack. The old positions were occupied again. The enemy extended his attack to the sector of "Kampfgruppe von Ribbentrop" as well. A breakthrough near Pamet, into the positions of the Großjohann Kompanie, was cleared up in a counterattack, supported by a Panzer IV which destroyed an enemy anti-tank gun.[42]

In the right sector of Divisional Kampfgruppe "HJ" (at Regimental Kampfgruppen 25 and 26, as well as "Kampfgruppe Bremer"), 17 April 1945 remained a quiet day. Repeated enemy attacks at the boundary with Divisional Kampfgruppe "LAH" to the east and northeast of Neuhaus were repelled, some through counterattacks. The enemy attacked St. Corona a number of times but was fought off. In the morning, the Soviets attacked the

Schöpfl hill from the south, however, without success. Finally, the position on the hill came under simultaneous attacks from the north, east, and west. The weak force there was unable to hold the position and withdrew. Hauptsturm-führer von Reitzenstein had no battle reserves available. Again, he was forced to pull men out of the positions to form an assault squad, and bring in every man who seemed dispensable at the time. By 15.30 hours, he had captured the hill in a counterattack and ordered the old positions manned again. In the evening, "Kampfgruppe Groß" cleared the forested terrain around the Totenköpfl hill (703 meters) and the Wittenbachberg hill (846 meters) southeast of Wöllersdorf where the enemy had broken through on 14 April.[43]

From the bulge in his front line southeast of Pölten, the enemy mounted an attack to the south with strong forces on the left wing of the I. SS-Panz-erkorps. Wilhelmsburg a.d. Traisen changed hands several times. In the evening, the Soviets were inside the city. From the district around Wald (7.5 kilometers northeast of Wilhelmsburg), the enemy advanced, in battalion strength and with tank support, to the south. To the rear of the blocking positions of "Kampfgruppe Peiper" on both sides of Perschenegg, at the cross-connection from the Perschling valley to the Michelbach valley, the enemy swung to the east. A counterattack was mounted. The threat of a Soviet breakthrough between the Vienna Woods and Traisen into the rear of the I. SS-Panzerkorps became apparent. Its forward line ran approximately west of Hohe Wand via Berndorf-Pottenstein-Neuhaus-Dörfl-St. Corona-Schöpfl-Laaben-Brand and in a generally westerly direction from there. It also bulged far to the east. The I. SS-Panzerkorps flanked the Soviet forces sit-uated between Vienna and the Traisen river south of the Danube. In order to strengthen the particularly threatened left wing, Regimental Kampfgruppe 26 was to be moved into the region around St. Corona, after being relieved by elements of Divisional Kampfgruppe "LAH".[44]

On 18 April 1945, Regimental Kampfgruppe 26 was relieved at 05.00 hours. Kampfgruppe Möbius remained in position on Hill 638 for the time being. The troops, which had been relieved, marched to St. Corona. The Korpssicherungskompanie, in position at the left boundary of the Division, was to be relieved in the morning. An enemy attack, which started at 07.00 hours, delayed that. The hand-over was completed at 11.30 hours. A few enemy assault and reconnaissance squads were repelled near St. Corona. That town came under repeated enemy shelling from the Corona creek val-ley which led toward it from the northwest. At the left neighbor of "Kampf-gruppe von Reitzenstein", violent fighting was under way in the vicinity of the Schöpfl hill. It appeared that the enemy had gained a foothold there. In the bitter battles since 13 April, the Kampfgruppe had suffered considerable losses which could not be replenished. It had no reserves which could be sent into action for a counterattack. Regimental Kampfgruppe 26 had not yet arrived. For the time, the situation could not be cleared up.

At "Kampfgruppe von Ribbentrop", the enemy attacked in the sector of the staff company and was repulsed. Enemy assemblies on the Neustift-Audorf road were observed. On the left wing of I. SS-Panzerkorps, the enemy continued his attack to the south. With thirty-eight tanks, he captured the area around Michelbach. In the evening, he was on the advance to Stollberg and toward the Kasberg hill (five kilometers east-southeast and 3.5 kilometers southeast of Michelbach, respectively). Farther to the west, the enemy by-passed Schwarzenbach (three kilometers northwest of St. Veit, in the Gölsen valley) in a southeasterly direction. From the high terrain northwest of Hainfeld (in the Gölsen valley), a counterattack in northerly and northwesterly directions was mounted. The only supply route, running behind the front line of the I. SS-Panzerkorps in the Gölsen and Triesting valleys in a west-east direction, was threatened.[45]

In the daily report of Heeresgruppe Süd on 18 April 1945, the name of the town of Ober-Grafendorf appeared for the first time. It is located eight kilometers southwest of St. Pölten. At Korps von Bünau (the former military commander of Vienna, General der Infanterie von Bünau, had taken over Korps Schulz) repeated enemy assaults northeast of Ober-Grafendorf were repelled. It is possible that "Kampfgruppe Chemnitz" saw first action there. In addition to the Panzer-less crews of the mixed I. Abteilung of Panzerregiment 12, two battle replacement companies of the Regiment were situated in Fallingbostel. The 1. Kompanie, equipped with four not fully operational Panthers, was led by Obersturmführer Jürgen Chemnitz. The 2. Kompanie, which was commanded by Obersturmführer Eggers, had three Panzer IVs which were also designated and usable only for training purposes. From approximately 7 April 1945 onward, the two companies moved to Lower Austria by rail transport and unloaded in Wilhelmsburg shortly before the Soviets captured it. The elements of the two companies equipped with Panzers were combined into a Kampfgruppe under the command of Obersturmführer Chemnitz. Added to them were a complete Zug of Panzer IVs of the II. Abteilung (probably from the repair company) and one Panzer IV of SS-Panzerregiment 2. The Kampfgruppe was ordered to cooperate with the Kampfgruppe of Hauptsturmführer Resch, and assigned to the heavy Panzerjägerabteilung 560 for supply purposes. It fought in the district around Ober-Grafendorf until 29 April. The Panzer-less crews of the two companies were combined into a Grenadier company under the command of Obersturmführer Eggers and probably attached to "Kampfgruppe Groß".[46]

At the same time, a larger and more massive threat to the eastern front in Austria arose. The spearhead units of the American forces had reached the area around Regensburg. With a further advance, they would push into the rear area of Heeresgruppe Süd. The provision of the fighting forces with ammunition and fuel would then deteriorate significantly. Hence, the Heeresgruppe planned to pull out individual divisions or Divisional combat groups out of its front line and hold them in readiness for action in the west, if it were to become necessary. Among others, Divisional Kampfgruppe "HJ" was designated for that. With the existing situation on the left wing of the I. SS-Panzerkorps, that was not yet possible. As another prerequisite, the front of the Panzerkorps would have to be pulled back to a shorter line.[47]

In order to be able to hold the positions near St. Corona (the town was the backbone of the defenses in the Vienna Woods) the situation in the area around the Schöpfl hill had to be cleared up. During the night from 18 to 19 April 1945, Regimental Kampfgruppe 26, without "Kampfgruppe Möbius", attacked from Hill 880 (this is presumably 882, Mitterschöpfl hill) toward Point 840 (unclear in the manuscript, not shown on map 1:50,000). Without encountering resistance, it succeeded in closing in on the Bildstock hill, located between the two hills. There, the attacking Kampfgruppe came under heavy fire, in particular from the left flank. It appeared that the enemy was located on the Schöpfl hill and on the ridge running from there to the southwest. The attack was halted for the time, to be re-started after the arrival of "Kampfgruppe Möbius". Leutnant Möbius, with his men, reached Neuwald (1.7 kilometers southwest of St. Corona) at 04.00 hours. At 10.00 hours, he started out from there in order to reach the starting position for the attack on the Schöpfl hill. A difference in elevation of 350 meters had to be overcome. The Soviets attacked Hill 880 (882) in the afternoon and achieved a breakthrough which was immediately sealed off. In the meantime, "Kampfgruppe Möbius" continued its attack on Hill 890 (893) by way of 777. Approximately 800 meters from the top of the hill, it encountered enemy resistance. Contact to Leutnant Möbius was lost.

The Soviets attacked, simultaneously and after massive preparatory fire, along the road which led from the northeast to St. Corona. The positions of "Kampfgruppe von Reitzenstein" ran on both sides of Point 551. From there, the road initially climbs in switchbacks to a saddle and then drops off to the village in the same manner. The two companies in action at Point 551, among them a Luftwaffe company, were dispersed. The enemy pushed into St. Corona. At 18.30 hours, it was completely captured. Hauptsturmführer von Reitzenstein collected the companies at the western exit and sent them to set up a line of blocking positions from Hill 554 west of the Reutelsgraben via the Hirschenstein hill (785 meters) to 150 meters southeast of the road fork at the southeastern entrance to St. Corona, then along the slope southwest of the village, to the western exit from St. Corona, then along the Coronabach creek to Miesenberg hill (785 meters). There was no contact with the artillery located in the region around Kleinmariazell. The enemy prepared for defense in the town. He set up heavy anti-tank guns in positions at the exits from the village. The Division had ordered "Kampfgruppe Bremer" to send two armored reconnaissance vehicles and four armored personnel carriers to St. Corona to reinforce the Kampfgruppe. They arrived after the village had already been taken and took up blocking positions southeast of St. Corona in a farm located at the road.

While the enemy attacked St. Corona, Regimental Kampfgruppe 26 continued its own attack on the Schöpfl hill. By 22.00 hours, "Kampfgruppe Möbius" had cleared up the breakthrough near Hill 880 (882). The group mounting the attack against Hill 890 (893) was located 500 meters west of the top of the hill at that time.[48]

While the enemy attempts to break through in the area around St. Corona were being repelled, bitter defensive fighting was also under way on the left wing of the Korps against strong enemy forces attacking on a wide front. At Kompanie Jauch of "Kampfgruppe von Ribbentrop" and to the west of there, the enemy succeeded in initially breaking through and then capturing Brand-Laaben in a pincer-like attack. Kompanie Großjohann pulled back its left wing, but held its other positions. Attacks mounted from the region around Stössing and from Michelbach against Stollberg were repulsed, with significant losses to the enemy. However, the enemy managed to occupy, farther to the west, Schwarzenbach (three kilometers northwest of St. Veit). St. Veit was then recaptured through a counterattack. In order to protect the Wöllersdorf-Hainfeld road, a line of blocking positions was set up between Stollberg and the hill north of Hainfeld. Taking advantage of the darkness, the enemy continued his attacks in the rugged, hilly and wooded terrain. On the attack from the Brand-Laaben district and west of there, he broke through a blocking position on both sides of Stollberg, pushing to the south. The enemy penetrated into Hainfeld from the north. "Kampfgruppe von Ribbentrop" withdrew, as ordered, to the south at the fall of darkness. A four-barrel Flak-Panzer, in action with Kompanie Großjohann, had to be blown up since the road through Laaben was in enemy hands and the broken terrain was impassable. The Kompanie initially withdrew to Hochberg (1.2 kilometers east-northeast of Wöllersdorf). Reconnaissance, sent out from there at 02.00 hours, determined that Wöllersdorf was occupied by the enemy. Near the Totenköpfl hill (703 meters), the Kompanie came upon the guards of a unit of the Hungarian Waffen-SS which was in the process of withdrawing. The Kompanie continued to withdraw to the south by way of Hill 766.[49]

In the right sector of Divisional Kampfgruppe, the enemy remained generally quiet. He attacked only in the sector of "Kampfgruppe Bremer" in the late afternoon with infantry and tanks north of the road. Pak, and Panzerjägers of the Heer brought in from Hafnerberg, knocked out two T-34s, the others withdrew. In occasional hand-to-hand combat and with the support of several armored personnel carriers, the accompanying infantry was thrown back at Nagglhof. A renewed attack during darkness was fought off.[50]

Contact to the neighbor on the left ("Kampfgruppe Großjohann") had been broken by the enemy breakthrough on both sides of Laaben. The Divisionsbegleitkompanie received orders to reconnoiter toward Hainfeld. The scouting party returned on 20 April 1945 at 00.30 hours. It reported that the enemy, who had pushed into Hainfeld in the evening of 19 April, had been thrown back. A new line of resistance had been established in front of Hill 624 (627?) north of Hainfeld. At 11.45 hours, a scouting party of the Aufklärungsabteilung reported enemy forces in the western section of Hainfeld. The stretch between Hainfeld and Rohrbach was free of the enemy, there was already fighting inside Rohrbach. The situation between Rohrbach and Lilienfeld was unclear at best. Individual blocking positions existed there.[51]

The Großjohann Kompanie first reached Wienhof on 20 April (3.5 kilometers southeast of the Klammhöhe hill on the road to the Kaumberg railroad station). It then marched on to Götzhof (1.5 kilometers southwest of the Klammhöhe hill). It was held in readiness there as reserve for "Kampfgruppe Groß".[52]

"Kampfgruppe von Reitzenstein" recaptured Point 648 in a counterattack during the night. In the morning, the Soviets mounted another attack on St. Corona, took Point 648 after bitter fighting, and pushed into the town. Hauptsturmführer Hauschild continued the attack toward the top of the Schöpfl hill in the morning, and captured it. A scouting party, sent by Hauptsturmführer von Reitzenstein to establish contact on the right, encountered an enemy force of some 240 men strong south of the Großer Hollerberg hill (three kilometers east of St. Corona). It was marching through the forest to the south. A forward German artillery observer spotted a strong enemy assembly near Point 648, while St. Corona appeared only sparsely occupied. The communications intelligence Zug reported that the enemy's intention was to push ahead toward Altenmarkt along the Gsteiner-Altenmarkt road. At approximately 17.30 hours, the enemy attacked the village of Wimmer (2.4 kilometers southeast of Gsteiner) and seized it. Two armored personnel carriers of the III./26 prevented him from advancing farther.[53]

At Regimental Kampfgruppe 25, the enemy attacked Hill 600 at 02.00 hours, but was repelled. In the late afternoon, he again attacked that hill and Hill 555 (one kilometer east of Nöstach) and was fought off. Two assault guns, in action with Regimental Kampfgruppe, had to be moved to Kaumberg. On 18 April, Obersturmbannführer Wilhelm Weidenhaupt had taken over the leadership of Regimental Kampfgruppe for a period of ten days.[54]

In the sector of "Kampfgruppe Groß", the situation developed unfavorably in the course of the afternoon. The enemy broke through, in a southeasterly direction, near the Klammhöhe hill, but was repulsed outside of Wienhof. Parts of Regimental Kampfgruppe 26 were sent out toward Gruber (1.2 kilometers south of Wienhof), which monitored enemy radio communications indicated seized by the enemy. At 19.30 hours, it was reported clear of the enemy. Blocking positions were set up along the line northwest of the chapel at Gruber to northwest of Wienhof. With that development, it was not sensible to hold on to the far-forward position on the Schöpfl hill. "Kampfgruppe Hauschild" was pulled back, and received orders to advance from Neuwald toward Kleinlindner (two kilometers southeast of the Klammhöhe hill) in order to establish contact with "Kampfgruppe Groß". Obersturmban-nführer Groß prepared a counterattack to recapture the Klammhöhe hill.

Scouting parties of the Divisionsbegleitkompanie were sent out to reconnoiter throughout the whole sector of Divisional Kampfgruppe. Nöstach was reported free of the enemy at 18.00 hours. Enemy forces with mortars, at scouting party strength, were spotted in Wimmer. A scouting party, which had been sent out toward the Klammhöhe hill, returned at 19.15 hours. The hill could not be reached by vehicle since Neuwald and Hainfeld were occupied by the enemy. The enemy advanced farther to the south near Neuwald. Enemy forces were spotted on the Klammhöhe hill. At 20.30 hours, the Divisionsbegleitkompanie set up a blocking position on Hill 585, 500 meters north of the eastern exit of Altenmarkt. The Divisional command was located in the town.[55]

"Kampfgruppe Groß" mounted an attack on the Klammhöhe hill at three o'clock on 21 April 1945. The attack stalled in the face of a strong anti-tank gun line. "Kampfgruppe von Ribbentrop" moved into a blocking line from Schreiberhof (500 meters south of the Klammhöhe hill) via Unter Götzhof-Ober Götzhof to Kuminerer (2.6 kilometers southwest of the Klammhöhe hill). At 05.55 hours, "Kampfgruppe Hauschild" started an attack on Kleinlindner. It initially advanced quickly but, after 800 meters, stalled in front of a strong enemy. "Kampfgruppe Möbius" also took part in that attack. With Leutnant Möbius in the lead, it captured an enemy rocket launcher position in an assault. During the continuation of the attack on a column of trucks, Leutnant Möbius was killed. The attack then faltered in the Soviet fire from the flank. The leader-less Kampfgruppe tried to withdraw to the starting position. Only a few men survived that battle in the Hetzgraben valley. The medical officer of the Kampfgruppe, Unterarzt Dr. Kleinmann, was killed during the rescue of a wounded man. In the St. Corona cemetery, 121 unknown German soldiers are buried. Most of them were killed during that battle, or wounded and shot later, but the enemy, too, suffered heavy losses. The Soviets took the pay-books and identity discs from all the killed men so that they could not be identified later. The brave men of the staff of the I. Bataillon of Panzergrenadierregiment 26, the Sanitäts-abteilung 12, and the band of the "HJ" Division fought outstandingly in the Triesting valley and the Vienna Woods under the exemplary leadership of the extremely gallant Leutnant Möbius.[55a]

Two assault guns and four armored personnel carriers were scheduled to support the attack by "Kampfgruppe Hauschild" along the road. However, they were unable to get across the bridge outside Koglbauer. The enemy advanced farther to the southeast to the south of Kleinlindner. A scouting party of the Divisionsbegleitkompanie spotted enemy forces near a farm immediately southwest of Jura (three kilometers southeast of Kleinlindner) at approximately 10.00 hours. It then came upon German blocking positions

500 meters south of there. Another scouting party approached to within 10 m of Jura. No German troops were located there. Instead, fifty to eighty sleeping Soviet infantrymen were found in the forest 400 meters southeast of Jura and fired at with assault rifles. From Vorer (1.2 kilometers northeast of Jura), enemy columns moved, without interruption, partly on foot, partly in trucks, in the direction of Jura. The Hegemann group set up a blocking position on the hill 800 meters north of Kaumberg and harassed the enemy advance with MG fire. At 14.00 hours, the enemy attacked from the direction of Jura towards Kaumberg and entered the town along the railroad embankment. He suffered considerable losses under the MG fire from the blocking positions of the Begleitkompanie. The outflanked group moved into a new blocking position 500 meters east of Kaumberg, at the rail line and the road, reinforced by a Jagdpanzer. The hills north of the Kaumberg-Altenmarkt road were reported clear of the enemy between 13.00 and 16.00 hours. In the late afternoon, a scouting party was spotted at Reisbergerhof (1.2 kilometers northwest of Tenneberg), but it withdrew again. During the noon hours, the enemy attacked the blocking positions east of St. Corona from the rear, having swung across the Steinriegel hill (743 meters, 1.5 kilometers south of St. Corona). The positions were overrun, the remaining men assembled in Faschingbauer. "Kampfgruppe von Reitzenstein" was pulled back to Gadinger (2.3 kilometers southeast of St. Corona). The Pionierbataillon occupied Wimmer again. To the north of the St. Corona-Altenmarkt road, the enemy advanced on Kleinmariazell.[56]

While the enemy advanced to the south through the woods in the sector between Altenmarkt and Hainfeld, slowly gaining ground, his attacks in the right sector of Divisional Kampfgruppe "HJ" were repulsed. In the morning, enemy forces assembled between Beringer and Pankrazi. The assembly was smashed by the fire of the Artillerieregiment which had, in the meantime, moved its position from the area around Kleinmariazell to the south. In the evening, the Soviets attacked from the region around Schwarzensee and Neuhaus to the south and threatened to cut the Altenmarkt-Pernitz road near Weißenbach. That was the only connecting road to the rear for the Divisional Kampfgruppe, after the east-west connecting road from Altenmarkt via Hainfeld to Lilienfeld had been cut at Kaumberg and Hainfeld. Under pressure from the enemy, Regimental Kampfgruppe 25 withdrew to the line Thalhof-Festenberg-hills west of Hafnerberg (3.8 kilometers southeast, 2 kilometers east, and 2.2 kilometers east-northeast of the road fork at the western exit from Altenmarkt, respectively). At "Kampfgruppe Bremer", the positions on Hill 602 were under massive artillery and rocket launcher fire, which had started at dawn. In the afternoon, the Soviets attacked the hill from the north and seized it. The line of resistance had to be pulled back to Nöstach. The enemy did not continue his attack.[57]

Since stronger enemy forces were firmly established in Kaumberg, the attack on the Klammhöhe hill had been repelled, and the Soviets had broken through in many locations in the area between Kaumberg and the Klammhöhe hill, the attack by Regimental Kampfgruppe 26 on Kleinlindner had to be broken off. Contact to "Kampfgruppe Groß" was not established. Regimental Kampfgruppe 26, which had been taken over by Obersturmbannführer Sandig of the officer reserve of the Armee on 21 April, was ordered to withdraw behind the Hainfeld-Kaumberg road. At "Kampfgruppe Groß", which was again attached to Divisional Kampfgruppe "HJ" since 12.30 hours, the enemy again pushed into Hainfeld, which he had temporarily lost, around 20.00 hours. Near Gerichtsberg (3.5 kilometers west of Kaumberg), the enemy crossed the road to the south. From Kaumberg, too, he advanced in a southerly direction. "Kampfgruppe von Reitzenstein" was ordered to abandon its line of blocking positions southeast of St. Corona and to move into a new line of positions south of the Hainfeld-Altenmarkt road. The Kampfgruppe disengaged from the enemy unnoticed. Hauptsturmführer von Reitzenstein, with his adjutant, once more walked along the old line of blocking positions in order to make certain that the order had reached all the groups. They observed strong enemy forces on the march from St. Corona along the road to Gadinger. Through the woods, the "rearguard" of the Kampfgruppe reached the Mayerhof farm (two kilometers southwest of Kaumberg). The new line of blocking positions, which the Kampfgruppe, also marching on foot through the woods, had reached, ran from the Schachnerberg hill (three kilometers southeast of Kaumberg) in the direction of Mayerhof and from there to Kollmannhof (1.5 kilometers west of Mayerhof).[58]

The commanding general, Gruppenführer Priess, ordered that Kaumberg be recaptured and the gap to "Kampfgruppe Groß" be closed. The artillery was to remain in its old positions, the Panzers of "Kampfgruppe Groß" were to be brought in from the west for the action. That was not possible since the bridge near Gerichtsberg had already been blown up. The commanding general placed the responsibility for that on Obersturmbannführer Groß and ordered him relieved of his duties. Hauptsturmführer von Ribbentrop took over the leadership of the Kampfgruppe; his previous position was transferred to Hauptsturmführer Minow. Flakabteilung 12, which had last been located in Hainfeld, moved to Ramsau (4.2 kilometers southeast of Hainfeld).[59]

On 22 April 1945, Regimental Kampfgruppe 26 mounted an attack on Kaumberg from the Lohmühle district. Almost simultaneously, enemy forces pushed into the assembly area. They were driven back, but the troops had to assemble one more time. Immediately outside of Kaumberg, the attack came to a halt under the defensive enemy fire. The Kampfgruppe suffered high losses. In addition, two German assault guns, four armored personnel carriers and one 7.5 cm Pak were lost.

Since the morning, the enemy also attacked in the area around Altenmarkt. A critical situation developed. Ober-scharführer August Zinßmeister was in action there with his eight-wheel armored reconnaissance vehicle. He noted the events in his diary as follows:

> . . . In the early morning, back to Lohmühle. Even before reaching it, fire from Russian tanks. I drove back to Tenneberg where I met the Divisional commander Kraas in an armored personnel carrier at the bridge (1.3 kilometers west of the road fork Altenmarkt West, Author). He issued a new order: Once more through the anti-tank fire from the hills along the Triesting valley to carry orders to an infantry battalion near Lohmühle. Back through enemy fire and through Altenmarkt which had already been captured by 'Ivan'. From the Abteilung command post, we knocked out, with our third shell, a Russian armored personnel carrier on the hill above Altenmarkt. It had been hammering our infantrymen with its gun as they advanced for a counterattack, led by the Ia. In the afternoon, new orders took us from Weißenbach via Furth, in the mountains, to the road in the direction of Kaumberg. Terrible rain. Our fire drove 'Ivan' from a captured 'Wespe' and 'Grille' battery (east of Saghäusel, west of Furth, Author). Several 'Urraa' attacks down the hill to the vehicles broke down under our fire. Unter-scharführer Höhns of the Wittenburg Panzer was hit in the upper arm by shrapnel from an explosive shell. In the evening, our ammunition had run out. Re-supply at Regiment 26. We fell asleep over our pan-fried potatoes. But, we had to get out again to the edge of town, blocking toward Kaumberg . . .[60]

Theo Rossiwall wrote on the battles for Altenmarkt:

> . . . Altenmarkt a.d. Triesting was ultimately occupied by the Soviets after 14 days of fighting, while the Germans withdrew to the south and blew up the road bridge at Hafnerberg . . . The advancing Russians shot dead the village priest in the church . . . Neuhaus in the Triesting valley had changed hands several times before it finally was in Soviet possession; almost all the houses were destroyed or damaged . . . Tenneberg was encircled from the north, east and west . . . The Germans withdrew south by way of Hocheck and blew up four railroad and road bridges in the municipal district . . .[61]

The Divisional command post was first moved to the command post of "Kampfgruppe Bremer" in Hafnerberg, then via Weißenbach to Furth on the Triesting river (4.8 kilometers south of Altenmarkt). The Divisionsbegleitkompanie attacked Russians, who had broken through, near Saghäusel, two kilometers west of Furth, at 15.00 hours and drove them back. It took up position 200 meters east of the road fork near Saghäusel and blocked to the west. There was no contact with the right wing of "Kampfgruppe von Reitzenstein" at the Schachnerberg hill. The Begleit-kompanie was repeatedly attacked in the evening. It cleared up one breakthrough and held its position through the night, without enemy contact. "Kampfgruppe Bremer" was forced to give up its positions near Nöstach after the loss of Altenmarkt, and pulled back to Weißenbach. The enemy attacking from Neuhaus was fought off.[62]

"Kampfgruppe Minow" moved into a line of blocking positions south of the Kaumberg-Hainfeld road, with Kompanie Großjohann located near Gerstbach (3.7 kilometers east of Hainfeld), Kompanie Nölk (previously Minow) near Edelhof (1.3 kilometers southwest of Gerstbach). The command post of "Kampfgruppe von Ribbentrop" was located in Ramsau. In accordance with orders, "Kampfgruppe Taubert" also withdrew to the south and moved into a blocking line on both sides of the Hocheck mountain (1.037 meters, 3 kilometers northwest of Furth).[63]

Beginning on 21 April, the enemy expanded his attacks on the I. SS-Panzerkorps also into its right sector. He attacked toward Berndorf from the area west and southwest of Baden and pushed Divisional Kampfgruppe "LAH" back. Elements, coming from Pottenstein, marched through Weißenbach to the south on 22 April, according to information provided by Rossiwall.

During the night from 22 to 23 April, enemy forces advanced along the Steinbach valley which leads from Rehhof (2.7 kilometers east of Kaumberg) in a southwesterly direction to the rear of the Hochriegel hill. Enemy scouting parties, sent out into several directions, were repelled by "Kampfgruppe von Reitzenstein". At "Kampfgruppe Taubert", the enemy had already in the morning reached the slopes below the shelter hut on Hocheck mountain. He was fought with hand grenades and Panzerfausts and withdrew with considerable losses. From the top of the mountain, the Kaumberg-Altenmarkt road could be observed. Heavy vehicular traffic was noticed and reported to the Divisional staff. The artillery was ordered to aim harassing fire on the road. Hauptsturmführer Taubert directed the fire from Hocheck mountain, with good effect. The left neighbor of "Kampfgruppe von Reitzenstein", "Kampfgruppe Minow", moved its blocking line to the hill on both sides of Kämpf. Contact to "Kampfgruppe von Reitzenstein" at Kollmannhof could not be established.[65]

Toward noon, the enemy attacked the Gemeindeberg hill (769/772 meters), one kilometer south of Altenmarkt, from the town, and from several directions. The majority of the blocking forces there were massacred, approximately twenty men were able to retreat to the south. In the afternoon, the enemy advanced from the Gemeindeberg hill to Hill 792 (Kienberg hill?), and attacked simultaneously near Tasshof (2.5 kilometers northwest of Weißenbach) along both sides of the Altenmarkt-Weißenbach road. He was brought to a halt through a counterattack. Regimental Kampf-

gruppe 25 was ordered to move into a new blocking line from Furth to
Hocheck mountain, but it had first to keep the Pottenstein-Fahrafeld-
Weißenbach road open for Divisional Kampfgruppe "LAH". Later, the neighbor on the right was to maintain contact to Regimental Kampfgruppe 25
during the withdrawal.

Oberscharführer August Zinßmeister had reported that enemy forces
had pushed forward into the firing positions of self-propelled guns near
Saghäusel on 22 April, and that his scouting party had effectively fought the
enemy following behind. One of the two "Grillen" (heavy infantry guns on
Panzer chassis) in position there could be towed away on 23 April, the other
one had to be blown up. Furth and the blocking positions of the Divisionsbegleitkompanie near Saghäusel were under violent enemy artillery fire
throughout the day. The enemy brought in strong infantry forces from the
north. He obviously planned to break through to Pernitz where the withdrawal routes from the sector of Divisional Kampfgruppe "LAH" joined up.
A further withdrawal to the west (for Divisional Kampfgruppe "HJ", as well)
was possible only from there. In the morning, the Divisionsbegleitkompanie
had pushed its blocking positions to within fifty meters of Saghäusel. It was
relieved by a company of Regiment 26 in the afternoon. A combat-ready
scouting party of the Begleitkompanie, ordered to reconnoiter by way of Im
Moos along the valley to Harras in the west, came under heavy fire from
machine guns and bazookas at the western exit from Saghäusel at 20.30
hours. It was not possible to destroy the enemy, some 150 to 200 men strong
and firmly dug-in for defense, in an encircling attack, or to drive him back.
With support from four armored personnel carriers, equipped with 2 cm
triplet guns, Saghäusel was captured at 23.00 hours and the blocking positions were pushed forward to the western exit. A scouting party of the III./26
with four armored personnel carriers encountered Russians in the Rohrbach
valley, north of Furth. The Divisional command post was moved from Furth
to Riegelhof, one kilometer northwest of Muggendorf (2.5 kilometers northwest of Pernitz). A road of the third class condition led from Furth to the
edge of the Steinwandgraben valley at the Steinwandklamm gorge; from
there, across the mountains to Riegelhof, led a narrow track. At the time, the
road conditions were unfavorable. When Ober-scharführer Zinßmeister
crossed the hill at noon, it was snowing there.[66]

During the night from 23 to 24 April 1945, the Soviets attacked Ramsau
in "Kampfgruppe Minow's" sector. Kompanie Großjohann, located in a prepared rear position there (the Kompanie command post was situated in
Großbichler, 1.2 kilometers west of Ramsau) was pushed back to the cemetery. It repulsed two attacks of company-strength enemy forces, supported by
anti-aircraft guns. In the morning, twenty-five killed enemy soldiers were
counted in front of the position.[67]

On 23 April, the Soviets captured or occupied Ober-Piesting, Pottenstein, and Weißenbach in the sector of Divisional Kampfgruppe "LAH".[68]

At Korps von Bünau, after the capture of St. Pölten on 15 April, the enemy remained generally quiet. On 24 April 1945, however, he continued his concentric attacks against the bulge in the front line of the I. SS-Panzerkorps. In the sector of Divisional Kampfgruppe "HJ", the focal point of the enemy attacks was again south of Altenmarkt and south of Hainfeld.

The gap between the right wing of "Kampfgruppe von Reitzenstein" near Schachnerberg and the blocking positions of "Kampfgruppe Taubert" at the Hocheck mountain caused the Divisional command deep concern.

The Divisionsbegleitkompanie was ordered to again send out the combat-ready scouting party of Unterscharführer Hegemann toward Harras. At 01.45 hours, only 300 meters west of Saghäusel, it came upon enemy positions which it could not get around. The group returned to the Kompanie at 03.00 hours. After a short preparatory fire, the Soviets attacked Furth, defended by elements of "Kampfgruppe Hauschild", with strong forces at 08.10 hours. They captured it after a short battle. Supported by an armored personnel carrier with 2 cm triplet gun, the Divisionsbegleitkompanie mounted a counterattack at 08.45 hours. It reached (at time in hand-to-hand combat) the center of the town against determined resistance. At 10.00 hours, the enemy again attacked the town with strong infantry forces. The Begleitkompanie withdrew at 11.00 hours to the south into the Ebelthal valley and assembled at the Divisional command post in Riegelhof at 17.00 hours.[69]

"Kampfgruppe von Reitzenstein", still without contact either on the right or left, observed, from the Schachnerberg hill, the approach of very strong enemy columns with horse-drawn heavy weapons from the Höfnerbach valley (south of Rehhof) in the direction of Hocheck mountain and the Brunntal valley (southeast of Hochriegel hill). Individual scouting parties sent against the blocking line of the Kampfgruppe were repelled. Enemy battle reconnaissance by-passed the left wing, moving south. The threat of an encirclement became apparent. Contact between the Divisional staff and the Kampfgruppe had been lost since the enemy had advanced to Saghäusel and outside of Ramsau. Hauptsturmführer von Reitzenstein, on his own decision, prepared for defense on the hills on both sides of the exit of the Mariental valley: the Feigl Kogel, Kölchberg and Sonnstein hills. He also set up a blocking position to the rear in the town of Mariental.[70]

"Kampfgruppe Minow" came under repeated enemy attacks on both sides of Ramsau. It pulled back its blocking line by a short distance. Farther to the west, the enemy attacked from the area around Hainfeld to the south and southwest, but gained only little ground.[71] During the night, the Divisional operations staff moved, together with the Begleitkompanie, via Pernitz, Gutenstein, Rohrer Sattel (864 meters), Rohr in the mountains, to Reintal (2.5 kilometers east of Rohr).[72]

On 25 April 1945, Regimental Kampfgruppe 25, to which "Kampfgruppe von Reitzenstein had also been attached, and "Kampfgruppe von Ribbentrop" were holding the north—facing blocking line of Divisional Kampfgruppe "HJ". At the same pace at which Divisional Kampfgruppe "LAH" withdrew under enemy pressure to the west, the north-facing front line was shortened. The forces, thus freed up, were moved to the west along difficult mountain roads. Reconnaissance sent out by "Kampfgruppe von Reitzenstein" observed, from the Schachnerberg mountain, undiminished strong columns of enemy traffic from the Triestingtal valley, near Rehhof, to the south. Kompanie Großjohann repelled enemy scouting parties near Ramsau and temporarily recaptured abandoned positions in a counterattack.[73]

During the night from 25 to 26 April, the III./26, which was blocking the road to Muggendorf and Pernitz near Furth, received orders to withdraw to Rohr in the mountains. It reached Pernitz in the early morning hours. Unfortunately, a German Pak, which had not been identified as such, was overrun. A T-34, sitting next to the church, fired at the armored personnel carriers, but missed. The Bataillon drove back to the exit toward Muggendorf. In a ravine, three armored personnel carriers got stuck and were blown up. The remaining seventeen drove along the Raimundspfad trail to the road leading to Gutenstein. The road was under heavy artillery fire. Blocking forces of Divisional Kampfgruppe "LAH" were in position along the rail line. The Bataillon reached Rohr without stopping. The Flakabteilung moved from Adamstal (four kilometers south of Ramsau) by way of Hölle, Kalte Kuchel (four kilometers west of Rohr) along the road with many detours, via Untermitterbach to Hohenberg in the valley of the Unrechttraisen creek. The town is located exactly thirty-two kilometers south of St. Pölten, on the Traisen river, in approximate extension of the front line of Korps von Bünau.[74]

The Soviets attacked the blocking line of Divisional Kampfgruppe "HJ" at several points, in particular at the Araberg hill, at "Kampfgruppe von Reitzenstein", but were repulsed. An enemy patrol reached the area immediately north of -Mariental where the command post of Regimental Kampfgruppe 25 was situated. "Kampfgruppe Minow" repelled several scouting parties. Hauptsturmführer Minow was killed by a shell fragment. Hauptsturmführer Großjohann took over the leadership of the Kampfgruppe. "Kampfgruppe Taubert", which had repeatedly been attacked unsuccessfully on Hocheck mountain on 24 and 25 April, withdrew to Rohr, as ordered and in the process of shortening the front line, via the Hochriegel hill (2.5 kilometers west of the Hocheck mountain), the Kieneck hill (seven kilometers northwest of Muggendorf) and the Unterberg hill (eight kilometers northeast of Rohr).[75]

In the course of the day, Divisional Kampfgruppe "HJ" received orders to assemble, after being relieved by elements of Divisional Kampfgruppe "LAH", in the area Lilienfeld-Rabenstein-Tradigist, and to take over the sector of the 10. Fallschirmjägerdivision there. The relief operation began at 21.30 hours. The combat groups reached the roads, where their vehicles were waiting for them, after rather extensive foot marches.[76]

In the course of 27 and 28 April 1945, the combat troops of the "HJ" Division marched into the assembly area by way of Kalte Kuchel, Hohenberg, Schrambach and Tradigist. The Divisionsbegleitkompanie took over the directing of traffic. The Divisional command post was located in Tradigist. The units, originating with many different organizations, were returned to their regiments, battalions and Abteilungen, except those formed from supply troops. "Kampfgruppe Groß-johann" remained in existence. Replacements, which had arrived, were incorporated. Wounded men returned to their units from the hospitals. Some, who had not fully recovered, "discharged" themselves since they preferred to be with their units. After a period of rest, the weapons were cleaned and the uniforms repaired. Since renewed action was in the future, the replacements (e.g. at the Divisionsbegleitkompanie) were trained in the field and prepared through lectures. The commanders and unit leaders explored the sectors assigned to them, in which the 10. Fallschirmjägerdivision was to be relieved. It became apparent that the relief operation in the Lilienfeld-Hill 883 (Lorenzi-Pechkogel) sector could be carried out only at night. A scouting party of the Divisionsbegleit-kompanie reconnoitered in the area around Schrambach (2.5 kilometers southwest of Lilienfeld) in the morning of 28 April. It reported at 10.15 hours that the Soviets had advanced along the road to Tradigist up the bend in the road 2.5 kilometers northwest of Schrambach. The Fallschirmjägers cleared up the breakthrough in a counterattack.[77]

The bulk of the Fallschirmjägerdivision was relieved on 29 April 1945. Delays during the approach had made a relief during the previous night impossible. Panzergrenadier-regiment 25 took over the right sector even before noon. Under enemy observation, the I./25 was able to relieve only one-at-a time in the Lilienfeld-Hill 883 sector; that required the whole day. "Kampfgruppe Großjohann" moved into positions on the crest of Hill 883 and scouted toward Eschenau. By the fall of darkness, the Division had taken over all sectors, except for the I./26.[78]

"Kampfgruppe Chemnitz", which had been fighting in the district east of Ober-Grafendorf since 18 April, disengaged and was moved to Panzer-regiment 12. It arrived there on 1 May and handed over the remaining Panzers to the mixed II. Abteilung. The newly Panzer-less crews were reorganized into an infantry company under the command of Obersturm-führer Bormuth; Obersturmführer Jürgen Chemnitz was forced to enter a hospital for the treatment of serious after effects from a previous wound.[79]

The day of 30 April 1945 remained generally quiet. The units reconnoitered in front of their sectors, but no fighting broke out. The scouting parties observed the enemy building entrenchments and barbed wire obstacles at a brisk pace. One party brought back a Russian NCO who had defected. The Ic asked the deserter for the reason for the construction. He gave the astounding reply: "We will be awaiting the Americans in this position". That information conformed with observations in the Russian rear area facing the sector of Korps von Bünau. There, too, the Soviets had been constructing trenches at a rapid pace. Forests were cut down. The civilian population was brought in for that, or was evacuated. Loudspeakers,which had been set up by the Soviets in the no-man's land in that sector of the front, broadcast messages such as:

> . . . Comrades, the greatest treason in the history of the world lies ahead. Do not let yourselves be pushed into a new war. Defect to the Red Army! . . .[80]

Those observations, to some extent, fed the expectation that a break in the pact of the Allies might, indeed, be possible. The commander and the Ia of the "HJ" Division considered such hopes to be misleading.

During the night from 30 April to 1 May 1945, the Hauschild (I./26) and Großjohann battalions were scheduled to attack and capture Hill 877. Reconnaissance determined that the enemy positions were so strong that available forces would, in no way, be adequate for the task. Regiment 25 reconnoitered toward "Wh. Hasen" [country inn, named 'Rabbit'] (three kilometers east of Lilienfeld) in the morning. The scouting party surprised the Soviets during an assembly and opened fire. The enemy suffered significant losses. The scouting party returned without casualties.[81]

The news of the death of Adolf Hitler and the proclamation by Großadmiral (admiral of the fleet) Dönitz, his successor, arrived at the "HJ" Division during the night from 1 to 2 May 1945. That outcome could be foreseen for some time. Still, it struck the troops suddenly and moved them deeply. An era of German history was coming to an end but the battles were not yet over. It could be expected that Großadmiral Dönitz, the highly reliable soldier, would do everything imaginable in order to save what could be saved. During the first days of the withdrawal into the mountains, many civilians had fled to the west, so as not to fall into Soviet hands. Others stayed behind and hung white or red pieces of cloth from the windows as a sign of surrender, or of friendship with the Soviets expected to arrive. It depressed the withdrawing troops that they could not safeguard the population. The men knew that in Hungary many civilians had been murdered, women raped, and houses looted. The white and red pieces of cloth were not felt to be provocative by the withdrawing soldiers. Compassion with the desperate people was felt. The "comrades' would get to know the other side soon enough. Refugees, who crossed the front line during the following days, reported how worthless the pieces of cloth were. In particular, the inhabitants of houses from which red cloth was flying, were treated the worst by the Soviets. Would "Every man for himself!" now become the supreme law? More than ever, it was important to preserve the spirit of comradeship which held the troops together, and to remain united.

CHAPTER 11.2
The Division as Armee Reserve—Capitulation on 8 May 1945

The "HJ" Division received orders to assemble in the area around Kilb (seventeen kilometers northwest of Lilienfeld), at the disposal of the 6. SS-Panzerarmee. Its bulk was relieved during the night of 2 to 3 May 1945. Bataillon von Ribbentrop (Obersturm-bannführer Martin Groß had again taken over the command of the Regiment) remained in its position as the only unit of the Division. The Divisional command post was kept in Tradigist until further notice. By dawn on 3 May, the relief operation was completed.[1] Thus, combat action for the 12. SS-Panzerdivision "Hitlerjugend" had come to an end. Once more, it had given its best. After great initial successes against the Soviet Gran bridgehead and during the offensive at Lake Balaton, its strength was exhausted. The rearguard battles in Hungary, in Burgenland and in Lower Austria had been endured in wooded mountainous terrain and under the most unfavorable tactical circumstances for armored units. The replacements, brought in from other branches of the Wehrmacht, and not trained for infantry combat, had, in most cases proved to be not of help but, rather, an encumbrance. The mainstay of the fighting was the, more and more shrinking battle-tested core of the units. Panzer-less crews, artillerymen without guns, and members of the support and supply troops had fought excellently as infantry under the most difficult conditions, and had stood the test in a remarkable manner. As well, the repair and supply units fulfilled their duties under extremely tough circumstances. Thus, in Lower Austria, the previously motorized vehicle companies had to bring ammunition from the Danube barges, unloading in Melk, to the front by horse-drawn carts. The untiring labor by the repair and maintenance units brought, time and again, damaged Panzers, Jagdpanzers, armored personnel carriers, guns and motor vehicles back to combat-ready condition. Hence, despite constant enemy attacks, the front line had finally stabilized to some extent while the Division was at the focal points of those battles throughout. That last action had caused heavy losses. The following figures show the total losses, the number of killed is given in brackets. From 10 February to 8 May 1945, the "Hitlerjugend" Division lost: 96 (53) officers, 380 (125) NCOs, and 3,900 (1,320) men—a total of 4,376 casualties. Total losses amounted to: 32 Panzer IVs, 35 Panthers, 1 Wespe, 11 light field howitzers, 1 heavy field howitzer, 1 10 cm gun, and 6 15 cm rocket launchers. At the conclusion of the fighting, the following were still, or again, combat-ready: 6 Panzer IVs, 9 Panthers, 1 Wespe, 17 light field howitzers, 4 heavy field howitzers, 2 10 cm guns, 7 15 cm rocket launchers, and 7 captured Russian 7.62 cm guns. The difference in the available numbers of guns on 10 February 1945 resulted from transfers to other units because of the lack of tractor capacity.[2]

On 7 May 1945, the Division (without Bataillon von Ribbentrop) moved into the district around Steinakirchen, fourteen kilometers southeast of Amstetten. The Ia was ordered to report to the headquarters of the 6. SS-Panzerarmee in Gresten, nine kilometers south of Steinakirchen. There, the chief of staff, Gruppenführer Fritz Kraemer, notified him that Generaloberst Jodl, on behalf of Großadmiral Dönitz, had offered, at the headquarters of General Eisenhower in Reims/France, the surrender of all German armed forces and had signed the document on 7 May at 02.41 hours. General Eisenhower had promised him the cessation of hostilities by 01.00 hours German summer time on 9 May. By that time, all troops had to be across the demarcation line between the Americans and the Soviets, which ran along the Enns river. Until then, that was valid only for the troops in action on the western front. However, the attempt was being made to achieve silent agreement for the crossing over of the troops still situated on the eastern front. The Ia was ordered to offer surrender at the 65th US Infantry Division in Steyr on 7 May 1945 in the afternoon. During that, he was to expressly point out that the Division was held in readiness in the area around Steinakirchen, as Armee reserve, for action on the western front. In accordance with directives from the Americans, the Division was to move into captivity on 8 May 1945. Gruppenführer Kraemer requested that the thanks of Oberstgruppenführer Sepp Dietrich (who was not present) for its outstanding action, as well as his best wishes for the future be conveyed to the Division. He, himself, thanked the Ia for the excellent cooperation and wished him the best of luck. Obersturmbannführer Meyer sincerely returned both thanks and best wishes.

After his return to the Divisional command post, the Ia reported to the Divisional commander. They deliberated on how the move to captivity could best be carried out from the Division's point of view. It was important, above all, that the Americans accepted the surrender, since the Division had, to the end, been fighting against the Soviets. Also, a capture of elements of the Division by possibly pursuing Soviet troops had to be prevented.

Gruppenführer Kraemer had been unable to answer the question of what the future, after the surrender, would hold. Captivity was unavoidable since almost all of Germany was occupied by the Allies. Those small areas, such as those in Lower and Upper Austria, would doubtlessly also fall into their hands in the course of the surrender. Everything else was uncertain. Staying together and maintaining the spirit, that had to be the goal for the near future.

In the afternoon of 7 May 1945, Obersturmbannführer Meyer, Untersturmführer Kurt Rinne (one of the orderly officers of the Divisional staff) and Unterscharführer Helmut Schmieding, as the driver of the VW-Kübelwagen, set out for Steyr. Just before they reached the Enns river, they met Sturmbannführer Stürzbecher, the Ia of the "Hohenstaufen" Division, who was returning from Steyr. The Americans had accepted the surrender, but he felt humiliated and was depressed. After a few minutes the car of the negotiators from the "HJ" Division reached the demarcation line on a hill at the east bank of the Enns. A narrow lane had been opened up through a mine field, marked by white tape. An American jeep guided the car to a sentry at the entrance to a factory. The Ia requested to be taken to the command post of the regiment in the city. Approval was obtained by telephone. The pistols were handed over, Unterscharführer Schmieding and the car had to stay behind in the factory yard. The Ia and the orderly officer were driven into the city in an American jeep, with an escort. It stopped in front of a hotel at the market square, the command post was located there. The American escort led the two Germans into the building. The American guard at the entrance said, in German: "Don't worry, everything will work out!" That was a comforting, friendly gesture, or was it more? At least, it diminished the tension somewhat.

The negotiators were led into a room on the first floor. In its center stood a large table, covered with maps. Other than that, there was no furniture in the room. Three of four American officers were sitting on the floor. A staff officer stood up, the Ia introduced himself and his companion and advised that he had orders to offer the surrender of his Division. He was requested to indicate on the map the area where the Division was located. Then came the question, how many men the Division had. The answer: "Ten thousand" was taken in with great delight by the officers sitting on the floor. Bottles and glasses standing around gave an indication that the victory had already been celebrated. That was understandable, but it was deeply painful to the negotiators.

The American staff officer announced the conditions:

The "HJ" Division will cross the demarcation line in the Upper Austrian city of Enns on the Enns river on 8 May 1945, from 08.00 hours to 24.00 hours American time. Anyone arriving later will go into Russian captivity. All weapons will be unloaded two kilometers from the river, small-arms are to be removed. The ammunition for Panzers and guns will follow behind them on trucks. The Panzers will point their guns sky-ward. All vehicles will have to fly white flags.

These conditions were accepted. Finally, the American chief negotiator informed that a motorized American scouting party was missing east of the demarcation line since the previous day. He requested that it be guided back and provided with help, if necessary. That was promised. The German negotiators took their leave and were taken back to the sentry post at the demarcation line. Unterscharführer Schmieding pulled up with his VW. The pistols were demanded to be returned. The Americans had thrown them unto a large heap of pistols in a room of the gate-keeper's lodge. Pistols, which appeared suitable, were picked out and taken along. Along the same path on which they had arrived, the three men drove back to the Divisional command post in Steinakirchen. Once more, they deeply breathed the air of freedom, probably for the last time in a long while.

The negotiators' arrival was awaited with tension at the Divisional staff. The Ia reported to Brigadeführer Hugo Kraas. The conditions were clear. They had to be accepted, but white flags would not be shown. In order to be able to defend against pursuing Soviets, the weapons would be unloaded as late as possible. The Ia reported the result of the surrender negotiations to the Armee. The commanders of the Divisional units were ordered to the command post and briefed. Brigadeführer Kraas thanked all members of the Division for their valor, loyalty, and comradely spirit. He requested that the principled attitude and spirit of camaraderie be maintained, in memory of those who were killed, during captivity and, thereafter, during the rebuilding of the destroyed fatherland, which was bleeding from many wounds. The preservation of the human substance of the German people was the objective for the near future. He closed with the words:

> . . . We set out on the bitterest journey of our life as soldiers with our heads held high. In quiet composure, we will march toward our destiny. We have fought bravely and with integrity on all theaters of war, still, the war is lost. Long live Germany.[3]

The comrades-in-arms during great and during bitter times felt particularly close and dependent on each other during that most sad hour. The commanders returned to their -regiments and battalions, to call them together for a last inspection.

In the morning of 8 May 1945 at 04.30 hours, Brigade-führer Hugo Kraas and Obersturmbannführer Hubert Meyer drove with the operations staff of the Divisional staff and the Divisionsbegleitkompanie via Amstetten to Enns. They stopped approximately 1,000 meters from the Enns river, where the road leads down from the ridge to the river. Along both sides of the road were deep gravel pits. At the left edge of the road (there was a high embankment on the right) stood the Divisional commander, his adjutant, and the first general staff officer, and awaited the approach of the columns of the Division. The Begleitkompanie buried its weapons in the gravel pits and assembled close to the Divisional staff. Then, the regiments, the battalions and the Abteilungen approached. The commanders reported their units, the troops marched past, mounted, as if on parade, with perfect bearing.

Suddenly, a few Wehrmacht vehicles came out of Enns. Sitting on them were former prisoners of the close-by Mauthausen concentration camp, with weapons at the ready. They drove along the column and started looting the vehicles. In order to prevent such further abuse, an approaching Panther was parked in the left driving lane so that no vehicles could drive down the column. With the agreement of the commander, the Ia drove to the American staff, located in Enns, to request protection of the disarmed troops, as ordered, against abuses by armed men. Despite his protests, he was detained in a school where a staff of the 65th US Infantry Division was located. Only after repeated protests was he led to the CIC officer of the American staff who listened to the complaint and promised remedial measures. As had already happened the previous day in Steyr, the American officer requested a search for the missing American scouting party. The VW had, in the meantime, been confiscated. On orders of the CIC officer it was finally handed over so that the Ia and Unterscharführer Schmieding were able to drive back. The troops were not molested anymore. The American regimental commander had, in the meantime, been to the departure point and had discussed the situation with Brigadeführer Kraas, showing great understanding. He promised fair treatment of the troops in captivity.

Around noon, a small number of American ambulances drove as fast as possible along the column of the Division, which alternately moved slowly or stopped, toward the east in the direction of Amstetten. After some time, the ambulances returned along the same route. Soon, it became known what had happened. An American advance unit had arrived in Amstetten and had been joyously welcomed by the population in the market square. Suddenly, seven Soviet combat aircraft attacked the gathering of people in low level flight. Numerous civilians and American soldiers were wounded. At that time, no members of the "HJ" Division were in the city anymore. In addition, there was a truce. Rauchensteiner reported that the event was not mentioned with one word in the After Action Report of the XX US Corps and the 65th Infantry Division. Birjukov, the commander of the Soviet XX Guards Rifle Corps, wrote on it:

> . . . It became apparent that Amstetten was the collection center for German units which wanted to withdraw to the north into Czechoslovakia. They greeted our advance units with concentrated artillery and tank fire. Our men, however, were helped by the air force. Approximately one hundred combat aircraft. . .delivered an extremely heavy blow to the assembly of fascist troops with bombs and rockets . . .[4]

Before evening, still, the last vehicles of the column crossed the Enns near the city of Enns. The troops made camp in fields and pastures next to the road. The vehicles, guns, and Panzers were assembled in separate areas. Lines of American sentries guarded the camps on the inside and outside.

Bataillon von Ribbentrop crossed the Enns shortly before midnight near Steyr. The last five kilometers had to be covered on foot since the road was totally congested. The Divisional supply troops crossed the river near Großraming, eight kilometers northwest of Weyer Markt. Individual groups reached the Enns only after 24.00 hours and were turned back. They swam across the river at other locations.

Thus, the Enns was crossed on 8 May 1945 by 328 officers, 1,698 NCOs, and 7,844 men, a total of 9,870 men of the 12. SS-Panzerdivision "Hitlerjugend", on their way into American captivity.[5]

PART V

The Post-War Period

SECTION 12

Captivity

The units of the "Hitlerjugend" Division which had crossed the demarcation line near the Upper Austrian city of Enns were left to their own resources during the first days of captivity. They lived on the last of the supplies they had brought along. American sentries guarded the carrying of water from close-by farms. Tents were set up in fields and pastures. Fortunately, the weather was warm and sunny. Everyone was waiting for what was to come next. After a few days, the rumor spread that German troops which had fought against the Americans north of the Danube, and surrendered to them, had been turned over to the Soviets. As was confirmed later, that was indeed true for members of the 3. SS-Panzer-division "Totenkopf".

There was fear that the "HJ" Division would also be handed over. As a result of deliberations of the inner Divisional staff, it was recommended that anyone who dared, and who thought himself capable, should escape from captivity and disappear somewhere. Brigadeführer Hugo Kraas decided to stay under all circumstances in order to represent the members of his Division who could or would not flee. Anyone who originated from the German Eastern Territories, from Central Germany, the Sudetenland, the eastern Austrian states, from Hungary, Yugoslavia, and Rumania, the areas occupied by the Soviets, could not go back. Those who wanted to escape had first to find their way through the American line of sentries, and then get across the area immediately adjacent which was swarming with former prisoners from the concentration camps. Many of them were armed. During day and night, shots could be heard. They were thought to stem from those activities. Under such circumstances, almost all captured members of the Division preferred to await developments for the time being. Only few men managed to escape in small groups. Even clad in semi-civilian clothes, they could still be recognized as former soldiers. Thus, they moved only at night and stayed away from roads and villages. During the day, they hid in the woods. They preferred terrain which was difficult to reach for motorized patrols. In order to eliminate the sinister activities of the armed gangs, the Americans imposed curfews and prohibited entry to the woods at the pain of death. American troops combed the forest close to the camp. During those days, the life of a former German soldier was not worth very much in "freedom". Not all who escaped managed to get home.

The elements of the "HJ" Division which had crossed the Enns river in Steyr, in Groflraming, in Altenmarkt near St. Gallen, and at other locations, were also assembled in an open field and then moved into the area around Mauerkirchen (ten kilometers southeast of Braunau on the Inn river). There, the Americans separated the members of the Waffen-SS and distributed them to several special camps. Some were sent to the former concentration camp Ebensee, others to Altheim, fifteen kilometers east of Braunau. The move from Mauerkirchen to Altheim continues to live on in the local population as the "Death March of the Waffen-SS". The American guard details forced the exhausted prisoners of war, time and again, to jog along the thirteen-kilomter-long route, in the heat and dust. Women who wanted to give them water were driven back with rifle butts. The encampment was in a wet meadow at the bank of a creek, surrounded by barbed wire, and guarded by tanks. The prisoners of war vegetated out in the open or in holes in the ground.

As victims of the "March of Death" and of the inhumane conditions in the Altheim camp, twenty-nine soldiers of the Waffen-SS are buried in a cemetery at the edge of the former camp terrain. Several are buried in the cemetery in St. Florian, 2 kilometers south of Mauerkirchen. The date of their death is given as 7 June 1945.[1]

Until 21 May 1945, the bulk of the "HJ" Division was located in the open along the Enns-Lind road and in Haid (ten kilometers southwest of Linz) in make-shift shelters. A number of members of the Division, among them its commander, were moved to the permanent camp "Kleinmünchen", immediately south of Linz, together with members of other units and civilians. Brigadeführer Hugo Kraas kept a diary from then on. The following excerpts surely characterize the situation accurately, not only in that camp:

> . . . 22 May 1945. Now we are really in captivity! Inside a cramped camp of shacks, between two rivers, situated immediately on the Danube. Any view is blocked off. Three-meter high electric barbed wire fences, with flanking machine gun towers, surround us. . . . We have now been branded as criminals! We have ended up in the concentration camp! . . .
>
> 26 May 1945. My five-day fever returns, as scheduled, and every time more serious than before . . . Between the bouts of fever, there is little recuperation because of the scarce food . . . For the first time in our lives we go hungry . . .

5 June 1945. On orders of the American camp commander, Lieutenant Henning, all war decorations are to be collected and handed over today. That is a blow for us all—dishonoring! That is the way it goes, step by step. I finally obtained approval so that we could keep our decorations provided that we removed all swastikas from them . . .

7 June 1945. The 51st fever attack happened some days ago, maybe it will be the last. . . . The food provided in the camp is not enough to live on, too much to die on. Now we have to train ourselves to go hungry. The food consists of: in the morning (about eight o'clock) $1/2$ liter of coffee; at noon (about twelve noon) $3/4$ liter of 'thin soup'—made up of vegetables, sometimes a little flour, sometimes a handful of peas; in the evening (about 18.00 hours) 60 to 100 grams of bread [one ounce equals approximately twenty-eight grams], 10 to 20 grams of margarine, 20 to 50 grams of cottage cheese, $3/4$ liter of coffee . . .

16 June 1945. Today, the whole camp was frisked by American soldiers. Much went along with them: 46 watches, 5,000 Reichsmarks, and many 'souvenirs'. We are defenseless, without rights . . . That will last us for days! . . . Daily, the numbers of men fainting from loss of strength are increasing, especially during hot days. Men are sick from hunger and malnutrition, in particular the young and the old look terrible. The menu: [same as on 5 June] that are 600 calories, and a person requires a minimum of approximately 2,000 to live . . .

1 July 1945. From today on, we are working. Get out of the lethargy, that is the motto. Our group of roommates has decided to do something (physically and mentally), from 1 July onward. We take over a small piece of land between the shacks and plant vegetables. The first bed has already been seeded . . . There is quite a bit to do. It brings about different ideas . . . Every day, we now receive the "Linzer Zeitung' (newspaper), sometimes the one from Munich. We follow each news item eagerly, as if we could find a glimmer of hope somewhere. But we know, there is no more hope for us . . . All of Germany is nothing but a prison camp . . .

3 July 1945. We were frisked again today. It was a raid by the American soldiers. We had to line up outside in the square. The shacks were searched, i.e. plundered. Watches were ripped directly from the wrists. When they refused, two commanders of my Division, old front line soldiers, were kicked and beaten. That was as if I had been beaten myself!—Altogether, among other things, 102 watches and 46,000 Reichsmarks were taken.

4 July 1945. We now have almost 300 malnourished men, i.e. men who have already suffered serious damage from hunger; also the

first dead from starvation! Finally, the Americans realize it and provide extra food for the ill and malnourished. Altogether four dead, two at the electric fence (suicide?), one from hunger, one shot, since, allegedly, he had come too close to the wire fence. The morale in the camp has dropped to a low point.

5 July 1945. Complaints about the events and the treatment in the camp have apparently reached the right man: Colonel Georges, commander of the 259th Infantry Regiment. He is the noble man who met us in such a gentlemanly manner at the bridge across the Enns on 8 May 1945. I describe the events to him, on my officer's word of honor. He is upset and promises redress and changes. We will see?! On 6 July 1945, the previously accused American guards were brought face to face with us so that the guilty could be picked out. That is a lot! More than we had expected. The important thing is that this standard now remains, since the degrading treatment caused worse suffering than the hunger.

7 July 1945. We have become cautiously optimistic. Colonel Georges inspects quite frequently himself. It appears that he is able to institute a new approach. We can only hope for that, since, what happened to us during the last months, could not be endured much longer. At the beginning of the month, the bread ration dropped to a total of sixty grams per day, i.e. only one slice per day, and at noon, only a thin watery soup. Now, the bread ration climbs to 120 grams, and it is promised that it will climb to 200 grams. . . . The many smells in the camp are terrible . . . No newspaper anymore, no radio-but for what, anyway? I do not believe that they will let us go free anytime soon . . .

22 July 1945. We have opened a busy camp school. Many of the men feel the urge to join it after these weeks of aimlessness and doing nothing, but still, it requires considerable effort each time to work seriously, considering the situation and the future. There is a great selection of lectures: Russian, French, English, mathematics, German—up to philosophy . . .

1 August 1945. Colonel Georges of the 259th Regiment had me called in. He likes to talk with me and tries to instill courage and confidence in me. How much a drowning person likes to grasp for straws! . . . What can we do?—Nothing, but wait and practice patience . . .

3 August 1945. The conference of the "Big Three" in Potsdam is over. We are drinking the vessel of defeat to the last drop!

3 August 1945. In the late afternoon, we are handed a form to notify our family. We only fill in the address and our name. I write to my wife and my mother. I do not know where my family is . . .

14 August 1945. Since yesterday, a new ration plan has been introduced. Provided, per day and men, will be: 250 grams of bread, 15 grams of margarine, 30 grams of cheese. That is still not much for a normal person; we are all very run-down. But, four weeks ago!—the treatment now is invariably correct, the weekly searches are also done properly. In the afternoon, the first 'gifts' arrived in the camp. They are donations from the population and collected by the Catholic church: potatoes, bread, even some bacon, and one egg per man! We accept gratefully.

15 August 1945. The first committee to muster/release? those born in 1926 or later is working in the camp today. Hope is growing. For myself, I have no illusions, I have prepared for at least one year of captivity . . .

17 August 1945. This is our daily routine: The day starts around 10.00 to 11.00 hours, since there is no breakfast, and we have to conserve calories. A short walk in the camp. One waits for the 'frugal' lunch at twelve noon. Subsequently, to digest the copious luncheon, rest until 15.00 hours. At 15.00 hours, coffee is provided, half of which is drunk to fill the stomach, the other half saved for the evening meal. From 16.00 to 18.00 hours, some work is done: one hour of lectures, read some English text, write in the diary, water the 'garden', and then, waiting longingly for the men fetching our food. 18.00 hours, shower. And then it is generally time for the evening, and main, meal. Today: 250 grams of bread = 5 slices (!), 11 grams of margarine (enough for two slices), 30 grams of cheese (maybe cottage cheese) for one slice, 2 cigarettes (every day!), 3–4 radishes from our garden! That is the routine of my days, for the first time in my life without reason and aim . . .

20 August 1945. Most of us dream themselves at home at Christmas. I do not, although hopeful, allow myself to become tied to that thought . . .

Going home, who would not think of that? What is left at home? Our families, all our thoughts center on them. If only we had news from them for the first time . . .

26 August 1945. Finally, we have set up a small camp library, having collected all privately owned books, a real hodgepodge . . .

On Sunday, 2 September 1945, at 10.00 hours, there is a repeat performance in the school shack behind the kitchen of the

Musical Morning Celebration "Affection"
Directed by: Oberstleutnant Waizenegger
Program:

Allegretto from the string quartet in D-Major	by W.A. Mozart

Restless Love poem	by J.W. von Goethe
Life Brings Great Joy	folk song
Gretchen at the Spinning Wheel	poem by J.W. von Goethe
Little Rose on the Heath	song by Franz Schubert
Straight Ahead!	poem by Eduard Möricke
Serenade	by Franz Schubert
It Must be Something Wonderful	two songs for bass
	by Franz Liszt
And One Day the Door Will Open	
from "Letters of Two Lovers"	by W. Kefller
Larks' Quartet	from Opus 64, No. 5
	by Joseph Haydn
It Will Be! poem	by M. Schmückle
Molto Adagio	from Opus 59, No. 2
	by L. van Beethoven

Completion of the program at approximately 11.15 hours.

3 September 1945. Effective immediately, approximately 2,000 men (of a total of 3,000) are sent to Linz daily, organized in so-called labor columns under the leadership of German officers, to clear the rubble. Immediately, the mood has changed. The men get out, hear and see a lot, have work and are properly tired again in the evening. The guards behave correctly and generously . . .

7 September 1945. Musical Morning Celebration "Homeland" . . .

10 September 1945. Finally, we are allowed to write! Five letters of twenty-five lines each per month. I only hope that this first letter will arrive quickly, so that the painful uncertainty regarding our fate will be lifted from our families. Of course, from now on, I will be waiting longingly for the first mail from the loved ones. What news will it bring? . . .

18 September 1945. Twenty-eight generals and general staff officers are brought in today, among them Generaloberst Rendulic, the last commander of Heeresgruppe Süd. It appears that the situation is growing more tense. The generals have to report twice a-day, i.e. they have to line up for individual roll calls by name, carried out by the American commander. The American sergeant who controlled the procedure carried it out in a very degrading manner. One's blood stood still, but we had learned already to remain calm . . .

4 October 1945. Since yesterday, the camp can only be compared to an anthill. All officers, NCOs and men whose home or destination is located in the American-occupied zone in Germany were alerted yesterday and left the camp within a few hours, as a group. I assume that they were all hauled off to southern Germany as con-

script labor. Only few officers and NCOs now remain in the camp, they all want to go to the English-occupied zone . . .

8 October 1945. Yesterday, I once more invited all former members of the "HJ" Division to a comradely evening. We spent the evening in good and traditional fashion. There was a mood of parting. One feels the unrest and knows that this last community may be ripped apart any day now . . .

24 October 1945. The transport from Kleinmünchen Camp to Germany takes place today . . .[2]

The selected notes from the diary of Brigadeführer Hugo Kraas can illustrate the events and the conditions in American captivity during the first months only in broad terms. Some additional information will supplement them. During the rearguard battles, personal documents were lost. Reports on these losses were assembled and submitted to the International Red Cross. Thus, the 5. Kraftfahrkompanie (motor vehicle company) of the Divisionsnachschubtruppen 12 (supply troops) reported from "Camp 1" on 14 May 1945: 2 killed on 22.3.1945, 7 missing in the actions in Austria since 28 March 1945, and 35 missing since 8 May 1945.

The war diaries, which the units had kept during the last months, had been destroyed as ordered. Based on reports and orders received, and on personal notes, documents were reconstructed in a few cases. For instance, the adjutant of the II. Bataillon of SS-Panzergrenadierregiment 26, Obersturmführer Harro Lübbe, once more wrote the war diary of the Bataillon for the period from 3.9.1944 to 8.5.1945, with assistance from several comrades. Others noted down details about their units which ended up in a collection of documents by Brigadeführer Kraas. They found their way into this book through his estate.

Brigadeführer Kraas mentioned in his diary on 3 August 1945 that forms were handed out in the Kleinmünchen Camp to inform the families. That did not occur everywhere at the same time. Since summer 1945, the Author had been in the "P.W.E. Auerbach No. 24" which had been set up at the Grafenwöhr training grounds. Several thousand soldiers of the Waffen-SS were located there. Only on 9 October 1945, as all the other prisoners of war in that camp, could the Author send information to his family for the first time. The form designed for that is indicative of the mentality and the intentions of the victors at that time. The printed form started with the following sentence: "A member of the defeated Wehrmacht is looking for his closest relative".

It was obviously part of the victors' plan to degrade and morally unsettle the enemy they had overcome after almost six years of bitter fighting. The postcard arrived at the addressee on 5 December 1945 and was answered on "Part VII' of the form on the same day. That part began with the sentence:

Communication from the closest relative
(Capital letters—Not more than 25 words).

Part III   No stamp required

Last known address of the
closest relative
IN CAPITAL LETTERS

Part IV   In the American Zone, send to . . . Central Referral Office
In case addressee   Frankfurt/Main
cannot be located   In the British Zone, send to. . . .
                     Central Referral Office
                     Hamburg

Part V
For official use only by the Central
Referral Office for onward mailing
                     Part I

First letter of sender's   A MEMBER OF THE DEFEATED
family name   WEHRMACHT IS LOOKING FOR HIS
                              CLOSEST RELATIVE

I am still alive and am, at this time, in American hands
   healthy

I am _____. My address is as below. Please return
this card in hospital immediately!

Date: _____ 1945   Signed _____

     PoW Number _____

     Place and Date of Birth _____

Two experiences of the Author in Camp Auerbach are indicative of the policies of the Americans toward the German prisoners of war. In his position as the most senior member of the community in one of the shacks in one of the numerous camp districts (cages) he submitted a complaint on the unbearable treatment of seriously disabled comrades to the camp's German senior member. In the office of the cage commander, an American CIC officer listened to the complaint. When the spokesman presenting the complaint referred to the Geneva Convention, he received a short and unambiguous reply:

"What do you mean, Geneva Convention? You seem to have forgotten that you lost the war!"

One day, the supreme commander of the 3rd American Army, General George S. Patton Jr., visited Camp Auerbach. He satisfied himself of the correctness of the complaints submitted to him and immediately rectified the situation. Among other measures, instead of the starvation diet, portions of American "C-Rations" were handed out. After the sudden death of the General in December 1945, caused by a car accident, his directives were quickly cancelled. The previous conditions prevailed once again. They obviously represented the occupation program of the US government. But, in addition to General Patton, there were also staff officers (such as Colonel Georges) subaltern officers, NCOs and men who, in the face of the realities they saw, shook off the hate propaganda of the war time period. They attempted, as best as they could, to lighten the lot of the prisoners of war, and avoided any degrading treatment.

One day, the military government ordered that those born in 1926 and after were to be released on a preferential basis. Sturmmann Hans Harder of 4. Kompanie of SS-Panzergrenadierregiment 25 also belonged to that group. He had crossed the demarcation line on 8 May 1945 near Steyr and had been moved to the Ebensee Camp from there. After some time, the prisoners of war were sent to prison camps in the relevant occupation zone, according to their place of residence. Hans Harder had lived in the Soviet occupation zone, and had provided that information. He was transported to Lichtenfels in Upper Franconia, close to the border between the occupation zones. The prisoners of war feared that they would be handed over to the Soviets. However, during the next days they were driven south again and ended up in a camp in Winkel near Berchtesgaden. In May 1946, Hans Harder was moved to the Auerbach Camp. In the meantime, he had volunteered for agricultural labor in Bavaria, in order to be released on a preferential basis. On 24 May 1946, he walked through the camp gate into freedom.[3]

Otto Helmut Müller, also sixteen years old at the time, had volunteered for the "Hitlerjugend" Division in 1943. He was called up only in September 1944 since in 1943 he was 2 cm short of the minimum height. With the Divisional combat school he went into action on the western front in spring 1945. He entered American captivity after the surrender, near Kiefersfelden at the border between the Tyrol and Bavaria. By way of the camps in Erding, Fürstenfeldbruck and Dachau, he ended up in the British occupation zone and was moved from there to England in the spring of 1946. He was sent to Camp 180 in Saffron Walden in County Essex. The prisoners of war (members of the Waffen-SS, the Afrikakorps, and U-Boat crews) worked on farms. In the fall of 1946, Dr. Kurt Schuhmacher, chairman of the SPD (German Social-Democratic Party), and Cardinal Frings visited that model camp. In April 1947, Otto Helmut Müller was moved back to Munsterlager. He was released on 10 May 1947.[4]

Sturmmann Christel Graen, born in 1926, had joined the artillery training and replacement regiment on 5 July 1943. From October 1943 until the
surrender he was a member of 10. Batterie of SS-Panzerartillerieregiment 12
as a radio operator at forward observation posts. By way of the American
prison camps Mauerkirchen, Altheim, Ebensee, and Babenhausen, he
arrived at Chambery/France, in Camp 144, for labor service. He was
released to go home only on 20 November 1948.[5]

Overall, the developments in captivity were as different as the process of
captivity experienced by those three young volunteers. By the end of 1948,
most of the members of the Division, in captivity with the Western Allies, had
been released.

Only a few soldiers of the "HJ" Division had ended up in Soviet captivity.
Among them was Sturmmann E. who had been saved from the worst fate in
a Hungarian hospital by the physicians, nurses and Hungarian soldiers there.
That has already been reported on. Sturmmann E. wrote about his captivity:

> . . . What would become of us? The chief physician, who had appar-
> ently established good relations with the Russian major, believed
> that he could guarantee our safety as long as we stayed in his hospi-
> tal. However, he demanded our word of honor that we would not
> leave it on our own, since he had to warrant that with his word. As
> long as we were suffering from our shot-up bones, we were glad of
> that development since, above all else, we were doing not too badly:
> we had simple, but adequate, food, were treated and cared for prop-
> erly, and increasingly, we had visitors—visitors from the small city
> and the villages in the vicinity! Once the word had spread there that
> a few German soldiers were in hospital in the county town, pockets
> were filled with goods, and hardly a day passed when there was not a
> knock on our door. Whole families came, old women, young girls,
> and if conversation was sometimes difficult because of a lack of
> knowledge of the language on both sides, then it was simply the
> enjoyment of being able to help a little and of seeing us.
>
> The religious sisters, who still administered the hospital, as well as
> the school and the library during the first months after the end of
> the war, also visited us often, brought us German reading material,
> and provided us with our first lessons in the Hungarian language.
>
> But we knew that it could not continue like that for long. One
> evening in June, our four Austrians disappeared, never to be seen
> again. The lure of the near-by homeland had been stronger than
> their promise, for which, our promise was renewed. There was no
> question of a joint 'action' by myself and Untersturmführer F., since
> he was still almost completely immobile. In addition, we felt strongly
> bound by our word given to the physician, to the point where we
> would rather take a risk than get him into difficulties. He advised us,

equipped with medical certificates he provided, to surrender to the Russians. Surely, we would soon be sent home.

Hence, our small gang marched in the morning of 31 July 1945, with harmless divisional and regimental numbers memorized, to the Russian commander's office. We were ceremoniously received there. Our personal details were taken down, and we were handed over to the Communist local police. They put us into jail immediately. It was situated opposite the hospital from where we had just come. The warden must have had nothing more urgent to do than to inform our old friends of our arrival there since, an hour later, the first loaves of bread and bowls of soup were handed over at the prison gate for us. After two days, badly bitten by fleas, the transport to the camp began. Our two Russian military policemen had problems finding accommodations for us. We were sent away from the first camp and were forced to overnight in the small local prison of a village near the Neusiedler lake. It, too, must have been swarming with fleas. In the morning, before our two Russians showed up, six women, alerted by the local police, were waiting for us with bags and baskets full of warm and cold food for us. Our guards later asked us for a few half-ripe plums. They had not been given anything, as they admitted, with curses.

Two hours later, however, everything changed for us as well. We were in a camp. Our hair was cut off, and we had our first acquaintance with the ruling mentality there. The bulk of the prisoners was transported from that camp in batches in the direction of Russia. Is it possible that the well-meant certificates from our Hungarian physician helped us there? Certainly, our flea bites initially saved us. The Russian female medic diagnosed them as scabies and directed us, disgusted, to the isolation station. Thus, we lived, cut off, in pig sties and were then moved to yet another camp, from where transports indeed left for home. My four comrades left with the last one, a German. I was kept behind, being healthy, strong and well cured, for 'clean-up work'. It lasted for well over four years and provided me with a trip to 'paradise'. In the middle of September, my train rolled from Preflburg through Hungary and Rumania into the Ukraine. At the end of October 1949, I returned by way of Frankfurt/Oder . . .[6]

No soldier of the "Hitlerjugend" Division who had gone into American captivity was handed over to the Soviets. In contrast, the Ukrainian nurses aids of SS-Feldlazarett 501 (field hospital), who came from Charkow and vicinity, were turned over to the Soviets by the Americans.[7] Unimaginable suffering awaited them. The auxiliary personnel serving with the Division, and who also originated from the Ukraine, had attempted to go under cover with the assistance of the troops. Those of them who did not succeed in the long run, had to walk the same path as the nurses and Cossacks who were handed over to the Soviets by the English occupation force in Austria.

The prisoners of war from the "HJ" Division, who had been sent to foreign countries, kept their status as prisoners of war until they were transported to one of the occupation zones in Germany. The soldiers of the Waffen-SS and a few "selected" members of the Wehrmacht, located in one of the prisoner of war camps in the western occupation zones in Germany, were released from captivity, by a directive from the military government, on 1 November 1946 and, simultaneously, taken into "automatic arrest". That conveyed the status of civilian internees upon them.

On 12 January 1946, the "Allied Control Council" decided on guidelines to remove National-Socialists and militarists from the administration and other agencies. For the American zone of occupation, the military government issued, on 5 March 1946, the "Law for the liberation from national-socialism and militarism". From then on, only those who had been "denazified" by a tribunal could be released from the internment camps. In accordance with that law, all officers of the Waffen-SS, down to Sturmbann-führers inclusive, were initially classified as "major perpetrators", all other members were classified as "incriminated". The only exception were those liable to military service who had been drafted into the Waffen-SS. However, if they had subsequently been promoted to NCO, they were also judged to be "incriminated". The volunteers of the Waffen-SS, that means the overwhelming majority of those who joined in 1943, were excepted from the amnesty for juveniles which had been decreed soon after the start of the "denazification process". As well, the juvenile amnesty was not valid for those who had been drafted, and promoted to NCO.[8] Those who had been released before the law was handed down, were "denazified" by the tribunals of their place of residence. Basis for grading were not punishable activities but merely the membership in the Waffen-SS and rank. During the decision on "sanctions", war decorations and promotions based on valor in the face of the enemy were detrimental factors. The British and French military governments acted, in their zones of occupation, similar to the American.

The soldiers of the "Hitlerjugend" Division were released from the internment camps, after years of dedicated combat action, full of sacrifices, and of captivity, labeled as "major perpetrators", "incriminated" and "fellow-travelers". Among the "sanctions" imposed were labor service in internment camps, monetary fines, prohibition to work in one's profession, and loss of the right to vote or to be elected, either for life or for a limited period. Despite all that, the soldiers of that "army of outlaws" began, without reservation, to build a new existence for themselves and to rebuild their fatherland which lay in ruins. They contributed a significant portion to what has been achieved.

During the first months of captivity it became noticeable that members of certain units, among them those of the Panzeraufklärungsabteilung 12, were sought out and transported off to unknown destinations. Initially, there was no obvious explanation for that. On 7 December 1945, the German camp administration in Auerbach Camp published Proclamation No. 1 of the International Military Tribunal. According to it, the whole of the Waffen-SS was accused of being a "criminal organization". The inmates of the prisoner of war camp P.W.E. 24 protested against that with a letter by the German camp leadership, on 8 December 1945, to the president of the International Military Tribunal. They requested that indictment be made available to them and that their elected representatives be heard. Later, it became known that individual soldiers and even certain companies of the "HJ" Division were accused of having shot prisoners of war. Secret orders were to have existed that, as a matter of principle, no prisoners would be taken. That seemed to explain the selection proceedings. The Author collected 159 affidavits in the camp from members of the units concerned, as well as from other units of the Division, who could be reached, and submitted them to the defense of the Waffen-SS in Nuremburg.[9]

Indeed, neither the Division nor the regiments and battalions/Abteilungen have ever ordered that no prisoners be taken. Rather, hundreds of prisoners were taken by the Division during the offensive fighting in Normandy, in the Ardennes and in Hungary, and were handed over at the collection points. The Divisional command had no knowledge of even one incident where prisoners were shot by the troops. The command would have, immediately, started investigations and prosecuted any offenses in accordance with martial law. During the fighting for Caen in summer 1944, a French mayor reported a punishable offense committed by a member of the Division to the Divisional staff. In a court-martial, the accused was convicted and sentenced to death. The sentence was carried out in the presence of the mayor.

Three trials of members of the "HJ" Division took place during the years 1945 to 1949 before Allied courts. The proceedings will not be reopened here. That would not be possible, in any case, since the documentation of the trial proceedings have been sealed by the former Allies. Since these trials were frequently mentioned in war history literature, or the events on which they were based, were described—mostly in a one-sided manner—they will be reported on here as objectively as is possible.

In April 1944, when the "HJ" Division was being moved from Belgium to Normandy by numerous rail transports, an explosives attack was carried out on a transport train of the Aufklärungsabteilung on 1 April 1944 at 22.45 as it entered the station at Ascq near Lille. Several cars were derailed and the train came under fire from small arms. Since two attacks had already been carried out on trains a few days previously, a guard unit, provided by the senior field command in Lille, was located in the Ascq railroad station. It had not been able to prevent the renewed attack. In numerous other locations in France, as well, attacks were being carried out since some time previously, on the troops, the German administration and their establishments, at a threateningly increasing rate. Consequently, the Supreme Commander West had issued orders to the troops, on 3.2.1944, how to behave in such circumstances. The order stated, inter alia:

> . . . If the troops are attacked in any manner, the leader is obliged to take countermeasures independently and according to his own judgment.
> Among these will be:
>   a) Fire will be returned immediately!
>   Should innocent people be hit during that, it is regrettable but exclusively the responsibility of the terrorists.
>   b) Immediate sealing-off of the site of the crime and detention of all civilians in the vicinity, regardless of their position or person.
>   c) Immediate burning-down of houses from which shots originated.
>   Only after these or similar measures will a report be provided . . .
> 4. When judging the actions by decisive troop leaders, their determination and speed of action must be given priority under all circumstances. Only the weak and indecisive troop leader must be penalized severely since he, thus, endangers the safety of the subordinate troops and the respect for the German Wehrmacht. In view of the present situation, measures which are too severe cannot be a reason for punishment . . .[9a]

As directed, the troops had been informed of that order.

The commander of the transport under attack immediately had the village of Ascq searched for weapons, and had all males detained. They were led to the transport train and guarded, in order to be handed over to the responsible investigative authorities. Nobody was injured or even killed during that search operation. When several of the detained men tried to escape, the guards opened fire. A panic broke out during which eighty-six men were killed and eight wounded.

After arriving in the billet area in Normandy, the troop commander initially provided a verbal, then a written, report on the occurrence. The report went, through channels, to the Supreme Commander West. The French ambassador de Brinon submitted a written protest in the name of the French government. Generalfeldmarschall von Rundstedt, the Supreme Commander West, rejected the protest. The investigation by the senior field command in Lille led to the arrest of several Frenchmen who had taken part in acts of sabotage in Ascq. On 16 June 1944, the court of the senior field command Lille sentenced seven of the accused to death. Six of the sentences were carried out by firing squad. After the war, a trial against members of the transport of the Aufklärungs-abteilung took place before the French military court in Metz. On 6 August 1949, eight attending and eight absent members of the Abteilung were sentenced to death, one to fifteen years of forced labor. The sentences were not based on proven personal guilt, but, rather, on the "Lex Oradour" because of collective guilt. The brave advocacy of the French defending attorneys, in particular Maître de la Pradelle, against the use of the collectivity law, twice achieved a pardon. The last five men were released to Germany in 1954.

After an interval of almost forty years, the painful events of Ascq make it clear that fighting in the underground could not be carried out with traditional means. Its planners unleashed passions which they, soon, no longer knew how to contain. In the same manner, the German command authorities found themselves unable to fight off those attacks with the usual means of open combat. Their strength, as well as that of the troops, were overtaxed in the defense against that war in the dark. Those who suffered from that fighting were mainly uninvolved civilians whom one had always tried to spare. The legalization of underground fighting after the Second World War has, in no way, diminished the hardships of war, rather to the contrary, they were increased. The wars in Indochina and many other locations in the world have shown that only too clearly. It is all-the-more important that Germany and France, across the trenches which divided them for centuries, have reconciled and decided on a common path into the future.

In a second trial, which took place in 1945 in Aurich/Eastern Friesland, Brigadeführer Kurt Meyer was accused, as commander of the SS-Panzer-grenadierregiment 25, of being responsible for the shooting of seven Canadian prisoners of war during the first days of the invasion fighting. It was claimed that he had stated, during his address at a swearing-in of recruits in Beverloo: ". . . prisoners will not be taken! . . ." In addition, he was accused to have personally ordered the shooting of the seven prisoners of war. The first accusation was to be proven by the statements from two witnesses. One of them had deserted in April 1944 and dictated his statement to a Belgian resistance group. A photocopy of the English translation of the Flemish text was submitted to the court as evidence. The witness "could not be found". The second witness retracted his previously made deposition on the witness stand. The witness, who had testified on the second point of the indictment, was also a deserter of Polish origin. His accounts during the trial proved to be incredible. The testimony by former Canadian prisoners of war and German officers, in particular by General der Panzertruppen Eberbach, completely exonerated Brigadeführer Kurt Meyer. Despite that, he was sentenced to death by the Canadian court martial on 28 December 1945. On the urging from Canadian officers, the death sentence was commuted to lifelong incarceration on 13 January 1946. Later, after public attacks on the court statute, the sentence was reduced to fourteen years imprisonment. In 1951, Brigadeführer Kurt Meyer was transferred to Germany, to the Werl penitentiary. There, the federal chancellor, Konrad Adenauer, visited him in his cell. On 6 September 1954, the Brigadeführer was released into freedom after 10 years of captivity and imprisonment.[10] Soldierly spirit and genuine consciousness of justice on the part of the previous enemy had conquered the aftereffects of war propaganda and victor's arbitrariness.

In the third trial against members of the "Hitlerjugend" Division, Obersturmbannführer Bernhard Siebken, Untersturm-führer Dieter Schnabel and two men of II. Bataillon of SS-Panzergrenadierregiment 26 were accused of being responsible for the shooting of three Canadian prisoners of war in le Mesnil-Patry during the first days of the invasion fighting. That event and its prehistory has been reported on in Chapter 1.5 of Volume I. In the trial, Obersturmbannführer Siebken was accused of having ordered the shooting of the prisoners. Untersturmführer Schnabel was accused of having carried out the order; the two co-accused were to have taken part in that. The Author participated in the trial, which took place in summer 1948 in the "Curio-Haus" in Hamburg, as a witness for the defense. The court did not accept witness statements regarding unequivocally established shootings of German prisoners of war by Canadian soldiers. Nor did it take note of the testimony by Graf (count) Clary-Aldringen concerning the shooting of members of Panzerartillerieregiment 130 by a scouting party of the Inns of Court Regiment during which he, himself, had been seriously wounded. The court stated that it was not Canadian, but four German soldiers, who were the accused. The shooting of three Canadians remained undisputed. It remained doubtful, who had given the order for that. The court sentenced Obersturmbannführer Bernhard Siebken and Untersturmführer Dieter Schnabel to death by hanging. The two co-accused were men acquitted. The witnesses for the defense attending the trial were firmly convinced of Bernhard Siebken's innocence. Submissions, which were meant to prove that, could not even bring about a mitigation of the sentences. The sentences were carried out on 20 January 1949 in the Hameln prison.

The former first orderly officer of the Divisional staff, Bernhard-Georg Meitzel, also attended the trial in the "Curio-Haus". Under the devastating impact of the victors' justice practiced there, he approached the two great British military historians General Fuller and Liddell Hart. In his answering letter of 9 November 1948, Liddell Hart confirmed a case of shooting of German and Italian prisoners of war by American soldiers in Sicily which had come to his knowledge. He, too, felt the injustice of the trials which were directed, exclusively, against Germans. He had already attempted, in public protests, to have them stayed. He continued in his efforts and found growing public support. Sincere thanks are due to these two highly regarded soldiers even though they were unable to save Bernhard Siebken and Dieter Schnabel from death. Liddell Hart's letter is reproduced below.

In some of the chapters of this book, violations of the laws of the conduct of war, i.e. war crimes, by soldiers of the opposite side have been reported on. Those were, partly, acts by individuals, partly, they were based on orders, as several witnesses in the "le Mesnil-Patry case" testified. In all wars of the past (before and after the Second World War) war crimes have been committed by members of all armies, and that will, regrettably, continue to be the case in the future. They are the deeds of individuals, they cannot be blamed on the entirety of an armed force. That, however, is what happened in the so-called "war criminal trials" against German soldiers after the Second World War. On that score, the concept of the "criminal organization" was invented and utilized exclusively during those trials. During the trials against Brigadeführer Kurt Meyer and Obersturmbannführer Bernhard Siebken, the prosecution attempted, in vain, to establish that the regimental and battalion commanders of the 501 HJ Division had ordered that, as a matter of principle, no prisoners were to be made. In the end, a conviction of the two commanders was possible only by holding them responsible for everything which happened in their operations areas. Canadian officers, who brought Brigadeführer Kurt Meyer from his cell to their mess a few days before the sentence was handed down, and celebrated his birthday with him there, said to him during that occasion:

> . . . If you are found guilty, and if the sentence is to stand in the face of the world and of history, then the Canadian army will have no generals left the next day. All generals would have to walk the same path as you . . .[11]

It has been mentioned that a member of the "HJ" Division was sentenced by the Divisional court-martial for having committed a crime during combat actions, and that the sentence was carried out. It remains to be seen if the opposite side acted in the same manner. Those responsible for the shooting of the members of the staff of the Artillerieregiment of the Panzer-Lehr-Division have certainly not been brought to trial by the British side. That would surely have been brought forward by the British court in the "Curio-Haus" in order to devaluate the testimony by Graf Clary-Aldringen. In other cases also, nothing of that nature has become known. After the war, the Western Allies enacted an amnesty for all offenses committed by members of their armed forces. However, numerous "war crimes trials" were conducted against Germans. The realization, that the application of two kinds of justice for victors and vanquished had to reflect on the originators, regrettably prevailed only too late.

SECTION 13

Meetings and Friendships

Time heals wounds—not only those ripped into the body by bullets and shells, but also those inflicted on the soul. For a long period of time after the surrender of the German Wehrmacht on 8 May 1945, the world was still divided into victors and vanquished. The first to overcome the trenches which separated them were the soldiers who had fought against each other in terrible battles. French, British and Americans sought contact with their former enemies in Germany. Germans visited the battlefields where they had fought, the graves of their killed comrades in the German war cemeteries, and the people who had been forced to endure the fury of war, as helpless civilians at the time, and who had shared many a hardship with them. Numerous ties of friendship were formed.

Thus, E. also visited the place in Hungary where he was wounded in March 1945, as well as several other locations which had lived on in his memory. He wrote about it:

> . . . In all the years after, my thoughts revolved around what was our personal fate during those drama-filled weeks, but, above all, around the country and the people who had so gallantly and selflessly stuck up for us. There was no doubt in my mind that I would return to Hungary at some time. It was the autumn of 1967 before the plan could be realized. With only a Hungarian visa, and without hotel reservations or help from a travel agency, I drove off in my small VW and visited one after the other of the long-known places, and then some others. Anyone who has ever undertaken a similar journey will understand that I very often approached these places with anxiety and a throbbing heart. Also, time has changed that country much less in the meantime than it changed Germany, much could be recognized again at first glance. As a German, in particular coming from the Federal Republic, one finds a friendly welcome and inter-

est everywhere. The fact that I remembered enough of the Hungarian language to converse fairly well, particularly helped to establish contacts. Such effort is highly appreciated and recognized in any small country. Much in Hungary is gray and poor. Even if some things have changed and improved after 1956, one cannot help but notice the unavoidable pressures of a totalitarian state and their consequences. One thing which the Hungarians have kept alive and thriving is the love of their country, pride in their small nation, and loyalty to their language and their customs. All that helps them, with determination, cunning and humor, to still make the best of frequently adverse circumstances.

Of all places, it was in the small village on the Raab, where I had been wounded, that I again met someone I knew. She was one of the girls who had visited us in the hospital at the time; today she is the mother of a family. Within seconds, her memory had also returned, and there followed a greeting of indescribable cordiality. I just had to stay there for the remaining two days of my stay in Hungary. Together, we visited the cemetery where the German and Hungarian soldiers, killed during the battles there, are buried; lost and forgotten, without legible name plates anymore, but at least, the graves were kept up by the population and even decorated with flowers for the holidays. In the village, I was able to learn a few of the names of the Germans resting there, and I provided those to the National Association for the Care of War Graves after my return.

When I took my leave, I left behind everything I could spare. Every little thing is valuable there and highly welcome. The village street was full of people, everyone had tried to remember things that happened in the past. I also was told that of thirty-two young soldiers who were reported to have shot themselves after they were encircled by the Russians and out of ammunition. The leader of our Kampfgruppe was reported killed by the enemy, and almost none of the defenders likely got away alive. I drove home, full of these impressions and full of thanks . . .[1]

During 1947, a group of members of the American "Second (Indian Head) Division Association, led by its president, Dr. John P. Wakefield, visited the battlegrounds of the two world wars in Europe. The former soldiers, accompanied by their ladies, had fought in the Ardennes in the winter of 1944–1945. Their 2nd Infantry Division had played (unintentionally and without realizing it) a decisive role in the attack sector of the 6. Panzerarmee, even in the whole of the German operation. The group visited the former battlefields in the Wahlerscheid-Elsenborn-St. Vith-Rocherath/Krinkelt area. In a roundabout way, they made contact with the Author. He was invited to an evening of exchanging thoughts in Bonn. Both sides were looking forward to that first encounter with the former enemy with eager expectation. The American visitors were most interested in hearing how the heavy fighting, in particular for the twin-village of Rocherath/Krinkelt during the period of 16 to 19 December 1944, was viewed by their former enemy. Both sides obtained surprising insights and important information. Thus, the artillerymen were pleased to have the extraordinary, possibly decisive, impact of their weapons confirmed to them, even if the infantry, tank crews and tank destroyers had to carry the main burden of the fighting. President Wakefield concluded the exchange of thoughts with the remark that his battle-hardened and well-tried division—"Second to none in three wars"—had to withdraw, for the first time in its history, near Rocherath/Krinkelt where it was fighting against the 12. SS-Panzerdivision "Hitlerjugend".

During conversations in a small circle, which lasted deep into the night, the former enemies on the battlefield also got closer to each other on a human level. Subsequently, the American gentlemen provided material on the action of their division, the divisional history being part of it, for this book. Contact was also established with Richard Schulze-Kossens. He had been in action, with the II. Bataillon of the SS-Panzergrenadierregiment 25, in the focal point of the battle for Rocherath/Krinkelt. An honorable membership in the "Second (Indian Head) Division Association" was offered to him and to the Author. Both were very pleased to accept it. Several years later, a meeting took place, in the course of another visit, in Boppard. Both gentlemen took part and the get-together proceeded in the same comradely, even cordial, spirit.

During three battlefield inspections in the area around Rocherath/ Krinkelt, around Bütgenbach, near Sadzot and near Bastogne, former members of the "Hitlerjugend" Division tried successfully to clear up open questions on the spot for this Divisional history. Only a few weeks before his death on 20 February 1980, Brigadeführer Hugo Kraas took part in the second visit. Many very friendly and informative conversations were held with the inhabitants of the territories which had been fought for more that thirty years ago. The inspections concluded with visits to the graves of killed comrades in the German war cemetery in Recogne near Bastogne. The text carved into the memorial is engraved in the memories of all the visitors:

> We all must read it,
> carved into the silent rock:
> You have been faithful,
> May we also be thus.

At the end of the 1960s, several French citizens interested in war history visited the Author in order to discuss certain details of the invasion battles in summer 1944. During these talks it became apparent how large the existing gaps in information on the action by the "Hitlerjugend" Division were, since no war diaries survived, except for that of one Bataillon, and even that only covered four weeks of the fighting. That reinforced the Author's intention to write a Divisional history which would delve into detail. His first visit to Normandy in 1969 led to personal encounters with several Frenchmen who were, themselves, working on war historical studies and books. The former battlefields awakened many, often painful, memories. Particularly impressive was the visit to the house in Venoix where the Divisional command post had been located during the first days of the invasion fighting. Brigadeführer Fritz Witt, the first Divisional commander, and two comrades had been killed there. The owners of the house, who had been evacuated as children at the time, displayed sincere interest in the events at that place where war history had been made and which they had, until then, not known about. A visit by the Author and his wife to the British war cemetery in St. Manvieu was an experience which brought about a hopeful mood, since German soldiers had found their last resting place there next to British soldiers. All the graves, without exception, were arranged in the same manner and carefully looked after. More encounters were added to those first ones in the following years. Cordial personal relationships, even real friendships, developed.

In 1974, the Author was invited by the British Staff College Camberley to a battlefield tour in Normandy. That college trains the future general staff of the Commonwealth armies. The annual battlefield inspections in Normandy are meant to familiarize the young officers with the course of the fighting and the problems of a conventional war on the former battleground. Participants in those battles describe their -experiences to the students in the courses, prepared on the theory, in the place where the fighting occurred. Individual combatants from the "other side" were invited to take part. The objects of the inspection were the British-Canadian parachute operation near Caen on 6 June 1944, Operation "GOODWOOD" on 18 and 19 July 1944, and several battles by elements of the 50th Infantry Division on the day of the landing—6 June 1944—the battle near Cristot on 11 June and, the battle of Lingèvres on 14 June 1944.

During the time of the meeting, the participants of the battlefield tour lived in a seaside resort at the Channel coast near Caen. When the former Ia of the "HJ" Division entered the room, in which the active British training officers had assembled, he was welcomed in an unexpectedly friendly, even comradely manner. Here, soldiers were meeting for whom it was a matter of course to fight "decently", in the service of their country with total personal devotion, in wars which are brought about by politicians, and not by soldiers.

The task of the former Ia in Cristot was to report on the battle of 11 June 1944 from the German point of view. The German liaison officer, Oberstleutnant i.G. Graf Stauffenberg, asked him in the morning of the first day, on the request of the British officers, if his participation really appeared reasonable to him, since the British participants in the war would be speaking quite frankly about the course of the battles, and that would surely awaken painful memories. The answer was that the question was an appreciated and considerate one but, after all, both sides were in the same situation. And that was the manner in which the discussions in the terrain also took place. The reports from "this side and the other" resulted in noteworthy discoveries which had been missing until then. The same agreeable and comradely atmosphere dominated the more than three days of the get-together. The group departed with mutual respect and was glad that the battles it had lived through once again in the discussions belonged to the past, and that a common future faces the younger soldiers, standing shoulder to shoulder under a treaty.

During the following year, a larger number of comrades from various units of the "HJ" Division (some accompanied by their wives and children) visited Normandy. In addition to revisiting the country, it was the first encounter for the ladies and children, that tour was meant to clarify questions concerning the history of the Division. The gathering started with a visit to the British war cemetery in Fontenay-le Pesnel where nine comrades from SS-Panzergrenadierregiment 26, SS-Panzerregiment 12 and SS-Panzerpionierbataillon 12 are also buried. A wreath was laid during a commemoration dedicated to the killed German and British soldiers. The Ardennes monastery, the towns of M,lon, Buron, Rots, St. Manvieu, PutÙt, Brouay, Cristot, Fontenay, Rauray, Cheux, Hill 112, and Esquay, Carpiquet, Verson, Venoix, Vimont, le Tombeau de Marie Joli, Jort, Falaise, Chambois, St. Lambert and Hill 262 were visited, one after the other, and some more than once. Important facts for the Divisional history were discovered. The stops at Ardennes, St. Manvieu, Hill 112, Esquay and Venoix were particularly impressive to all participants; beyond that, they each revisited especially valued memories by themselves. The German war cemeteries in la Cambe and Champigny/St. André de l'Eure, where Brigadeführer Fritz Witt found his last resting place, were also visited. Everywhere, the French citizens showed not only a vivid interest, they also recognized, very quickly in most cases, what kind of visitors these were. They joined the discussions and frequently provided useful information. In several houses, the visitors were treated with considerable hospitality, such as, for instance, by a family which Sturmbannführer Bernhard Krause had arranged to be taken to safety in an ambulance of his battalion. It was gratifying to note that the men of the Division were accepted everywhere in the former theater of combat, and that they were received by those, who had suffered so severely from the war at the time, in a friendly and, sometimes, touchingly cordial manner. Their spirit in combat, their willingness to sacrifice, and their understanding for the hardships of the population had not been forgotten. Both the visitors and the numerous women and men of Normandy with whom they spoke, also felt that the past war had not separated them, rather, that they belonged together. Further visits by both sides deepened and consolidated the bonds. Many men of the former Division and their families will be drawn, time and again, to that beautiful country, where the fate of so many came to its conclusion, and to its sympathetic people.

The work on this Divisional history created many relationships. They are of high value since they serve to reconcile the former enemies and point to a European future full of hope. This Divisional history describes the horrors of war in an unadulterated way. Since the history must be truthful, that cannot be left out. It is all-the-more valuable that no feeling of hostility exists between the former foes, rather, that they can look into each others' eyes and shake hands, despite the shortcomings and and the failures of some individuals. The letter from a combatant from the "other side" is quoted here at the conclusion as an example of that.[2] The reason for the letter was the work on this book. May it contribute to bring together the living and the future generations. Mr. Robert H. Broughton wrote:

My dear Colonel,

My son showed me your kind answer to his request concerning military uniforms and organizations. I learned that you are working on the history of your division. The battalion in which I served in June 1944, the 11th H.L.I., was an element of the 'Polar Bear' Division. During the fighting, which concentrated on the village of Rauray, it was facing units of the 12. SS-Division. I thought that the attached report, taken from the diary of the regiment, might be helpful to you. I am of the opinion that it is always useful to know how the events were seen 'on the other side of the hill'. The emotional description of the enemy is a consequence of the intent of the reports at the time. Today, we would, for instance, replace the word 'fanaticism' by the word 'valor'.

As a very young officer at the time, it was my first battle. When I led the scouting party to Rauray during the night of 26 June (1944), I was wounded and captured by your men. I remained as their prisoner there in a stone farmhouse at the extreme edge of the village until it was captured the following afternoon. Thus, I had the unusual, and somewhat exciting, opportunity to observe an attack by my own battalion from a favorable location in the middle of the enemy main line of resistance!

I cannot conclude this letter without expressing my appreciation of the valiant defense by your men, and the gentlemanly and generous treatment I experienced by them. All that happened a long time ago, but I think of it with gratitude and am happy that fate has allowed me to provide my testimony to your historian . . .

Victory or defeat rest in God's hand,
of honor we are, ourselves, master and king.

(from the Edda)

SECTION 14

Addendum

Readers of the first German edition of this book have provided numerous complementary and confirming comments, as well as corrections. The corrections have been incorporated, the complementary information will find its place in the German Federal Archives/Military Archives, together with all documentation used for this book.

I thank all contributors for their participation and interested collaboration.

Reports and new information regarding four events, which were of particular impact on many readers, follow here as an Addendum.

Hubert Meyer

TO CHAPTER 2.5 DEATH OF BRIGADEFÜHRER FRITZ WITT ON 14 JUNE 1944

One of the two clerks of the Ia, Sturmmann Hans Nepomuck, was one of those who experienced the artillery attack on the Divisional command post in Caen-Venoix. In a letter to the Author, he wrote:

> Brigadeführer Witt, together with Obersturmführer Meitzel, was in your room. During the fire attack he then rushed, with Untersturmführer Hausrath, to the bunker located in the garden. The bunker was covered with wooden planks. Meitzel remained, as reported, in the house. I threw myself behind the relatively thick wall which ran along the property line on the road to Caen. After the artillery attack, I jumped up and was probably the first to see the smashed planks across the bunker (slit trench). A lifeless arm led to expect the worst, and I think that I ran, crying, to Obersturmführer Meitzel in order to report the inconceivable event. I want to indicate with this that the fragments of a shell exploding in the tops of the trees could not have had that effect, in particular

since Untersturmführer Hausrath was also mortally wounded. Be that as it may, the tragic impact is not lessened by that.[1]

TO CHAPTER 5.5 THE CANADIAN-BRITISH OPERATION "TOTALIZE". THE DEFENSIVE BATTLES NEAR ST. SYLVAIN AND AT THE LAISON SECTOR FROM 8 TO 11 AUGUST 1944

Until the start of the year 1983, Hauptsturmführer Michael (called Michel) Wittmann, the most successful Panzer commander of the Second World War, was considered as missing. Until then, the search for him had been in vain. On 23 March 1983, farmer Samson of Cintheaux was tilling his field near Gaumesnil for spring seeding. On 8 August 1944, four German "Tigers" had been fighting in the field and were destroyed there. Very close to the spot where the knocked-out Tiger 007 was sitting after the conclusion of the fighting (as the farmer knew in his own mind) he encountered human bones. He immediately advised the administrator of the German war cemetery in la Cambe, Herr Otto, who was an employee of the German Association for the Care of War Graves.[2] Employees of the Association recovered the skeletons of four killed men. Also found were remnants of a black Panzer uniform, a leather jacket, an officer's collar patch cord, an officer's belt buckle, a 6.35 mm pistol, a Waffen-SS belt buckle with the inscription "Meine Ehre heiflt Treue" (my honor is loyalty), an ear piece from a headphone, a Waffen-SS identity tag, remnants of leather clothing, belt and uniform buttons of the Heer. At another location, an identity tag of the Luftwaffe/Flak was found together with some skeleton parts.

Through cooperation between the German Association for the Care of War Graves in Kassel, the section for the record of graves of the German Office for the Notification of Closest Relatives of the Killed of the Former German Wehrmacht in Berlin, the search experts of the Comrades' Association of Soldiers of the I. Panzerkorps of the former Waffen-SS, Heiner Kugel, and Frau Hilde Helmke, the widow of Michael Wittmann, the names of the crew of Michael Wittmann's Tiger could be determined:

Commander	Hauptsturmführer Michael Wittmann	
		born 22.4.1914
Driver	Unterscharführer Heinrich Reimers	
		born 11.5.1924
Gunner	Unterscharführer Karl Wagner	born 31.5.1920
Radio Operator	Sturmmann Rudolf Hirschel	born 3.1.1924
Loader	Sturmmann Günther Weber	born 21.12.1924

Sturmmann Günther Weber had been transferred from the Luftwaffe-Flak to the Waffen-SS. The Luftwaffe identity tag which had been found, had been his.[3]

Michael Wittmann and the other comrades of his Tiger crew, very likely the vehicle 007, were buried in the German war cemetery in la Cambe near

Bayeux in a common grave. On 3 June 1983, together with Frau Hilde Helmke, comrades of the "HJ" Division and their German and French friends assembled in honor of their memory at their grave.

Untersturmführer Willi Ihrion, the commander of one of the other three Tigers knocked out near Gaumesnil, is also buried in la Cambe. The names of the other members of his crew are not yet known.

A former member of the Schwere SS-Panzerabteilung 101, Untersturmführer Heinz Höflinger, drew a sketch for Frau Hilde Wittmann while he was in an internment camp in 1946. It indicates that the commanders of the other two Tigers were Hauptsturmführer Heurich (the technical officer of the Abteilung) and Untersturmführer Dollinger (the communications officer). On the sketch, Höflinger also noted the last orders which Hauptsturmführer Michel Wittmann had issued during the attack by radio:

"March!"—

"Attention! Attention! Pak from the right!"—

"Pull back . . ."

The only survivor of the four Tiger crews who could be found until now, Sturmmann Alfred Bahlo, reported on his experiences during that battle:

I was the radio operator on medium frequency (contact with the Division) and MG gunner in the Dollinger Panzer. My commander Dollinger was an Untersturmführer and the communications officer of the Panzerabteilung. Ober-scharführer Schott was the radio operator on very high frequency (contact to the other Panzers) and the loader. That distribution of tasks was true only for the so-called 'staff-Panzers'. The driver and gunner were Unterschar-führers whose names I have forgotten.

The hit which our Panzer took slammed through the right side wall. The shell exploded inside the fighting compartment and seriously wounded Oberscharführer Schott. I received a minor wound to the neck. I do not know from where that defensive fire came. Later, there was talk about a Canadian anti-tank gun position.

Untersturmführer Dollinger, the driver and I bailed out. Oberscharführer Schott, greatly impeded by his serious wound, followed later and I helped him to climb out. I tried to get a withdrawing Panzer to take Oberscharführer Schott along. I was unsuccessful since Untersturmführer Ihrion (3rd Panzer) did not open the hatch, and the fourth Panzer was knocked out in front of my eyes immediately there-after. Untersturmführer Dollinger and I carried Oberschar-führer Schott on a make-shift stretcher to the Caen-Falaise road where we loaded him into a Kübelwagen which then drove off. During that march we walked past the knocked-out Panzer of Hauptsturmführer Wittmann, its turret had been ripped off. I then made my way on foot to the field dressing station.

From what I have heard, Untersturmführer Dollinger was killed in Hungary at the start of 1945.[4]

Based on the combat reports in the first edition of this book, the English magazine "After The Battle" researched which Allied armored unit knocked out the four Tiger Panzers. It came to the conclusion that it had been the "A"-Squadron of the 1st Northamptonshire Yeomanry, a tank battalion, which was part of the independent 33rd Armored Brigade (tanks). For that attack, the Brigade had been attached to the 51st British Infantry Division. In the morning of 8 August, the infantry battalion Black Watch had captured the village of St. Aignan-de Cramesnil with the support of the tank battalion, and had initially prepared for defense there. The "A"-Squadron of the tank battalion was located in an orchard south of the village. From there, the British observed the Tigers attacking in a northerly direction from Falaise toward Caen, approximately parallel to Route Nationale No. 158. The acting chief of the squadron, Captain Boardman, knew that the shells from the short 7.5 cm gun, with which most of the Shermans were equipped, could break through the armor of the Tigers only at close range. Hence, he used the only "Firefly" of his unit to fight the Tigers. The Sherman M4A4 "Firefly" was equipped with a 7.62 cm gun, with a barrel length of 58. Using anti-tank shells of the type APDS, it could penetrate an armor thickness of 192 mm at 1,000 meters. The Tiger I had a frontal armor of 100 mm, and side armor of 80 mm thickness.

At 800 yards (730 meters), the tank opened fire at 12.40 hours at the rearmost of the three Tigers visible to it. The gunner, trooper Joe Ekins, fired two shells in quick succession which set the Tiger on fire. The second Tiger swung to the right and fired three shots at the "Firefly" which was just rolling back into cover. Thus, the shells did not hit it, but a ricochet glancing off the cover of the turret hatchet hit the commander in the head. Totally dazed, he bailed out and was wounded. Lieutenant James took over the command and brought the tank into a new firing position. At 12.47 hours, Ekins fired a shell at the second Tiger, which exploded in a flash flame. The front Tiger had apparently been hit by the fire of the other tanks with their short 7.5 cm guns in the drive sprocket and was turning in circles. Two shells from the "Firefly" set that Tiger on fire at 12.52 hours. The various reports do not indicate how the fourth Tiger (probably that of Michel Wittmann) was knocked out.

It is certain that the English tanks in St. Aignan-de Cramesnil, which had prepared for defense there since the morning and were well camouflaged, had not been spotted. In addition, when the Tigers passed Gaumesnil, a hedge blocked the visibility to the village. The attention of the attacking Tigers was concentrated on the Canadian tanks of the 2nd Canadian Armored Brigade which were advancing on both sides of the Route Nationale. Thus, they fell victim to the flanking fire from St. Aignan.

The war diary of the 1st Northamptonshire Yeomanry notes, for 13.30 hours, that the 1st Polish Armored Division had mounted a breakthrough attack on its left (east), had been stopped and was retreating. This book reports on that battle in Chapter 5.5.

The war diary of the British tank battalion notes, for 13.40 hours, that the German counterattack, which was directed at the advancing tanks of the 4th Canadian Armored Division and the 1st Polish Armored Division, had been fought off, with high German losses. The British tank battalion reported the destruction of five Tigers, four Panthers, six Panzer IVs, and five self-propelled guns.[5] The losses of the II. Panzerabteilung of Sturmbannführer Prinz which was attacking there and which had thirty-nine combat-ready Panzer IVs, are not known, but may have been correctly stated as six vehicles. Panthers were not in action there. The Jagdpanzer IVs of SS-Panzerjägerabteilung 12 (if they were referred to as the self-propelled guns) were in battle near St. Sylvain, beyond the range of the British tanks. Guns of the I. Abteilung of SS-Panzerartillerieregiment 12 were not in combat either in such a forward location.

According to its war diary, the British tank battalion lost twenty tanks, twelve killed and fifty-one wounded. The Poles had lost (as reported) forty tanks. No information is available on the Canadian losses in that battle and in that sector.

Suffering heavy losses, the vastly numerically inferior Panzer crews, Panzerjägers, Panzergrenadiers, artillerymen, and Flak gunners of the "HJ" Division, the Schwere SS-Panzerabteilung 101, and rocket launchers of the Waffen-SS and the Heer, had succeeded in preventing a deep breakthrough of two Allied armored divisions, of two infantry divisions, and of two tank brigades with a total of more that 600 tanks. On the German side, thirty-nine Panzer IVs, approximately ten Tigers and fourteen Panzerjäger IVs faced that huge armada of tanks. The city of Falaise, the objective of Operation "TOTALIZE", was only captured by the Canadians on 17 August.

TO CHAPTER 5.6 THE DEFENSE OF FALAISE FROM 16 TO 18 AUGUST 1944

This chapter reports that, in the opinion of Rottenführer Paul Hinsberger, the Kampfgruppe of the I./26, encircled inside the Ecole Supérieure de Jeunes Filles of Falaise, had attempted a breakout during the night of 17 to 18 August 1944. The attempt had, however, failed. That information is contrary to descriptions in the war diary of the 6th Canadian Infantry Brigade and in the book "Grenadiere" by Panzermeyer. A confirmation of the reports from Paul Hinsberger could not be located before this book was published.

In the fall of 1983, a former member of the then-encircled Kampfgruppe, Sturmmann Karl-Heinz Decker, came forward. He had previously belonged to the II. Bataillon of Panzergrenadierregiment 25. He had joined Kampfgruppe Krause through circumstances which can no longer be determined.

After the end of his captivity, he had settled in England since he could not return to East Prussia, his homeland, which was occupied by the Soviets. He reported that a Kampfgruppe had tried to break out of the burning school during the night from 17 to 18 August. He wrote:

> It was still dark when we entered the street. There we came under terrible fire. We ran into the houses, in order to find cover, and stayed there until dawn. During a German air attack, we managed to steal through the enemy positions. There were eighteen of us.

After crossing the railroad line (probably south of the city) they tried, in vain, to make contact with German troops. Totally exhausted and hungry, they finally sought cover in a farm. There, they were surprised by Allied soldiers and captured.[6]

That partly contradictory information can likely be traced back to the fact that the large building complex of the Ecole Supérieure and the adjoining grounds were defended by several small Kampfgruppen. The group, to which Karl-Heinz Decker belonged, fought in a detached building in the garden. Contact between the various groups was surely, at least partly, lost in the course of the fighting. It can be assumed that the small Kampfgruppe, to which Karl-Heinz Decker belonged, broke out of the burning building on their own decision. The others, who remained behind in the school building and the other buildings, perished fighting, as was noted in the war diary of the 6th Canadian Infantry Brigade.

TO CHAPTER 8.4 THE ATTACK ON 16 DECEMBER 1944—FIGHTING TO BREAK THROUGH THE AMERICAN FRONT LINE

It was reported that the heavy Panzerjägerabteilung 560 (Heer), the SPW-Bataillon III./26, and the bulk of Regiment 26 had not been sent into action on 18 December. They had to be ready to march forward along Advance Route C as soon as the obstructions had been removed, and Mürringen and Hünningen had been taken.

It was only in 1985 that contact could be established with former members of Schwere Panzerjägerabteilung 560. Obergefreiter (corporal) Lothar Giebeler was radio operator, loader and MG gunner in a Jagdpanzer IV of the 3. Kompanie. At the time, he had noted important dates and events in key phrases in a small diary. He wrote about his action on 18 and 19 December:

> Our Kompanie had already advanced, with Grenadiers mounted, to the wooded area on 17 December. There, Grenadierregiment 989, reinforced by the Grenadier-regiment of the H.J. Division, was still in battle. Bitter fighting for each bunker was taking place. After several attempts to push into the woods, our attack was called off again. In any case, we could not have advanced through the wet and

marshy terrain, and would very probably have got stuck. The risk posed by advancing along the forest trail was still too high at that time. In addition to artillery, the enemy had also sent armor-piercing weapons into action there. Hence, we drove back to our starting positions and waited there. In the evening and during the night, there was bitter fighting ahead of us. The next morning, a radio message arrived that the wooded area had been cleared of the enemy. The path through the forest was now open for Panzers and heavy vehicles. But, the enemy had gained time and probably also figured out our plan.

In the early morning of 18 December, young SS-Grenadiers moved approximately 100 captured Americans past our vehicles. Many wounded, Germans and Americans, were also brought back, either on foot or on vehicles. It had snowed during the night, the terrain and the roads were covered with slush. We hear loud Panzer noises in front of us. The Pantherabteilung of the SS-Panzer-regiment drove in the direction of Krinkelt to mount an attack. A short time later, we heard the harsh barks of Panzer guns being fired, and heavy artillery fire. We were slowly getting somewhat restless, since we were in those waiting positions for the second day by then.

However, our company also received the order to attack Krinkelt in the afternoon. No Grenadiers accompanied us. Again, we pushed into the wooded terrain. There was only one improved trail through the forest available for the vehicles.

It was just wide enough that our Panzer tracks could roll on it. We kept a predetermined distance from the vehicle ahead and had strict orders not to open the hatches. Thus, I was able to see and observe the terrain on the right, where the heaviest fighting had taken place, through the periscope. The battles had left some signs behind. One could see shot-up trees and destroyed vehicles, as well as bunkers, some of which had been blown up. Frequently, the column had to stop. Then, I lifted my hatch cover a little and could still hear sporadic rifle and pistol shots. The young Grenadiers tried to break into the undamaged bunkers, since provisions and even cigarettes could be found there. Quite a few paid for that with their lives, or were maimed, when they stepped on a mine.

When we left the forest at the fall of darkness, we were welcomed by heavy enemy anti-tank and artillery fire. The enemy obviously knew exactly at which spot we would leave the woods. Also, he must have heard the din from the tracks and the engines. The distance to the village was approximately one kilometer. The terrain in-between was crossed by many hedges and bushes. In the beginning, we had the feeling that we were fired on from each of those hedges. We received orders to immediately spread out to both sides and to advance widely staggered. Half-right, along the road and in the terrain, sat a number of knocked-out Panthers of the I. Abteilung which had attacked in the morning. The sight of those abandoned vehicles did give us a fright. Some of them were burnt out, and the turret hatches still stood open. They had, obviously, driven frontally into the heavy American defensive fire. The losses and number of damaged vehicles must have been high. The rapidly falling darkness came to our rescue. Just before we reached the village of Krinkelt, it was completely dark. Inside the village, a spooky activity was going on. The shadows from vehicles passing by moved in the reflection from burning houses. No-one really knew where the enemy was moving. We came under concentrated enemy tracer fire, and returned fire in that direction. But, the deeper we entered into the streets, the more confused the situation became. We no longer had a field of fire. The enemy, vastly superior there also, was well camouflaged. The enemy artillery concentrated its fire on the terrain behind us so that the Grenadiers were unable to come across from the edge of the forest.

Oberfeldwebel [1st sergeant] Rudloff of our Kompanie, with his Panzer, almost collided with a Sherman at a crossroads. Since neither could fire in that situation, both pulled their vehicles back. Our whole radio communications almost collapsed then since the Americans were talking in fluent German on the same frequency. Coded phrases were hardly used any more, which increased the confusion even more. For instance, a message came in on the radio: 'Assemble at the water tower', then again 'Assemble at the church'. The water tower was located in the Rocherath section of the village, the church in the Krinkelt section. Then, a warning was broadcast: 'Attention, enemy is listening in. Stop spoken communications immediately, enemy monitoring and interference is taking place.' The Americans had really caused some confusion with that. There were hardly any spoken messages after that.

In the narrow streets of the village we hardly knew anymore where friend or foe was. The Panzer of Leutnant Freyer had got stuck in a narrow hollow which was under heavy enemy fire. Despite that, we were able to back up close to it. Tracers were whistling above us at hair's breadth. Our commander, Oberfeldwebel Franz Scheller, finally managed to open the hatch and to climb out. He shouted at us from the outside: 'We will try to tow the Panzer away.' But, that did not succeed even after several attempts. Our tracks were spinning in place, and we did not move at all. After some time, Leutnant Freyer climbed in on my side. The other crew members had also left the vehicle and joined other vehicles. Suddenly, we came under heavy artillery fire. We determined that it came from our own guns whose fire was much too short. The hits landed exactly in our positions and constantly became more intensive. It was a terrible feeling to be shelled by our own artillery.

Consequently, when our comrades did not move their fire forward, we terminated 'Operation Krinkelt'. We drove back to the edge of the forest from where we had come. It was no longer under enemy fire.

Once the dark forest had engulfed us, it became more and more silent in our cramped Panzer. Hardly a word was spoken, since no-one was satisfied with that, our first, combat action. We had achieved nothing, the enemy still sat in Krinkelt-Rocherath as before. How high had our own losses been? None of us could answer that question.[7]

The reports on losses from the Abteilung indicate that one NCO and three men were wounded in Krinkelt. It is not known whether Jagdpanzers were lost. However, since the casualties were distributed through several companies, it is hardly likely.

Since the Schwere Panzerjägerabteilung 560 only arrived in Krinkelt at dusk on 18 December and barely became involved in the fighting inside the village, it could be pulled out as the first unit and moved forward on 19 December to Büllingen. From there, it attacked the Schwarzenbüchel hill and the Bütgenbach estate, together with the I./26, during the night from 19 to 20 December. Those battles are described in Chapter 8.5.

SS-PANZERGRENADIER-AUSBILDUNGS-UND ERSATZBATAILLON 12

While the "HJ" Division was fighting in Austria, the SS-Panzergrenadier-Ausbildungs-und Ersatzbataillon 12 (SS-Panzergrenadier training and replacement battalion) was taking part in the battles in the northern German theater. Its garrison town, since the end of October 1943, had been Nienburg/Weser. When British troops approached the region of its garrison, it was incorporated into the very fragmented defensive front line. The Bataillon took part in the fighting for the Weser river crossings, at the Aller river, on the Lüneburg Heath, and the in Hamburg district. In his booklet "Endkampf" ("Final Battle"), Wolfgang Buchwald reports on those actions. New results of research on the fighting for the Aller bridgehead near Essel are recorded by Oberstleutnant Ulrich Saft in his publication "Krieg in der Heide" (war on the heath), author's private publication, Munster/Örtze.

Appendix 1

Order for the Formation of the Division, June 24, 1943.

Supreme SS Command   Berlin-Wilmersdorf, 24 June 1943
Command of the Waffen-SS   Kaiserallee 188
Organization Diary No.784/43

Secret Command Matter

<u>Concerns</u>:   Formation of SS-Panzer Grenadier Division "Hitlerjugend"
<u>Attachments</u>: -3- (sent only to the respective authorities)

<u>Distribution</u>: Special Distribution   <u>70</u> <u>copies</u>
                                           Prf. No. 1 Attach 2+3

1.) On orders of the Führer, with immediate effect, the formation at the troop training area Beverloo (northwest of Brussels) of SS-Panzer-Grenadier-Division "Hitlerjugend" (SS-Panz.Gren.Div. "Hitlerjugend") is ordered.

2.) <u>Structure</u> <u>and</u> <u>Equipment</u>
see attachments 1 and 2.
     The formation of the Feldgend.Kp. [military police company] has already been ordered through Directive SS-FHA, Kdo.Amt d.W.-SS, Org.Tgb.Nr.II/4028/43 geh. [secret] of 8 June 43. The additionally approved positions, weapons, vehicles and field kitchen—see attachment 3.

3.) <u>Officers-</u>, <u>NCO-</u>, <u>and</u> <u>enlisted</u> <u>positions</u> <u>staffing</u> will take place through SS-FHA, Amt V, Abt.IIa and IE, and Amtsgr.D and Personalamt [personnel office] of the SS-W. V-Hauptamt, respectively, in cooperation with Gen.Kdo. [chief command] of I.SS-Panz.Korps "Leibstandarte".

4.) Regarding the provision of <u>weapons, equipment and vehicles</u>, special orders will be issued through SS-FHA, Abt.Ib and Amt X, respectively.

5.) Assignment of <u>field post numbers</u> will take place through SS-FHA, Amt II, Abt.Ic/Fp.

6.) <u>Kst</u> and <u>KAN</u> will be assigned automatically through SS-FHA, Amt II, Org./StAN. Regarding the provision of <u>regulations</u>, special orders will be issued through SS-FHA, Vorschriften [regulations] and Lehrmittel [teaching aids] Abteilung.

7.) The transferred personnel are to be issued uniforms and equipment in accordance with V.Blatt [regulation leaflet] W.-SS Nr.16, article 348 of 1 September 1941.

8.) Responsible for the formation is the commander of SS-Panz.Gren.Div. "Hitlerjugend".

9.) Responsible replacement unit for all Panzer Grenadiers, including staff and staff company, of SS-Panz.Gren.Div. "Hitlerjugend", is the SS-Panz.Gren.Ausb.u.Ers.Btl.12 [training and replacement battalion], Arnheim. (For specialists see special units).

signed: Jüttner

SS-Obergruppenführer and

F.d.R.   General of the Waffen-SS

SS-Obersturmbannführer

Appendix 2

Order for Reorganization as a Panzer Division, October 30, 1943

SS-Führungshauptamt   Berlin-Wilmersdorf, 30 Oct. 1943
Amt II Org.Abt.Ia/II   Kaiserallee 188
Tgb.Nr.1660/43 g.Kdos

Secret Command Matter

<u>Concerns</u>:   Reorganization of SS-Panz.Gren.Div. "Hitlerjugend"
<u>Attachments</u>: - 2 - (sent only to respective authorities)

<u>Distribution</u>: Special distribution   <u>70 copies</u>
                                             2.Copy 1+2 Attach

1.) The Führer has ordered the following structure for SS-Panz.Gren.Div. "Hitlerjugend" and its re-naming to 12. SS-Panzer-Division "Hitlerjugend".

2.) The reorganization has to take place with existing personnel, weapons and equipment.

3.) a) Structure: see attachment 1
    b) Kst and KAN: see attachment 2
    c) Regarding the formation of the Flamm-Zug in the Stabs-Kp. of Panz.Gren.Rgt.25 (gp), a timely special order will be issued.

4.) Kst and KAN, unless already available, will be issued automatically. After issue of the new KSt and KAN, with the same paragraph numbers, these will go into effect. In view of the issue of the new KStN, the total strength of 12.SS-Panz.Div."Hitlerjugend" is to be reduced by 10%.

5.) Responsible for the reorganization is the division commander.

signed: Jüttner

F.d.R.

SS-Hauptsturmführer

Appendix 3

List of Units of 12. SS Panzer Division 'Hitlerjugend'

Units	Field Post Number	Date of Formation (+) or Dissolution (-) (Month / Year)	Comments
12.SS-Pz. Div.			
Stab	59900	- 5.45	
Begl.Kp.(Sich.Kp.)	59900A		
Kdt.Stab. Qu.	59900B		
Musikzug	59900C		
Kriegsber. Zug	56965	- 5.45	
Unterführer Lehr Kp.	59805	+ 3.44	
Aufstellungs-Stab	27861	8.43 - 8.44	Already dissolved earlier
Genes.Kp.	22126	+ 8.44	
SS-Feldgend.Kp.12	57150	- 5.45	
SS-Felders.Btl.12			
Stab	59805A	+ 3.44	
1.Kp.	59805B		
2.Kp.	59805C		
3.Kp.	59805D		
4.Kp.	59805E		
5.Kp.	59805F		
6.Kp.	59805G		
7.Kp.	59805H		
8.Kp.	59805J		
9.Kp.	59805K		
SS-Pz.Gren.Rgt.25 **(SS-Pz.Gren.Rgt.1)**			
Rgts.Stab	56840	- 5.45	
I.Btl.	58048	- 5.45	
II.Btl.	57377	- 5.45	

Units	Field Post Number	Date of Formation (+) or Dissolution (-) (Month / Year)	Comments
III.Btl.	59601	- 5.45	
13.Kp.	59367	- 5.45	
14.Kp.	57714	- 5.45	
15.Kp.	58829	- 5.45	
16.Kp.	56986	- 5.45	
SS-Pz.Gren.Rgt.26			
(SS-Pz.Gren.Rgt.2)			
Rgts.Stab	58077	- 5.45	
I.Btl.	57403	- 5.45	
II.Btl.	59760	- 5.45	
III.Btl.	56804	- 5.45	
13.Kp.	58130	- 5.45	
14.Kp.	57553	- 5.45	
15.Kp.	56954	- 5.45	
16.Kp.	57615	- 5.45	
SS-Pz.Rgt.12			
Rgts.Stab	59230	- 5.45	
I.Abt.	59043	- 5.45	
II.Abt.	58698	- 5.45	
Pz.Werkst.Kp.	56903	- 3.44	
Pi.Kp.	57292	- 3.44	Dissolved before 6.44
	56903	+ 3.44	
1.Kol.	57418	- 5.45	
2.Kol.	56125	- 5.45	
SS-Pz.Art.Rgt.12			
Rgts.Stab	59611	- 5.45	
I.Abt.	56762	- 5.45	
II.Abt.	58343	- 5.45	
III. Abt.	57766	- 5.45	
SS-Sturmgesch.Abt.12.	59805	- 3.44	
SS-Flak Abt.12	59572	- 5.45	
SS-Werfer Abt.12			
Stab	10443	+ 8.43	
1.Bttr.	14052	+ 8.43	
2.Bttr.	15541	+ 11.43	
3.Bttr.	12394	+ 9.43	
4.Bttr.	10823	+ 9.43	
Kol.	13008	+ 1.44	

Units	Field Post Number	Date of Formation (+) or Dissolution (-) (Month / Year)	Comments
SS-Pz. Aufkl.Abt.12	58286	- 5.45	
SS-Pz.Jäg.Abt.12			
Stab	12611	+ 3.44	
1.Kp.	13427	+ 2.44	
2.Kp.	14046	+ 2.44	
3.Kp.	15775	+ 2.44	
SS-Pz.Pi.Btl.12	58497	- 5.45	
SS-Pz.Nachr.Abt.12	57824	- 5.45	
SS-Nachsch.Tr.12			
Stab	59425	+ 43	
1.Kraftf.Kp.	56568	+ 43	
2.Kraftf.Kp.	58570	+ 43	
3.Kraftf.Kp.	57974	+ 43	
4.Kraftf.Kp.	56423	+ 43	
5.gr.Kw.Kol.	59771	+ 43	
6.gr.Kw.Kol.	58627	+ 43	
7.gr.Kw.Kol.	56313	+ 43	
8.gr.Kw.Kol.	59234	+ 43	
9.gr.Kw.Kol.	56095	+ 43	
Waffen Werkst.Kp.	58761	+ 43	
Nachsch.Kp.	59388	+ 43	
SS-Instands.Abt.12	57032	+ 43	
SS-Wirtsch.Btl.12			
Stab	59195A	+ 43	
Bäcker.Kp.	59195B		
Schlächter.Kp.	59195C		
Verw.Kp. (Verpfl.Amt)	59195D		
SS-Feldpostamt 12	58910	- 5.45	
SS-San.Abt.12	58817	- 5.45	

Appendix 4

Guidelines for Firearms Training under Combat Conditions

12.SS-.Pz.Div."Hitlerjugend"   Div.St.Qu., 10 Nov. 1943
Abt. Ia

Attached are guidelines for rifle training under combat-like conditions. They are to be used as a basis for firearms training by all units. Suggestions for improvement are to be directed to the Division, Abt. Ia. After completion of basic rifle training, the following training must be carried out:

1. Close-combat firearms training with rifle, pistol and submachine-gun,
2. Firearms training with machine gun, also close-combat fire training,
3. Combat firing as a group, Zug, company, etc.

For 12.SS-Pz.Div. "Hitlerjugend"
Senior General Staff Officer
(signed // Meyer)

SS-Panzer-Grenadier-Division   O.U., 30 October 1943
        "Hitlerjugend"
15.(Aufkl.-)SS-Pz.Gren.Rgt.25

Guidelines for combat-like basic rifle training

It must be the aim of every unit, which is being given the task to train recruits at the present stage of the war, to produce combat-ready soldiers in a few weeks of training time. The traditional peace-time firearms training, as laid down in its basics in HDV. 240, is geared to a much longer training period and can thus no longer satisfy the requirements of the war. It is not reasonable to teach the recruit, during long lectures on the science of ballistics, the various stages of a trajectory with all the difficult technical details, and then to teach the recruit to fire on targets during the traditional pre-fir-

546

ing training period, since nearly all these matters present themselves in a significantly different manner later on the field of battle. This must be the desirable objective: firearms training away from the barrack-square; combination of firearms training with combat training. The young recruit must, from the start, become familiar, in addition to the traditional firearms training (i.e. firing on targets), with firing on combat-like targets.

It has become particularly apparent, during the short-duration firearms training that the (too sudden) change-over from traditional firearms training to simulated combat firing, and combat firing, has caused significant problems to the recruit. Consequently, the results achieved during simulated combat firing have been dismal. The objective of the firearms training schedule below is to bridge this gap and to organize the whole of the firearms training in a manner more reflective of the war environment.

With this firearms training it is important, from the start, to remove all matters which are not war-like or to reduce them to the greatest extent. Among these, above all, is the too-frequent use, and in the initial weeks of training, almost exclusive use, of blank cartridges. Experience has shown that blanks lead the recruit, time and again, to non-war like behavior and carelessness, since they are <u>only</u> blanks. Above all, it is important that training with live ammunition should start as early as possible during firearms training. Only the use of live ammunition trains the recruit within a short period of time to employ the desired manner of calm, deliberate and responsible firing, as well as to instill the firing discipline which is even more important with the new narrow and deep formation of the group during combat than it was with the old, wide formation.

A) The following text details the proposed training schedule of "Firing practice
for rifle and light machine gun at 5 training stations in terrain" with the recruit prone and the weapon supported.

<u>1st</u> <u>Station</u>: Controlled aiming.

1. In a prone position, the rifleman aims the rifle which is supported on grass-covered ground at the indicated point of aim on the target with the black 5 cm (later 2 cm) Balken cross. The rifle is initially adjusted in the perpendicular, then in the horizontal and then onto the point of intersection.

2. The firing instructor (Gruppenführer) then carries out the following controls:

He rests his head on both arms, with the elbows firmly pressed into the ground, and has a white piece of paper held in front of the muzzle of the rifle so that the target can no longer be seen. He then, again, checks for medium sight. There can be no error in aiming since the target cannot be seen. When the firing instructor is satisfied that he has medium sight, his assistant removes the white paper to the side on the instructor's signal. This extends the line of sight to the target and the point of aim at which the line of sight is really directed becomes apparent. The result of the aiming exercise is not initially provided to the rifleman. Instead, the instructor allows him to check the result in the same manner and then discusses any errors in aiming (with this: use of the usual aids—sights made of cardboard, etc., repetition of the concepts of point of aim, line of sight).

At this first station, the recruit is to be given the basics of firearms training: Here, he must learn to move his rifle with the sight edge horizontal and the bead in the center of the notch in the perpendicular and horizontal so that the line of sight is directed at the point of aim.

The most frequently appearing aiming errors here are:
a) The bead is either brought too much or too little into the notch which causes high- (over) or short firing.
b) The sight edge is not horizontal but is angled to one side or the other. The bullet will stray to the side towards which the rifle is angled and will land somewhat short.
c) The bead is not exactly centered in the notch, but slightly to the side. A bead to the left of center results in the bullet straying to the left, a bead to the right of center results in the bullet straying to the right.

Any errors made by the rifleman in aiming the rifle are to be explained to him through use of the traditional wooden or cardboard aids which represent notch and bead. The concepts of line of sight and point of aim are to be repeated continually. Advantages over the triangular method of aiming: It is less complicated, requires less preparation and equipment, and can be carried out more combat-like than triangular aiming.

2nd Station: Aiming the rifle at three combat targets (70, 100 and 150 m; kneeling, prone rifleman with machine gun support plate).

1. The Gruppenführer aims the rifle at the point of aim on the combat target. Each rifleman looks along the line of sight.

   The following difficulty must be overcome at this second station: At the first station, the rifleman could be ordered to aim the line of sight of his rifle at a clearly outlined and defined point of aim. The rifleman has no longer such a definite point of aim when he must now aim his rifle at the combat target. This difficulty is overcome by the firing instructor definitely indicating the respective point of aim of the combat target with the aid of a miniature exact replica of the target which the instructor has available.

2. The Gruppenführer repeats the concepts of line of sight and point of aim and draws the attention of the rifleman to the possible errors in aiming.

<u>3rd</u> <u>Station</u>: Methodical execution of all individual activities of firing with the rifle in the aiming position, supported, and the rifleman prone, under direct instruction and control of the Gruppenführer: charge the rifle—bring the rifle forward—grasp the small of the stock—pull back the rifle while properly inhaling and exhaling, at the same time taking up the slack—holding the breath after half exhalation—aiming at the target (point of aim)—slowly pulling the trigger until the shot is fired—observing through the muzzle flash—eye open, finger stretched—slowly putting down the rifle.

Of crucial importance is, in particular at this station, the direct instruction by the firing instructor of the individual activities to be carried out by the recruit. The firing instructor lies—without crowding the recruit—next to the recruit in the camouflaged position and slowly talks him through each activity which he must carry out while lying prone with the rifle loaded and supported. This allows the rifleman the time to carry out the recited activity immediately, under the control of the firing instructor, even while the words of the instructor still echo in his ear.

What is usual in other areas of instruction, and often justified there, the dressing down, must never be used here as a means to reprimand mistakes which are so common in particular at the start of firearms training. The firing instructor does not use harsh language, rather, he draws the attention of the rifleman repeatedly to his mistakes in a quiet tone of voice and with much patience. This confidence and superior calm of the firing instructor will be transferred in this manner to the practicing recruit. It is important that this station, in particular, is staffed by an especially competent firing instructor who will quickly earn the trust of the men through his teaching methods. A shouting loudmouth will ruin everything here. Calmness, confidence and self-assurance are in a much larger measure the basics of well-executed firing than the technical preparedness which is unquestionably required at the same time.

4th Station: Combining of all individual activities practiced at Station 3 with firing at targets (100–150 m) using blank cartridges. Now that the rifleman has become confident in aiming the rifle after practice at the previous stations, aiming and pulling the trigger are now being combined. The pulling of the trigger is initially practiced on the rifle which is put down to the right. The index finger makes contact with the trigger with either the root of the first segment or with the second segment. It then pulls back the trigger in one movement by bending the two top segments until resistance is felt, i.e. the rifleman feels first pressure. The bending of the finger then continues immediately at a constant rate.

A very frequent mistake of the beginner, tearing the trigger, must be stopped here. "Tearing the trigger" means the jerky and hasty pulling of the trigger, after properly taking aim, out of fear of missing the favorable moment for firing.

In addition to tearing the trigger, another frequent mistake is caused by the fear of the bang and the recoil which causes the head to be inclined forward, closing of the right eye and pushing the right shoulder forward. The most promising method to overcome these mistakes is by no means that the instructor yells into the ear of the recruit: 'You flinched!'— Once the recruit has been made aware of his mistake repeatedly in such manner, and he knows that he is inclined to tear the trigger or to flinch, his fear of repeating these mistakes will prevent his attention from being centered on aiming the rifle and bending the finger, rather it will be on the trigger and the instant of the crack. Thus he will never achieve calm and confident firing.

Both these mistakes cannot be overcome by shouting but only through repeated and calm instruction. While constantly watching the right eye (the firing instructor is again lying to the right of the rifleman) it is recommended that the instructor place his finger on that of the recruit, takes first pressure and then continues to bend the finger in order to give the recruit the proper feeling for bending the finger. Conversely, the instructor will let his finger be moved back by that of the recruit together with the trigger. From the start, and time and again, the recruit must be trained to simultaneously carry out the two activities of aiming and bending the finger, even after the shot has been fired. It is recommended that the recruit be reminded of the two activities by repeating the words 'Aim—continue bending', spoken in a slow manner, until they have become automatic.

The recruit is to be weaned of flinching with the following remark: 'You have quit aiming at the moment of firing. You must force your eye to look steadily through the notch, take medium sight, and try to observe the impact of the bullet in the target.' The tearing of the trigger is to be overcome by the remark: 'You bent the finger too quickly and jerkily. That caused the muzzle to pull to the side. You must always think of the constant and slow bending of the index finger while aiming. Then, the line of sight will continue to the steadily directed at the point of aim.'

These first 4 stations were staffed by Gruppenführers.

5th Station: The 5th Station is staffed by a Zugführer. It brings a repeat of the activity of Station 4, but with live ammunition at a target with camouflage paint, and the rifleman in prone position. The marker is located in a foxhole in front of the target. The Zugführer checks the firing in accordance with the aspects described in Station 4, and ensures that any individual errors, which still exist, are overcome.

It goes without saying that maximum possible safety must be paramount at this station. This training process which continues to increase in difficulty from station to station must be brought together in location and time. It is only when the recruit has the opportunity to make use of knowledge gained at one station immediately during practice at the next-higher that the desired improvement effort is possible.

This process of using stations during pre-firing training will be carried out Zug by Zug within the Kompanie. The Zug will be guided through the five stations in such a manner that each individual man will be moved to next station as soon as he is finished at the present one.

It is important that the last of the five stations be staffed by the Zugführer. Apart from the supposition that the Zugführer is also the best firing instructor in his Zug, the recruit will work very hard at the first four Gruppenführer stations so as not to make a bad impression on his Zugführer who tests the rifleman at the last station where live ammunition is used.

The first and second firing exercises of II.Schießklasse (firing course), 150 m prone supported and prone without support, will be practiced in pre-firing training with the use of blanks (rifle is supported naturally, no platform).

B.) <u>Firing during twilight and night.</u>
The experiences in Russia have shown that more emphasis must be placed on night combat training during the training of recruits. The small pamphlet "Schütze und Gruppe im Nachtgefecht" (Rifleman and group during night combat), issued by the OKH, can be used as the basis for night combat training.

This pamphlet is a collection and analysis of our experiences in night combat in Russia, in particular of the Russian methods of night combat. In order to familiarize our recruits with the totally different circumstances of night combat, the usual training demonstration is no longer sufficient. It only shows the 'rights' and 'wrongs' in a superficial manner (rattling of the mess kit, loud talking and issuing of orders, loud digging, rustling of leaves, breaking branches, demonstrating the various revealing light sources, etc.). In addition, the recruit must be made familiar with realistic combat-like impressions of night fighting. He must learn to properly identify and evaluate suspicious noises of a stealthy approach, breaking of branches, coughing, e.g. the non-war-like behavior of an enemy scouting party. He must learn to properly aim his rifle at enemy muzzle flashes, suspicious noises, etc., in accordance with elevation and direction. He must learn to make clever and quick use of short light flashes in order to see and fire. Above all, he must learn proper behavior and firing during the artificial illumination of the forefield by flares. The rifleman must learn to move at night in a cat-like and noiseless manner, and to use all available ruses of war (e.g. setting up alarm wires hung with cans, strewing around glass shards, use of straw men to draw enemy fire or to draw out the enemy, etc.). Exact delineation of the observation areas in front of the group sector. Determination of important distances with the help of individual outstanding markers in the terrain even during the day (of course, calculation and determination of basic firing values for mortars and heavy machine gun). Firing with fixed bayonet.

Night is the time of close combat. Thus, close combat training is required at night, as well as getting used to firing with fixed bayonet.

Mention of the fact that, in general, one tends to fire high at night since one cannot distinctly see the bead, and that it is more efficient to fire somewhat low rather than over the enemy since one has the chance to at least endanger the enemy through ricochets when firing low, while any bullets passing high over the enemy are lost in all cases.

Instructional firing at night using 3 stations.
1st Station: Listening and observation practice at night.
a) The rifleman (in a foxhole) identifies various noises (e.g. from muzzle fire, etc.) to his Gruppenführer according to their cause, direction and distance.
b) The rifleman learns to distinguish bushes, shrubs, tree stumps, dirt piles which stand out against the horizon from the outlines of enemy riflemen etc. Subsequently, always the use of a flare so that the practicing rifleman can see the cause of the noises and identify the bush or tree stump which he had thought to be an enemy rifleman.

2nd Station: Aiming practice.
The rifleman aims his rifle at muzzle fire, at the cause of the various noises in accordance with elevation and direction. The Gruppenführer checks the aimed rifle using a flashlight.

3rd Station:
a) Firing at ringed targets in the terrain at 70, 100 and 150 m during darkness. Muzzle fire noise and other suspicious enemy noises, at which fire is opened, are caused by the marker who sits under the target in a foxhole. Hits are indicated by red light from a flashlight on a mount.
b) Firing at combat targets during artificial illumination of the forefield. The rifleman fires during the short period of illumination by white flare at medium-sized terrain targets at 30, 50, 70, 100 and 150 m which he has not seen previously. Tracer ammunition is to be used if possible. Despite the short period of illumination, the rifleman is expected to fire, as rapidly as possible, well-aimed and observed shots.

C) Defensive fire against low-level aircraft.
It is necessary to familiarize the infantryman, who is only used to ground fighting, with the peculiarities of firing at aircraft targets - following the target with the rifle, amount of required lead, letting the aircraft fly into the front ring sight of the machine gun. The following three typical flight path images are to be used: passing to the side, passing at an angle, passing overhead.

1st Station: The recruit is made familiar with the required amount of lead through use of the following targets: passing to the side target (black), 2 lengths ahead of it is the outline of the aircraft is depicted by tiny dots, not visible to the recruit, where the shots have to land if the proper amount of lead is used.

Rifle is mounted on aiming support with ball-and-socket joint.

2nd Station: At this station, firing at aircraft targets is practiced using blank ammunition.

Setting up the target: Two approximately 6 to 8 m high masts are connected by a horizontal wire. The aircraft model (25 to 30 cm wing span) is suspended on two vertical wires which, in turn, run along the horizontal wire by means of two rollers. In the case of passing to the side, the model can be pulled from left to right of the rifleman. In the case of passing at an angle or passing overhead, the model can be pulled toward the rifleman. Firing distance in the first instance is 15–20 m, in the second instance 20–10 m.

3rd Station: Repetition of Station 2—firing at aircraft target from cover—using live ammunition.

Appendix 5

Officer Positions and Names of Occupants in 12. SS Panzer Division 'Hitlerjugend'

Unit	Invasion, 6.6.1944	Ardennes Offensive, 16.12.44	Hungary, 17.2.1945
Divisionsstab			
Divisionskommandeur	Brig.Fhr. Fritz Witt * 14.6.44 (ab 14.6.44	Staf. Hugo Kraas	Oberf. Hugo Kraas (Brig.Fhr. 20.4.1945)
Staff Kurt Meyer,	Brig.Fhr. 1.9.44)		
4. Ordonnanzoffizier, O4	Ustuf. Hausrath * 14.6.1944		
Führungsabt. Ia			
1.Gen.St.Offz.	Stubaf. H. Meyer	Ostubaf. H. Meyer	Ostubaf. H. Meyer
1.Ord.Offz., O1	Ostuf. Meitzel	Hstuf. Hesselmann	Hstuf. Hesselmann
3.Gen.St.Offz., Ic	Ostuf. Doldi	Ostuf. Doldi	Ustuf. Bredehorst
3.Ord.Offz., O3	Ustuf. Trommer	Ustuf. Bredehorst	
Div. Kartenstelle	Uscha. Kriegge	Oscha. Kriegge	Oscha. Kriegge
Leiter d. Nachrichtend. LdN	Ostuf. v. Brandis		
Divisionsbegleitkompanie	Ostuf. Guntrum	Ostuf. Stier	Ostuf. Stier
Feldgend. Komp.	Ostuf. Buschhausen	Ostuf. v. Drateln	Ostuf. v. Drateln
Abt. VI. Weltansch. Schulung u. Tr. Betr.			
Adjutantur: Abt. IIa	Hstuf. Rothemund	Hstuf. Höfler	Hstuf. Höfler IIa
Abt. IIb	Ustuf. Krause	Ostuf. Krause	Ostuf. Krause
Abt. III, Div. Gericht			
Kdt. Stabsquartier	Hstuf. Schuch	Hstuf. Tiefengruber	Hstuf. Tiefengruber
TFK	Ustuf. Dirks		
Gräber-Offz.			

Unit	Invasion, 6.6.1944	Ardennes Offensive, 16.12.44	Hungary, 17.2.1945
Quartiermeisterabt. Ib	Ib		
2.Gen.St.Offz.	Stubaf. Buchsein	Stubaf. Buchsein	Stubaf. Buchsein
2.Ord.Offz., O2	Ustuf. Lübbe	Ustuf. Zentgraf	Ostuf. Zentgraf
WaMun.	Stubaf. Schürer	Stubaf. Schürer	Hstuf. Sporer
Abt. IVa, Div. Intendant	Stubaf. Dr. Kos	Hstuf. Reichenbach	Stubaf. Reichenbach
Abt. IVb, Div. Arzt	Ostubaf. Dr. R. Schulz	Staf. Dr. R. Schulz	Staf. Dr. R. Schulz
Div. Zahnarzt	Hstuf. Dr. Rogge		
Abt. V, Div. Ing.	Stubaf. Manthey	Stubaf. Manthey	Stubaf. Manthey
SS-Panzerregiment 12			
Rgt.-Kommandeur	Ostubaf. Wünsche	Stubaf. Kuhlmann	Ostubaf. M. Groß
Adjutant	Hstuf. Isecke	Ostuf. v. Ribbentrop	Hstuf. Büttner
Ord. Offz.	Ustuf. Nerlich	Ustuf. Jungbluth	
Nachr. Offz.	Hstuf. Schlauß		
Verw. Fhr.	Hstuf. Lütgert		
Rgt. Arzt	Hstuf. Dr. Stiawa		
Rgt. Zahnarzt	Hstuf. Neinhardt	Hstuf. Neinhardt	Hstuf. Neinhardt
TFK	Ostuf. Sammann	Hstuf. Sammann	
Stabskompanie, Chef			
Versorgungskompanie, Chef		Ostuf. Donaubauer	
I. Abteilung			
Abt. Kdr.	Stubaf. Jürgensen	Stubaf. Jürgensen * 23.12.44	Hstuf. v. Ribbentrop
Adjutant	Ustuf. Nadler	Ustuf. Nadler	
Ord. Offz.	Ustuf. Hogrefe		
Nachr. Offz.	Ustuf. Jauch	Ustuf. Jauch	Ostuf. Jauch
Verw. Fhr.			
Tr. Arzt	Ostuf. Dr. Daniel		
TFK	Ostuf. Surkow		
TFW	Lt. Schulenburg		
Stabskompanie, Chef			
1. Kompanie, Chef	Hstuf. Berlin	Hstuf. Bormuth	Ostuf. Gaede
2. Kompanie, Chef	Ostuf. Gaede	Ostuf. Gaede	Hstuf. Minow
3. Kompanie, Chef	Ostuf. v. Ribbentrop	Ostuf. Brödel	
4. Kompanie, Chef	Hstuf. Pfeiffer * 11.6.44	Ostuf. Pohl	
Werkstattkp., Chef	Ustuf. R. Maier	Ostuf. R. Maier	Ostuf. R. Maier
II. Abteilung			
Abt. Kdr.	Stubaf. Prinz * 14.8.44	Hstuf. Siegel	Stubaf. Siegel (20.4.45 bef.)

Unit	Invasion, 6.6.1944	Ardennes Offensive, 16.12.44	Hungary, 17.2.1945
Adjutant	Ostuf. Hartmann		
Ord. Offz.	Ustuf. Walther		
Nachr. Offz.	Ustuf. Kommadina		
Verw. Fhr.	Ustuf. Schwaiger		
Tr. Arzt	Hstuf. Dr. Jordan		

Unit	Invasion, 6.6.1944	Ardennes Offensive, 16.12.44	Hungary, 17.2.1945
Tr. Zahnarzt	Ustuf. Hofner		
TFK	Ostuf. Breitenberger		
TFW	Lt. Pfannkuch		
Stabskompanie Chef	Hstuf. Großjohann		
5. Kompanie, Chef	Ostuf. Bando * 27.6.44	Ostuf. Jeran	Ostuf. Jeran
6. Kompanie, Chef	Hstuf. Ruckdeschel	Hstuf. Großjohann	Hstuf. Großjohann
7. Kompanie, Chef	Hstuf. Bräcker	Ostuf. Gasch	Ostuf. Gasch
8. Kompanie, Chef	Ostuf. Siegel		
9. Kompanie, Chef	Ostuf. Buettner		
Werkstattzug	Ostuf. D. Müller		

SS-Panzerjägerabteilung 12

Unit	Invasion, 6.6.1944	Ardennes Offensive, 16.12.44	Hungary, 17.2.1945
Abt. Kommandeur	Stubaf. Hanreich	Hstuf. Brockschmidt	Hstuf. Brockschmidt (Stubaf. 20.4.45)
Adjutant	Ostuf. Winkler	Ustuf. Probst	Ustuf. Rabe
Ord. Offz.	Ustuf. Wigand		
Nachr. Offz.	Ostuf. Siegert		
Verw. Fhr.			
Tr. Arzt			
TFK	Ostuf. aus der Wiesche	Ostuf. aus der Wiesche	Ostuf. aus der Wiesche
TFW	Ustuf. Gille		
Stabskompanie, Chef	Ostuf. Winkler		
1. Kompanie, Chef	Ostuf. Hurdelbrink	Ostuf. Zeiner i.V.	Ostuf. Zeiner
2. Kompanie, Chef	Ostuf. Wachter	Ostuf. Wachter * 17.12.44	
3. Kompanie, Chef	Hstuf. Wöst		

SS-Panzergrenadierregiment 25

Unit	Invasion, 6.6.1944	Ardennes Offensive, 16.12.44	Hungary, 17.2.1945
Rgt. Kommandeur	Staf. Kurt Meyer (bis 14.6.44)	Stubaf. S. Müller	Stubaf. S. Müller
Adjutant	Ostuf. Schümann * 8.7.44	Ostuf. Dr. Bäder	
Ord. Offz.	Ostuf. König (?)		
Nachr. Offz.	Ustuf. Stejskal	Ustuf. Stejskal	Ustuf. Stejskal

Unit	Invasion, 6.6.1944	Ardennes Offensive, 16.12.44	Hungary, 17.2.1945
Verw. Fhr.			
Rgt. Arzt	Stubaf. Dr. Gatternigg		
Rgt. Zahnarzt	Ostuf. Dr. Stift		
TFK			
Stabskompanie, Chef	Ostuf. Hoffmann * 8.6.44		
13. (S.I.G.) Kompanie, Chef		Oblt. Kaminski	Oblt. Kaminski
14. (Flak) Kompanie, Chef	Hstuf. Brantl	Ostuf. Wagner	
15. (Aufkl.) Kompanie, Chef		Hstuf. v. Büttner * 8.6.44	
16. (Pionier) Kompanie, Chef		Ustuf. Werner	
I. Bataillon			
Btl. Kdr.	Stubaf. Waldmüller * 8.9.44	Hstuf. Ott	Hptm. F.
Adjutant	Ustuf. Klein	Ostuf. Klein	Ostuf. Striebinger
Ord. Offz.	Ustuf. Exner		
Verw. Fhr.	Ustuf. Striebinger	Ostuf. Striebinger	
Tr. Arzt	Ostuf. Dr. Hermann * 8.7.44		
TFK	Ustuf. Päster		
1. Kompanie, Chef	Oblt. F.	Ustuf. Welzin	Ustuf. Wilkening
2. Kompanie, Chef	Ostuf. Knössel	Ustuf. Hansen	Ustuf. Hansen
3. Kompanie, Chef	Hstuf. Peinemann	Lt. Schäfer	Lt. Schäfer
4. Kompanie, Chef	Ostuf. Wilke	Ostuf. Fehrmann	
II. Bataillon			
Btl. Kdr.	Stubaf. Scappini * 7.6.44	Ostubaf. R. Schulze	Hstuf. Markus (?)
Adjutant	Ostuf. Pfeffer		
Ord. Offz.	Ustuf. Wentzlau * 24.6.44	Ustuf. Buchmann	
Verw. Fhr.	Ustuf. Gardeike		
Tr. Arzt	Ostuf. Dr. Sedlacek	Ostuf. Dr. Sedlacek	
TFK			
5. Kompanie, Chef	Hstuf. Kreilein * 25.6.44	Ustuf. Eichler	
6. Kompanie, Chef	Hstuf. Dr. Thirey * 8.7.44	Ostuf. König	Ostuf. König
7. Kompanie, Chef	Hstuf. Schrott * 2.9.44	Ustuf. Stuhr	
8. Kompanie, Chef	Hstuf. Breinlich *	Ustuf. Wunderlich	Ustuf. Wunderlich * 4.45

Unit	Invasion, 6.6.1944	Ardennes Offensive, 16.12.44	Hungary, 17.2.1945
III. Bataillon			
Btl. Kdr.	Ostubaf. Milius	Hstuf. Brückner	Hstuf. Dehne
Adjutant	Ustuf. Bergmann	Ustuf. Schäuble	

Unit	Invasion, 6.6.1944	Ardennes Offensive, 16.12.44	Hungary, 17.2.1945
Ordn. Offz.	Ustuf. Breiholz	Ustuf. Seidel	
Verw. Fhr.	Ostuf. Pohlmann		
Tr. Arzt	Ostuf. Dr. Lampel	Ostuf. Dr. Eder	
TFK	St.O.Jk. Hartung		
9. Kompanie, Chef	Oblt. Fritsch	Ustuf. Tanneberger	Ustuf. Breiholz
10. Kompanie, Chef	Oblt. Dietrich	Oblt. Dietrich	Ostuf. Klein
11. Kompanie, Chef	Ostuf. Stahl	Ustuf. Lang * 21.12.44	
12. Kompanie, Chef	Oblt. Wörner	Ustuf. Hubbes	
SS-Panzergrenadierregiment 26			
Rgt. Kommandeur	Ostubaf. Mohnke	Stubaf. Krause	Ostubaf. Krause * 19.2.45
Adjutant	Hstuf. Kaiser	Ostuf. Hölzl	Hptm. Glosser
Ord. Offz.			
Nachr. Offz.	Ostuf. Griebel		
Verw. Fhr.	Ostuf. Klünder	Ostuf. Klünder	
Rgt. Arzt	Ostuf. Dr. Lauchart	Ostuf. Dr. Lang	Ostuf. Dr. Lang
Rgt. Zahnarzt	Hstuf. Dr. Köpf	Hstuf. Dr. Köpf	
T.F.K.	Hstuf. Winter	Hstuf. Winter	
Stabskompanie, Chef			
13. (s.J.G.) Kompanie, Chef		Ostuf. Polanski	Ostuf. Polanski
14. (Flak) Kompanie, Chef	Hstuf. Stolze	Hstuf. Stolze	Hstuf. Stolze * 14.3.45
15. (Aufkl.) Kompanie, Chef		Oblt. Bayer	
16. (Pionier) Kompanie, Chef		Ostuf. Trompke	
I. Bataillon			
Btl. Kdr.	Stubaf. Krause	Hstuf. Hein	Stubaf. Kostenbader
Adjutant	Ustuf. Hölzel	Ustuf. Bergmann	Ustuf. Bergmann * 16.3.45
Ord. Offz.			
Verw. Fhr.	Ostuf. Klünder		
Tr. Arzt	Unterarzt Jesnaniadt	Dr. Remplik	
T.F.K.	Ustuf. Förster		

Unit	Invasion, 6.6.1944	Ardennes Offensive, 16.12.44	Hungary, 17.2.1945
1. Kompanie, Chef	Hstuf. Eggert * 12.7.44	Ostuf. Ludwig	Ostuf. Ludwig
2. Kompanie, Chef	Ostuf. Gröschel * 27.6.44	Ostuf. Brockmann	Ostuf. Brockmann * 17.2.45
3. Kompanie, Chef	Ostuf. Düvel	Ostuf. Düvel	
4. Kompanie, Chef	Ostuf. Hartung	Ostuf. Hartung	Ostuf. Hartung
II. Bataillon			
Btl. Kdr.	Stubaf. Siebken * 20.1.49	Hstuf. Hauschild	Hstuf. Ott
Adjutant	Ostuf. Andersen * 6.5.45	Ostuf. Lübbe	Ostuf. Lübbe
Ord. Offz.	Ustuf. Schnabel * 20.1.49	Oscha. Winkler	Oscha. Winkler
Verw. Fhr.	Ostuf. Paierl	Ostuf. Paierl	
Tr. Arzt	Stabsarzt Dr. Schäfer	Unterarzt Dr. Löffler	
TFK	Ustuf. Nagel	Ustuf. Ribbert	
Versorg.Kp.	Ustuf. B. Kaiser	Ustuf. B. Kaiser	Ustuf. B. Kaiser
5. Kompanie, Chef	Ostuf. Gotthard * 17.6.44	Ostuf. Bütschek	Ustuf. Gruber * 23.2.45
6. Kompanie, Chef	Ostuf. Schmolke	Ustuf. Lehmann	Ustuf. Lehmann
7. Kompanie, Chef	Lt. Henne	Ostuf. Löbzien	Ostuf. Löbzien * 13.3.45
8. Kompanie, Chef	Hstuf. Fasching	Ostuf. Brinkmann	Hstuf. Brinkmann
III. Bataillon (gep.)			
Btl. Kdr.	Stubaf. Olboeter * 2.9.44	Hstuf. Urabl	Stubaf. Brand
Adjutant	Ustuf. Kugler	Ostuf. Kugler	Ostuf. Kugler
Ord. Offz.			
Verw. Fhr.			
Tr. Arzt	Ustuf. Dr. Steiner	Oblt. Dr. Rathmann	Oblt. Dr. Rathmann
TFK	Hscha. Klein		
Versorgungskompanie	Ostuf. Mader	Ostuf. Mader	
9. Kompanie, Chef	Oblt. Göbel	Hstuf. Ernst	Ostuf. D. Schmidt
10. Kompanie, Chef	Oblt. Pallas	Ostuf. Latter	Ostuf. Guntrum * 20.3.45
11. Kompanie, Chef	Ostuf. Hauser	Ostuf. Burkhardt	Ostuf. Burkhardt
12. Kompanie, Chef	Ostuf. Riede	Hstuf. Riede	Hstuf. Riede
SS-Panzeraufklärungsabt. 12			
Abt. Kdr.	Stubaf. Bremer	Stubaf. Bremer	Stubaf. Bremer
Adjutant	Ostuf. Buchheim		

Unit	Invasion, 6.6.1944	Ardennes Offensive, 16.12.44	Hungary, 17.2.1945
Ord. Offz.	Ustuf. Gauch		
Nachr. Offz.	Ustuf. Schenk		
Verw. Fhr.			

Unit	Invasion, 6.6.1944	Ardennes Offensive, 16.12.44	Hungary, 17.2.1945
Tr. Arzt	Ostuf. Dr. Schudok		
TFK			
Stabskompanie	Ostuf. Buchheim	Ostuf. Doldi	
1. (Pz.Späh) Kompanie, Chef		Ostuf. Hansmann	Ostuf. Berg * 2.1.45
2. (Pz.Späh) Kompanie, Chef		Ostuf. Hauck	
3. (Aufkl.) Kompanie, Chef		Ostuf. Keue	Ostuf. Flanderka
4. (Aufkl.) Kompanie, Chef		Ostuf. Beiersdorf * 26.6.44	Ostuf. Flanderka
5. (schw.) Kompanie, Chef	Hstuf. v. Reitzenstein	Hstuf. v. Reitzenstein	Hstuf. v. Reitzenstein

SS-Panzerartillerieregiment 12

Unit	Invasion, 6.6.1944	Ardennes Offensive, 16.12.44	Hungary, 17.2.1945
Rgt. Kommandeur	Ostubaf. Schröder	Ostubaf. Drexler	Ostubaf. Drexler
Adjutant	Ostuf. Henßler	Hstuf. Macke	Hstuf. Macke
Ord. Offizier	Ustuf. Anger		
Nachr. Offz.	Ustuf. Studier	Ustuf. Studier	
Verw. Fhr.			
Rgt. Arzt			
Rgt. Zahnarzt			
TFK	Ustuf. Gesell		
TFW			
Stabsbatterie, Chef			

I. Abteilung

Unit	Invasion, 6.6.1944	Ardennes Offensive, 16.12.44	Hungary, 17.2.1945
Abt. Kdr.	Stubaf. Urbanitz	Stubaf. K. Müller	Stubaf. K. Müller
Adjutant			
Ord. Offz.			
Nachr. Offz.			
Verw. Fhr.			
Tr. Arzt			
TFK			
TFW			
Stabsbatterie, Chef			
1. Batterie, Chef	Hstuf. Gille		
2. Batterie, Chef	Ostuf. Timmerbeil	Ostuf. Schachtebeck	
3. Batterie, Chef	Ostuf. Heller	Ostuf. Heller	

Unit	Invasion, 6.6.1944	Ardennes Offensive, 16.12.44	Hungary, 17.2.1945
II. Abteilung			
Abt. Kdr.	Stubaf. Schöps * 27.6.44	Stubaf. Neumann	Stubaf. Neumann
Adjutant	Ustuf. Engemann		
Ord. Offz.	Ustuf. Schwarze		
Nachr. Offz.			
Verw. Fhr.	Ostuf. Franze		
Tr. Arzt			
TFK			
TFW			
Stabsbatterie, Chef	Ostuf. Schmidt		
4. Batterie, Chef	Oblt. Haller * 27.6.44	Ustuf. Pfaffinger	Ustuf. Grether
5. Batterie, Chef	Ostuf. Kurzbein		
6. Batterie, Chef	Ustuf. Kilchling	Ustuf. Kilchling	Ostuf. Kilchling
III. Abteilung			
Abt. Kdr.	Stubaf. Bartling	Hstuf. Fritsch	Hstuf. Fritsch
Adjutant	Ostuf. Göricke	Ustuf. Wirisch	
Ord. Offz.	Ustuf. Querfurth	Ostuf. Fuchs	
Nachr. Offz.	Ustuf. Amler	Ostuf. Amler	
Verw. Fhr.	Ustuf. Böhr	Ustuf. Menke	
Tr. Arzt	Hstuf. Dr. Busch		
TFK	Ustuf. Zelsmann		
TFW	Oscha. Heinze		
Stabsbatterie, Chef	Ustuf. Amler	Ostuf. Amler	
7. Batterie, Chef	Ostuf. Etterich	Ostuf. Etterich	
8. Batterie, Chef	Ustuf. Peschel	Ustuf. Peschel	Ostuf. Peschel *
9. Batterie, Chef	Ostuf. Balschuweit	Ostuf. Heller	
10. Batterie, Chef	Hstuf. Heydrich	Ustuf. Schwolow * 24.1.45	
SS-Werferabteilung 12			
Abt. Kdr.	Stubaf. W. Müller	Stubaf. W. Müller	Hstuf. Ziesenitz
Adjutant	Ostuf. Lämmerhirt	Ostuf. Lämmerhirt	Ostuf. Lämmerhirt
Ord. Offz.	Ustuf. Schulte	St.O.Jk. Behrens	
Unit	Invasion, 6.6.1944	Ardennes Offensive, 16.12.44	Hungary, 17.2.1945
Nachr. Offz.			
Verw. Fhr.	Ostuf. Sander		
Tr. Arzt	Hstuf. Dr. Busch		
TFK	Ostuf. Meyering		
Stabsbatterie, Chef	Hstuf. Weitkamp		

Unit	Invasion, 6.6.1944	Ardennes Offensive, 16.12.44	Hungary, 17.2.1945
1. Batterie, Chef	Hstuf. Macke		
2. Batterie, Chef	Hstuf. Ziesenitz		
3. Batterie, Chef	Ostuf. Bay	Ostuf. Bay	
4. Batterie, Chef	Ostuf. Dr. Erhart	Ostuf. Dr. Erhart	Ostuf. Dr. Erhart
SS-Flakabteilung 12			
Abt. Kdr.	Stubaf. Fend	Stubaf. Dr. Loenicker	Stubaf. Dr. Loenicker
Adjutant	Ustuf. Kolb	Ustuf. Kolb	Ustuf. Kolb
Ord. Offz.	Ostuf. Thoma		
Nachr. Offz.	Ustuf. Hüholt	Ustuf. Bachis	
Verw. Fhr.	Hstuf. Fischer	Hstuf. Fischer * 29.1.45	
Tr. Arzt	Hstuf. Dr. Wölke	Hstuf. Dr. Wölke	
TFK	Hstuf. Trost	Hstuf. Trost	
TFW	Ostuf. Grimm	Ostuf. Grimm	
Stabsbatterie, Chef	Ustuf. Hüholt	Ustuf. Wilhelm	
1. Batterie, Chef	Hstuf. Ritzel * 8.7.44	Ustuf. Görz	
2. Batterie, Chef	Ostuf. Riedel	Ostuf. Bulla	
3. Batterie, Chef	Hstuf. Dr. Weygand	Hstuf. Fischer	Ostuf. Schüller
4. Batterie, Chef	Ostuf. Ritscher	Ostuf. Ritscher	Ostuf. Ritscher
5. Batterie, Chef	Ostuf. Kranen	Ostuf. Kranen	
SS-Panzerpionierbataillon 12			
Btl. Kommandeur	Stubaf. S. Müller	Hstuf. Taubert	Hstuf. Taubert (Stubaf. 20.4.45)
Adjutant	Ustuf. Betz	Ostuf. Trötscher	Ostuf. Trötscher
Ord. Offz.			
Nachr. Offz.	Ustuf. Studier		
Verw. Fhr.	Hstuf. Pinkernell	Hstuf. Pinkernell	Ostuf. Dargel
Tr. Arzt	Hstuf. Dr. Zistler	Stabsarzt Dr. Zöberlein	Hstuf. Dr. Preißel
Tr. Zahnarzt	Oscha. Zickelbein		
TFK	Ustuf. Hornbogen	Ostuf. Hornbogen	Ostuf. Hornbogen
TFPi	Ustuf. Lorenz	Ostuf. Lorenz	Ostuf. Lorenz
Stabsbatterie, Chef	Hstuf. Pinkernell		
1. (gep.) Kompanie, Chef	Oblt. Toll * 10.6.44	Ustuf. Betz	Ustuf. Betz
2. Kompanie, Chef	Ostuf. Kuret	Ostuf. Richter	
3. Kompanie, Chef	Hstuf. Tiedke	Ostuf. Lauterbach	Ostuf. Lauterbach
4. Kompanie, Chef	Ostuf. Bischof	Hstuf. Bischof	Hstuf. Bischof
Brückenkdonne B, Chef	Ustuf. Richter		
SS-Panzernachrichtenabt. 12			
Abt. Kdr.	Stubaf. Pandel * 20.8.44	Hstuf. Krüger	Hstuf. Krüger (Stubaf. 20.4.45)

Unit	Invasion, 6.6.1944	Ardennes Offensive, 16.12.44	Hungary, 17.2.1945
Adjutant	Ustuf. Poetschke	Ostuf. Poetschke	
Verw. Fhr.	Ustuf. Schenking	Hstuf. Ferstl	Hstuf. Ferstl
Tr. Arzt	Oblt. Gurk * Juli 44		
Tr. Zahnarzt			
TFK			
TFN	Ustuf. Grothkop	Ustuf. Grothkop	Ostuf. Grothkop
1. (Fe) Kompanie, Chef	Ostuf. Dinglinger	Hstuf. Brauer	Hstuf. Brauer
2. (Fu) Kompanie, Chef	Hstuf. Krüger	Ostuf. Studier	Ostuf. Studier

SS-Panzerdivisionsnachschubtruppen 12

Unit	Invasion, 6.6.1944	Ardennes Offensive, 16.12.44	Hungary, 17.2.1945
Abt. Kdr.	Stubaf. Kolitz	Stubaf. Kolitz	Stubaf. Kolitz
Adjutant	Ustuf. Schlüter	Ostuf. Schlüter	Ostuf. Schlüter
Ord. Offz.	Ustuf. Rosin		
z.b.V.	Ostuf. Robel		
Verw. Fhr.	Ostuf. Rogler		
Tr. Arzt	Stabsant Schmidt		
Tr. Zahnarzt			
TFK	St.Ob.Jk. Heiermann		
1. Kraftf. Kompanie, Chef	Oblt. Weiß	Hstuf. Weiß	Hstuf. Weiß
2. Kraftf. Kompanie, Chef	Lt. Schäfer	Lt. Schäfer	Lt. Schäfer
3. Kraftf. Kompanie, Chef	Ustuf. Tiefengruber	Ustuf. Ewert	Ustuf. Ewert
4. Kraftf. Kompanie, Chef	Oblt. Müller	Ostuf. Hübner	Ostuf. Hübner
5. Kraftf. Kompanie, Chef	Ustuf. Bald	Ustuf. Bald	Ostuf. Bald
6. Kraftf. Kompanie, Chef	Ostuf. Althoff		
Nachschubkompanie, Chef	Ustuf. Reuter	Ostuf. Siedler	Ostuf. Siedler

Unit	Invasion, 6.6.1944	Ardennes Offensive, 17.2.1945 16.12.44	Hungary,

SS-Panzerinstandsetzungsabteilung 12

Unit	Invasion, 6.6.1944	Ardennes Offensive, 16.12.44	Hungary, 17.2.1945
Abt. Kdr.	Stubaf. Manthei	Stubaf. Manthei	Stubaf. Manthei
Adjutant	Ostuf. Kohlhagen	Ostuf. Kohlhagen	Ostuf. Kohlhagen
Ord. Offz.			
Verw. Fhr.	Ostuf. Laue		
Tr. Arzt	Ustuf. Dr. Schäfer	Ustuf. Dr. Schäfer	Ustuf. Dr. Schäfer
TFK			
1. Werkst. Kompanie, Chef	Hstuf. Magunna	Hstuf. Magunna	Hstuf. Magunna
2. Werkst. Kompanie, Chef	Hstuf. Sprick	Hstuf. Sprick	Hstuf. Sprick

Unit	Invasion, 6.6.1944	Ardennes Offensive, 16.12.44	Hungary, 17.2.1945
3. Werkst, Kompanie, Chef	Ostuf. Trinkhaus	Ostuf. Trinkhaus	Hstuf. Trinkhaus
4. (Waffen) Werkst.Kp., Chef		Hstuf. Klein	Hstuf. Klein Hstuf. Klein
5. (Ersatzteil) Kp., Chef	Hstuf. Löll	Hstuf. Löll	Hstuf. Löll
SS-Wirtschaftsbataillon 12			
Btl. Kdr.	Stubaf. Dr. Kos	Hstuf. Reichenbach	Hstuf. Reichenbach
Adjutant	Ustuf. Paschke	Ustuf. Paschke	Ustuf. Paschke
1. Mitarbeiter	Hstuf. Reichenbach	Hstuf. Stollhoff	Hstuf. Stollhoff
2. Mitarbeiter	Ustuf. Wunderlich	Ustuf. Krafft	Ustuf. Krafft
Verw. Fhr.	Ostuf. Hesse	Ostuf. Laue	Ostuf. Laue
Tr. Arzt	Ostuf. Dr. Klingler	Unterarzt Dr. Wüst	Unterarzt Dr. Wüst
Zahnarzt	Ostuf. Dr. Stadelmann		
TFK	Ustuf. Kunath	Ustuf. Kunath	Ustuf. Kunath
Bäckereikompanie, Chef	Ostuf, Schaksmeier	Ostuf. Schacksmeier	Ostuf. Schacksmeier
Schlächtereikompanie, Chef	Hstuf. Dr. Metsch	Hstuf. Dr. Kiehas	Hstuf. Dr. Kiehas
Div. Verpflegungsamt, Chef	Ostuf. Pischel	Ostuf. Pischel	Ostuf. Pischel
Feldpostamt, Leiter	Hstuf. Schlebusch	Hstuf. Schlebusch	Hstuf. Schlebusch
SS-Sanitätsabteilung 12			
Abt. Kdr.	Ostubaf. Dr. R. Schulz	Staf. Dr. R. Schulz	Staf. Dr. R. Schulz
Adjutant	Ustuf. Baierlein	Ostuf. Bunert	Ostuf. Bunert
Verw. Fhr.	Ostuf. Streit	Ostuf. Streit	
Div. Apotheker	Ostuf. Petry	Ostuf. Petry	Ostuf. Petry
TFK	Ostuf. Amend	Hstuf. Amend	Hstuf. Amend
1. Sanitätskompanie, Chef	Stubaf. Dr. Kirschner		
1. Hauptverbandsplatz-Zug	Hstuf. Dr. Triendl	Stubaf. Dr. Triendl	Stubaf. Dr. Triendl
2. Hauptverbandsplatz-Zug	Hstuf. Dr. App	Hstuf. Dr. App	Hstuf. Dr. App
2. Sanitätskompanie, Chef	Hstuf. Dr. Vieweg		
1. Hauptverbandsplatz-Zug	Hstuf. Dr. Dienstbach	Stubaf. Dr. Vieweg	Stubaf. Dr. Vieweg
2. Hauptverbandsplatz-Zug	Stabsarzt Dr. Oborny	Stabsarzt Dr. Oborny	Stabsarzt Dr. Oborny
Krankenkraftwagen-kompanie,	Ostuf. F. Müller	Ostuf. F. Müller	Ostuf. F. Müller

Unit	Invasion, 6.6.1944	Ardennes Offensive, 16.12.44	Hungary, 17.2.1945
Chef			
Versorgungskompanie, Chef		Ostuf. Knoll	Ostuf. Knoll

Feldersatzbataillon 12

Btl. Kdr.	Hstuf. Urabl		

Appendix 6

The Wartime Establishment of the German, British/Canadian, and US Armoured Divisions, and the British/Canadian and US Infantry Divisions, 1944

12.SS-Pz.Div."HJ"	Strength	Brit./Can. Panzerdivision	Strength	US-Panzerdivision	Strength
Divisionsstab	533	**Divisionsstab**	220	**Divisionsstab**	287
Panzerregiment 12	2.301	**Panzerbrigade**	2.817	**Combat Command A u. B**	
6 Pz III, 103 Pz IV, 81 Pz V		33 leichte Tanks, 193 mittlere Tanks,		Stab	
I. Panzerabteilung (Panther)		3 Tank-Regimenter		3 Tank Bataillone	je 184
II. Panzerabteilung (Pz IV)		1 Mot-Infanterie-Bataillon		159 mittlere Tanks	2187
Panzergrenadierregiment 25	3.316	**Infanteriebrigade**	2.944		
1 Kp.schw.Infanteriegeschütze		1.Kp.schw.Maschinengewehre			
1.Kp.2cm-Flak					
1 Kp.Aufklärer					
1 Kp.Pioniere					
3 Panzergrenadierbataillone mot		3 Infanteriebataillone mot		3 Infanteriebataillone gep.	3.000
Panzergrenadierregiment 26	3.316				
1.Kp.schw.Infantenegeschütze					
1.Kp.2cm-Flak					
1.Kp.Aufklärer					
1.Kp.Pioniere					
2 Panzergrenadierbataillone mot					
1 Panzergrenadierbataillon gep.					
Panzeraufklärungsabteilung 12	938	**Panzeraufklärungs-Regiment**	666	**Aufklärungs-Regiment**	931
11 Pz.Sp.Wg., 116 SPW		11 leichte Tanks, 61 mittlere Tanks		54 Pz-Späh-Wg.	
Panzerjägerabteilung 12	516	(siehe Divisionsartillerie)			
45 Panzerjäger IV					
Panzerartillerieregiment 12	2.499	**Divisions-Artillerie**		**Divisions-Artillerie**	
I. Abteilung gep.		1 Feldartillerie-Regiment			
12 le.F.H., 6 s.F.H. Selbstfahrlafetten		24 25pdr-Geschütze mot Z			
II. Abteilung mot Z		1 Artillerieregiment mot		3 Bataillone	
				45 10,5cm-Haubitzen	
				auf Selbstfahrlafetten	

12.SS-Pz.Div."HJ"	Strength	Brit./Can. Panzerdivision	Strength	US-Panzerdivision	Strength
Divisionsstab	533	Divisionsstab	220	Divisionsstab	287
18 le.F.H. III. Abteilung mot Z 12 s.F.H., 4 10cm Kan.		24 25pdr-Selbstfahrlafetten			
Werferabteilung 12 24 15cm-Nebelwerfer	ca. 675				
Flakabteilung 12 12 8.8 cm Flak 9 3,7 cm Flak	ca. 940	Flak-Regiment 54 40mm Flak			
		Anti Tank-Regiment 24 17pdr Pak mot Z 24 17pdr M10			
Panzerpionierbataillon 12	ca. 1050	Pionierbataillon	1000	Pionierbataillon	698
Panzernachrichtenabteilung 12	519	Nachrichten-Regiment	728	Nachrichten-Kompanie	302
Versorgungstruppen	2.490	Versorgungstruppen		Versorgungstruppen	1.372
Panzerdivisions-Nachschubtzuppen 12	976				
Panzer-Instandsetzungs-Abteilung 12	543				
Wirtschafubataillon 12	311				
Sanitätsabteilung 12	660				
kämpfende Truppe Versorgungstruppen	16.600 2.490				
Total Strength	19.090	Total Strength	14.964	Total Strength	10.668

12.SS-Pz.Div."HJ"	Strength	Brit./Can. Infanteriedivision	Strength	US-Infanteriedivision	Strength
Divisionsstab	533	Divisionsstab	220	Divisionsstab	287
		1 Infanteriebrigade	2.529	1 Infanterieregiment	3.562
		3 Schützenbataillone	je 821	1 Kp. Granatwerfer	
		1 Infanteriebrigade	2.529	1 Kp. Panzerabwehr	
		3 Schützenbataillone	je 821	3 Infanteriebataillone	je 1.014
		1 Infanteriebrigade	2.529	1 Infanterieregiment	3.562
		Schützenbataillone	je 821	wie oben	
				1 Infanterieregiment	3.562
				wie oben	
		Divisionsartillerie		Artillerieregiment	2.273
		3 Feldartillerie-Regimenter		3 Feldartillerie-Bataillone	
		je 24 25pdr-Geschütze		je 12 10,5cm Haubitzen	
		1 Anti Tank-Regiment		1 Mittleres Artilleriebataillon	
		32 17pdr Pak mot Z		12 15cm Haubitzen	
		1 Flak-Regiment			
		54 40mm Flak			
		Aufklärungsregiment	796	Aufklärungszug	149
		Pionierbataillon	1.000	Pionierbataillon	621
		Nachrichten-Regiment	728	Nachrichten-Kompanie	306
		Maschinengewehr-Bataillon	697		
		Versorgungstruppen		Versorgungstruppen	
		Total Strength	18.347	Total Strength	15.289

References

PART II
Chapter 5.4
1) War diary Supreme Command West, appendices from 1.8.–10.8.1944, pp. 78/79, F/M
2) War diary Panzergruppe West Ia, from 10.6.–8.8.1944
3) Study MS-B-012 by Oberst Neitzel: "89. Infanterie-division, Bewegungen nach dem Eintreffen in Frank-reich vor dem Einsatz an der Invasionsfront" (89. Infanteriedivision, movements after the arrival in France before the action at the invasion front), Research Institute for Military History, Freiburg (MH)
4) M. Dufresne, loc. cit., Cipher Message No. D/10/31
5) Stacy, loc. cit., p. 204 and following pages
6) M. Dufresne, loc. cit., 21st Army Group, M 516 of 4.8.1944
7) As 5), p. 209, and II Canadian Corps Operation Instruction No. 4 of 5.8.1944
8) As 6), M 715 of 6.8.1944
9) 53rd Infantry Division Intelligence Summary No. 37 until 6.8.1944 at 23.59 hours
10) XII Corps Operation Instruction No. 3, without date, and War Diary 53rd Infantry Division
11) Study B-256 of 1.10.1946 by Generalleutnant Dann-hauser: "Einsatz der 271. Infanteriedivision" (March-13 August 1944), and War Diary 34th Tank Brigade
12) Ellis, loc. cit., p. 411
13) Personal Report by Heinz Förster to the Author on 29.10.1978, report by Hermann Asbach to the Author on 6.12.1979, and War Diary 34th Tank Brigade
14) "Die Dritte Kompanie", loc. cit.
15) Report by Friedrich Heubeck to the Author on 6.6.1980
16) Lists of losses
17) As 2)
18) As 2)

Chapter 5.5
1) First Canadian Army Intelligence Summary No. 38 of 6.8.1944, quoted after Stacy, loc. cit., p. 214
2) War diary Panzer AOK 5, addendum to the daily report of 3.8.1944, and Report by Georg Isecke, loc. cit.
3) Stacy, pp. 215/216, and Outline of Instructions issued by GOC 4th Canadian Armoured Division of 7.8.1944, 13.00 hours

4) Allied Expeditionary Air Force Daily Intelligence Operations Summary No. 202 of 9.8.1944, quoted after Stacy

5) Study B-425, Oberst Neitzel: "89. Infanteriedivision in den Kämpfen an der Invasionsfront und während des Rückzuges auf den Westwall" (The 89. I.D. in the battles at the invasion front and during the withdrawal to the Westwall), part 1, Allendorf 1947

6) Stacy and Colonel Robert J. Icks in: "Truppendienst" (operational service), 4/1965

7) Stacy, p. 218, and as 5)

8) Study B-702, Generalleutnant Friedrich August Schack: "Die Kämpfe der 272. Infanteriedivision in Nordfrankreich vom 28. Juli bis 28. August 1944" (The battles of the 272. I.D. in Northern France from 28 July to 28 August 1944), and as 2), noon report of 8.8.1044, appendix 284, and evening report of 8.8.1944, appendix 285

9) Stacy, pp. 219/220

10) As 9)

11) As 9)

12) War diary Supreme Command West, appendices orders and reports from 1.8.–1.10.1944, daily report of 7.8.1944

13) Panzermeyer: "Grenadiere", 5th edition, pp. 281/282

14) Map from the possessions of Karl Vosloh, former member of 3. Batterie of Werferregiment 83, copy in the hands of the Author

15) Stacy, p. 222

16) As 15), pp. 222/223

17) Wladyslaw Dec "Narvik i Falaise", 1958 (translation by Hans Stöber)

18) Stacy, p. 223

19) As 18), p. 222

20) As 17), and Stacy pp. 223/224

21) As 20)

22) As 13), p. 228 and following pages

23) Report by Helmut Wiese to the Author on 19.11.1979

24) Stacy, p. 224

25) Letter from Dr. med. Wolfgang Rabe of 6.9.1979 to the Author

26) Report by Horst Borgsmüller to the Author on 8.2.1980

27) Report by Herbert Debusmann to the Author on 4.3.1980, and letters by Mr. M.D. of 5.1.1977 and Mr. S.V. of 16.10.1977 to the Author

28) Personal report by Willi Klein to the Author, and Stacy, p. 224

29) Unpublished history of SS-Werferabteilung 12

30) War diary Panzer AOK 5, part II from 9.8.1944 to Sept. 1944

31) As 30)

32) Personal report by Willi Klein to the Author

33) Front situation Supreme Command West, condition in the morning of 9.8.1944, and B-256, General-leutnant Dannhauser, sketch 10

34) As 33), and war diary Panzer AOK 5, appendix 1 of 9.8.1944

35) Study B-702, as 8)

36) Report by Bernhard Meitzel in: Canadian Army Journal, V4, April, May, June 1950 "Caen-Falaise" (translated by Frau Tekla Meitzel)

37) Stacy, pp. 225/226

38) Stacy, p. 228

39) As 17)

40) Stacy, p.228

41) Report by Leo Freund to the Author on 3.1.1977

42) Diary of the Divisionsbegleitkompanie, loc. cit.

43) As 8)

44) As 5)

45) Study B-256, Generalleutnant Dannhauser: "Einsatz der 271. Infanteriedivision, März bis 13. August 1944" of 1.10.1946

46) As 30), appendix 3 of 9.8.1944

47) As 46), appendix 3a

48) Stacy, pp. 229/230

49) As 13), p. 295, and report by Borgsmüller, loc. cit.

50) As 30), p. 6

51) Stacy, pp. 230/231

52) As 17)

53) Report by Walter Gömann to the Author on 12.3.1974

54) Diary of Helmut Zeiner, copy in the hands of the Author

55) Study B-846 by Oberstleutnant i.G. Schuster: "Aufstellung und Einsatz der 85. Infanteriedivision im Westen, Februar-November 1944" (Creation and action of the 85. Infanteriedivision in the west, February-November 1944), part II, May 1948

56) Letter from Paul Kamberger of 17.9.1977 to the -Author

57) Letter by Heinrich Peyers of 29.12.1965, copy in the hands of the Author

58) As 6)

59) Study B-528 by Generalleutnant Dannhauser, supplement to Study B-256, and war diary Panzer AOK 5, appendix 6, daily report of 10.8.1944

60) War diary Panzer AOK 5, appendix 6, daily report of 10.8.1944

61) As 60), appendix 9, noon report of 11.8.1944, and appendix 6a, addendum to the daily report of 10.8.1944

62) As 55)

63) As 60), appendix 11a, addendum to the daily report of 11.8.1944

64) Lists of losses

Chapter 5.6

1) 21st Army Group, M 518, General Operational Situation and Directive, M. Dufresne, loc. cit.

2) WFSt.Op(H) West, 3rd situation west of 12.8.1944, and Study B-529 be Generalleutnant Dannhauser

3) Studies by Oberstleutnant i.G. Kurt Schuhmacher: No. B-244 of 5.10.1946, B-424 of 15.3.1947, and B-864 of May 1948

4) As 3)

5) 4th Canadian Armoured Division, Outline of Instructions by GOC of 13.8.1944

6) II Canadian Corps Intelligence Summary No. 33 of 13.8.1944, Part I

7) Stacy, loc. cit., p. 237 and following pages, and 5)

8) As 5)

9) War diary Panzer AOK 5, appendix 14 of 12.8.1944

10) As 7), p. 238, and 3)

11) Diary of the Divisionsbegleitkompanie, and 3)

12) Diary of August Zinßmeister, copy in the hands of the Author

13) War diary Panzer AOK 5, Ia, part II from 9.8. to 9.9.1944, and of 13.8.1944

14) As 7), p. 240

15) As 7), pp. 240/241

16) Study B-702 by Generalleutnant Friedrich August Schack, commander of the 272. Inf.-Div.

17) As 7), pp. 240/241

18) As 7), p. 241

19) Studies B-528, 529, and addendum to Study B-256 by Generalleutnant Dannhauser

20) As 13)

21) As 16)

22) As 3)

23) As 19)

24) Blumenson: "The Patton Papers", pp. 508/509

25) As 7), p. 249, and diary of the Divisionsbegleit-kompanie

26) Will Fey, manuscript for: "Panzer im Brennpunkt der Schlachten" (Panzers in the focal points of the battles)

27) Combat report of 2./Schwere Panzerabteilung 102, copy in the hands of the Author

28) Panzermeyer: "Grenadiere", pp. 300/301

29) as 3)

30) Wladyslaw Dec: "Narvik i Falaise" (translation by Hans Stöber)

31) As 16)

32) As 19)

33) As 13)

34) As 9), appendix 23

35) As 3)

36) As 7), pp. 249/250

37) As 30)

38) As 16)

39) As 9), appendix 27

40) Report by Horst Borgsmüller to the Author on 7.5.1980

41) As 39)

42) II Canadian Corps Intelligence Summary of 16.8.1944

43) As 17) and as 9), appendix 27

44) War diary Supreme Command West, Ia orders and reports from 11.9. to 20.8.1944, teletype message to OKW of 16.8.1944

45) As 9), appendix 24

46) As 44), appendices Ia No. 726/44 g.K. chiefs

47) As 9), appendix 27

48) As 47)

49) As 16)

50) As 7), p. 250, and Dr. Paul German: "Histoire de Falaise", Falaise 1966, p. 288

51) Dr. Paul German, and War Diary 6th Canadian Infantry Brigade of 16.8.1944

52) As 27)

53) War Diary 6th Canadian Infantry Brigade of 16.8.1944

54) Report by Heinrich Bassenauer to the Author on 29.7.1975

55) Report by Leo Freund to the Author on 3.1.1977

56) As 53)

57) As 50), p. 294

58) As 50), pp. 293/294

59) As 50), p. 296, and as 53)

60) As 11)

61) As 27)

62) As 53)

63) As 50), p. 297

64) As 53

65) As 50), p. 297

66) As 53)

67) As 28), p. 303

68) Various reports by Paul Hinsberger to the Author

69) AS 53)

70) Eversley, Belfield and Essame: "The Battle for -Normandy", London 1965, p. 212

71) As 53)

72) II. Canadian Corps Intelligence Summary No. 35 of 16.8.1944

73) Diary of the Divisionsbegleitkompanie

74) Report by Alfred Schulz to the Author on 16.11.1977

75) As 27)

76) As 73)

77) Study B-536 by Oberst Neitzel, loc. cit.

78) As 19)

79) Study B-631 by Generalmajor Feuchtinger, with dates corrected by Werner Kortenhaus

80) J. Kamar: "Sladami gasieniec pierswszej Diwitzji -panvernej" (Following in the tracks of the 1st Polish Tank Division), p. 104, (translated into German by Hans Stöber)

81) As 79)

82) As 7), p. 252, and War Diary 4th Canadian -Armoured Brigade

83) As 13), p.19

84) As 83), and appendix 31

85) As 83), appendix 34

86) Report by Leo Freund to the Author on 3.1.1977

87) As 73), and 27)

88) As 30)

89) As 7), and map 5 in 7)

90) Reports by Karl Kolb of 1954 and by Kurt Göricke of 6.10.1980 to the Author

91) As 83), appendix 35

92) As 7), p. 259, and map Op(H) 4th situation west of 18.8.1944

93) As 79), letter by Eberhard Köpke of 20.10.1946 to St., copy in the hands of the Author, and personal report by Willy Klein to the Author

94) Report by Fritz Freitag, loc. cit.

95) Report by Leo Freund to the Author on on 3.1.1977

96) "Normandy-Battle of the Falaise Gap", loc. cit.

97) As 27)

98) Report by Hans Krieg of March 1977, copy in the hands of the Author

99) As 7), p. 259

100) As 99)

101) As 73)
102) As 30)
103) Report 90th Us Infantry Division 182300B of August 1944
104) Général de Langlade: "En suivant Leclerc" (Following Leclerc), Paris, no year given, pp. 178/179
105) As 104), p. 180 and following pages
106) Study A-923 by General der Flieger Meindl
107) As 106)

Chapter 5.7

1) Study A-923, General der Flieger Meindl
2) Tieke: "Feuersturm", loc. cit., pp. 267/268
3) Reconstructed war diary 2. SS-Panzerdivision "Das Reich", and report by Heinz Werner
4) Report by Leo Freund to the Author on 3.1.1977
5) Report by Theodor Waischat to the Author on 2.9.1979
6) Report by Willy Kretzschmar to the Author on 5.11.1979
7) Report by Willy Schnittfinke to the Author on 16.12.1979
8) Letter by Karl Musch of 3.10.1973 to the Author
9) Report by Max Anger to the Author on 19.6.1975
10) Verbal report by Hugo Kraas to the Author on 12.4.1977
11) Note by Oberstgruppenführer Paul Hausser of 1952, archives of the MUNIN-Verlag, Osnabrück
12) Reports by Günter Neumann of 5.4.1977, Hans Hartmann and Christian Graen of 9.4.1980 to the Author
13) Letter from Werner Halbroth to Frau Pandel of 19.11.1947, copy in the hands of the Author
14) Deutsche Dienststelle, Berlin
15) As 1)
16) Report by Fritz Freitag to Max Wünsche of 1980, copy in the hands of the Author
17) Report by Max Wünsche to the Author on 22.1.1980
18) Evaluation of the lists of losses by Wolfgang Lüdicke
19) War diary Panzer AOK 5 from 10.6.–8.8.1944, -appendix 158
20) 21st Army Group, General Operational Situation M 517 of 6.8.1944, and Situation Map 12th Army Group of 19.8.1944, 21st Army Group, M 518 of 11.8.1944, M. Dufresne
21) 12th Army Group, Letter of Instructions No. 5 of 17.8.1944, M. Dufresne
22) Report by Czarnecke to M. Dufresne

Section 6

1) Study MS-A-922 by General der Panzertruppen Eberbach: "Panzergruppe Eberbach bei Alençon und beim Durchbruch aus dem Kessel von Falaise" (Panzergruppe Eberbach near Alençon and during the break-out from the Falaise encirclement)
2) Stöber, Hans: "Die Sturmflut und das Ende" (The tidal wave and the end), Osnabrück 1976

3) 21st Army Group, General Operational Situation and Directive M 519 of 20.8.1944
4) Report by Harro Lübbe to the Author on 27.8.1978
5) Letter by Eberhard Köpke of 20.10.1946 to H.St., copy in the hands of the Author
6) Report by Hans Siegel to the Author of 14.10.1979
6a) War diary Heeresgruppe B of 21.8.1944, F/M, RH19/19 IX-88
7) War diary 5. Panzerarmee from 9.8.–9.9.1944, appendix 44, F/M
8) As 7), appendix 36
9) As 7), appendix 41
10) Diary of August Zinßmeister, copy in the hands of the Author
11) As 7)
12) As 8)
13) As 10)
14) Report by Emile Maître to the Author of 8.11.1971
15) As 7)
16) Letter from Harro Lübbe of 27.12.1979 to the Author
17) War diary 5. Panzerarmee of 24.8.1944
18) As 7)
19) As 17), 25.8.1944
20) As 10)
21) Diary of Paul Baier, copy in the hands of the Author
22) Report by Karl Leitner to the Author on 1.6.1977

Section 7

1) War diary Panzer AOK 5, Ia, part II from 9.8.–9.9.1944, p. 35, and appendix 47 of 25.8.1944, F/M
2) Diary of the Divisionsbegleitkompanie
3) As 1), appendix 56 of 27.8.1944, and as 2)
4) As 1), appendix 58 of 28.8.1944
4a) 9.11.1944, promotion to SS-Brigadeführer and General-major der Waffen-SS, with an effective date of 1.9.1944
5) Report from 12. SS-Panzerdivision to General-inspekteur (chief of staff) der Panzertruppen of 4.9.1944
6) Report by Hans Kesper to the Author on 14.7.1977
7) Report by Heinz Berger to the Author on 20.3.1980
8) War diary Heeresgruppe B of 30. and 31.8.1944, and map front situation of 30.8.1944; personal report by Dr. H. Jarczyk; lists of losses
9) Diary of August Zinßmeister, copy in the hands of the Author
10) War diary Divisionsbegleitkompanie, and report by Hermann Buchmann to the Author on 1.10.1979; information on days of close combat of the I./25 based on the pay-book of Willi Klein
10a) Reports by Dr. H. Jarczyk and members of the III./26
11) Stamp of the customs office Hestrud in the Author's pay-book
12) As 9)
13) Report by Hermann Buchmann, see 10)
14) As 2)
15) Report by Leo Freund to the Author on 26.2.1977

16) Diary of Hermann Laudenbach, copy in the hands of the Author
17) As 9)
18) As 8), F/M, RH19 IX/89
19) As 2), lists of losses I./25, II./26; letter by General-major retd. Heinz Guderian of 28.7.1980 to the -Author; letter by Franz X. Pfeffer of 20.1.1980 to the Author; map front situation of 4.9.1944 evening
20) As 9), letter by Günter Neumann of 22.6.1978 to the Author
20a) War diary Heeresgruppe B, appendix operation orders, teletype messages, F/M, RH19 IX/5; the Panther mentioned in this report was no longer with the Divisional Kampfgruppe on 4.9.1944
21) Letter by Eberhard Köpke of 20.10.1946 to St., copy in the hands of the Author
22) As 2)
23) As 8), and frontal situation of 4.9.44 evening
24) M 160 TOPSEC Personal to Eisenhower and Eyes Only from Montgomery of 4.9.1944
25) Chester Wilmot, loc. cit., p. 513
26) Report of Operations of the 9th US Infantry Division of 1.10.44 for the period from 1 to 30.9.1944, -National Archives, Washington
27) As 1), 4.9.1944
28) As 15)
29) As 9)
30) As 1) and 8)
31) Report by Teo Flanderka to the Author on 22.6.1982
32) As 2)
33) As 9)
33a) Letter from Rudolf von Ribbentrop of 22.10.1979 to the Author
34) Panzermeyer: "Grenadiere", Munich 1965, p. 315 and following pages
35) Verbal reports by former members of the Aufklärungs-abteilung to the Author
36) As 34), p. 319 and following pages
37) As 15)
38) As 21
39) As 2)
40) As 8), 6.9.1944
41) Letter from Karl-Heinz Milius of 26.11.1979; Report by Günter Neumann p. 20; Report by Alfred Dosenbach of 26.2.1976 to the Author, Klietmann: "Die Waffen-SS", Osnabrück 1965
42) Report by Alfred Dosenbach, and letter from K.H. Milius, p. 41
43) Lists of losses, and evaluation by Wolfgang Lüdecke, April 1969

PART III
Chapter 8.1
1) SS-Führungshauptamt, Amt II, Org.Abt. Ia/II, diary No. 3037/44, g.K. of 13.9.1944
2) As 1), diary No. 3250/44, g.K. of 22.9.1944
3) Notes of Sturmmann Paul Baier, 4. Batterie Flak-abteilung 12, and action report II./26, copies in the hands of the Author
4) As 3)
5) As 1), diary No. 3486/44, g.K. of 14.10.1944

6) War diary of the III./SS-Pz.-Gren.-Rgt. 25 for the period from 17.11. to 16.12.1944, copy in the hands of to the Author

7) Activity report of the II./SS-Pz.-Gren.-Rgt. 26 for the period of 3.9. to 5.12.1944, copy in the hands of the Author

8) As 7)

9) Letter by Z. of 7.4.1978 to the Author

10) Letter from Untersturmführer X of 19.9.1944, copied by the Author

11) Personal Report by Untersturmführer Willi Klein to the Author, and statement by Wolfgang Vopersal

12) According to file-card OKW diary No. I/20078 g.K. of 20.10.1944, copy in Vopersal working archives

Chapter 8.2

1) Questionnaire Generalfeldmarschall Keitel and Generaloberst Jodl, MS-A-928 of 20.7.1945

2) War diary Generaloberst Jodl of 9.10.1944; war diary OKW, IV/1., p. 432 and following pages

3) Büchs: "Die Ardennenoffensive", Study MS-K 977, p. 35

4) Appendix 2 of Chef WFST. No. 20/44, g.K. chiefs, of 1.11.1944

5) War diary Supreme Command West, Ia No. 00108/44, g.K. chiefs, of 3.11.1944

6) Monograph by the chief of the general staff of Heeresgruppe B, General der Infanterie Krebs, Ia 0008/44, g.K. chiefs of 5.11.1944

7) Supreme Command of the Wehrmacht No. 31/44, g.K. chiefs St.WFST/Op(h); regarding "Wacht am Rhein" (watch on the Rhine), of 10.11.1944

8) Supreme Command West, Ia, No. 00121/44 g.K. chiefs of 11.11.1944

9) Supreme Command Heeresgruppe B, Ia, No. 0051/44 g.K. chiefs of 20.11.1944

10) OKW/WFST/Op(H) No. 774185/44 g.K. chiefs of 22.11.1944

11) General der Panzertruppen Hasso von Manteuffel: "Die Schlacht in den Ardennen 1944/1945" (The battle in the Ardennes); in "Entscheidungsschlachten des Zweiten Weltkrieges" (Decisive battles of the Second World War), p. 537 and following pages

12) Appendix to Supreme Command Heeresgruppe B, Ia, No. 0180/44 g.K. chiefs

12a) As 12)

13) Heeresgruppe B, Ia, No. 0180/44 g.K. chiefs, appendices 1 and 2

14) As 13)

15) According to index, OKW diary No. I/20411 of 6.11.1944, loc. cit.

15a) According to index, OKW I/20632 g.K. of 17.11.1944

15b) As 15a), I/21036 g.K. of 17.11.1944

16) Activity report II./26; war diary III./25; notes by Sturmmann Baier, 4./Flak-Abt. 12, loc. cit.

17) Preparatory study by Brigadeführer Kraas of 6.8.1945 and of 1.5.1947

17a) Letter bei Hein Springer of 13./14.8.1980 to the -Author

18) Study by Standartenführer Rudolf Lehmann, B-577; and preparatory study by Brigadeführer Kraas of 1.5.1947

19) See also frontal situation Supreme Command West of 13, 14, and 15 December 1944

19a) Letter from Rudolf Lehmann of 13.7.1982 to the Author

19b) Tessin: "Verbände und Truppen der deutschen Wehrmacht und Waffen-SS" (Units and troops of the German armed forces and the Waffen-SS); study B-

273, Generalmajor Wilhelm Viebig: "Einsatz der 277. Volksgrenadierdivision im November und Dezember 1944" (Action by the 277. Volksgrenadierdivision in November and December 1944)

19c) Study by Standartenführer Rudolf Lehmann B-577

19d) Study Lehmann, loc. cit.

20) The following maps were used to examine the evaluation, at the time, of the road conditions and to describe them: general map of Central Europe 1:300,000, sheet J 51 Aachen, edition 1940; map of the German Reich 1:100,000, sheet 107a, issue 1940, and topographical map 1:25,000 Kreis (county) Schleiden of 1949; map of Belgium 1:100,000 No. X Malmedy of 1940.

The course of the advance routes is taken from a sketch by SS-Gruppen-führer and Generalleutnant der Waffen-SS Hermann Prieß, commanding general I. SS-Panzerkorps, which is an attachment to Manuscript No. A-877 "Commitment of I. SS-Panzerkorps During the Ardennes Offensive (16 December 1944–25 January 1945)" (National Archives and Records Office, Modern Military Branch, Military Archives Division). It cannot be determined on what documentation this information is based. In the interview with General-major Kraemer—see 24)—the course of the routes is given in broad outlines. The interview indicates that a captured German map was available at the time, but the map is not identified. On the basis of a comparison of the details on roads, it can be assumed that it was a map 'situation France OKW-West Op(H) West'. The marking of the advance routes on those OKW maps vary, in part, considerable from the information provided by SS-Gruppenführer Prieß. The routes point farther to the northwest in the western section. Route A leads from Camp Elsenborn via Mont Rigi in the direction of Verviers—instead to Sart—and, thus, toward the Maas sector north of Liège, which was expressly forbidden to Panzer units and was, in addition, outside the sector of the I. SS-Panzerkorps. On the OKW map, Routes B and C between Bütgenbach and Belair are drawn separated, but, in reality, together. The same is true for Routes D and E in Trois Ponts. That would be unreasonable and would certainly not conform with the planning. Hence, we consider the information provided by Prieß as probably the correct one.

As well, there are differences on the two maps regarding the dividing line between the two Armees. According to Prieß, Vielsam belonged to the 6. Panzerarmee, according to the OKW, it belonged to the 5. Panzerarmee. Since it is certain that St. Vith was located in the sector of the 5. Panzerarmee, it appears logical that Vielsam was also. While, on the OKW map, Advance Route ran partly to the north, partly to the south of the dividing line between the two Armees, it cannot be ruled out that Vielsam could be used by the I. SS-Panzerkorps, at least after agreement was obtained, in particular since the LXVI. A.K., adjacent to the left, had not assigned a Panzer unit to the 5. Panzerarmee.

21) Study B-273, Generalmajor Wilhelm Viebig, loc. cit.

22) Study by Obersturmbannführer Hubert Meyer: "Die 12. SS-Panzerdivision 'Hitlerjugend' in der Ardennenoffensive Winter 44/45"

23) As 19b)

24) Ethint 21, Interview with Generalmajor Fritz Kraemer, 6. Panzerarmee, 16 November 1944–4 January 1945; conducted by 1st Lt. Robert G. Merriam on 14 and 15 August 1945; Generalmajor retd. Professor Freiherr von der Heydte:

"Der letzte deutsche Sprungeinsatz" (The last German paratroop action), in "Zwischen den Fronten" (Between the fronts), war diary of the Kreis (county) Monschau, Monschau 1959, p. 252 and following pages

25) Ethint 65, 69, 75; interview with Obersturmbann-führer Otto Skorzeny, Oberursel 1945

26) Ethint-21; interview with Generalmajor Kraemer (refer to 24)

27) As 25)

28) Appendix 17 to General der Panzertruppen West, Ia No. 1775/44 g.K. of 19.12.1944, Division 'Hitler-jugend', condition on 8.12.1944

29) Report by 12. SS-Panzerdivision "Hitlerjugend" concerning the level of refitting, appendix to Ia 1406/44 g.K. of 1.12.1944; inventory chief of staff of the Panzer forces 001534/44 g.K.

29a) Hermann Jung: "Die Ardennen-Offensive 1944 und 1945", Göttingen 1971

30) Letter from Karl H. Brockschmidt of March 1977 to the Author

31) As 17a)

32) Report by Brigadeführer Hugo Kraas, recorded by his brother, Helmut Albert Kraas, on 12.4.1978

33) Helmut Heiber: "Lagebesprechungen im Führerhauptquartier" (Discussions on the situation in the Führer headquarters), Berlin-Darmstadt, Wien 1963, p. 281 and following pages

Chapter 8.3

1) Handwritten notes of an officer of Artillerieregiment 12 of August 1945 in Kleinmünchen Camp near Linz, from the estate of the Divisional commander Hugo Kraas

2) Study by Standartenführer Rudolf Lehmann of May 1947, copy of the draft in the hands of the Author, p. 7

3) As 1)

4) War diary No. 2, III./SS-Panzergrenadierregiment 25, started on 17.11.1944, concluded on 16.12.1944; original in F/M, microfilm in the hands of the Author

5) Marching order office field post number 59572 E of 13.12.1944, in the possession of Sturmmann Paul Baier, 4./Flak 12; copy in the hands of the Author

6) "Die 3. Kompanie SS-Panzer-Regiment 12, 12. SS-Panzerdivision 'Hitlerjugend'", Pr.-Oldendorf 1978, pp. 74/75

7) As 4)

8) Diary of August Zinßmeister, copy in the hands of the Author

9) Interview with Brigadeführer Fritz Kraemer, chief of staff of 6. SS-Panzerarmee on 14. and 15,8.1945, conducted by 1st Lt. Robert E. Merriam; Ethint 21

10) Study by Standartenführer Rudolf Lehmann, part II, p. 9, loc. cit.

11) War diary Supreme Command West from 1.12.– 31.12.1944, p. 49

12) As 11), p. 54

13) As 11), p. 56

14) War diary Supreme Command West, front situation as on 13.12.1944, scale 1:1,000,000

15) Map 'enemy situation' of 15.12.1944, 20.00 hours; F/M, RH19 IX/34K

16) MacDonald, Charles B.: "The Siegfried Line Campaign"; Office of the Chief of Military History, United States Army, Washington, D.C., p. 596 and following pages

17) As 16), p. 598 and following pages
18) As 16), p. 603 and following pages
19) As 16), p. 607
20) As 16), p. 607 and following pages; "Combat History of the Second Infantry Division in World War II", The Battery Press, Nashville, reprint of 1979, p. 82 and following pages
21) War diary Supreme Command West from 1.12.– 31.12.1944, p. 56
22) Cole: "Battle of the Bulge", Office of the Chief of Military History, United States Army, Washington, D.C., p. 59 and following pages

Chapter 8.4

1) War diary Supreme Command West, appendices orders and reports from 11.12.–20.12.1944; F/M, RH19 IV/84 D, Ia, No. 10697/44 geheim (secret)
2) "Die 3. Kompanie", loc. cit., p. 77
3) Study by Standartenführer Rudolf Lehmann, loc. cit., 15/16 December 1944
4) Interview Brigadeführer Fritz Kraemer, Ethint 21, loc. cit.; Study by Standartenführer Lehmann, loc. cit., of 16.12.1944
5) Studies by Generalmajor Viebig, B-237, 1.; General-leutnant Engel, B-733, "Die Ardennenoffensive in der Zeit vom 16. Dezember bis 29. Dezember 1944" (The Ardennes offensive during the period from 16 to 29 December 1944), Neustadt 1947
6) Personal information from Karl Bartling to the Author on 28.8.1980
7) As 1), p. 62
8) Study by Generalleutnant Engel, loc. cit.
9) 393rd Infantry Regiment, After Action Report of 4 January 1945, National Archives 407–399 JNF (393)-0.3–10165, p. 2
9a) Cole, loc. cit., p. 96
10) As 9), p. 4
11) As 8), pp. 2/3
12) Study by Generalmajor Viebig, loc. cit.
13) As 12)
14) As 3), 4), and 8)
14a) As 3)
15) As 1), p. 137
16) War diary No. 2, III./SS-Panzergrenadierregiment 25 from 17.11.–16.12.1944
16a) According to the report from Alfons Ott to the Author on 30.3.1980
17) As 8), and Cole, loc. cit. (According to the study by Generalleutnant Engel, Füsilier Regiment 27 had reached the edge of the forest 1 km east of Honsfeld in the evening. We are using here the information from Cole who also had other sources available)
18) As 8)
19) As 8)
20) As 1), p. 156 and 163 respectively, F/M, RH19 IV/84
21) Cole, loc. cit., p. 86
22) As 3)
23) Cole, loc. cit., pp. 90/91
24) Lt. Mitteilung Alfons Ott report to the Author on 30.3.1980
25) Omitted
26) Omitted

27) As 1)

28) Report by Ernst Stuhr, 7./25, to the Author on 8.3.1980

28a) Report on strength and losses II./25, F/M, RS3–12/35

29) From Ernst Stuhr's documents regarding his wounds

30) Concerning the mortars, see Cole, loc. cit., p. 97, also, the result of a battlefield tour in 1977

31) Report by H. Brockschmidt to the Author on 2.7.1977

32) Report by Helmut Heiner to the Author on 25.12.1976

33) As 31)

34) Report by Richard Schulze-Kossens to the Author on 13.9.1970

35) Cole, loc. cit., p. 97

36) As 9), p. 4, and Cole, loc. cit., p. 98

37) Cole, loc. cit., pp. 98/99

38) As 9), p. 4

39) Cole, loc. cit., p. 99

40) As 9), p. 3

41) Cole, loc. cit., pp. 100/101

42) Cole, loc. cit.

43) Unit Journal 9th Infantry, 17.12.1944

44) Cole, loc. cit., p. 111

45) Journal 38th Infantry, 17 December 1944

46) Journal 38th Infantry, 17 December 1944

47) After Action report 38th Infantry, 7 January 1945, p. 4

48) As 47), p. 4

49) As 26a)

50) Cole, loc. cit., pp. 91/92

51) Cole, loc. cit., pp. 265/266

52) Cole, loc. cit., p. 93

53) Oberstleutnant retd. Professor von der Heydte: "Der letzte deutsche Sprungeinsatz" in "Zwischen den -Fronten", Monschau 1959

54) As 43) of 17.12.1944, p. 2

54a) 18th Infantry After Action Report, December 1944, p. 2

54b) War diary Supreme Command West, noon report of 19.12.1944, p. 2 (p. 238)

55) As 53)

55a) After Action reports for December 1944, 26th Infantry Regiment, pp. 2/3; 18th Infantry Regiment, pp. 1/2; 16th Infantry Regiment, p. 2

56) As 42) of 17.12.1944, p. 3

57) Cole, loc. cit., p. 113

58) As 32)

58a) Letter by Benno Zoll of 12.12.1977 to the Author

58b) As 58)

59) Report by Götz Großjohann to the Author on 8.8.1980

60) Cole, loc. cit., p. 116, and as 47), p. 5

61) "Die 3. Kompanie, SS-Panzerregiment 12", loc. cit., pp. 87/88

62) Report by Max Söllner of 8.8.1980, copy in the hands of the Author

63) Report by Hannes Simon of August 1980, original in the hands of the Author

64) Cole, loc. cit., p. 117

65) As 61), p. 89 and following pages

66) Cole, loc. cit., p. 115

67) Cole, loc. cit., p. 105
68) As 47) of 18 December 1944
69) As 8), and "Schwungvoller Angriff bleibt stecken. Die Panzerjäger 12 bei der Ardennenoffensive" (Bold attack stalls. Panzerjäger 12 during the Ardennes offensive), magazine "Alte Kameraden" (Old comrades), December 1982, by Major retd. Holz
70) Report by Major retd. Holz, see 69)
71) As 1), p. 231; daily report of 18.12.1944
72) As 70)
73) As 1), p. 231
74) As 46) of 19 December 1944
75) As 61), p. 88
76) As 62)
77) "Panzerangriff ohne Infanterie auf zwei Ortschaften" (Panzer attack without infantry on two villages), in "Wehrausbildung in Wort und Bild" (Military instruction in word and picture), 12/72, pp. 569/570
77a) As 1), p. 238, noon report of 19.12.1944
78) As 46) of 19 December 1944
79) Report by Heinz Nußbaumer, 6. Kompanie, Panzerregiment 12, to the Author on 5.8.1980
80) As 9), p. 8; as 47), p. 6; Cole, loc. cit., pp. 125/126

Chapter 8.5

1) War diary Supreme Command West from 1.12.–31.12.1944; 19.12.1944: morning report, appendices 1564 and 1571, F/M, RH19 IV/84 D
1a) Cole, loc. cit., and letter from Ralph G. Hill Jr. of 12.3.1981 to the Author, published in "The Checkerboard", Rootstown, Ohio, January 1982
2) After Action Report 26th Infantry Regiment, 1st US Infantry Division, pp. 2/3, National Archives, Washington
3) Cole, loc. cit., p. 128
4) Map "Lage Frankreich" (situation in France), OKW/WFSt. Op(H) West, and war diary Supreme Command West, appendices orders and reports from 11.–20.12.1944, p. 220, F/M
5) Diary of August Zinßmeister, copy in the hands of the Author
6) As 1), p. 232
7) Report by Erwin Dittmann during the battlefield tour on 2.2.1980
8) Report by Günther Burdack in February 1977 to the Author
9) Report on losses of the III./26 to Deutsche Dienststelle of 5.1.1945
10) Letter from Günter Neumann of 23.3.1980
11) As 1), p. 265
12) As 1), p. 273 and following pages
13) As 2), pp. 4/5
14) As 1), pp. 288, 295, 307, 308
14a) Report on losses Schwere Panzerjägerabteilung 560
14b) As 3)
14c) Notes by Dr. Wolfgang Loenicker, excerpt copy in the hands of the Author
15) As 3a)
16) After Action Report 18th Infantry, December 1944, p. 3, National Archives, Washington

17) After Action Report 16th Infantry, December 1944, National Archives, Washington
18) Report by an unnamed artillery commander, from the estate of Brigadeführer Hugo Kraas, copy in the hands of the Author
19) Cole, loc. cit., p. 131
20) "Die 3. Kompanie/SS-Panzerregiment 12", Preußisch-Oldendorf 1978, p. 86 and following pages
21) Letter by Heinz Müller of 17.6.1980 to the Author
22) Letter by Willy Kretzschmar of 27.10.1980 to the Author
23) Letter by Karl Leitner of 1.6.1977 to the Author
24) Omitted
25) As 2), p. 5
26) Cole, loc. cit., pp. 131/132
27) War diary Supreme Command West from 21.12.– 28.12.1944, appendices, pp. 17/18
28) As 27), pp. 22/23
29) Journal 26th Infantry of 22 December 1944, and as 16)
30) Report by Günther Burdack, as 8)
30a) As 8)
30b) Study by Generalleutnant Engel, loc. cit.
31) As 9)
32) As 27), p. 62
33) As 27), pp. 87, 93, 106, 125

Chapter 8.6

1) War diary Supreme Command West from 1.12.– 31.12.1944, p. 107
2) As 1), p. 108
3) Report by August Zinßmeister, manuscript in the hands of the Author
4) Report by Dr. Wolfgang Loenicker on 18.11.1980; excerpts from his pocket calendar
5) Diary of the Divisionsbegleitkompanie, p. 19
6) As 3)
7) Diary notes by Oberscharführer Heinz Thomas, copy in the hands of the Author
8) As 4)
9) War diary II./26 from 14.12.1944–8.5.1945
10) Study by Standartenführer Lehmann, loc. cit., pp. 22/23
11) As 1), p. 112
12) As 1), p. 115
13) The development of the overall situation between 22 and 26 December 1944 is also described with the war diary of Supreme Command West and its appendices as a basis
14) As 1), p. 116
15) W. Tieke: "Im Feuersturm letzter Kriegsjahre", Osnabrück 1975, p. 435 and following pages
15a) War diary Supreme Command West, appendices from 27.12.–31.12.1944, p. 3; addendum to the noon report Heeresgruppe B of 27.12.1944 and p. 16; evening report of 27.12.1944
16) As 15a)

17) Study by Generalmajor Rudolf Langhäuser, MS No. B 027 of 15.5.1946: "560. V.G.D. und 12. V.G.D.; Angriffs- und Abwehrschlacht in den Ardennen vom 16.12.1944 bis 17.1.1945" (560. V.G.D. and 12. V.G.D.; attack and defense in the Ardennes from 16.12.1944 to 17.1.1945)

18) As 16), pp. 16 and 25

19) "Spearhead in the West", history of the 3rd US Armored Division, p. 227

20) As 16), additionally p. 25

20a) Weidinger, Otto: "Division Das Reich", volume V, Osnabrück, based on the manuscript

21) Report by Werner Damsch to the Author on 9.6.1980

22) Report by Richard Schulze-Kossens to the Author on 13.9.1970

23) As 19), p. 227

24) As 19), p. 228

25) As 21), and results of a battlefield tour on 5.9.1981

25a) As 20a)

26) As 16), pp. 39, 44, 48, 49

27) War diary II./26, loc. cit.

28) Report by Günther Burdack to the Author in April 1974

29) As 19), p. 228

30) As 16), pp. 58, 73, 77, 78

31) As 17)

32) As 16), p. 103

33) As 5), p. 20

Chapter 8.7

1) OKW, order for the initial and final assembly for the attack of 10 November 1944; No. 31/44 g.K. chiefs WFSt/Op(H), item 3b)

2) Appendices to the war diary Supreme Command West from 21.12.–26.12.1944, p. 122; report by the chief of the general staff Heeresgruppe B of 24.12.1944

3) War diary Supreme Command West from 1.12.– 31.12.1944, pp. 113/114

4) as 3), p. 116

5) Appendices to the war diary Supreme Command West from 27.12.–31.12.1944, p. 25; daily report of 27.12.1944

6) As 5), pp. 44 and 49; evening and daily report of 28.12.1944

7) As 5), p. 38, Supreme Command West: Ia No. 12309/44 g.K.

8) As 5), p. 78, daily report of 29.12.1944

9) As 5), p. 98, evening report of 30.12.1944

10) As 5), pp. 102/103, daily report of 30.12.1944

11) As 3), p. 113

12) As 3), p. 139

13) ??

14) As 5), p. 113; briefing on the situation by Heeresgruppe B on 31.12.1944, 12.15 hours and p. 123: daily report of 31.12.1944

15) War diary II./26 from 14.12.1944–8.5.1945, p. 10

16) As 15), pp. 9/10

17) Combat Record Sixth Armored Division, p. 145

18) As 17), p. 147

19) Cole, loc. cit., pp. 628/629

20) Cole, loc. cit., pp. 629/630

21) Study by Standartenführer Lehmann, loc. cit.

22) War diary Divisionsbegleitkompanie, p. 20

23) As 15), p. 10

24) The 68th Tank Battalion in Combat, The National Archives, record group No. 407–606TK(68)-9, p. 30

25) AAR Combat Command B, 1–31 January 1945, -National Archives, record group No. 407–606–CCB-0.3 p. 3

26) Cole, loc. cit., p. 633; AAR 50th Armored Infantry Battalion, National Archives, record group No. 407–606Inf.(50)-0.3, and as 22), p. 20

27) As 24), pp. 30/31

28) 69th Tank Battalion, Summary of Operations 1–31 January 1945, National Archives, record group No. 407–606TK(69)-0.3, p. 1

29) As 13), p. 633

30) As 21) The date of 4 January 1944 mentioned in the Study is probably a lapse of memory. See also the Study by Oberstleutnant i.G. Hans Voigt (340.V.G.D.), loc. cit.

31) CG VIII Corps, 2 January 1945, 18,30,F01; National Archives record group No. 407, Office of the Adjutant General, WWII Operations Reports, 3101–0.8 Journal File 18 December 1944–April 1945, Box 14338

32) Tieke: "Im Feuersturm letzter Kriegsjahre", Osnabrück 1975, pp. 441/442

33) AAR VIII Corps, National Archives, record group No. 407, Office of the Adjutant General, WWII Operations Reports 3101–0.8 Journal File 18 December 1944–April 1945, Box 14338

34) As 32)

35) Study by Oberstleutnant i.G. Hans Voigt, first general staff officer V.G.D., B-678 of 1.11.1947

36) Report by Günther Burdack, 9./26, of February 1977, manuscript in the hands of the Author

37) As 15), p. 11

38) As 15), p. 12

39) As 15), p. 12

40) As 15), pp. 12 and 36

41) Report by Ewald Rien, 7./26, manuscript in the hands of the Author

42) AAR 50th Armored Infantry Battalion, compare also 26), p.2

43) As 24), p. 31

44) As 25), p. 4, and 6th Armored Division, Summary of Operations, 1–31 January 1945, p. 4

45) As 15), pp. 13 and 36

46) As 41)

47) As 36)

48) As 15), p. 13

49) As 35) and as 41)

50) Daily Report Supreme Command West of 4.1.45

51) As 33)

52) As 42), p. 2

53) 6th Armored Division, see 44) and 28)

53a) War diary of OKW, IV/2, p. 1346

54) As 21)

55) As 35)

55a) As 36)
56) Daily reports Supreme Command West from 1.9.1944–31.1.1945, F/M, RHZ v. 494
57) Report by Werner Damsch to the Author on 29.1.1980 regarding action in the period 15.12.1944 to 5.1.1945
58) As 24), p. 32
59) As 15), p. 14
60) Report by Alfred Schulz, 2./SS-Panzerjägerabteilung 12, to the Author on 30.3.1977
61) As 24), p. 32
62) As 41)
63) Report by Hans Richter to the Author on 10.5.1977
64) As 22), p. 20
65) As 62)
66) As 22), pp. 20/21
67) As 24), p. 32
68) Hq 68th TK Bn, Unit History: "Battle of the Bulge", p. 29, National Archives, record group No. 407, 606TK(68)-0.1
69) Report by W. Bald of June 1982 to the Author
70) As 56)
71) Study by Generalmajor Hans Kokott: "Die 26. Division (V.G.) in der Ardennen-schlacht 1944/45" (The 26. Division in the Ardennes battle 1944/45), parts II, III, IV and IX, MS P-032 d of 15 October 1949. This study can be used only with qualification since it contains, in addition to incorrect information, non-factual and emotional accounts.
    Letter from Obersturmführer Rudolf von Ribbentrop of 30.6.1980 to the Author
72) "Die 3. Kompanie/SS-Panzerregiment 12", loc. cit., pp. 111/112
73) As 15, p. 15a
74) As 15. p. 16
75) As 15), p. 17 and following pages
76) Notes by Dr. Wolfgang Loenicker, commander SS-Flakabteilung 12; excerpt copies in the hands of the Author

PART IV
Chapter 9.0
Note: The Panzerarmee led by Oberstgruppenführer Sepp Dietrich was officially designated as "6. Panzerarmee", although it consisted mainly of Panzerdivisions of the Waffen-SS. In Part IV (except in the documents), it is referred to as "6. SS-Panzerarmee" in order to avoid confusing it with the German "6. Armee" and the Soviet "6. Guards Tank Army". (Author)

1) Report by Otto Günsche of 1.2.1982, copy in the hands of the Author
2) SS-Führungshauptamt, Amt II Org. Abt. Ia/II, diary No. 355/45 g.K. of 16.1.1945, F/M

Chapter 9.1
1) Activity report II./26; diary Divisionsbegleitkompanie; reports by Dr. Wolfgang Loenicker, Karl Kolb, Paul Baier, Hans Lierk to the Author

2) Letter from Georg Maier of 28.2.1977 to the Author
3) Activity report II./26, recorded by the Bataillon adjutant, Obersturmführer Harro Lübbe
4) Report by Günther Burdack of February 1977 to the Author.

Chapter 9.2
1) Report on condition of 12. SS-Panzerdivision "HJ" of 1.2.1945 and notes from the estate of Hugo Kraas (abbreviations written out in full by the Author)
2) As 1)

Chapter 9.3
1) Gosztony, Peter: "Endkampf an der Donau 1944/45" (Final battle on the Danube), Wien 1969, notes Nos. 19 and 20, pp. 311/312
2) as 1), p. 130
3) War diary Heeresgruppe Süd, MA, and as 1), p. 155

Chapter 9.4
1) AOK 8, operation order for operation "Südwind" (south wind) of 13.2.1945, F/M
2) As 1)
3) Teletype message KR HLZX/FUE 03684 of 15.2.1945, 2010 from AOK 8 to Heeresgruppe Süd, F/M, RH19 V/60
4) Teletype message KR HLZX/QEK 03669 13/2 2350 from AOK 8 to Heeresgruppe Süd, F/M
5) As 1)
6) Activity report II./26 and diary of the Divisionsbegleit-kompanie
7) War diary Heeresgruppe Süd
8) Activity report II./26 and as 7)
9) As 7)
10) As 7), activity report II./26, and report by Günther Burdack to the Author on 29.5.1977
11) As 7)
12) As 6) and 7), report by Dr. Wolfgang Loenicker to the Author on 18.11.1980
13) As 7)
14) As 12)
15) As 7), and situation map of 22.2.1945
16) Diary of August Zinßmeister
17) Report by Günther Burdack to the Author on 29.5.1977
18) Report by Hans-Jürgen Ross to the Author on 16.9.1976
19) Activity report II./26. The report erroneously states 20.2.1945 as the date of the attack on Bart, instead of 21./22.2.1945
20) As 7), 16), and 17)
21) As 7)
22) Activity report II./26, and as 17) and 18)
23) As 7)
24) As 7)
25) Appendix to war diary of AOK 8, Military Archives, RH19 V/69
26) As 7)

Planning and Assembly for the Offensive

1) War diary Heeresgruppe Süd, F/M, and Peter -Gosztony, loc. cit., p. 219
2) Gosztony, loc. cit., p. 220 and following pages
3) War diary Heeresgruppe Süd, F/M
4) Personal notes of Hugo Kraas
5) As 3), report on strength Heeresgruppe Süd of 7.3.1945, condition on 3.3.1945
6) Letter from R. Richter of 21.7.1982 to the Author
7) As 5)
7a) Activity Report II./26
8) Notes by Dr. Wolfgang Loenicker, copy in the hands of the Author; notes by Paul Baier for 4. Batterie Flakabteilung 12

The Offensive

1) War diary Heeresgruppe Süd, quoted after Wilhelm Tieke: "Vom Plattensee bis Österreich" (From Lake Balaton to Austria), Gummersbach 1975
2) Activity report II./26; report by Hans Siegel and working group II. Panzer-abteilung; report by Günther Burdack and working group III./26; report by Hannes Taubert to the Author on 5.1.1981; diary of Heinz Thomas, copy in the hands of the Author, notes by Dr. W. Loenicker, loc. cit.
3) Activity report II./26 and notes by Dr. W. Loenicker
4) Report by Hans-Jürgen Ross to the Author on 3.11.1976
5) Activity report II./26; in error, the date of the start of the attack was given as 5.3.1945
6) Days of close combat for I./25; report by Günther Burdack, loc. cit.
7) As 1), and report by Günther Burdack, loc. cit.
8) As 1)
9) As 1)
10) As 1)
11) Peter Gosztony, loc. cit., p. 223
12) Activity report II./26; report by Günther Burdack, loc. cit., days of close combat for I./25
13) As 1), and report by Günther Burdack, loc. cit.
14) Activity report II./26
15) Reports by Hans Siegel to the Author on 7.11. and 10.11.1977
16) As 15)
17) As 1); reports by Hans Siegel of 7.11. and 10.11.1977 to the Author; activity report II./26; report by Günther Burdack, loc. cit.
18) As 1)
19) As 1) and report on losses
20) Report by Dr. Elmar Lochbihler to the Author on 27.3.1981
21) As 1)
22) As 1)
22a) Activity report II./26; as 1)
23) Report by Günther Burdack, loc. cit.
23a) As 23)
24) Report by Willy Kretzschmar to the Author on 27.10.1980
25) Report by Heinz Müller to the Author on 19.9.1980
26) As 1)
27) As 1)

28) As 1)

29) As 4)

30) As 14)

31) As 1)

32) As 14)

33) Diary of the Divisionsbegleitkompanie

34) As 1)

35) As 1)

35a) Report by Martin Glade on 28.11.1978

35b) As 1)

36) As 33)

37) War diary Heeresgruppe Süd KR Blitz (flash) HRAX 336 of 15.3., 15.15 hours, F/M

38) As 1)

39) As 11), p. 230

40) As 1)

41) As 14)

42) As 1) and as 14)

43) As 33)

44) As 1)

45) As 11), p. 231 and following pages

46) War diary Heeresgruppe Süd

47) As 1)

48) As 33)

49) As 1) and as 14)

Section 10

1) War diary Heeresgruppe Süd, loc. cit.

2) As 1)

3) As 1)

4) As 1)

5) War diary II./26, loc. cit.

6) Diary of the Divisionsbegleitkompanie; note by Karl Kolb; notes from the estate of Hugo Kraas

7) As 1)

8) As 5)

9) Reports by Hans Siegel on 16.2. and 4.9.1978, letter of 20.9.1978 to the Author

10) Report by Hermann Asbach to the Author on 16.11.1978

11) War diary Heeresgruppe Süd, quoted after Tieke, loc. cit.

12) As 1)

13) Letter from Hans Lierk of 27.8.1980 to the Author; days of close combat Willi Klein and Helmut -Hackmann

14) As 1)

15) As 1), and Gosztony, loc. cit., p. 239 for tank strength of 6. Soviet Guards Tank Army

16) As 11)

16a) Report by Hans Siegel to the Author on 16.2.1978

17) Letter from Hans Siegel of 20.9.1978 to the Author and report of 1.9.1978; as 4) with wrong dates and erroneous sketch from memory

17a) Garbade, Hinrich: "Aufstellung, Ausrüstung und -Einsatz der ehemaligen schweren SS-Korps-Artillerie-Abteilung 501" (Creation, equipment and action of the former heavy SS-Korps-Artillerie-Abteilung 501), no date; "Schwere SS-Korps-Artillerie-Abteilung 101/501—Einsatz", without further information

18) As 6), and diary of Heinz Thomas, 1. Fernsprech-kompanie (telephone company) Nachrichten -Abteilung 12, copy in the hands of the Author; as 11)

19) Diary of Dr. Wolfgang Loenicker, loc. cit.

20) Diary of Karl Kolb, loc. cit.

21) Estate of Hugo Kraas, loc. cit.

22) As 1)

23) Days of close combat Regiment 25, loc. cit.; report by R. Richter to the Author on 9.6.1982

24) Report by Hannes Taubert to the Author on 5.1.1981; diary of Kurt Pörtner

25) Report by Martin Glade to the Author on 28.11.1978

26) Letter from Herbert Pospich to Kurt Pörtner, original in the hands of the Author

27) As 6), and diary of Heinz Thomas, loc. cit.

28) As 5)

29) As 19) and 20)

30) As 5), and letter from Hans Siegel of 1.9.1978 to the Author

31) As 11)

32) As 21)

33) As 1)

34) As 6)

35) As 19) and 20)

36) As 5)

37) As 11)

38) Report by H. Saal to Albert Schlüter, copy in the hands of the Author

39) As 1)

40) As 5), and report by Hans Siegel to the Author on 1.9.1978

41) Report by Wolfgang Lincke of April 1977, copy in the hands of the Author

42) Report by Hans Siegel to the Author on 1.9.1978

43) As 42)

44) Diary of the Divisionsbegleitkompanie and war diary II./26

45) Diary of the Divisionsbegleitkompanie; instead of a Jagdpanzer, it was likely a Panther with the explosives squad, since an SS-Führer is named as the commander. A Jagdpanzer would not have been able to fire to the rear if required

46) As 44), and the estate of Hugo Kraas

47) Close combat days Willy Klein and Helmut -Hackmann

48) As 1) and 11)

49) As 1)

50) As 1); war diary II./26; estate of Hugo Kraas

51) Report by Hannes Taubert to the Author on 5.1.1981, and as 1)

52) Estate of Hugo Kraas, and diary of the Divisionsbegleit-kompanie

53) As 1)

54) Estate of Hugo Kraas; war diary II./26; diary of Heinz Thomas

55) As 1)

56) As 1)

57) Report by Hannes Taubert to the Author on 5.1.1981

58) As 5)
59) As 1), and days of close combat Regiment 25
60) As 5)
61) As 1)
62) Diary of the Divisionsbegleitkompanie and estate of Hugo Kraas
63) As 1)
64) As 5); diary of the Divisionsbegleitkompanie; estate of Hugo Kraas
65) As 1)
66) As 5), and estate of Hugo Kraas
67) As 11)
68) Diary of the Divisionsbegleitkompanie
69) That book was scheduled for publication in 1983
70) Report on 5.1.1969 to the Author
71) Estate of Hugo Kraas; diary of Wilhelm Kolf, excerpts in the hands of the Author; report by Hannes Taubert to the Author on 5.1.1981
72) As 5) and as 11)
73) As 11); estate of Hugo Kraas; war diary II./26; diary of the Divisionsbegleitkompanie

Chapter 11.1

1) Estate of Hugo Kraas; letter from Helmut Mader of 19.10.1980 to the Author; diary II./26
2) As 1), and diary of the Divisionsbegleitkompanie
3) Letter from Martin Glade of 28.11.1978, and personal information of 16.6.1986
3a) As 1)
4) OKH/Gen.St.d.H./Op.Abt., war diary from 2.4.– 8.4.1945, morning report of Heeresgruppe Süd of 3.4.1945, F/M. RH2/v.325
5) As 4), daily report of Heeresgruppe Süd of 3.4.1945
6) As 4), and report by Hans Krieg to the Author on 20.7.1981; days of close combat Helmut Hackmann
7) Rauchensteiner, Manfred: "Krieg in Österreich 1945" (War in Austria), Wien 1970, map p. 97 and p. 175; diary of August Zinßmeister, loc. cit.
8) Diary of the Divisionsbegleitkompanie; days of close combat Helmut Hackmann; report by Willi Wagner to the Author on 27.12.1981, war diary II./26
8a) Report by Günther Burdack of 1976
9) Diary of the Divisionsbegleitkompanie, and report by Willi Wagner, San.Abt.12, of 27.12.1981
10) As 4), daily report of Heeresgruppe Süd of 6.4.1945
11) Report by R. Richter to the Author on 9.6.1982
12) As 4), daily report of Heeresgruppe Süd of 6.4.1945, and morning report of 7.4.1945; day of close combat Walter Hohmann; report by Willi Wagner, as under 8)
13) As 1), morning report of 7.4.1945
14) Estate of Hugo Kraas; as 4), morning report of Heeresgruppe Süd of 8.4.1945; diary of the Divisionsbegleitkompanie; as 4), assessment of the situation 6. SS-Panzerarmee of 7.4.1945, F/M, RH2/v.335
15) As 4), daily report of Heeresgruppe Süd of 8.4.1945; estate of Hugo Kraas
16) War diary II./26

17) Estate of Hugo Kraas, and as 4) war diary from 9.–15.4.1945, daily report of Heeresgruppe Süd of 9.4.1945, F/M, RH2/v.326

18) As 17)

19) Estate of Hugo Kraas; war diary as 17), daily report of 10.4.1945; report by Günther Burdack of 1976 to the Author

20) Report by Hans Krieg to Paul Baier on 15.12.1945, copy in the hands of the Author

21) As 17), daily report of Heeresgruppe Süd of 11.4.1945

22) Estate of Hugo Kraas; diary of August Zinßmeister, loc. cit.; day of close combat Walter Hohmann; report by Günther Burdack of 1976

23) Diary of the Divisionsbegleitkompanie

24) Estate of Hugo Kraas

25) Diary of the Divisionsbegleitkompanie; report by Hannes Taubert to the Author on 28.1.1981

26) Report by Gerd Freiherr von Reitzenstein to the -Author on 8.6.1981

27) Excerpt from the diary of Karl Hollander, copy in the hands of the Author; report by Götz Großjohann of late 1979 to the Author

28) "Die 3. Kompanie", loc. cit., p. 120 and following pages; as 27); diary of the Divisionsbegleitkompanie; report by Leopold Lengheim to the Author on 16.12.1979; report on losses 1. Kompanie of 13.4.1945 in the St. Corona action area to the Wehrmacht-sauskunftstelle (Wehrmacht information office)

29) As 28), p. 125 and following pages

30) Diary of the Divisionsbegleitkompanie; as 26); as 17), daily report Heeresgruppe Süd of 13.4.1945

31) Estate of Hugo Kraas; as 20)

32) Estate of Hugo Kraas

33) As 32) and as 17), daily report Heeresgruppe Süd of 13.4.1945; as 26)

34) Rauchensteiner, loc. cit.

35) Estate of Hugo Kraas; diary of the Divisionsbegleit-kompanie; report by Günther Burdack of 1976

36) As 26), and estate of Hugo Kraas

37) As 27), 28), and 17), daily report Heeresgruppe Süd of 14.4.1945

38) Estate of Hugo Kraas; diary of the Divisionsbegleit-kompanie

39) As 17), daily report Heeresgruppe Süd of 15.4.1945

40) Estate of Hugo Kraas

41) Report by Ivo Dane to the Author on 9.6.1981 and estate of Hugo Kraas

42) Estate of Hugo Kraas; as 26); as 4), war diary from 16.–24.4.1945, daily report Heeresgruppe Süd of 16.4.1945, F/M, RH2/v.327

43) Estate of Hugo Kraas

44) As 43), and as under 42), daily report of Heeresgruppe Süd of 17.4.1945

45) As 43), and as under 42), daily report of 18.4.1945; as 26)

46) Reports by Alois Morawetz of 17.12.1976 and 26.6.1980; letters by Dr. Jürgen Chemnitz of 11.7.1976 and 14.9.1980 to the Author; letter by Dr. Chemnitz of 14.10.1979 to A. Morawetz

47) Rauchensteiner, loc. cit., p. 184

48) Estate of Hugo Kraas; as 26); diary of August -Zinßmeister, loc. cit.; report by Fritz Gottzmann in "Der Freiwillige" (The volunteer), Osnabrück, -September 1977

49) Estate of Hugo Kraas; as under 42), daily report of 19.4.1945, and morning report of 20.4.1945 of Heeresgruppe Süd; as 27)
50) Report by Günther Burdack of 1976 to the Author
51) Diary of the Divisionsbegleitkompanie; estate of Hugo Kraas
52) As 27)
53) Estate of Hugo Kraas; as 26); as 50)
54) Estate of Hugo Kraas; personal information from Wilhelm Weidenhaupt
55) As 54); as 27); diary of the Divisionsbegleitkompanie
55a) Report by Karl Garrecht to the Author on 25.6.1966
56) Estate of Hugo Kraas; as 27); diary of the Divisions-begleitkompanie
57) As 54); report by Günther Burdack of 1976 to the Author
58) Estate of Hugo Kraas; as 26)
59) Estate of Hugo Kraas
60) Diary of August Zinßmeister, loc. cit.
61) Rossiwall, Theo: "Die letzten Tage—Die militärische Besetzung Österreichs 1945" (The last days—the military occupation of Austria 1945), Wien 1969
62) Diary of the Divisionsbegleitkompanie; as 59); as 50)
63) As 27); as 28), p. 13; report by Hannes Taubert to the Author on 28.1.1981
64) Rauchensteiner, loc. cit., pp. 189/190; as 61)
65) As 59); as 26); as 27); report by Hannes Taubert to the Author on 28.1.1981
66) Diary of August Zinßmeister, loc. cit.; diary of the Divisionsbegleitkompanie; as 50)
67) As 27)
68) Rauchensteiner, loc. cit., p. 190
69) Diary of the Divisionsbegleitkompanie
70) As 26)
71) As 27), and as under 42), daily report Heeresgruppe Süd of 24.4.1945
72) As 69)
73) As 26) and 27)
74) As 50), and report by Karl Kolb, loc. cit.
75) As 59); as 26); as 27); report by Hannes Taubert, as under 65)
76) As 59)
77) As 59) and as 69)
78) As 59)
79) Letter from Dr. Jürgen Chemnitz of 14.10.1979 to the Author
80) Rauchensteiner, loc. cit., pp. 189 and 193
81) As 59) and as 27)

Chapter 11.2

1) Estate of Hugo Kraas, and as 27)
2) Estate of Hugo Kraas; "Divisionsnachschubtruppen" (Divisional supply troops), collected reports by Albert Schlüter and comrades, copy in the hands of the Author
3) Report by Hans Siegel of 15.6.1981
4) Rauchensteiner, loc. cit., p. 316; Birjukov, N.J.: "Trudnaja nauka probezdat" (The difficult science of victory), Moscow 1968, quoted after Rauchensteiner, loc. cit.; "Die 3. Kompanie", loc. cit., p. 133
5) As 1)

PART V
Section 12

1) Reports by Hans Lierk of 21.5.1975 and 8.11.1982 to the Author; Kammüller, Heinz: "Bericht über einen Besuch in Ungarn . . ." (Report on a visit to Hungary . . .) in "Der Freiwillige", issue 6, Osnabrück 1981, p. 22
2) Diary of Brigadeführer Hugo Kraas, copy in the hands of the Author
3) Letter from Hans Harder of 3.3.1963 to Heinz Fehmer, copy in the hands of the Author
4) Report by Otto Helmuth Müller to the Author on 16.11.1976
5) Report by Christel Graen to the Author on 9.4.1980
6) Report by E., loc. cit.
7) Report by Willi Wagner and comrades to the Author on 27.12.1981
8) Hausser, Paul: "Soldaten wie andere auch der Weg der Waffen-SS" (Soldiers as the others—the path of the Waffen-SS), Osnabrück 1966
9) Copies of the submissions in the hands of the Author
9a) Appendices to the war diary Supreme Command West, Ia, from 1.1. to 31.3.1944, p. 131, F/M, RH 19/IV/27
10) Panzermeyer: "Grenadiere", loc. cit., p. 353 and following pages
11) As 10), p. 375

Section 13

1) Report by E., loc. cit.
2) Letter by Robert H. Broughton of 1.2.1978 to the Author

Section 14

1) Letter by Hans Nepomuck of 8.3.1985 to the Author
2) Letter by S.V. to the Author
3) Letter from the federal office of the association caring for war cemeteries of 10.1.1984 to the Author
4) Letter by Alfred Bahro of 18.3.1986 to the Author
5) After the Battle, issue 48/1985
6) Letter by Karl-Heinz Decker of 17.11.1983 to the Author
7) Letter by Lothar Giebler of 16.8.1986 to the Author

Index

Page numbers in italics indicate tables and illustrations.

597